CRISIS *of* CONSCIENCE

Fifth Edition

RAYMOND FRANZ

1922 - 2010

Former member of the
Governing Body of Jehovah's Witnesses

NU**LIFE**
P R E S S

2018

The body of this work is based on the 2008 printing of the Fourth Edition of *Crisis of Conscience*, by Raymond Franz with additional pages added to the Appendix from *In Search of Christian Freedom* written by Raymond Franz and the entire booklet *"Where is The "Great Crowd" Serving God?"* by Jon A. Mitchell. The 'Table of Contents', Index and the footnotes have been updated to reflect the added pages to the Appendix and current resources. Additionally a *Foreword* by David Henke has been added at the beginning of the book and *The Copyright Owners Story* at the very end of the book.

Unless otherwise noted, Scripture quotations are taken from the New World Translation of the Holy Scriptures, published by the Watchtower Bible and Tract Society of New York, Inc. | Scripture quotations marked JB are taken from The Jerusalem Bible © 1966 by Darton Longman & Todd Ltd and Doubleday and Company Ltd. | Scripture quotations marked NEB taken from the New English Bible, copyright © Cambridge University Press and Oxford University Press 1961, 1970. All rights reserved | Scripture quotations marked NIV are taken from the Holy Bible, New International Version®, NIV®. Copyright © 1973, 1978, 1984 by Biblica, Inc.™ Used by permission of Zondervan. All rights reserved worldwide. The "NIV" and "New International Version" are trademarks registered in the United States Patent and Trademark Office by Biblica, Inc.™ | Scripture quotations marked RSV are taken from the Revised Standard Version of the Bible, copyright 1952 [2nd edition, 1971] by the Division of Christian Education of the National Council of the Churches of Christ in the United States of America. Used by permission. All rights reserved. | Scripture quotations marked NRSV are taken from the New Revised Standard Version Bible, copyright 1989, Division of Christian Education of the National Council of the Churches of Christ in the United States of America. Used by permission. All rights reserved. | Scripture quotations marked NLT are taken from the Holy Bible, New Living Translation, copyright ©1996, 2004, 2007, 2013, 2015 by Tyndale House Foundation. Used by permission of Tyndale House Publishers, Inc., Carol Stream, Illinois 60188. All rights reserved.

Wherever possible, and for the sake of authenticity, an effort has been made within this book to present quotations from other publications by direct photocopies. Since certain of these publications may go back over one hundred years in the past, the quality of the type may not always be of the highest standard.

Crisis of Conscience, Fifth Edition
Copyright © 2018 Deborah Dykstra

Published by NuLife Press™
www.NuLifePress.com

HARDCOVER: 978-0-9994992-0-7
PAPERBACK: 978-0-9994992-1-4
EBOOK: 978-0-9994992-2-1

When persons are in great danger from a source that they do not suspect or are being misled by those they consider their friends, is it an unkindness to warn them? They may prefer not to believe the warning. They may even resent it. But does that free one from the moral responsibility to give that warning?

—*The Watchtower* magazine,
January 15, 1974.

Life is uncertain and when a man dies what he knows dies along with him— unless he passes it on while still in life.

What this book contains is written out of a sense of obligation to people whom I sincerely love. In all good conscience I can say that its aim is to help and not to hurt. If some of what is presented is painful to read, it was also painful to write. It is hoped that the reader will recognize that the search for truth need never be destructive of faith, that every effort to know and uphold truth will, instead, strengthen the basis for true faith. What those reading this information will do with it is, of course, their own decision. At least it will have been said, and a moral responsibility will have been met.

IN THE HISTORY of a religious organization there can be defining moments, particular times and circumstances that allow for seeing beyond external appearance and recognizing the true character and essential spirit of the organization. The organization's own self- image, its dominant cast of mind and outlook, its motivating force and its pattern of response to disagreement or challenge, can then be seen more clearly. The factors that come to light may have actually been there all along, at the inner core of the organization, but were beneath the surface, even at odds with external appearances and professed principles. The defining moment may produce a portrait that is disturbingly different from the image the organization holds in the minds of its membership, and that defining period may even escape their notice if those at the organization's center can effectively suppress awareness of it.

Most readers of the book that follows will have at least some familiarity with the religion of Jehovah's Witnesses. Consider, then, the following statements and ask yourself as to the possible source of these expressions, and also as to their validity:

> The natural man can see that a visibly organized body, with a definite purpose, is a thing of more or less power; therefore they esteem the various organizations, from which we have come out, in obedience to the Master's call. But the natural man cannot understand how a company of people, with no organization which they can see, is ever going to accomplish anything. As they look upon us, they regard us simply as a few scattered skirmishers—a "peculiar people"—with very peculiar ideas and hopes, but not worthy of special notice.

> Under our Captain, all the truly sanctified, however few or far separated in person, are closely united by the Spirit of Christ, in faith, hope

and love; and, in following the Master's command, are moving in solid battalions for the accomplishment of his purposes. But, bear in mind, God is not dependent upon numbers (See Judges 7, as an illustration).

. . . We always refuse to be called by any other name than that of our Head—Christians—continually claiming that there can be no division among those continually led by his Spirit and example as made known through his Word.

Beware of "organization." It is wholly unnecessary. The Bible rules will be the only rules you will need. Do not seek to bind others' consciences, and do not permit others to bind yours. Believe and obey so far as you can understand God's Word today, and so continue growing in grace and knowledge and love day by day

. . . by whatsoever names men may call us, it matters not to us; we acknowledge none other name than "the only name given under heaven and among men"—Jesus Christ. We call ourselves simply CHRISTIANS and we raise no fence to separate from us any who believe in the foundation stone of our building mentioned by Paul: "That Christ died for our sins according to the Scriptures"; and those for whom this is not broad enough have no right to the name Christian

If asked to assess these statements and characterize the principles they advance, among Jehovah's Witnesses today most would certainly classify them as of an "apostate" source. The actual source is, however, the *Watch Tower* magazine—of an earlier time.[1] The rejection and discarding of the principles espoused in those published statements were factors in a major transformation within a body of people initially joined together in free affiliation, having no visible organizational structure, and their transposition into a highly centralized organization with a distinctive name and the claim to the exclusive right to be viewed as genuinely Christian.

---

1 See the *Watch Tower* magazines of March 1883, February 1884, and September 15, 1885. For photocopies of the actual material see the book *In Search of Christian Freedom*, pages 72-76, which have been inserted into Appendix B of this 2018 edition of *Crisis of Conscience.*

That transformation took place many decades ago. Yet the pattern it established remains in effect to this day and exercises a controlling force.

Similarly with the events and circumstances set forth in *Crisis of Conscience*, they point to a defining moment in more recent times, one that for many may be as unfamiliar as the previous quotations from the *Watch Tower* magazine. The evidence presented in this edition demonstrates the continuing impact of that period's developments through the succeeding years and into this 21st century. Rather than diminish their relevance, the years that have passed have instead served to enhance the significance of that period and its events, to validate the picture that unfolds, and provide living examples of the accompanying effect on people's lives. It is against the background of that defining period that one can discern a reality that is as meaningful and crucial today as it was at the time of the original writing of the book.

TABLE OF CONTENTS

FOREWORD

Can I read this book? Let me answer this question with another question. Did you know that the primary control method in dictatorial countries is control of the press? By controlling the information people receive you gain control of the way they think about issues. The Watchtower Society has historically promoted this personal right to investigate truth claims, but sadly they have not practiced it. In their book *The Truth That Leads To Eternal Life*, page 13, they say, "We need to examine not only what we personally believe, but also what is taught by any religious organization with which we may be associated." It is this sense of personal responsibility that led to Raymond Franz' own *Crisis of Conscience*.

Taking a path of personal investigation will lead to both blessings and struggles. The blessing will be in knowing the truth and that truth will set you free. The struggle often comes in a sense of loss in finding things that disappoint you and fail to meet your expectations. Mark Twain made the comment that "A cat that walks on a hot stove will never walk on a hot stove again. But neither will it walk on a cold stove." That is a very appropriate mental image of the response of so many who leave "high control" and "high demand" religions. When anyone becomes disillusioned with his or her religion, the most common reaction is to keep one's distance from all religious organizations. Reading *Crisis of Conscience* could cause the reader to have his doubts confirmed or it could cause his doubts to begin. What will be the proper reaction? Is organized religion as a whole something to avoid? Is the Bible trustworthy? Where was God when I was hurting?

My hope is that this book will help to set you free from the past but not hinder your quest for a relationship with God. Most would agree

1

that trust should be earned. But the converse of that is that in our trust of people and organizations we have a healthy level of skepticism. "And the people of Berea were more open-minded than those in Thessalonica, and they listened eagerly to Paul's message. They searched the Scriptures day after day to see if Paul and Silas were teaching the truth." (Acts 17:11, NLT). If people let you down, it was people, and not God.

The emotional damage done by religious disillusionment can be deep. In their book, *The Subtle Power of Spiritual Abuse*, David Johnson and Jeff VanVonderen, describe the symptoms of a spiritual abuse victim as being identical to the symptoms of an incest victim. The reason the symptoms are identical is that religious faith is at the very core of a person's being. It is just as deep as family trust and expectations. That being the case, one can understand the hesitancy of thinking about another religious group. Because disillusionment is emotionally felt, the tendency can be to let those emotions outweigh rational thought.

Stephen Arterburn said in his book, *Toxic Faith*, that a harmful faith will have these ten characteristics:

1   Special claims for itself
2   Dictatorial authority
3   An us verses them mentality
4   Punitive in nature
5   Overwhelming service
6   The followers are in pain
7   Closed communication
8   Legalism
9   No objective accountability
10   Labeling

Arterburn was not speaking of a particular religion. These are the common denominators of any religion that is authoritarian in nature. I would add to that list the control of information, as discussed above. It is essential to controlling a group of people. It has been called "group think." This is why all high control religions prohibit their members from reading any contrary literature. That you have this book in your hands is the beginning of breaking that control. Jesus said, "And you will know the truth, and the truth will set you free." (John 8:32, NLT). The Apostle Paul said, "So Christ has truly set us free. Now make sure that you stay free, and don't get tied up again in slavery to the law." (Galatians 5:1, NLT).

Moving on after a harsh legalistic religion can be as hard as wandering lost in a wilderness, or it can grow you in ways you could not have imagined, making you stronger emotionally, spiritually and giving you extraordinary peace. The choice will be yours.

My four decades of counseling survivors of spiritual abuse has led me to advise two things. Study the Bible as the Word of God written to you personally, and ask God in prayer to reveal Himself to you. The prophet Jeremiah said, "If you look for me wholeheartedly, you will find me." (Jeremiah 29:13, NLT) And Jesus said, "Keep on asking, and you will receive what you ask for. Keep on seeking, and you will find. Keep on knocking, and the door will be opened to you." (Matthew 7:7 NLT)

David Henke
Founder, Watchman Fellowship, Inc.
Author of *Spiritual Abuse Recovery Workbook*
Columbus, Georgia, USA
www.watchman-ga.org

1

PRICE OF CONSCIENCE

Whether we like it or not, moral challenge affects each of us. It is one of life's bittersweet ingredients from which there is no successful escape. It has the power to enrich us or impoverish us, to determine the true quality of our relationships with those who know us. It all depends on our response to that challenge. The choice is ours—it is seldom an easy one.

We have the option, of course, of surrounding our conscience with a sort of cocoon of complacency, passively "going along," shielding our inner feelings from whatever might disturb them. When issues arise, rather than take a stand we can in effect say, "I'll just sit this one out; others may be affected—even hurt—but I am not." Some spend their whole life in a morally 'sitting' posture. But, when all is said and done, and when life finally draws near its close, it would seem that the one who can say, "At least I stood for something," must feel greater satisfaction than the one who rarely stood for anything.

Sometimes we may wonder if people of deep conviction have become a vanishing race, something we read about in the past but see little of in the present. Most of us find it fairly easy to act in good conscience so long as the things at stake are minor. The more that is involved, the higher the cost, the harder it becomes to resolve questions of conscience, to make a moral judgment and accept its consequences. When the cost is very great we find ourselves at a moral crossroads situation, facing a genuine crisis in our lives.

This book is about that kind of crisis; the way people are facing up to it and the effect on their lives.

Admittedly, the story of the persons involved may have little of the high drama found in the heresy trial of a John Wycliffe, the intrigue of the international hunt for an elusive William Tyndale, or the horror of the burning at the stake of a Michael Servetus. But their struggle and suffering are, in their own way, no less intense. Few of them could say it as eloquently as Luther, yet they take very much the same stand he took when he said to the seventy men judging him:

> Unless I am convinced by the testimonies of the Scriptures or by evident reason (for I believe neither pope nor councils alone, since it is manifest they have often erred and contradicted themselves), I am bound by the Scriptures I have quoted, and my conscience is held captive by the word of God; and as it is neither safe nor right to act against conscience, I cannot and will not retract anything. Here I stand; I cannot otherwise; God help me. Amen.[1]

Long before any of these men, the apostles Peter and John of nineteen centuries ago confronted essentially the same issue when they stood before a judicial council of the most respected members of their lifelong religion and frankly told them:

> Whether it is right in the sight of God to listen to you rather than to God, you must judge; for we cannot but speak of what we have seen and heard.[2]

The people I write of are from among those I know most intimately, persons who have been members of the religious group known as Jehovah's Witnesses. I am sure, and there is evidence to show, that their experience is by no means unique, that there is a similar stirring of conscience among people of various faiths. They face the same issue that Peter and John and men and women of later centuries confronted: *the struggle to hold true to personal conscience in the face of pressure from religious authority.*

---

1   These were Luther's concluding words in making his defense at the Diet of Worms, Germany, in April of 1521.
2   Acts 4:19, 20, *RSV.*

For many it is an emotional tug-of-war. On the one hand, they feel impelled to reject the interposing of human authority between themselves and their Creator; to reject religious dogmatism, legalism and authoritarianism, to hold true to the teaching that Christ Jesus, not any human religious body, is "the head of every man."[3] On the other hand, they face the risk of losing lifelong friends, seeing family relationships traumatically affected, sacrificing a religious heritage that may reach back for generations. At that kind of crossroads, decisions do not come easy.

What is here described, then, is not merely a "tempest in a teapot," a major quarrel in a minor religion. I believe there is much of vital benefit that any person can gain from considering this account. For if the numbers presently involved are comparatively small; the issues are not. They are far-reaching questions that have brought men and women into similar crises of conscience again and again throughout history.

At stake is the freedom to pursue spiritual truth untrammeled by arbitrary restrictions and the right to enjoy a personal relationship with God and his Son free from the subtle interposition of a priestly nature on the part of some human agency. While much of what is written may on the surface appear to be distinctive of the organization of Jehovah's Witnesses, in reality the underlying, fundamental issues affect the life of persons of any faith that takes the name Christian.

The price of firmly believing that it is "neither safe nor right to act against conscience" has not been small for the men and women I know. Some find themselves suddenly severed from family relationships as a result of official religious action—cut off from parents, sons and daughters, brothers and sisters, even from grandparents or grandchildren. They can no longer enjoy free association with longtime friends for whom they feel deep affection; such association would place those friends in jeopardy of the same official action. They witness the blackening of their own good name—one that it has taken them a lifetime to earn—and all that such name has stood for in the minds and hearts of those who knew them.

---

3 1 Corinthians 11:3.

They are thereby deprived of whatever good and rightful influence they might exercise on behalf of the very people they have known best in their community, in their country, in all the world. Material losses, even physical mistreatment and abuse, can be easier to face than this.

What could move a person to risk such a loss? How many persons today would? There are, of course (as there have always been), people who would risk any or all of these things because of stubborn pride, or to satisfy the desire for material gain, for power, prestige, prominence, or simply for fleshly pleasure. But when the evidence reveals nothing indicating such aims, when in fact it shows that the men and women involved recognized that just the opposite of those goals was what they could expect—what then?

What has happened among Jehovah's Witnesses provides an unusual and thought-provoking study in human nature. Besides those who were willing to face excommunication for the sake of conscience, what of the larger number, those who felt obliged to share in or support such excommunications, to allow the family circle to be broken, to terminate long-standing friendships? There is no question about the sincerity of many of these persons, or that they felt and still feel distress from carrying out what they deemed a necessary religious duty. What convictions and reasoning motivated them?

Notably, as regards the cases here dealt with, many if not most of those involved are persons who have been associated with Jehovah's Witnesses for twenty, thirty, forty or more years. Rather than a "fringe element" they have more frequently been among the more active, productive members of the organization.

They include persons who were prominent members of the Witnesses' international headquarters staff at Brooklyn, New York; men who were traveling superintendents and elders; women who spent long years in missionary and evangelistic work. When they first became Witnesses, they had often cut off all previous friendships with persons of other faiths, since such "outside" associations are discouraged among Jehovah's Witnesses. For the rest of their life their only friends have been among those of their religious community. Some had built their whole life plans around the goals set before them by the organization, letting these control the amount of education they sought, the type of work they did, their decisions as to marriage, and whether they had children or remained childless. Their "investment" was a large one, involving some of life's most precious assets. And now they have seen all this disappear, wiped out in a matter of a few hours.

This is, I believe, one of the strange features of our time, that some of the most stringent measures to restrain expressions of personal conscience have come from religious groups once noted for the defense of freedom of conscience.

The examples of three men—each a religious instructor of note in his particular religion, with each situation coming to a culmination in the same year—illustrate this:

One, for more than a decade, wrote books and regularly gave lectures presenting views that struck at the very heart of the authority structure of his religion.

Another gave a talk before an audience of more than a thousand persons in which he took issue with his religious organization's teachings about a key date and its significance in fulfillment of Bible prophecy.

The third made no such public pronouncements. His only expressions of difference of viewpoint were confined to personal conversations with close friends.

Yet the strictness of the official action taken toward each of these men by their respective religious organizations was in inverse proportion to the seriousness of their actions. And the source of the greatest severity was the opposite of what one might expect.

The first person described is Roman Catholic priest Hans Küng, professor at Tübingen University in West Germany. After ten years, his outspoken criticism, including his rejection of the doctrinal infallibility of the Pope and councils of bishops, was finally dealt with by the Vatican itself and, as of 1980; the Vatican removed his official status as a Catholic theologian. Yet he remains a priest and a leading figure in the university's ecumenical research institute. Even students for the priesthood attending his lectures are not subject to church discipline.[4]

---

4   They simply receive no academic credit for such attendance.

The second is Australian-born Seventh Day Adventist professor Desmond Ford. His speech to a layman's group of a thousand persons at a California college, in which he took issue with the Adventist teaching about the date 1844, led to a church hearing. Ford was granted six months leave of absence to prepare his defense and, in 1980, was then met with by a hundred church representatives who spent some fifty hours hearing his testimony. Church officials then decided to remove him from his teaching post and strip him of his ministerial status. But he was not disfellowshipped (excommunicated) though he has published his views and continues to speak about them in Adventist circles.[5]

The third man is Edward Dunlap, who was for many years the Registrar of the sole missionary school of Jehovah's Witnesses, the Watchtower Bible School of Gilead, also a major contributor to the organization's Bible dictionary (*Aid to Bible Understanding* [now titled *Insight on the Scriptures*]) and the writer of its only Bible commentary (*Commentary on the Letter of James*). He expressed his difference of viewpoint on certain teachings only in private conversation with friends of long standing. In the spring of 1980, a committee of five men, none of them members of the organization's Governing Body, met with him in secret session for a few hours, interrogating him on his views. After over forty years of association, Dunlap was dismissed from his work and his home at the international headquarters and disfellowshipped from the organization.

Thus, the religious organization that, for many, has long been a symbol of extreme authoritarianism showed the greatest degree of tolerance toward its dissident instructor; the organization that has taken particular pride in its fight for freedom of conscience showed the least.

Herein lies a paradox. Despite their intense activity in door-to-door witnessing, most people actually know little about Jehovah's Witnesses aside from their position on certain issues of conscience. They have heard of their uncompromising stand in refusing to accept blood transfusions,

---

5   In conversation with Desmond Ford at Chattanooga, Tennessee, in 1982, he mentioned that by then more than 120 ministers of the Seventh Day Adventist church had either resigned or been "defrocked" by the church because they could not support certain teachings or recent actions of the organization.

their refusal to salute any flag or similar emblem, their firm objection to performance of military service, their opposition to participation in any political activity or function. Those familiar with legal cases know that they have taken some fifty cases to the Supreme Court of the United States in defense of their freedom of conscience, including their right to carry their message to people of other beliefs even in the face of considerable opposition and objections. In lands where constitutional liberties protect them, they are free to exercise such rights without hindrance. In other countries they have experienced severe persecution, arrests, jailing, mobbing, beatings, and official bans prohibiting their literature and preaching.

How, then, is it the case that today any person among their members who voices a personal difference of viewpoint as to the teachings of the organization is almost certain to face judicial proceedings and, unless willing to retract, is liable for disfellowshipment? How do those carrying out those proceedings rationalize the apparent contradiction in position? Paralleling this is the question of whether endurance of severe persecution and physical mistreatment at the hand of opposers is, *of itself,* necessarily evidence of belief in the vital importance of staying true to conscience, or whether it can simply be the result of concern to adhere to an organization's teachings and standards, violation of which is known to bring severe disciplinary action.

Some may say that the issue is really not as simple as it is here presented, that there are other crucial matters involved. What of the need for religious unity and order? What of the need for protection against those who spread false, divisive and pernicious teachings? What of the need for proper respect for authority?

To ignore those factors would admittedly show an extreme, blindly unbalanced, attitude. Who can challenge the fact that freedom, misused, can lead to irresponsibility, disorder, and can end in confusion, even anarchy? Patience and tolerance likewise can become nothing more than an excuse for indecision, non-action, a lowering of all standards. Even love can become mere sentimentality, misguided emotion that neglects to do what is really needed, with cruel consequences. All this is true and is what those focus on who would impose restraints on personal conscience through religious authority.

What, however, is the effect when spiritual "guidance" becomes mental domination, even spiritual tyranny? What happens when the desirable qualities of unity and order are substituted for by demands for institutionalized conformity and by legalistic regimentation? What results when proper respect for authority is converted into servility, unquestioning submission, and an abandonment of personal responsibility before God to make decisions based on individual conscience?

Those questions must be considered if the issue is not to be distorted and misrepresented. What follows in this book illustrates in a very graphic way the effect these things have on human relationships, the unusual positions and actions persons will take who see only one side of the issue, the extremes to which they will go to uphold that side. The organizational character and spirit manifest in the 1980s, continued essentially unchanged in the1990s, and remains the same in this year 2008.

Perhaps the greatest value in seeing this is, I feel, that it can help us discern more clearly what the fundamental issues were in the days of Jesus Christ and his apostles, and understand why and how a tragic deviation from their teachings and example came, so subtly, with such relative ease, in so brief a span of time. Those who are of other religious affiliations and who may be quick to judge Jehovah's Witnesses would do well to ask first about themselves and about their own religious affiliation in the light of the issues involved, the basic attitudes that underlie the positions described and the actions taken.

To search out the answers to the questions raised requires going beyond the individuals affected into the inner structure of a distinctive religious organization, into its system of teaching and control, discovering how the men who direct it arrive at their decisions and policies, and to some extent investigating its past history and origins. Hopefully the lessons learned can aid in uncovering the root causes of religious turmoil and point to what is needed if persons trying to be genuine followers of God's Son are to enjoy peace and brotherly unity.

2

CREDENTIALS AND CAUSE

I am speaking the truth as a Christian, and my own conscience, enlightened by the Holy Spirit, assures me it is no lie. . . . For I could even pray to be outcast from Christ myself for the sake of my brothers, my natural kinsfolk.
— Romans 9:1, 3. *New English Bible.*

WHAT has thus far been said gives, I believe, good reason for the writing of this book. The question may remain as to why I am the one writing it.

One reason is my background and the perspective it gives. From babyhood up into my sixtieth year, my life was spent in association with Jehovah's Witnesses. While others, many others, could say the same, it is unlikely that very many of them had the range of experience that happened to be my lot during those years.

A reason of greater weight is that circumstances brought to my knowledge information to which the vast majority of Jehovah's Witnesses have absolutely no access. The circumstances were seldom of my own making. The information was often totally unexpected, even disturbing.

A final reason, resulting from the previous two, is that of conscience. What do you do when you see mounting evidence that people are being hurt, deeply hurt, with no real justification? What obligation do any of us have—before God and toward fellow humans—when he sees that information is withheld from people to whom it could be of the most serious consequence? These were questions with which I struggled.

What follows expands on these reasons.

In many ways I would much prefer passing over the first of these since it necessarily deals with my own "record." The present situation seems to require its presentation, however, somewhat in the way circumstances obliged the apostle Paul to set out his record of personal experiences for Christians in Corinth and afterward to say to them:

> I am being very foolish, but it was you who drove me to it; my credentials should have come from you. In no respect did I fall short of these superlative apostles, even if I am a nobody [even though I am nothing, *New International Version*].[1]

I make no pretense of being a Paul, but I believe that my reason and motive at least run parallel with his.

My father and mother (and three of my four grandparents) were Witnesses, my father having been baptized in 1913 when the Witnesses were known simply as Bible Students. I did not become an active Witness until I was sixteen in 1938. Though still in school, I was before long spending from twenty to thirty hours a month in "witnessing" from door to door, standing on street corners with magazines, putting out handbills while wearing placards saying "Religion is a snare, the Bible tells why. Serve God and Christ the King."

That year, 1938, I had attended a Witness assembly in Cincinnati (across the Ohio River from our home) and listened to Judge Joseph F. Rutherford, the president of the Watch Tower Society, speak from London, England, by radiotelephone communication. In a major talk entitled "Face the Facts," Rutherford's opening words included this:

---

1   2 Corinthians 12:11, *NEB*; compare 3:1, 2; 5:12, 13; 6:4-10; 11:21-29.

> Because the full statement of facts tends to
> shock the susceptibilities of some persons
> furnishes no excuse or justification to withhold
> from the public any part thereof, particularly
> when the public welfare is involved. When pre-
> sented to the people, those hearing should face
> the facts with calmness and sobriety and then
> sincerely take the course which is for their best
> interest. Previous belief or opinion should never
> be permitted to hinder one in receiving and con-
> sidering a statement of facts. [2]

That appealed to me as a worthwhile principle to follow in life. I felt receptive to the facts he would present.

World War II had not yet begun as of that year, but Nazism and Fascism were growing in power and posing an increasing threat to democratic lands. Among major points emphasized in the Watch Tower president's talk were these:

> God has made it clearly to be seen by those who diligently seek the truth that religion is a form of worship but which denies the power of God and turns men away from God. . . . *Religion and Christianity are therefore exactly opposite to each other.* . . .[3]

> According to the prophecy of Jesus, what are the things to be expected when the world comes to an end? The answer is world war, famine, pestilence, distress of nations, and amongst other things mentioned the appearance of a monstrosity on the earth. . . . *These are the indisputable physical facts* which have come to pass *proving that Satan's world has come to an end,* and which facts cannot be ignored. . . .[4]

> Now Germany is in an alliance with the Papacy, and Great Britain is rapidly moving in that direction. The United States of America, once the bulwark of democracy, is all set to become part of the totalitarian rule. .

2   *Face the Facts*, p. 3.
3   Ibid., pp. 7, 8. (Jehovah's Witnesses now view "religion" as an acceptable term for true worship.)
4   Ibid., p. 9. (The teaching then was that, since Satan's lease of power ended in 1914, the "world ended" in that sense. The Society's publications no longer teach this.)

. . Thus the indisputable facts are, that there is now in the earth Satan's dictatorial monstrosity, which defies and opposes Jehovah's kingdom. . . . *The totalitarian combine is going to get control of England and America. You cannot prevent it. Do not try.* Your safety is on the Lord's side. . . .[5]

I have italicized statements that particularly engraved themselves on my mind at that time. They created in me an intensity of feeling, of near agitation that I had not experienced before. Yet *none* of them today form part of Witness belief.

Rutherford's other major talk, "Fill the Earth," developed the view that as of 1935 God's message, till then directed to persons who would reign with Christ in heaven, a "little flock," was now being directed to an earthly class, the "other sheep," and that after the approaching war of Armageddon these would procreate and fill the earth with a righteous offspring. Of these he said:

> They must find protection in God's organization, which shows that they must be immersed, baptized or hidden in that organization. The ark, which Noah built at God's command, pictured God's organization. . . .[6]

Pointing out that Noah's three sons evidently did not begin to produce offspring until two years after the Flood, the Watch Tower president then made an application to those with earthly hopes in modern times, saying:

> **Would it be Scripturally proper for them to now marry and to begin to rear children? No, is the answer, which is supported by the Scriptures.**
>
> **It will be far better to be unhampered and without burdens, that they may do the Lord's will now, as the Lord commands, and also be without hindrance during Armageddon.** [7]

---

5   Ibid., pp. 16, 17, 27. (As is well known, the Second World War ended in the defeat of the Nazi-Fascist "dictatorial monstrosity," the exact opposite of what is here predicted.)

6   Ibid., pp. 40, 41. (This view of the ark's symbolic significance has changed, though the role of the organization as essential to salvation as presented is basically the same.)

7   Photocopies from *Face the Facts*, pp. 46, 47.

Joseph Rutherford spoke forcefully and with a distinctive cadence of great finality. These were *facts*, even "*indisputable facts*," solid truths on which to build life's most serious plans. I was deeply impressed with the importance of the organization as essential to salvation, also that the work of witnessing must take precedence over, or at least militate against, such personal interests as marriage and childbearing.[8]

In 1939 I was baptized and in June, 1940, on graduating from high school I immediately entered full-time service in witnessing activity. That year was a turbulent one for the world and for Jehovah's Witnesses. World War II was under way, the work of Jehovah's Witnesses came under governmental ban in several countries and hundreds of Witnesses were imprisoned; in the United States large numbers of children of Jehovah's Witnesses were being expelled from school for refusal to salute the flag (viewed as a form of image worship); the Witnesses' stand of neutrality toward war often inspired violent antagonism on the part of those priding themselves on their loyalty and patriotism; vicious mob attacks were starting to spread.

That summer of 1940 our family went to Detroit, Michigan, to attend a major Witness convention. A spirit of tense anticipation prevailed, a sense of being under siege. At the close of the assembly Judge Rutherford indicated that 'this might be the last assembly we would have before the great tribulation struck.' When the autumn of 1940 came and I put my summer clothes away, I remember thinking that I would likely never take them out again—that either Armageddon would have come or we would by then all be in concentration camps, like many Witnesses in Nazi Germany.

Mob violence reached a crescendo during the early 1940's. In Connersville, Indiana, I attended a court trial of two women Witnesses charged with seditious activity ("riotous conspiracy"), simply because they studied Watch Tower publications as part of a home study group. The trial ran five days and on the last day, after night had fallen, the jury brought

---

8   It was not until 1959, when I was 36 that I finally married; my wife and I are childless, having been vigilant in birth control for most of our marriage.

in its verdict of guilty. On leaving the courthouse, the defense attorney (a Witness named Victor Schmidt) and his wife were violently assaulted by a mob and were forced to walk, in a driving rain, the entire distance to the city limits. On the way the horror of the situation caused Schmidt's wife suddenly to begin to menstruate.

I had in my car group a Witness representative (Jack Rainbow) who had earlier been threatened with death by some of these men if he returned to "their city." On arriving at the city limits and there seeing Schmidt and his wife, followed by a remnant of the mob, I felt obliged to take the risk of picking them up and was able to do so. Another Witness had attempted this but only got a broken car window for his efforts. Schmidt's wife broke out into hysterical screaming when we got her into the car; her husband's face was bruised and covered with blood from deep cuts where he had evidently been hit with brass knuckles.[9] To experience firsthand such raw and callous intolerance left a vivid impression on my young mind. I felt all the more convinced of the rightness of my course with those who were quite evidently the true servants of God.

Later, as a tactic recommended by the Watch Tower Society's legal counsel, Hayden Covington, a large group of seventy-five Witnesses from the Cincinnati, Ohio area, including my parents, my two sisters and myself, traveled to Connersville in a "blitzkrieg" witnessing effort. With one exception, we all, men, women and children, were arrested and wound up in various jails, being locked up for one week until bail could be worked out. Still in my teens, it was my first time at experiencing the feeling that comes with seeing a massive metal door swing shut, hearing the bolt shoved in place and realizing that your freedom of movement is now taken from you.

---

9   See the *1975 Yearbook of Jehovah's Witnesses*, pp. 186-188. The photo above, from my personal files, shows the way Victor Schmidt looked after we brought him to his home and helped him from his bloodstained clothes.

Some months later I was in Indianapolis, Indiana, for a superior court hearing involving the Connersville events. My uncle, Fred Franz, a member of the Watch Tower headquarters staff since 1920 and a close associate of Judge Rutherford, was also there from Brooklyn as sort of an expert witness on the Society's behalf. The local congregation asked him to speak to them one evening. During the course of his talk he began discussing the attitude of so many that the work of witnessing was nearing its end, just about finished. To put it mildly, I was stunned to hear my uncle speak to the contrary, saying that at Brooklyn they were not expecting to close down, that 'anyone who wanted to send in a subscription for the *Watchtower* magazine needn't send it in for just six months—he could send it in for a full year or for two years if he wanted!'

The thrust of his remarks was so contrary to the comments of the Society's president at the Detroit assembly that it seemed clear to me that my uncle was speaking on his own, not presenting some duly authorized message from the Society. I actually felt like going to him and urging caution lest his remarks get back to Brooklyn and be viewed as disloyal, as having a dissipating, undermining effect on the sense of extreme urgency that had developed. Although then in his late forties, my uncle was a relatively young man compared to Judge Rutherford and I found myself uncertain as to whether to accept his remarks as proper or discount them as the product of an independent, somewhat brash attitude.

Leaving home that year to become the partner of a young fellow Witness in the coal mining region of West Virginia and eastern Kentucky, I found myself in an area where the threat of violence was faced almost on a daily basis. Some mining camps consisted of long wooden "row houses" strung along the highway. At times, upon reaching the last of such a section of houses, we could look back to the point where we had begun our calls and see men and boys excitedly running about gathering a mob.

At the "Octavia J" mining camp in Kentucky, our old "Model A" Ford car was surrounded by a group of angry miners and we were told to 'get out of there and out of the State of Kentucky and not come back if we valued our lives.' Attempts to reason only provoked greater anger. We did return a couple of months later and before we got out were shot at and pursued, escaping only by a ruse that led us over back roads and across a mountain until we could finally make our way home. More so than patriotic fervor, religious bigotry seemed to have been the force motivating the miners. Our disbelief of the teaching of a literal hell fire torment (causing young boys to yell out "no-hellers" as we drove by) weighed almost as heavily as our stand toward war.

I found that close-minded bigotry appalling then. I was happy to be part of an organization free from such intolerance.

The summer of 1941 came and, contrary to my expectation, I found myself attending another assembly, held in St. Louis, Missouri. I still remember seeing crowds gather around as Judge Rutherford was driven up to the assembly site in a large car with Hayden Covington and Vice President Nathan Knorr, both men of large build, standing on the running boards as bodyguards. On the final day of the assembly, Rutherford had all the children from five to eighteen years of age seated before the platform. After his prepared speech, he talked to them extemporaneously.

A tall man of usually stern appearance and stern tone, Rutherford now spoke with almost fatherly persuasion and recommended to these children that they put marriage out of their minds until the return of Abraham, Isaac, Jacob and other faithful men and women of old who would soon be resurrected and would guide them in their selection of mates.

A free copy of a new book entitled *Children* was given each child. As a vehicle for developing the material, it presented a fictional young Witness couple, John and Eunice, who were engaged but who had decided to postpone their marriage until the arrival of the New Order so near at hand. In the book, John said to Eunice:

> Our hope is that within a few years our marriage may be consummated and, by the Lord's grace, we shall have sweet children that will be an honor to the Lord. We can well defer our marriage until lasting peace comes to the earth. Now we must add nothing to our burdens, but be free and equipped to serve the Lord. When THE THEOCRACY is in full sway it will not be burdensome to have a family. 10

---

10   Photocopy from the book *Children*, published in 1941, p. 366.

I was then nineteen, and today in my eighties I can still remember the inner emotional stirrings, a strange mixture of agitation and depression, those expressions generated in me. At my age back then, to be confronted with statements of that kind that, in essence, called upon me to make a decision and set aside interest in marriage for an indefinite time, had an unsettling effect. I could perhaps appreciate better what young men contemplating entering the priesthood of Catholicism experience. Of course, the force of the Watch Tower president's urgings lay in the shortness of time till Armageddon. As the September 15, 1941, *Watchtower* magazine in describing the occasion later said:

> Receiving the gift [the book *Children*], the marching children clasped it to them, not a toy or plaything for idle pleasure, but the Lord's provided instrument for most effective work <u>in the remaining months before Armageddon</u>.[11]

Years later I learned that Judge Rutherford was at that point dying of cancer. He had been separated for many years from his wife, who was also a Witness and who lived as an invalid in California; his one son on reaching adulthood had shown no interest in the religion of his father. My uncle, Fred Franz, said that the Judge's failing condition, coupled with his strong desire that the "end" come while he was still alive to see it, motivated many such expressions as those made in 1940 and 1941.

I have thought since that, had the couple in the book been real instead of fictional, their engagement period would have been rather long, in fact, would still be in effect. All the young girls present at that assembly would be well past the childbearing age now, being at least in their late sixties or early seventies. Some of those who were then present as children, however, did loyally follow through on the counsel heard and remained single through what might be called their normal marriageable years on into bachelorhood and spinsterhood.

In 1942, a "special pioneer" assignment in Wellston, Ohio, brought other experiences.[12] Another young Witness and I lived in a small trailer

---

11   See the *Watchtower* of September 15, 1941, p. 288 [underlining mine].

12   "Special pioneers" are full-time representatives ("pioneers") given special assignments by the Society, with a higher quota of hours and a monthly allowance to aid in expenses.

 house, a homemade "box on wheels" six feet wide and fourteen feet long (1.8 meters by 4.3 meters). It had no insulation whatsoever in the walls and our small coal stove held a fire for at most a few hours. Many wintry nights saw the water in the pail *inside* the trailer freeze over and it was not uncommon to awaken and then be unable to get back to sleep because of feet throbbing with pain from the cold. We could afford nothing better since, aside from our share of the contributions people gave for literature, we each received as a monthly allowance from the Society a maximum of fifteen dollars.[13] During the better part of a year, our main meal of the day usually consisted of boiled potatoes, oleomargarine and day-old bread (half the cost of fresh bread). My partner had an old car but we rarely had the money to put fuel in it.

In this town, too, animosity flared. At one time or another young boys broke every window in the trailer. One night I returned home to find it thrown completely over on its side. I again experienced arrest and spent a night in the local jail. The place literally crawled with bed bugs and, unable to bring myself to lie on the jail bunk, I spent the entire night sitting on an empty tin can someone had left in the cell.

In 1944, an invitation came to attend a missionary school, the Watchtower Bible School of Gilead, for a five-months course. Upon graduation and while awaiting a missionary assignment, I spent a year and a half in traveling work, visiting congregations in a "Circuit" that took in the state of Arizona and a large section of California. When visiting congregations in the San Diego, California, area I spent five nights at "Beth Sarim" (meaning "House of Princes"). This was a large home built by the Society and said to be 'held in trust' for the faithful men of old, from Abel

---

13   The request form for this allowance had spaces to indicate what had been received from contributions for literature, what had been spent, and the difference. Since at times the difference did not come quite to fifteen dollars, I felt the right thing to do was to ask for less. But this resulted in my consistently winding up short of funds and then requesting smaller and smaller amounts. As I realized later, most "special pioneers" just asked for the straight fifteen dollars.

onward, to be used by them upon their resurrection.[14] Judge Rutherford, who had had some lung problems, spent the winters there during his life. I recall that the place gave me somewhat of a sense of unreality. San Diego was a nice city; the home was a fine, upper-class residence. But I could not see why the men I had read about in the Bible would have any interest in being placed there; something did not seem to fit.[15]

Assigned first to France as a missionary, I was unable to go due to the refusal of my draft board to grant me permission to leave the country. (Though I had gained exemption from military service as a "minister," they justified their refusal on the basis of my still being within the age limit covered by the military draft.) Thereafter I was assigned to the island of Puerto Rico (viewed as still within the USA). Before leaving, in 1946, Nathan Knorr, now president of the Society (Rutherford having died in early 1942), talked to a group of us, all young men being sent out to do supervisory work in different countries as "Branch Overseers." Among other things he strongly stressed that if we wished to remain in our missionary assignments we should avoid anything that might lead to courtship and marriage. The policy was: *Loss of singleness means loss of assignment.*[16]

In Puerto Rico it was not long before our "missionary home" group in San Juan consisted of one married couple, seven young girls in their twenties and me, all living in a two-story, six bedroom house. Though I followed Knorr's counsel and kept very busy (sometimes conducting more than fifteen home Bible studies a week), the announced policy on marriage and the circumstances in the close quarters of the home created pressure that wore ever more heavily on me. Bouts with dysentery, then a paratyphoid infection with its intense spasms of intestinal pain and passage of stools of blood, and later a case of infectious hepatitis did nothing to help. (I worked in the office right through the cases of dysentery and paratyphoid infection and was off only one week as a result of

---

14   See the book *Salvation*, published in 1939, pp. 311, 312.

15   Not many years later Beth Sarim was sold. The belief in the return of the "faithful men of old" before Armageddon was also set aside.

16   Basically the same rule applied at the international headquarters and all Branch Offices; in the mid-1950s this rule was changed; Knorr himself married.

the hepatitis, though I felt so weak I could hardly climb the stairs to the office.) After eight years the combined strain brought me near to a nervous breakdown.

Upon writing the president, I was relieved of my Branch responsibilities (I had not requested this) and was given the option of returning to the States to do traveling work there. I asked to be allowed instead to remain in my assignment in Puerto Rico and was transferred to another town. Though the town, Aguadilla, was one for which I felt no attraction, I had requested it since it seemed the need was greater there.

Within a year or so I was assigned to do traveling work, visiting congregations in the island and in the neighboring Virgin Islands (lying to the east of Puerto Rico).

An added feature was that periodically the Society asked me to make trips to the Dominican Republic where the work of Jehovah's Witnesses had been banned by the government of dictator Rafael Trujillo. The pur-

Dominican Dictator Rafael Trujillo

pose was primarily to smuggle in copies of Watch Tower literature.[17] I did so a number of times and then, in 1955, was asked to try to deliver a petition personally to the dictator. Knowing that people who incurred his disfavor had a way of simply disappearing, I accepted the assignment with a measure of apprehension.

Arriving in Ciudad Trujillo (now Santo Domingo), I sent a telegram to the Generalissimo presenting myself solely as a "North American educator with information of great importance to you and your country." The interview was granted at the National Palace and

---

17   Though of medium height, my average weight while in the Caribbean was only 117 pounds (53 kilos). I could place several magazines around my body beneath a double set of undershirts and also slip an opened, 384-page book inside my shorts and still look normal. The only problem was that while seated on the plane the corners of the opened book cut into my thighs causing some discomfort.

I was able to deliver the petition into his hands.[18] To my surprise I was not expelled and continued to make my periodic "smuggling" trips without being apprehended.

Then in 1957 all the American missionaries of the Witnesses were expelled from the Dominican Republic in the wake of a wave of violent persecution, many local Witnesses being brutally beaten and imprisoned. A major issue had been the refusal of male Witnesses to do "marching" as required by military training laws, but there was also considerable religious opposition expressed, priests and others making inflammatory statements in the newspapers.

The Society asked me to go in and check on the conditions of the native Dominican Witnesses. I had been in just shortly before to deliver instructions to the missionaries and had brought out detailed accounts of the harsh persecution and these were prominently featured in Puerto Rican newspapers. As we learned from a source close to him, this adverse publicity enraged Trujillo.

Feeling like a marked man, I recall that my first night at a hotel in Ciudad Trujillo I was given a room on the ground floor with French windows right next to the bed. My sense of real danger was strong enough to move me to rig up the appearance of a form on the bed while I slept on the floor behind it. Again, however, I was able to make it in and out without incident and made other trips in the following years.

Later the Society changed its policy on marriage and, thirteen years after arriving in Puerto Rico and now approaching 37 years of age, I married. Cynthia, my wife, joined me in traveling work. Economic conditions in the islands were poor, considerably beneath today's level. We lived with the people we served, sharing their little homes, sometimes with running water and electricity, sometimes not; sometimes with a measure of privacy, often with very little. Relatively young, we adjusted, though my wife's health was due to be seriously affected.

---

18   The Generalissimo received me in full uniform with all his medals on (many, if not most, of these being self-bestowed). When he found out what my mission actually was, the interview ended fairly soon. It apparently created a favorable impression; nonetheless, since some time later the ban was lifted for a period of about a year and then was reimposed.

Only a few months after our marriage, while serving in the small island of Tortola my wife fell ill with a severe case of gastroenteritis, evidently from bad water or tainted food. The home we were staying in belonged to a fine West Indian couple with lovable children. Unfortunately the house they were renting was overrun with roaches, a creature that inspires near panic in my wife. At night we regularly checked our bed for any roaches before letting the mosquito netting down. Suspecting that a large box in a corner containing clothes was the creatures' headquarters, one day I took some insect spray and went to the box and lifted the top garment. I quickly let it down, for the box was alive with what looked to be hundreds of small roaches and I feared the spray could send them everywhere. For added measure a large rat each night entered the kitchen (next to our room and next to the only bathroom), its size being enough to make the tins of food on the shelves move.

In these circumstances my wife now began to experience the gastroenteritis, developing extreme diarrhea and regular vomiting. I was able to get her to the island's one doctor and an injection temporarily stopped the vomiting. Late that night it began again and this, coupled with the constant diarrhea, brought Cynthia to the point of dehydration. I ran about a mile in the dark to rouse the doctor from sleep and we carried her in his jeep to a little clinic. Her veins had nearly collapsed and the nurses tried again and again before they could finally insert a needle to administer saline solution. She was able to leave a few days afterward but her health was never quite the same. A later parasite infection (whipworm) added to the problem.

We continued in traveling work until 1961 and then were transferred to the neighboring Dominican Republic. The dictator Trujillo had been assassinated shortly before our arrival.

During our nearly five years there, we saw the fall of four separate governments and in April of 1965 experienced a war that centered around the capital where we were located. Most Americans and other foreign residents fled the country. Our missionary group felt no inclination to abandon the Dominican Jehovah's Witnesses and our assignment, and so we learned what war-time life is like.

Army tank across the street from the missionary home.

Nights were filled with the crack of hundreds of rifles, the rattle of machine guns, the boom of bazookas and other heavier weapons. Lulls came in the fighting during the day and we were able to get outside and carry on some activity, though sometimes almost pinned down by the eruption of gunfire. To this day I have wondered just how close bullets must come for the distinct buzzing sound like that of angry bees to be heard as they fly past your head. One soldier comfortingly told me, "There's no need to worry about those. You won't hear the one that hits you."

The remaining fifteen years of full-time service were quite different, as they were spent at the international headquarters in Brooklyn, New York. My reason for describing in some detail the earlier years up to 1965 is that their content seems to be more of the fabric (though greatly inferior in quality) of the experiences the apostle focuses on in setting forth the evidence of the genuineness of his service to God and Christ, saying:

> We prove we are servants of God by great fortitude in times of suffering: in times of hardship and distress.

In the words that follow, he makes no mention of his speeches, gives no figures of great audiences he addressed, cites no examples of organizational feats in building up large numbers of believers.[19]

---

19   2 Corinthians 6:4-10, *JB.*

I make no claim that what I went through was any more than what many others have experienced, either as missionaries of Jehovah's Witnesses or of other religions. The record is simply set out for the reader to decide upon its relative worth, particularly as regards assessing the validity and integrity of the information supplied in the rest of this publication.

CIRCUMSTANCES AND CONSEQUENCES

We cannot but speak of what we have seen and heard.
— Acts 4:20, *Revised Standard Version.*

What I saw, heard and experienced during the next fifteen years had a great impact on me. Whether the reaction of the reader will coincide with mine, I have no way of knowing, but one thing is certain and that is that no one could understand what brought me to a crisis situation without knowing these developments. The proverb is apt: "When anyone is replying to a matter before he hears it, that is foolishness on his part and a humiliation."[20]

The year before the war in the Dominican Republic, and following an attack of dengue fever which left my nerve endings hypersensitive, I had attended a ten-month course at Gilead School.[21] At the close, the Society's president, N. H. Knorr, asked me to leave my missionary service in the Caribbean and come with my wife to the international headquarters (called "Bethel") in Brooklyn, where I would serve in the Writing Department. Though doubtless this would have been viewed as an honor by others, I frankly had no interest in leaving the place where I was. Speaking to Brother Knorr in his office I explained how much I enjoyed my current assignment, enjoyed the people, enjoyed the work. This apparently was viewed as a lack of appreciation for the opportunity offered; he seemed visibly offended. I then told him I simply had wanted him to know my feelings, my love for missionary activity, and that I would accept the change of assignment.

---

20 Proverbs 18:13.
21 Dengue fever is like malaria in being transmitted by mosquitoes but is self-limiting. Its permanent effect on me may have been due to an earlier, childhood case of scarlet fever.

A few months after our arrival and after I had done some work in writing, President Knorr showed me into an office containing a table piled high with stacks of typed papers and asked me to undertake the development of a Bible dictionary. The papers were the result of assignments that had been parceled out to 250 men around the world. Those assignments, however, were generally made on the basis of the person's organizational position (as Branch Office personnel, factory overseers, and so forth). Few of the men had writing experience and fewer still had either the experience, the time or the library facilities for doing research. I believe it can be conservatively said that at least ninety percent of the submitted material was not used.

I began with "Aaron" and continued with "Aaronites," "Ab," "Abaddon," and so on but the impracticality of one writer undertaking the task soon became obvious. First, a director of the Watch Tower Society, Lyman Swingle, was assigned to aid in the project; shortly thereafter Edward Dunlap, the Registrar of Gilead School was also assigned. Eventually Reinhard Lengtat and John Wischuk, of the Service and Writing Departments respectively, joined the project group. Others shared intermittently for varying periods but the five persons mentioned carried the project through until the 1,696-page reference work, called *Aid to Bible Understanding*, was completed five years later.[22]

Near the start, President Knorr made a statement that proved a key factor in our approach to the project. It was not intended the way we understood it but that undoubtedly was fortuitous. Talking to those of us then assigned, he said, "We just want to present what the Bible says; there is no need to look up everything in the Society's publications."

His intent in saying this, as we realized later, was so that the project could get done quickly and so that it would produce something relatively small, a "handbook" as he later expressed it. By just restating what was in the particular Bible verses relating to a subject, with very little additional clarification, there would be only a minimal amount of time needed for research.

---

22   Subjects were assigned to us by Karl Adams, the writing department overseer. *Insight on the Scriptures* a two-volume set with very minor revisions, replaced *Aid to Bible Understanding* in 1988.

We misunderstood him to mean that we should strive always to present what the Bible *actually* said rather than feel obliged to present things the way the Watch Tower publications presented them. A considerably different kind of publication resulted than would otherwise have been the case. The material sent in by the 250 men almost without exception presented information according to the "accepted viewpoint" of the Society's publications. Our research often revealed differences.

The Society's vice president, Fred Franz, was acknowledged as the organization's principal Bible scholar. On a number of occasions I went to his office to inquire about points. To my surprise he frequently directed me to Bible commentaries, saying, "Why don't you see what Adam Clarke says, or what Cooke says," or if the subject primarily related to the Hebrew Scriptures, "what the Soncino commentaries say."

Our Bethel library contained shelf after shelf after shelf filled with such commentaries. Since they were the product of scholars of other religions, however, I had not given much importance to them and, along with others in the department, felt some hesitancy, even distrust, as to using them. As Karl Klein, a senior member of the Writing Department, sometimes very bluntly expressed it, using these commentaries was "sucking at the tits of Babylon the Great," the empire of false religion according to the Society's interpretation of the great harlot of Revelation.[23]

The more I looked up information in these commentaries, however, the more deeply impressed I was by the firm belief in the divine inspiration of the Scriptures the vast majority expressed. I was impressed even more so by the fact that, though some were written as early as the eighteenth century, the information was generally very worthwhile and accurate. I could not help but compare this with our own publications, which often within a few years became "out of date" and ceased to be published. It was not that I felt these commentaries to be without error by any means; but the good certainly seemed to outweigh the occasional points I felt to be mistaken.

I began to appreciate more than ever before how vitally important *context* was in discerning the meaning of any part of Scripture, and that

---

23 I find it hard to believe he meant this as seriously as it sounded, since he made use of the commentaries himself and knew that Fred Franz used them quite frequently.

realization seemed to be true of others of the group who were working regularly on the *Aid* project. We also came to realize the need to let the Bible define its own terms rather than simply taking some previously held view or letting an English dictionary definition control. We began to make greater use of the Hebrew and Greek lexicons in the Bethel library, and concordances that were based on the original language words rather than on English translations.

It was an education and it was also very humbling, for we came to appreciate that our understanding of Scripture was far less than we had thought, that we were not the advanced Bible scholars we thought we were. I personally had been on such a "treadmill" of activity over the previous twenty-five years that, although reading through the Bible several times, I had never been able to do such serious, detailed research into the Scriptures, in fact never felt great need to do so since it was assumed that others were doing it for me. The two courses at Gilead School I had attended were so tightly programmed that they gave little time for meditation, for unhurried investigation and analysis.

Having now both time and access to the extra Bible helps, the lexicons, commentaries, Hebrew and Greek concordances, and so forth, was an aid. But above all it was seeing the need always to let the context guide, always to let the Scriptures themselves control, that made the major difference. There was no overnight change of viewpoint but rather, over a period of years, a gradual deepening of appreciation of the crucial need to let God's Word speak for itself to the fullest extent possible. I could see why those one-hundred and two-hundred-year-old commentaries in our Bethel library were comparatively timeless in their value. The very fact of their verse-by-verse approach more or less obliged them to stay within the contextual meaning and thereby considerably restricted them from taking excursions into sectarian views or interpretative flights of fancy.

Among the subjects assigned to me by Karl Adams, overseer of the Writing Department, were those of "older man [elder]" and "overseer." All I received were those words; there was no accompanying instruction or recommendation as to the development of the topics. Note, then, how the Watch Tower's 1993 organizational history book, *Jehovah's Witnesses— Proclaimers of God's Kingdom*, on page 233, represents the matter:

Gearing Up for Explosive Growth

When research was being done under the supervision of the Governing Body in preparation of the reference work *Aid to Bible Understanding*, attention was once more directed to the way in which the first-century Christian congregation was organized. A careful study was made of such Biblical terms as "older man," "overseer," and "minister." Could the modern-day organization of Jehovah's Witnesses conform more fully to the pattern that had been preserved in the Scriptures as a guide?

Jehovah's servants were determined to continue to yield to divine direction. At a series of conventions held in 1971, attention was directed to the governing arrangements of the early Christian congregation. It was pointed out that the expression *presby′te-ros* (older man, elder), as used in the Bible, was not limited to elderly persons, nor did it apply to all in the congregations who were spiritually mature. It was especially used in an official sense with reference to overseers of the congregations. (Acts 11:30; 1 Tim. 5:17; 1 Pet. 5:1-3) These received their positions by appointment, in harmony with requirements that came to be part of the inspired Scriptures. (Acts 14:23; 1 Tim. 3:1-7; Titus 1:5-9) Where enough qualified men were available, there was more than one elder in the congregation. (Acts 20:17; Phil. 1:1) These made up "the body of older men," all of whom had the same official status, and not one of whom was the most prominent or powerful member in the congregation. (1 Tim. 4:14) To assist the elders, it was explained, there were also appointed "ministerial servants," in accord with the requirements set out by the apostle Paul. —1 Tim. 3:8-10, 12, 13.

Arrangements were promptly put into operation to bring the organization into closer conformity to this Biblical pattern.

The picture here drawn is remarkably distorted to create a false impression. It speaks of the research that went into *Aid to Bible Understanding* as "being done under the supervision of the Governing Body," and conveys the idea of smoothness of direction from a body of men motivated by intense concern to hold to the Scriptures. In reality, the *Aid* book project was neither initiated by nor supervised by any Governing Body of that time, but by the Watch Tower corporation president, Nathan Knorr. And though he initiated the project, any *actual* direction by him was a very detached and limited one, since any real direction was done through Karl Adams, the overseer of the Writing Department. Knorr neither developed the list of subjects to be included in the book nor supervised the assigning of them nor their development. All assignments of subjects were originated by and made by Karl Adams.

Adams was neither a member of the Governing Body nor for that matter of those called the "anointed." Of those who shared personally and directly in the actual research and writing of articles for the *Aid* book, Lyman Swingle, from the corporation's Board of Directors, was the only one who could be considered a "Governing Body member." And his assignments came from Karl Adams and he worked under Adams' supervision, turning in whatever he wrote to Karl for editing and

Karl Adams

approval, as was true of the rest of us working on the project. Nathan Knorr and Fred Franz eventually read some of the finished articles, but Knorr left it up to Karl Adams to select whatever articles Karl felt they ought to read. These were remarkably few.

As stated, when the subjects of "older man [elder]" and "overseer" were assigned to me all I received in the assignment were those titles, nothing more. I was not then a member of the Governing Body and what developed was not the result of guidance by any Governing Body, nor even by Karl Adams. My uncle, Fred Franz, had some input, but only as a result of my personal initiative, and his subsequent actions seemed almost a denial of that input. It was quite evident that the result of my research was something unexpected, even viewed as not particularly desirable, by either Nathan Knorr or Fred Franz.

That research revealed that the arrangement relating to elders and the congregational direction in Bible times was very different from the position then held by Jehovah's Witnesses, where a more or less "monarchical" arrangement prevailed. Each congregation was under the supervision of a single individual, a "congregation servant" or "congregation overseer." The term "overseer" applied only to him and any others were viewed as his assistants. The Scriptural arrangement of bodies of elders had been summarily ended in 1932 by Judge Rutherford due to a lack of cooperation on the part of some elders with the Society's programs and policies.[24] His position as President gave Rutherford the necessary authority to take such a stand and all congregations were invited to vote for the disbanding of bodies of elders and their replacement by a Society-appointed "Service Director." For the next forty years there were no bodies of elders in the congregations. That is why the *New World Translation* of the Bible published by the Society in the 1950s regularly used the rendering "older men" rather than "elders," a then officially discredited term.[25]

Somewhat disturbed by what my research revealed, I approached my uncle with the evidence. His response took me by surprise. "Don't try to understand the Scriptures on the basis of what you see today in the organization," he said, and added, "Keep the *Aid* book pure." I had always looked upon the organization as God's one channel for dispensing truth and so this counsel sounded unusual to say the least. When I pointed out that the Society's *New World Translation* rendering of Acts, chapter fourteen, verse 23, evidently inserted the words "to office" in connection with the appointment of elders and that this somewhat altered the sense, he said, "Why don't you check it in some other translations that may not be as biased."[26] I walked out of his office wondering if I had actually heard what I had heard. In future days I was to remind him of these statements on more than one occasion during Governing Body sessions.

Admittedly, that conversation strongly affected my approach to Scripture. I deeply appreciated the integrity toward Scriptural truth his remarks indicated. That made his later reaction to the final results all the more puzzling, disturbing.

---

24 Generally, in justifying this action, focus is placed on the lack of cooperation by some elders in sharing in the door-to-door witnessing which was now being strongly promoted. They are represented as men who were only interested in conducting meetings and giving talks. It is never mentioned that the Watch Tower president, Judge Rutherford, followed exactly that same course. The explanation given was that his responsibilities did not allow for him to share in the door-to-door activity.

25 Later editions of the *New World Translation* use "elder" but only in Revelation in texts referring to the 24 elders by God's throne.

26 Later editions of the *New World Translation* also dropped this added phrase. The first editions had read: "Moreover, they appointed older men to office for them in the congregation and, offering prayer with fastings, they committed them to Jehovah."

After completing the subjects "Older Man" and "Overseer" I submitted these. Normally, President Nathan Knorr and Vice President Fred Franz would not have read the articles. However, Karl Adams, as head of the Writing Department, told me that upon reading the information he went to Brother Knorr and said, "I think you should read this. It changes a lot of things."

Go back, now, to the presentation made in *Jehovah's Witnesses—Proclaimers of God's Kingdom.* The second paragraph under the subheading "Gearing Up for Explosive Growth" is essentially a résumé of the content of the articles I submitted, as a comparison with those articles in the *Aid* book will show. (The only exception would be the emphasis this paragraph places on the concept of an "official status" of elders.) I would obviously not expect the writer or writers of the book to mention who wrote those articles for the *Aid* book. But from this paragraph and the start of the following one, the reader would understand that the articles led to a willing and almost immediate decision to bring everything into conformity to the Scriptural arrangement pointed to. What actually did happen?

As Karl Adams related to me, after reading the material, Knorr went into Fred Franz's office and, with considerable vehemence, said, "What does this mean? Does this mean we have to change everything at this late date?" Fred Franz replied, No, that he did not think that would be necessary—that the existing arrangement could be continued without problem.

When Karl later passed this information on to me, I found it hard to believe, particularly in view of my uncle's earlier expressions to me. I felt obliged to go to his room one evening to inquire about it. He confirmed that he felt no need to make adjustments. Knowing that the *Aid* book was to be released to the brothers in completed form that summer at the District Assemblies, I asked what effect he thought it would have on them to read the evidence that there were bodies of elders in the first-century congregation, that *all* elders served as overseers, and then to find out that we had no intention of following this Scriptural example?

He said calmly that he did not think it would cause any problem, that the existing arrangement could be "accommodated" to the information in the *Aid* book. I expressed deep concern that this setting aside of the Scriptural precedent could be very unsettling to the brothers. Holding to his position, he related how brothers of earlier decades had reasoned that, since Christ had taken Kingdom power in 1914, there could rightly be changes in the way things were administered on earth. He added that he had believed and still believed that Christ Jesus would direct and administer the affairs of his servants earthwide by the use of, or through the office of, just a single individual, and that this would be the case until the New Order came. The tenor of these expressions seemed so different from those he had made on earlier occasions that I found it difficult to reconcile them.

Sometime later, however, the vice president prepared some convention material that indicated that a change in the congregational direction *would* take place. When the copy of this material reached Karl Adams he saw the implications and immediately contacted President Knorr, saying to him, "I think you had better talk with Brother Franz again. I believe he has changed his mind." Brother Knorr did and Brother Franz had. And the forty-year-old arrangement changed as a consequence.

To present the development of this change as the book *Jehovah's Witnesses—Proclaimers of God's Kingdom* does, representing a "Governing Body" as supervising the research and "careful study" of Biblical terms, their sole concern being how to "conform more fully to the pattern" set out in Scripture, "determined to continue to yield to divine direction," and promptly "to bring the organization into closer conformity" to that pattern, is to present an idealized picture that is simply untrue. It either manifests ignorance on the part of the writer or writers of the material as to how matters actually developed, or else is duplicitous, designed to elevate the role of a group of men in the view of the membership. The reality reveals instead how heavily control was vested in a few individuals, and how one man's rather idiosyncratic decision (that of Fred Franz) could affect the direction a worldwide organization could take.

When the subject "Chronology" was assigned to me this similarly led to serious questions.[27] A major teaching of Jehovah's Witnesses is that

---

27   I was also assigned most of the historical subjects, dealing with the rulers and history of Egypt, Assyria, Babylon (rulers only), Medo Persia and others.

Bible prophecy had pointed to the year 1914 as the end of the "Gentile Times" of Luke chapter twenty-one, verse 24, and that in that year Christ Jesus actively took up his Kingdom power and began to rule invisibly to human eyes. In Daniel chapter four, references to a period of "seven times" were the foundation for the calculations leading to that date and, by use of other texts, these "seven times" were translated into a period of 2,520 years beginning in 607 B.C.E. and ending in 1914 C.E. The starting date, 607 B.C.E., was held to be the time of the destruction of Jerusalem by Babylonian conqueror Nebuchadnezzar. I knew that the 607 B.C.E. date seemed to be peculiar to our publications but did not really know why.

Months of research were spent on this one subject of "Chronology" and it resulted in the longest article in the *Aid* publication.[28] Much of the time was spent endeavoring to find some proof, some backing in history, for the 607 B.C.E. date so crucial to our calculations for 1914. Charles Ploeger, a member of the headquarters staff, was at that time serving as a secretary for me and he searched through the libraries of the New York City area for anything that might substantiate that date historically.

We found absolutely nothing in support of 607 B.C.E. All historians pointed to a date twenty years later. Before preparing the *Aid* material on "Archaeology" I had not realized that the number of baked-clay cuneiform tablets found in the Mesopotamian area and dating back to the time of ancient Babylon numbered into the tens of thousands. In all of these there was nothing to indicate that the period of the Neo-Babylonian Empire (in which period Nebuchadnezzar's reign figured) was of the necessary length to fit our 607 B.C.E. date for the destruction of Jerusalem. Everything pointed to a period twenty years shorter than our published chronology claimed.

Cuneiform tablet

---

28   It covered 27 pages (322-348). In its most extensive change, the 1988 revised edition reduced this to about 20 pages, eliminating any acknowledgment of problems regarding 607 B.C.E.

Though I found this disquieting, I wanted to believe that our chronology was right in spite of all the contrary evidence, that such evidence was somehow in error. Thus, in preparing the material for the *Aid* book, much of the time and space was spent in trying to weaken the credibility of the archeological and historical evidence that would make erroneous our 607 B.C. E. date and give a different starting point for our calculations and therefore an ending date different from 1914.

Charles Ploeger and I made a trip to Brown University in Providence, Rhode Island, to interview Professor Abraham Sachs, a specialist in ancient cuneiform texts, particularly those containing astronomical data. We wanted to see if we could obtain any information that would indicate any flaw or weakness whatsoever in the astronomical data presented in many of the texts, data that indicated our 607 B.C.E. date was incorrect. In the end, it became evident that it would have taken a virtual conspiracy on the part of the ancient scribes—with no conceivable motive for doing so—to misrepresent the facts if, indeed, our figure was to be the right one. Again, like an attorney faced with evidence he cannot overcome, my effort was to discredit or weaken confidence in the witnesses from ancient times who presented such evidence, the evidence of historical texts relating to the Neo-Babylonian Empire.[29] In themselves, the arguments I presented were honest ones, but I know that their intent was to uphold a date for which there was no historical support.

So, despite our heightened appreciation of certain principles, the *Aid* book nonetheless contained many examples of our efforts to be loyal to the Society's teachings. In many respects, what we learned through our experience did more for us than it did for the publication. Still, the *Aid to Bible Understanding* book did serve to quicken interest in the Scriptures among many Witnesses. Perhaps its tone, its approach, the effort put forth by most of the writers to avoid dogmatism, to acknowledge that there might be more than one way of seeing certain matters, not to make more of something than the evidence honestly allowed—these things may have been of principal benefit, though in these too we certainly fell short at times, allowing preconceived ideas to control, failing to hold as

---

29   See *Aid to Bible Understanding,* pp. 326-328, 330, 331.

firmly as we should have to the Scriptures themselves. I know this was true in my own case in preparing such subjects as the "Appointed Times of the Nations," "Faithful and Discreet Slave," and "Great Crowd," all of which contain arguments designed to uphold current teachings of the Watch Tower publications. Simply because in my mind those teachings were then equivalent to "fact," I found myself doing what the "Foreword" I later wrote said was not intended. On page 6 under the heading "Its Aim," the words appear, "*Aid to Bible Understanding* is not intended to be a doctrinal commentary or an interpretive work." Also, that whatever application was made of figurative and symbolic expressions, this was not done "arbitrarily or to conform to a creed." In the main, that was true. But ingrained beliefs sometimes overrode our efforts to hold to that standard.

The year the completed *Aid* book was released, I was invited to become a member of the Governing Body of Jehovah's Witnesses, the Body that now directs the activity of Jehovah's Witnesses in some 230 countries of the world. Up to that point it had been composed of seven members who were identical with the seven members of the Board of Directors of the corporation called the Watch Tower Bible and Tract Society, a corporation founded originally in Pennsylvania by Charles Taze Russell, the first president. On October 20, 1971, along with three others, I was appointed as a member of the now expanded Governing Body. This circumstance, perhaps more than any other, brought me face to face with some realities that I had never expected to encounter.

Many of Jehovah's Witnesses took exception to a statement that appeared in a *Time* magazine article (February 22, 1982) in which my name figured prominently. The writers of the article referred to the organization of Jehovah's Witnesses as "secretive." It may seem odd to use a term like that about an organization that encourages vigorously a work of the most public kind—house-to-house activity in cities, towns and countryside around the world. The *Time* reporters evidently wrote what they did because they found it extremely difficult to obtain any comment from the international headquarters about the situation described in the first chapter of this book.

Religion

Witness Under Prosecution

A secretive and apocalyptic sect shuns a former leader

For 40 years Raymond Franz devoted his whole being to the Jehovah's Witnesses. The religion responded by raising him to the very top, as a member of its worldwide Governing Body. But it was a difficult period for the leadership. In 1975 the sect faced a debacle: the present world did not vanish as Witness publications had all but guaranteed. In a faith in which doubt is not tolerated, questions inevitably arose in the minds of some believers. Gradually Franz began to question other teachings, and now, in a downfall as dramatic as an excommunication within the College of Cardinals, he has been ostracized, or as the Witnesses say, "disfellowshipped." The result is that the former leader is being shunned by almost everyone he has ever worked with, cut off from all relatives except his wife, and denied any hope of eternal life.

Officials of the Watch Tower Society, as the religious organization of 2,257,000 followers is formally known, refused all comment on the unprecedented case. But Franz, 59, reluctantly agreed to break his silence and explain to TIME the accusations against him. In doing so, he provides a rare glimpse inside the secretive headquarters of the tightly organized faith.

Franz is a third-generation Witness. His uncle, Frederick W. Franz, 88, has been the religion's top ideologue for decades and, since 1977, its head. Raymond Franz began full-time work for the sect as soon as he finished high school. He suffered penury during 20 years as a missionary in the Caribbean, became a trusted writer of official publications, and joined the 17-member Governing Body in 1971.

Known to outsiders for their persistent door-to-door proselytizing, Jehovah's Witnesses exist within what Franz calls a "hermetically sealed" community; every doctrinal blip or scintilla of sin is closely monitored. Nowhere is this more true than at Bethel, the sect's Brooklyn headquarters. By Franz's account, reading or studying of the Bible is considered "evil" unless conducted in authorized discussions following Watch Tower doctrinal guides, lest staffers veer into error.

Because of his own work as an author of an official volume about the Bible and a growing feeling that Watch Tower discipline was too harsh, Franz privately concluded that the religion emphasized human organization rather than biblical teachings. Says he: "While producing people who were outwardly moral, they subverted the essential qualities of humility, compassion and mercy."

Franz never hinted at his uncertainties as he delivered speeches in 50 nations through the 1970s. But to ease his internal strain, he took a leave of absence from his Bethel duties early in 1980. Meanwhile, the Governing Body had begun a secret investigation of heresy rumors, and it used star-chamber tactics. Initially there were no direct confrontations. Instead, staff members were allegedly threatened with disfellowshipping to get their testimony about doctrinal discussions with others. On May 21, Franz was summoned to Brooklyn for a fateful grilling by his Governing Body colleagues. Did he doubt that Jehovah had only one chosen organization? Did he question the official End-times chronology? Franz sought to avoid confrontation but could "only bend so far." It was not enough. Opponents were unable to get a two-thirds majority for his disfellowshipping on the spot, but he was forced to resign from Bethel. In all, about a dozen officials were purged, almost certainly the worst doctrinal crisis Watch Tower headquarters has ever faced.

But the pursuit of Franz was not over. As a refugee from Bethel and his life's work, he found himself with few marketable skills. A $10,000 settlement from headquarters and $600 in personal savings. He turned to an old friend in the faith, Peter Gregerson of Gadsden, Ala., who runs a regional supermarket chain. Gregerson loaned Franz and his wife a house trailer to live in and gave him work as a handyman. By 1981 Gregerson too had begun to question Watch Tower dogma and resigned from the faith.

Six months later, the official Watch tower newspaper announced that the policy of shunning disfellowshipped Witnesses included shunning those like Gregerson who were "disassociated." Not long afterward, Franz was seen in a restaurant eating a meal with his benefactor Gregerson. That single sighting provided the technical infraction for which Franz was finally disfellowshipped by the Gadsden leaders two months ago. "By one stroke they eliminated all my years of service," says Franz. "I frankly do not believe there is another organization more insistent on 100% conformity."

From the leaders' viewpoint, however, it was obviously imperative to strike at Franz and the others. The dissenters' Luther-like emphasis upon "Scripture alone" rather than official interpretation was only one threat to the foundations of the religion. Many other central Watch Tower doctrines were also at stake.

For one, Witnesses believe that only 144,000 of the faithful (a number taken from *Revelation 14: 1-3*) will be "born again" and go to heaven. The faith's rulers, among whom Raymond Franz was once numbered, come from this elite. The "other sheep" who are loyal to the Watch Tower are promised an earthly paradise. Jehovah will shortly annihilate the rest of the human race. The dissenters reject this class system. They contend that the figure of 144,000 is symbolic and that all believers since Christ's day will go to heaven.

The Witnesses also teach that the Second Coming occurred secretly in 1914, a date reached by complex historical and biblical rationales; the end of the world system must occur during the present generation (an interpretation of *Luke 21: 32*: "This generation will not pass away till all has taken place"). The dissidents have come to believe that Christ's kingdom and the "last days" were inaugurated at about A.D. 33, and that Christ's Second Coming is a future event.

The dissenters, in other words, have moved toward conventional Christianity, except for continuing to reject Christ's divinity. For his part, Franz has not become a bitter Watch Tower antagonist. "There is no life outside the organization" is all he will say about the pain of his shunning. But other ex-Witnesses have launched a barrage of protests, publications and lawsuits. These dissidents contend that roughly 1 million people have left the Watch Tower ranks over the past decade. The Witnesses report that they are still growing, thanks to nonstop recruiting. Still, that success may not go on for long. They have necessarily backed off the 1975 date, but the End must occur during the lifetime of people who still remember the earthly events of 1914. With the rapidly thinning ranks of such oldsters, the Witnesses confront an increasingly troublesome, self-imposed and absolute deadline. *— By Richard N. Ostling. Reported by Anne Constable/Atlanta*

TIME, FEBRUARY 22, 1982

Ex-Jehovah's Witness Raymond Franz
Leaving heaven over one restaurant meal.

66

But the fact is that even among Jehovah's Witnesses very few have any clear idea as to how the central part of the organization functions. They do not know how decisions as to doctrinal teachings are reached, how the Governing Body that directs all their activities worldwide conducts its discussions, whether decisions are consistently unanimous or what is done if there is disagreement.

All this is cloaked in secrecy as the Governing Body meets in closed sessions. I can only recall two or three occasions in the nine years that I was a part of the Body when persons other than appointed members were allowed to be present at a regular session of the Body. And on those occasions their presence was simply to give a report requested by the Governing Body, after which they were dismissed and the Governing Body then carried on its deliberations in private—the importance of their reports did not qualify those persons to share in the discussion. Also, no specific information is ever given to Witnesses as a whole as to the Society's income, expenditures, assets or investments (although they have received a brief expense report in the annual *Yearbook*).[30]

---

30   In 1978 a financial report to the Governing Body itself listed $332 million in assets (properties, deposits and so forth). Even on the Governing Body, few members knew much about the nature of the financial holdings of the Society. Beyond doubt, the present-day assets far exceed this amount.

Thus numerous factors that are relatively common knowledge in many religious organizations are known only vaguely, if at all, by the vast majority of Jehovah's Witnesses. Yet the decisions made by the small group of men forming that Body can, and often do, affect their lives in a most intimate way and are supposed to be applied globally.

Which brings me to the final reason for writing, the most important since without it the previous ones are of little consequence.

OBLIGATION

Whatever you wish that men would do to you, do so to them; for this is the law and the prophets.
— Matthew 7:12, *Revised Standard Version.*

That principle stated by Jesus Christ binds any of us claiming to be Christian, in whatever we do. No honest person can claim to carry out those words perfectly and I make no such claim. But I believe I can say that what is here written owes to a sincere desire to follow that principle.

The apostle Paul spoke of himself as a "debtor" to persons of all kinds.[31] He felt an obligation toward them, and I feel a similar sense of obligation. If someone else had knowledge of facts that could be of value to me in making vital decisions, I would want him to make these available to me—not to make my decision for me, but to supply the information, leaving it to me to weigh its value or significance. If he were a friend, a genuine friend, I believe he would do that.

The nine years spent on the Governing Body had great impact on me and particularly on my conscience. I found myself facing a major crisis in my life, a crossroads situation I had never expected to encounter. The decision I made was my own and the resulting cost was considerable. But I do not regret it nor do I regret having gained the information that contributed toward it. Others might decide differently; some have. That is their privilege, something between them and God.

After I resigned as a member of the Governing Body in May 1980, I received numerous calls from newspapers and magazines wanting

---

31   Romans 1:14.

information about the situation existent within the organization. I consistently directed the inquirers to the headquarters in Brooklyn. The inquirers, in turn, consistently said that they had tried that avenue with no success: "No comment." My reply was simply that I could not be their source of information. I maintained that position for nearly two years. What happened in those two years, not merely as regards myself but as regards others, caused me to reassess that position.

During those two years, the motives, character and conduct of persons who conscientiously disagreed with the organization were portrayed in the worst of terms. Their concern to put God's Word first was represented as the product of ambition, rebellion, pride, as sin against God and Christ. No allowance was made for the possibility that any of them acted out of sincerity, love of truth or integrity to God. No effort to distinguish was made, but all were "lumped" together. Any misconduct or wrong attitude on the part of some who had left the organization was attributed to all who have left. For those who did display a wrong attitude, no effort was made to appreciate the part that frustration, disappointment and hurt may have played in that conduct. An enormous amount of rumor and even gutter-level gossip circulated among Witnesses, internationally. Faithful Christians with high standards of morality were spoken about as being wife swappers, homosexuals, hypocrites, egoists interested in establishing their own personal cult. Older ones were often dismissed as being "mentally disturbed" or "senile."

The only ones who could have restrained such talk, simply by pointing out the possibility that such persons *could* be genuinely sincere, *could* have true concern for conscience—as well as by reminding the sowers of rumor how repugnant false testimony is to God—these persons in reality contributed to the spread of rumor by what they published.[32]

Consider, for example, this material found in the August 15, 1981, *Watchtower* (pages 28, 29), circulated in the millions of copies in many languages around the earth:

---

32   Exodus 20:16; Leviticus 19:16; Psalm 15:3; 1 Peter 2:21-23

¹¹ From time to time, there have arisen from among the ranks of Jehovah's people those who, like the original Satan, have adopted an independent, faultfinding attitude. They do not want to serve "shoulder to shoulder" with the worldwide brotherhood. (Compare Ephesians 2:19-22.) Rather, they present a "stubborn shoulder" to Jehovah's words. (Zech. 7: 11, 12) Reviling the pattern of the "pure language" that Jehovah has so graciously taught his people over the past century, these haughty ones try to draw the "sheep" away from the one international "flock" that Jesus has gathered in the earth. (John 10:7-10, 16) They try to sow doubts and to separate unsuspecting ones from the bounteous "table" of spiritual food spread at the Kingdom Halls of Jehovah's Witnesses, where truly there is 'nothing lacking.' (Ps. 23:1-6) They say that it is sufficient to read the Bible exclusively, either alone or in small groups at home. But, strangely, through such 'Bible reading,' they have reverted right back to the apostate doctrines that commentaries by Christendom's clergy were teaching 100 years ago, and some have even returned to celebrating Christendom's festivals again, such as the Roman Saturnalia of December 25! Jesus and his apostles warned against such lawless ones.—Matt. 24:11-13; Acts 20:28-30; 2 Pet. 2:1, 22.

Thus, in one paragraph, persons are described as *like Satan, independent, faultfinding, stubborn, reviling, haughty, apostate* and *lawless.* What had they actually done to earn this array of charges? Among the "wrongs" mentioned is that of disagreeing in some unspecified way with some unspecified part of the organization's teachings; also, holding that God's inspired Word alone is sufficient and that large meetings in a building are a nonessential.

Could these things *of themselves* place a person in the Satan-like category described? Nothing is said to indicate otherwise and, incredible as it may seem, in the minds of many Witnesses, including elders and traveling representatives, this has been considered enough to so categorize them and to deal with them accordingly.

Compare this blanket condemnation with articles in the June 22, 2000 issue of *Awake!* They warn that "generalizations tend to obscure important facts about the real issues in question, and they are frequently used to demean entire groups of people." A paragraph on page 6 reads:

Name-Calling

Some people insult those who disagree with them by questioning character or motives instead of focusing on the facts. Name-calling slaps a negative, easy-to-remember label onto a person, a group, or an idea. The name-caller hopes that the label will stick. If people reject the person or the idea on the basis of the negative label instead of weighing the evidence for themselves, the name-caller's strategy has worked.

Re-read the *Watchtower* material on the preceding page and compare it with this statement. The thrust of the *Awake!* article is to defend Jehovah's Witnesses against labels such as "sect." Certainly the label of "apostate" is equally or more demeaning. Yet Witnesses are expected to apply it to any member who may disagree with positions taken by the leadership. The practice of "tarring everyone with the same brush" is unfair and therefore unchristian. The reasons why people separate from the Witness organization are many and varied. And the number who do leave on a yearly basis is remarkable.

Tabulating the world reports for the years 1970 through 1999 one finds that a total of 6,587,215 persons were baptized worldwide. The organization customarily estimates that 1% of those associated die each year. Figuring this out year by year, it would mean an estimated 985,734 members were lost through death. If we reduce the baptismal figure by that amount it leaves 5,601,481 as the increase gained in that 30-year period if all surviving persons remained in the organization.

What do we find? The year previous to this 30-year period (1969) the report showed a total of 1,256,784 persons actively associated. Adding 5,601,481 to that number gives a total of 6,858,265 that should be associated in 1999. But the report for that year shows only 5,912,492 associated. That means that during the 30-year period some 945,773 persons left the organization or ceased activity. This is equal to 14% of the total number of new members baptized.

Specific examples from the 1999 world report illustrate graphically the situation currently prevailing in many countries, particularly the industrialized nations.

For the 12 major western European countries and for the British Isles the report provides the following figures:

Baptized in 1999:	21, 376
Average publishers reporting in 1998:	933,043
Average publishers reporting in 1999:	923,143

Although 21,376 new persons were baptized, there was a *decrease* in total publishers of 9,900. That means that over 31,000 persons either left of became "inactive" during that period.

For 3 major Pacific Rim countries (Japan, Korea and Australia) the following figures result:

Baptized in 1999:   12,162
Average publishers reporting in 1998: 325,316
Average publishers reporting in 1999: 325,972

Again, 12,162 entered as newly baptized persons, yet the growth was only 656 persons. Hence, 12,162 entered and 11,506 left or became "inactive."

For the United States and Canada, similar results are seen:

Baptized in 1999:   34,123
Average publishers reporting in 1998: 1,055,950
Average publishers reporting in 1999: 1,051,124

Although 34,123 were baptized, the number of "publishers" *decreased* by 4,826, meaning that 38,949 left or became "inactive" between 1998 and 1999.

If we combine the figures for all these 19 major countries listed, we reach a total of 67,661 baptized, but rather than a growth of equal numbers, the 1999 figures show a decrease of 14,070, meaning that in those 19 major countries 81,731 left or became "inactive."

Since worldwide the 1999 report showed a 2% increase, it is clear that some countries did experience growth. But the "revolving door" situation in the major countries listed is not only notable, it is striking. Particularly since, aside from Japan and Korea, they represent the countries that figure earliest in the history of the Watch Tower Society, the countries of its initial development and growth.

The reasons for persons leaving or ceasing activity are multiple. I have no illusions that all of the nearly one million persons who left the organization during the thirty-year period from 1970 to 1999 did so for reasons of conscience or that every one of them is necessarily a humble, rightly motivated person, more concerned about truth than about self. Many quite evidently are not; some have pursued a course of immorality either before or after leaving; some who left because of disagreement have become guilty of the same wrongs they objected to, expressing vindictiveness, using ridicule, half-truths and exaggerations. Some have even created disturbances at meetings or assemblies of Jehovah's Witnesses, conduct that I find deplorable. But I know personally many, many persons who are not like that, who give every indication of being decent, God-fearing, compassionate persons. If viewed from a selfish standpoint, they had everything to lose and nothing to gain from the stand they took and the course they have followed thereafter.

In many cases it was not some unkind treatment they themselves experienced that disturbed them; it was seeing such treatment meted out to others, seeing people suffer because of the rigidity, narrow-mindedness, even arrogance of men in charge, elders and others, or recognizing the hurtful effects of certain edicts of the organization that did not rest on a solid Scriptural foundation. Rather than disgruntled, vindictive complainers, they have simply pleaded for greater compassion, a closer adherence to the example of God's own Son, the Master of the Christian household of faith.

This *feeling for others* is, I believe, a decisive factor as to the genuineness of motive. Similarly, a concern for truth, a concern not to be guilty of misrepresenting God's own Word, a concern not to be hypocritical in appearing to believe what they do not believe, support what they cannot conscientiously support, condemn what they cannot see that Scripture itself condemns—such concern is, I think, also determinative as to genuineness of motive of any taking such a stand. I know many persons who clearly evidence such concern, yet who are labeled as "apostates," "anti-christs," "instruments of Satan." In case after case after case, the sole basis for such condemnation is that they could not honestly agree with all the organization's teachings or policies.

I feel an obligation toward such persons. In virtually every instance, a small group of three to five men (a "judicial committee") met with them in secret meetings, where those who came as witnesses could only give their testimony but not stay to witness the discussion. Later a brief disfellowshipping announcement was read to the congregation that presented none of the testimony and none of the evidence in support of the disfellowshipping action. After the reading of that announcement no Witness was supposed to talk with the persons disfellowshipped, thereby shutting down any possibility of their expressing themselves by way of an explanation to friends and associates. For them to have done so *before* the disfellowshipping would have been counted as 'proselytizing,' 'undermining the unity of the congregation,' 'sowing dissension,' 'forming a sect.' For anyone to talk to them afterward would jeopardize that person's own standing, make him liable for similar disfellowshipment.

An effective "quarantining" is thus accomplished; a "lid" is placed on any discussion of the matter. The record of the disfellowshipping hearing and any claimed evidence now resides in one of the many voluminous files at the Brooklyn Service Department (or the files of a Branch Office), stamped "Do Not Destroy." This file containing the charges made against them, like their hearing, is also secret, not subject to review.

The Scriptures tell us that, "A true companion is loving all the time, and is a brother that is born for when there is distress."[33] I once thought I had many, many such genuine friends. But when the crisis reached a decisive point I found I had only a few. Still, I count those few precious, whether they said little or much on my behalf. Because of past prominence, people inquire about me. However, almost no one ever inquires about the others who lack such prominence, although they have suffered through the same experience with essentially the same costs and agonies.

What must it mean to a mother, who has seen a baby daughter come forth from her own body, has nursed that baby, cared for it through illness, has trained the young girl through the formative years of life, living her problems with her, feeling her disappointments and sadnesses as if they were her own, shedding tears along with her tears—what must it mean to that mother to have her daughter, now an adult, suddenly reject her, and do so simply because her mother sought to be true to her conscience and to God?

What must it do to a father or mother to see a son or daughter marry and be told, for the same reason, that 'it would be best if they did not

---

33   Proverbs 17:17.

appear at the wedding,' or know that a daughter has given birth to a child and be told that they should not come to see their grandchild?

This is not imagination. Exactly those things are happening to many parents who have been associated with Jehovah's Witnesses.

Consider here just one example, from a mother in Pennsylvania who writes:

> I have children in the organization, married, who at the time of my disassociation even offered for me to come to their home, for a rest, and their opinion of me as a person was not altered. When the information came through later [in the September 15, 1981, *Watchtower* which set forth detailed instructions as to association with any who thus disassociated themselves] I've been shunned by them ever since and they will not talk to me on the phone or have contact with me. I've got to do something about it but I don't know what. I make no move lest it be a wrong move and alienate them further. I don't phone them for fear they'll get an unlisted number, and I don't write, as I said, for fear of saying anything they might construe as offensive. I've been hospitalized during this time for emotional exhaustion and I suffered an additional crisis all within a short time of each event which proved, unfortunately, overwhelming.
>
> Perhaps you share this experience. I do not know how I am going to handle the loss of my children (and future grandchildren). The loss is monumental.

If my past prominence could now contribute in some way to the conscientious stand of such persons being considered with a more open mind and could aid others to revise their attitude toward persons of this kind, I feel that such prominence would thereby have served perhaps the only useful purpose it ever had.

I think here of Paul's words when he says:

> What we are is plain to God, and I hope it is also plain in your conscience. We are not trying to commend ourselves to you again, but are giving you an opportunity to take pride in us, so that you can answer those who take pride in what is seen rather than in what is in the heart.
>
> Make room for us in your hearts. We have wronged no one, we have corrupted no one, we have exploited no one. I do not say this to condemn

you; I have said before that you have such a place in our hearts that we would live or die with you.[34]

If the information presented in this book could help toward one such mother being viewed by her children, not with shame, but with pride for staying by her conscience, all the effort involved would be worth it.

That is basically why this book will present things that I saw, heard and experienced during my nine years on the Governing Body of Jehovah's Witnesses. It is evidently necessary in order to get at the root of what is a heartbreaking problem for many, on both sides of the issue.

What is presented is not intended as some kind of "exposé." While it is true that some things were shocking to me, they are not presented for their shock value. Their presentation is because they illustrate and exemplify very fundamental problems, very serious issues. They demonstrate the extremes to which "loyalty to an organization" can lead, how it is that basically kind, well-intentioned, persons can be led to make decisions and take actions that are both unkind and unjust, even cruel. Names along with times and places will generally be cited because that seems necessary for a credible, factual presentation. I am quite sure that without these many would doubt or deny the factualness of what is said. Where these features seem unnecessary and where they could, by their use, cause needless difficulty for individuals involved, names or other identifying factors will not be stated.

I have sought to be fair in whatever quotations are made, not taking them out of context, not seeking to give them a meaning that is not there. I believe the quotations made are typical of the persons quoted, not something out of character with their usual outlook, approach and personality. Nonetheless, I have kept a few quotations anonymous, because of wishing to avoid unnecessary difficulty for the individual or those closely related to that person. It is, obviously, impossible to do this in all cases or the account would become meaningless. I believe, too, that none of us can expect to receive total exemption from the responsibility indicated by Jesus' statement: "I tell you that men will have to give account on the day of judgment for every careless word they have spoken. For by your words

---

34   2 Corinthians 5:11, 12; 7:2, 3, *NIV.*

you will be acquitted, and by your words you will be condemned."[35] We may seek, and gain, forgiveness for wrong or hurtful things said. But we are still responsible for them.

Some will likely condemn certain information as an 'airing of our dirty linen before the public.' Strangely, these same ones generally do not object to the airing of the 'dirty linen' of other religions and may, in fact, take great interest in it, even publicize it widely. But they feel that what happens within their own religious organization should not be discussed outside its confines.

The hard fact is, however, that within the community of Jehovah's Witnesses today there is simply no possibility for such discussion to take place. Anyone's attempting to do so would be viewed as showing a rebellious spirit and would only result in further disfellowshipping. Since the information cannot be discussed within, and if it is not to be discussed outside the structure, that means that it must be left un-discussed, ignored. Some, of course, would like it to remain that way, but is it right that it should?

It is true that the Christian rightly relies on God to see all things and to be the true and final Judge of all matters. Undeniably, He alone can fully and finally right all wrongs committed. There is never any justification for angry retaliation, spiteful recrimination. There is no room for 'smear tactics.' The Scriptures leave no doubt in that regard.[36] Does this, however, call for maintaining total silence about injustice? Does it require keeping silent when error is propagated in the name of God? Is, perhaps, the discussion thereof evidence of 'disrespect for divinely constituted authority'?[37]

The position of the organization is that no injustice exists. That what has been, and is being, done is in full harmony with the Scriptures, in fact that the Scriptures *require* such action to be taken. If that is so, then there should be no objection to a frank discussion of things. Such discussion

---

35   Matthew 12:36, 37, *NIV*

36   Psalm 37:5-9, 32, 33; Romans 12:17-21; 1 Peter 2:21-23.

37   The August 15, 1982, *Watchtower* in discussing Jude's remarks regarding those "speaking abusively about glorious ones" (verse 8) states that those glorious ones include "appointed Christian overseers" and warns against the "tendency to disregard God-given authority." See also the boxed information on page 29 of that issue.

should actually result in the rightness of the organization's position becoming more evident, should vindicate it of any charge of injustice. Only persons truly responsible for injustice prefer silence and seek to impose it, as has long been the case with dictatorial governments and authoritarian religions in past as well as recent times.

Do Scriptural examples themselves urge against disclosure of wrongs where these involve those in high places of authority? It does not seem so, since the work of the Hebrew prophets frequently focused on such ones, those prophets making known the ways in which Israel's leaders and men in authority, even high priests, had strayed from God's standards with resulting problems. Jehovah's Witnesses have often pointed to such candor and openness as one of the evidences that the Bible is truthful, genuinely God's Book.[38]

What, too, of Jesus' apostles and disciples? It was the very authority structure of God's covenant people—its Sanhedrin, its elders, and the divinely constituted priestly authority—that objected strenuously to the publicizing done by the apostles of the unjust handling of Jesus' case.[39] In both cases, that of the Hebrew prophets and that of the Christian disciples, those publicizing the wrongs did so out of respect for, and in obedience to, a *higher* authority, and in the interests of the people who needed to know.

Obviously, no one today has a divine commission as a prophet or an apostle. But one does not have to be a prophet to take a course that follows the *example* of God's prophets. Otherwise Jesus' words would lose their meaning when, speaking to those who were reproached and about whom every sort of wicked thing was being said, he encouraged them to rejoice, saying, "for in that way they persecuted the prophets before you."[40] It was because they were following a parallel course that those Christians were receiving parallel treatment. One does not have to be an apostle to follow the example of the apostles, nor does he have to be, or pretend to be, a Messiah in order to walk in the footsteps of Jesus Christ.[41]

---

38   See the book *"All Scripture Is Inspired of God and Beneficial,"* published in 1963, page 341.
39   Acts 4:5-23; 5:17-40
40   Matthew 5:11, 12, compare James 5:10, 11.
41   1 Corinthians 11:1; Ephesians 5:1; 1 Peter 2:21.

There is, of course, an enormous difference between the treatment accorded God's Son—as to importance, significance and consequence—and that accorded to the persons involved in this modern-day situation. But it would seem that the principle of open disclosure that God approved in the above examples has force in this present-day situation, gives some indication at least that He is by no means averse to having injustice and misrepresentation uncovered, provided that the motivation is that of helping, of alerting people to realities that can aid them in arriving at right conclusions. The saying that "evil prevails when good men remain silent" seems to have some validity here.

Regardless of the seriousness of the matters here made known, they alone did not lead me to a decision. But they did cause me to ponder more seriously than ever before the meaning of major portions and teachings of the Bible—why the apostle Paul could stress salvation by faith, "not owing to works, in order that no man should have grounds for boasting," what the real difference is between the righteousness produced by law keeping and the righteousness resulting from God's grace or undeserved kindness, the importance of the role of God's Son as Head of the Christian congregation, what the true purpose of the congregation is, the reason for God's granting authority therein and how that authority can be misused. The things that I saw, heard and experienced as a member of the Governing Body of Jehovah's Witnesses, part of the inner executive circle, brought home to me more than ever before the crucial importance of those teachings.

Many others of Jehovah's Witnesses, not having the information I here supply, arrived at the same crossroads and made their own decision, doing so simply on the basis of what they had read in the Scriptures. Others, however, face a serious crisis of conscience and do so with uncertainty, with a sense of confused anguish, even of guilt. My hope is that what is presented in this book may be of help and I feel it is owed to them. It is offered to be applied in whatever way their conscience may lead, as they submit to the guidance of God's spirit and word.

3

GOVERNING BODY

Not that we are the masters over your faith, but we are fellow workers for your joy, for it is by your faith that you are standing. — 2 Corinthians 1:24.

THE above-quoted statement of Paul repeatedly came into my mind during the nine years of my participation in the Governing Body of Jehovah's Witnesses. I could wish that all Witnesses might have the experience of participation. Perhaps then they could understand what words alone cannot convey.

To clarify what the Governing Body is:

Jehovah's Witnesses understand that Christ Jesus, as Head of the congregation, feeds and governs his congregation by means of a "faithful and discreet slave" class. This class is now said to be composed of a remnant of the 144,000 persons anointed as heirs of Christ's heavenly kingdom.[1] But from among such class there is a small number of men who act as a Governing Body and perform all administrative functions for the global congregation, not only for the present number of about 9,100 "anointed ones" out of whom these men are drawn, but also for the approximately 6.1 million other persons associated who are not considered to be among the heavenly heirs.[2]

It seemed an awesome responsibility for me when I became one of eleven members of the worldwide Governing Body in 1971 (the number

---

1   The term "faithful and discreet slave" is drawn from Jesus' parable at Matthew 24:45-47, the number 144,000 is taken from Revelation 7:4 and 14:1, 3.

2   See the January 1, 2004 *Watchtower,* page 21.

later grew to as many as eighteen in 1977 and as of the year 2008 now stands at nine).[3] The first sessions of the weekly meetings (held every Wednesday) that I attended, however, proved quite different from what I had expected.

A rotational chairmanship had recently been put into effect and Vice President Fred Franz was that year's chairman. But the matters to be discussed were determined by the corporation president, Nathan Knorr. Whatever he considered advisable for the Body to discuss he brought to the meeting and generally that was the first time we had any knowledge of the matter under discussion.

During some weeks the meetings consisted simply of a consideration of lists of recommendations for traveling representatives in different countries—the name, age, date of baptism, whether of the "anointed" or not, the years of full-time service being read out. In the vast majority of cases these were no more than names to us; we seldom knew any of the individuals involved. So after listening to such readings of lists from Suriname or Zambia or Sri Lanka, we would vote on the appointment of these men.[4] I recall that Thomas Sullivan (usually called "Bud") was then in his eighties, nearly blind and in poor health. He repeatedly would give in to sleep during these sessions and it seemed a shame to wake him to vote on things

---

3   At that time the eleven members were: Nathan Knorr, Fred Franz, Grant Suiter, Thomas Sullivan, Milton Henschel, Lyman Swingle, John Groh (these seven also being the Directors of the Watch Tower Society), then, William Jackson, Leo Greenlees, George Gangas, Raymond Franz. Of these eleven men, I am the only person surviving at this time in 2008.

4   Some Witnesses doubtless had the idea that appointment of congregational elders is done by the Governing Body itself. Initially, a couple of Governing Body members did sit with a staff member of the Service Department and review and pass on all appointments of elders in the United States. This practice was discontinued after a relatively short time; however, all appointments were thereafter left up to the Service Department staff members. In other countries appointments of elders were from the start handled entirely by the Watch Tower's branch offices. The only appointments made since by the Governing Body, in the U.S. or elsewhere, were those of traveling representatives and of Branch Committee members. I believe this was in order that these men might present themselves as "representatives of the Governing Body" in a special sense, one that carries greater weight and implies greater authority than that of the local elders.

he knew little about. At times the entire meeting lasted but a few minutes; one that I recall lasted only seven minutes (including the opening prayer).

Then from time to time President Knorr would bring some "problem correspondence" involving questions as to certain conduct by individual Witnesses, and the Body was to decide what policy should be adopted regarding these, whether the particular conduct called for disfellowshipping, some lesser discipline, or no action at all. During that period (and on up until 1975) all decisions were expected to be unanimous. After discussion, a motion would be made, seconded, and then the Chairman called for a show of hands. If a unanimous vote was not obtained, as occasionally different ones would not vote for a motion, generally some compromise solution was developed that could gain unanimity.

As is but natural in those circumstances, there was a certain sense of pressure to go along with the majority rather than take a lone stance on matters and thus appear as independent or out of harmony. There were votes where I did not raise my hand, but as a rule I conformed. In the few instances where my not having voted resulted in someone's proposing a compromise motion, even though the compromise motion still did not seem fully right to me I would concede and vote with the majority. It appeared necessary to conform if matters were to be decided and expedited rather than stalemated. However, issues began arising that made this more and more difficult for me.

As weeks went along discussions were held on such subjects as whether a father qualifies as an elder if he allows a son or daughter to marry when only eighteen years of age; whether one qualifies as an elder if he approves of his son or daughter taking higher education;[5] whether one qualifies as an elder if he does shift work and sometimes (while on night shift) misses congregational meetings; whether elders can accept circumstantial evidence of adultery, or the testimony of a wife that her husband confessed adultery to her, and whether this is sufficient to allow for Scriptural divorce and remarriage; whether a divorce is Scripturally acceptable if, even where adultery has been committed, the one obtaining the divorce

---

5   Higher education was, and to some extent still is, generally frowned upon as conducive to loss of faith and as providing an atmosphere likely to contribute to immorality.

is the guilty mate rather than the innocent mate;[6] what validity a divorce has when obtained on grounds other than adultery if, after the divorce is granted, evidence of *pre*-divorce adultery comes to light; what the situation is if such a divorce is obtained and there is *post*-divorce adultery; whether an innocent mate's having sex relations with an adulterous mate (subsequent to learning of the adultery) cancels out the right to divorce that mate and be free to remarry; whether it is proper for a Witness to pay a fine if that fine is imposed because of an infraction of law resulting from his witnessing activity or because of some stand he had taken in order to adhere to Witness beliefs;[7] whether it is proper to send food or other assistance to persons by means of the Red Cross (the main issue here being that the cross is a religious symbol and so the Red Cross organization might be quasi-religious; this discussion was quite lengthy and was carried over to a subsequent meeting); issues about the Society's then-existing practice of using irregular channels to funnel money into certain countries (Indonesia as one example) in a way that would gain greater value for the American dollars involved, doing this even though the particular country had laws ruling this illegal; also as to getting certain equipment into some countries without having to pay the heavy import tax imposed by law; whether Witnesses belonging to labor unions can accept strike duty assignments or can accept a union order to do cleaning work on the union premises in lieu of accepting such assignments as picketing; whether Witnesses could respond to military conscription simply to do work in cotton fields (this from Bolivia).

These are only a partial sampling of things discussed during the first two years or so of my being on the Body. The effect of our decisions was considerable in its impact on the lives of others. In matters of divorce, for example, the congregation elders serve as a sort of religious court and if they are not satisfied as to the validity of a divorce action, the individual

---

6   At that time the ruling was that only if the innocent mate got the divorce was it Scripturally valid.

7   The policy had been that the fine should not be paid, that in these circumstances it would be an admission of guilt and hence a compromise of one's integrity. This policy has changed.

who goes through with such a divorce and then later remarries becomes subject to disfellowshipping.

A matter, not among those just mentioned, but which brought considerable discussion involved a Witness couple in California. Someone had seen in their bedroom certain literature and photographs dealing with unusual sex practices. (I do not recall that we learned just how or why the Witness individual reporting this happened to have access to the couple's bedroom.) Investigation and interrogation by the local elders confirmed that the couple did engage in sexual relations other than simple genital copulation.[8] Correspondence from the elders came in to Brooklyn and the Governing Body was called upon to rule as to what action if any should be taken toward the couple.

Until the correspondence was read to us that morning, none of us aside from the president had had any opportunity to think about the subject. Yet within a couple of hours the decision was reached that the couple was subject to disfellowshipping. This was thereafter set out as a formal published policy, applicable to any persons engaging willfully in similar practices.[9]

The published material was understood and applied in such a way that marriage mates generally felt obliged to report to the elders if any such practice existed or developed in their marriage, whether mutually agreed upon or done solely at the initiation of one of the mates. (In the latter case the non-initiating mate was expected to come forward and convey this information to the elders if the initiating mate was unwilling to do so.) To fail to come forward generally is viewed as indicative of an unrepentant attitude and as weighing in favor of disfellowshipping. The belief that disfellowshipping cuts one off from the one organization where salvation can be found, as well as from friends and relatives, exercises heavy pressure on the person to conform, no matter how difficult confession (or reporting) to the elders may be.

---

8   An article in the December 15, 1969, *Watchtower* (pp. 765, 766) had first focused attention on such sexual relations, discussing them at considerable length, and this doubtless served to sensitize the elders to reports of such conduct, in fact, was likely responsible for this report about people's private bedroom matters being made in the first place.

9   See the *Watchtower,* December 1, 1972, pp. 734-736; also November 15, 1974, pp. 703, 704.

The Governing Body's decision in 1972 resulted in a sizeable number of "judicial hearings" as elders followed up on reports or confessions of the sexual practices involved. Women experienced painful embarrassment in such hearings as they responded to the elders' questions about the intimacies of their marital relations. Many marriages where one of the mates was not a Witness underwent a turbulent period, with the non-Witness mate objecting strenuously to what he or she considered an unwarranted invasion of bedroom privacy. Some marriages broke up with resulting divorce.[10]

An unprecedented volume of mail came in over a period of five years, most of it questioning the Scriptural basis for the Governing Body members inserting themselves into the private lives of others in such a way, and expressing inability to see the validity of the arguments advanced in print to support the stand taken. (The principal portion of Scripture relied upon was Romans, chapter one, verses 24-27, dealing with homosexuality, and those writing to the Society pointed out that they could not see how it could rightly be applied to heterosexual relations between man and wife.) Other letters, often from wives, simply expressed confusion and anguish over their uncertainty as to the properness of their "sexual foreplay."

One woman said she had talked to an elder and he had told her to write to the Governing Body "for a sure answer." So she wrote, saying that she and her husband loved each other deeply and then she described the "certain type of foreplay" they were accustomed to, stating, "I believe it's a matter of conscience, but I am writing you to be sure." Her closing words were:

> I am scared, I am hurt, and I am more worried at this time about [my husband's] feeling for the truth. . . . I know you will tell me what to do.

In another typical letter an elder wrote, saying that he had a problem he wanted to get straightened out in his mind and heart and that to do

---

10   In a memorandum to the Governing Body, dated August 9, 1976, a headquarters staff member handling correspondence states: "Many, many problems have resulted from the position taken, often where there is an unbelieving [meaning a non-Witness] husband. Wives have refused to allow such husbands to stimulate them in this way or to stimulate the husbands in this way. As a result marriages have broken up."

this he felt "it's best to contact the 'mother' for advice."[11] The problem dealt with his marital sex life and he said that he and his wife were confused as to "where to draw the line in the act of foreplay before the actual act of sex." He assured the Society that he and his wife would "follow any advice you give us to the letter."

These letters illustrate the implicit trust these persons had come to place in the Governing Body, the belief that the men forming that Body could tell them where to "draw the line" in even such intimate aspects of their personal lives, and that they should rightly hew to that line "to the letter."

Many letters went out from the Society in response. Often they endeavored to provide some limited clarification (saying without *exactly* saying) as to what sexual foreplay fell within the bounds of condemned actions, other foreplay thereby being exempt.

A memo from a member of the Society's Service Department, in June of 1976, discusses a telephone conversation with an Instructor of seminars (held with elders). The memo relates that the Instructor had phoned about an elder attending the seminar who confessed to certain disapproved sexual practices within his marriage. The memo states:

> Brother [here giving the name of the Instructor] closely discussed the matter with him to determine whether it was really oral copulation that was involved. . . . [The Instructor] had told him in view of the circumstances that he ought to go to the other members of the committee and it happened that the other two members of the committee were in the class and so he went and talked with them. Now [the Instructor] was wondering what else should be done. . . . It was suggested to [him] that he write a full report on this to the Society so that in the future when he has any such case come up he will have direction on how to handle the matter and he will not have to call.

---

11   Many Witnesses refer to the organization as "our mother," and this is because the *Watchtower* magazine has used this term in such way, as in the February 1, 1952, issue, p. 80, and the May 1, 1957, issue, pp. 274, 284; see also the April 1, 1994 *Watchtower*, p. 32.

This illustrates the extent to which interrogation went in intimacy and the extent to which the headquarters organization supervised the whole situation.

Letter after letter revealed that the persons involved felt positively responsible before God to report to the elders any deviance from the norm established by the Governing Body. A man in a Midwestern state who confessed to an infringement of the Governing Body's decision as regards his marital relations with his wife was told by the elders that they were writing about this to the Society; he also wrote an accompanying letter. Eight weeks passed and finally he wrote again to Brooklyn, saying that "the waiting, anxiety and anticipation is almost more than I can bear." He said that he had been removed from all congregational assignments, including offering prayer at the meetings, and that "almost weekly I am losing something that I have worked and prayed for for thirty years." He pleaded for an early answer, saying:

> I do need some mental relief as to how I stand with Jehovah's organization.

Some elders endeavored to take a moderate approach to the matter. Doing so, however, could make them liable for reprimand from the headquarters' offices in Brooklyn. Consider the following letter. It is a photocopy of that sent by the Society's Service Department to one body of elders (names and specific places have been blocked out).[12]

Interestingly, some elders actually felt that the Governing Body's position was, if anything, somewhat lenient or limited. A letter sent by an elder in the United States says:

> Some of the older brothers felt that the Governing Body could have gone even further in condemning unnatural practices among married couples to include assuming certain positions when performing the sexual act. . . .

---

12   This copy is of the carbon copy of the letter and hence bears no stamped Watch Tower signature. The symbol "SCE" identifies the writer of the letter as Merton Campbell of the Brooklyn Service Department.

SCB:SSE   August 4, 1976

Body of Elders of the
W████ Congregation
of Jehovah's Witnesses, M████
c/o ████████████
W████ M████████

Dear Brothers:

    We have a copy of the letter dated July 21 from the committee
of the S████████ Congregation in California in which they write
about matters involving J████████.

    Please let us know if any of the elders in the congregation
have been giving incorrect advice with regard to matters involving
oral sex. If any of the elders in the congregation have advised
married persons that it would not be improper for them to engage
in oral sex, then on what basis was such counsel given? If wrong
counsel was given, then let us know if appropriate steps have been
taken to correct any misunderstanding on the part of individuals
who were given wrong counsel and let us know if the elders concerned now are in agreement with what has been stated in the
Society's publications with regard to oral sex.

    If any of you brothers as elders have been advising in-
dividuals that oral sex would be permissible as foreplay prior
to having actual sex relations, then such advice was not correct.

    Thank you for your attention to the above matter. May
Jehovah's rich blessing go with you as you endeavor always to
care for your responsibilities as elders in an exemplary manner.

                         Your brothers,

cc: Judicial Committee of the
     S████████ Congregation
     of Jehovah's Witnesses, Ca

Later this elder expressed *his own* feelings saying:

Since Jehovah went into great detail in this chapter [18] of Leviticus as
well as other chapters on sexual behavior, why is there no statement made
to married couples as to acceptable or unacceptable forms of copulation?
Would it not be likely that Jehovah would have done so if he wanted
this personal and private area of the marriage union open to the scrutiny
or opinions of the "Judges" or "Older men" of Israel so that appropriate
action could be taken against offending individuals?

Some of those affected by the organization's ruling were persons whose normal sexual functions had been seriously impaired by an operation or by an accident. Some of these expressed dismay at the position in which the Governing Body's decision placed them.

One such person who had become impotent in this way, had, during the years that followed, been able to perform a sexual role through one of the means now condemned by the organization. Before the Governing Body's ruling he said he had been able to stop feeling like half a man, because he could still please his wife. Now, he wrote saying that he could not see the Scriptural proof for the stand taken in the *Watchtower* magazine but that his wife felt duty bound to obey, and because he loved her he acceded. He said he knew that he was the same as before, yet emotionally he was crumbling since he feared their marriage would be seriously affected. He pleaded to be told if there was not some "loophole" in God's will that would allow him the satisfaction of pleasing his wife.

All of these situations put considerable strain on the conscience of elders called upon to deal with those offending against the Governing Body's decision. At the conclusion of the earlier-mentioned letter from one elder, that elder states:

> I find I can only use what Bible laws and principles I understand with any degree of sincerity and conviction in representing Jehovah and Christ Jesus, and if I have to administer these laws and principles in exercising my responsibility as an elder in the congregation I want to do it not because I have come to take for granted that this is Jehovah's organization and I'm going to follow it no matter what it says, but do it because I truly believe it to be scripturally proven and correct. I truly want to continue believing as Paul admonished the Thessalonians in the second chapter, verse 13, to accept the word of God, not as of men, but as it truthfully is, as the word of God.

His position is notable. I frankly doubt that many elders today would feel free to express themselves in this manner, declaring their position in such clear, frank terms.

Though I find the sexual practices involved to be definitely contrary to my personal standards, I can honestly say that I did not favor the disfellowshipping decision made by the Body. *But that is all that I can say.* For when the vote came I conformed to the majority decision. I felt dismayed when the Body assigned me to prepare material in support of the decision, yet I accepted the assignment and wrote it as was desired by the Body, in conformity with its decision. Thus I cannot say that I acted according to the same fine outlook expressed by the elder just quoted. My belief in the organization as God's only agency on earth caused me to do what I did at that time without particularly great qualms of conscience.

The bulk of the correspondence on this subject never reached the Governing Body, being handled by the staff members assigned to "correspondence desks" or by the members of the Service Department. I am sure, however, that the various Governing Body members must have been made aware, likely through personal contacts and conversations, that many felt they had improperly invaded people's private lives.

When finally, after some five years, the matter came up again on the agenda, the disfellowshipping policy was reversed and the Governing Body in effect now withdrew itself from that intimate area of others' lives. Again the Body assigned me to prepare material for publication, this time advising of the change. I found it personally satisfying to be able to acknowledge, even though rather obliquely, that the organization had been in error.

The February 15, 1978, *Watchtower*, pages 30 and 32, carried the material and included the following points:

> A careful further weighing of this matter, however, convinces us that, in view of the absence of clear Scriptural instruction, these are matters for which the married couple themselves must bear the responsibility before God and that these marital intimacies do not come within the province of the congregational elders to attempt to control nor to take disfellowshiping action with such matters as the sole basis.* Of course, if any person chooses to approach an elder for counsel he or she may do so and the elder can consider Scriptural principles with such a one, acting as a shepherd but not attempting to, in effect, "police" the marital life of the one inquiring.

> This should not be taken as a condoning of all the various sexual practices that people engage in, for that is by no means the case. It simply expresses a keen sense of responsibility to let the Scriptures rule and to refrain from taking a dogmatic stand where the evidence does not seem to provide sufficient basis. It also expresses confidence in the desire of Jehovah's people as a whole to do all things as unto him and to reflect his splendid qualities in all their affairs. It expresses a willingness to leave the judgment of such intimate marital matters in the hands of Jehovah God and his Son, who have the wisdom and knowledge of all circumstances necessary to render the right decisions.

Actually, I felt that way about a whole host of matters that came before us, that there was really no basis in Scripture for taking dogmatic stands on the vast majority of things we were ruling on. I expressed that view here and it was accepted by the Body on this point. I expressed that same view again and again in the future but it was rarely accepted.

Looking over the letters at hand, some of which have been presented, whatever satisfaction it brought to write that corrective material seems rather hollow. For I know that no matter what was said, it could never in any way compensate for or repair all the damage in embarrassment, mental confusion, emotional distress, guilt pangs, and broken marriages that resulted from the earlier decision—a decision made in a few hours by men almost all of whom were approaching the matter 'cold,' with no previous knowledge, thought, meditation, specific prayer on the matter or searching of Scriptures, but whose decision was nonetheless put in force globally for five years and affected many people for a lifetime. None of it needed ever to have occurred.[13]

Another issue that arose, somewhat linked to the above, involved a Witness in South America whose husband had confessed to having had sexual relations with another woman. The problem was that he said that the relations were of the kind involved in the issue earlier described, in this particular case anal and not genital copulation.

The decision of the Governing Body was that this did not qualify as adultery; that adultery required strictly genital copulation 'capable of producing children.' Therefore the man had not become "one flesh" with the other woman and hence the decision was *that the wife had no grounds for Scriptural divorce and future remarriage.*

The existing rule of voting required unanimity of decision and I conformed. I felt genuinely disturbed, however, at thinking about this woman and her being told that she could not Scripturally choose to become free from a man guilty of such an act. The decision also meant that a husband who engaged in homosexual acts with other men or who even had relations with a beast was not subject to "Scriptural divorce," since a man could not, with any procreative possibilities, become "one flesh" with another man or with an animal. A *Watchtower* magazine earlier that year had, in fact, specifically ruled this way.[14]

---

13 A few years after my resignation from the Governing Body, the organization in effect reinstated basic elements of its earlier policy on "unnatural sex practices." The March 15, 1983 *Watchtower* (pages 30, 31), while stating that it was not up to elders to "police" the private marital matters of congregation members, nonetheless ruled that the advocacy *or the practice* of what was classed as "unnatural sex relations" among married persons not only would disqualify a man for eldership or other Society-appointed position but "could even lead to expulsion from the congregation." Lloyd Barry had not been present when the 1972 policy had been effectually canceled by a Governing Body decision and upon his return he expressed his disapproval of the cancellation. Since he headed the Writing Department and oversaw the production of *Watchtower* material, his influence may have contributed toward this shifting back to much of the earlier position. Whatever the case, this 1983 material did not produce the great surge of judicial hearings that accompanied the initial announcement of that policy in 1972, perhaps because that earlier experience had produced sufficient bad fruitage to restrain the zeal for inquiry on the part of elders.

14 See the *Watchtower* of January 1, 1972, pp. 31, 32.

The emotional upset I felt moved me to make a study of the original language terms (in Greek) used in Matthew, chapter nineteen, verse 9. The Society's *New World Translation* there presents Jesus as saying:

> I say to you that whoever divorces his wife, except on the ground of fornication, and marries another commits adultery.

Two different words are used, "fornication" and "adultery," yet the *Watchtower* publications for many decades had taken the position that they both referred essentially to the same thing, that the "fornication" meant a man's having adulterous relations with a woman other than his wife (or a wife's having such relations with a man not her husband). Why then, I asked myself, did Matthew, in recording Jesus' statement, use two different words (*porneia* and *moikheia*) if the same thing, adultery, was actually meant in both cases?

Searching through the many translations, Bible dictionaries, commentaries and lexicons in the Bethel library, the reason became obvious. Practically every book I opened showed that the Greek term *porneia* (rendered as "fornication" in the *New World Translation*) was a very broad term and applied to ALL types of sexual immorality and for this reason many Bible translations simply render it as "immorality," "sexual immorality," "unchastity," "unfaithfulness."[15] Lexicons clearly showed that the term was also applied to homosexual relations. The conclusive point to me, however, was realizing that in the Bible itself *porneia* is used at Jude, verse 7, to denote the notorious homosexual conduct of people in Sodom and Gomorrah.

I prepared fourteen pages of material containing the results of the research and made copies for each member of the Body. But I felt very uncertain as to how this would be received and so I went to Fred Franz's office and explained what I had done, expressing my doubt that the material would be favorably accepted. He said, "I don't believe there will be any difficulty." Though very brief, the words were spoken with a tone of

---

15   In the original Greek of Matthew 19:9, the word rendered "adultery" is *moikheia* and, unlike *porneia,* is not broad but very limited in meaning, being restricted to adultery in the ordinary sense of the word.

confidence. When I inquired if he would like to see what had been found, he declined and again said he thought there would be "no problem."

My impression was that he was already aware of some of the points my research had revealed, though for how long I had no way of knowing. Since he had been the principal translator of the Society's *New World Translation* I felt he must surely have at least been apprised of the true sense of the word *porneia* ("fornication").[16]

When the matter came up in the Governing Body session, the material I submitted was accepted, Fred Franz having expressed his support, and I was assigned to prepare articles for publication in the *Watchtower* presenting the changed stand this would bring about.[17]

I still remember, some time after the articles appeared, a letter that came in from a Witness who some years before had discovered her husband having sexual relations with an animal. As she said, "I couldn't live with a man like that," and she divorced him. Later she remarried. The congregation then disfellowshipped her for so doing as she was not "Scripturally free." After the *Watchtower* articles appeared, she now wrote and asked that, in view of the changed position, something be done to clear her name of the reproach she had suffered as a result of the disfellowshipping action. I could only write her that the articles published were themselves a vindication of her course.

Though again it had been satisfying to prepare the material acknowledging the organization's erroneous view and rectifying it, the sobering thought remained that this could never undo whatever harm the previous position had caused over decades of time and—only God knows—to how many people.

The Governing Body at that time was, in reality, both a judicial court and also—because its decisions and definitions had force of law for all

---

16 The *New World Translation* bears no translator's name and is presented as the anonymous work of the "*New World Translation* Committee." Other members of that committee were Nathan Knorr, Albert Schroeder and George Gangas. Fred Franz, however, was the only one with sufficient knowledge of the Bible languages to attempt translation of this kind. He had studied Greek for two years at the University of Cincinnati but was only self-taught in Hebrew.

17 See the *Watchtower* of December 15, 1972, pp. 766-768.

Jehovah's Witnesses—a legislative body. It was a "Governing Body" in the sense that the Sanhedrin of Bible times might be called such, its functions being similar. Just as all major questions involving Jehovah's name people of that period were brought to the Sanhedrin in Jerusalem for settlement, so with the Governing Body of Jehovah's Witnesses in Brooklyn.

But it was *not* an administrative body in any sense of the word. The administrative authority and responsibility rested exclusively with the corporation president, Nathan H. Knorr. I had not expected this because the same year of my appointment Vice President Franz had given a speech, later carried in the December 15, 1971, *Watchtower*, in which he described the role of the Governing Body, contrasting this with that of the corporation, the Watch Tower Bible and Tract Society. The Vice President's language was unusually bold and frank, as he stated again and again that the corporation was simply an "agency," a "temporary instrument" used by the Governing Body (pages 754, 760):

> [29]This worldwide evangelizing organization is not tailored according to any present-day legal corporation that may be required under the laws of man-made political governments that now face destruction in the "war of the great day of God the Almighty" at Har-Magedon. (Rev. 16:14-16) No legal corporation of earth shapes the evangelizing organization or governs it. Rather, it governs such corporations as mere temporary instruments useful in the work of the great Theocrat. Hence it is patterned according to His design for it. It is a theocratic organization, ruled from the divine Top down, and not from the rank and file up. The dedicated, baptized members of it are under Theocracy! Earthly legal corporations will cease when the man-made governments that chartered them perish shortly.

> ──────────

> So the Society's voting members see that this governing body could most directly use that "administrative agency" as an instrument in behalf of the work of the "faithful and discreet slave" class by having members of the governing body on the Board of Directors of the Society. They recognize that the Society is not the administrative body, but is merely an agency for administering matters.

Hence the Society's voting members do not desire that there be any basis for conflict and division. They do not want to cause anything like a situation where the "administrative agency" controls and directs the user of that agency, which user is the governing body as representing the "faithful and discreet slave" class. No more so than to have the tail wag a dog instead of the dog's wagging its tail. A legal religious instrument according to Caesar's law should not attempt to direct and control its creator; rather, the creator of the legal religious instrument should control and direct it.

Because of the simile used, the talk was spoken of by some as the "tail wagging the dog talk." Unquestionably it contained powerful expressions. The problem was that they presented a picture that was completely contrary to fact.

The Governing Body did not control the corporation, not at the time that the aforementioned talk was given by the vice president, nor at the time the material was published, nor for some four years thereafter.

The picture presented eventually did come to be true, but only as the result of a very drastic adjustment, one unpleasantly fraught with heated emotions and considerable division. Strange as it may seem to most Jehovah's Witnesses today, the kind of Governing Body described in that talk had never existed in the whole history of the organization. It took over ninety years for it to come into being and its present existence dates only from January 1, 1976, or about one-fifth of the organization's history. I will explain why I make such a statement and why it is factual.

THREE MONARCHS

You know that in the world, rulers lord it over their subjects,
and their great men make them feel the weight of authority;
but it shall not be so with you.
        — Matthew 20:25, 26, *New English Bible.*

The history of Jehovah's Witnesses becomes one of record particularly with the publication of the first issue of the *Watch Tower* magazine on July 1, 1879. The corporation called the Watch Tower Bible and Tract Society was formed in 1881 and incorporated in 1884. It is certainly true that back there the corporation did not 'shape, govern, control or direct' (to use the words of the vice president) the governing body of those associated with the Watch Tower. It did not, and in fact could not do so, for the simple reason that no "governing body" existed.

Charles Taze Russell personally started the Watch Tower as his own magazine and was its sole editor; during his lifetime all those associated with the Watch Tower Society accepted him as their one and only Pastor. It is true, of course, that the Society, once formed, had a Board of Directors (Russell's wife, Maria, originally being one of these). But that Board was not viewed as a governing body nor did it serve as such. Yet the *Watchtower* of December 15, 1971, pages 760 and 761, had made this statement:

Charles Taze Russell

HOW THE GOVERNING BODY CAME TO EXIST

How did this governing body make its appearance in recent times? Evidently under the direction of Jehovah God and his Son Jesus Christ. According to the facts available, the governing body became associated with the Watch Tower Bible and Tract Society of Pennsylvania. C. T. Russell was patently of that governing body back there in the last quarter of the nineteenth century.

It is difficult for me to understand how Fred Franz could write this as being "according to the facts available" inasmuch as he became affiliated with the Watch Tower organization during Russell's life and knew personally what the reality then was. What do the "facts available" actually show?

Concerning the Board of Directors, Russell himself states in a special edition of *Zion's Watch Tower* dated April 25, 1894, page 59:

> Having, up to Dec. 1, '93, thirty–seven hundred and five (3,705) voting shares, out of a total of sixty–three hundred and eighty–three (6,383) voting shares, Sister Russsell and myself of course elect the officers, and thus *control* the Society; and this was fully understood by the directors from the first. Their usefulness, it was understood, would come to the front in the event of our death. [18]

That Russell clearly did not view the Directors (or any others) as a governing body along with himself is obvious from the course he consistently followed. The *Watch Tower* of March 1, 1923, page 68, says:

> Often when asked by others, Who is that faithful and wise servant?—Brother Russell would reply: "Some say I am; while others say the Society is."

The article then goes on to say:

> Both statements were true; for Brother Russell was in fact the Society in a most absolute sense, in this, that he directed the policy and course of the Society without regard to any other person on earth. He sometimes sought advice of others connected with the Society, listened to their suggestions; and then did according to his own judgment, believing that the Lord would have him thus do.

In answer to a question from some *Watch Tower* readers, C. T. Russell wrote in 1906:

> No, the truths I present, as God's mouthpiece, were not revealed in visions or dreams, nor by God's audible voice, nor all at once, but gradually, especially since 1870, and particularly since 1880. Neither is this clear unfolding of truth due to any human ingenuity or acuteness of perception, but to the simple fact that God's due time has come; and if I did not speak, and no other agent could be found, the very stones would cry out. [19]

18 Mrs. Russell resigned as associate editor of the *Watch Tower* in October 1886, due to disagreement with her husband and on November 9, 1897, she separated from her husband. She remained a Director of the Society, however, until February 12, 1900. In 1906 she obtained a divorce.

19 The *Watch Tower,* July 15, 1906, p. 229.

Believing himself to be "God's mouthpiece" and His agent for revelation of truth, it is understandable why he would see no need for a governing body. The year after this statement, Russell prepared a "Last Will and Testament" which was published in the December 1, 1916 *Watch Tower* magazine following his death in that year. Since nothing illustrates more clearly the total control Charles Russell exercised over the *Watch Tower* magazine, the full text of his Will is presented in Appendix A. We may here note what is said in the second paragraph of this published Will:

> However, in view of the fact that in donating the journal, ZION'S WATCH TOWER, the OLD THEOLOGY QUARTERLY and the copyrights of the MILLENNIAL DAWN SCRIPTURE STUDIES Books and various other booklets, hymn-books, etc., to the WATCH TOWER BIBLE AND TRACT SOCIETY, <u>I did so with the explicit understanding that I should have full control of all the interests of these publications during my life time, and that after my decease they should be conducted according to my wishes.</u> I now herewith set forth the said wishes—my will respecting the same—as follows:

Although he donated the Watch Tower magazine to the corporation (at its incorporation in 1884), he clearly considered it *his* magazine; to be published according to his will even after his death. He directed that, upon his death, an Editorial Committee of five men, personally selected and named by him, should have entire editorial charge of the Watch Tower magazine.[20] He also willed all his corporation voting shares to five women named by him as Trustees, and provided that if any member of the Editorial Committee should be impeached, these women would serve along with the other corporation trustees (evidently the Directors) and the remaining Editorial Committee members in acting as a Board of Judgment to decide the case of the Editorial Committee member accused.[21]

Since one person cannot form a collective body, the facts show that during C. T. Russell's lifetime, that is up until 1916, there was not even a

---

20   Russell did not list Rutherford among these five but placed him in a second group of five who might serve as replacements if occasion required.

21   The book *Jehovah's Witnesses in the Divine Purpose,* published in 1959, p. 64, says that by law Russell's votes died with him.

semblance of a governing body. That continued to be the case during the presidency of his successor, Joseph F. Rutherford. One might assume that the members of the Editorial Committee, along with the Board of Directors, would compose such a governing body. But the facts show that that assumption would be wrong.

At the annual corporation meeting in January 1917, Rutherford was elected to replace Russell as president of the Watch Tower corporation. Early in his presidency, four of the seven Directors (a majority) took issue with what they viewed as arbitrary action on the part of the president. He was not recognizing the Board of Directors and working with it as a body but was acting unilaterally, taking actions and informing them later of what he had decided to do. They did not feel that this was at all in harmony with what Pastor Russell, the "faithful and wise servant," had outlined as the course to follow. Their expressing objection led to their swift elimination.[22]

Joseph F. Rutherford.

Rutherford found that, though they were personal appointees of C. T. Russell as Directors for life, the directorship of these four had never been confirmed at an annual corporation meeting. According to A. H. MacMillan, then a prominent member of the headquarters staff, Rutherford conferred with an outside lawyer who agreed that this allowed for dismissing the men—on a legal basis, that is.[23]

---

22 Typical of this course was Rutherford's decision to publish a book titled *The Finished Mystery*, presented as the 'posthumous work of Russell,' but actually written by Clayton J. Woodworth and George H. Fisher. Rutherford not only had not consulted with the Directors about the writing of the book, they did not even know it was being published until Rutherford released it to the "Bethel Family," the headquarters staff. Later Watch Tower publications, including the book *Jehovah's Witnesses in the Divine Purpose* (pp. 70, 71), give the impression that this was the initiating and primary cause of the objections of the four Directors. This distorts the facts, since Rutherford announced the dismissal of these four men as Directors the same day (July 17, 1917) that he presented the book *The Finished Mystery* to the headquarters staff. The announcement of the dismissal of the Directors was, in fact, made before the book was presented.

23 A. H. MacMillan, *Faith on the March* (Englewood Cliffs: Prentice-Hall, Inc., 1957), p. 80. The Foreword to the book is by N. H. Knorr.

Rutherford thus had an option. He could acknowledge the objections of the majority of the Board and seek to make amends. (If he had viewed these men as the majority of a "Governing Body" of the kind described in the 1971 *Watchtower* he would have been morally bound to do so.) Or, he could avail himself of the legal point mentioned and use his presidential authority to dismiss the Directors who disagreed with him.

He chose the latter course, appointing Directors of his own choice to replace them.

What of the Editorial Committee? *The Watchtower* of June 15, 1938, page 185, shows that in 1925 the majority of this Committee "strenuously opposed" the publication of an article titled "The Birth of The Nation" (meaning "the kingdom had begun to function" in 1914). *The Watchtower* states the result to those who disagreed with the president:

> . . . but, by the Lord's grace, it [the article] was published, and that really marked the beginning of the end of the editorial committee, indicating that the Lord himself is running his organization.

The Editorial Committee was now eliminated. Rutherford had effectively excised any opposition to his full control of the organization.

An interesting feature about all this is that during this entire time, not only *The Finished Mystery* book (a major bone of contention in 1917), but also the *Watch Tower* magazine had been forcefully teaching that Pastor Russell was indeed the "faithful and wise servant" foretold in Scripture, whom the Master would make "ruler over his household."[24] The way in which this teaching was used to insist upon everyone's full conformity is well illustrated in these statements from the *Watch Tower* of May 1, 1922, page 132:

---

24 See *The Finished Mystery,* pp. 4, 11; the Watch Tower, March 1, 1922, pp.72, 73; May 1, 1922, p. 131; March 1, 1923, pp. 67, 68.

FAITHFULNESS IS LOYALTY

To be faithful means to be loyal. To be loyal to the Lord means to be obedient to the Lord. To abandon or repudiate the Lord's chosen instrument means to abandon or repudiate the Lord himself, upon the principle that he who rejects the servant sent by the Master thereby rejects the Master.

There is no one in present truth today who can honestly say that he received a knowledge of the divine plan from any source other than by the ministry of Brother Russell, either directly or indirectly. Through his prophet Ezekiel Jehovah foreshadowed the office of a servant, designating him as one clothed with linen, with a writer's inkhorn by his side, who was delegated to go throughout the city (Christendom) and comfort those that sighed by enlightening their minds relative to God's great plan. Be it noted that this was a favor bestowed not by man, but by the Lord himself. But in keeping with the Lord's arrangement he used a man. The man who filled that office, by the Lord's grace, was Brother Russell.

Again, in the March 1, 1923, *Watch Tower*, pages 68 and 71, in an article titled "Loyalty the Test," conformity to Russell's teachings and methods was equated with conformity to the Lord's will:

> [8]We believe that all who are now rejoicing in present truth will concede that Brother Russell faithfully filled the office of special servant of the Lord; and that he was made ruler over all the Lord's goods.

> [38]Every fellow servant has shown his ability or capacity and has increased the same in proportion as he has joyfully submitted to the Lord's will by working in the harvest field of the Lord *in harmony with the Lord's way*, which way the Lord used Brother Russell to point out, because Brother Russell occupied the office of that "faithful and wise servant." He did the Lord's work according to the Lord's way. If, then, Brother Russell did the work in the Lord's way, any other way of doing it is contrary to the Lord's way and therefore could not be a faithful looking after the interests of the Lord's kingdom.

The issue was quite clear. Either one could loyally line up with and conform to the teachings and way of this 'ruler over the Master's household' (Russell) or he could become guilty of repudiation of Christ Jesus, hence, an apostate. Rarely has appeal to human authority been more strongly stated.

That is what makes it so notable that, within a few years of Russell's death, and during the very time these claims about him were made, the provisions he made in life and his personal selections of men for the office of supervision were set aside by the new president. Russell's expressions contained in his "Will" were discounted as having no legal force and, evidently, no moral force either. The *Watchtower* of December 15, 1931, page 376, says of it:

> 24 The facts which are well known to exist and which apply to the prophetic words of Jesus are these: In 1914 Jehovah placed his King upon his throne. The three and one-half years immediately following afforded the opportunity to test those who had responded to the call to the kingdom, as to whether or not they were selfish or unselfish. In 1916 the president of the Watch Tower Bible and Tract Society died. A paper writing was found which he had signed and which was called his "last will and testament", but which in fact was not a will. It then appeared that Brother Russell, some years before his death, had concluded that he could not make such a will. The work of God's organization is not subject to the control of man or to be controlled by the will of any creature. It was therefore not possible to carry on the work of the Society to the Lord's glory and honor as outlined in that paper writing, called a "will".

Just eight years before, the *Watch Tower*, the "Lord's channel," had insisted that Russell "did the Lord's work according to the Lord's way" and therefore "any other way of doing it is contrary to the Lord's way." Now, eight years later, any who objected to Rutherford's setting aside of the directions given by the one the *Watch Tower* had so adamantly argued was the "faithful and wise servant" were portrayed as motivated by ill will and malice, as workers of iniquity:

> This gathered out or rejected class, however, do weep and wail, and they gnash their teeth against their brethren, because, they say, "Brother Russell's will is being ignored, and *The Watchtower* is not being published as he directed"; and they hold up their hands in holy horror and shed crocodile tears because the Lord's organization on earth is not being used according to the will of a man. In other words, they make these pretenses as a cause for weeping and wailing and sorrow. They wail, complain and weep because they have not charge of the Society. They gnash their teeth against those who are engaged in the Lord's work, and they give expression to all manner of ill will, malice and lying statements against those whom they once claimed to be their brethren. Jude mentions the same class, and his words definitely fix the time when this wailing and weeping begins, to wit, at the time the Lord Jesus Christ comes to the temple of Jehovah for judgment. He says: "These are murmurers, complainers, walking after their own lusts [selfish desires]; and their mouth speaketh great swelling words [claiming themselves to be God's favored ones], having men's persons in admiration because of advantage [in other words, they express their admiration for the person of man and desire admiration for themselves, and their conduct and course of action exactly fit the words of the apostle]." They make great pretense of love and devotion to a man, namely Brother Russell, but it is manifest they do so with a view of gaining some selfish advantage. The purpose, therefore, of mentioning these matters, and manifestly the purpose of the Lord in permitting his people to understand them, is that they might avoid such workers of iniquity.

It is difficult to explain such fickle, unstable, erratic course. Yet this was supposedly the channel the Lord Jesus Christ had found so worthy of being made his sole means of direction to people on earth.

In actuality, by 1925 J. F. Rutherford exercised unquestioned direction of the Society and the years that followed only strengthened his control over all organization functions.[25]

This included full control of what would be published through the channel of the *Watch Tower* and other publications used to provide spiritual food for the congregations earthwide. I recall my uncle's telling me one day in his office of an occasion when Rutherford presented a certain issue, a new viewpoint, to the Bethel Family for discussion.[26] My uncle related that in the discussion he expressed himself negatively about the new view being advanced, doing so on the basis of Scripture. Afterward, he said, President Rutherford personally assigned him to prepare material *in support of* this new view, although he, Fred Franz, had made clear that he did not consider it Scriptural.

On another occasion he related that the "Judge" (Rutherford) later in his presidency made it a firm policy that the *Watch Tower* magazine would carry only articles that stressed prophecy or the preaching work. For that reason a period of years passed in which articles on subjects such as love, kindness, mercy, longsuffering and similar qualities simply did not appear in the magazine.

Thus, during the nearly sixty-year period of the presidencies of Russell and Rutherford, each man acted according to his own prerogative in exercising his presidential authority, with no hint of a governing body.

In 1993 the organization produced a new history book, titled *Jehovah's Witnesses—Proclaimers of God's Kingdom*, replacing a previous work titled *Jehovah's Witnesses in the Divine Purpose*. It seems evident that at various points the book seeks to counter the effect

---

25 A. H. MacMillan in *Faith on the March*, p.152, says: "Russell had left it much to the individual as to how we were to fulfill our responsibilities . . . Rutherford wanted to unify the preaching work and, instead of having each individual give his own opinion and tell what he thought was right and do what was in his own mind, gradually Rutherford himself began to be the main spokesman for the organization. That was the way he thought the message could best be given without contradiction."

26 The point at issue was either the new view that the "higher powers" of Romans 13:1 were not the governmental authorities of earth but were Jehovah God and Jesus Christ, or the decision regarding the elimination of bodies of elders, which of the two I do not now recall.

of information that has appeared in published form in recent years, including the original 1983 printing of this book, *Crisis of Conscience*, the 1991 printing of its sequel, *In Search of Christian Freedom*, and in Carl Olof Jonsson's book *The Gentile Times Reconsidered* (which first appeared in 1983.) Certain facts are admitted for the first time in this new history book, perhaps with a view to muting the effect if members were to become aware of them through other sources. At its start the book's editors assure readers of their endeavor "to be objective and to provide a candid history."[27]

The vast majority of Jehovah's Witnesses have no access to the records of the past and no personal knowledge of the events relating to the organization's development. The operations of the central authority structure or of the men forming that inner authority structure are likewise unknown to them. They are thus essentially at the mercy of the editors of this 1993 publication's supposedly impartial, "candid history."

I have seldom read a more "sanitized" less "objective" presentation. Its depiction of organizational history and policy paints a picture that differs measurably from reality. This is the case in its discussion of the presidencies of both Russell and Rutherford.

With regard to the identification of the "faithful and wise servant" of Matthew 24:45-47, this book finally acknowledges (on pages 142, 143, 626) that, "for a number of years" the *Watch Tower* magazine did indeed set forth the view that Charles Taze Russell was that chosen "faithful and wise servant," and that, from 1896 on, Russell himself acknowledged "the apparent reasonableness" of this view. It does not acknowledge the fact that Russell not only viewed as "reasonable" the application to an individual (himself) as the specially chosen "faithful and wise servant" but that (in the very *Watch Towers* the book lists in its footnote) he actually *argued*

---

27   See the "Foreword" to the book *Jehovah's Witnesses—Proclaimers of God's Kingdom*. As but one illustration of presenting information already made available by another source, this book, on page 200, presents a picture of the Brooklyn headquarters staff celebrating Christmas in 1926. That photo was published in 1991 in the book *In Search of Christian Freedom*, page 149, which has been inserted into Appendix B of this 2018 edition of *Crisis of Conscience*. Two years later the new history book presented it for the first time in a Watch Tower publication. Yet that photo had been in their possession for 67 years.

for it as the true Scriptural application, rather than the position he had taken back in 1881. Rather than acknowledge this, the new history book misleadingly continues to place emphasis on Russell's 1881 statement in which he applied the figure to the entire "body of Christ."

The book does not inform its readers that in the October 1, 1909 issue of the *Watch Tower* Russell described as his "opponents" those who would apply the term "faithful and wise servant" to "all the members of the church of Christ" rather than to an individual. Nor does it tell its readers that the special issue of the *Watch Tower* of October 16, 1916 stated that, while not openly claiming the title, Russell "admitted as much in private conversation."

And while acknowledging finally that for years after his death the *Watch Tower* magazine itself promoted the view of Russell as "that servant," the book gives the reader no idea of the *insistence* with which this was done, as in stating that everyone having a knowledge of God's divine plan must truthfully admit that "he derived that knowledge from studying the Bible in connection with what Brother Russell wrote; that before such time he did not even know that God had a plan of salvation"; or in describing those questioning any of Russell's teaching as having "rejected the Lord" because of rejecting his special servant.[28]

Likewise it does not explain the paradox created by the Watch Tower's own teaching: on the one hand, the present-day teaching that in 1919 Christ Jesus definitely selected, approved and identified a "faithful and wise servant *class*," and, on the other hand, the fact that in that very same year of 1919 and for years thereafter the very ones supposedly so chosen believed the "faithful and wise servant" was *not a class* but an *individual,* Charles Taze Russell, selected many decades before 1914 by a reigning Christ who had become "present" since 1874.

Effort is made (on pages 220, 221 of the Watch Tower's new history book) to deny that the second president, Joseph F. Rutherford, sought

---

28   See Chapter 8 of this book, under the section *Millions Now Living Will Never Die;* also pages 78-84 of *In Search of Christian Freedom,* which has been inserted into Appendix B of this 2018 edition of *Crisis of Conscience.*

to gain full and total control of the organization. A quotation from Karl Klein is presented to show him as actually an essentially humble man, 'childlike in prayer to God.'

Yet the historical record demonstrates that anyone, including any member of the Board of Directors or of those on the Editorial Committee, who expressed disagreement with Rutherford was quickly eliminated from whatever organizational position that person occupied. One has only to talk with others who were at the headquarters during his presidency to know that the picture of humility conveyed by Karl Klein does not conform to the reality, and that, to all intents and purposes, the "Judge's" word was law.

I was actively associated with the organization during the last five years of his presidency and know the clear effect the man had upon me and the viewpoint that others expressed. Most Witnesses today have not had that experience. But God's Son said that 'out of the heart the mouth speaks,' and that 'by your words you will be justified or judged.' (Matthew 12:34, 37) I believe that anyone who simply reads the material found in the *Watch Tower* magazine from the 1920s on through to 1942 can clearly see the spirit, not of humility, but of dogmatism and authoritarianism the articles breathed, articles admittedly written principally by Rutherford. Deprecating, even harsh language is employed against any who dared to question any position; policy or teaching that came forth from the organization of which he was the head.

On these same pages of the book *Jehovah's Witnesses—Proclaimers of God's Kingdom*, effort is made to demonstrate that Rutherford was not looked upon by the membership as "their leader" and his personal denial of such position, made in 1941 just before his death, is quoted as proof. The caption beneath the photo shown on the next page was placed there by the writer or writers of the Watch Tower's history book. The words are there but the facts are not.

While admittedly Watch Tower adherents viewed Christ as their *invisible* leader, the fact is that they *did* look upon Rutherford as their *visible* earthly leader, contrary to Christ's injunction at Matthew 23:10: "Neither be called leaders, for your Leader is one, the Christ." Rutherford cannot fail to have *known* that the membership viewed him in that light.

Consider the following photos and captions from *The Messenger*, a Watch Tower convention report, of July 25, 1931, describing large conventions held that year in major European cities. The captions shown underneath are the original captions found in *The Messenger*. Compare them with the caption the writer or writers of the Society's history book placed beneath that book's photo of J. F. Rutherford, shown here to the right, claiming that "the Witnesses knew that he was not their leader."

J. F. Rutherford in 1941. The Witnesses knew that he was not their leader

The first photo in *The Messenger*, of a 1931 convention in Paris, in its caption underneath describes Rutherford *explicitly* as "Their Visible Leader."

The International European Conventions
Planned by Brother Rutherford for the Convenience of Our Brethren Across the Atlantic Who Could Not Come to Columbus

Their Visible Leader—About to Give Instructions to the Paris Division of "Une Grande Armee."

In the next two, from London and from Magdeburg (Germany), the captions refer to Rutherford as "The Chief."

The Bethel Family at London. See 'em Grinning? The Chief Had Just Finished Telling Them Something in the "Colored Language."

The Chief Inspects the Cleaning of "Kopf Salat", Just Gathered from the Garden. It Takes Only Four Bushels for a Meal!

President of the Watch Tower Bible and Tract Society and Generalissimo of the Convention.

A fourth designates him "Generalissimo of the convention."

This convention report was printed *ten years before* Rutherford's 1941 statement quoted in the Watch Tower's new history book. There is no reason to believe that Rutherford was not aware of the way he was actually viewed by Watch Tower adherents throughout most of his presidency and he clearly did nothing to change that image. The evidence, including the whole history of his administration, makes his disavowal of that image—made when nearing death—seem hollow.

When Judge Rutherford died on January 8, 1942, Nathan H. Knorr was unanimously elected president by the

Board of Directors. The organizational structure continued basically the same, though with some adjustments, as Knorr did field out some responsibility. (Circumstances actually made this a necessity, for the number of Witnesses grew from only 108,000 at the time of Rutherford's death to more than two million during Knorr's presidency.)

Not a writer, nor particularly a student of Scripture, Knorr relied on Fred Franz (the vice president) as more or less the final arbiter on Scriptural matters and the principal writer of the organization. Questions such as those discussed at Governing Body sessions (related earlier in this chapter) were, for decades, submitted to Fred Franz for decision. If President Knorr felt that the decision might have some critical effect on the Society's operation in certain countries of the world, he would usually discuss it personally with Fred Franz and would not hesitate to make known what he felt the circumstances made advisable in a pragmatic way, overruling the vice president if necessary. As has been noted earlier, this basic relationship continued up into the 1970s as illustrated in the decision to return to having bodies of elders in the congregations. That particular decision hinged largely upon the view and opinion of one person, the vice president, and when he changed his mind and favored the return to bodies of elders, the president acceded.

The same was basically the case with all published material. The president selected the main articles for the *Watchtower* from material submitted by various writers and he then passed these on to the Writing Department for proofreading and any necessary editing or polishing. Then these were finally read by the vice president and the president and, if approved, were published. Karl Adams, who was in charge of the Writing Department when I entered it in 1965, explained to me that the president by then had given the department considerable latitude as to the reworking of such material. He pointed out the one exception, namely, any material written by the vice president, stating that "what comes from Brother Franz is viewed as 'ready for publication,' with no adjustments to be made."

Here again, nonetheless, the president himself could overrule. As an example, in 1967, President Knorr sent to Karl Adams, Ed Dunlap and myself, copies of a "Questions from Readers" that Fred Franz had prepared and turned in for publication.[29] Just the year before, a book had been published, authored by Fred Franz, in which it was pointed out that the year 1975 would mark the end of 6,000 years of human history. Likening those 6,000 years to six days of a thousand years each, he had written:

> So in not many years within our own generation we are reaching what Jehovah God could view as the seventh day of man's existence.
>
> [43] How appropriate it would be for Jehovah God to make of this coming seventh period of a thousand years a sabbath period of rest and release, a great Jubilee sabbath for the proclaiming of liberty throughout the earth to all its inhabitants! This would be most timely for mankind. It would also be most fitting on God's part, for, remember, mankind has yet ahead of it what the last book of the Holy Bible speaks of as the reign of Jesus Christ over earth for a thousand years, the millennial reign of Christ. Prophetically Jesus Christ, when on earth nineteen centuries ago, said concerning himself: "For Lord of the sabbath is what the Son of man is." (Matthew 12:8) It would not be by mere chance or accident but would be according to the loving purpose of Jehovah God for the reign of Jesus Christ, the "Lord of the sabbath," to run parallel with the seventh millennium of man's existence.[30]

Not for many decades had there been such a sense of excitement among Jehovah's Witnesses as these statements generated. A tremendous surge of expectation developed, far surpassing the feeling of the end's nearness that I and others had experienced in the early 1940s.

That is why we were amazed to see that the "Question from Readers" Fred Franz had worked up now argued that the end of 6,000 years would actually come *one year earlier* than had just been published in the new book, namely that it would come in 1974 instead of 1975. As Knorr told Karl Adams, when he received this material he went to Fred Franz and

---

29   Of the three receiving copies, at the time I was the only one professing to be of the "anointed" class, having made such profession since 1946.

30   *Life Everlasting in Freedom of the Sons of God,* published in 1966, pp. 29, 30.

asked why the sudden change. Franz replied with definiteness, "This is the way it is. *It's 1974.*"

Knorr did not feel at ease with the change and that is why he sent the three of us copies with his request that we submit our individual observations. The vice president's argumentation was built almost entirely upon the use of a cardinal and an ordinal number in the account of the Flood at Genesis, chapter seven, verses 6 and 11 ("six hundred years" and the "six hundred*th* year"). The argument endeavored to show that the count of time set out in the new book was off one year as to the time of the Flood and that one more year needed to be added, with the result that the end of 6,000 years would come up one year earlier, in 1974 instead of 1975.

Each of the three of us respectfully wrote that we did not think the material should be published, that it would have an extremely unsettling effect on the brothers.[31] The president evidently agreed, since the material prepared by the vice president was never published and this was quite a rare occurrence.

It was during Knorr's presidency that the term "governing body" first began to be used with a measure of frequency.[32] The literature now began to tie such a body in with the Board of Directors of the Watch Tower Society. In the Society's book, *Qualified to Be Ministers,* published in 1955, page 381, the statement appears:

> During the years since the Lord came to his temple the visible governing body has been closely identified with the board of directors of this corporation.

Thus the seven members of the Board of Directors were considered to be the seven members of the "governing body." The fact is, however,

---

31 In the letter I submitted, I pointed out that the argument rested heavily on a portion of Scripture that is difficult to be definite about, and that the reasons given for the change were, at best, tenuous.

32 In the *Watchtower* of June 1, 1938, p. 168, in an article on "Organization" the expressions "central body" and "central authority" are used but only with reference to the body of apostles and those who were their immediate associates, with no modern application made. The term "governing body" first appears in its current usage in the *Watchtower,* October 15, 1944, page 315, and November 1, 1944, pages 328-333.

that their situation was much as had been the case with the Directors in Russell's and Rutherford's day.

Marley Cole, a Witness who wrote a book (with the full cooperation of the Society) entitled *Jehovah's Witnesses—The New World Society,* points this out.[33] In a section headed "Internal Rebellion," he first describes the controversy in 1917 between Rutherford and the Board, saying:

> Four directors wanted a reorganization. . . . As things stood the president was the administration. He was not consulting them. He was letting them know what he was doing only after it was done. He was putting them in the position of advisers on legal corporate matters.
>
> Rutherford made no bones about 'going ahead.' The Pastor before him had worked that way. The Pastor made decisions. The Pastor issued administrative orders without the Board's prior sanction.

Then, in a footnote, Cole states:

> That the president of the Society thereafter continued to exercise such unrestricted freedom may be seen by the following account of N. H. Knorr's actions in relation to bringing forth a new Bible translation.[34]

The *Watchtower* of September 15, 1950, pages 315 and 316, is then quoted. It reveals that the Directors of the Board were first informed by the president of the existence of the *New World Translation* (probably one of the biggest projects ever engaged in by the organization) only after the translation of the Greek Scripture portion had already been completed and was ready for printing.

Right up until 1971 when the "tail wagging the dog talk" was given, the Board of Directors did not meet on any regular schedule but only as the president decided to convene them. Sometimes months went by

---

33   Marley Cole, *Jehovah's Witnesses—The New World Society* (New York: Vantage Press, 1955). pp. 86-89. Cole wrote the book as if he were a non-Witness writing an objective account. The idea was that by having the book published by an outside publishing firm it might reach persons who normally would not take Society literature. Thus it was a form of public relations tactic.

34   Ibid., p.88.

without any meetings, the most frequent agenda evidently being such corporate matters as the purchase of property or of new equipment. As a rule, they had nothing to say about what Scriptural material would be published, nor was their approval sought.

Vice President Franz made this clear when testifying before a court in Scotland in 1954 in a case known as the Walsh Case. Questioned as to what was done if some major change in doctrine was made and whether such had to be first approved by the Board of Directors, the vice president replied (the material here being reprinted from the official court transcript with "Q" representing the question of the counselor and "A" the response given by Fred Franz):

> **Q.** In matters spiritual has each member of the Board of Directors an equally valid voice? **A.** The president is the mouthpiece. He pronounces the speeches that show advancement of the understanding of the Scriptures. Then he may appoint other members of the headquarters temporarily to give other speeches that set forth any part of the Bible upon which further light has been thrown. **Q.** Tell me; are these advances, as you put it, voted upon by the Directors? **A.** No. **Q.** How do they become pronouncements? **A.** They go through the editorial committee, and I give my O.K. after Scriptural examination. Then I pass them on to President Knorr, and President Knorr has the final O.K. **Q.** Does it not go before the Board of Directors at all? **A.** No.[35]

I personally knew that presentation of matters to be true as regards the Board of Directors. Before 1971, I was in a meeting with several Writing Staff members called by Karl Adams, and the question arose as to how to get the president's approval of certain proposed improvements in the *Watchtower* magazine. Someone suggested that Lyman Swingle, who was present as one of the writers, broach the matter to Knorr. Swingle's reply

---

35   Although the vice president makes reference to an "editorial committee" he later identifies only himself and President Knorr as on that committee from among the Board members. In actuality there was no official "editorial committee" aside from these two. In 1965 Karl Adams was the only other one whose signature was regularly required on material to be published and he was not on the Board of Directors nor does he profess to be of the "anointed" class.

was brief but spoke volumes as to the reality of the situation. He said: "Why me? What can I do? I'm only a Director."

Not only do the statements by the vice president at the Scotland trial bear on the issue of the existence of a genuine "governing body" at that time, they also show how fictitious the claim is that the "spiritual food" provided proceeds from a "faithful and discreet slave *class*." Two, or at best, three men determined what information would appear in the *Watchtower* magazine and other publications—Nathan Knorr, Fred Franz and Karl Adams, the last of these not of the so-called "anointed class." As the vice president's statements clearly show, not even the members of the Board of Directors, all supposedly members of the "faithful and discreet slave class," were invited to express approval of the "spiritual food" to be presented.

Thus, even as Russell up until the year 1916 exercised full and unique control over what was published by the Watch Tower Society, and just as Rutherford did so throughout his presidency until 1942, similarly during Knorr's presidency the exercise of authority as to the preparation and serving up of the "spiritual food" for the Witness community was limited to two or three men, not something carried out by a "class" of persons, supposedly assigned by Christ to be "over all his belongings."[36]

The situation remained the same even after the enlargement of the Governing Body to include more than the seven Directors. In 1975 during one session some material the vice president had prepared for use as a convention talk came up for discussion. It dealt with the parable of the mustard seed and the parable of the leaven (found in Matthew chapter 13) and argued in detail that the "kingdom of the heavens" Jesus referred to in these parables was actually a "fake" kingdom, a counterfeit. One member of the Body who had read the material felt unconvinced by the argumentation.

After discussion, of the fourteen members present only five (including Knorr and Fred Franz) voted in favor of using the material as a convention talk, the other nine did not. So it was not used—as a talk—but the material appeared in a book released at the convention and within a few

---

36   Matthew 24:47.

months also appeared in the *Watchtower* magazine.[37] The fact that nearly two-thirds of the Body members present had expressed at least some lack of confidence in the material did not affect the president's decision to go ahead with publishing it.

Not only the contents of the magazines and other literature, but every other feature of the worldwide activity of Jehovah's Witnesses —the direction of the 90 or more Branch Offices (each Overseer of a Branch being described as the "presiding minister of Christianity for and within the territory to which he has been appointed"), the supervision of all the work of all traveling representatives, the direction of the missionary School of Gilead and the assignment and work of all missionaries, the planning of conventions and convention programs—all this and much more ultimately were the sole prerogative of one person: the president of the corporation. Whatever the Governing Body discussed or did not discuss in any of these areas was strictly as the result of his decision and at his discretion.

All this was difficult to reconcile with the articles published after the vice president's "tail wagging the dog talk." The language there had been so forceful, so conclusive:

> (Acts 20:28) Thus, too, even though there were no apostles of Christ on hand in the nineteenth century, God's holy spirit must have been operative toward the formation of the governing body for his anointed remnant of the "faithful and discreet slave" class. The facts speak for themselves. There came on the scene a body of anointed Christians who accepted and undertook the responsibilities of governing the affairs of Jehovah's dedicated, baptized, anointed people who were following in the footsteps of Jesus Christ and endeavoring to fulfill the work stated in Jesus' prophecy at Matthew 24:45-47.

---

37 See the book *Man's Salvation Out of World Distress At Hand!,* published in 1975, pp. 206-215; also the *Watchtower,* October 1, 1975, pp. 589-608.

> Facts speak louder than words. The gov-
> erning body is there. Thankfully Jehovah's
> Christian witnesses know and assert that
> this is no one-man religious organization,
> but that it has a governing body of spirit-
> anointed Christians. [38]

Unfortunately the picture presented simply was not true. The facts *do* "speak for themselves," and the facts, already presented from the Watch Tower Society's own approved publications and from statements of Directors, clearly show there was no governing body in any factual sense in the nineteenth century during Russell's presidency, none in the twentieth century during Rutherford's presidency, and there had been none in the sense described in this same *Watchtower* article during Knorr's presidency.

It was an impressive-sounding picture presented but it was illusory, fictional. The fact is that a monarchical arrangement prevailed from the very inception of the organization (the word "monarch" being of Greek origin and meaning "one who governs alone," also defined in dictionaries as "one holding preeminent position and power"). That the first president was benign, the next stern and autocratic, and the third very businesslike, in no way alters the fact that each of the three presidents exercised monarchical authority.

The great majority of Witnesses forming what the 1971 *Watchtower* article had referred to as the "rank and file"—and including most of the "anointed" composing the "faithful and discreet slave class"—were totally unaware of this. Those in positions close enough to the seat of authority knew it to be the case; the closer they were the more they were aware of the facts.

This was particularly true of the members of the Governing Body and in 1975 the "dog" decided it was time to "wag the tail." Most of the members felt that it was time that the facts finally started matching the words being spoken and published.

---

38   The *Watchtower,* December 15, 1971, p. 761.

Interestingly, what was done was essentially *the same as what the four Directors in 1917 had proposed,* a reorganization, an effort on their part that had consistently been described thereafter in the Watch Tower publications as an 'ambitious plot' and 'a rebellious conspiracy,' one that, 'by God's grace, did not succeed!' Fifty-five years later basically the same proposition did succeed, but only after months of turmoil for the Governing Body.

4

INTERNAL UPHEAVAL
AND RESTRUCTURE

*So never make mere men a cause for pride. There is nothing
to boast about in anything human.*
— 1 Corinthians 3:21. *New English Bible and Jerusalem Bible.*

THE information the book *Aid to Bible Understanding* presented
about elders doubtless began the process. Till then congregations
had been under the supervision of a single person, the "Congregation
Overseer." His replacement by a body of elders of necessity raised questions about Branch organizations where one man was the "Overseer" for
a whole country, much as a bishop or archbishop has under his supervision a large region composed of many congregations. And the central
headquarters had its president, to whom I had personally referred (in
addressing a seminar for Branch Overseers in Brooklyn) as "the Presiding
Overseer for all congregations earthwide."[1]

Evidently the apparent anomaly, the contrast between the situation
in the congregations and that at the international headquarters is what
led to the "tail wagging the dog" talk and *Watchtower* articles, since these
endeavored to explain away the difference existing between the situation
in the congregations and that at the central headquarters. It is almost certain that at the same time these articles were meant to send out a signal
to voting members of the corporation that they should not try to express

---

1   President Knorr was sitting on the platform at the time and expressed no disagreement with
     the description.

themselves through vote to effect some change in the headquarters structure or to express themselves as regards the membership of the Governing Body and its administration.

The year of that talk, 1971, President Knorr decided to allow the Governing Body to review and pass judgment on a book entitled *Organization for Kingdom-Preaching and Disciple-Making*, a form of church manual setting out organizational structure and policy governing the entire arrangement, from the headquarters through to the branches, districts and circuits, and on to the congregations. The Governing Body was not asked to supply the material for the book. The president had assigned the project of the book's development to Karl Adams, the overseer of the Writing Department (not a Governing Body member nor one professing to be of the "anointed"). He in turn had assigned Ed Dunlap and myself to collaborate with him in the manual's development, each of us writing about one-third of the material.[2]

The material we developed presented the relationship of the Governing Body and the corporations in harmony with the *Watchtower* articles stressing that the "dog should wag the tail" and not vice versa. When certain points relating to this came before the Body, they provoked rather heated discussion. President Knorr expressed himself clearly as feeling that there was an effort to "take over" his responsibility and work. He stressed that the Governing Body was to concern itself strictly with the "spiritual matters" and that the corporation would handle the rest. But, as the Body members knew, the "spiritual matters" allotted to them at that stage consisted almost entirely of the near ritual of approving appointments of largely unknown persons to traveling overseer work and the handling of the constant flow of questions about "disfellowshipping matters."

---

2   I was assigned chapters on "Your Service to God," 'Safeguarding the Cleanness of the Congregation," and "Endurance That Results in Divine Approval."

Governing Body members in 1975. **First row:** *Ewart Chitty, Fred Franz, Nathan Knorr, George Gangas, John Booth, Charles Fekel.* **Second row:** *Dan Sydlik, Raymond Franz, Lloyd Barry, William Jackson, Grant Suiter, Leo Greenlees.* **Back row:** *Theodore Jaracz, Lyman Swingle, Milton Henschel, Karl Klein, Albert Schroeder.*

At certain points in the discussion I expressed my understanding that other matters of a spiritual nature were likewise the responsibility of the Body. (I could not personally harmonize the existing monarchical arrangement with Jesus' statement that "all you are brothers" and "your Leader is one, the Christ"; that "the rulers of the nations lord it over them and the great men wield authority over them," but "this is not the way among you."[3] It simply did not seem honest to say what had been said in the 1971 *Watchtower* articles and then not carry it out.)

In each case of my doing so, however, the president took the remarks very personally, speaking at great length, his voice tense and forceful, saying that 'evidently some were not satisfied with the way he was handling his job.' He would go into great detail as to the work he was performing and then would say, "now apparently some don't want me to handle things anymore" and that perhaps he should "bring it all down here and turn it over to Ray Franz and let him handle it."

---

3   Matthew 23:8, 10; 20:25, 26.

I found it hard to believe that he could so totally miss the essential point of my comments, that I was expressing myself in favor of a *body* arrangement, not in favor of a transferal of authority from one individual administrator to another individual administrator. Each time I would explain this to him, making plain that what was said was never meant as any kind of personal attack, that I did not feel that ANY one individual should take on the responsibilities under discussion, but rather that my understanding from the Bible and from the *Watchtower* was that they were matters for a body of persons to deal with. I said again and again that if it were a matter of one person handling everything, then he would be my choice; that I felt he had simply been doing what he felt he should do and what had always been done in the past; that I had no complaint about his doing so.

This did not seem to make any impression, however, and, realizing that anything I said along this line would simply provoke anger, after a few attempts I gave up. On these occasions the remainder of the Body members sat, observed and said nothing. What happened a few years later therefore came as a surprise.

Nothing further developed until the year 1975. Consider now what the organization's 1993 history book *Jehovah's Witnesses—Proclaimers of God's Kingdom* relates as to what then took place, an event described as "one of the most significant organizational readjustments in the modern-day history of Jehovah's Witnesses." On pages 108 and 109, we read:

Organizational Readjustments

By 1976, Brother Knorr had worked diligently as president of the Watch Tower Society for over three decades. He had traveled the globe many times over, visiting and encouraging missionaries, teaching and instructing branch-office personnel. He was privileged to see the number of active Witnesses increase from 117,209 in 1942 to 2,248,390 in 1976.

But by the summer of 1976, 71-year-old N. H. Knorr had noticed that he had a tendency to bump into things. Subsequent tests indicated that he was suffering from an inoperable brain tumor. He struggled to continue to carry a work load for some months, but his physical prognosis was poor. Would his failing health impede the forward movement of the work?

Enlargement of the Governing Body had already begun in 1971. During 1975, there were 17 members. Throughout much of that year, the Governing Body had given serious and prayerful consideration to how they could best care for all that is involved in the global preaching and teaching work outlined in God's Word for our day. (Matt. 28:19, 20) On December 4, 1975, the Governing Body had unanimously approved one of the most significant organizational readjustments in the modern-day history of Jehovah's Witnesses.

Starting January 1, 1976, all the activities of the Watch Tower Society and of the congregations of Jehovah's Witnesses around the earth had been brought under the supervision of six administrative committees of the Governing Body. In harmony with that arrangement, on February 1, 1976, changes had been put into effect in all branch offices of the Society around the earth. No longer was each branch supervised by one branch overseer, but three or more mature men served as a Branch Committee, with one member serving as the permanent coordinator.* After the committees had been operating for some months, the Governing Body observed: "It has proved beneficial to have a number of brothers taking counsel together to consider the interests of the Kingdom work.—Prov. 11:14; 15:22; 24:6."

The book thus leads the reader to believe that the failing health of the Society's third president, Nathan Knorr, in late 1975 was somehow involved in this major event in the organization's history, was perhaps a motivating reason for it. All the men who were on the Governing Body at that time know that this picture is not true. Knorr's health problem in reality became evident *after* the issue had arisen leading to the change, and hence was purely coincidental. It neither gave rise to the issue nor was it a factor in the Governing Body discussions and decisions. There is a clear lack of candor in the picture presented.

What then did happen?

In 1975, two Bethel Elders (Malcolm Allen, a senior member of the Service Department and Robert Lang, the Assistant Bethel Home Overseer) wrote letters to the Governing Body expressing concern over certain conditions prevalent within the headquarters staff, specifically referring to an atmosphere of fear generated by those having oversight and a growing feeling of discouragement and resultant discontent.

At that time anyone applying for service at headquarters ("Bethel Service") had to agree to stay a minimum of four years. Most of the applicants were young men, 19 and 20 years of age. Four years equaled one-fifth of the life they had thus far lived. When at the meal tables, I often asked the person next to me, "How long have you been here?" In the ten years I had by now spent at headquarters I had never heard one of these young men respond by saying in round figures, "About a year' or "about two years." Invariably the answer was, "One and seven," "two and five," "three and one" and so forth, always giving the year or years and the exact number of months. I could not help but think of the way men serving a prison sentence often follow a similar practice of marking off time.

Generally it was difficult to get these young men to express themselves about their service at headquarters. As I learned from friends who worked more closely with them, they were unwilling to say much in an open way since they feared that anything they said that was not positive would cause them to be classed as what was popularly called a "B.A.", someone with a "bad attitude."

Many felt like "cogs in a machine," viewed as workers but not as persons. Job insecurity resulted from knowing that they could be shifted at any time to another work assignment without any previous discussion and often with no explanation for the change made. "Management-employee" lines were clearly drawn and carefully maintained.

The monthly allowance of fourteen dollars often barely covered (and in some cases was less than) their transportation costs going to and from Kingdom Hall meetings. Those whose family or friends were more affluent had no problems as they received outside assistance. But others rarely could afford anything beyond bare necessities. Those from more distant points, particularly those from the western states, might find it virtually impossible to travel and spend vacations with their families, particularly if they came from a poor family. Yet they were regularly hearing greetings passed on to the Bethel Family from members of the Governing Body and others as they traveled around the country and to other parts of the world giving talks. They saw the corporation officers driving new Oldsmobiles bought by the Society and serviced and cleaned by workers like themselves. Their work schedule, then consisting of eight hours and forty minutes each day, and four hours on Saturday morning, combined with attendance at meetings three times a week, plus the weekly "witnessing" activity, seemed to many to make their lives very cramped, routine, tiring. But they knew that to lessen up in any of these areas would undoubtedly put them in the "B.A." class and result in their being called to a meeting designed to correct their attitude.

The letters by the two Bethel Elders touched on these areas but without going into detail. The president again seemed to feel, unfortunately, that this constituted criticism of his administration. He expressed himself to the Governing Body as wanting a hearing to be held on the matter and on April 2, 1975, this was done. A number of Bethel Elders spoke and many of the earlier-mentioned specifics were there aired. Those speaking did not indulge in personalities and made no demands, but they stressed the need for more consideration of the individual, for brotherly communication and the benefit of letting those close to problems share in decisions and solutions. As the Assistant Bethel Home Overseer, Robert Lang, put it, "we seem more concerned about production than people." The staff doctor, Dr. Dixon, related that he frequently received visits from married couples distressed due to the inability of the wives to cope with the pressures and keep up with the demanding schedule, many of the women breaking into tears when talking to him.

A week later, April 9, the official "Minutes" of the Governing Body session stated:

> Comments were made on the relationship of the Governing Body and the corporations and what was published in the *Watchtower* of December 15, 1971. It was agreed that a committee of five made up of L. K. Greenlees, A. D. Schroeder, R. V. Franz, D. Sydlik, and J. C. Booth go into matters concerning this subject and the duties of the officers of the corporations and related matters and take into consideration the thoughts of N. H. Knorr, F. W. Franz and G. Suiter who are officers of the two societies, and then bring recommendations. The whole idea is to strengthen the unity of the organization.

At a session three weeks later, April 30, President Knorr surprised us by making a motion that thenceforth all matters be decided by a two-thirds vote of the active membership (which by then numbered seventeen).[4] Following this, the official "Minutes" of that session relate:

---

4   The College of Cardinals of the Catholic Church requires a similar two-thirds majority when voting for a papal successor. I think it quite possible that Knorr and Fred Franz felt it unlikely that such a decisive majority of members would vote for a change.

L. K. Greenlees then began his report from the committee of five on Brother Knorr's request to tell him what he should do.[5] The committee considered the *Watchtower* of December 15, 1971, paragraph 29 very carefully, also page 760. The committee feels that today the Governing Body should be directing the corporations and not the other way around. The corporations should recognize that the Governing Body of seventeen members has the responsibility to administer the work in the congregations throughout the world. There has been a delay of putting the arrangement into effect at Bethel as compared to the congregations. There has been confusion. We do not want a dual organization.

There followed a lengthy discussion of questions relating to the Governing Body and the corporations and to the president, with comments by all members present. At the close of the day a motion was proposed by N. H. Knorr, followed by a comment by E. C. Chitty. L. K. Greenlees also presented a motion. It was agreed that the three should be Xeroxed and copies given to all members and meet again the next day at 8 a.m. There would be time to pray over the matter which is so important.

The Xeroxed motions referred to read as follows:

N. H. Knorr: "I move the Governing Body take over responsibility of looking after the work directed in the Charter of the Pennsylvania Corporation and assume the responsibilities set out in the Charter of the Pennsylvania Corporation and all other corporations throughout the world used by Jehovah's Witnesses."

E. C. Chitty said: "To 'take over' means relieve the other party. I believe for my part the responsibility stays as it is. Rather it would be right to say 'supervise the responsibility.'"

L. K. Greenlees said: "I move that the Governing Body undertake in harmony with the Scriptures the full responsibility and authority for the administration and supervision of the worldwide association of Jehovah's

---

5   It was President Knorr who had nominated the five of us serving on this committee. At the first meeting of the "Committee of Five" it was voted, on my motion, that Leo Greenlees serve as Chairman.

Witnesses and their activities; that all members and officers of any and all corporations used by Jehovah's Witnesses will act in harmony with and under direction of this Governing Body; that this enhanced relationship between the Governing Body and the corporations go into effect as soon as can reasonably be done without hurt or damage to the Kingdom Work."

On the next day, May 1, 1975, there was again a long discussion. In particular the vice president (who had written the *Watchtower* articles referred to) objected to the proposals made and to any change in the existing setup, any reduction of the corporation president's authority. (This brought to mind, and was in harmony with, his remarks to me back in 1971 that he thought Jesus Christ would direct the organization through a single person on down to the time when the New Order came.) He made no comment on the evident contradiction between the presentation made in the *Watchtower* articles (and their bold statements about the Governing Body using the corporations as mere instruments) and the three motions made, each of which showed that the makers (including the president himself) recognized that the Governing Body did not at that time supervise the corporations.

Discussion went back and forth. A turning point seemed to come with remarks made by Grant Suiter, the crisp-speaking secretary-treasurer of the Society's principal corporations. Different from the comments made till then by those favoring a change, his expressions were quite personal, seemingly the release of a long pent-up feeling about the president, whom he directly named. While discussing the authority structure he made no specific charges, except as regards the right to make a certain change in his personal room that he had requested and had been denied, but as he went on his face became flushed, his jaw muscles flexed and his words became more intense. He closed with the remark:

Grant Suiter

> I say if we are going to be a Governing Body, then let's get to governing! I haven't been doing any governing till now.

Those words hit me hard enough that I am satisfied that I have remembered and recorded them as said. Whether they were meant to convey the sense they did is, of course, beyond my knowing and they may well have been merely a momentary outburst, not indicative of any heartfelt motive. At any rate they served to make me think very seriously about the matter of right motivation and I felt considerable concern that whatever should come of this whole affair might be the result of a sincere desire on the part of all involved to hold more closely to Bible principles and patterns and not for any other reason. I found the whole session disturbing, mainly because the general spirit did not seem to conform to what one would expect of a Christian body. However, shortly after these last-mentioned comments by the secretary-treasurer, Nathan Knorr evidently reached a decision and made a lengthy statement, taken down in shorthand by Milton Henschel, who had made certain suggestions himself and who then acted as secretary for the Body.[6] As recorded in the official "Minutes" the president's statement included these expressions:

> I think it would be a very good thing for the Governing Body to follow through along the lines that Brother Henschel has mentioned and design a program having in mind what the *Watchtower* says, that the Governing Body is Governing Body of Jehovah's Witnesses. I am not going to argue for or against it. In my opinion it is not necessary. The *Watchtower* has stated it.
>
> It will be the Governing Body who will have overall guiding power and influence. They will take their responsibility as Governing Body and direct through different divisions they will set up and they will have an organization.

At the end he said, "I make that a motion." Somewhat to my surprise, his motion was seconded by F. W. Franz, the vice president. It was adopted unanimously by the Body as a whole.

---

6   Milton Henschel, tall and of generally serious mien, spoke fairly seldom in discussions but when he did it was usually with considerable firmness, definiteness. In his younger years he had been President Knorr's personal secretary; at the time here being discussed, he was in his middle fifties.

The bold language of the *Watchtower* of four years previous seemed about to change from mere words into fact. From the expressions made by the president it appeared that a smooth transition lay ahead. That is the picture of harmonious unity the book *Jehovah's Witnesses—Proclaimers of God's Kingdom* portrays. It was, instead, only a lull preceding the stormiest period of all.

In the months that followed, the appointed "Committee of Five" met with all members of the Governing Body individually and with thirty-three other longtime members of the headquarters staff. By far the majority favored a reorganization. The Committee drew up detailed proposals for an arrangement of Governing Body Committees to handle different facets of the worldwide activity. Of the seventeen Governing Body members personally interviewed, eleven indicated basic approval.

Of the remaining six, George Gangas, a warm and effervescent Greek, and one of the oldest members of the Body, was very uncertain, changeable in his expressions according to the mood of the moment. Charles Fekel, an eastern European, had been a Society Director many years before but had been removed under the charge of having compromised his integrity by the oath he took when obtaining American citizenship. He was now among the most recent appointees to the Body and, of a very mild nature, rarely shared in the discussion, consistently voting whichever way the majority went, and he had little to say on this issue. Lloyd Barry, a New Zealander and also a recent addition to the Body, had come to Brooklyn after a number of years as Branch Overseer of Japan, where Witness activity had seen phenomenal growth. He expressed very strong misgivings about the recommendations, particularly the decentralizing effect it would have as regards the presidency; in a letter dated September 5, 1975, he characterized the recommended change as "revolutionary." Bill Jackson, a down-to-earth, unassuming Texan (not as rare as some would make it appear), had spent most of his life at headquarters, and, like Barry, he felt that things should be left very much as they were, especially since such good numerical increases had come under the existing administration.

The strongest voices of opposition were those of the president and vice president, the maker and seconder of the motion earlier quoted! They were, in fact, publicly vocal in their opposition.

During the period the appointed "Committee of Five" was interviewing longtime staff members to get their viewpoint, the president's turn to preside at the head of the Bethel table for one week came up. For several mornings he used the opportunity to discuss before the 1,200 or more "Bethel Family" members in the several dining rooms (all tied in by sound and television) what he called the "investigation" going on (the Committee of Five's interviews), saying that "some persons" favored changing things that had been done a certain way for the whole life of the organization. He asked again and again, "Where is their proof that things aren't working well, that a change is needed?" He said that the "investigation" was endeavoring to "prove this family is bad," but said he was confident that "a few complainers" would not "overwhelm the joy of the majority." He urged all to "have faith in the Society," pointing to its many accomplishments. At one point he said with great force and feeling that the changes some wanted to make as to the Bethel Family and its work and organization "will be made over my dead body."[7]

In all fairness to Nathan Knorr, it must be said that he undoubtedly believed that the then-existing arrangement was the right one. He knew that the vice president, the organization's most respected scholar and the one he relied upon to handle Scriptural matters, felt that way. Knorr was basically an affable person, capable of warmth. When he was not in his president's "uniform" or role, I genuinely enjoyed my association with him. However, his official position, as is so often the case, did not generally let that side of him be seen and (again, doubtless due to his feeling that the role he carried out was according to God's will) he inclined to react very quickly and forcefully to any apparent infringement upon his presidential authority. People learned not to do this. For all that, I seriously doubt that Nathan would have gone along with some of the harsh actions that were later to come from the collective body that inherited his presidential authority.

---

7   Words in quotations are from notes written down at the time the words were spoken; they were, of course, heard by over a thousand persons in each case.

I can empathize with his feelings and reaction, having served for many years as a Branch Overseer in both Puerto Rico and the Dominican Republic where I was to be, according to the prevailing organizational viewpoint, the "top man" in the country, the president's personal representative. My efforts to act in accord with this viewpoint made me constantly aware of "position" and the need to uphold that "position." I found by hard experience, however, that trying to live up to that organizational concept did not contribute to pleasant relations with others and that it made my own life unpleasant; the confrontations it produced were not something I felt at all suited for by nature and, after a while, I simply gave up trying to emulate what I had seen at headquarters. My life became much more enjoyable as a result and I found the overall effect far more productive and beneficial.

The president's last-mentioned words ("over my dead body") nearly proved prophetic. At the time of saying them he evidently had already developed a malignant tumor on his brain, though this did not become known until after the reorganization was definitely a *fait accompli,* its completion taking place officially on January 1, 1976, and Knorr's death occurring a year and a half later, on June 8, 1977.

The president's quite vocal opposition was matched, perhaps even surpassed, by that of the vice president. At the September 7, 1975, graduation program for the missionary school of Gilead, attended by the Bethel Family members and invited guests (largely relatives and friends of the graduating class), the vice president gave a talk, a customary feature of each graduation program.

Fred Franz had an inimitable, often dramatic (even melodramatic) speaking style. What follows is from an exact copy of his talk, but the written words cannot convey the inflections, the spirit, the "flavor," even the occasional sarcasm, that came through in the talk itself.[8]

F. W. Franz

---

8   A recording of this entire talk, with accompanying brief observations, is available through NuLife Press. See contact page at the end of this book.

His opening words gave a clear indication as to where the talk was headed. Having in mind that a committee duly appointed by the Governing Body was at that very time making a proposal that the training, assignment and supervision of missionaries be directed by the Governing Body rather than by the corporations, we may note his opening expression. He began saying:

> This class is being sent forth in collaboration with the Watchtower Bible and Tract Society of New York, Incorporated, by the Watch Tower Bible and Tract Society of Pennsylvania. Now the question is raised today, What right does the Watch Tower Bible and Tract Society have to send missionaries out into the field? . . . Who authorized the Watch Tower Bible and Tract Society of Pennsylvania to send missionaries all around the globe?
>
> Now, such a challenging question may be raised with an earlier circumstance. And that is based on the fact that the Watch Tower Bible and Tract Society was founded by a man who became an evangelizer of world note, one of the most eminent evangelizers of this twentieth century and who especially attained global fame when he made his trip around the world in the year 1912. That man was Charles Taze Russell of Allegheny, Pennsylvania.

The focus was clearly on the corporation; the Governing Body was not mentioned. Of course no one had raised the "challenging question" he was here describing; the real issue in the Governing Body was whether the talk he had given four years before about the relationship between the Body and the corporation was to be taken seriously. However, he went on to say in his distinctive manner:

> Now I've wondered about this matter. Maybe you have too. Just how did Russell become an evangelizer? Who made him an evangelizer? . . . the various religious establishments of Christendom were in operation. For instance, there was the Anglican Church with its ruling body, and the Protestant Episcopal Church with its ruling body. There was the Methodist Church with its Conference; there was also the Presbyterian Church, to which Russell used to belong, with its Synod. There was

also the Congregational Church, which Russell joined, with its Central Congregation.

But by none of these controlling organizations . . . was Russell made an evangelizer or missionary.

Without directly or openly referring to the Governing Body he had managed to introduce it into the discussion indirectly by referring to these "ruling bodies," under their various names. (He could also have mentioned the Jesuits, who have an administration bearing this name: Governing Body.) But the point made was that no such a Governing Body had anything to do with or exercised any authority toward this founder of the Watch Tower corporation. Russell was an "independent," not subject to any of them.

The Governing Body had appointed the "Committee of Five" and that committee was recommending that permanent committees be formed to care for the direction of the work worldwide. Thus these following words of the vice president's talk take on added significance as, after speaking of the seventy disciples Jesus sent out, he told the graduating class:

> Now we're not to imagine that by sending the seventy evangelizers . . . by sending them forth by twos, the Lord Jesus Christ was not making each two a committee, so that for the seventy evangelizers there were thirty-five committees of two. . . . You're being sent forth today after your graduation as missionaries . . . two being sent to Bolivia, and then there are others who are being sent, maybe four or six or eight, to a different country as assignment for work. Now, don't you missionaries think because you are being sent forth two together, or maybe four or six or maybe eight, that you are being sent forth as a committee to take over the work for the land to which you are assigned. No such thing! You are being sent forth as individual missionaries to cooperate together and to cooperate with the Branch of the Watch Tower Bible and Tract Society which is operating and directing the work in the land to which you are assigned to act as an evangelizer. So don't get this committee idea into your head.

In all this, the Governing Body remained "conspicuous by its absence," eclipsed by the corporation. Not a single person had suggested that the missionaries be sent out as "committees" or that they "take over the work" in their assigned lands, and the idea of their doing so had undoubtedly never entered their minds, but this served as a means for introducing the idea of committees and discrediting the concept.

The talk then went on to discuss Philip "the evangelizer," raising once more the question as to "who made him an evangelizer or missionary?"[9] The vice president referred to the account in Acts, chapter six, where the apostles as a body found it necessary to appoint seven men, including Philip, to care for food distribution so as to end complaints being made of discrimination against certain widows. He then said:

> Well, now, if you look up the *McClintock and Strong's Cyclopedia of Religious Knowledge* you'll find that the work that the apostles assigned to these seven men is called a "semi-secular work." But the apostles didn't want that semi-secular work; they unloaded it onto these seven men and said "you take care of that. Well, *we're* going to specialize on prayers and teaching." Now were these twelve apostles of the Lord Jesus Christ, by unloading this responsibility for taking care of tables, were they making of themselves mere *figureheads* in the congregation of God and of Jesus Christ? They certainly were not making themselves figureheads because they specialized on spiritual things.

To those Governing Body members who had heard the president emphasize that the Governing Body should care for the "strictly spiritual things" and leave the rest to the corporation, the vice president's words had a familiar ring. Strangely, however, about half of the men on the Body were spending their eight hours and forty minutes of each day in just such "semi-secular work." Dan Sydlik and Charles Fekel worked in the factory; Leo Greenlees handled insurance and related matters for the Secretary-Treasurer's office; John Booth had oversight of the Bethel kitchen; Bill Jackson handled legal matters and documents; Grant Suiter was daily occupied in financial matters, investments, stocks, wills; and Milton Henschel and the president himself (who controlled all these assignments

---

9   See Acts 8:5-13; 21:8.

of work) spent considerable time in the kind of "semi-secular" work that the vice president said should be "unloaded" for others to care for.

The vice president's exposition now took a strange turn, one that actually contradicted the official teaching as to the divine authority for a governing body from the first century onward. The history of Paul, the converted Saul, was first related; that, after his conversion, when he went to Jerusalem he saw only two of the apostles, not the whole body of them; how he eventually came to Antioch in Syria. Having remarked that, in selecting and appointing Saul of Tarsus, Christ "took direct action without consulting any man or body of men on earth," the vice president now presented a sort of "Tale of Two Cities," in which the role of Antioch was set over against that of Jerusalem as regards the missionary activity of Paul and Barnabas. In what follows, keep in mind the existing official Watch Tower teaching that there was a governing body *based in Jerusalem* that exercised supervisory direction over all congregations of Christians in all places and that in this it was the model for the present-day governing body of Jehovah's Witnesses.

In relating the holy Spirit's calling of Paul and Barnabas to missionary activity, the vice president continually emphasized that all this was done through the *Antioch* congregation (hence *not* through Jerusalem where the apostolic body was located).[10] He said:

> And then, all of a sudden as he [Paul] was serving in Antioch, in Syria, not in Israel but in Syria, why God's spirit spoke to that congregation there in Antioch and said, "Now of all things, you set aside, YOU, this congregation in Antioch, you set aside these two men, namely Barnabas and Saul for the work for which I have commissioned them." And so the Antioch congregation did that and they laid their hands upon Paul (or Saul) and Barnabas and sent them forth . . . and they went forth by the holy spirit operating through the Antioch congregation and they went out on their first missionary assignment.

10   It should be remembered that the whole basis for the Witnesses' teaching of a "governing body" arrangement and authority is that there was such an arrangement operating from Jerusalem in Bible times.

So, you see the Lord Jesus Christ was acting as the Head of the congregation and taking action directly, without consulting anybody here on earth what he could do and what he could not do. And he acted in that way in regard to Saul and Barnabas and they were both apostles of the Antioch congregation.

At this point of the talk I recall sitting there and saying to myself, "Does the man realize what he is saying? I know what his goal is, to de-emphasize the Governing Body so as to maintain the authority of the corporation and its president, but does he realize the implication of what he is saying? In the process of attaining his goal he is undermining the whole teaching and claim about the existence of a centralized, first-century governing body operating out of Jerusalem with earthwide authority to supervise and direct all congregations of true Christians everywhere in all matters, a concept that the Society's publications have built up in the minds of all of Jehovah's Witnesses and to which the vast majority hold today."

But the vice president had by no means finished and he drove the idea home with even greater force. Describing the completion of Paul and Barnabas' first missionary tour, he continued with growing intensity and dramatization:

> . . . and where did they go, where did they report? There's the record, you read it for yourself in the closing verses of the fourteenth chapter of Acts. They went back to *Antioch*, to the congregation there, and the account says that they related things in detail to them; to this congregation that had committed them to the undeserved kindness of God for the work they had performed. So there's where they reported.
>
> So the record also says they stayed in Antioch not a little time. Now, what happened? All of a sudden something occurred and Paul and Barnabas, they go up to Jerusalem. Well, what's the matter? What brings them up to Jerusalem?
>
> Well, is it the body of apostles and of other elders of the Jerusalem congregation that summoned them up there and say, "Look here! We have heard that you two men have gone out on a missionary tour and finished it and you haven't come up here to Jerusalem to report to us. DO YOU KNOW WHO WE ARE? We are the council of Jerusalem.

DON'T YOU RECOGNIZE THE HEADSHIP OF THE LORD JESUS CHRIST? If you don't come up here in a hurry, we're going to take disciplinary action against you!"

Is that what the account says? Well, if they had acted that way toward Paul and Barnabas because they reported to the congregation by means of which the holy spirit had sent them out, then this council of apostles at Jerusalem and other elders of the Jewish congregation would have put themselves above the headship of the Lord Jesus Christ.

His points were completely valid. They were also completely contrary to the view presented in the Society's publications, which present a picture of Jerusalem as the seat of a governing body exercising full authority and direction over all Christians as Christ's agency, acting with divine authority. That is doubtless why, unlike other talks the vice president had given, this one was never used as the basis for articles in the *Watchtower* magazine.

For any individual Witness to present such an argument today would be counted as heretical, rebellious speech. If actually applied as stated, his words would mean that any congregation on earth could send out its own missionaries if they believed Christ Jesus and holy Spirit so directed, doing so without consulting anyone else, whether in Brooklyn or in a Branch Office. There was no question in my mind as to the quick and adverse reaction this would provoke from the Society's headquarters and its offices. It would be viewed as a threat to their centralized authority and any congregation doing this would in so many words be asked, "Do you know who we are? Don't you recognize the headship of the Lord Jesus Christ operating through us?" All that he said in this area was true, perfectly true. But it was evidently no more meant to be applied in full force than the points that he made about four years earlier in the "tail wagging the dog" talk, *except* that, by the references to Antioch, he was clearly endeavoring to establish a parallel with the corporation as operating apart from the Governing Body.

The talk went on to show that the *real reason* Paul and Barnabas went to Jerusalem, as recorded in Acts, chapter fifteen, was because *Jerusalem itself* had been the *source* of a serious problem for the Antioch congregation, men coming down from Jerusalem and stirring up trouble over the issue of law keeping and circumcision. Hence the trip to Jerusalem was, not an evidence of submission to a governing body, but for the purpose of overturning the effect of the teaching of these Jerusalem troublemakers.

Continuing the argument, he dealt with the second missionary tour of Paul and his new partner Silas and emphasized again that it was from the *Antioch* congregation that they went forth, so that "again, the Antioch congregation was being used to send out missionaries of great eminence in Bible history." That they returned to *Antioch* and that from *Antioch* Paul embarked on his third tour. Winding up the account from the book of Acts, the vice president said:

> And so as we examine this account of these two most outstanding among the missionaries recorded in Bible history, we find that they were sent out especially by the Lord Jesus Christ, the Head of the church, a fact which the Watch Tower Bible and Tract Society has upheld and accepted ever since the Society was formed. So, we see how the Lord Jesus Christ is the Head of the church and has a right to act direct, without whatever other organizations in view, no matter who they are. He is the Head of the church. We can't challenge what HE DOES.

Those last three sentences spoken by the vice president represent the position that had been taken in recent times by a number of Witnesses. For taking that identical position, they were and are now labeled "apostates."

Again, however, those statements, seemingly expressing deep respect for the superior authority of Christ, actually conveyed a different concept, one placing emphasis on a different source of authority. For the vice president was at the very same time saying that to challenge the authority of the Watch Tower Bible and Tract Society and the authority of its president was to challenge the Lord Jesus Christ. He did not believe the thinking or action of the Governing Body-appointed "Committee of Five" could in any way be representative of the direction of the Head of the church, for the simple reason that He, Jesus Christ, had caused the corporation to be formed and was dealing through it. This seemed to me to be a case of mixed-up reasoning.

That this was the whole thrust of his talk could be seen in that, coming to the crux of the matter, he now applied all these points to modern times. He spoke of the raising up of Charles Taze Russell, his starting a new religious magazine, the *Watch Tower,* and, "Who authorized this man to do that?" Then, on to Russell's incorporating Zion's Watch Tower Bible and Tract Society, and here he added:

> And mind you, friends, when he founded that Society, the Watch Tower Bible and Tract Society, he was not founding a DO-NOTHING society or organization.

The Lord Jesus Christ and God's spirit had raised Russell up, he said, and also backed the formation of the corporation, "this active, *do-something* Society." The vice president then described the origin of the Gilead School; that it had been the corporation president's idea; that, when informed, the Board of Directors had given its backing and that the president was to have supervision of the School. Nathan Knorr was sitting on the platform while the vice president gave his talk and Fred Franz gestured toward him in the course of these following remarks:

> So you see, dear friends, that the Boards of Directors of the New York corporation and of the Pennsylvania, as constituted back there, they had *respect* for the office of the president and they did not treat the president of these organizations as a *poker-faced, immobilized figurehead* presiding over a society, *a do-nothing* society.

From the start of the talk I had thought this was the goal aimed at and so it came as no surprise to me, though the language used did. From this stage of the presentation, the tone of the talk now softened and he went on to highlight that particular day, September 7, 1975, saying:

> And do you know what that means? According to this diary, Hebrew diary, from the land of Israel [referring now to a small booklet he held in his hand], why this is the *second day* of the month Tishri of the lunar year 1976, and do you know what that means? That here on this day of your graduation, why it is the *second day of the seventh millennium* of man's existence here on earth. Isn't that something? Isn't that something grand

[applause here] that the opening day of the seventh millennium of mankind's existence is signalized by the operation of the Watch Tower Bible and Tract Society in full compliance of the terms of its charter sending out the 59th class of the Gilead School for missionaries.

Jehovah God certainly has blessed it, and by its fruit, why, it has become known as an approved agency in the hand of Jehovah God and so that there is no need to challenge the right and the authority of this Society to send out missionaries.

And, friends, notice this, that just as God used the Antioch congregation to send out the two of the most outstanding missionaries of the first century, Paul and Barnabas, so today Jehovah God is using the Watch Tower Bible and Tract Society of Pennsylvania, in collaboration with the New York corporation, to send out further missionaries and they are determined to keep on in that course. That's something very, very gratifying.[11]

There could be no question but that in the vice president's mind someone had "thrown down the gauntlet" in a challenge to the corporation presidency. By this talk the battle lines had been carefully and emphatically drawn. The corporation had its sovereign terrain and it was off limits to the Governing Body. The sad effect of all this was that many of his fellow members of the Governing Body were distinctly cast in the role of aggressor and openly displayed as disrespectful of the authority of the Lord Jesus Christ vested in this "approved agency," the corporation.

The guests present, parents and friends of the graduating class, were generally mystified by many of the things said and by the whole thrust of the talk, the biting language at times employed. The Bethel Family members, though having a vague idea of difficulties because of comments made by the president and vice president when acting as head of the table, now had reinforced their suspicion that there was indeed a quarrel going on in the Governing Body, apparently a power struggle.

The contrast between this talk and the talk using the metaphor of the dog and its tail, given four years previously (in which the "dog"

---

11 Following the talk. President Knorr spoke, visibly moved and almost choked with emotion. He expressed great appreciation for what had been said. And I am sure he was thoroughly sincere in his feelings. He then gave a pleasant talk on "Wholesomeness of Speech."

"represented the Governing Body and the "tail"—which should be wagged and not do the wagging—represented the corporation) could hardly have been greater. They were given by the same man, yet they seemed to go in totally opposite directions. I would be less than honest if I did not admit that I left the auditorium that day feeling not only deeply disturbed but also somewhat ill. It seemed that God's Word was something that could be made to fit one argument when circumstances made it advisable, and an opposite argument when circumstances were different. This disturbed me more than any other aspect of the matter.

As in Nathan Knorr's case, so, too, certain factors help in understanding Fred Franz's actions. In late 1941, when Judge Rutherford lay on his deathbed at Beth Sarim in San Diego, California, he had called three men to his side: Nathan Knorr, Fred Franz and Hayden Covington. Rutherford told them that he wanted them to carry on after his death and that they should "stick together" as a team. That action was reminiscent of Pastor Russell's "Will," though here given orally rather than in writing. Twenty years later, in 1961, in writing the book *Let Your Name Be Sanctified,*" Fred Franz alluded to that occasion when discussing the account of the passing on of Elijah's prophetic mantle ("official garment" in the *New World Translation)* to his successor Elisha.[12] He presented this as a prophetic drama and stated:

> ♦ Rutherford was abed on the Pacific Coast when the United States of America was plunged into World War II Sunday, December 7, 1941. Two men of the anointed remnant (one since 1913 and one since 1922) and one of the "other sheep" (since 1934) were summoned from Brooklyn headquarters out to Rutherford's bedside at the home called "Beth-sarim," San Diego, California. On December 24, 1941, he gave these three his final instructions. For years he had been hoping to see the faithful prophets, including Elijah and Elisha, resurrected from the dead and installed as Kingdom "princes in all the earth" in God's new world. (Psalm 45:16) But on Thursday, January 8, 1942, Rutherford died at seventy-two years of age, as a faithful witness of Jehovah God, completely devoted to the interests of God's kingdom. He had proved himself fearless in support of Jehovah's side of the paramount issue of Universal Domination.

12   2 Kings 2:8, 11-14.

> [5] As viewed from our present time, it appears that there the Elijah work passed, to be succeeded by the Elisha work. It was as when Elijah and Elisha had crossed the Jordan River by means of a dividing of the waters to the east shore and were walking along, awaiting the removal of Elijah.

> Elisha became heir to Elijah's official garment that had fallen from him. With it went its powers. [13]

When the Governing Body discussed the proposed reorganization, the vice president made direct reference to this assignment from the dying Judge Rutherford. I have no doubt that Fred Franz felt that a certain "mantle-izing" had occurred at that time. As has been stated, Nathan Knorr succeeded Rutherford to the presidency. Hayden Covington, the big Texas lawyer who defended Jehovah's Witnesses in many cases before the U.S. Supreme Court, was asked by Knorr to become vice president, this despite the fact that Covington made no profession then of being of the "anointed" class. (This shows that neither Judge Rutherford nor, initially, Nathan Knorr felt that being of the "anointed" was essential for directing the work worldwide.) Covington's own testimony, given during the Walsh case in Scotland, indicates that it was not until some correspondence came in a couple of years later asking how this could be, that he and Knorr talked about his not being of the "anointed" and Covington decided he should resign.[14] Relations between the two deteriorated as time went on and Covington eventually left the headquarters staff to go into private practice.[15] Fred Franz was elected as vice president following Covington's resignation in 1944.

Though the three heirs to Rutherford's deathbed transference of responsibility (which, incidentally shows there was no "governing body"

---

13   "Let Your Name Be Sanctified," published in 1961, pp. 335-337.
14   From the official court record, pp. 387, 388.
15   Covington had had a severe struggle with alcoholism and had undergone one "drying out" treatment while still in headquarters service. He went through another at Speers Hospital in Dayton, Kentucky, after being disfellowshipped in the 1970s, and finally conquered the problem. He was reinstated and continued association until his death.

in operation) had now reduced to two, there was evidently still a definite feeling that a role in fulfilling prophecy was in effect. In 1978, at a large convention in Cincinnati, Ohio, when Fred Franz, now the Society's president, was asked to speak to the audience of over 30,000 persons about his life experience as a Witness, he chose to spend the bulk of the time discussing his relationship with the now deceased Nathan Knorr, particularly emphasizing Judge Rutherford's dying words to them. It can very truthfully be said that the talk took on the aspect of a eulogy as Fred Franz described Knorr's qualities and stressed that he had stuck by Nathan Knorr right to the end "just as the Judge had urged" and that he was proud of having done so.

Perhaps even more illuminating as regards this view of being "mantleized" was an expression made that same year, 1978, during a session of what was now the Writing Committee of the Governing Body. Present were Lyman Swingle, Ewart Chitty, Lloyd Barry, Fred Franz and myself. A commentary on the Letter of James was being written by Ed Dunlap, and Fred Franz had asked for an adjustment to Dunlap's discussion of James, chapter three, verse 1, where the disciple says:

> Not many of you should become teachers, my brothers, knowing that we shall receive heavier judgment.

The material Dunlap had prepared said that this evidently was a warning against unqualified individuals seeking to serve as teachers simply because of a desire for prominence. Fred Franz asked for the elimination of most of the material but gave no particular explanation for his objections except to ask in writing:

> If Jesus gave some to be teachers, how many was he to give? And since Jesus does the giving, how could James tell the men "not *many* of you should become teachers"? How did James himself become a teacher?

Since I had been assigned to oversee the project of the commentary's development, at the Committee hearing I asked Fred Franz to clarify his objection and tell us just what *he* thought was meant by this text. He stated that he believed it meant that it was God's will that there be just a few men in the entire Christian congregation who could rightly be called "teachers." I inquired who such would be in our time. Speaking very calmly his reply was:

> Well, I believe that I am. I have been here at headquarters for over fifty years and have been involved in the field of writing and research during most of that time, so I believe that I am. And—there are some other brothers throughout the earth who are.

This response was another occasion when the effect was so startling that the words were, in effect, burned into my memory. I was not the only witness to them since they were spoken before the other three members of the Writing Committee. By his remark we had had identified for us only one teacher on earth by name: Fred Franz. Who the others were, we were left to speculate. As I told Lyman Swingle on more than one occasion thereafter, I regretted not having pursued the matter further by asking for names of the other "teachers" of our time. But the response left me momentarily speechless.

In the same material in which he presented his objection to Dunlap's material, President Franz had also suggested the addition of the following points in the forthcoming commentary (here presented in a photocopy from page 2 of his write-up, containing his initials):

```
         CORRECTIONS AND CHANGES THAT SHOULD BE MADE ON JAMES 3 COMMENTARY
James 3, page 2

     After paragraph 5 I would insert the following paragraph:
      How James himself became a teacher we do not know, except
that his half brother, Jesus Christ, appeared to him after his
resurrection. (1 Cor. 15:7; Acts 1:14) Not every dedicated,
baptized Christian man who may want to 'become a teacher' does so
out of a selfish, ambitious motive.  Such a rightly motivated
teacher was seen in the case of the 27-year-old "Editor and
Publisher" of the magazine Zion's Watch Tower and Herald of
Christ's Presence in July of 1879.
```

This brought memories of his Gilead Graduation talk in 1975 when he had made clear his conviction that Christ Jesus had personally raised up Pastor Russell to carry out a special role. This material three years later indicated that he felt such personal, individual selection by Christ was continuing in other cases, with the result that only a few select persons were raised up as special "teachers" for the congregation.[16]

The above-suggested material bringing Russell into the picture was not used, however, and the information found on pages 99 to the top of 102 in the *Commentary on the Letter of James* is a replacement of Dunlap's material, which I wrote so that President Franz's objections would be met. It was in a certain sense a refutation of his view since Jesus' words at Matthew, chapter twenty-three, verse 8, "But you, do not you be called Rabbi, *for one is your teacher, whereas all you are brothers*," seemed to be completely contrary to the idea of a very small number of men forming a somewhat exclusive group of specially selected "teachers," the chosen few. The rewrite I submitted was approved in committee and published.

There is another reason why there was such an evident contradiction between certain bold, forceful statements made in print and the comparatively timid, puny reality actually existing at the time. The reason is that the officers of the corporation could rationalize that a small, representative change or reform would suffice as substitution for, or a "token" of, a larger, genuinely meaningful change.

As an example of this, the mere fact that in 1971 President Knorr had decided to relinquish his monopoly of the chairmanship at the Bethel dining tables, sharing it with the other members of the Board of Directors and also had decided to allow them to serve on a rotational basis as chairmen of the Governing Body sessions was viewed as all that was needed to demonstrate that the corporations (and their officers) were in fact directed by and submissive to the Governing Body and that the 'dog was indeed wagging the tail.' No other tangible action or significant change had taken

---

16   Karl Klein on several occasions during Governing Body sessions referred to Fred Franz as having been the "oracle" of the organization for many years. Though generally said with a smile, his repeated use of the term implied more than mere jesting.

place in the authority structure, nor was it viewed as necessary to fulfill the impressive picture painted.

That Fred Franz could so view matters seems evident, particularly so since, surprisingly, *over twenty years earlier,* back in 1944 he had written articles for the *Watchtower* that contained all the *basic* points on elders and overseers that appeared in the *Aid* book.[17] Despite this, *no change whatsoever* took place back then in the congregational arrangement. But it had been *said,* it had been *published,* and this was viewed as enough.

In those articles, 1944 was presented as a marked year in Bible prophecy, and this mainly because an amendment had been passed whereby voting rights in the corporation would no longer be based on a $10 donation as previously. Instead a maximum number of 500 persons, selected by the corporation's Board, would be the only ones with a right to vote. Anyone who has attended an annual meeting of the Watch Tower Society where elections of Directors take place knows that it is extremely routine and that voting is mainly a mere formality. The bulk of the voting members know virtually nothing of the inner workings of the organization and have neither influence, voice or control as to the policies and programs of the organization. The actual *business* part of the meeting usually takes no more than one hour; then it is over until another year passes.

Yet the adoption of this amendment as to voting members was presented in articles in the *Watchtower* of December 1, 1971 (written by Fred Franz) as being an occasion of such significance and magnitude that it became a focal point in the explanation of the prophecy of Daniel 8:14, regarding the 2,300 prophetic days connected with the 'bringing of the sanctuary into its proper condition.' I doubt that one Witness in a thousand, if shown that verse today, would ever connect it up with 1944 and the corporation amendment made then. Yet that remains the official explanation of that prophecy to this day. It was another example of the ability to take an event of relatively minor effect and then to clothe it with symbolic value as being of great significance.

---

17   The *Watchtower.* October 15. 1944. See the book *Pay Attention to Daniel's Prophecy* (1999), pp. 178, 179.

On August 15, 1975, the Committee of Five finally presented its findings and recommendations. On behalf of the committee I prepared a document of 45 pages, setting out the historical and, particularly, the Scriptural reasons for recommending that the basically monarchical structure should change, plus 19 pages outlining a system of Governing Body Committees for directing the different areas of activity. The initial document ended with the following paragraph:

> All the deliberations of the committee of five have been made with much prayer and careful thought. We sincerely hope that God's spirit has guided in the results and pray that they will be of some assistance to the body in reaching a decision. It is hoped that the adjustments recommended, if approved, will contribute toward an even more pleasant, peaceful relationship among the members of the Governing Body, helping to eliminate the tension that at times has surfaced in our meetings. (Ps. 133:1; Jas. 3:17, 18) It is also hoped that the recommended adjustments will, if accepted, serve to enhance and make yet more prominent the headship of Christ Jesus and the spirit of genuine brotherhood found among his disciples—Mark 9:50.

Those words expressed my sincere feelings and hope. I could not see how they could be viewed as a challenge to Christ Jesus' direction of his congregation.[18]

The material came before the Governing Body, and in the session on September 10, 1975, it was now obvious that by far the majority favored the basic change recommended. However, a second Committee of Five was assigned to make final adjustments.[19] The Body did not select either the president or vice president to serve on this committee since their opposition had been clearly stated.

---

18 A covering letter, written by Leo Greenlees, accompanied the document and included this statement: "Our recommendations are not motivated by dissatisfaction with the work as it has been administered heretofore, but mainly out of concern for the direction indicated by the Bible and *Watchtower* articles, we believe that once the Scriptural principles are brought to bear on the matter, then the direction we should take is evident."

19 The second committee was composed of Milton Henschel, Ewart Chitty, Lyman Swingle, Lloyd Barry and Ted Jaracz.

The president's comments at this point mainly expressed doubt as to the practicality of the change. The vice president, however, made plain that he viewed the presentation as an "attack on the presidency." When the president's own motion was read out to him, he replied that Brother Knorr had made that statement "under duress."

Lyman Swingle expressed himself as feeling that all members of the Body had respect for the president and did not view him as a "poker-faced, immobilized figurehead of a do-nothing Society," here using the vice president's language at the graduation exercises. He stressed that the president could still use his energy, drive and initiative within the proposed arrangement. Later in the discussion, the vice president insisted that the Committee of Five's document did just what he had said was being done. He stated that at the coming annual meeting his vote would be for the corporation powers to continue and said that his talk at the Gilead Graduation owed to a feeling of obligation to let the brothers know this so that they would not feel that a "hoax" had been practiced on them.

After the second committee completed its recommendations and submitted these on December 3, 1975, the matter came down to a final vote.[20] The Chairman called for a show of hands. All but two raised their hands in favor of the motion to implement the recommendations.

The two who did not raise their hands were the president and the vice president.

The following day the Body met again. The vice president said he had taken no part in the discussion the day before since he "didn't want to have anything more to do with it"; to participate would mean he was in favor and he "conscientiously could not do so." He referred repeatedly to Nathan Knorr as the "chief executive" of the Society, the "chief executive of the Lord's people on earth," and said that "Jesus Christ is not down here on earth and so is using agents to carry out his will."

Dan Sydlik, a square-built, deep-voiced man of Slavic descent, said he would have been "happy to see Brother Knorr or Brother Franz turn

---

20   About the only major change the second committee made in the recommendations of the first committee was that, in addition to a rotating chairmanship of each proposed Governing Body Committee, there should be a permanent "Coordinator" for each Committee.

to the Scriptures or even to the *Watchtower* publications to support their position but that was not the case." Leo Greenlees remarked that if all the congregations were glad to submit to the direction of the Governing Body, why not the corporations also?

The president basically confined his remarks to saying that he thought the corporation would act "parallel" to the Governing Body but that, instead, the proposed arrangement subordinated the corporation, adding, "which is probably correct." The vice president said he too thought the two organizations were going to run parallel (perhaps like Antioch and Jerusalem?) and said: "I never had in mind what the Governing Body wants to do now."

It was obvious that the president and vice president were maintaining their opposition. Lloyd Barry, his voice strained and shaking with emotion, now pleaded with them that they make the matter unanimous since it was obvious that it would pass anyway.

Another vote was taken and this time President Knorr raised his hand and the vice president followed suit.

Four years later, in 1979, in a Governing Body session, Fred Franz, now president, stated that his vote for the change back then was made "under duress." I would agree. When Nathan Knorr conceded, Fred Franz felt compelled to join him. He went on to say that he had not been in favor of the change then and that from that point forward he had "just been watching" to see what would result.

Contrast the above information with the idealistic picture Watch Tower publications seek to convey. Quoting Isaiah 60:17, which gives Jehovah's promise to replace 'bronze with gold,' 'iron with silver,' and to appoint "Peace as your overseer and Righteousness as your taskmaster," the *Watchtower* of March 15, 1990 contains articles describing "progressive improvements" and "continual refinements" in organization, as if organizational changes have come smoothly, in an atmosphere of peace and harmony. They present the fiction that a governing body was operative throughout Watch Tower history.

As has been shown, the reality is quite different. During the first seven decades of the organization's history no one spoke of, or thought in terms of, a governing body. Russell had arranged that after his death committees would handle matters and share authority and responsibility. Rutherford promptly and effectively eliminated these, crushed any opposition, and for the following two decades autocratically exercised total control as corporation president. While moderating the existing atmosphere, Knorr retained that total control until a sort of "palace revolution" stripped the corporation presidency of its power. As of 1976, the authority passed from one man to a number of men, and, after nearly half a century, committees once again became operative. This back-and-forth scenario hardly fits the picture of a harmonious process of "progressive improvements" and "continual refinements."

The Watch Tower's 1993 history book, *Jehovah's Witnesses—Proclaimers of God's Kingdom,* in its "Foreword" comments that while others have written about Jehovah's Witnesses, this was "not always impartially." It then states:

> The editors of this volume have endeavored to be objective and to present a candid history.

The book, on pages 108, 109, describes the 1975/1976 major restructuring of the administration as "one of the most significant organizational readjustments in the modern-day history of Jehovah's Witnesses." (See page 83 of this chapter for the text of those pages.) How "objective" and "candid" is their presentation of that major event?

The change is presented as if achieved in peaceful harmony. If the anonymous "editors" of the book were themselves ignorant of the months of acrimonious inner struggle that preceded this change, it is certain that every one of the hundreds of men and women who were members of the Brooklyn headquarters staff at the time, and who heard the angry expressions of the president in morning text discussions, knew that the change did not come peacefully. Of all these, the members of the Governing Body knew most intimately the intensity of the struggle. As of 1993, when the history book was published, all those then members of the Body had personally lived through that experience. They knew that the change from a one-man rule to that of a body rule was achieved in the face of intense, even caustic opposition from both the president and the vice president, and that the 'unanimous approving' of the change the history book refers to was achieved only as a result of these two men, Knorr and Fred Franz, being faced with obvious defeat and finally capitulating (reluctantly and "under duress," as the vice president himself expressed it). Any candor in this published account is clearly conspicuous for its absence. To allow this fictional picture of peaceful, harmonious change to be published does not speak well for the moral standards of those knowing the reality.

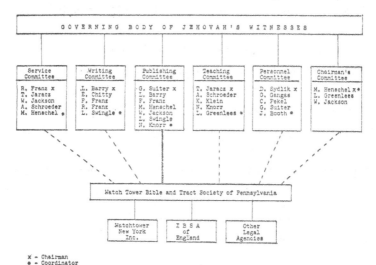

The preceding chart, prepared by the second Committee of Five, shows the arrangement that went into effect on January 1, 1976.

John Booth, a member of the first Committee of Five, and in early life a farmer from upstate New York, a gentle man who thought deeply but normally had difficulty in expressing those thoughts well, seemed to have best described what now became the case with the corporation. In one of the Committee of Five's first meetings, he had said:

> A corporation is just a legal tool. It's like a pen lying on the desk. When I want to use the pen I pick it up. When I'm finished I just lay it down until I want to use it again.

That now became the position of the Watch Tower Bible and Tract Society of Pennsylvania and its subsidiary corporations. Inevitably that meant that the power of the presidency was decimated and virtually disappeared, that office now serving an almost purely legal function.

When Nathan Knorr died, the Governing Body considered the matter of his successor. The most likely candidates were Vice President Franz and Milton Henschel, who had worked closely with Knorr in Administration. Henschel moved that Fred Franz become president and this was unanimously approved. When replacement for Knorr's position as "Coordinator" of the Publishing Committee then came up, Henschel seemed the logical successor, but Fred Franz, now president, spoke in favor of Lloyd Barry. Relations between Knorr and Henschel had been poor in recent years and in one interview with the first Committee of Five, Knorr had implied that he felt Barry could take over his job (his presidential work) if necessary. Evidently Fred Franz viewed this somewhat in the light of Judge Rutherford's deathbed instructions and felt that some transfer of "mantle" to Barry was thus in order, but the Body voted Henschel into the position.

An article in *Time* magazine, reporting the election of Fred Franz as the new president, stated:

> Though few people know his name, he has acquired more-than-papal power over 2.2 million souls around the world.[21]

That statement could hardly have been more wrong. It would have been true a year or so earlier, but the office of president, though still carrying a measure of prestige and prominence, was no longer the earthwide power base it had been. Few persons outside the Body could appreciate how drastic a change had taken place.

If the president previously had indeed had power of papal scope, though with none of the trappings and pomp of the papacy, the Branch Overseers had been equivalent in domain to archbishops, each being the "presiding minister of Christianity for and within the territory to which he has been appointed."[22] Here, too, a change entered as Branch Committees took on this responsibility.

---

21   *Time,* July 11, 1977, p. 64.
22   Quoted from pages 5 and 6 of the *Branch Office Procedure* book, a manual for all Branch Offices in effect at the time.

The years of 1976 and 1977 brought some pleasant moments. A very different climate seemed to be in evidence at the international head-quarters, a spirit of greater brotherliness, openness and equality. Some compared it to the "window" that Pope John XXIII had opened in the Catholic Church to 'let a breath of fresh air in.'

The new Governing Body Committees put into effect a number of changes to improve Bethel Family circumstances, both in Brooklyn and among the more than ninety Branches. Greater consideration was given to financial needs of the so-called "rank and file" members, to the special needs of women and to those who were older. During 1976 a series of meetings was held with respected and esteemed men in various categories: representatives from the Branches around the world were first brought in; then traveling representatives across the United States; finally congrega-tion elders representing the different sectors of the country were invited to Brooklyn. In all cases there was a freedom of discussion and expression that most found refreshingly different from any experienced in the past.

On the congregational level, I doubt that much of this was felt, since the many suggestions made by the men in these meetings were not implemented to any major extent. Still, many Witnesses expressed appreciation that, for a time at least, published material gave stronger emphasis to the authority of the Scriptures and the headship of Jesus Christ and less to the authority of a human organization. They felt overall that a more moderate, balanced, compassionate approach was being taken. As one longtime Witness put it, "I used to feel like I *had* to do things; now I'm beginning to feel like I *want* to do them."

The sessions of the Governing Body manifested this changed atmo-sphere in some measure. The passing of the much publicized year of 1975 without the hoped-for arrival of a millennial jubilee doubtless had a some-what humbling effect, as dogmatism diminished perceptibly. More cau-tion as to imposing new rulings on the lives of people and less inclination to categorize specific actions as "disfellowshipping offenses" were reflected in the voting, though never in a complete sense.

It was during this year (1976), that Nathan Knorr's health began to deteriorate. Yet, as long as he was able to attend, he shared in discus-sions and, though clearly not happy with changes made, showed a gener-ally cooperative and helpful attitude. His expressions at times helped to overcome extreme points of view. Though rarely based on Scriptural argument, they reflected his common sense approach to matters.

Throughout most of this period Vice President Franz preferred to sit and listen, only occasionally participating in discussions and, almost without fail, what he had to say would come toward the close of the discussion, just before voting took place. By that point the general consensus of thinking was fairly evident (based on the individual comments made) and often his remarks were opposite to the trend of the majority. Perhaps nothing illustrates more strikingly the changed thinking of the Body during this period, as does the fact that the voting, while sometimes showing a shift due to the influence of the vice president's last-minute remarks, often went contrary to his expressions. In the main, however, during this period he gave no indication of his thinking until the customary show of hands was called for and, as the official "Minutes" record, there were numerous cases where the vote read "Sixteen [or whatever the figure might be] in favor; one abstention," that one being the vice president. This was generally where issues involved moderations of policy regarding so-called "disfellowshipping matters." Matters in the secular or semi-secular field (such as purchases of property, office procedures) or appointments to membership in Branch Committees were usually unanimous.

When the new arrangement was voted in, I found it hard to believe that such a major change in the authority structure had actually taken place, particularly in view of the intense opposition it had met from the most prominent men in the organization, as well as from some of their close associates outside the Body. My earnest hope was that the "leveling" and equalizing effect of the change would allow for greater moderation, a reduction of dogmatism, a greater concern for individuals and their individual circumstances and problems, and perhaps, some day, the elimination of the authoritarian approach that produced so many rules and assumed such great control over the personal lives of people.

As has been noted, some of that came. It came for a while. Then, within about two years, like a chilling breeze in late autumn that signals the approach of winter coldness, evidence of a very clear swing back to earlier approaches began surfacing again and again.

5

TRADITION AND LEGALISM

*Thus you nullify the word of God for the sake of your tradition.
. . . their teachings are but rules made by man.*
— Matthew 15:6, 9. *New International Version.*

Most of Jehovah's Witnesses envision Governing Body sessions as meetings of men who spend a great amount of their time in intense study of God's Word. They think of them as meeting together to consider humbly how they can better help their brothers understand the Scriptures, to discuss constructive and positive ways to build them up in faith and love, the qualities that motivate genuine Christian works, doing all this in sessions where Scripture is always appealed to as the only valid and final and supreme authority. Since all Governing Body sessions are completely private, only its members are witnesses of what actually occurs in those sessions.

As has been noted, the Governing Body members, better than anyone, knew that the *Watchtower* articles describing the relationship between the corporation and the Governing Body presented a picture that did not accord with reality. So, too, members of the Governing Body know, better than anyone else, that the picture described in the preceding paragraph differs measurably from reality.

I spent nine years on the Governing Body. Going over the records of meeting after meeting after meeting, the most prominent, constant and time-occupying feature found is the discussion of issues ultimately coming down to this question: "Is it a disfellowshipping matter?"

I would liken the Governing Body (and in my mind I often did) to a group of men backed up against a wall with numerous persons tossing

131

balls at them for them to catch and throw back. The balls came so frequently and in such number that there was little time for anything else. Indeed, it seemed that every disfellowshipping ruling made and sent out only brought additional questions thrown at us from new angles, leaving little time for thought, study, discussion and action of a truly positive, constructive nature.

Over the years I sat through many, many sessions where issues that could seriously affect the lives of people were discussed, yet where the Bible did not come into the hands or even on the lips of practically any of those participating. There were reasons, a combination of reasons, for this.

Many Governing Body members admitted that they found themselves so occupied with various matters that there was little time for Bible study. It is no exaggeration to say that the average member spent no more time, and sometimes less, in such study than many Witnesses among the so-called "rank and file." Some of those on the Publishing Committee (which included the officers and directors of the Pennsylvania corporation) were notable in this regard, for a tremendous amount of paper work came their way and they evidently felt that they could not or should not delegate this to anyone else to review and present conclusions or recommendations.

On the few occasions when some purely Scriptural discussion was programmed it was generally to discuss an article or articles for the *Watchtower* that an individual had prepared and to which there was some objection. In these cases it regularly occurred that, even though notified a week or two in advance of the matter, Milton Henschel, Grant Suiter or another member of this Committee felt obliged to say, "I only had time to look this over briefly, I've been so busy."

There was no reason to doubt that they were truly busy. The question that came to mind was, How then can they vote in good conscience on approval of the material when they have not been able to meditate on it, search the Scriptures to test it out? Once published it was to be viewed as "truth" by millions of people. What paper work could equal this in importance?

But these brothers were by no means alone, for the discussions themselves clearly demonstrated that by far the majority of the Body had done little else than read the material written. The subject was often one that had originated and developed in the mind of the writer without consultation with the Body, even though it represented some "new" understanding of Scripture, and often the writer had then worked up all his arguments and put the material in final form without having talked things over, tested his thinking, with even one other person. (Even during Nathan Knorr's lifetime this was the normal procedure followed by the Society's principal writer, Fred Franz. Only when put in completed form did anyone else—and usually only the president—have opportunity to consider and discuss the ideas or interpretations developed.) The argumentation was frequently complex, involved, of a kind that no superficial reading could ever allow for sufficient analysis to test its validity and determine if it was Scripturally solid or just a case of 'acrobatical logic,' a skillful juggling of texts that made them say something other than what they really said. Those who had only read the material usually voted in favor; those who had done extra study and research were those most likely to raise serious questions.

Thus, after one discussion of an article by Fred Franz which presented the view that the "festival of the harvest ingathering" (celebrated, according to the Bible, at the *close* of the harvest season) pictured a circumstance in the history of the Witnesses at the *start* of their spiritual harvesting, sufficient members voted in favor for it to be accepted.[1] Lyman Swingle, who had not voted in favor and who was currently serving as Coordinator of the Writing Committee, then said: "All right, if that's what you want to do I'll send it over to the factory for printing. But that does not mean that I believe it. It is just one more stone piled on the enormous monument of testimony that the *Watchtower* is not infallible."

A second reason for lack of real Bible discussion, follows obviously, I believe, from the preceding one. And that is that most of the Body were actually not that well versed in the Scriptures, for their "busyness" was not something of recent origin. In my own case, right up until 1965 I had been on such a "treadmill" of activity that I had found little time for truly serious study. But I think the matter goes deeper than that. I believe that

---

1   See the *Watchtower* of February 15, 1980, pp. 8-24.

the feeling prevailed that such study and research were really not all that essential, that the policies and teachings of the organization—developed over many decades—were a reliable guide in themselves, so that, whatever motion might be made in the Body, as long as it conformed satisfactorily to such traditional policy or teaching, it must be all right.

The facts point to this conclusion. At times a long discussion on some "disfellowshipping" issue would suddenly be resolved because one member had found a statement related to the matter in the Society's *Organization* book, or, more likely, in the book called "Aid to Answering Branch Office Correspondence," a compendium of policies arranged alphabetically on a broad range of subjects—employment, marriage, divorce, politics, military matters, labor unions, blood and scores of others. When such statement was found, even though no Scripture was cited in support of the particular point of policy, this seemed to settle the matter for most of the Body members and they would usually vote without hesitation in favor of any motion that conformed to the printed policy. I saw this happen on several occasions and I never ceased to be impressed by the way that kind of printed policy statement could effect such a sudden transformation in the progress and resolution of a discussion.

A final reason for the Bible's playing little part in such discussion is that in case after case the issue involved something on which the Scriptures themselves were silent.

To cite specific examples, the discussion might be to decide whether the injection of serums should be viewed the same as blood transfusions, or whether platelets should be considered just as objectionable for acceptance as packed red blood cells. Or the discussion might center on the policy that a wife who committed one act of unfaithfulness was obliged to confess this to her husband (even though he was known to be extremely violent in nature) or else her claim of repentance would not be considered valid, leaving her liable for disfellowshipping. What scriptures discuss such matters?

Consider this case that came up for discussion and decision by the Governing Body. One of Jehovah's Witnesses, driving a truck for the

Coca-Cola Company, had as his route a large military base where numerous deliveries were made. The question: Could he do this and remain a member in good standing or is this a disfellowshipping offense? (The crucial factor here being that *military* property and personnel were involved.)

Again, what scriptures discuss such matters—in a way that can be clearly and reasonably seen, in a way that obviates the need for involved reasoning and interpretations? None were brought forward, yet the majority of the Body decided that this work was not acceptable and that the man would have to obtain another route to remain in good standing. A similar case came up involving a Witness musician who played in a "combo" at an officers' club on a military base. This too, was ruled unacceptable by the majority of the Body. The Scriptures being silent, human reasoning supplied the answer.

Generally, in discussions of this type, if any appeal *was* made to Scripture by those favoring condemnation of the act or conduct, that appeal was to very broad statements such as, "You are no part of the world," found at John, chapter fifteen, verse 19. If a Governing Body member personally scrupled against the action or conduct under discussion and could think of no other argument against it, often he would fall back on this text, extending it and applying it to fit whatever the circumstances were. The need to let the rest of the Scriptures define what such a broad statement means and how it applies often seemed to be considered unnecessary or irrelevant.

A major factor in Governing Body decisions was the two-thirds majority rule. This produced some strange effects at times.

The rule was that a two-thirds majority (of the total active membership) was needed to carry a motion. I personally appreciated the opportunity this allowed for a member to vote differently from the majority or simply to abstain without feeling that he was, in effect, exercising "veto power." On minor matters, even when not in complete agreement, I generally voted with the majority. But when issues came up that genuinely affected my conscience I frequently found myself in the minority—seldom alone but often with only one, two or three other members expressing conscientious objection by not voting for the motion.[2] This was not so often the case during the first two years or so after the major change effected in the authority structure (officially put in motion on January 1, 1976). In the final two years of my membership, however, a strong trend toward a "hard line" approach obliged me either to vote differently from the majority—or to abstain—with greater frequency.

But consider now what sometimes happened when the Body was quite divided in its viewpoint, not nearly so uncommon an occurrence as some might think.

An issue might be under discussion involving conduct that had, somewhere in the Society's past, been designated a "disfellowshipping offense," perhaps a person's having a particular blood fraction injected to control a potentially fatal ailment; or possibly the case of a wife who had a non-Witness husband in military service and who worked in a commissary on her husband's military base.

At times in such discussions the Body might be quite divided, sometimes even split right down the middle. Or there might be a majority who favored removing the particular action, conduct or type of employment from the "disfellowshipping offense" category. Consider what might happen because of the two-thirds majority rule:

If out of fourteen members present, nine favored removing the disfellowshipping offense "label" and only five favored retaining it, the majority was not sufficient to change the disfellowshipping label. Though a clear majority, the nine were not a *two-thirds* majority. (Even if there were ten of them favoring change this was still not enough, for though they would be two-thirds majority of the fourteen *present,* the rule was two-thirds majority of the *total active membership,* which during much of the time was seventeen.) If someone from the nine favoring removal of the disfellowshipping category advanced a motion it would fail, because twelve votes were needed for it to pass. If someone from the five favoring retention of the disfellowshipping offense category advanced a motion that the policy be maintained, the motion would, of course, fail also. But even the failure

2   I can recall, and my records indicate, only a couple of occasions in over eight years where I found myself completely alone in voting contrary to the majority or in abstaining.

of the motion in favor of retaining the category would not result in the removal of that disfellowshipping category. Why not? Because the policy was that some motion had to *carry* before any change would be made in previous policy. In one of the first of these instances of such a divided vote, Milton Henschel had expressed the view that, where there was no two-thirds majority, then "status quo should prevail," nothing should change. It was quite uncommon in these cases for any member to change over on his vote and so a stalemate usually resulted.

That meant that the Witness taking the particular action or having the particular employment involved would continue to be subject to dis-fellowshipping, *even though a majority of the Body had made clear their feeling that he or she should not be!*

On more than one occasion when a sizeable minority or even a major-ity (though not two-thirds) felt that a matter should not be a disfellow-shipping offense, I voiced my feelings that our position was unreason-able, even incomprehensible. How could we let things go on as before, with people being disfellowshipped for such things, when right within the Governing Body there were a number of us, sometimes a majority, who felt that the action involved did not merit such severe judgment? How would the brothers and sisters feel to know that this was the case and yet they were being disfellowshipped?[3]

To illustrate, if five congregational elders forming a "judicial com-mittee" were to hear a case and three of the five did not believe that the person's action or conduct called for disfellowshipping, would the fact that they were only a three-fifths majority and not a two-thirds majority make their position invalid?[4] Would the person then be disfellowshipped? Surely not. How could we, then, let a mere procedural rule of voting cause a traditional stand on disfellowshipping to prevail when most of the Body members felt otherwise? Should we not at least take the position that, *in all disfellowshipping matters,* when even a considerable minority (and

3   The secret nature of Governing Body sessions, of course, allows little likelihood for any to come to know this. The "Minutes" of the meetings are never opened for other Witnesses to see them.

4   Three out of five is only 60%, not 66²/₃%, as in a two-thirds majority.

especially a majority, however small) felt that there were not sufficient grounds for disfellowshipping, then no disfellowshipping ruling should be sustained?

These questions put to the Body brought no response, but again and again in such cases the previously-established traditional policy was kept in force, and this was done as a matter of course, as normal. The effect on people's lives somehow did not carry enough weight to make the members feel moved to set aside their "standard" policy in such cases. Somewhere in the past history of the organization a disfellowshipping policy had been formulated (often the product of one man's thinking, a man all too often pathetically isolated from the circumstances being dealt with) and that policy had been put into effect; a rule had been adopted and that rule controlled unless a two-thirds majority could overturn it.

In all these controversial cases the "disfellowshipping offense" was not something clearly identified in Scripture as sinful. It was purely the result of organizational policy. Once published, that policy became fixed on the worldwide brotherhood for them to bear, along with the consequences of the policy. Is it wrong in such circumstances to feel that Jesus' words apply: "They tie up heavy loads and put them on men's shoulders, but they themselves are not willing to lift a finger to move them"?[5] I leave that to the reader to decide. I only know what my conscience told me and the stand I felt compelled to take.

Nonetheless, I feel that in these various disputed issues the Governing Body members favoring disfellowshipping generally believed they were doing the right thing. What thinking could cause them to hold to a disfellowshipping stand in the face of objection from a sizeable minority or possibly from half or more of their fellow members?

In one case where prolonged discussion had made such a situation predictable, Ted Jaracz voiced a view that may well reflect the thinking of others. Of Slavic descent (Polish) like Dan Sydlik, Jaracz was different both in build and in temperament. Whereas Sydlik often was moved by a "gut" feeling as to the rightness or wrongness of an issue, Jaracz was of a

---

5   Matthew 23:4, *NIV.*

more dispassionate nature. In this particular session he acknowledged that 'the existing policy might work a measure of hardship on some individuals in the particular situation being discussed,' and said, "It is not that we don't feel for them in the matter, but we have to always keep in mind that we are not dealing with just two or three persons—we have a large, worldwide organization to keep in view and we have to think of the effect on that worldwide organization."[6]

This view, that what is good for the organization is what is good for the people in it, and that the interests of the individual are, in effect "expendable" when the interests of the large organization appear to require it, seemed to be accepted as a valid position by many members.

Additionally, some might advance the argument that any softening of position could "open the way" to a floodtide of wrongdoing. If one or more extreme examples of bad conduct were known that could be related to the issue under discussion, these were presented as strong evidence of the potential danger. The ominous specter of such danger was usually brought forth in those cases where, even before a motion had been offered, it was fairly evident that a considerable number of the Body inclined toward a change. In one such case, Milton Henschel seriously urged caution, making the point that, "If we let the brothers do this, there is no telling how far they will go."

I believe that he, and others who made the same point on other occasions, doubtless felt convinced that it was necessary to hold firmly to certain longtime policies in order to 'keep people in line,' to hold them within a protective "fence" so that they would not stray off.

If the protective "fence" of these policies had actually been one plainly outlined in God's Word, I would have had to agree and would gladly have voted accordingly. But so often that was not the case, and that it was not was clearly indicated by the fact that the particular elders (often men on Branch Committees) who had written in about the subject had found nothing in Scripture dealing with the matter, and by the fact that

---

6   These points may also have been substantially what Milton Henschel meant when he frequently commented on the need to "be practical" in our approach to such matters, for in voting his position and that of Ted Jaracz regularly coincided.

the Body itself had not found anything either. Thus the members had to resort to their own reasoning in a prolonged discussion, in many respects, a debate.

On the occasion earlier mentioned, following Milton Henschel's expression, my comment was that I did not believe that it was up to *us* to "let" the brothers do anything. Rather, I believed that God is the One who "lets" them do certain things, either because his Word approves it or because it is silent on the matter, and that He is the One that prohibits, when his Word clearly condemns the action, either explicitly or by clear principle. That I did not believe that as imperfect, error-prone men we were ever authorized by God to decide what should be allowed or disallowed for others. My question before the Body was, "When the matter is not clear in Scripture, why should we try to play God? We do so poorly at it. Why not let Him be the Judge of these people in such cases?" I repeated that view on other occasions when the same line of argument was being advanced, but I do not feel that the majority saw it in that light and their decisions indicated that they did not.

To paint a foreboding picture of potential unrestrained wrongdoing on the part of the brothers simply because we, as a Governing Body, removed some existing regulation, appealed to me as saying that we suspected our brothers of lacking true love of righteousness, of inwardly *wanting* to sin and being held in check only by organizational regulations.

An article published some years earlier in the Society's magazine *Awake!* came to mind. It described a police strike in Montreal, Canada, and showed that the absence of the police force for a day or so led to all kinds of lawless deeds by usually law-abiding citizens. The *Awake!* article pointed out that genuine Christians did not have to be subject to law enforcement in order to act in a lawful manner.[7]

Why, then, I wondered, was the position taken by the Governing Body that it was dangerous to remove a traditional regulation, in the belief that this could "open the way" for widespread immorality and misconduct on the part of the brothers? What did that say about our attitude toward, and our confidence in, those brothers? How different did we feel that these

---

7   See *Awake!*, December 8, 1969, pp. 21-23.

brothers were from those individuals who violated laws during the police strike in Montreal, and how deep and genuine did we believe their love of righteousness really was? At times it seemed that the prevailing sentiment within the Body was, trust no one but ourselves. That, too, did not seem to reflect commendable modesty to me.

The results that came out of these divided decisions were by no means inconsequential. Failure to conform to a Governing Body decision once published or made known could, and did, bring disfellowshipping, being cut off from congregation, family and friends. To conform, on the other hand, might require giving up a certain employment, sometimes when jobs were scarce and costs of caring for a family were great. It could mean taking a stand against a marriage partner's wishes, a stand that could, and sometimes did, lead to divorce, the breaking up of marriage, home and family, separating children from father or mother. It could mean feeling compelled to refuse to obey a certain law and then being arrested and sent away from family and home to a place of imprisonment. It could, in fact, mean loss of life itself, or what can be even more difficult to bear; to see loved ones lost in death.

To illustrate the difficulties that might arise even when a change *was made* in some earlier ruling, consider the organizational position taken regarding hemophiliacs and the use of blood fractions (such as Factor VIII, a clotting factor) to control against fatal bleeding.

For many years inquiries sent by hemophiliacs to the headquarters organization (or its Branch Offices) received the reply that to accept such blood fraction *one time* could be viewed as not objectionable, as, in effect, "medication." But to do so *more than once* would constitute a "feeding" on such blood fraction and therefore be considered a violation of the Scriptural injunction against eating blood.[8]

Years later this ruling changed. Those staff members who worked at answering correspondence knew that in the past they had sent out letters to the contrary and that hemophiliacs who had taken their "one time" injection were still under the impression that to do so again would be

---

8   Texts referred to included Genesis 9:3, 4; Leviticus 17:10-12; Acts 15:28, 29.

counted as a violation of Scripture. They could bleed to death because of holding to such a stand.

The administration was not in favor of publishing the new position in print since the old position had never been put in print but only conveyed to the particular individuals inquiring. To publish something would require first explaining what the old position had been and then explaining that it was now obsolete. This did not seem desirable. So the staff workers made a diligent search through their files to try to find the names and addresses of all those persons who had written inquiries and another letter was sent to each advising of the change. The staff workers felt better about this.

Then they realized that many of the inquiries had come in by phone and that they had no record of such phone calls and absolutely no way of determining who such inquiring hemophiliacs were. Whether, in the interim between the old ruling and the new, some had died, they did not know; whether some whom they had not been able to contact would yet die because of holding to the old ruling, they did not know. They only knew that they had followed instructions, being loyally obedient to their superiors in the organization.

This change in policy was made official at the June 11, 1975, session of the Governing Body. It was not until three years later, in 1978, however, that the change was finally put into print, though rather obscurely stated and, strangely, listed in with the issue of the use of serum injections to combat disease (whereas hemophilia is not a disease but a hereditary defect), in the June 15, 1978, issue of the *Watchtower.* It still was not acknowledged that this represented a change in the previous policy as to multiple use of blood fractions by hemophiliacs.

Another clue to the thinking of Governing Body members in such cases was the emphasis often placed on the long-standing nature of a particular policy. This meant that through the years thousands had abided by the Society's policy even though it created a severe burden for them, perhaps leading to imprisonment or other suffering. To change now, it was argued, might make such ones feel that what they had undergone had been unnecessary and, whereas they had found personal satisfaction in suffering in such way, viewing it as 'suffering for righteousness sake,' now they might feel disillusioned, possibly even feel it unfair that they had endured a form of martyrdom while others now could escape such.

I found that potential attitude a poor reason for holding back on making a change where there was sound evidence in favor of it. It seemed that such ones who had suffered could rejoice in knowing that others would not be called upon to undergo that burden in order to stay in good standing in the organization. If, as an illustration, an individual had lost a farm due to heavy—even unjust—taxation, should he not rejoice on behalf of friends, faced with a similar loss, if he learned that the heavy tax was lifted? Should not a coal miner suffering with a lung ailment be happy if conditions in mines improved, even though he could no longer benefit from this? It seemed that a genuine Christian would. Particularly so if the source of the unjust policy accepted its responsibility and expressed regret for harm done. It appeared to me that we needed to ask ourselves how much of the concern expressed might not actually be traceable to a concern over the Governing Body's own "image," its credibility, and its hold on people's confidence, being affected by fear that admitting error could weaken this.

Listening to some of the arguments presented in the Governing Body sessions brought to mind the many cases that Jehovah's Witnesses had carried before the Supreme Court of the United States. Opposing lawyers had used arguments similar in many respects to those used by men on the Governing Body. Such lawyers stressed *potential* dangers. They claimed that there was a strong danger that door-to-door visitation might become a serious nuisance or a blind for thievery and other criminal activity and that this justified placing restrictions on the Witnesses' freedom to carry on this activity. They said that to allow the Witnesses freedom to carry on their public activity or to give talks in parks in certain communities could lead to mob violence, due to the adverse and hostile attitude of the community as a whole, and therefore that restrictions should be placed. They argued that to allow the Witnesses to express their views on such subjects as saluting the flag, or their attitude toward worldly governments as being "part of the Devil's organization," could be detrimental to the interests of the larger community, could tend to create widespread disloyalty, hence be seditious; restrictions were necessary.

The Supreme Court justices in many cases showed remarkable insight and clarity of mind in cutting through such arguments, demonstrating them to be specious. They did not agree that the rights of the individual or of a small unpopular minority could properly be curtailed just because the fear of *possible* or imagined danger or because the claimed interests of the larger majority made this appear desirable. They held that before any rightful restriction could be applied limiting such freedoms, the danger must be more than a "fear," something *presumed* to be likely to develop. It must be proven a *"clear* and *present* danger," one actually existing[9]

How many favorable decisions would the Witnesses have received if the Supreme Court justices had not shown such judicious wisdom, such ability to see where the real issue lay, such concern for the individual? Their decisions were applauded in the Society's publications. Sadly, however, the high standards of judgment and the approach to emotionally charged issues shown by these judges often appeared to be on a higher level than that manifested in many Governing Body sessions. The expression of one Supreme Court justice in a particular Witness case comes to mind. He stated:

> The case is made difficult not because the principles of its decision are obscure but because the flag involved is our own. Nevertheless, we apply the limitations of the Constitution with no fear that freedom to be intelligently and spiritually diverse or even contrary will disintegrate the social organization. . . . freedom to differ is not limited to things that do not matter much. That would be a mere shadow of freedom. The test of

---

9   See the Society's publication *Defending and Legally Establishing the Good News,* p. 58.

its substance is the right to differ as to things that touch the heart of the existing order.[10]

The confidence that the justice expressed in the 'existing social order' and the freedoms it espoused seemed considerably greater than the confidence expressed by some Governing Body members in their fellow Witnesses and the effect their freedom of conscience, if exercised, could have on the existing "Theocratic order." If the Supreme Court justices had reasoned as some of the Governing Body members reasoned, the Witnesses would likely have lost case after case.

Court decisions are judged by history. The Scriptural declaration that, on a day certain to come, each Christian elder will "render an account" to the Supreme Judge regarding his dealings with, and treatment of, God's sheep, should surely give those exercising great authority among Christians a serious reason for weighing carefully what they do.[11]

The way in which recent major changes of policy have been presented in the organization's official publications demonstrates that concern over the effect of the change indeed has not been so much for the individuals who had suffered needlessly but concern for the "image" of the organization as God's channel and of the Governing Body as a body of divinely appointed and divinely guided administrators. Perhaps the most striking example of this is with regard to the major change as to acceptance of "alternative service."

"Alternative service" describes civil service (such as hospital work or other forms of community service) offered by a government as an alternative for those who conscientiously object to participation in compulsory military service. Many enlightened countries offer this alternative to such ones among their citizens. What developed within the Witness organization and its Governing Body in this connection is of particular interest in view of a policy change in 1996.

---

10   Ibid., p. 62.
11   Hebrews 13:17.

The official position of the Watch Tower Society, developed in the early 1940s during the Second World War, was that if one of Jehovah's Witnesses accepted such alternative service he had "compromised," had broken integrity with God. The reasoning behind this was that because this service was a "substitute" it therefore *took the place of* what it substituted for and (so the reasoning apparently went) came to stand for the same thing.[12] Since it was offered in place of military service and since military service involved (potentially at least) the shedding of blood, then anyone accepting the substitute became "bloodguilty." This remarkable policy developed before the Governing Body became a genuine reality and was evidently decided upon by Fred Franz and Nathan Knorr during the period when they produced all major policy decisions. Failure to adhere to this policy would mean being viewed automatically as "disassociated" and being treated the same as if disfellowshipped.

The May 1, 1996, *Watchtower* reversed this policy. In an article titled "Paying Back Caesar's Things to Caesar," the paragraphs shown in Appendix A (for Chapter 5) appeared. These gave the readers none of the history of the policy that had existed up to this point, a policy that had been in effect *for more than 50 years*. Similarly, they told the readers nothing of what had taken place within the Governing Body some two decades earlier regarding this same policy. Perhaps nothing illustrates so forcefully the effect of the "two-thirds majority" voting rule on people's lives as does that information. Consider:

It was over thirty years ago, in November 1977, that a letter arrived in Brooklyn from a Witness in Belgium, Michel Weber, questioning the reasoning on which this organizational policy was based. See the following page for some of the points his letter raised:

---

12   As late as the November 1, 1990 *Watchtower* this was alluded to as a "compromising substitute" for an unscriptural service.

What are the arguments which can be considered in connection
with this law?

The civil service is a substitution of the military service.
This is quite evident. However it is not a reason to refuse.
When we refuse a blood transfusion, we are gratefull to the
doctors when they give us a product which is able to replace
the volume of the blood. Or when offered meat with blood we
refuse but are happy to accept any other meat.

If a war should occur, the conscientious objector should join
the army. It is not true. On the contrary, the conscientious objector will never more allowed to have or to wear a weapon, or
to work in a weapon factory, etc. What concerns the brother who
have been condemned and have been in prison, they will be among
the first ones to be called to join the army.

During the civil service, the young christian will never participate to any war effort. He wears no uniform and is completely
free to go back home after the normal working hours. That means
he could manage to participate to the meetings, if not with his
own congregation with another one. He can still participate to
the predication, except if he was a pioneer.

Personnaly, I do not see why why it would be against the christian law to accept this solution.

To summarize, do you, brothers, consider that the question to
decide whether or not to accept this law of 1969 is a matter
of personal decision? If your answer is affirmative, this should
be urgently communicated to the congregations. Many brothers
do think indeed that they will be excluded when they accept these
opportunities instead of going in prison. The overseers should
know exactly what attitude to adopt when a member of the congregation takes such a decision. They should be able to explain that
their decision is a matter of personal conscience.

I hope brothers you will understand that it is urgent to help our
young brothers. I pray Jehovah to bless the efforts which will
be done to help young Witnesses of his Name to grow in maturity.

I remain,

Your brother Michel Weber.

This led to the alternative service issue being dealt with by the
Governing Body in a number of lengthy and intense discussions, first on
January 28, 1978, then on March 1, and again on September 26, October
11, October 18 and November 15. A worldwide survey was made and letters were received from some 90 branch offices.

As documentation shows, many Branch office committees, including those from several major countries, indicated that the Witness men
affected did not understand either the logic or the Scripturalness of the

organization's position. In a number of cases the Branch committees themselves raised questions as to the rightness of the policy and presented Scriptural reasons for allowing the matter to be one of conscience. The Branch Committee in Belgium, the country from which Michel Weber's letter originated, made this expression:

TEL. 02/31.17.50

WATCH TOWER
BIBLE AND TRACT SOCIETY
ASSOCIATION SANS BUT LUCRATIF
VERENIGING ZONDER WINSTOEVEND DOEL

C.C.P.: 969.76
P.C.R.:

RUE D'AROILE 60 — POTAARDESTRAAT 60, B - 1950 KRAAINEM Belgium
AB   July 14, 1978   N° 171

Watch Tower Bible and Tract Society
of Pennsylvania
Attention: Governing Body - Writing Committee
124 Columbia Heights
Brooklyn, New York, 11201, USA

Dear Brothers:

After receiving your letter of June 8, 1978 requesting additional information about the matter of Christian neutrality our Branch Committee has given prayerful consideration on the points mentioned.

Yes, where the law provides for the acceptance of alternative civilian work rather than military service, most of the brothers understand it is considered wrong to accept this if ordered to do so by an induction center, draft board or other governmental agency. As we wrote in our previous letters of March 8, 1978 and April 25, 1978, some youths and elders have difficulties to understand that when the alternative civilier work is enforced in order to satisfy the military authorities. They say that accepting the civil service is a matter of conscience. But as we write, most of the brothers understand that it is wrong to accept the alternative civil service.

After being sentenced to two years in prison, the brothers are assigned to various works in the prison like kitchen, cleaning, office work, maintenance or farming work. Some are even working outside of the jails to take care of State's buildings but they are not sentenced to perform the alternative civilian work proposed instead of the military service. If, after being sentenced, they would be assigned by the prison or the court to accomplished some humanitarian works as those pertaining to the civilian service they would not view that as a compromise.

Can they explain and support this position Scripturally? Few brothers are really in position to explain with the Bible why they refuse to accept the alternative civilier work rather than military service. As far as military service and political affairs are concerned, they can explain that the Bible condemns these activities but regarding the civilier service very few are really able to demonstrate with the Holy Scriptures that such a service cannot be accepted instead of the military service. Not only the youths but also some elders have difficulties to explain that position. We have heard that some brothers were unable to explain their neutral position before the judges who sometimes play with them like a cat with a mouse. Nevertheless, the brothers refuse the civilian service proposed in lieu of active military service because, basically, they know it is wrong and that the Society views it as such. For that reason some courts said to the brothers that they were pushed by the Society to refuse the provision of the civil service.

Watch Tower Bible and Tract Society
Attention: Writing Committee
July 14, 1978 (171) Page Two

We have been approached by several brothers who came at the
Branch to discuss the matter of Christian neutrality. Some of these
brothers were disturbed by some elders or youths who tried to convince
them that the civil service could be accepted especially when humanitarian activities could be performed. We have made clearly known that
everyone has to make his own decision and that it is not possible
for us or the Society to tell anyone what he should do. In reading
the regulations in connection with the civil service we have seen
with the brothers that such a service was a parcel of the military
service law because the whole basis for the existence of the civil
service provision was the prior and primary existence of the military
service law. It was clearly seen that the civilian service is in lieu
of the military service. According to our understanding we have said that
the problem has not to be considered first in viewing the humanitarian
work but why such a work is proposed or choioed. When an activity is
requested by Cesar in lieu of the military service those accepting
this work are compromising their Christian neutrality.

We would like to inform you that our brothers incarcerated in
the prison at Saint Gilles-Brussels were not allowed to celebrate the
Memorial on March 23, 1978. When the elders visiting them and some
members of their families have contacted us about that problem we
gave the suggestion that the parents of the brothers write a letter
of protestation to the Minister of Justice because the refusal to
hold that religious meeting was a violation of the Belgian Constitution.
We enclose a translation of the letter sent to the Minister of Justice.
Happily, the permission was granted and the brothers had their Memorial
meeting 30 days later.

We pray Jehovah to guide you in the decision to be made and
please accept our warm love and best wishes.

Your brother,

Willet

The letter from the Belgian Branch committee, signed by the Branch
Coordinator, makes clear to what it was that "loyalty" was being shown. It
recounts the committee's efforts loyally to uphold *organizational policy*. It
also shows that it was not a case of "loyally upholding Christian principles
as they understood them," nor of "responding to the proddings of conscience" that caused the young men to reject alternative service and thereafter be imprisoned for two years. The truth is that "few," in fact "very
few" of the brothers affected could explain with the Bible the basis for that
policy. The letter states that nonetheless they refused alternative service
because "they knew it was wrong and that the Society views it as such."
Since they could not explain it Scripturally, their 'knowing it was wrong'
can actually mean only that for them whatever the Society in Brooklyn

said determined the rightness or wrongness of the matter—not what the Scriptures themselves said. They suffered two years imprisonment, not because of a decision based on personal conscience and personal conviction, but because of adherence to a humanly originated ordinance.

The Branch Committee in Canada clearly indicated that they did not believe the then-current Watch Tower position was truly explainable from the standpoint of logic or Scripture. Discussing the problems on justifying that position both to governmental authorities and to the young Witness men affected by it, they wrote:

Watch Tower Bible and Tract Society
Governing Body

July 28, 1978, No. 341

Page 3

point of view, they might concede that they appreciate our desire to have nothing to do with the military, but that if the actual work assigned is the same, regardless of the agency ordering it, then what's the difference? We would find that a problem to argue successfully. Either we need more clarification on this ourselves or we need to reexamine whether we explain our neutrality as to what we participate in or as to agencies dealt with.

Of course, it may be argued that we do not want our brothers to 'take orders' from the military, because that would be getting a bit close to the military setup. But is not the type of work ordered the basis for refusal to cooperate with them? For example, would we 'take orders' from a court that assigned us to a Scripturally objectionable work? So, again, we come back to the activity as the basis for a conscientious reaction rather than the agency of origin of the work order. This way, we are always on the same ground in all places, including lands where it is nigh to impossible to separate even the courts from the military.

Hence, we sincerely feel that we need a clean-cut, clear position defined for us, one that the brothers can everywhere react to with understanding, proving it from the Bible on the basic stand of Christian neutrality and one that officials can grasp easily without having to take a course in each religion's individual views--a bother to them. A simplified stance would carry much more weight with the superior authorities and still leave the individual brother to react according to his own conscience. This would also make it easier for the brothers to base their decisions on simple principles in any country, not having to make numerous and fine-line decisions that will vary from place to place because of the particular political and military setup. Thus, whether our brothers are in touch with branch offices or Brooklyn or not for some special interpretation on an "agency" dealt with (with all the confusing possibilities there), they would still be able to decide the way to go. This would take into account varying circumstances in many lands that are so different from the American system.

But would this effort toward having a simplified, standardized position be in harmony with the Scriptures? Would we have Bible backing for this position?

Well, we would still be respecting Caesar. (Romans 13) But we would respectfully decline to engage in any activities ordered by anyone that would require us to disobey God or to not give Him what is due. (Matt. 22:21; Acts 5:29; Rev. 1:9) The Caesar-borne "sword" in the first century often was publicly manifest in the form of the military, but the Christian's respect for Caesar in that manifestation in no way meant that the Christian became a part of the military establishment. Yet he often had to 'take orders' from the military authority.

Watch Tower Bible and Tract Society
Governing Body

July 28, 1978, No. 341

Page 4

   The Roman penal system included slave labor, often in mines.
Quarries were in such places as Patmos. Though John was likely too
old to do such work and was perhaps treated as an exile there, what
about other Christians who were younger and physically able to work'
Do we know what they did under those circumstances? Is it not
likely that these mines were run by the military? Under that human
government, how much could our early brothers escape direction from
the military? Where did they draw the line? We have not been able
to find here any historical work that reveals much about this matter
but it would seem reasonable to us that what they must have done was
simply refuse to compromise Christian principles as to what they were
ordered to do or make or produce. They may not have had much choice
as to where the orders came from. Should they then have been (or ou
brothers now be) disadvantaged simply by being under a system that
affords no choice or possibility of getting an order from a secular
body rather than a military one? Should a brother suffer more than
others because he happens to live in a land where the military run
everything, while others do not because they live in a land where th
military are not in control? Is that political situation our basis
for decision? Thus, has our position in the past been one resulting
from the American situation of the orders coming from both a secular
and a military source? Does that stance fit the world situation
for our brothers?

   Today, courts, councils, police, induction centers and the
military are all manifestations of "Caesar's" authority. All are,
in one way or another, his agencies. Where the Christian would
Scripturally decline cooperation would be in the nature of the work
ordered. For example, if in a disaster the military came into a
community and organized all the available citizens to help sandbag
a dike or river bank, we could work under the direction of the
military establishment representing Caesar, but we would not partic'
in any nationalistic ceremonies they might also introduce and observ
on that site, or otherwise compromise Christian principles in carry'
out any orders. They might, to illustrate, 'order' blood donations
for disaster victims, but we would not obey in that case. Yet, in
all areas where we would, in this situation, cooperate with the
military, we would not be "in" the army and would not have accepted
'induction' into the armed forces, nor would we be compromising with
the military. The individual Christian would make his decisions at
the time and under the circumstances on the basis of Christian
neutrality and obedience to the commands of God as to human conduct
and behavior.--Acts 4:19, 20.

   To summarize, would it simplify matters to have the matter
proceed thus:

(A) A Christian is called for military service. He conscientiously
refuses. He might have already registered or gone through other
legally required procedures, in some lands even doing so with the
military authorities. But he declines induction. Once he makes

Watch Tower Bible and Tract Society
Governing Body

July 28, 1978, No. 341

Page 5

that position clear, Caesar is going to react.

(B) Now, the government 'orders' (through the courts, the police,
the military, or other agency) that the one refusing must perform
some work thought to be essential. Or, they might order him to
prison for a sentence of so many years. In either case, whatever
work he is asked to do--either at a work camp, a farm, a hospital,
a prison--he must now consider if his conscience permits him to do
that work and whether he wants to suffer the consequences of refusing
to do that work if it is contrary to Christian principles.

The same procedure could be followed in lands that seem to
respect the Christian position and that do not even try to draft
the Christian. But they do order him to perform certain work they
think he can do as an "alternative." So does "alternative" just
become a term without special significance, if in the end it is the
same work?

So, whether we see a prison sentence as different from what
might be viewed as a compromise with the military in what is
termed "alternative" service, is to us not as important as what kind
of work one might be ordered to do in either prison or in a work
camp or other location. The ordering agencies, locations of work
and management of work sites are all variables that we cannot
control. The Christian's conscientious reaction to these allows him
to follow through under all these variables.

Thus, what happened in Canada, ending up doing the same work
anyway (different from the U. S. experience), may have shown the need
to keep the conscience clean on basic principles and not get bound
up with a confusing "agency" approach.

On the other hand, there may be something in our grasp of matters
that is deficient and, if so, we will await your assistance.

Please be assured of our Christian love and best wishes.

Your brothers,

BRANCH COMMITTEE

per _____
       for K. LITTLE (ALAN)

The Branch in Spain wrote a five-page letter.

These are some of the points raised in their letter:

;h Tower Bible and Tract Society of Pennsylvania
;n.: Governing Body
4 Columbia Heights
rooklyn, New York   11201   U.S.A.
/2 254   July 28, 1978

Page 2

cooperating with this program, their consciences rebelling against
being so closely associated with a martial organization. It has
not been too difficult to reason with young people on the point of
substitute service under this present law. In fact, even Catholic
objectors (whose position is ideological, not religious) have pro-
tested the present arrangement and some of them have been in prison for refusing to comply.

Right now this legislation is under review and different
substitute service provisions will soon be set up. During this
transition period objectors are being sent home until further
call up after the new law is on the books. A few are asked to
sign a statement promising to obey any law concerning performance
of civic and social service that might be adopted in the future.
Although no one knows exactly what provisions will be included
in future legislation, more than one have signed, unwisely, such
a promise.

When an elder discusses the matter of substitute service
with someone, that person generally accepts that substitution
amounts to equivalence. But this idea is not usually truly understood. Rather, it is taken to be the organizations's viewpoint,
and the elders present it as well as they can and the brothers
loyally follow through as they know is expected of them. But it
seems to us that many brothers find our reasoning somewhat artificial. They do not clearly appreciate on what basis we cannot
accept civil work as directed by a conscription board operating
under law, and we can, on the other hand, properly accept the
very same work as a penalty prescribed by a court acting under
law. Of course, the elder will say that the former case is a
service rendered and considered by Caesar as equivalent to military service, and the latter case is punishment. But the work
remains the same. (We must remember too that a court's imposing
objectionable service of a political or warlike nature does not
make it acceptable, since a Christian would refuse it under whatever guise it was required.) It is hard for the brothers here to
understand that the motive of Caesar in requiring civil service
of the individual (namely to substitute for service under arms)
makes any service unsuitable, even though the work itself and
its results be inoffensive.

This dilemma is more difficult to reconcile because the
modern-day Christian in Spain recognizes his obligation to obey
Caesar's commands to the extent possible, up to the point that
he is asked to do something against his godly conscience and
his relationship to Jehovah is threatened. This is why brothers
travel all the way across the country to present themselves for
induction, knowing that they will be unable to follow through

Watch Tower Bible and Tract Society of Pennsylvania
Attn.: Governing Body, Writing Committee
124 Columbia Heights
Brooklyn, New York 11201   U.S.A.
NQ 254   July 28, 1978

Page 3

once they arrive and are asked to join the ranks. So it is hard
for them to see any valid objection to obeying Caesar when he
requires non-warlike service of them.

     It is also noticeably difficult to help brothers to see
clearly why in some other countries brothers can of their own
volition seek certain work to avoid problems with military conscription, but that it would be unchristian to accept assignment
to the very same type of work as a substitute for military service. One reasons and reminds them of the way substitute service
programs are usually administered, citing the text that bids us
not to be slaves of men (1 Corinthians 7:23), but in their eyes
it is just a technicality for such a brother to seek work before
being asked to perform it. His real motive is to carry out a
service that will be accepted as a substitute for service in the
armed forces.

     As a part of the research for this report, a member of the
branch committee spoke extensively with three brothers who were
exemplary in their neutral stand years ago. He also conversed
with three mature elders, two of them from other countries, who
have not personally faced the neutrality issue in Spain. Varying
viewpoints surfaced on many aspects of this matter, but there
was complete agreement on one point: Practically none of our
young brothers really understand why we cannot accept "substitute
service" if it is of civic nature and not under the control of
the military. It seems clear that most of the elders do not
understand it, either, and therefore they often send youngsters
to the office to get information. So the question comes up,
Why don't they understand? Is it a lack of personal study? Or
is it because the arguments and reasonings we are using are not
convincing enough or do not have a clear and firm Bible basis?

     For the purpose of clarifying our position and its foundation,
and thus being able to help our brothers to make sound decisions
in this field, we think the following questions should be thrashed
out:

     If citizens are assigned to help in road work because of
some disaster, we do not refuse to cooperate. But if the same
work is offered as an alternative to military service, we will
not accept it. We would consider it a violation of our Christian
neutrality. But why? What violates one's neutrality? Is it not
the identifying of oneself with a political movement or with the
war machine? Does performing such a substitute civil service
result in this identification?

Watch Tower Bible and Tract Society of Pennsylvania
Attn.: Governing Body, Writing Committee
124 Columbia Heights
Brooklyn, New York 11201 U.S.A.
No 254   July 28, 1978

Page 4

     In reasoning on the subject of substitute civil service in
anticipation of the time when such would be offered here in Spain,
many brothers have based their stance on the idea that by performing civil duties assigned by the government one would be freeing
another person to bear arms and to serve as a part of the war
machine. But this is not usually true in a literal sense, and
we can ask if it applies at all when the civil service consists
of work done in hospitals, institutions for the elderly, or many
other tasks of social value.

     There is no doubt in the minds of our brothers in regard to
the proper position to take if substitute civil service really
means direct support of an organization that is condemned in the
Bible. But in cases where the activities are of benefit to other
people, far removed from the destructive, harmful and political
aspects that are objectionable to students of God's Word, does
substitution (for military service) really constitute equivalence
(with military service)?

     When a young man reaches the age of 20 years, the civil
government obligates him to give a great part of two or three
years of his life as a service to Ceesar. (And this is especially
the case in Spain, where there is a large army and military personnel care for any number of non-military duties for which the
government insists it could not pay normal wages.) If the individual's conscience does not allow him to do military service, the
civil government offers an alternative service in an effort to
accommodate his Christian conscience and to avoid offending public
opinion by "letting some off lightly." Would it not be similar to
paying taxes to which a government has a right? Would it not be
part of our rendering tribute "to him who calls for tribute"?
(Romans 13:7) Is it really so different from the case of being
"impressed into service" as mentioned in Matthew 5:41?

     How can we convincingly claim and show that an objector that
seeks out work that he knows will bring him exemption from military
service is not violating his Christian neutrality and that one
that accepted the very same work by assignment in lieu of military
service is disassociating himself from the congregation?

     We apply to ourselves Bible texts that show that Christians
are serving as ambassadors or envoys and therefore must maintain
their neutral position. At the same time we do not renounce
either country or citizenship or passport. We are foreigners,
but not stateless persons. Are we really justified in making
such an extensive application of these Scriptures?

```
Watch Tower Bible and Tract Society of Pennsylvania
Attn.: Governing Body, Writing Committee
124 Columbia Heights
Brooklyn, New York  11201  U.S.A.
NR 254    July 28, 1978

Page 5

     In relation to the above questions, all the members of the
Spain branch committee present for the consideration of this
matter of substitute service agree,and we feel that our present
position needs to be reexamined, and either reinforced or modified.
We are conscious of the fact that the material on neutrality cannot
be considered in depth in the publications for reasons of prudence.
That means that there may be other principles, or different aspects
of the well-known principles that could be more fully explained.

     There is another point which we have discussed, without until
now arriving at a unanimous point of view.  It has to do with
military administration of a civic substitute service.  In certain
countries the military establishment cares for many parts of the
country's activities, supervising in some cases harvests, highway
maintenance, and so on.  It is always possible that, even though
the work done is of civil nature and is in itself inoffensive to
the Christian, it be assigned or perhaps the workers be paid
through military channels.  If a law made by civil authority
empowered the Ministry of Defense or even the Army to administer
a program of civil construction, hospital or social benefit work,
without any oath, warlike or political activities or proximity
to the same, would bowing to this arrangement made by the civil
government constitute a violation of Christian neutrality?

     We have complete confidence in Jehovah and His organization
and we are looking forward to receiving any clarification from
the Governing Body in order to adjust our own thinking or to help
our brothers to continue faithfully in their service to God and
go on enjoying His approval.

     Receive a fervent expression of love and best wishes.

                    Your brothers,

                    Asociación de los
                    Testigos de Jehová [13]
```

I personally had already presented to the Body some fourteen pages of historical, Scriptural and lexicographical evidence pointing in the same direction (See Appendix A "For Chapter 5"). Consider, then, what took place in the last three of the six Governing Body sessions referred to:

13　See also the book *In Search of Christian Freedom*, pages 255-270 which has been inserted into Appendix B of this 2018 edition of *Crisis of Conscience,* for added documentation and quotations demonstrating the degree to which this policy presented serious problems for both the male Witnesses affected and the Branch Committee members of several countries.

At the October 11, 1978, meeting, of thirteen members present, *nine* voted in favor of changing the traditional policy so that the decision to accept or reject alternative service would be left to the conscience of the individual; four did not vote for this. The result? Since there were then sixteen members in the Body (though not all were present) and since nine was not two-thirds of sixteen, no change was made.

On October 18 there was discussion on the subject but no vote taken. On November 15, all sixteen members were present and eleven voted for changing the policy so that the Witness who conscientiously felt he could accept such service would not be automatically categorized as unfaithful to God and disassociated from the congregation. This *was* a two-thirds majority. Was the change made?

No, for after a brief intermission, Governing Body member Lloyd Barry, who had voted with the majority in favor of a change, announced that he had changed his mind and would vote for continuance of the traditional policy. That destroyed the two-thirds majority. A subsequent vote taken, with fifteen members present, showed nine favoring a change, five against and one abstention.[14]

Six sessions of the Governing Body had discussed the issue and, when votes were taken, *in every case* a majority of the Governing Body members had favored removal of the existing policy. The one vote with the two-thirds majority lasted less than one hour and the policy remained in force. As a result Witness men were still expected to risk imprisonment rather than accept alternative service—even though, as the letters coming in from the survey showed, they might conscientiously feel such acceptance was proper in God's sight. Incredible as it may seem, this was the position taken, and most members of the Body appeared to accept it all as nothing to be disturbed about. They were, after all, simply following the rules in force.

---

14 Lloyd Barry had left. According to my records, those voting in favor of a change were: John Booth, Ewart Chitty, Ray Franz, George Gangas, Leo Greenlees, Albert Schroeder, Grant Suiter, Lyman Swingle and Dan Sydlik. Those voting against were: Carey Barber, Fred Franz, Milton Henschel, William Jackson and Karl Klein. Ted Jaracz abstained.

A year later, on September 15, 1979, another vote was taken and it was evenly divided, half for a change, half against.

For *another 16 years* the policy remained in effect, until the May 1, 1996 *Watchtower* abruptly decreed that acceptance of alternative service was now a matter of conscience. During those 16 years, thousands of Witnesses, mainly young men, spent time in prison for refusing to accept assignments to perform various forms of community service as an alternative to military service. As late as 1988, a report by Amnesty International stated that in France, "More than 500 conscientious objectors to military service, the vast majority of them Jehovah's Witnesses, were imprisoned during the year." For the same year, in Italy, "Approximately 1,000 conscientious objectors, mostly Jehovah's Witnesses, were reported to be imprisoned in 10 military prisons for refusing to perform military service or the alternative civilian service."[15]

That is just a partial picture. If that one Governing Body member had not changed his vote in 1978, virtually none of these men would have gone to prison—for the branch office committees' reports give clear evidence that it was not the personal, individual consciences of these young men that produced the imprisonment. It was the *compulsion to adhere to an organizationally imposed policy.*

The policy change is unquestionably welcome. Nonetheless, the fact that it took some 50 years for the organization's to finally remove itself from this area of personal conscience surely has significance. One cannot but think of all the thousands of years collectively lost during half a century by Witness men as to their freedom to associate with family and friends, or to contribute to their own economy and the economy of those related to them, or pursue other worthwhile activities in ways not possible within prison walls. It represents an incredible waste of valuable years for the simple reason that it was unnecessary, being the result of an unscriptural position, imposed by organizational authority.

----

15   In several European countries the Watch Tower Society has recently experienced some difficulty in attaining or retaining a certain status with the government. The change in policy with regard to alternative service may be related to their concern in this area.

Had there been a frank acknowledgment of error, not merely doctrinal error, but error in wrongfully invading the right of conscience of others, and of regret over the harmful consequences of that intrusion, one might find reason for sincere commendation, even reason for hope of some measure of fundamental reform. Regrettably, the May 1, 1996 *Watchtower nowhere* deals with these factors and contains not even a hint of regret for the effects of the wrong position enforced for over half a century. It does not even offer any explanation as to why the mistaken policy was rigidly insisted upon for over fifty years. In a couple of sentences it makes the change, doing so as if by edict, one that in effect says, "Your conscience may now be operative in this area."

In place of apology, the organization instead seems to feel it deserves applause for having made changes it should have had the good sense (and humility) to have made decades earlier, changes that were resisted in the face of ample evidence presented from the Scriptures, both from within the Body and from Branch Office committees. Some of these Branch committees presented not only all the Scriptural evidence found in the May 1, 1996 *Watchtower,* but even *more extensive* and *more carefully reasoned* Scriptural evidence. They did this back in 1978 but what they wrote was, in effect, shrugged off or discounted by those of the Governing Body who held out for maintaining the traditional policy then in place.

Paragraph 17 of the article, for example, points out that "compulsory service was practiced in Bible times" and contains a brief quotation from a history book that describes the "corvée" labor under Roman rule and the example of Simon of Cyrene being compelled to carry Jesus' cross. The memorandum I submitted to the Governing Body 18 years before (in 1978) contained *fourteen pages of evidence* of this identical evidence, as also extensive documentation of the fact that the Biblical term for "tax" (Hebrew *mas;* Greek *phoros*) was commonly used to describe payment *in the form of compulsory service.* (See Appendix A.) The major Biblical texts cited in the 1996 *Watchtower* in support of viewing compulsory service as acceptable, such as Matthew 5:41; 27:32; 1 Peter 2:13; Titus 3:1, 2, are all found (along with numerous other texts) not only in the memorandum I had provided but also in many of the letters written by branch committees whose members reasoned that alternative service had Biblical acceptance. The Scriptural evidence had thus been presented back in 1978 but was simply not given weight by those Governing Body members voting against any change in policy. For 18 years the traditional position continued to receive greater consideration.

Even error—if it is *Watch Tower* error—is presented as somehow beneficial. This same 1996 *Watchtower* discusses the organization's earlier erroneous interpretation of the "higher powers" or "superior authorities" of Romans chapter 13, which interpretation rejected the clear evidence that these referred to human governmental authorities and insisted that the "higher powers" referred only to God and Christ. This wrong interpretation had replaced an even earlier, correct view and was taught from 1929 until 1962. The May 1, 1996 *Watchtower* (page 14) says of this wrong understanding:

> Looking back, it must be said that this view of things, exalting as it did the supremacy of Jehovah and his Christ, helped God's people to maintain an uncompromisingly neutral stand throughout this difficult period [that is, the period of World War II and of the Cold War].

This in effect says that to have had the *right* understanding, the understanding the apostle Paul intended when he wrote his counsel, would either not have been sufficient in guiding, or would not have been as *effective* in protecting against unchristian action, as was the erroneous view taught by the Watch Tower organization! There is nothing to show that God guides his people by means of error. He strengthens them with truth, not error, in time of crisis.—1 John 1:5; Psalm 43:3; 86:11.

More recently the August 15, 1998 *Watchtower* also dealt with the issue of alternative service in place of military service, as shown here:

Feelings of Having Suffered Needlessly

[6] In the past, some Witnesses have suffered for refusing to share in an activity that their conscience now might permit. For example, this might have been their choice years ago as to certain types of civilian service. A brother might now feel that he could conscientiously perform such without overstepping his Christian neutrality regarding the present system of things.

[7] Was it unrighteous on Jehovah's part to allow him to suffer for rejecting what he now might do without consequences? Most who have had that experience would not think so. Rather, they rejoice that they had the opportunity of demonstrating publicly and clearly that they were determined to be firm on the issue of universal sovereignty. (Compare Job 27:5.) What reason could anyone have to regret having followed his conscience in taking a firm stand for Jehovah? By loyally upholding Christian principles as they understood them or by responding to the proddings of conscience, they proved worthy of Jehovah's friendship. Certainly, it is wise to avoid a course that would disturb one's conscience or that would likely cause others to be stumbled. We can think in this regard of the example that the apostle Paul set.—1 Corinthians 8: 12, 13; 10:31-33.

[8] In order to please Jehovah, the Jews were required to obey the Ten Commandments and also a wide variety of about 600 additional laws. Later, under the Christian arrangement, obedience to these laws as such was no longer a requirement for serving Jehovah, not even for fleshly Jews. The laws no longer binding included those dealing with circumcision, keeping the Sabbath, offering animal sacrifices, and observing certain dietary restrictions. (1 Corinthians 7:19; 10:25; Colossians 2:16, 17; Hebrews 10:1, 11-14) Jews—including the apostles—who became Christians were released from the obligation to keep laws that they were required to obey when they were under the Law covenant. Did they complain that God's arrangement was unrighteous in having formerly required of them things that were no longer necessary? No, they rejoiced in the broadened understanding of Jehovah's purposes.—Acts 16:4, 5.

[9] In modern times, there have been some Witnesses who were very strict in their view of what they would or would not do. For that reason they suffered more than others. Later, increased knowledge helped them to expand their view of matters. But they have no reason to regret having earlier acted in harmony with their conscience, even when this possibly brought extra suffering. It truly is commendable that they demonstrated their willingness to suffer in faithfulness to Jehovah, to "do all things for the sake of the good news." Jehovah blesses that kind of godly devotion. (1 Corinthians 9:23; Hebrews 6:10) The apostle Peter wrote with insight: "If, when you are doing good and you suffer, you endure it, this is a thing agreeable with God."—1 Peter 2:20.

Once again there is no shouldering of responsibility for the harm done to people's lives by the imposition of a policy that had no Biblical basis. The suffering undergone, which over a period of half a century meant imprisonment for thousands of young men, is presented as if purely the result of the individuals feeling obliged to reject "certain types of civilian service," due to "loyally upholding Christian principles as they understood them or by responding to the proddings of conscience."

There is no reason to doubt that many, probably most, of these young men felt clear in their minds and hearts as to "Christian principles" if the issue were regarding participation in the bloodshed connected with war, or the issue of entrance into the military, with its emphasis on force and violence. But the issue they faced was not either of these matters. The "alternative service" provision was there *precisely because their government gave consideration to conscientious objection in those areas.*

Perhaps the writer of the *Watchtower* article presented was in ignorance of the reality of the situation. But the article had to have been read and approved by at least five members of the Governing Body, those forming the then current Writing Committee. They of all persons knew how inaccurate the picture here presented is, for they knew that Branch committee after Branch committee stated that the young men in their countries did not understand the Biblical basis for the policy, and submitted to it, not out of 'loyalty to Christian principles,' but out of submission to an organizational directive. They knew that many of the Branch committee members themselves advanced reasons why Christian principles actually allowed for acceptance of such "types of civilian service."

Quotations from the 1978 letters of Branch committee members in such countries as Austria,, Brazil, Chile, Denmark, Italy, Norway, Poland,, and Thailand can also be found in the book *In Search of Christian Freedom,* pages 259-266, 398, 399, demonstrating these points.

Statements comparable to these are found in numerous other letters from Branch committees. They show how falsely the matter is presented in the August 15, 1998 *Watchtower,* when it says of a person who suffered due to holding that policy:

> Was it unrighteous on Jehovah's part to allow him to suffer for rejecting what he now might do without consequences? Most who have had that experience would not think so. Rather, they rejoice that they had the opportunity of demonstrating publicly and clearly that they were determined to be firm on the issue of universal sovereignty. (Compare Job 27:5) What reason could anyone have to regret having followed his conscience in taking a firm stand for Jehovah? By loyally upholding Christian principles as they understood them or by responding to the proddings of conscience, they proved worthy of Jehovah's friendship.

The August 15, 1998 *Watchtower* article compounds the wrongness of its presentation by thereafter attempting to find an analogy for this situation in the experience of Jews who had been under the Mosaic Law and its requirement for obedience, and who later as Christians were no longer bound to that requirement. The article follows this with the question:

> Did they complain that God's arrangement was unrighteous in having formerly required of them things that were no longer necessary?

The analogy is completely without basis, since God himself *did* provide the Law covenant with its requirements, which served a beneficial purpose, but He did *not* provide the Watch Tower's arbitrary policy requiring refusal of alternative service, with its imposition of sanctions for failing to adhere to that policy. In the words of God's Son, it was a "tradition of men," a "human precept," one that "made void the word of God" on the issue involved.[16]

One cannot but think here of published statements such as these in the October 15, 1995 *Watchtower* in its article "Watch Out for Self-Righteousness." On pages 29, 30 the following paragraphs appear:

> What are some of the traits that we must "watch out" for? Self-righteous individuals usually "speak, and stand, and look as if they had never done a wrong," explains the *Encyclopædia of Religion and Ethics.* The self-righteous are also boastful and self-promoting, which was a major problem with the Pharisees.

By attempting to divert attention from themselves to God, as if He needed defending for the responsibility for the "needless suffering," the Governing Body again makes evident that, rather than expressing sincere regret for a wrong course and its harmful consequences, primary concern is to protect its image and avoid any diminishing of its organizational authority and control.

Because of the power of control the organization exercises over its members through its decisions, and because of the enormous effect that these can have on people's lives, it seems proper here to review what I

---

16   Matthew 15:6-9.

consider one of the greatest examples of inconsistency experienced in my nine years on that Body. It still seems difficult to believe that men who voiced such strong concern for "an uncompromising stand," could simultaneously gloss over a circumstance that can only be described as shocking. You may judge the appropriateness of that term by what follows.

6

DOUBLE STANDARDS

The doctors of the law and the Pharisees sit in the chair of Moses; therefore do what they tell you; pay attention to their words. But do not follow their practice; for they say one thing and do another.
— Matthew 23:2, 3. *New English Bible.*

MANY worthwhile and helpful discussions can be found in the publications of the Watch Tower Society. Frequently articles supply support for belief in a Creator, encourage wholesome family life, exhort to honesty, stress the importance of humility and other virtues, doing this on the basis of Scripture. Other articles speak out strongly against religious deception and hypocrisy. Consider, for example, the portion of an article published in the *Watchtower* magazine reproduced on the following page.

The Watch Tower Society has, throughout its entire history, never been guilty of what it describes as "condoning and 'whitewashing' the wrongdoing and violation of God's righteous standards and way" on the part of the various religious organizations and their leaders. The Watch Tower publications have taken the lead in boldly publicizing worldwide any misconduct or evidence of hypocrisy within these organizations. They have pointed out the parallel between the deceptiveness of such religious leaders and the Pharisees of Jesus' day. They have stated repeatedly their own declared position of strict adherence to righteous standards, moral integrity and upright and honest dealings with all.

It is precisely this that made so disturbing certain information that came to light at the same time the issue of alternative service was being debated within the Governing Body of Jehovah's Witnesses.

Can You Be True to God, YET HIDE THE FACTS?

WHAT results when a lie is let go unchallenged? Does not silence help the lie to pass as truth, to have freer sway to influence many, perhaps to their serious harm?

What happens when misconduct and immorality are allowed to go unexposed and uncondemned? Is this not like covering over an infection without any effort to cure it and keep it from spreading?

When persons are in great danger from a source that they do not suspect or are being misled by those they consider their friends, is it an unkindness to warn them? They may prefer not to believe the warning. They may even resent it. But does that free one from the moral responsibility to give that warning?

If you are among those seeking to be faithful to God, the issues these questions raise are vital for you today. Why? Because God's servants in every period of history have had to face up to the challenge these issues present. They have had to expose falsehood and wrongdoing and warn people of dangers and deception—not just in a general way, but in a specific way, in the interest of pure worship. It would have been far easier to keep silent or say only what people wanted to hear. But faithfulness to God and love of neighbor moved them to speak. They realized that "better is a revealed reproof than a concealed love."—Prov. 27:5.

THE CONTINUING PATTERN

Consider the situation in ancient Israel and the example that God's prophets then set. Wrongdoing became rampant in that nation. Dishonesty, violence, immorality and hypocrisy disgraced the name of the God whom the Israelites claimed to worship. Did the people welcome divine correction? To the contrary, the Bible shows that they said this to God's prophets:

" 'You must not see,' and to the ones having [inspired] visions, 'You must not envision for us any straightforward things. Speak to us smooth things; envision deceptive things. Turn aside from the way; deviate from the path.' "—Isa. 30:9-11.

The majority of the religious leaders sought popularity by doing just that, condoning and "whitewashing" the wrongdoing and violation of God's righteous standards and ways. But God's instructions to his true prophets are exemplified by what he said to the prophet Ezekiel:

"Now as regards you, O son of man, a watchman is what I have made you to

WOULD YOU RATHER HAVE THE TRUTH COVERED OVER . . . ?

THE WATCHTOWER — JANUARY 15, 1974

. . . OR DO YOU WANT TO KNOW THE FACTS?

35

The information came from Mexico. As startling as the information itself was, what I found far more disquieting was the stark contrast it revealed between the organizational position adopted toward that country as compared with that adopted in another country—the East African country of Malawi (formerly Nyasaland).

To appreciate this it is important to know certain background. Beginning in 1964, Jehovah's Witnesses in Malawi began to experience persecution and violence on a scale rarely equaled in modern times. Successive waves of vicious countrywide attacks and brutality by savage mobs swept over them in 1964, 1967, 1972 and again in 1975. In the first attack, 1,081 Malawian families saw their little homes burned or otherwise demolished, 588 fields of crops destroyed. In the 1967 attacks Witnesses reported the rapings of more than one thousand of their women, one mother being sexually violated by six different men, her thirteen-year-old daughter by three men. At least forty of the women were reported to have suffered miscarriages due to this. In each wave of violence, beatings, torture and even murder went virtually unchecked by the authorities and reached such intensity that thousands of families fled their homes and fields to neighboring countries. In 1972 authoritative estimates were that 8,975 fled to Zambia, 11,600 to Mozambique. When violence subsided, in time the families filtered back to their homeland. Then a new wave forced them to flee again. Adding to the tragedy of all this were the reports coming out of the camps of small children dying because of lack of medicine and medical treatment.[1]

---

1   Details of these attacks and the conditions in the refugee camps are found in the *1965 Yearbook of Jehovah's Witnesses*, p. 171; *Awake!* magazine, February 8, 1968, pp. 16-22; the *Watchtower*, February 1, 1968, pp. 71-79; *Awake!*, December 8, 1972, pp. 9-28; December 8, 1975, pp. 3-13.

What was the issue around which this recurrent storm of violence revolved? It was the refusal of the Witnesses to purchase a party card of the ruling political party. Malawi was a one-party state, ruled by the Malawi Congress Party through its head, Dr. H. Kamuzu Banda, who was "president for life" of the country. Jehovah's Witnesses who inquired were informed by the Society's Branch Office that to buy such a party card would be a violation of their Christian neutrality, a compromise, hence, unfaithfulness to God. The Branch position was upheld by the world headquarters organization and presented in detail in the Watch Tower Society's publications. The vast majority of Malawian Witnesses held firm to that position even though at enormous cost to themselves.

The brutality that was practiced upon defenseless people in Malawi can never be justified. There is no question in my mind about that. The government and party officials were determined to attain a state of total conformity to their policy that all persons should possess a party card; it was viewed as tangible evidence of loyalty to the governmental structure. The methods used to attain that goal were depraved, criminal.

There is, however, a serious question in my mind about the position taken by the Branch Office and supported by the central headquarters in Brooklyn. There are a number of reasons for such question.

In 1975, I was assigned to write material on the latest campaign of terror being carried on against the Malawian Witnesses. In explaining why Jehovah's Witnesses viewed the purchase of the party card so seriously, I employed information that had been published earlier, tracing a parallel between their stand and that of Christians in early centuries who refused to put a pinch of incense on an altar as a sacrifice to the "genius" of the Roman emperor.[2] At the time of doing so, I felt a sense of uncertainty—was the parallel *completely true?* There was no question but that the placing of the incense on the altar was viewed as an act of worship. Was purchasing a party card just as clearly an act of *worship?* I could not

---

2   This argument was presented in the *Awake!* magazine of December 8, 1972, p. 20. The article I wrote appeared in the December 8, 1975 issue of the same publication.

really see any strong argument in that direction. Was it, then, a violation of Christian neutrality, a breaking of integrity with God?

I cannot say that my thinking on the matter fully crystallized at that time, nor am I dogmatic on the point today. But the following thoughts came to mind, making me wonder how solid a basis the organization, of whose Governing Body I was now a member, had for taking an intransigent, unbending position of condemnation of such card purchase as an act of unfaithfulness to God:

The issue hinged on the fact that the card was a "political" card representing membership in a "political" party. To many, and particularly to Jehovah's Witnesses, the word "political" is viewed as describing something inherently bad. Corrupt politicians have, over the centuries, contributed toward the unsavory connotation the term often carries today. The same might be said, however, of such terms as "pious," which frequently calls up visions of sanctimoniousness and feigned holiness due to the hypocrisy of some religious persons. Yet the term "pious" actually relates to dutiful reverence and earnest devotion to God; that is its *basic* meaning. Similarly, the word "political" carries this basic definition:

> Having a fixed or regular system or administration of government; relating to civil government and its administration; concerned in state affairs or national measures; pertaining to a nation or state, or to nations or states, as distinguished from *civil* or *municipal;* treating of politics or government; as, *political* parties.[3]

I knew that the word "political" as well as "politics" came from the Greek word *polis* meaning simply a *city* (as in the word "metropolis"). In Greek *polites* meant a "citizen" (the English word "citizen" being drawn from a Latin term likewise meaning "city"), and the adjective *politikos* (from which our English "political" is derived) meant "of the citizens, of the state." The English language received these terms through Latin and the Latin term *politia* means simply "citizenship, government, administration." Such words as "police," and "policy" all derive from the same source.

---

3   *New Webster's Dictionary,* Deluxe Encyclopedic Edition.

Obviously, all government is *political* in this fundamental sense of the word. Every government on earth is a political entity; every people organized under a particular form of government form a "polity" (from Greek *politeia*). To be a *citizen* of any country is to be a *member* of such a political state, enjoying the benefits and bearing the responsibilities this membership brings. The *extent* to which one may submit to the demands of such a political state may vary; but the membership is still a fact.

It is of such political states and their rulers that the apostle Paul writes at Romans chapter thirteen, exhorting Christians to be submissive to these as unto "God's servant" or "minister." True, political activity may become corrupt—and there is no question but that the political state of Rome became extremely corrupt—yet that of itself does not make everything political inherently evil. Nor does it make national citizenship—membership in a political state or nation—something inherently bad. Political parties in their competition for power are largely responsible for the added, subordinate (not the *basic* or *fundamental*) meaning which the word "politics" may come to have, that of "the plotting or scheming of those seeking personal power, glory, position, or the like." This *is* evil, but not because everything related to political activity is evil, for the absence of political activity is, in its secular sense, the absence of government.

Which leads to the second reason for my questioning. I can understand why a person could conscientiously desire to be separate from the political strife and fierce competition that generally characterize *party* politics. The factors that made me think seriously about the situation in Malawi, however, was that it was and remained until recent times, a *one-party state.* The Malawi Congress Party was the country's ruling party with no other parties allowed. It thus became, in a *de facto* sense, equivalent to the government itself, the "superior authority." If a person could be a citizen, and hence a member of the national political community, without violating integrity to God, where was the evidence to show that being submissive to the government's insistence (expressed from the head of state on down) that *everyone* purchase a card of the ruling party would constitute such a violation of integrity to God? I wondered then, and I still wonder, how major is the difference?

Most of all I have asked myself whether, if found in a similar circumstance in Bible times, Abraham, Daniel, Jesus and his apostles, or early Christians, would have viewed submission to such government demands in the way the organization has presented it? Granted, there was no actual *law* passed in Malawi requiring the purchase of the card, but would such a technicality have been viewed by Christ Jesus as crucial in the face of the statements made nationwide by the ruling authorities?[4] How would Christians of the first century have viewed it in the light of the apostle's exhortation, "Render to all their dues, to him who calls for the tax, the tax; for him who calls for the tribute, the tribute; to him who calls for fear, such fear; to him who calls for honor, such honor"?[5]

To submit to such demands, then as now, would certainly be condemned by some as "compromise," a "caving in" to the demands of the political authorities. But I am sure that in Jesus' day there were many devout Jews who felt that to accede to the demands of a military officer of the hated Roman Empire that one carry certain baggage for a mile would be just as detestable; many would have suffered punishment and mistreatment rather than submit. Yet Jesus said to submit and to go, not just one mile, but two![6] To many of his listeners this counsel was doubtless repugnant, smacking of craven surrender instead of unbending adherence to a position of no collaboration with alien, Gentile powers.

Of one thing I eventually became certain and that was that I would want to be very confident that the position adopted was solidly founded on God's Word, and not on mere human reasoning, before I could think of advocating it or promulgating it, particularly in view of the grave consequences it produced. I no longer felt confident that the Scriptures did give such *clear* and *unequivocal* support to the policy taken toward the situation in Malawi. I could see how one might feel impelled by conscience to refuse to purchase such a card and, if that were the case, then one *should* refuse, in harmony with the apostle's counsel at Romans, chapter

---

4   Compare Matthew 17:24-27, where Jesus states that a certain tax did not rightly apply to him, but he nevertheless tells Peter to pay it so as 'not to offend the authorities.'

5   Romans 13:7.

6   Matthew 5:41.

fourteen, verses 1 to 3 and verse 23.[7] But I could not see the basis for anyone's imposing his conscience on another in this matter, nor of presenting
such position as a rigid standard to be adhered to by others, particularly
without greater support from Scripture and fact.

Against such background of circumstances relating to Malawi, consider
now the information that came to light during the Governing Body's discussion of the alternative service issue. Many of the statements made by
members arguing this issue reflected the strict, unyielding attitude encouraged on the part of the Malawian Witnesses. Statements such as these were
made by those opposing change in the existing alternative service policy:

> Even if there is the slightest suggestion of compromise, or a doubt, we
> should not do it.
>
> There must be no compromise. . . . Again, it needs to be made clear
> that a stand of neutrality, as "no part of the world," keeping clear of those
> arms of the world—religion, politics and the military—supporting them
> neither directly nor indirectly, is the stand that will be blessed by Jehovah.
> We want no grey areas, we want to know exactly where we stand as non-
> compromising Christians.[8]
>
> . . . doing civilian work in lieu of military duty is . . . a tacit or implied
> acknowledgement of one's obligation to Caesar's war machine. . . . A
> Christian therefore cannot be required to support the military establish-
> ment either directly or indirectly.[9]
>
> For one of Jehovah's Witnesses to tell a judge that he is willing to
> accept work in a hospital or similar work would be making a "deal" with
> the judge, and he would be breaking his integrity with God.[10]

---

7   These verses say: "Welcome the man having weaknesses in his faith, but not to make deci-
    sions on inward questionings. One man has faith to eat everything, but the man who is weak
    eats vegetables. Let the one eating not look down on the one not eating, and let the one not
    eating not judge the one eating, for God has welcomed that one." "But if he has doubts, he
    is already condemned if he eats, because he does not eat out of faith. Indeed, everything that
    is not out of faith is sin."

8   From the memorandum submitted by Governing Body member Lloyd Barry.

9   From the memorandum by Governing Body member Karl Klein.

10 From statements made by Governing Body member Fred Franz and spelled out in a letter by
    William Jackson to Paul Trask.

DOUBLE STANDARDS   173

To accept the alternative civil service is a form of moral support to the entire arrangement.[11]

We should have a united stand all over the world. We should be decisive in this matter. . . . If we were to allow the brothers this latitude we would have problems. . . . the brothers need to have their consciences educated."[12]

If we yield to Caesar then there is no witness given.[13]

Those who accept this substitute service are taking the easy way out.[14]

What I find amazing is that at the same time these strong, unyielding statements were made, those making them were aware of the situation then existing in Mexico. When I supplied each member of the Governing Body with a copy of the survey of Branch Committee reports on alternative service, I included material sent in by the Branch Committee of Mexico. It included this portion dealing with the "Identity Cartilla for Military Service" ("cartilla" means a certificate):

> The "Identity Cartilla for Military Service"
> should be obtained by carrying out military service during one year. Those
> who have a Cartilla have the obligation to present themselves when the nation
> calls them, be it by movilization of forces or at least by effecting an act
> of presence. (Articles 136 to 139, page 6)
>
> However, although the law prohibits the military or members of the
> Draft Offices to make out "Cartillas" by illegal means, such as payment, the
> great majority of the officials violate these laws. (Articles 50 and 51, page
> 21; Article 3, page 29; Instructive number 1, of September 16, 1977, page 2,
> paragraphs 3 and 4)
>
> Almost any person, under any pretext, can avoid military service
> and pay an official to note down supposed attendances for the weekly instruction,
> (giving appearance of regular attendance) or paying at the same time so that

---

11   From the Denmark Branch Committee letter (Richard Abrahamson, Coordinator), quoted in Lloyd Barry's memorandum.
12   From statements made by member Ted Jaracz.
13   From statement made by member Carey Barber.
14   From statement made by member Fred Franz.

the document is given to them correctly legalized. In Mexico this is very
common. The Mexican government is trying to stop the officials making
out documents of military service for persons not having rendered such
service, when there is no valid justification according to law. Recently
a general said, when the President of the Republic, Licenciado Jose Lopez
Portillo, was at the ceremony of pledging allegiance to the flag, on May
5, 1978, before close to 100,000 young men, draftees, that "the army will
not tolerate illegal operations to obtain Military Service 'Cartilla.'" The
general said: "we have made ourselves responsible, so that in a brief
period of time, the last protuberances of unlawfulness in the service will
be erradicated and we will succeed in that all young men can go to the
Municipal Draft Boards to obtain their 'Cartillas'." (See El Heraldo,
May 6, 1978)

What was the position of Jehovah's Witnesses as to such "illegal operations" in connection with this law? The Branch Committee's letter goes on to say:

Young publishers in Mexico have had no difficulty in relation to
military service. Although the laws on military service are very specific,
generally they are not enforced strictly. If a publisher, upon arriving at
military age, does not present himself voluntarily before a draft board,
they do not call him to do so. On the other hand, those who have their
"cartilla" and are in one of the reserves have never been called. They only
have to go in order to have their "cartilla" stamped when they transfer
from one reserve to the other, but this does not involve any ceremony,
but only presenting themselves in an office having to do with the stamping
of the "cartilla."

The "cartilla" has become a document of identification. It is used
as identification when one requests employment, although it is not indispensable.

In order to obtain a passport, this document is indispensable. One cannot
leave the country without the "cartilla" unless a special permit is obtained
from the military authorities. Publishers who wish to obtain a "cartilla"
go to one of the Draft Boards, to register to receive immediately their
"cartilla" but of course this is not complete, that is, it is not legalized.
Then in order to legalize it they go to someone they know with influence or
directly to an official. For this they have to pay a certain amount of money
(according to what may be asked). In this way the publishers obtain their
"cartilla" or the majority of them that have it.

Put briefly, in Mexico men of draft age were required to undergo a
specified period of military training during a period of one year. Upon
registration the registrant received a certificate or "cartilla" with places for
noting down attendance at weekly military instruction classes. It was illegal and punishable for any official to fill in this attendance record if the
registrant had not actually attended. But officials could be bribed to do so
and many men in Mexico did this bribing. According to the Branch Office
Committee this was also a common practice among Jehovah's Witnesses
in Mexico. Why? Note what the Branch statement goes on to say:

The position of the brothers in Mexico related to this matter was
considered years ago by the Society and we have information that we
have followed since then when the brothers have come to the Society
to inquire on this matter. (See the enclosed photostatic copy.)

What was the information provided by the Society that the Branch
Office in Mexico had been following for years? How was it supplied? How
did the information provided compare with the position taken in Malawi
and with the strong, unbending statements made by Governing Body
members against even "the slightest suggestion of compromise," against
any form of "moral support," either "directly or indirectly," of the military
establishment?

I made a trip to Mexico within a few days of the November 15,
1978, Governing Body session which had resulted in a stalemate on the

alternative service issue. I was assigned to visit the Mexico Branch Office as well as those of several Central American countries. During my meeting with the Mexico Branch Committee they brought up the practice described in their report. They said that the terrible persecution endured by Jehovah's Witnesses in Malawi due to their refusal to buy a party card had caused many Witnesses in Mexico to feel disturbed in their conscience. They made clear, however, that their counsel to the Mexican Witnesses was fully in accord with the counsel the Branch Office had received from the world headquarters. What was that counsel? It may be difficult for some to believe that the counsel given was actually given, but this is the evidence presented by the Branch Committee. First comes this letter:

<pre>
                              February 4, 1960   No. 123
N. H. Knorr
124 Columbia Heights
Brooklyn 1, New York

Dear Brother Knorr:

     We have two questions that we would like the Society's policy
on. First we have a case where the father of the girl is congregation
servant. The girl is married and her husband as well as she were pub-
lishers and living with the father who is congregation servant. The
son-in-law is disfellowshiped because he had another woman. Over a
period of some years this son-in-law raises two families - one by his
legal wife and sister in the truth and lives with her in the home of
his father-in-law who is congregation servant and at the same time
has his other woman and raises a family by her. Of course he is
disfellowshiped all this time. Because of the father-in-law of this
wicked man permitting him to live with his daughter in his own house
has caused much confusion and dissention in the congregation until
the number of publishers has dropped over the years and the congregation
(unit) is in a very bad condition. The question is, does the daughter
have the right to live with this man? He is her legal husband it is
true but at the same time retains another family. Is the father-in-law
doing right to permit this man to live with his daughter (a sister)
in his house? We would like the Society's policy in such a case so
we can handle this case.

     Another thing that has to be contended with here is the law to
march as part of the military training program. After "marching" for
1 year you get a card showing you have marched your 1 year and this
card is your basic document to secure a passport, driver's liscence
and in fact many legal transactions. The brothers understand the
Christian's position of neutrality with regard to such matters but
many brothers pay money to certain officials and they arrange for
their marching card. Is this action right? If a brother actually
marches we apply the policy that they have comprimized and we will
not appoint them as servants for at least 3 years. But here a brother
who probably is a servant or circuit servant has his marching card
which he uses now and then in such legal transactions but he has not
marched. What is correct in this regard? It is and has been the
custom amoung the brothers to pay this sum of money and secure their
marching cards and many of them are now serving as circuit servants
and congregation servants. Are they living a lie? Or is it just
one of those things in this crooked system of things? Shall we
pass it by or should something be done about it? There are so many
irregularities in this country. A cop pulls you over for some traffic
violation and works for his "mordida" or little bribe of 40 cents.
Everyone knows he has no right to do it but they give him the 5 pesos
in order to avoid going to the police station and be charged 50 pesos
and waste much time. It is a habit here, common practice. Is the marching
card the same? Your counsel on this will be appreciated.

                    With you serving Jehovah,
</pre>

What you have just read is a copy of a letter from the Mexico Branch to the president of the Society, the second paragraph of which shows the question the Branch presented for answer on the paying of bribes for a falsified military document. (The copy is of the carbon copy retained by the Branch which, unlike the original, customarily did not bear a signature.)

What reply did their inquiry receive? The Society's answer came in a two-page letter dated June 2, 1960. The second page dealt with the military issue written about. This is that page as presented to me by the Mexico Branch Committee, containing the Society's counsel on their questions.

La Torre Del Vigia
Calzada Melchor Ocampo No. 71
Mexico 4, D.F.
Mexico

June 2, 1960 (157) Page Two

course as that described above would not be necessary. The major stumblingblock, namely, the man's adultery, would be removed. Consequently the matter will have to be presented very straight and unmistakenably to both the congregation servant and his daughter. The congregation servant will have to make the first move in the right direction in the interests of the congregation to which he by his course is a stumblingblock now if he refuses to eject the adulterous son-in-law and continues to furnish offense to the congregation, disturbing its unity and peace of heart and mind. If he chooses not to follow this course, then he must be removed from his position as congregation servant.

As to those who are relieved of military training by a money transaction with the officials who are involved therewith, this is on a par with what is done in other Latin American countries where brothers have paid for their relief through some military official in order to retain their freedom for theocratic activities. If members of the military establishment are willing to accept such an arrangement upon the payment of a fee then that is the responsibility of these representatives of the national organization. In such a case the money paid does not go to the military establishment, but is appropriated by the individual who undertakes the arrangement. If the consciences of certain brothers allow them to enter into such an arrangement for their continued freedom we have no objection. Of course, if they would get into any difficulties over their course of action then they would have to shoulder such difficulties themselves, and we could not offer them any assistance. But if the arrangement is current down there and is recognized by the inspectors who do not make any inquiries into the veracity of the matter then the matter can be passed by for the accruing advantages. Should a military emergency arise and confront these brothers with their marching card it would oblige them to make a decision by which they could not extricate themselves by a money payment and their mettle would be tested and they would have to demonstrate outright where they stand and prove that they are in favor of Christian neutrality in a determinative test.

Faithfully yours in the Kingdom ministry,

Watch Tower B.& T. Society
OF PENNSYLVANIA

Although the Branch's letter had been directed to President Knorr, the reply, bearing the stamped corporation signature, was evidently written by Vice-President Fred Franz, who, as stated earlier, was regularly called upon by President Knorr to formulate policy on matters of this type. The language is typically that of the vice president, not that of the president.

The expressions this letter contains are worth noting. It would be worthwhile to take the time to go back and compare them with the earlier listed statements by Governing Body members arguing the alternative service issue, statements made then that neither minced words nor sought nicety of language but which were often blunt, even hard-hitting.

In this Society reply to the Mexico query, the word "bribe" is avoided, replaced by euphemistic reference to "a money transaction," the "payment of a fee." Emphasis is placed on the fact that the money went to an individual rather than to the "military establishment," apparently indicating that this somehow improved the moral character of the "transaction." The letter speaks of the arrangement being "current down there" and says that as long as inspectors do not inquire about the "veracity of matters" it can be "passed by" for the "accruing advantages." It ends with mention of maintaining integrity in some possible future "determinative test."

If this same message were put in the kind of language heard from Governing Body members in the sessions debating alternative service, I believe it would read more like the following:

> Paying bribes to corrupt officials is done by Jehovah's Witnesses in other Latin American countries. If the men of the war machine are willing to be bribed, the risk is theirs. At least you are not paying the bribe to the actual war machine itself—only to a colonel or other officer who pockets the bribe for himself. If brothers' consciences will let them make a 'deal' with some official who is 'on the take,' we will not object. Of course, if there is trouble they should not look to us for help. Since everyone down there is doing it and inspectors make no issue about the faked documents, then you at the Branch Office can just look the other way too. If war comes that will be time enough to worry about facing up to the issue of neutrality.
>
> Faithfully yours in the Kingdom ministry,

It is not my intent to be sarcastic and I do not believe what is set out constitutes sarcasm. I believe it to be a fair presentation of the Society's counsel to the Mexican Branch Office put in down-to-earth language, free from euphemisms—language more like that used in the Governing Body sessions mentioned.

One reason why this information was so personally shocking to me was that, at the very time the letter stating that the Society had "no objection" if Witnesses in Mexico, faced with a call to military training, chose to "extricate themselves by a money payment," there were scores of young men in the Dominican Republic spending precious years of their life in prison—because they refused the identical kind of training. Some, such as Leon Glass and his brother Enrique, were sentenced two or three times for their refusal, passing as much as a total of nine years of their young manhood in prison. The Society's president and vice president had travelled to the Dominican Republic during those years and had even been made visits to the prison where many of these men were detained. How the situation of these Dominican prisoners could be known by them and yet such a double standard be applied is incomprehensible to me.

Four years after that counsel was given to Mexico the first eruption of violent attacks against Jehovah's Witnesses in Malawi took place (1964) and the issue of paying for a party card arose. The position taken by the Malawi Branch Office was that to do so would be a violation of Christian neutrality, a compromise unworthy of a genuine Christian. The world headquarters knew that this was the position taken. The violence subsided after a while and then broke out again in 1967, so fiercely that thousands of Witnesses were driven into flight from their homeland. The reports of horrible atrocities in increasing number came flooding in to the world headquarters.

What effect did it have on the men leading the organization and on their consciences as regards the position taken in Mexico? In Malawi Witnesses were being beaten and tortured, women were being raped, homes and fields were being destroyed, and entire families were fleeing to other countries—determined to hold to the organization's stand that to pay for a party card would be a morally traitorous act. At the same time, in Mexico, Witness men were *bribing* military officials to complete a certificate falsely stating that they had fulfilled their military service obligations. And when they went to the Branch Office, the staff there followed the Society's counsel and said nothing to indicate in any way that this practice was inconsistent with organizational standards or the principles of God's Word. *Knowing this,* how were those in the position of highest authority in the organization affected? Consider:

Nine years after the Mexico Branch wrote their first letter they wrote a second letter, dated August 27, 1969, also addressed to President Knorr. This time they emphasized a particular point they felt had been overlooked. Set out are pages three and four of the letter provided me by the Branch Committee. I have underlined the main point the Branch focuses on.

Watch Tower Bible and Tract Society
Office of the President
124 Columbia Heights
Brooklyn, New York 11201

August 27, 1969   Page 3   No. 182

        Gilead Graduate. Brother Wayne Preble, a graduate of
Gilead, has written us concerning his plans to marry in January,
1970. Brother Preble is marrying a special pioneer who is not
a graduate of Gilead and has mentioned to us that he has
notified your office. However, we are mentioning the matter
since he is a Gilead graduate and his status will probably change
by this step. Brother Preble at present is serving as a circuit
servant and is doing well and since the special pioneer, Joy
Konnett, has progressed well in the Spanish language she will
be able to accompany him in this service. We look forward to
hearing from you on this matter.

        Brother Pedro Arias is with us and he has had three weeks
of training with a local circuit servant so as to become somewhat acquainted with the manner of carrying on the work here and
the terms we use. He has been assigned a circuit in Monterrey
where he is fairly near the border. We are not recommending
a brother to take the place of Brother Contreras who has been
recommended for Bethel because with the coming of Brother Arias
we have our number of circuit servants complete.

        Question. During the branch meetings in June the matter
was discussed which is presented on pages 34 and 35 of the
"Aid to Answering." Due to the way the military question has
been handled over the years here I brought the matter to the
attention of some of the brothers there but since I thought I
might not have some of the details of the matter in mind it was
thought best to wait and write from here and then get an answer.
<u>After checking back in the files we have found a letter dated
February 4, 1960, No. 123, in which the question was asked as
to what to do because many were paying a sum of money to obtain
the legal document given to those of draft age. However, it was
not mentioned in the question that when this document is obtained
it places the receiver in the first reserve subject to being
called if and when an emergency should arise which the army in
uniform could not handle. So our question is this: Does this
change the policy set out in your letter of June 2, 1960 (157)</u>
Page Two which answered our letter mentioned above? Your
letter said this: "As to those who are relieved of military
training by a money transaction with the officials who are
involved therewith, this is on a par with what is done in other
Latin American countries where brothers have paid for their
relief through some military official in order to retain their
freedom for theocratic activities. If members of the military
establishment are willing to accept such an arrangement upon the
payment of a fee then that is the responsibility of these
representatives of the national organization. In such a case the

Watch Tower Bible and Tract Society
Office of the President
124 Columbia Heights
Brooklyn, New York 11201

August 27, 1969   Page 4   No. 182

money paid does not go to the military establishment, but is
appropriated by the individual who undertakes the arrangement.
If the consciences of certain brothers allow them to enter into
such an arrangement for their continued freedom we have no
objection. Of course, if they would get into any difficulties
over their course of action then they would have to shoulder such
difficulties themselves, and we could not offer them any assistance. But if the arrangement is current down there and is
recognized by the inspectors who do not make any inquiries into
the veracity of the matter then the matter can be passed by for
the accruing advantages. Should a military emergency arise and
confront these brothers with their marching card it would oblige
them to make a decision by which they could not extricate themselves by a money payment and their mettle would be tested and
they would have to demonstrate outright where they stand and
prove that they are in favor of Christian neutrality in a
determinative test." What has been quoted from your letter is
what has been followed but it seems that there would be some
modification in this when it is considered that these brothers
are in the first reserves. Of course, it appears that Jehovah's
blessing has been on his servants here because the work has
progressed very well over the years and this even though the
majority of the circuit and district servants and those in the
Bethel family have followed this procedure. We would very much
appreciate having some information from you on this matter if
a change should be made or not. If a change is made and this
procedure is not followed then the brothers could not obtain a
passport but they can always attend an assembly in the country.
If a change is made what will be the position of those in the
first reserves? How should this be handled? We will await
your answer on the matter.

The construction of our new building is progressing very
well and we look forward to seeing it finished and in use to
Jehovah's praise and to build up the brothers by the assemblies
to be held there. Be assured of my love and best wishes.

Your brother and fellow servant,

The reply sent, dated September 5, 1969, and shown on the next page,
bears the stamp of the New York Corporation but the symbol before the
date indicates that it was written by the president through a secretary ("A"
being the symbol for the president, and "AG" being the symbol held by
one of his secretaries). Keeping in mind that the world headquarters was
fully informed of the horrible suffering Jehovah's Witnesses in Malawi had
already undergone in 1964 and in 1967 because they steadfastly refused
to pay for the party card being actively promoted by the government of
their country, consider the reply of September 5, 1969, sent to the Mexico
Branch's inquiry.

WATCHTOWER

TELEPHONE (212) 625-1240   BIBLE AND TRACT SOCIETY   CABLE WATCHTOWER
OF NEW YORK, INC.

117 ADAMS STREET, BROOKLYN, NEW YORK 11201, U.S.A.

A/AG September 5, 1969

Mexico Branch

Dear Brothers:

We have your letter of August 27 (182) in which you ask
a question about brothers who had registered in Mexico and are
now in the first reserves.

The letter that you quoted of February 4, 1960 (123)
covers the whole matter. There is nothing more to be said.
The responsibility will be upon these individuals if they
are ever called up as to what they are going to do and that
is soon enough to take any action. In the meantime these
brothers who have registered and who have paid a fee are free
to go ahead in the service. Not that we are giving our approval
in this matter, but it is their conscience, not ours, that has
allowed them to take the course of action that they have taken.
If their conscience allows them to do what they have done and
they are not compromising in any way then you just lay the
matter on the shelf. There is no reason for you to answer any
questions or give comment to individuals, nor to enter into a
discussion. Someday we may have to face the issue and they
may have to make a decision, as the letter points out, and
then it will be for them to decide. We cannot decide the lives
of everyone in the world. If the consciences of these persons
allowed them to do what they did and to be registered in the
reserves that is for them to worry about, if they are worried.
It is not for the Society's office to be worried about it.

The Society has always said that people should comply with
the law and if the individual has done what you have described
in your letter and it does not hurt his conscience then we
leave the matter just as it is. There is no reason for us to
decide another man's conscience, nor to get into an argument
or controversy over the matter. If the individuals are not
compromising in the sense of taking up arms, and what they
are doing continues to allow them to beat their swords into
pruning shears, then the decision rests with them. If they
change that position in their lives that is soon enough for
the overseers in the congregation to take action. So leave
things stand as they are and have been since February of 1960
with no further comment.

May Jehovah's rich blessing go with you.

Your brothers,

Watchtower B. & S. Society
OF NEW YORK, INC.

What makes all this so utterly incredible is that the organization's position on membership in the military has always been identical to its position on membership in a "political" organization. In both cases any Witness who enters such membership is automatically viewed as "disassociated." Yet the Mexico Branch Committee had made crystal clear that all these Witnesses who had obtained the completed certificate of military service (by means of a bribe) were now placed *in the first reserve of the military.* The Witnesses in Malawi risked life and limb, homes and lands, to adhere to the stance adopted by the organization for their country. In Mexico there was no such risk involved, yet a policy of the utmost leniency was applied. There, Witness men could be members of the first reserves of the army and yet be Circuit or District Overseers, members of the Bethel family! The report from the Branch Committee in response to the survey makes this clear (as well as showing how common the practice of bribing to get the certificate was among the Witnesses). It goes on to say:

> As indicated in the above mentioned letter from Brooklyn, the brothers
> have to use their own conscience on this matter. Something that nevertheless
> would be good to clarify is that it has become so common in the organization
> in Mexico to obtain the "cartilla" in this way (paying). The inconveniences
> caused by not obtaining the "cartilla" are that one cannot leave the country
> (which the brothers of this country frequently do going to the United States
> to assemblies) or having a little difficulty obtaining work when this document
> is required. Aside from that young men would have no strong reason
> to try to obtain the document. But it is so easy to obtain it and consulting
> with other young men who have obtained it, they tell them how it can be
> done, and these young men do not even think if it is all right for them
> in itself, individually, to obtain this document in the above mentioned way.
> There is no other objection for the brothers to continue obtaining

Literally thousands of Witnesses in Mexico knew the truth of the situation as described. All the members of the Mexico Branch Committee knew it. And all those then members of the Governing Body of Jehovah's Witnesses knew what the stated position of the world headquarters was on the matter. Yet outside of Mexico very few people had any idea of what was said. Probably no one among the Witnesses in Malawi was aware of this remarkable policy.

I cannot imagine a more obvious double standard. Nor can I conceive of more twisted reasoning than that which allowed for the position taken in Mexico and at the same time argued so strenuously and so dogmatically that to accept alternative service is condemnable because it is "viewed by the government as fulfillment of military service' is a "tacit or implied acknowledgement of Caesar's war machine." The same men who made those statements in Governing Body sessions and insisted that "we want no grey areas" and that "the brothers need to have their consciences educated," said this knowing that the common practice among Jehovah's Witnesses in Mexico for over twenty years had been to pay a bribe for a certificate saying they had fulfilled their military service, a practice that the world headquarters had officially stated was 'up to their conscience.'

Despite this, some members (and, happily, in several of the sessions it was only a minority) strenuously argued for the traditional position— a position that labeled a man as "disassociated" if he answered a judge's question about working in a hospital by responding simply and truthfully that his conscience would allow this. They favored that traditional policy while knowing that in Mexico men who were elders, Circuit Overseers, District Overseers and Branch Office staff personnel, had bribed officials to get their completed military service certificate stating that they were now in the first reserves of the military, the "war machine."

One Governing Body member, arguing for the traditional stand, had quoted a member of the Denmark Branch Committee, Richard Abrahamson, as having said regarding alternative service, "I shudder to think of putting these young men on their own choice." Yet the official counsel sent by the headquarters organization to the Mexico Branch was that young brothers' paying a bribe for a falsified document placing them in the first reserves was "for them to worry about, if they are worried. It is not for the Society's office to be worried about." Later the letter stated that, "There is no reason to decide another man's conscience."

Why was not the same position taken toward those in Malawi? I seriously doubt that the majority of Witnesses there would have arrived at the same conclusions as the Branch Office personnel did. It is equally doubtful that there was a single native of Malawi (then Nyasaland) among those Branch representatives, who formulated that policy decision, to be obeyed by the Malawian Witnesses.

Is there no responsibility resting upon those in authority within the organization for what amounts to a grotesque disparity of direction given?

Notably, as regards the failure of the Malawian authorities to uphold the high principles of their Constitution, the Watch Tower Society had stated that the "ultimate responsibility" for the injustice must be placed on President Banda, saying:

> If he knows and allows it to continue, then surely he as the leader of the country and the Malawi Congress Party must bear the responsibility for what is happening in his country and in the name of his political party.
>
> Likewise, members of Parliament and party members who have either incited the young people to violence or turned a blind eye to what is happening cannot be exempted from responsibility. Can civil servants, police officers, the legal profession and other responsible officials who because of concern for their security of position condone by silence what is happening in Malawi absolve themselves from responsibility? [15]

The same standard by which the organization judged the actions of the Malawian authorities should certainly apply to the Watch Tower organization also. If the Governing Body, not only knowing what had been said about the Malawian authorities and their responsibility, but also knowing of the organization's stand taken in Mexico, really believed that the position promulgated among the brotherhood in Malawi was the right one,

---

15   *Awake!*, February 8, 1968, pp. 21, 22; compare Matthew 7:1-5.

then they should certainly have felt impelled to reject the position taken in Mexico. To uphold the rigid position taken in Malawi they should have been positively convinced of the rightness of that stand, with no doubts about it as being the only stand for a true Christian to take, one soundly and solidly based on God's Word. To countenance in any way the position taken in Mexico would be to deny that they held such a conviction.

If on the other hand they believed the position taken in Mexico, allowing men to exercise their personal conscience as to obtaining the military certificate (even by illegal means), was right or at least acceptable, then they certainly should have accorded to the brotherhood in Malawi the same right to exercise their conscience in a matter that involved *no bribing, no illegality, no falsification.* Any fence-straddling, and 'turning of a blind eye to the facts,' 'condoning by silence' a double standard, perhaps out of "concern for their security of position," would mean following the same course they condemned on the part of Malawian officials, from top to bottom.

What was actually said by the Governing Body during the sessions in which the information from Mexico was called to their attention? The policy for Mexico had been developed primarily by only two men, Nathan Knorr and Fred Franz, but now the entire Body knew of it.[16] What responsibility did they feel and how did they react to the obvious disparity between this position and that taken in Malawi?

When I brought up the matter, not one word of disapproval or of moral indignation was heard from those who had argued in such forceful, uncompromising terms against alternative service. There was no call for some action to change the existing policy in Mexico for one boldly declaring against even the "suggestion" of compromise. Though the third and fourth waves of violence had hit Malawian Witnesses (in 1972 and 1975), I heard no expression of dismay at the disparity in the standard there and the one applied in Mexico. Most of the members apparently found

---

16   By this time (1978) Nathan Knorr had died; however, Fred Franz, now president, was at all the sessions involving the discussion of alternative service.

they could accept the Mexico policy while simultaneously insisting upon a totally different standard for people elsewhere.

Once more, I do not think the matter simply resolves down to personalities, the individual members involved. I have come to the conclusion that this outlook is in reality a typical product of any authority structure that takes a legalistic approach to Christianity, enabling those sharing in the authority structure to see double standards exist without feeling strong qualms of conscience. To their credit, brothers in Mexico were disturbed in their consciences at learning of the intense suffering of Witnesses in Malawi who refused to pay a legal price in a lawful way for a party card of the government running the country; while in Mexico they themselves were illegally obtaining a military certificate through bribes. Those in Brooklyn, at the "top," in the so-called "ivory tower," however, seemed strangely detached from such feelings, insensitive to the consequences to people from such double standard. This, too, I believe is an effect of the system, which is one reason why I find such a system so personally repelling.

All Governing Body members were fully aware of the policy in Mexico by the fall of 1978. Almost a *year later,* in September of 1979, the Governing Body again resumed discussion of the undecided issue of alternative service, this time brought to the fore by a letter from Poland.

Warning that alternative service could be a "trap for indoctrinating the brothers," Milton Henschel urged extreme caution, speaking in favor of the practice of many Polish Witnesses who were taking the expedient course of going to work in coal mines to avoid induction. Lloyd Barry again urged that we hold to the position that Witnesses "should keep free from the entire military organization." Ted Jaracz said that "our brothers are going to have problems and they look to Jehovah's organization for direction," that there was need to avoid diversity of opinions, that we should not give the brothers the idea that the Governing Body was saying, 'go ahead and submit' to alternative service orders. Carey Barber voiced the view that "there is no room here for exercising conscience, it is something where we just have to go right on through" without yielding. Fred Franz said our "conscience has to be Bible trained" and stated again his support for the traditional position against any acceptance of alternative service.

By now, Ewart Chitty was no longer a member of the Body, having submitted his resignation in accord with the Governing Body's wishes. Grant Suiter was absent from the session, both he and Chitty having voted for a change in policy at the November 15, 1978, meeting. But there were two new members on the Body, Jack Barr (from England) and Martin Poetzinger (from Germany), and they were present at the September 15, 1979, session. When a motion was finally presented, the vote was split right down the middle, eight in favor of changing the policy, eight (including the two new members) against doing so.

In 1980, on February 3, the subject was once more placed on the agenda. By this time more than a year had elapsed since my visit to Mexico and Albert Schroeder had made another annual visit there. The Mexico Branch Committee members again expressed to him their concern about the practice of bribing to obtain falsified documents of military service, and Schroeder related this continuing situation to the Body after his return. Remarks by the various members during the session made it evident that no two-thirds majority would be attained either way on the alternative service issue and there was not even a motion made.

The matter was "shelved." From the time the letter from Michel Weber, the elder in Belgium, was received in November 1977, until February, 1980, the Governing Body of Jehovah's Witnesses had tried on *six separate occasions* to resolve the issue without success.[17]

What, though, of the *people* affected by the policy that continued in force, those of what the *Watchtower* had called "the rank and file"? Could they also "shelve" the issue? To the contrary, the inability of the Body to achieve that indispensable two-thirds majority meant that male Jehovah's Witnesses in any country of the world who acted according to their conscience and accepted alternative service as a proper government requirement, could still do so only at the cost of being viewed as outside the organization, equivalent to expelled persons. It also meant that the Governing Body as a whole was willing for the twenty-year-old policy in

---

17 For further details on this issue, see the sequel to *Crisis of Conscience*, titled *In Search of Christian Freedom*, pages 255 to 270, which has been inserted into Appendix B of this 2018 edition of *Crisis of Conscience*.

effect in Mexico to continue in effect while a totally different policy in Malawi remained unchanged.

TWO SORTS OF WEIGHTS FOR MEASURING

Two sorts of weights are something detestable to Jehovah, and a cheating pair of scales is not good. — Proverbs 20:23.

It may help to understand the reasoning of some Members if other circumstances then prevailing among Jehovah's Witnesses in Mexico are reviewed. As a result of the Mexican revolution, and because of the Catholic Church's long history of holding immense quantities of land and other property in the country, the Mexican Constitution until recently forbid any religious organization the right to own property. Churches and church property were, in effect, held in custody by the government, which allowed the religious organizations to use these. Due to past exploitation by foreign clergy, no foreign missionaries or ministers were allowed to function as such in Mexico. What did this result in for the Witness organization?

The administration of the headquarters organization of Jehovah's Witnesses many decades ago decided that, because of the existing law, Jehovah's Witnesses in Mexico would present themselves, not as a religious organization, but as a "cultural" organization. The local corporation there formed, La Torre del Vigia, was so registered with the government of Mexico.[18] So, Jehovah's Witnesses in Mexico for many decades did not speak of having religious meetings or Bible meetings but of having "cultural" meetings. At these meetings they had no prayers or songs, and this was also true of their larger assemblies. When they engaged in door-to-door activity they carried only Watch Tower literature (which they said the Watch Tower Society provided them as an "aid to them in their cultural activity"). They did not carry the Bible while in such activity since that would identify them as engaging in religious activity. A group of

---

18   The registration was dated June 10, 1943, in which the Secretariat of Foreign Affairs *(Secretaría de Relaciones Exteriores)* authorizes the registration of La Torre del Vigía as a "Non-Profit Civil Association Founded for Scientific, Educational and Cultural Dissemination" *("Asociación Civil Fundada para la Divulgación Científica. Educadora y Cultural No Lucrativa")*. This arrangement remained in effect over a period of some 46 years.

Witnesses in a given area was not called a "congregation" but a "company." They did not speak of having baptisms but did the same thing under the name of performing the "symbol."

This "double talk" was not done because of living in some totalitarian country that took repressive measures against freedom of worship.[19] It was done largely to avoid having to comply with government regulations regarding ownership of property by religious organizations.[20] Nor should it be thought that the arrangement was something originating with and decided upon by the Mexican Witnesses themselves; it was an arrangement worked out and put into effect by the international headquarters at Brooklyn.

It is interesting to contrast the deliberate elimination of prayers and songs at Witness meetings in Mexico with the action of the Watch Tower Society in the United States, where they were willing to fight case after case all the way up to the Supreme Court of the country rather than give up certain practices, such as offering literature from door to door without a license and without having to register with the police, the right to use sound cars, distribute literature on street corners, and many other such practices which are covered by Constitutional rights. The organization did not want to relinquish any of these things. It fought to hold on to them, even though these particular practices are certainly not things that were done by early Christians in the first century and hence cannot be counted as among primary Christian practices.

But congregational or group prayer *was* a primary religious practice in early Christian meetings and has been among servants of God from time immemorial. The Mexican government said nothing against prayer at religious meetings. Jehovah's Witnesses, however, were instructed to

---

19   The government of Mexico, in reality, showed considerable leniency toward Jehovah's witnesses, for it must have been known that their presentation of themselves as a non-religious "cultural" organization was simply a subterfuge.

20   In the 1970s, my wife and I attended an international assembly in Mexico City and we were lodged at the Society's Branch office. President Knorr was also there and during our stay he conducted a group of us on a tour of the various buildings of the Mexican branch. During the tour, he commented directly on the legal status of a "cultural organization" held in Mexico and he specifically mentioned as a primary reason for this unusual status the fact that it allowed the organization to keep control of its properties in that country.

say that their meetings were *not* religious. Few things could be viewed as more completely related to worship of God, as more purely spiritual, than prayer. When an imperial decree in Persia prohibited prayer to anyone except to the king for a period of thirty days, the prophet Daniel considered the issue so crucial that he risked position, possessions and life itself in violating the decree.[21]

The headquarters organization, however, considered it expedient to sacrifice congregational prayer among Jehovah's Witnesses throughout Mexico. With what benefit, what "accruing advantage"? By giving up congregational prayer and song and the use of the Bible in public witnessing activity, the organization could retain ownership of Society property in Mexico and operate free from governmental regulations that other religions complied with. They were willing to say that their organization was not a religious organization, that their meetings were not religious meetings, that their witnessing activity was not religious activity, that baptism was not a religious act—when in every other country of the world Jehovah's Witnesses were saying just the opposite.

Since they knew of this arrangement, some Governing Body members may have been inclined to accept the paying of bribes for falsified documents as being not far out of line with the overall policy for Jehovah's Witnesses in that country. This may explain in part how they could at the same time speak so adamantly for "no compromise" in other lands. It seems evident that in the minds of some members it was not a question of a double standard. In their minds there was just the one standard. That standard was: *doing whatever the organization decided and approved.* The organization made decisions regarding Mexico and the practice of bribing there, leaving it to the individual conscience, and so that was acceptable and a man could pay such bribe for a military certificate and still be used in the most responsible way, with no need for particular concern before God on the part of those directing the work there. The organization decided otherwise regarding alternative service (as it also did regarding

---

21   Daniel 6:1-11.

the situation in Malawi), and so any man who failed to follow that decision was unworthy of occupying any position at all in the congregation, was in fact a breaker of integrity with God.

I could not understand then how Christians could adopt such a viewpoint and I can not understand it now. For me it made all the bold, almost strident, calls of some for 'staying clean from the world' sound hollow, like mere rhetoric, as impressive language that did not fit reality. I could not relate in any way to the reasoning that allowed for such expressions in the face of facts that were well known to all members speaking and hearing those expressions.

I lived in Latin American countries for nearly twenty years and paid no bribes. But I know full well that there are some places, not just in Latin America but in various parts of the earth, where, although the law is on your side and what you seek is perfectly legitimate, it is almost impossible to get certain things done without money being paid to an official who has no right to such. It is not hard to see that a person confronted with this situation may view this as a form of extortion, even as in Bible times tax-collectors and also military men might exact more than was due and thus practice extortion. It does not seem fair to me to judge adversely persons who feel obliged to submit to such extortion. More than that, I am not presuming to judge those in Mexico who, not having the law on their side, acted against the law, who did not simply submit to extortion but instead deliberately *solicited* the illegal actions of an official through an offer of money to get a falsified, illegal document. This is *not* what I find so shocking and even frightening about the whole affair.

It is instead the way that religious men in high authority can allow supposed "organizational interests" to be counted as of such enormous importance as compared to the interests of ordinary people, people with children and homes and jobs, individuals many of whom give evidence of being every bit as conscientious in their devotion to God as any man among those men who sit as a court to decide what is and what is not within the realm of conscience for such people.

It is men in authority who accord to *themselves* the right to be of divided opinion, but who exact uniformity from all others; men who express mistrust of others' use of Christian freedom of conscience, but who expect such others to put implicit trust in them and their decisions, while they grant to themselves the right to exercise their conscience to condone illegal maneuvering and obvious misrepresentation of fact.

It is men in authority who, because the change of one vote reduces a majority down from 66 $^2/_3$ % to 62 $^1/_2$ %, are willing to allow this to keep in force a policy that can cause other men to undergo arrest, be separated from family and home for months, even sent to jail for years, when those men do not understand the Scriptural basis for the policy they are asked to follow and, in some cases, believe that the policy is wrong.

It is men in authority who can apply a policy that calls on ordinary people, men, women and children, to face loss of home and lands, endure beatings, torture, rape and death because of refusal to pay a legal fee for the card of the organization that is, to all intents and purposes, the ruling power of their country, while at the same time telling men in another country that it is acceptable for them to bribe military officers for a card that falsely says they fulfilled their military service and are in the first reserves of the army.

All *this* is what I find shocking. And, however sincere some may be, I still find it frightening.

I could not personally comprehend how grown men could fail to see inconsistency in all of this, could fail to be repelled by it, could not be deeply moved by its effect on people's lives. In the end it simply convinced me that "organizational loyalty" can lead people to incredible conclusions, allow them to rationalize away the grossest of inequities, relieve them from being particularly affected by any suffering their policies may cause. The desensitizing effect that organizational loyalty can produce is, of course, well documented, having been demonstrated again and again throughout the centuries, both in religious and political history, as in the extreme cases of the Inquisition and during the Nazi regime. But it can still produce a sickening effect when seen at close quarters in an area where one never expected it. To my mind, it illustrates forcefully the reason why God never purposed that men should exercise such excessive authority over fellow humans.

It may be noted that, after nearly a half century of holding the status of a "cultural" organization in Mexico, the Watch Tower organization finally changed to that of a religious organization. The *Watchtower* magazine of January 1, 1990 (page 7) announced that a "change of the status" of Jehovah's Witnesses had taken place in 1989. It described the Mexican Witnesses as *for the first time* being able to use the Bible when going from house to house, and *for the first time* being able to open meetings with prayer.

The magazine described how "thrilling" this change was to Mexican Witnesses and that it brought "tears of joy" to them. It attributed an immediate jump in "publishers" by over 17,000 to this change.

The article told the reader absolutely nothing as to what the *previous* status had been, why it prevailed, or how the change in status came about. Anyone reading the article would assume that the change in status, with the benefits described, was something the organization had wanted all along. From reading the article one would assume that it was the government of Mexico or its laws that had till now prevented the Witnesses from praying at meetings or using the Bible in their door-to-door activity. It never told the reader that the reason the Mexican Witnesses were deprived of these things—for at least a half century—was because *their own headquarters organization chose to have it so,* voluntarily opted in favor of another status. It did not tell the reader that these "thrilling" changes that brought "tears of joy" had been available all along, for many decades, requiring only an organizational decision to abandon its pretense that the Witness organization in Mexico was not a religious organization but a "cultural" one. The only reason the Mexican Witnesses had not engaged in these things before was because the headquarters organization *instructed* them not to do so, in order to protect the status chosen of a "cultural" organization. These are facts known by those in responsible positions in the Mexican Witness organization. They are not known by the vast majority of Witnesses outside that country and the January 1, 1990, *Watchtower* let them remain in the dark on the subject. It presented a "sanitized" picture of the occurrence, one that was as misleading as the pre-1989 practice of pretending to be something other than a religious organization while knowing full well that they were.

As more recent articles both in the July 22, 1994 *Awake!* and in the 1995 *Yearbook of Jehovah's Witnesses* show, the Watch Tower organization's willingness to abandon its decades-long pretense was connected with the amendments to the Mexican constitution that have been progressively adopted by the legislative bodies there. The *Yearbook* (page 212) acknowledges that ownership of property was a factor in the decision to adopt the pretense of being—not a religious organization—but a civil society back in 1943, resulting in replacing the term "congregation" with "company," calling meeting places "Halls for Cultural Studies," eliminating audible prayers and "every appearance of a religious service" at meetings there, as well as avoiding "direct use of the Bible" in their door-to-door activity. It states (pages 232, 233) that in the 1980s the organization came under increasing governmental pressure. It acknowledges (page 249) that from December 1988 "one could foresee that there would be a change in policy regarding religion. The conclusion was drawn that it would be advantageous from the standpoint of relations with the government to come out into the open, dropping the pretense of not being a religious organization, and that this was subsequently done in 1989 with Governing Body permission. Under new constitutional amendments, churches were once again allowed to own buildings and property. This was true not only of the Catholic Church but of all denominations." In view of all this, the evidence is that the opting for a change in status by the Watch Tower organization was made, not primarily because of concern over spiritual issues and principles, but for pragmatic reasons.

The years that have intervened give no evidence of improvement in this area. Recent information has come to light as regards the Watch Tower Society's affiliation with the United Nations through its Department of Public Information, doing so as a "Non-Governmental Organization [or NGO]." This was done in 1991 and only when it became publicly known and produced adverse reaction did the organization, in October 2001 request that its association be withdrawn. See below:

UNITED NATIONS   NATIONS UNIES

POSTAL ADDRESS—ADRESSE POSTALE UNITED NATIONS, N.Y. 10017
CABLE ADDRESS—ADRESSE TELEGRAPHIQUE UNATIONS NEWYORK

REFERENCE: 11 October 2001

To Whom It May Concern:

Recently the NGO Section had been receiving numerous inquiries regarding the association of the **Watchtower Bible and Tract Society of New York** with the Department of Public Information (DPI). This organization applied for association with DPI in 1991 and was granted association in 1992. By accepting association with DPI, the organization agreed to meet criteria for association, including support and respect of the principles of the Charter of the United Nations and commitment and means to conduct effective information programmes with its constituents and to a broader audience about UN activities.

In October 2001, the **Watchtower Bible and Tract Society of New York** requested termination of its association with DPI. Following this request, the DPI has made a decision to disassociate the **Watchtower Bible and Tract Society of New York** as of 9 October 2001.

We appreciate your interest in the work of the United Nations.

Yours sincerely,

Paul Hoeffel
Chief
NGO Section
Department of Public Information

In a report in the British newspaper *The Guardian,* Paul Gillies, acting as spokesman for the Watch Tower's London Branch Office, is quoted as saying: "We do not have hostile attitudes to governing bodies and if we are making representations on issues to the UN we will do so. . . . There are good and bad bodies just as there are good and bad   politicians.   We believe what the Book of Revelation tells us but we do not actively try to change the political system."

His reference to the Book of Revelation was evidently due to the fact that Watch Tower publications have, since 1942, identified the League of Nations and its successor, the United Nations, with the scarlet-colored wild beast, upon which the harlot Babylon the Great is depicted as riding (See

Revelation 16:3-6.) It says of it: "The UN is actually a blasphemous counterfeit of God's Messianic Kingdom by the Prince of Peace, Jesus Christ."[22]

Japan, Germany, and Italy withdrew, and the Soviet Union was dropped from the League. In September 1939 the Nazi dictator of Germany launched World War II.* Having failed to keep peace in the world, the League of Nations virtually plunged into an abyss of inactivity. By 1942 it had become a has-been. Neither before this nor at some later date —but right at that critical time—did Jehovah interpret to his people the full depth of

* On November 20, 1940, Germany, Italy, Japan, and Hungary signed up for a "new League of Nations," followed four days later by the Vatican's broadcasting a Mass and a prayer for a religious peace and for a new order of things. That "new League" never materialized.

to God's prophetic Word.—Hebrews 2:1; 2 Peter 1:19.

⁴ What light did the talk "Peace—Can It Last?" throw on the prophecy? Clearly identifying the scarlet-colored wild beast of Revelation 17:3 as the League of Nations, President Knorr went on to discuss its stormy career on the basis of the angel's following words to John: *"The wild beast that you saw was, but is not, and yet is about to ascend out of the abyss, and it is to go off into destruction."—Revelation 17:8a.*

⁵ "The wild beast . . . *was.*" Yes, it had existed as the League of Nations from January 10, 1920, onward, with 63 nations participating at one time or another. But, in turn,

5. (a) How was it that "the wild beast . . . was" and then "is not"? (b) How did President Knorr answer the question, "Will the League remain in the pit?"

AN AWESOME MYSTERY SOLVED

As prophesied about the scarlet-colored wild beast, the League of Nations was abyssed during World War II but was revived as the United Nations

---

22   See the book *Revelation—It's Grand Climax at Hand,* pages 246-248.

Thus, the mental outlook that prevailed in the cases cited within this chapter continued. Seen against the background of the organization's stance regarding Malawi and the issue of alternative service, this association with what the Watch Tower Society deems "a blasphemous counterfeit of God's Messianic Kingdom" betrays a seriously warped concept of Christian integrity and conscience.

7

PREDICTIONS AND PRESUMPTION

When the prophet speaks in the name of Jehovah and the word does not occur or come true, that is the word that Jehovah did not speak. With presumptuousness the prophet spoke it. You must not get frightened at him.

— Deuteronomy 18:22.

WHEN it comes to attitudes about the promised return of Christ Jesus, eagerness is certainly to be preferred to apathy. Early Christians were definitely not apathetic about that hoped-for event.

Some years ago I watched a television broadcast in which a public relations representative of the Canadian Branch Office of Jehovah's Witnesses, Walter Graham, responded to questions about the failure of certain predictions regarding Christ's return. He said that if any fault was to be found with Jehovah's Witnesses in this respect, then it was only due to "our enthusiasm of seeing God's name vindicated and his Kingdom rule the earth."

Most persons, I think, will agree that it is only human to make the mistake of saying things on the spur of the moment, to let wishful thinking or perhaps strong desire and enthusiasm sway our judgment, causing us to jump to hasty conclusions. Somewhere in our lives we have all done that. Surely if that were all that is involved, no one should have cause for great concern.

Personally I do not believe that that is all that is involved here, however. The issues go deeper and the factors related have far greater significance than some common, incidental mistake that we all commit at times. This is particularly so because of the way the predictions involved have affected people's most vital interests.

A factor that cannot be treated lightly is that the Governing Body views Jehovah's Witnesses, at least those of the "anointed class" (to which the Governing Body members all belong), as cast in the role of a "prophet," assigned to that awesome responsibility by God.

Thus, the April 1, 1972, issue of the *Watchtower* magazine, page 197, carried an article titled, "They Shall Know that a Prophet Was Among Them." It raised the question as to whether in modern times Jehovah God has had a prophet to help the people, "to warn them of dangers and declare things to come." The answer given was, yes, that the record showed there was such a prophet.

IDENTIFYING THE "PROPHET"
These questions can be answered in the affirmative. Who is this prophet?

However, Jehovah did not let the people of Christendom, as led by the clergy, go without being warned that the League * was a counterfeit substitute for the real kingdom of God. He had a "prophet" to warn them. This "prophet" was not one man, but was a body of men and women. It was the small group of footstep followers of Jesus Christ, known at that time as International Bible Students. Today they are known as Jehovah's Christian witnesses. They are still proclaiming a warning, and have been joined and assisted in their commissioned work by hundreds of thousands of persons who have listened to their message with belief.

Of course, it is easy to say that this group acts as a "prophet" of God. It is another thing to prove it. The only way that this can be done is to review the record. What does it show?

---

* Reference is to the "League of Nations," the predecessor of the United Nations organization.

More recently, the May 1, 1997 *Watchtower*, on page 8, said:

> JEHOVAH GOD is the Grand Identifier of his true messengers. He identifies them by making the messages he delivers through them come true. Jehovah is also the Great Exposer of false messengers. How does he expose them? He frustrates their signs and predictions. In this way he shows that they are self-appointed prognosticators, whose messages really spring from their own false reasoning—yes, their foolish, fleshly thinking!

The first *Watchtower* quoted states that the proof of the role of modern-day prophet (filled by the body of anointed Jehovah's Witnesses) is to be found in the "record." The second provides the criteria that Jehovah identifies his true messengers by making their messages "come true.," while exposing false messengers by 'frustrating their signs and predictions.' Applying these standards, what do we find?

The "record" is worth reviewing. That it reveals mistakes even the headquarters organization will acknowledge. One morning in 1980, when serving as chairman for the daily text discussion at the Brooklyn Bethel home, Fred Franz, then the Society's president, recounted to the headquarters family his recollections of expectations held regarding the year 1925, forecast as the time when Christ's millennial rule would be fully manifest on earth. He quoted Judge Rutherford as having said afterward about his own predictions: "I know I made an ass of myself."[1]

The organization, however, treats these mistakes as mere evidence of human imperfection and also as evidence of great desire and enthusiasm to see God's promises fulfilled. I believe that the "record" shows there is more to it than that. It is one thing for a man to make an "ass" of himself because of wanting to see something happen. It is quite another thing for him to urge others to share his views, to criticize them if they do not, even to question their faith or impugn their motives if they do not see the matter as he sees it.

---

1   This statement by Rutherford is quoted in the October 1, 1984, *Watchtower*, page 24.

It is still more serious for an organization representing itself as God's appointed spokesman to all mankind to do this—and to do it, not for a few days or months, but for years, even decades, repeatedly, on an earth-wide basis. The responsibility for the results can surely not be shrugged off with simply saying, "Well, nobody's perfect."

No one is, but every one of us bears a responsibility for what we do. And that is especially so when our actions may dramatically affect something as important and personal as others' relationship with God.

No less serious is it when a group of men have divided views on predictions related to a certain date and yet present to their adherents an outward appearance of united confidence, encouraging those adherents to place unwavering trust in those predictions.

I suppose I must credit my experience with the Governing Body for also bringing home to me the reality of these matters. During the first twenty years or so of my active association with Jehovah's Witnesses, I had at most a hazy idea about any failures in past predictions and simply did not attach any great importance to them. I had no interest in literature attacking our teachings on this point. From the late 1950s onward, certain Society publications, such as *Jehovah's Witnesses in the Divine Purpose* (a history of the organization), and the Society-sponsored book *Faith on the March*, did mention these failures, but they did so in a way that made them appear as of minor consequence and I viewed them in that same light.

It was not until the late 1970s that I learned just how far the matter went. I learned it then, not from so-called "opposition literature," but from Watch Tower publications themselves and from active, respected Witnesses, including fellow members of the Governing Body.

1914 is a pivotal date on which a major portion of the doctrinal and authority structure of Jehovah's Witnesses rests. Jehovah's Witnesses today hold the following beliefs tied in with that date:

> That in 1914 Christ Jesus became "present," invisible to human eyes, but now beginning a judgment period for all his professed followers and for the world.

That in 1914 Christ Jesus now began active rulership toward all the world, his kingdom officially taking power.

That 1914 marks the start of the "last days" or the "time of the end" foretold in Bible prophecy.

That three and a half years after 1914 (in 1918) the resurrection of Christians sleeping in death, from the apostles onward, began.

That about that same time (in 1918) Christ's true followers then living went into spiritual captivity to Babylon the Great, being released the following year, 1919, at which time Christ Jesus acknowledged them collectively as his "faithful and discreet slave," his approved agency for directing his work and caring for his interests on earth, his sole channel for communicating guidance and illumination to his servants earthwide.

That from that time forward the final "harvest" work has been in progress, with salvation or destruction as ultimate destinies.

To weaken belief in the significance of the foundation date of 1914 would weaken the whole doctrinal superstructure (described above) that rests on it. It would also weaken the claim of special authority for those acting as the official spokesman group for the "faithful and discreet slave" class.

To *remove* that date as having such significance could mean the virtual collapse of all the doctrinal and authority structure founded on it. That is how crucial it is.

Yet few Witnesses today know that for nearly half a century—from 1879 to the late 1920s—the time prophecies published in the *Watch Tower* magazine and related publications were essentially *contrary to all the beliefs just outlined*. I for one did not realize it much of my life. Then I found that for nearly fifty years the "channel" of the *Watch Tower* had assigned different times and dates for every one of the things just listed, and that it was only the failure of all the original expectations regarding 1914 that led to an assigning of new dates to those claimed fulfillments of prophecy.

As discussed in a previous chapter, the research I had to do in connection with the book *Aid to Bible Understanding* brought home to me that the Society's date of 607 B.C.E. for Jerusalem's destruction by Babylon was contradicted by all known historical evidence. Still, I continued to put trust in that date in spite of the evidence, feeling that it had Scriptural backing. Without 607 B.C.E. the crucial date of 1914 would be placed in question. I took the view that the historical evidence was likely defective and argued that way in the *Aid* book.

Then, in 1977, one of Jehovah's Witnesses in Sweden, named Carl Olof Jonsson, sent to the Brooklyn headquarters a massive amount of research he had done on Biblically related chronology and on chronological speculation. Jonsson was an elder and had been actively associated with Jehovah's Witnesses for some twenty years.

Having had experience researching chronology myself, I was impressed by how deeply he had gone into the matter, also by the completeness and factualness of his presentation. Basically he sought to draw the Governing Body's attention to the weakness in the Society's chronological reckonings leading to the 1914 date as the end point of the "Gentile Times," referred to by Jesus at Luke, chapter twenty-one, verse 24 (called "the appointed times of the nations" in the *New World Translation)*.

Briefly stated, the 1914 date is arrived at by the following process:

In the fourth chapter of Daniel's prophecy, the expression "seven times" occurs, applied there to the Babylonian king Nebuchadnezzar and describing a period of seven times of insanity the king would experience.[2] The Society teaches that those "seven times" are prophetic of something greater, namely, of the period of time extending from Jerusalem's destruction (placed by the Society at 607 B.C.E.) down to the end of the "Gentile Times," explained as meaning the period during which the Gentile nations exercise "uninterrupted" dominion over all the earth.

The "seven times" are interpreted as meaning seven years with each year consisting of 360 days (12 lunar months of 30 days each). Seven multiplied by 360 gives 2,520 days. However, other prophecies are referred to that use the expression "a day for a year."[3] Employing this formula, the 2,520 days become 2,520 years, running from 607 B.C.E. to the year 1914 C.E.

---

2   Daniel 4:17, 23-33.
3   Numbers 14:34; Ezekiel 4:6

As noted earlier, the Society's present teachings about the beginning of Christ's kingdom rule, the "last days," the start of the resurrection and related matters are all tied in with this calculation. Not many Witnesses are able to explain the rather intricate application and combination of texts involved, but they accept the end product of this process and calculation.

Most of Jehovah's Witnesses for many decades believed that this explanation leading to 1914 was more or less unique with their organization, that it was initially understood and published by the Society's first president, Pastor Russell. On its inside cover, the Society's publication *Jehovah's Witnesses in the Divine Purpose*, published in 1959, contained these statements:

> 1870   Charles Taze Russell begins his study of the Bible with a small group of associates
>
> 1877   The book "Three Worlds" is published identifying the date 1914 as the end of "Gentile Times"

The impression given here, as well as that presented within the book, was that this book "The Three Worlds" (which Russell actually only financed) was the first publication to contain this teaching about 1914.

This is what I had thought, until the material from the Swedish elder came in to the world headquarters. Then I realized how many facts had been either ignored or glossed over by the Society's publications.

Jonsson first traced the long history of chronological speculation. He showed that the practice of arbitrarily applying the "year for a day" formula to various time periods found in the Bible was initially done by Jewish rabbis dating back to the first century C.E. In the ninth century C.E. a "string of Jewish rabbis" began making calculations and predictions utilizing this day-year formula in connection with the time periods of 1,290, 1,335 and 2,300 days found in Daniel's prophecy, in each case applying their results to the time for the appearance of the Messiah.[4]

---

4   Daniel 8:14; 12:11, 12. The complete text of Carl Olof Jonsson's research has been published under the title *The Gentile Times Reconsidered*.

Among professed Christians, the practice first surfaces in the twelfth century, beginning with a Roman Catholic abbot, Joachim of Floris. Not only the periods of days found in Daniel's prophecy, but also the period of 1,260 days mentioned in Revelation, chapter eleven, verse 3, and chapter twelve, verse 6, were now interpreted by employing the "year for a day" method. As time went along, a remarkable succession of dates was arrived at by the different interpreters, their predictions including the year 1260, then 1364 and, later, various dates in the sixteenth century. Changes and new interpretations were regularly made necessary as one date after another eventually passed without the foretold event taking place.

In 1796, George Bell, writing in a London magazine, predicted the fall of the "Antichrist" (according to his view, the Pope). This was to come in "1797 or 1813," his prediction being based on an interpretation of the 1,260 days, but using a different starting point than other interpreters (some had begun their count from the birth of Christ, others from the fall of Jerusalem, others from the start of the Catholic Church). His prediction was written during the French Revolution. Not long after he made it, a shocking event took place—the Pope was taken captive by French troops and forced into exile.

Many took this as a most remarkable fulfillment of Bible prophecy and 1798 was accepted by them as the end of the prophetic 1,260 days. From this developed the view that the following year, 1799, marked the beginning of the "last days."

Further upheavals in Europe produced a spate of new predictions. Among the predictors was a man in England named John Aquila Brown. In the early 1800s he published an explanation of the 2,300 days of Daniel, chapter eight, showing these as ending in 1844 C.E. This understanding was also adopted by the American pioneer of the Second Advent movement, William Miller.

We will see how these calculations later came to play a role in the history of Jehovah's Witnesses.

John Aquila Brown, however, developed another explanation that is intimately related to the year 1914 as that date figures in the beliefs of Jehovah's Witnesses. How so?

Carl Olof Jonsson's material presented the evidence that Brown was the real originator of the interpretation of the "seven times" of Daniel chapter four, the interpretation that produces the 2,520 years by means of the day-year formula.

Brown first published this interpretation in 1823 and his method converted the "seven times" into 2,520 years in *exactly the same way found today in Watch Tower publications.*

This was twenty-nine years before Charles Taze Russell was born, forty-seven years before he began his Bible study group and more than a half century before the book "The Three Worlds" appeared.

I was totally unaware of this before reading the material sent to the Society from Sweden. There was nothing in any of the Watch Tower Society's publications that acknowledged these facts. There was no mention at all of John Aquila Brown.

Carl Olof Jonsson finally published his material in 1983. Ten years after Jonsson's book appeared the Watch Tower Society for the first time acknowledged the actual origin of the 2,520-year-calculation by John Aquila Brown—made in 1823, 50 years before Russell appeared on the scene.[5]

John Aquila Brown, however, started his 2,520-year period in 604 B.C.E. and therefore had it ending in 1917 C.E. He foretold that then "the *full glory* of the kingdom of Israel shall be perfected."

Where, then, did the emphasis on the date of 1914 originate?

After the failure of expectations surrounding the year 1844, a split-up of various Second Advent groups resulted, most of them setting up new dates for Christ's return. One of these groups formed around N. H. Barbour of Rochester, New York.

---

5   See page 134 of *Jehovah's Witnesses—Proclaimers of God's Kingdom.* The book makes the erroneous statement that, although not 'clearly discerning' the date with which the 2,520 years would begin or end (evidently meaning that his dates for the beginning and the ending did not match those of Watch Tower teachings), Brown "did connect these 'seven times' with the Gentile Times of Luke 21:24." As Jonsson's book *The Gentile Times Reconsidered* correctly states "Brown did not himself associate this period with the Gentile Times of Luke 21:24." His 2,520-year calculation did, however, play a part in the later linking of the "seven times" with the Gentile Times in 1826.

Barbour adopted much of John Aquila Brown's interpretation, but changed the starting point of the 2,520 years to 606 B.C.E. and came up with the ending date of 1914 C.E. (Actually this was a miscalculation since that would only be 2,519 years.)

In 1873 Barbour began to publish a magazine for Second Adventist adherents first titled *The Midnight Cry* and later the *Herald of the Morning*. On the following page is a copy of the title page of the *Herald of the Morning* of July, 1878, the year before the publication of the first issue of the *Watch Tower* magazine. Note the statement found at the lower right-hand corner, "'Times of the Gentiles' end in 1914."

This copy was made from one kept on file at the Brooklyn headquarters, though not accessible for general use. Its existence there shows that some persons of the headquarters staff must have known that the *Watch Tower* magazine was clearly *not* the first magazine to advocate the 1914 date as the end of the Gentile Times. That teaching was actually adopted from the Second Adventist publication of N. H. Barbour.

It may also be noted that at that time, July, 1878, C. T. Russell had become "assistant editor" of this Second Adventist magazine, the *Herald of the Morning*. Russell himself explains how he came to be associated with N. H. Barbour and how he came to adopt Barbour's chronology, much of which, including the interpretation of the "seven times" of Daniel chapter four, Barbour had in turn adopted from John Aquila Brown. Russell's explanation is published in the July 15, 1906, issue of the *Watch Tower*.

It was about January, 1876, that my attention was specially drawn to the subject of prophetic time, as it relates to these doctrines and hopes. It came about in this way: I received a paper called *The Herald of the Morning*, sent by its editor, Mr. N. H. Barbour. When I opened it I at once identified it with Adventism from the picture on its cover, and examined it with some curiosity to see what time they would next set for the burning of the world. But judge my surprise and gratification, when I learned from its contents that the Editor was beginning to get his eyes open on the subjects that for some years had so greatly rejoiced our hearts here in Allegheny—that the object of our Lord's return is not to destroy, but to bless all the families of the earth, and that his coming would be thief-like, and not in flesh, but as a spirit-being, invisible to men; and that the gathering of his church and the separation of the "wheat" from the "tares" would progress in the end of this age without the world's being aware of it.

I rejoiced to find others coming to the same advanced position, but was astonished to find the statement very cautiously set forth, that the editor believed the prophecies to indicate that the Lord was already *present* in the world (unseen and invisible), and that the harvest work of gathering the wheat was already due,—and that this view was warranted by the time-prophecies which but a few months before he supposed had failed.

Here was a new thought: Could it be that the *time prophecies* which I had so long despised, because of their misuse by Adventists, were really meant to indicate when the Lord would be *invisibly present* to set up his kingdom —a thing which I clearly saw could be known in no other way? It seemed, to say the least, a reasonable, a very reasonable thing, to expect that the Lord would inform his people on the subject—especially as he had promised that the faithful should not be left in darkness with the world, and that though the day of the Lord would come upon all others as a thief in the night (stealthily, unawares), it should not be so to the watching, earnest saints.—1 Thes. 5:4.

I recalled certain arguments used by my friend Jonas Wendell and other Adventists to prove that 1873 would witness the burning of the world, etc.—the chronology of the world showing that the six thousand years from Adam ended with the beginning of 1873—and other arguments drawn from the Scriptures and supposed to coincide. Could it be that these *time* arguments, which I had passed by as unworthy of attention, really contained an important truth which they had misapplied?

Note that up to this point Russell states that he had had no regard for time prophecies, had in fact "despised" them. What did he now do?

Anxious to learn, from any quarter, whatever God had to teach, I at once wrote to Mr. Barbour, informing him of my harmony on other points and desiring to know particularly why, and upon what Scriptural evidences, he held that Christ's *presence* and the harvesting of the Gospel age dated from the Autumn of 1874. The answer showed that my surmise had been correct, viz.: that the *time arguments*, chronology, etc., were the same as used by Second Adventists in 1873, and explained how Mr. Barbour and Mr. J. H. Paton, of Michigan, a co-worker with him, had been regular Second Adventists up to that time; and that when the date 1874 had passed without the world being burned, and without their seeing Christ in the flesh, they were for a time dumbfounded. They had examined the time-prophecies that had seemingly passed unfulfilled, and had been unable to find any flaw, and had begun to wonder whether the *time* was right and their *expectations* wrong,—whether the views of restitution and blessing to the world, which myself and others were teaching, might not be the things to look for. It seems that not long after their 1874 disappointment, a reader of the *Herald of the Morning*, who had a copy of the *Diaglott*, noticed something in it which he thought peculiar, —that in Matt. 24:27, 37, 39, the word which in our common version is rendered *coming* is translated *presence*. This was the clue; and, following it, they had been led through prophetic *time* toward proper views regarding the object and manner of the Lord's return. I, on the contrary, was led first to proper views of the object and manner of our Lord's return and then to the examination of the *time* for these things, indicated in God's Word. Thus God leads his children often from different starting points of truth; but where the heart is earnest and trustful, the result must be to draw all such together.

> But there were no books or other publications setting forth the time-prophecies as then understood, so I paid Mr. Barbour's expenses to come to see me at Philadelphia (where I had business engagements during the summer of 1876), to show me fully and Scripturally, if he could, that the prophecies indicated 1874 as the date at which the Lord's *presence* and "the harvest" began. He came, and the evidence satisfied me. Being a person of positive convictions and fully consecrated to the Lord, I at once saw that the special times in which we live have an important bearing upon our duty and work as Christ's disciples; that, being in the time of harvest, the harvestwork should be done; and that *present truth* was the sickle by which the Lord would have us do a gathering and reaping work everywhere among his children.

Thus, the visit of the Second Adventist, N. H. Barbour, changed Russell's mind about time prophecies. Russell became an assistant editor of Barbour's magazine, the *Herald of the Morning*, published for Second Advent adherents. From this time forward, time prophecies formed a prominent feature of Russell's writings and of the *Watch Tower* magazine he soon founded.[6]

The "seven times" interpretation and the 1914 date that Russell picked up were all tied in with the date of 1874, given primary importance by Barbour and his adherents (1914 was still decades away whereas 1874 had just passed). They believed that 1874 marked the end of 6,000 years of human history and they had expected Christ's return in that year. When it passed they felt disillusioned. As the earlier-quoted material shows, a Second Adventist contributor to Barbour's magazine named B. W. Keith later noticed that a certain New Testament translation, *The Emphatic Diaglott,* used the word "presence" in place of "coming" in texts relating to Christ's return. Keith advanced to Barbour the idea that Christ had indeed returned in 1874 but *invisibly* and that Christ was now invisibly "present" carrying on a judging work.

---

6   It was *after* the meeting with Barbour that Russell wrote an article for *The Bible Examiner,* published by George Storrs, another Adventist, in which article Russell set forth the 1914 date Barbour had arrived at. Like so many of the Second Adventist magazines, the magazine that Russell began included the term "Herald" in its title, *Zion's Watch Tower and Herald of Christ's Presence* (which "presence" was believed to have begun in 1874).

An "invisible presence" is a very difficult thing to argue against or disprove. It is something like having a friend tell you that he knows that a dead parent invisibly visits him and comforts him, and then trying to *prove* to your friend that this is not really so.

The "invisible presence" concept thus allowed these Second Adventists associated with Barbour to say that they had, after all, had the "right date [1874] but had just expected the wrong thing on that date." That explanation was also accepted and adopted by Russell.[7]

Today the several millions of Jehovah's Witnesses believe and teach that Christ's invisible presence began in 1914. Very few realize that *for nearly fifty years* the Watch Tower Society announced and heralded, in their role as prophet, that such invisible presence began in 1874. As late as 1929, fifteen years *after* 1914, they were still teaching this.[8]

Jehovah's Witnesses today believe that Christ officially began his Kingdom rule in 1914. The *Watch Tower* taught for decades that this took place in 1878.[9]

Jehovah's Witnesses today believe that the "last days" and the "time of the end" also began in 1914. The *Watch Tower* magazine taught for *half a century* that the "last days" began in 1799 (accepting the interpretation by George Bell published in 1796).

They believe today that the resurrection of anointed Christians who died from Christ's time forward began to take place in 1918. For more than forty years the *Watch Tower* taught that it began in 1878.

Their present belief is that from and after 1914 and particularly from 1919 onward the great "harvest" work is under way, to be climaxed by the destruction of the present system and all those who have not responded to their preaching activity. From its beginning, the *Watch Tower* magazine taught instead that the "harvest" would run from 1874 to 1914, and that by 1914 the destruction of all human institutions of this world would take place.

---

7   The July 15, 1906, *Watch Tower*, earlier quoted, shows that they did advance that very argument.

8   See the book *Prophecy*, published in 1929, pp. 64, 65. The August 15, 1974, *Watchtower* makes mention of this belief, but gives no indication that it continued to be taught after 1914.

9   This view began to be changed in 1922 at the Cedar Point Convention, eight years *after* 1914.

The organization today places the fall of "Babylon the Great" (the "world empire of false religion") in 1919. For at least four decades the *Watch Tower* placed it in 1878, with Babylon's complete destruction due in 1914 or 1918.

What was responsible for the change in all these major prophetic teachings held to for so many decades and by so many people?

It was the same as in the case of all the long line of predictions from the thirteenth century onward—the failure of their published expectations to be realized.

Some may incline to discount this as a mere assertion. After all, hardly any of Jehovah's Witnesses now have access to older issues of the *Watch Tower* and today, even when discussing the organization's past history, the Society's publications either ignore or present only a partial, sometimes altered, view of these teachings advocated for so long a time. They give little idea of how *positively* and *confidently* these views were advanced.

Consider then a portion of the evidence from "the record" of this organization; a record that the *Watchtower* says will confirm the validity of the organization's claim to the role of modern-day prophet.

In reviewing the earliest issues of the *Watch Tower* magazine, from 1879 onward, a notable feature is that they were expecting major things to happen *right then*. Though believing that 1914 would mark the end of the "Gentile Times," that date figured relatively little in their thinking. They were thinking far more of 1874 and the belief that Christ had begun his invisible presence then, had thereafter entered his Kingdom rule. So they expected to experience their transferal to heavenly life very soon. With this, the opportunity to become part of the "bride of Christ" would be closed. They expected, as well, that long before 1914 the world would enter into a time of great trouble that would worsen and develop into a state of chaos and anarchy. By 1914 everything would be over, finished, and Christ Jesus would have taken full charge of earth's affairs, his Kingdom completely replacing all human systems of rule.

This is aptly illustrated in the following material from the January, 1881, issue of the *Watch Tower*, certain points being underlined here for the reader's convenience.

We see too that not only are the harvest of Jewish and Gospel ages parallel in point of beginning, but also in length of duration; theirs being in all 40 years from the time of Jesus anointing [at beginning of their harvest, A. D. 30.] to destruction of Jerusalem, A. D. 70. So, ours, beginning in 1874 closes with the end of the "day of wrath" and end of the "times of the Gentiles," 1914—a similar and parallel period of 40 years. The first seven years of the Jewish harvest was especially devoted to the gathering of ripe wheat from that church; three and one-half of it was while he was present as the Bridegroom and three and a half of it after he had come to them as king and had entered into glory, but it was all under his supervision and direction.

As John had said he purged his flood, gathered his wheat and burned the chaff. So here the parallel is being fulfilled: We find, [as heretofore shown—see "Day Dawn"] *the law and the prophets* declaring him present at the culmination of the "Jubilee cycles" in 1874. And the parallels show us that then the *harvest* began, and that the gathering of the bride into the place of safety, will occupy a parallel of seven years of time, ending in 1881. But how, when, and why did the "house of servants" stumble over Christ? If we can ascertain this it should give us a clue to how, when, and why, the Gospel house stumbles, especially in view of the fact that in so many particulars the closing work of that age is the *exact pattern* of this.

We believe that Christ is now present, in the sense of having commenced the work of taking to himself his great power and reigning. The work begins with the separating of tares from wheat in the living church and the association of the wheat of all ages with himself in the authority of his kingdom. "To him that overcometh will I grant to sit with me in my throne," and "to him will I give power over the nations," to continue until all things are subdued under him. It seems proper, too, that the work should begin thus, by taking his bride and the twain becoming one.

Rather than 1914, the real "anchor" date for the *Watch Tower* then was clearly 1874. As of that date, Christ was present. Within the following 40 years he would accomplish all his harvest work. Because of believing this, it was felt that dramatic events should be taking place very quickly, perhaps in that very year of 1881, as argued in the additional article headed "How Long, O Lord?" Note these points:

"HOW LONG, O LORD?"

This is a question doubtless that many ask themselves, viz. "How soon will our change come?" This change many of us have looked forward to for years, and we yet with much pleasure, think of the time when we shall be gathered unto Jesus and see him as he is. In the article concerning our change, in December paper, we expressed the opinion that it was nearer than many supposed, and while we would not attempt to prove our change at any particular time, yet we propose looking at some of the evidences which *seem* to show the translation or change from the natural to the spiritual condition, due this side or by the fall of our year 1881. The evidence that our change will be by that time, increases since we have seen that the change to spiritual bodies is not the marriage. While we thought the marriage to be the change, and knowing there was three and a half years of special favor to the nominal church (now left desolate) from 1878, we could not expect any translation this side of 1881, or during this three and a half years. But since we recognize that going into the marriage is not only being made ready (by recognizing his presence) for the change, but also, that going in includes the change itself, then the evidences that we go in (or will be changed) inside of the time mentioned are strong, and commend themselves to all interested as worthy of investigation. Aside from any direct proof that our change is near, the fact that the manner of the change can now be understood, is evidence that we are near the time of the *change*, for truth is "meat in due season," and understood only as due. It will be remembered that after the spring of 1878, (when we understand Jesus was due as King) that the subject of holiness or the wedding garment, was very much agitated. And aside from the parallel to the end of the Jewish age, and favor at that time being shown to the Jewish nation, which implied the presence of the King, the consideration of the wedding garment, was also proof of the correctness of the application for

"the King had come in to see the guests." [Matt. xxii. 11.] and hence all were interested in knowing how they stood before him. Now as the inspection of guests is the last thing prior to our change, which precedes the marriage and we are all now considering *the change*, it would seem that the time for it, is nigh.

We shall now present what we adduce from the types and prophetic points as seeming to indicate the translation of the saints and closing of the door to the high calling by 1881.

Detailed argumentation followed, with emphasis on the fall of 1881 as the likely time for their change to heavenly life and the time "when the door—opportunity to become a member of the bride—will close." This would be *35 years before 1914*, which to them was simply a terminal point, the time by which all things would wind up.

The expectation that the anointed Christians of the "Bride class" would undergo a transition to heavenly life by the fall of 1881 obviously did not materialize. As the years passed, the focus of attention began to lengthen and 1914 began to receive somewhat greater emphasis. It was still the *terminal* point, however, when the elimination of earthly ruler-ships and the destruction of "nominal Christendom" would be complete, for it was believed that Christ began to exercise his full Kingdom power in 1878, as shown in the book Russell published in 1889, titled *The Time Is At Hand*, pages 239 and 247.

Parallel Dispensations.   239

house he came as Bridegroom and Reaper in the beginning of their harvest (the beginning of his ministry); and just before his crucifixion he presented himself as their King, exercising kingly authority in pronouncing judgment against them, in leaving their house desolate, and in the typical act of cleansing their temple. (Luke 19:41–46; Mark 11:15–17.) Just so it has been in this harvest: Our Lord's presence as Bridegroom and Reaper was recognized during the first three and a half years, from A. D. 1874 to A. D. 1878. Since that time it has been emphatically manifest that the time had come in A. D. 1878 when kingly judgment should begin at the house of God. It is here that Rev. 14:14–20 applies, and our Lord is brought to view as the Reaper *crowned*. The year A. D. 1878, being the parallel of his assuming power and authority in the type, clearly *marks the time* for the actual assuming of power as King of kings, by our present, spiritual, invisible Lord—the time of his taking to himself his great power to reign, which in the prophecy is closely associated with the resurrection of his faithful, and the beginning of the trouble and wrath upon the nations. (Rev. 11:17, 18.)

THEY KNEW NOT THE TIME OF THEIR VISITATION.

LUKE 19 : 44 ; MATT. 24 : 38, 39.

OUR LORD PRESENTED IN THREE CHARACTERS—AS BRIDEGROOM, REAPER AND KING.

JOHN 3 : 29 ; 4 : 35, 38 ; MATT. 21 : 5, 9, 4 ; 2 COR. 11 : 2 ; REV. 14 : 14, 15 ; 17 : 14.

AN ADVENT MOVEMENT AT THE TIME OF JESUS' BIRTH, THIRTY YEARS PRIOR TO HIS ADVENT AND ANOINTING, AS MESSIAH, AT BAPTISM.	AN ADVENT MOVEMENT IN 1844, THIRTY YEARS PRIOR TO THE ACTUAL TIME OF HIS PRESENCE, TO AWAKEN AND TEST THE CHURCH.
MATT. 2 : 1-16 ; ACTS 10 : 37, 38.	MATT. 25 : 1.
ACTUAL PRESENCE OF THE LORD AS BRIDE-GROOM AND REAPER—OCTOBER, A. D. 29.	ACTUAL PRESENCE OF THE LORD AS BRIDE-GROOM AND REAPER—OCTOBER, A. D. 1874.
POWER AND TITLE AS KING ASSUMED THREE AND A HALF YEARS LATER—A. D. 33.	POWER AND TITLE OF KING ASSUMED THREE AND A HALF YEARS LATER—A. D. 1878.

FIRST WORK OF THE KING, JUDGMENT.

NOMINAL JEWISH HOUSE REJECTED; LITERAL TEMPLE CLEANSED.—MATT.20 : 18; 21 : 5-15; 23:37; 24:1.	NOMINAL CHRISTIAN HOUSE REJECTED; SPIRITUAL TEMPLE CLEANSED.—1 PET.4:17; REV.3:16; MAL 3:2.
ENTIRE DESTRUCTION OF JEWISH POLITY, ACCOMPLISHED IN 37 YEARS AFTER BEING CAST OFF—OR 40 YEARS FROM THE BEGINNING OF THE HARVEST —A. D. 70.	ENTIRE DESTRUCTION OF NOMINAL CHRISTENDOM, ACCOMPLISHED IN 37 YEARS AFTER BEING CAST OFF —OR 40 YEARS FROM THE BEGINNING OF THE HARVEST—A. D. 1914.

Even after the turn of the century, in the early 1900s, the focus was still largely on 1874 and 1878 as the key dates to which all thinking was geared. They were *in* the "last days" since 1799, *in* the "harvest" period since 1874, Christ had been exercising his kingly power since 1878 and the resurrection had then begun. The passing of the years did not change these claims. They all related to *invisible* events, unlike the prediction about the translation to heaven of the living saints' expected in 1881. With no visible evidence to discredit them, these claims could be, and were, maintained.

Within three years of 1914, in 1911, the *Watch Tower* still proclaimed the importance of 1874, 1878 and 1881. "Babylon the Great" had fallen in 1878 and her "full end" would come in October 1914. An 'adjustment' was made, however, as regards the "closing of the door" to the opportunity to be part of the heavenly Kingdom class, earlier placed in 1881. Now the *Watch Tower* readers are informed that the "door" still "stands ajar," in this material from the June 15, 1911, issue:

> Noting these parallels, we find 1874 as the beginning of this "harvest" and the gathering together of the "elect" from the four winds of heaven; 1878 as the time when Babylon was formally rejected, Laodicea spewed out—the time from which it is stated, "Babylon is fallen, is fallen"—fallen from divine favor. The parallel in 1881 would seem to indicate that certain favors were still continued to those in Babylon up to that date, notwithstanding the rejection of the system; and since that date we would understand that that relationship has been in no sense an advantageous one, but has been in many senses of the word a distinct disadvantage, from

which only with difficulty could any free themselves, the Lord's grace and truth assisting. And in harmony with this parallelism, October, 1914, will witness the full end of Babylon, "as a great millstone cast into the sea," utterly destroyed as a system.

Coming back: We concede it reasonable to infer that the close of the favors upon fleshly Israel represent the close of the special favor of this Gospel age, viz., the invitation to the high calling; accordingly, our understanding is that the open or general "call" of this age to kingdom honors ceased in October, 1881. However, as already shown in SCRIPTURE STUDIES, we make a distinction between the end of the "call" and the closing of the "door"; and believe that the door into the kingdom class is not yet closed; that it stands ajar for a time, to permit those who had already accepted the "call" and who fail to use its privileges and opportunities in self-sacrifice to be thrust out, and to permit others to enter to take their crowns, in harmony with Rev. 3:11. The present time, therefore, from 1881 until the door of opportunity for sacrifice in the Lord's service shall fully close, is a period of "sifting" as respects all who are already in divine favor, in covenant relationship with God.

The windup date of 1914 was now at hand. With its arrival the harvest would be over, the last days would have reached their culmination; their hopes would be fully realized. *Exactly what did the Watch Tower publications teach would take place by the time 1914 came?*

The book *The Time Is At Hand,* published twenty-five years before 1914, set out seven points, as follows:

In this chapter we present the Bible evidence proving that the full end of the times of the Gentiles, *i. e.*, the full end of their lease of dominion, will be reached in A. D.

Times of the Gentiles.   77

1914; and that that date will be the farthest limit of the rule of imperfect men.   And be it observed, that if this is shown to be a fact firmly established by the Scriptures, it will prove:—

Firstly, That at that date the Kingdom of God, for which our Lord taught us to pray, saying, "Thy Kingdom come," will obtain full, universal control, and that it will then be "set up," or firmly established, in the earth, on the ruins of present institutions.

Secondly, It will prove that he whose right it is thus to take the dominion will then be present as earth's new Ruler; and not only so, but it will also prove that he will be present for a considerable period before that date; because the overthrow of these Gentile governments is directly caused by his dashing them to pieces as a potter's vessel (Psa. 2:9; Rev. 2:27), and establishing in their stead his own righteous government.

Thirdly, It will prove that some time before the end of A. D. 1914 the last member of the divinely recognized Church of Christ, the "royal priesthood," "the body of Christ," will be glorified with the Head; because every member is to reign with Christ, being a joint-heir with him of the Kingdom, and it cannot be fully "set up" without every member.

Fourthly, It will prove that from that time forward Jerusalem shall no longer be trodden down of the Gentiles, but shall arise from the dust of divine disfavor, to honor; because the "Times of the Gentiles" will be fulfilled or completed.

Fifthly, It will prove that by that date, or sooner, Israel's blindness will begin to be turned away; because their "blindness in part" was to continue only "*until* the fulness of the Gentiles be come in" (Rom. 11:25), or, in other words, until the full number from among the Gentiles, who are to be members of the body or bride of Christ, would be fully selected.

Sixthly, It will prove that the great "time of trouble such

78   *The Time is at Hand.*

as never was since there was a nation," will reach its culmination in a world-wide reign of anarchy; and then men will learn to be still, and to know that Jehovah is God and that he will be exalted in the earth. (Psa. 46:10) The condition of things spoken of in symbolic language as raging waves of the sea, melting earth, falling mountains and burning heavens will then pass away, and the "new heavens and new earth" with their peaceful blessings will begin to be recognized by trouble-tossed humanity. But the Lord's Anointed and his rightful and righteous authority will first be recognized by a company of God's children

while passing through the great tribulation—the class represented by *m* and *t* on the Chart of the Ages (see also
pages 235 to 239, VOL. I.); afterward, just at its close, by
fleshly Israel; and ultimately by mankind in general.

Seventhly, It will prove that *before that date* God's Kingdom, organized in power, will be in the earth and then
smite and crush the Gentile image (Dan. 2:34)—and fully
consume the power of these kings.   Its own power and
dominion will be established as fast as by its varied influ-
ences and agencies it crushes and scatters the "powers that
be"—civil and ecclesiastical—iron and clay.

These statements are found in editions *up until 1914.* As can be noted
in the material quoted, these editions clearly stated that 1914 "will be the
farthest limit of the rule of imperfect men." It said that at that date the
Kingdom of God *"will have obtained* full, universal control, and that it
will then be 'set up,' or firmly established, in the earth." Note how a *post-
1914* edition (1924) covers this up by saying:

In this chapter we present the Bible evidence proving
that the full end of the times of the Gentiles, *i. e.*, the full
end of their lease of dominion, will be reached in A. D.

Times of the Gentiles.   **77**

1914; and that that date will see the disintegration of the
rule of imperfect men. And be it observed, that if this is
shown to be a fact firmly established by the Scriptures,
it will prove:—

Firstly, That at that date the Kingdom of God, for which
our Lord taught us to pray, saying, "Thy Kingdom
come," will begin to assume control, and that it will
then shortly be "set up," or firmly established, in the
earth, on the ruins of present institutions.

In point three, the editions prior to and up to 1914 stated that before
the end of 1914 the last member of the "body of Christ" would be glorified with the Head. Here, also, the post-1914 edition changes the wording
and eliminates any reference to the year 1914:

> Thirdly, It will prove that some time before the end of
> the overthrow the last member of the divinely recognized
> Church of Christ, the "royal priesthood," "the body of
> Christ," will be glorified with the Head; because every
> member is to reign with Christ, being a joint-heir with him
> of the Kingdom, and it cannot be fully "set up" without
> every member.

Thus, in later editions a clear effort was made to cover up the more obvious failures of the very positive claims made regarding 1914 once that date had passed without the predicted events occurring. Few Jehovah's Witnesses today have any concept of the magnitude of the claims made for that year or the fact that not a single one of the original seven points was fulfilled as stated. Those expectations now receive only the briefest of mention in the Society's publications; some are totally passed over.[10]

In fact, by reading the Society's recent publications one might gather that Russell, the Watch Tower president, did not speak specifically about just what 1914 would bring. They imply that any strong expectations or dogmatic claims were the responsibility of others, the readers. An example of this is found in what was for many years the official history of the organization, *Jehovah's Witnesses in the Divine Purpose,* page 52.

> There is no doubt that many throughout this period were overzealous in their statements as to what could be expected. Some read into the *Watch Tower* statements that were never intended, and while it was necessary for Russell to call attention to the certainty that a great change was due at the end of the Gentile times, he still encouraged his readers to keep an open mind, especially as regards the time element.

---

10   So, too, with the claims made about the years 1878 and 1881, which, along with those about 1799 and 1874, were all eventually discarded as in error.

The book quotes excerpts from *Watch Tower* magazines but when examined they simply do not support the statement made above. The only one dealing with a specific "time element" is from a *Watch Tower* of 1893, which says:

> A great storm is near at hand. Though one may not know exactly when it will break forth, it seems reasonable to suppose that it cannot be *more* than twelve or fourteen years yet future.ʳ

This does nothing to prove the claim made; it merely confirms what other writings of Russell show, that he definitely expected worldwide trouble to break out *before 1914 arrived,* not later than 1905 or 1907 according to the quoted material, and that this outbreak of trouble would lead up to the eventual destruction of all earth's governments by that terminal date.

Two years before 1914 arrived, the *Watch Tower* did urge some caution on the part of its readers.

The book *Jehovah's Witnesses in the Divine Purpose* (page 53) quotes Russell's statement in a 1912 *Watch Tower* as follows:

> There surely is room for slight differences of opinion on this subject and it behooves us to grant each other the widest latitude. The lease of power to the Gentiles may end in October, 1914, or in October, 1915. And the period of intense strife and anarchy "such as never was since there was a nation" may be the final ending of the Gentile times or the beginning of Messiah's reign.
> But we remind all of our readers again, that we have not prophesied anything about the Times of the Gentiles closing in a time of trouble nor about the glorious epoch which will shortly follow that catastrophe. We have merely pointed out what the Scriptures say, giving our views respecting their meaning and asking our readers to judge, each for himself, what they signify. *These prophecies still read the same to us. . . .* However, *some* may make positive statements of what they know, and of what they do not know, *we never indulge in this;* but we merely state that we believe thus and so, for such and such reasons.

This, then, is the picture the organization seeks to convey. Compare that with other statements made in the *Watch Tower* magazine and other publications, statements to which the Society's publications today make no reference whatsoever. Ask whether it is true that the responsibility for any dogmatic claims rests outside the Society, rests instead with those who "read into" the publications a certainty never intended, particularly as regards what 1914 would bring.

From *The Time Is At Hand* (pages 98 and 99), published in 1889, we read the following:

> True, it is expecting great things to claim, as we do, that within the coming twenty-six years all present governments will be overthrown and dissolved; but we are living in a special and peculiar time, the "Day of Jehovah," in which matters culminate quickly; and it is written, "A short work will the Lord make upon the earth." (See Vol. I., chap. xv.)

> In view of this strong Bible evidence concerning the Times of the Gentiles, we consider it an established truth that the final end of the kingdoms of this world, and the full establishment of the Kingdom of God, will be accomplished at the end of A. D. 1914. Then the prayer of the Church, ever since her Lord took his departure—"Thy Kingdom come"—will be answered; and under that wise and just administration, the whole earth will be filled with the glory of the Lord—with knowledge, and righteousness, and peace (Psa. 72:19; Isa. 6:3; Hab. 2:14); and the will of God shall be done *"on earth, as it is done in heaven."*

If you say, not merely that something is true, but that you consider it an *"established* truth," is that not the same as saying that you *know* it to be so? Is that not 'indulging in positive statements'? If there is any difference, how much of a difference is it?

In the same publication, on page 101, this statement appears:

> *Times of the Gentiles.*   101

> and the living saints, as well as many of the world, are now being used as the Lord's soldiers in overthrowing errors and evils. But let no one hastily infer a *peaceable conversion*

of the nations to be here symbolized ; for many scriptures,
Such as Rev. 11 : 17, 18 ; Dan. 12 : 1 ; 2 Thes. 2 : 8 ; Psalms
149 and 47, teach the very opposite.

Be not surprised, then, when in subsequent chapters we
present proofs that the setting up of the Kingdom of God
is already begun, that it is pointed out in prophecy as due
to begin the exercise of power in A. D. 1878, and that the
"battle of the great day of God Almighty " (Rev. 16:14.),
which will end in A. D. 1914 with the complete overthrow
of earth's present rulership, is already commenced.   The
gathering of the armies is plainly visible from the standpoint of God's Word.

If our vision be unobstructed by prejudice, when we get
the telescope of God's Word rightly adjusted we may see
with clearness the character of many of the events due to
take place in the "Day of the Lord"—that we are in the
very midst of those events, and that " the Great Day of His
Wrath is come."

Two years after this book was published, another book by Russell,
"Thy Kingdom Come" was published in 1891, and on page 153 we find
the following:

The Work of Harvest.   153

The fall, plagues, destruction, etc., foretold to come upon mystic Babylon, were foreshadowed in the great trouble
and national destruction which came upon fleshly Israel, and
which ended with the complete overthrow of that nation
in A. D. 70.   And the period of falling also corresponds ; for
from the time our Lord said, " Your house is left unto you
desolate," A. D. 33, to A. D. 70 was 36½ years ; and so from
A. D. 1878 to the end of A. D. 1914 is 36½ years.   And,
with the end of A. D. 1914, what God calls Babylon, and
what men call Christendom, will have passed away, as already
shown from prophecy.

The next year, 1892, in the January 15 issue, the *Watch Tower* stated that the final "battle" had already begun, its end to come in 1914:

> While it was an agreeable surprise to us (in view of the contrary sensational accounts so often published) to find the situation in Europe as we here describe it—in harmony with what the Scriptures had led us to expect—yet so great is our confidence in the Word of God and in the light of present truth shining upon it, that we could not have doubted its testimony whatever had been the appearances. The date of the close of that "battle" is definitely marked in Scripture as October, 1914. It is already in progress, its beginning dating from October, 1874. Thus far it has been chiefly a battle of words and a time of organizing forces—capital, labor, armies and secret societies.
>
> Never was there such a general time of banding together as at present. Not only are nations allying with each other for protection against other nations, but the various factions in every nation are organizing to protect their several interests. But as yet the various factions are merely studying the situation, testing the strength of their opponents, and seeking to perfect their plans and power for the future struggle, which many, without the Bible's testimony, seem to realize is the inevitable. Others still delude themselves, saying, Peace! Peace! when there is no possibility of peace until God's kingdom comes into control, compelling the doing of his will on earth as it is now done in heaven.
>
> This feature of the battle must continue with varying success to all concerned; the organization must be very thorough; and the final struggle will be comparatively short, terrible and decisive—resulting in general anarchy. In many respects the convictions of the world's great generals coincide with the predictions of God's Word. Then "Woe to the man or nation who starts the next war in Europe; for it will be a war of extermination." It will be abetted not only by national animosities, but also by social grievances, ambitions and animosities, and if not brought to an end by the establishment of God's kingdom in the hands of his elect and then glorified Church, it would exterminate the race.—Matt. 24:22.

This short item appearing in the July 15, 1894, issue of the *Watch Tower* reveals how they viewed world conditions of that time as clear proof that the world was then about to enter its final throes, with its last gasp coming in 1914:

> ## CAN IT BE DELAYED UNTIL 1914?
> Seventeen years ago people said, concerning the time features presented in MILLENNIAL DAWN, They seem reasonable in many respects, but surely no such radical changes could occur between now and the close of 1914: if you had proved that they would come about in a century or two, it would seem much more probable.

What changes have since occurred, and what velocity is gained daily?

"The old is quickly passing and the new is coming in."

Now, in view of recent labor troubles and threatened anarchy, our readers are writing to know if there may not be a mistake in the 1914 date. They say that they do not see how present conditions can hold out so long under the strain.

We see no reason for changing the figures—nor could we change them if we would. They are, we believe, God's dates, not ours. But bear in mind that the end of 1914 is not the date for the *beginning*, but for the *end* of the time of trouble. We see no reason for changing from our opinion expressed in the view presented in the WATCH TOWER of January 15, '92. We advise that it be read again.

It is true that the word "opinion" is here used, but how meaningful is this when at the same time God is brought into the picture as backing up the dates set forth? Who would be inclined to doubt "God's dates," as the *Watch Tower* calls them?

Today, the organization would say that these matters are all peripheral, minor when compared to what they would present as a major truth, namely that the Society was right about the "end of the Gentile times" as coming in 1914, the *one early belief* concerning 1914 that they still retain. But in saying this they commit probably the greatest misrepresentation of all. For the fact is that all that has been retained is the *phrase:* "the end of the Gentile times." The *meaning* they now assign to that phrase is *totally different* from the meaning assigned to it by the Watch Tower Society during the forty years up to 1914.

During all those forty years those associated with the Watch Tower Society understood that the "end of the Gentile times" would mean the complete overthrow of all earthly governments, their total elimination and replacement by the rule of the whole earth by Christ's kingdom. No human rule would remain. Recall the statement on pages 98 and 99 of *The Time Is At Hand,* that "within the coming twenty-six years [from 1889] *all present governments will be overthrown and dissolved."* That, "In view of this strong Bible evidence concerning the Times of the Gentiles, we consider it an *established truth* that the *final end of the kingdoms of this world,* and the full establishment of the Kingdom of God, will be accomplished by the end of A.D. 1914."

Today the meaning assigned to the phrase "end of the Gentile Times" (or "the appointed times of the nations") is quite different. It is not the *actual* end of rulership by human governments as a result of their destruction by Christ. Now it is said to be the end of their "uninterrupted rule" of the earth, the 'interruption' resulting from Christ's invisibly having taken Kingdom power and begun reigning in 1914 and directing his attention in a 'special way' toward the earth, (which actually is what had been earlier taught about the year 1874).

Since, again, the realm of the invisible is where this is said to have occurred, it is difficult to argue with such a theory. The fact that nothing whatsoever has changed since 1914 as regards the earthly governments' dominion of the earth does not seem to be viewed as of any consequence. Their "lease" of power has expired, it is now said, being invisibly cancelled by the invisible King, and thus the "end" of their appointed time has come.

All of which is something like proclaiming for forty years that on a certain date the undesirable occupant of a property is going to be completely expelled, removed for all time, and then, when that date comes and goes and the undesirable occupant is still there carrying on as usual, explaining this away by saying, "Well, I cancelled his lease and as far as I'm concerned it's the same as if he were actually moved out. And, besides, I'm keeping a much closer watch on things now."

Admittedly, the closer 1914 came, the more cautious the forecasts became. Whereas Russell had argued that the storm of trouble and universal anarchy would take place before October of 1914, later, in the July 1, 1904 issue of the magazine he said:

UNIVERSAL ANARCHY—JUST BEFORE
OR AFTER OCTOBER, 1914 A. D.

What seems at first glance the veriest trifle and wholly unrelated to the matter, has changed our conviction respecting the time when universal anarchy may be expected in accord with the prophetic numbers. We now expect that the anarchistic culmination of the great time of trouble which will precede the Millennial blessings will be after October, 1914, A. D.—very speedily thereafter, in our opinion—"in one hour," "suddenly."

In 1894 he had affirmed that the figures expounded were "God's dates, not ours." In the October 1, 1907, *Watch Tower,* with 1914 only seven years away, in an article titled "Knowledge and Faith Regarding Chronology," he now said:

> A dear Brother inquires, Can we feel absolutely sure that the Chronology set forth in the DAWN-STUDIES is correct?—that the harvest began in A. D. 1874 and will end in A. D. 1914 in a world-wide trouble which will overthrow all present institutions and be followed by the reign of righteousness of the King of Glory and his bride, the church?
>
> We answer, as we have frequently done before in the DAWNS and TOWERS and orally and by letter, that we have never claimed our calculations to be infallibly correct; we have never claimed that they were *knowledge,* nor based upon indisputable evidence, facts, knowledge; our claim has always been that they are based on *faith.*

This same article, however, goes on to imply that those doubting such calculations were lacking in faith, saying:

> We remind you again that the weak points of chronology are supplemented by the various prophecies which interlace with it in so remarkable a manner that *faith* in the chronology almost becomes *knowledge* that it is correct. The changing of a single year would throw the beautiful parallels out of accord; because some of the prophecies measure from B. C., some from A. D., and some depend upon both. We believe that God meant those prophecies to be understood "in due time"; we believe that we do understand them now—and they speak to us through this chronology. Do they not thereby seal the chronology? They do to *faith,* but not otherwise. Our Lord declared, "The wise shall understand"; and he told us to "Watch" that we might know; and it is this chronology which *convinces us* (who can and do receive it by faith) that the Parable of the Ten Virgins is now in process of fulfilment—that its first cry was heard in 1844 and its second cry, "Behold the Bridegroom"—present—was in 1874.

How beneficial is it—or, for that matter, how much humility does it demonstrate—to acknowledge fallibility while at the same time implying that only those who accept one's views are showing faith, are among 'the wise who shall understand'? Would not those failing to heed these "cries" of 1844 and 1874 be classed logically with the "foolish virgins" of the parable?

Earlier, in the same article, Russell had said:

> God's times and seasons are given in such a way as to be convincing only to those who, by acquaintance with God, are able to recognize his characteristic methods.

Thus, if any expressed doubts about the Society's chronology, the very quality of their relationship with God was subtly placed in question—along with their faith and wisdom. This is a form of intellectual intimidation; a practice that increased many fold once 1914 had passed by, failing to fulfill the expectations published worldwide.

As has been mentioned, in 1993, the Watch Tower Society published a new history of Jehovah's Witnesses, titled *Jehovah's Witnesses—Proclaimers of God's Kingdom.* Certain portions appear to be reactions to information published by other sources, apparently in an effort to blunt the effect of that information. As an example, the book by Carl Olof Jonsson *The Gentile Times Reconsidered,* published and distributed since 1983, clearly showed the Second Advent sources for many of Charles Taze Russell's distinctive teachings, including that regarding the year 1914. Watch Tower publications for decades have glossed over or simply ignored this reality, conveying the impression that most of these teachings and the date of 1914 were original with Russell, and that he and his *Watch Tower* magazine constituted a unique divine channel for the revealing of previously lost or unknown truths.

Now, *for the first time,* a measure of acknowledgment was made of the *extent* of the indebtedness to these other, earlier sources, as in the case of John A. Brown's development of the theory of the "seven times" of Daniel chapter 4 as representing a period of 2,520 years and relating this to the "times of the Gentiles" of Luke 21:24. (Until this book the name of John A. Brown had never even *appeared in any Watch Tower publication.*) Also that it was, not Russell, but Second Adventist N. H. Barbour who had targeted 1914 as the "end of the Gentile Times" in his magazine *Herald of the Morning* in 1875—four years before the first *Watch Tower* magazine appeared—and that it was from him that Russell obtained this date.

All of this information was available and known to the Watch Tower leadership for decades. All Governing Body members received the first 20 pages of Carl Olof Jonsson's material in 1979, where these facts had all been spelled out in great detail. Yet only at this late date has the Watch

Tower organization made any open acknowledgment as to the true originators of these views and concepts.[11]

This new history book also makes at least some acknowledgment of the earlier, long-held teachings regarding the date of 1874 as supposedly marking the start of Christ's "second presence," of 1878 as the time when Christ assumed Kingly power, of 1881 as the time when the heavenly calling would close, and of 1925 as the time when the "ancient worthies" would be resurrected, and the grand Jubilee would begin for this earth. All this information had been presented back in 1983 in the first printing of this book, *Crisis of Conscience.*

What the book does *not* do is to admit honestly and frankly the *intense importance* and *constant emphasis* placed on these dates, in many cases for more than 50 years, and the *positiveness* with which assertions and claims were made. In this book, as in recent *Watchtower* and *Awake!* articles, there is an ongoing effort to minimize the importance attached to these dates and to what was predicted to take place by 1914 at the very latest.[12] They often focus on one aspect among many claims (as in referring only to the "end of the Gentile Times" or in presenting 1914 as being looked to simply as a "crucial date" or "a marked year") and do not mention other major claims that were part and parcel of the prediction. Generally, readers are only presented with a few later cautionary statements that came when 1914 (or, subsequently, 1925) was drawing close, and the bold predictions are then portrayed as only tentative 'suggestions' of mere 'possibilities.' Since the vast majority of their readers have no access to the earlier publications, the articles can trade on their ignorance and can downplay the force of the predictions by a selective use of quotations and either gloss over or deliberately ignore other clear statements made.

Very frequently the tactic employed is that of emphasizing the absence of specific terminology, as if the nonuse of those particular words or phrases frees them from having made false predictions in the name of

---

11 See *The Gentile Times Reconsidered,* pages 19-29; *Jehovah's Witnesses—Proclaimers of God's Kingdom,* pages 45-47, 132-135.

12 See, for example, the *Watchtower,* November 1, 1993, pages 8-12; *Awake!* March 22, 1993, pages 3, 4.

God. The March 22, 1993, *Awake!* on page 3 under the heading "Why So Many False Alarms?" presents an example of this:

> There are some who make spectacular pre-
> dictions of the world's end to grab attention
> and a following, but others are sincerely con-
> vinced that their proclamations are true. They
> are voicing expectations based on their own
> interpretation of some scripture text or physi-
> cal event. They do not claim that their predic-
> tions are direct revelations from Jehovah and
> that in this sense they are prophesying in Je-
> hovah's name. Hence, in such cases, when their
> words do not come true, they should not be
> viewed as false prophets such as those warned
> against at Deuteronomy 18:20-22. In their hu-
> man fallibility, they misinterpreted matters.*

The accompanying footnote contains the following:

> * Jehovah's Witnesses, in their eagerness for Jesus' second
> coming, have suggested dates that turned out to be incorrect. Never
> in these instances, however, did they presume to originate
> predictions 'in the name of Jehovah.' Never did they say,
> 'These are the words of Jehovah.' *The Watchtower*, the of-
> ficial journal of Jehovah's Witnesses, has said: "We have *not*
> the gift of prophecy." (January 1883, page 425) "Nor would
> we have our writings reverenced or regarded as infallible."
> (December 15, 1896, page 306) *The Watchtower* has also said
> that the fact that some have Jehovah's spirit "does not mean
> those now serving as Jehovah's witnesses are inspired. It does
> not mean that the writings in this magazine *The Watchtower*
> are inspired and infallible and without mistakes." (May 15,
> 1947, page 157) "*The Watchtower* does not claim to be in-
> spired in its utterances, nor is it dogmatic." (August 15, 1950,
> page 263) "The brothers preparing these publications are not
> infallible. Their writings are not inspired as are those of Paul
> and the other Bible writers. (2 Tim. 3:16) And so, at times,
> it has been necessary, as understanding became clearer, to
> correct views. (Prov. 4:18)"—February 15, 1981, page 19.

The argument thus is that if one does not use expressions such as, "this is a direct revelation from Jehovah," and avoids applying such terms as "infallible" and "inspired" to himself, the things said and the claims made by him are to be viewed as essentially harmless voicing of mere opinion. The Bible recognizes no such simplistic criteria for determining the wrongness of presuming to speak in the name of God and foretelling things which fail to come to pass. We may not find the false prophets within Israel employing specific expressions such as "direct revelation," or speaking of themselves by such terms as "inspired" and "infallible." Yet the pretense was nonetheless there that their words were indeed from Jehovah. To "speak in God's name" means doing so as a representative of that one, as the Watch Tower publication *Insight on the Scriptures* (Vol. II, page 468) recognizes. Russell referred to himself as God's spokesman and presented the chronological predictions as the product of God's guidance upon his people. God's name and his Word were certainly involved in all that was presented.

Consider the two quotations in the earlier footnote (taken from 1883 and 1896 *Watch Towers*), offered as evidence of not "prophesying in Jehovah's name" and of an avoidance of dogmatism and presumption, and then compare these with the statements found in publication after publication previous to 1914, statements declaring the *Watch Tower* time calculations as being "God's dates, nor ours" that "it has been emphatically manifest that the time had come in A.D. 1878 when kingly judgment should begin at the house of God" that that year [1878] "clearly marks the time for actual assuming of power as King of kings." Or the repeated statements that the Bible evidence would "prove" as "a fact firmly established by the Scriptures" that 1914 would mark "the farthest limit of the rule of imperfect men," would "prove" that "before the end of A.D. 1914 the last member" of the body of Christ would "be glorified with the Head," would "prove" that "before that date God's Kingdom, organized in power" would smite and crush and "fully consume the power of these [Gentile] kings," crushing and scattering the "'powers that be'—civil and ecclesiastical." Or the claim that "within the coming twenty-six years [from 1889] all present governments will be overthrown and dissolved," and that "we consider it an <u>established truth</u> that the final end of the king-doms of this world, and the full establishment of the Kingdom of God will be accomplished by the end of A.D. 1914," and that the date of the clos-ing of the great final battle "is <u>definitely marked</u> in Scripture as October, 1914. <u>It is already in progress</u>, its beginning dating from October, 1874." These statements are all documented on preceding pages of this chapter.

Following this same pattern of enshrouding the facts in a semantical smoke screen, with regard to the prediction of the church's glorification to heaven in 1914, the new history book (page 635) quotes a 1916 *Watch Tower* statement that "We merely inferred it and, evidently, erred."   In the face of the plain statements already quoted, with their frequent use of such terms as "proof" and "proved," "firmly established," "established truth," "definitely marked," this can only be described as journalistic and intellectual dishonesty.

Frequently, in Watch Tower argumentation, a "red herring" is dragged across the path, as in drawing attention away from the failure of the predictions by switching the focus to the willingness of many to stick with and support an organization despite its having fed them false hopes, while representing those who opted not to do so as being "spiritually weak," as "having grown weary in God's service," or being governed by selfish motives.

This only accentuates what is perhaps the most distressing factor of the whole matter: the apparent lack of any genuine concern for the *effect* such predictions had on the lives of people, those *Watch Tower* readers who viewed the predictive messages as coming from a God-directed source, as His divinely provided "meat in due season" for them. They were openly encouraged to allow these predictive claims, built around particular dates, to serve as a basis for their hopes and expectations, and thus to mold their lives in conformity. It produced a warped and shortsighted view of life and of the future and inevitably led to disappointment, for illusion sooner or later met up with reality.

The material shown is from an issue of the *Bible Students Monthly,* published during World War I. It illustrates the way in which predictive statements by the Watch Tower spokesman, Russell, were presented—not as merely something suggested or as mere *opinion*—but something to be declared due to the prediction's being connected with God's "divine plan of the ages."

8

JUSTIFICATION AND INTIMIDATION

When men talk too much, sin is never far away; common sense holds its tongue.
— Proverbs 10:19 *New English Bible.*

CHARLES Taze Russell, who had referred to himself as "God's mouthpiece," died in 1916. He left behind a legacy of time prophecies not one of which had brought the results foretold. He also left behind thousands of confused followers.

The Watch Tower book *Light I,* published in 1930, page 194, describes the situation in this way:

> All of the Lord's people looked forward to 1914 with joyful expectation. When that time came and passed there was much disappointment, chagrin and mourning, and the Lord's people were greatly in reproach. They were ridiculed by the clergy and their allies in particular, and pointed to with scorn, because they had said so much about 1914, and what would come to pass, and their 'prophecies' had not been fulfilled.

With the passage of both 1914 and 1915 and no complete overthrow of all kingdoms and human institutions, no takeover of all earth's rule by Christ's kingdom, no transition of the anointed to heavenly life, no destruction of "Babylon the Great," no conversion of Israel to Christianity—all foretold to take place by 1914—serious doubts arose among Watch Tower adherents. True, there had been the outbreak of World War I but it had not resulted in the worldwide anarchy predicted.

In October, 1916, shortly before his death, Russell, in writing a foreword to a new edition of *The Time Is At Hand,* endeavored to play down the significance of the inaccuracy of what had been predicted for 1914. What follows is illustrative of the approach he took:

> The author acknowledges that in this book he presents the thought that the Lord's saints might expect to be with Him in glory at the ending of the Gentile Times. This was a natural mistake to fall into, but the Lord overruled it for the blessing of His people. The thought that the Church would all be gathered to glory before October, 1914, certainly did have a very stimulating and sanctifying effect upon thousands, all of whom accordingly can praise the Lord—even for the mistake. Many, indeed, can express themselves as being thankful to the Lord that the culmination of the Church's hopes was not reached at the time we expected; and that we, as the Lord's people, have further opportunities of perfecting holiness and of being participators with our Master in the further presentation of His Message to His people.

Involving God and Christ with the mistakes made, with God 'overruling' certain predictions, provides a very convenient escape from having to shoulder the true responsibility for having falsely presented as "God's dates" things that were not God's dates but simply the product of unauthorized human speculation. Merit is found even in false predictions because of the "stimulating and sanctifying effect" produced, so that one may "praise the Lord—even for the mistake." That approach allowed for still more false predictions with their "stimulating" effect. One is reminded of the true prophet's presentation of God's words, saying:

> Woe to those who are saying that good is bad and bad is good, those who are putting darkness for light and light for darkness, those who are putting bitter for sweet and sweet for bitter![1]

While he remained alive and for a few years after his death, Russell's followers remained hopeful. When the war ended and things began to normalize, the passing of each year caused more questions to surface about the chronology advanced.

---

1   Isaiah 5:20

That is the situation Judge Rutherford inherited. (He had been elected as president of the Society in January, 1917, at the annual corporation meeting.) He was faced with two choices: rectifying by frank admission of error, or trying to justify the predictions of his predecessor. He chose the course of justification.

Acting quickly to revive any flagging confidence on the part of *Watch Tower* readers, Rutherford arranged for a book called *The Finished Mystery* to be published in 1917, the year following Russell's death.

This book endeavored to move some of the things expected in 1914 up to 1918, doing this by drawing a parallel with the smashing of the Jewish revolt by the Romans. The Roman destruction of Jerusalem came in the year 70 C.E., but the end of the struggle did not come until three and a half years later, in the year 73 C.E. So, that same amount of time was added to the autumn of 1914 and *The Finished Mystery* now pointed to the spring of 1918 as a new date of dramatic significance.

The portions of the book here underlined show what was now fore-told to occur. On reading them, note the language used and ask whether it would be 'reading into the book things that are not there' to say that it contained outright predictions and deliberately aroused expectations that were never fulfilled:

62   *The Finished Mystery*   REV. 3

Mark 1:5; Luke 1:5, 65; 3:1; 7:17; Acts 11:29; Rom. 15:31, and *especially* John 7:1-3 and 1 Thes. 2:14-16.
   The data presented in comments on Rev. 2:1 *prove* that the conquest of Judea was not completed until the day of the Passover, A. D. 73, and in the light of the foregoing Scriptures, *prove* that the Spring of 1918 will bring upon Christendom a spasm of anguish greater even than that experienced in the Fall of 1914. Reexamine the table of the Parallel Dispensations in STUDIES IN THE SCRIP-TURES, Vol. 2, pages 246 and 247; change the 37 to 40, 70 to 73 and 1914 to 1918, and we believe it is correct and will be fulfilled "with great power and glory." (Mark 13:26.) It was entirely impossible to foresee whether our Lord meant that A. D. 70 or A. D. 73 should serve as our guide to the time when the Jewish polity came to an end, until after October, 1915, had passed. Moreover, we have seen the promised signs, "upon the earth distress of nations, with perplexity; men's hearts failing them for fear, and for looking after those things which are coming on the earth," and we have the Lord's words for it that having seen those things "the Kingdom of God is nigh at hand," "even at the doors," and our "redemption

draweth nigh." (Luke 21:25-36; Mark 13:27-30.) It is
possible that A. D. 1980 marks the regathering of all of
Fleshly Israel from their captivity in death. It is just 70
years beyond 1910, the date when Pastor Russell gave his
great witness to the Jewish people in the New York Hip-
podrome. See page 551 (1).

But if the time of nominal Zion's travail (Isa. 66:8) is
due to occur in the Spring of 1918, and if we are now but
the "one day" (one year) distant from that event which
the Prophet mentions, what should be our expectation
regarding the experience of the "little flock" meantime?
"The symbolic travail, in the above prophecy, is a reference to the great Time of Trouble—the travail that is to
come upon the nominal Gospel church, Great 'Babylon,'
from which some are to be counted worthy to escape.

1918 was thus to see the nations of Christendom suffer a "spasm of
anguish" greater than that experienced in 1914 when World War I started.
In reality, 1918 saw the end of the war in an armistice.

The book also foretold that the remnant of "anointed ones," the "last
of the Elijah class," would experience their transition to heaven in that
year, as page 64 states:

Forty days after Christ's resurrection His ascension
occurred. This confirms the hope of the Church's glorification forty years (a year for a day) after the awakening
of the sleeping saints in the Spring of 1878. The seven
days before the Deluge may represent seven years, from
1914 to 1921, in the midst of which "week of years" the
last members of the Messiah pass beyond the veil. The
Great Company class shall be cut off at its end—the
fact that we see the first half of this week so distinctly
marked would lead us to expect three and one-half years
more of witnessing by the Great Company class; for it
seems to be the Heavenly Father's way to accomplish
His work by weeks and half weeks, from the very beginning of creation until now. The covenant with Abraham,
2045 B. C., was half way (2081 years each way) between
the fall of Adam, 4127 B. C., and the conversion of Cornelius, A. D. 36. The last observance of a typical jubilee
by Israel, 626 B. C., was half way (2500 years each way)
from the end of Adam's Day, 3127 B. C., and the beginning
of the Times of Restitution, A. D. 1874. The captivity, 606
B. C., marks the beginning of the Times of the Gentiles,
half way (2520 years each way) between the end of
Adam's 1000-year day, 3127 B. C., and the end of Gentile
Times, A. D. 1914. The captivity, 606 B. C., marks
a point half way (3520 years each way) between the
fall of man, 4127 B. C., and his full restoration to Divine
favor, A. D. 2914. Christ's death, A. D. 33, marks a point
half way (1845 years each way) between the death of
Jacob, 1813 B. C., and the restoration of favor to Israel
in 1878 A. D. The death of Christ, A. D. 33, was half way
(three and one-half years each way) between His baptism,
A. D. 29, and the conversion of Cornelius, A. D. 36.
The awakening of the sleeping saints, A. D. 1878, was
just half way (three and one-half years each way) between the beginning of the Times of Restitution in 1874
and the close of the High Calling in 1881. Our proposition is that the glorification of the Little Flock in the
Spring of 1918 A. D. will be half way (three and one-half
years each way) between the close of the Gentile Times
and the close of the Heavenly Way, A. D. 1921.

As with the similar prediction regarding 1881, this one also failed. Perhaps the most forceful language used was in the predictions of a terrible destruction due to come on Christendom's churches and their members in 1918, with their dead bodies strewn about unburied. On pages 484 and 485 we find two of several examples of this prophecy:

THE CHURCHES TO CEASE TO BE

24:20, 21. Then I answered them, The word of the Lord came unto me, saying, Speak unto the house of Israel, Thus saith the Lord God; Behold, I will profane My Sanctuary, the excellency of your strength, the desire of your eyes, and that which your soul pitieth; and your sons and your daughters whom ye have left shall fall by the sword. —God gives the reason. It was as a picture or parable of what is to happen to Christendom. Until 1878 the nominal church had been in a sense God's sanctuary or Temple; but He was from then on, culminating in 1918, to remove it with a stroke or plague of erroneous doctrines and deeds Divinely permitted. The Church was the strength of Christendom, that about which its life centered, and around which its institutions were built. It was the desire of the eyes of the people, that which all Christians loved. Nevertheless, God was to make manifest the profanation which ecclesiasticism had made of the Christian Church, and to cause the church organizations to become to Him as one dead, an unclean thing, not to be touched, or mourned. And the "children of the church" shall perish by the sword of war, revolution and anarchy, and by the Sword of the Spirit be made to see that they have lost their hope of life on the spirit plane—that "the door is shut."
24:22. And ye shall do as I have done: ye shall not cover your lips, nor eat the bread of men.—So universal and dreadful will be the troubles that the dead will literally lie unburied and unwept. There can be no mourning for the dead in a period when the living are overwhelmed by troubles worse than death.

PASTOR RUSSELL DEAD, BUT SPEAKING AGAIN

24:25, 26. Also, thou son of man, shall it not be in the day when I take from them their strength, the joy of their glory, the desire of their eyes, and that whereupon they set their minds, their sons and their daughters. That he that escapeth in that day shall come unto thee, to cause thee to hear it with thine ears?—Also, in the year 1918, when God destroys the churches wholesale and the church members by millions, it shall be that any that escape shall come to the works of Pastor Russell to learn the meaning of the downfall of "Christianity."
24:27. In that day shall thy mouth be opened to him which is escaped, and thou shalt speak, and be no more dumb: and thou shalt be a sign unto them; and they shall know that I am the Lord.—Pastor Russell's voice has been stilled in death; and his voice is, comparatively speaking, dumb to what it will be. In the time of revolution and anarchy he shall speak, and be no more dumb to those that escape the destruction of that day. Pastor Russell shall "be a sign unto them," shall tell them the truth about the Divine appointment of the trouble, as they consult his books, scattered to the number of ten million throughout Christendom. His words shall be a sign of hope unto them, enabling them to see the bright side of the cloud and to look forward with anticipation to the glorious Kingdom of God to be established. Then "they shall know the Lord."

Not only Christendom's churches but her governments as well would meet up with catastrophe and oblivion:

31:14. To the end that none of all the trees by the waters exalt themselves for their height, neither shoot up their top among the thick boughs, neither their trees stand up in their height, all that drink water; for they are all delivered unto death, to the nether parts of the earth, in the midst of the children of men, with them that go down to the pit.—No other earthly system may follow her proud example; for all of them are delivered, as systems, into death, to a dishonored place among the lowest in society.

31:15. Thus saith the Lord God; In the day when he went down to the grave I caused a mourning: I covered the deep for him, and I restrained the floods thereof, and the great waters were stayed: and I caused Lebanon to mourn for him, and all the trees of the field fainted for him. —In the year 1918, when Christendom shall go down as a system to oblivion, (Sheol) to be succeeded by revolutionary republics, God will cause mourning. He will restrain and defer for a brief period the threatening waves of anarchy. He will cause the nations to mourn for Christendom, and all the man-made systems (trees) of the world (field) to become weak on account of her fall.—E392, 372.

31:16. I made the nations to shake at the sound of his fall, when I cast him down to hell (Sheol) with them that descend to the pit: and all the trees of Eden, the choice and best of Lebanon, all that drink water, shall be comforted in the nether parts of the earth.—God will cause the nations to shake with gigantic revolutions, when He shall cast worldly Christendom, as an organized system, down to oblivion (as He did the Jews in the Dives parable).

31:17. They also went down into hell (Sheol) with him, unto them that be slain with the sword; and they that were in his arm, that dwelt under his shadow in the midst of the heathen.—But they also shall go down to oblivion (Sheol) (E392, 372), with Christendom, as well as those that were her power, that dwelt under her defense among the people.

All these things were foretold for the year 1918. None of them took place. But the book also predicted stupendous events for the year 1920. The gigantic revolutions that were to begin in 1918 would reach a culmination in 1920 with the disappearance of all orderly government of any kind:

To give unto her the cup of the wine of the fierceness of [His] THE wrath.—The wine of the vine of the earth.—Rev. 14:17-20; Jer. 8:14; Isa. 51:17-20; Jer. 25:26-28; Rev. 18:6.

16:20. And every island fled away.—Even the republics will disappear in the fall of 1920.

And the mountains were not found.—Every kingdom of earth will pass away, be swallowed up in anarchy.

16:21. And there fell upon men.—Greek "The Men," the worshipers of the beast and his image, i. e., the clergy.

A great hail out of heaven.—Truth, compacted, coming with crushing force. A concluding statement of how the seventh volume of *Scripture Studies* appers to the worshipers of the beast and his image.—Rev. 11:19; Isa. 28:17; 30:30; Ezek. 13:11; Joshua 10:11.

Every stone about the weight of a talent.—113 lbs. (Mal. 3:10.) Another view of the seventh volume of *Scripture Studies*, as it appears to the worshipers of the beast and his image, is found in the last of the Egyptian plagues, the death of the first-born, Exodus 11th. and 12th. chapters. As soon as this plague came the Egyptians, from Pharaoh down, were anxious to speed the parting guest, and willing to give up all the jewels of silver (the Great Company) and the jewels of gold (the Little Flock). In connection with the statement that "there was not a house where there was not one dead," it is admitted that if any sects were overlooked in the lists cited in comments on Rev. 8th and 9th chapters the omission was unintentional and will be corrected in later editions. <u>The three days in which Pharaoh's host pursued the Israelites into the wilderness represent the three years from 1917 to 1920 at which time all of Pharaoh's messengers will be swallowed up in the sea of anarchy. The wheels will come off their chariots—organizations.</u>

Thus, even the radical elements that would produce the revolutions in Christendom in 1918 and give birth to the laborite and socialist governments were to see those movements meet their demise. This would be because, even as those movements were to bring about the downfall of Christendom's existing governments, they themselves would be brought down by anarchists in 1920:

542   *The Finished Mystery*   EZEK. 35

upon ecclesiasticism and Christianity in anger and fury and with hateful envy, <u>so God will do to the Socialistic, laborite order of things. As they aid in smiting down Christianity, so will the anarchists smite them down.</u>

35:12. And thou shalt know that I am the Lord, and that I have heard all thy blasphemies, which thou hast spoken against the mountains of Israel, saying, They are laid desolate, they are given us to consume.—The laborites, etc., will learn that God rules in the affairs of men, and that the Almighty will pay attention to their utterances against the nations (mountains) of Christendom (Israel), when, after ecclesiasticism's fall, the laborites shall say, "The nations have been desolated, and are given to us working people to divide up for ourselves."

35:13. Thus with your mouth ye have boasted against Me, and have multiplied your words against Me: I have heard them.—The Socialistic and kindred movements, while speaking savagely against capitalism, and covertly against Christianity, have in reality been speaking against an order permitted by God, and in which God was—in the indwelling of His Holy Spirit, in such true Christians as were in the systems. In expressing the determination to lead the world out of the darkness of evil economic, social and political conditions, they unwittingly boast against God by presuming to perform what God previously planned to be done by His faithful Church, and which by any lesser agency is absolutely impossible of accomplishment, God will not pass by unnoticed the words of Socialists, syndicalists, laborites, etc. He will hear them, and remember them for just recompense.

35:14. Thus saith the Lord God; When the whole earth rejoiceth, I will make thee desolate.—When the Times of Restitution of all things come, one of the things not to be restored is the Socialist, laborite movement. When all society rejoices in the new order of things ordained of God, the Socialistic state will have been utterly and forever desolated.

35:15. As thou didst rejoice at the inheritance of the house of Israel, because it was desolate, so will I do unto thee; thou shalt be desolate, O mount Seir, and all Idumea, even all of it: and they shall know that I am the Lord.—As the fleshly-minded apostates from Christianity, siding with the radicals and revolutionaries, will rejoice at the inheritance of desolation that will be Christendom's after 1918, so will God do to the successful revolutionary movement; it shall be utterly desolated, "even all of it." Not one vestige of it shall survive the ravages of world-wide all-embracing anarchy, in the fall of 1920. (Rev. 11:7-13.)

"Worldwide, all-embracing anarchy, in the fall of 1920." Despite all the striking language and the positiveness of the claims, none of it came.

Like 1914, the new dates of 1918 and 1920 passed without the foretold "spasm of anguish" upon Christendom, the overthrow of her governments and destruction of her churches, and the slaughter of millions of their members, or the transferal of the anointed to heaven.

Instead, 1918 saw President Rutherford and six other principal officers of the Society tried and sentenced to prison on wartime charges that *The Finished Mystery* book and other publications contained seditious statements. The following year, 1919, they were released and exonerated of all charges.

Thus, they were free to observe 1920, the year in which, by autumn time, all republics and "every kingdom of earth" would be "swallowed up in anarchy," according to *The Finished Mystery.*

By that year, however, new predictions were developed and proclaimed. Without even allowing 1920 to pass, a new date was now set forth to be anticipated.

"MILLIONS NOW LIVING WILL NEVER DIE"

I did not send the prophets, yet they themselves ran. I did not speak to them, yet they themselves prophesied.
— Jeremiah 23:21.

In 1920, Watch Tower president Rutherford published a booklet titled *Millions Now Living Will Never Die*. That catchy phrase has been used even in recent times. Back there, however, it was based on a new prediction that Rutherford had developed. The whole thrust of the claim that millions then living would never die was tied to a new date: 1925. Note what the underlined portions of the booklet say of that year:

---

88   *Millions Now Living Will Never Die*

seventy jubilees ·kept. (Jeremiah 25:11; 2 Chronicles 36:17-21) A simple calculation of these jubilees brings us to this important fact: Seventy jubilees of fifty years each would be a total of 3500 years. <u>That period of time beginning 1575 before A. D. 1 of necessity would end in the fall of the year 1925</u>, at which time the type ends and the great antitype must begin. What, then, should we expect to take place? In the type there must be a full restoration; therefore the great antitype must mark <u>the beginning of restoration of all things.</u> The chief thing to be restored is the human race to life; and since other Scriptures definitely fix the fact that there will be a resurrection of <u>Abraham, Isaac, Jacob and other</u> faithful ones of old, and that these will have the first favor, <u>we may expect 1925 to witness the return</u> of these faithful men of Israel from the condition of death, being <u>resurrected</u> and <u>fully restored</u> to perfect humanity and <u>made</u> the <u>visible, legal representatives</u> of the <u>new order</u> of things on earth.

Messiah's kingdom once established, Jesus
and his glorified church constituting the great
Messiah, shall minister the blessings to the
people they have so long desired and hoped for
and prayed might come. And when that time
comes, there will be peace and not war, as the
prophet beautifully states: "In the last days it
shall come to pass, that the mountain of the
house of the Lord shall be established in the top
of the mountains, and it shall be exalted above

Millions Now Living Will Never Die   89

the hills; and people shall flow unto it. And
many nations shall come, and say, Come, and
let us go up to the mountain of the Lord, and to
the house of the God of Jacob; and he will teach
us of his ways, and we will walk in his paths:
for the law shall go forth of Zion, and the word
of the Lord from Jerusalem. And he shall judge
among many people, and rebuke strong nations
afar off; and they shall beat their swords into
plowshares, and their spears into pruninghooks;
nation shall not life up a sword against nation,
neither shall they learn war any more. But they
shall sit every man under his vine and under his
fig tree; and none shall make them afraid; for
the mouth of the Lord of hosts hath spoken it."
—Micah 4: 1 - 4.

EARTHLY RULERS

As we have heretofore stated, the great jubilee cycle is due to begin in 1925. At that time
the earthly phase of the kingdom shall be recognized. The Apostle Paul in the eleventh chapter
of Hebrews names a long list of faithful men
who died before the crucifixion of the Lord and
before the beginning of the selection of the
church. These can never be a part of the heavenly class; they had no heavenly hopes; but God
has in store something good for them. They are
to be resurrected as perfect men and constitute
the princes or rulers in the earth, according to
his promise. (Psalm 45: 16; Isaiah 32: 1; Matthew 8: 11) Therefore we may confidently expect that 1925 will mark the return of Abraham,

90   *Millions Now Living Will Never Die*

Isaac, Jacob and the faithful prophets of old, particularly those named by the Apostle in Hebrews chapter eleven, to the condition of human perfection.

Millions Now Living Will Never Die   97

in due time after the establishment of the kingdom. Then it shall come to pass that every one who will keep the saying of the Lord shall never see death. This promise would not have been made by Jesus if he did not intend to carry it into full force and effect in due time.

Again he said: "Whosoever liveth and believeth in me shall never die". (John 11:26) Do we believe the Master's statement? If so, when the time comes for the world to know, then they who believe and, of course, render themselves in obedience to the terms have the absolute and positive statement of Jesus that they shall never die.

Based upon the argument heretofore set forth, then, that the old order of things, the old world, is ending and is therefore passing away, and that the new order is coming in, and that 1925 shall mark the resurrection of the faithful worthies of old and the beginning of reconstruction, it is reasonable to conclude that millions of people now on the earth will be still on the earth in 1925. Then, based upon the promises set forth in the divine Word, we must reach the positive and indisputable conclusion that millions now living will never die.

Of course, it does not mean that every one will live; for some will refuse to obey the divine law; but those who have been evil and turn again to righteousness and obey righteousness shall live and not die. Of this we have the positive statement of the Lord's prophet, as follows:

The Watch Tower's more recent history book, as well as other sources, such as the 1993 *Awake!* article quoted in the previous chapter, all seek to portray the focus on specific dates, and the claims as to what those dates would bring, as mere "expectations," presented in a non-dogmatic manner, with no pretense of certainty. They make very selective quotations of cautionary statements or disclaimers of infallibility or divine inspiration. What, however, is the real difference between, on the one hand, specifically using the phrase "in Jehovah's name" and, on the other hand, describing events predicted for 1925 as "based upon the promises set forth in the divine Word," so that the return of Abraham, Isaac and Jacob in 1925 was—not something that might be *hoped* for—but something that "we may confidently expect"? In whose name do they profess to speak, and on what basis do they encourage readers to place confidence in the claim? And what real difference is there between, on the one hand, specifically professing certainty or infallibility and, on the other hand, stating that—due to being based upon *divine promises*—therefore "we must reach the <u>positive</u> and <u>indisputable conclusion</u> that millions now living [that is, living in 1920 when the booklet was published], will never die"? The difference is only in semantics, not in the force and sense of what is claimed, or in the effect on those claims on human minds.

This information formed the basis for what was called the "Millions Campaign," a worldwide effort to call attention to the message of this booklet during a two-year period. Large billboard advertisements were erected in all the big cities with streaming letters, "Millions Now Living Will Never Die." That publicity was buttressed by newspaper advertisements. All public talks given by Watch Tower representatives focused on this theme.

The Society in the above mentioned history book relates the pronouncements and features of this all-out, worldwide effort as if they were simply items of historical interest. Yet the sensational claims centered on 1925 were presented as something founded upon the word—not of some man—but upon the *Word of God, solidly* founded thereon and because of this *meriting full confidence.* Neither this Watch Tower history book nor any of the articles published in other sources ever acknowledge the profound effect this had on people's hopes and lives, and the deep disillusionment its failure produced. They never express regret that God's Word was deliberately tied in with predictions that were nothing more than human speculation and imagination. The *moral implication* of those factors seems of little significance, worthy of essentially no consideration.

In 1921, Rutherford published his first full-sized book, *The Harp of God.* It reaffirmed the Society's confidence and faith in 1799 as the start of the "last days" and 1874 as the time when Christ began his "invisible presence." In the portions that follow, with key points underlined, note the way the developments that were distinctive of those times and world conditions were used as "indisputable" testimony in support of those dates:

236 *The Harp of God*

Scriptures. The purpose here is to call attention to certain important dates and then see how much, if any, prophecy has been fulfilled within these dates. Chronology, to some extent at least, depends upon accurate calculations and there is always some possibility of mistakes. <u>Fulfilled prophecy is the record of physical facts which are actually existent and definitely fixed. Physical facts do not stultify themselves. They stand as silent witnesses whose testimony must be taken as indisputable.</u>

400 There are two important dates here that we must not confuse, but clearly differentiate, namely, the beginning of "the time of the end" and of "the presence of the Lord". <u>"The time of the end" embraces a period from 1799 A. D.</u>, as above indicated, <u>to the time of the complete overthrow of Satan's empire and the establishment of the kingdom of the Messiah. The time of the Lord's second presence dates from 1874</u>, as above stated. <u>The latter period is within the first named, of course, and in the latter part of the period known as "the time of the end".</u>

404 <u>From that time forward there has been a great corresponding increase of knowledge in all the sciences; and in fact, in all lines of learning.</u> The common school, always opposed by the Papacy, has afforded a means of general education and increase of knowledge for people in all walks of life. Colleges and universities have sprung up throughout the world. With the increase of knowledge on various lines have come the numerous inventions that man now has, time and labor-saving machines, etc.

405 Before 1799 the means of transportation were such that a man could travel only a short distance in a day. He must go either by a vehicle drawn by horses or oxen, or afoot; and when he would cross the sea he must go in a sailboat that made little progress. In 1831 the first locomotive steam engine was invented. Such wonderful progress has been made in this regard that now one can travel through almost any part of the earth at a rapid rate upon a railway train. Later came the electric engines and electric motor cars and gas engines; and now there is a tremendous amount of travel in every part of the earth. It is no uncommon thing for one to travel at the rate of 75 and 100 miles an hour; and particularly is this true by means of the flying machine, which is a very modern invention.

406 The aforementioned inventions are related to 'the day of God's preparation' during Christ's presence.—Nahum 2:1-6.

407 In 1844 the telegraph was invented, and later the telephone. These instruments were first used with wires, and by electricity messages were conveyed throughout the earth; but now by later invention wires are dispensed with and messages are flashed through the air by the use of instruments all over the earth.

408 This great increase of knowledge and the tremendous running to and fro of the people in various parts of the earth is without question a fulfilment of the prophecy testifying as to "the time of the end". These physical facts can not be disputed and are sufficient to convince any reasonable mind that we have been in "the time of the end" since 1799.

409 The latter part of "the time of the end" Jesus designates as a time of harvest, because he says: "The harvest is the end of the world [age]." He stated that he would be present at that time. From 1874 forward is the latter part of the period of "the time of the end". From 1874 is the time of the Lord's second presence, as above stated. The Apostle Paul, enumerating many things done concerning Israel, states that "they are written for our admonition, upon whom the ends of the world [ages] are come". (1 Corinthians 10:11) It must be presumed, then, that these things would be understood at "the time of the end".

⁴¹⁰ The laboring classes have always been down-trodden and kept in subjection to the financial, ecclesiastical, and political princes. It was in the year 1874, the date of our Lord's second presence, that the first labor organization in the world was created. From that time forward there has been a marvelous increase of light, and the inventions and discoveries have been too numerous for us to mention all of them here, but mention is made of some of those that have come to light since 1874, as further evidence of the Lord's presence since that date, as follows: Adding machines, aeroplanes, aluminum, antiseptic surgery, artificial dyes, automatic couplers, automobiles, barbed wire, bicycles, carborundum, cash registers, celluloid, correspondence schools, cream separators, Darkest Africa, disk plows, Divine Plan of the Ages, dynamite, electric railways, electric welding, escalators, fireless cookers, gas engines, harvesting machines, illuminating gas, induction motors, linotypes, match machines, monotypes, motion pictures, North Pole, Panama Canal, pasteurization, radium, railway signals, Rœntgen rays, shoe-sewing machines, skyscrapers, smokeless powder, South Pole, submarines, subways, talking machines, telephones, television, typewriters, vacuum cleaners, and wireless telegraphy.

Note particularly that, after describing the development of such things as Bible Societies, increase of colleges and universities, steam, electric and gasoline modes of transportation, telegraph and telephone—all resulting in a great increase in knowledge and movement—the book, on page 239, states:

> [This] is without question a fulfillment of the prophecy testifying to the "time of the end." These physical facts can not be disputed and are sufficient to convince any reasonable mind that we have been in "the time of the end" since 1799.

That which is "without question" and beyond dispute is logically infallible. The word "infallible" is not used—but to all intents and purposes the claim is made. And if any doubt or are not convinced, well, they simply do not come within the category of those having a "reasonable mind." This is also intellectual intimidation, a weapon that solid truth never needs to employ.

Despite whatever "stimulating and sanctifying" effect these new forecasts and strong affirmations about some of the old dates may have had, by the year 1922, with 1914 now eight years in the past, the confidence that many had placed in the Society's time prophecies was wearing thin. The methods the headquarters organization resorted to in trying to overcome this problem are revealing. They also form a pattern seen again in recent times, since 1975.

Instead of becoming more moderate in its claims about its interpretations or taking a more modest view of its authority, the organization became far more insistent upon conformity, the claims about the accuracy of its chronology became more dogmatic. "Loyalty" to the teachings of the "faithful and wise servant" (then argued as applying definitely to Pastor Russell) was the watchword. Those who questioned the chronology based on his teachings (which chronology was in turn based on the teachings of N. H. Barbour, John Aquila Brown and others) were depicted as not only lacking in faith but also overly impressed with their own wisdom, as proud, egotistical, ambitious, self-willed, misled by the adversary, and guilty of repudiating the Lord. To give any weight to the testimony of ancient historians in contradiction of the organization's dates was to put confidence in "agents of Satan's empire."

If that seems difficult to believe, consider the statements made in a steady stream of *Watch Tower* articles during 1922 and 1923. Note the repeated use of terms such as "indisputable," "correct beyond a doubt," "divinely corroborated," "absolutely and unqualifiedly correct," "incontestably established," "proven certainty," "of divine origin"—terms applied to the whole chronological scheme including 1799 (the start of the last days), 1874 (the start of Christ's invisible presence), 1878 (the start of the resurrection of the anointed), 1881 (the time when Russell was fully appointed as the Lord's steward), as well as 1914, 1918 and the most recent prophetic date of 1925, said to have 'as much Scriptural support as 1914.' For the reader's convenience, sections are underlined.

From the March 1, 1922, *Watch Tower:*

THE TIME OF THE HARVEST

Jesus said that the age would end with a harvest. at which time he would be present, and that he would then send forth his messengers to gather together his elect. (Matthew 13: 24-30; 24: 31) It is to be expected that the Lord would have some witness in the earth at the time of the harvest to make announcement of the fact of his presence and of the harvest. Here is some more circumstantial evidence which is proof conclusive; some more physical facts that speak louder than audible words, to wit: It was Brother Russell who announced the time of the harvest and the presence of the Master of the harvest. It was he who first went forth throughout the land crying out, 'The harvest is here; go ye into the field and labor'. And thousands of others taking up the slogan joined in the proclamation of the message.

Jesus plainly said that during the time of his presence he would have a faithful and wise servant whom he would use to give meat to the household (of faith) in due season. Every one today who has a knowledge of the divine plan of the ages must truthfully answer that he derived that knowledge from studying his Bible in connection with what Brother Russell wrote; that before such time he did not even know that God had a plan of salvation. Every person who today is rejoicing in the light of the truth of God's Word realizes that the Lord brought to him that truth, unfolding it through the ministrations and work begun by Brother Russell shortly following the presence of the Lord.

Under the heading "Wise Toward God" (referring to Russell), the article speaks disparagingly of those who "believe they have greater wisdom than others" and says such ones typically "make statements in dogmatic form." A few paragraphs later it begins setting forth the "indisputable facts" about 1799 and 1874. What is "dogmatism" in others, is evidently considered "sincere conviction" when practiced by the writers of the magazine.

WISE TOWARD GOD

Was he wise? As the world understands that word, particularly as defined by worldly clergymen, *he was not.* And thank God he was not. Had he possessed great worldly wisdom, such as that employed by his defamers, the Lord would never have used him. Be it noted that these so-called learned clergymen charge against him

> that he was not learned in the Greek and Hebrew. That charge is true. The facts demonstrate beyond a doubt that the majority of men who possess a knowledge of Greek and Hebrew take themselves too seriously. They begin to think they know so much that they must bring forth something startling to upset what somebody else has done. They depart from the Lord's way and lean to their own understanding, contrary to his. Word. (Proverbs 3:5, 6) They usually speak and write in such phrase that the ordinary mind cannot grasp it; and this they do hoping to magnify their own wisdom in the eyes of others. Because they believe they have greater wisdom than others they make statements in a dogmatic form, regardless of whether right or wrong, depending on the matter being swallowed by others because not able to fathom this supposed wisdom.
>
> ───────────
>
> The indisputable facts, therefore, show that the "time of the end" began in 1799; that the Lord's second presence began in 1874; that the harvest followed thereafter and greater light has come upon the Word of God. In this connection, then, let us note the words of Jesus: "Who then is a faithful and wise servant, whom his lord hath made ruler over his household, to give them meat in due season? Blessed is that servant, whom his lord when he cometh shall find so doing." (Matthew 24:

Two months later the May 1, 1922, issue continued the campaign to rout out any thought of questioning the organization's teachings, using the same tactic:

> #### AMBITION'S FRUITAGE
>
> Ever and anon there arises some one who has been following the Lord, for a time at least, who possesses a measure of beauty of mind and character, and possibly of person—one who takes himself too seriously. He succeeds in convincing himself that the Lord has appointed him to look after things divine and to lead God's people out of the wilderness. As he goes on in this way, he becomes convinced in his own mind that the Lord made a mistake in selecting Brother Russell as that servant; and this doubt leads to the conclusion later on that Brother Russell was not "that servant" at all. He begins to doubt what Brother Russell wrote, and so expresses himself. Now he disregards the Lord's Word, which says: "Trust in the Lord with all thine heart; and lean not unto thine own understanding. In all thy ways acknowledge him, and he shall direct thy paths."

> Thus disregarding this admonition, and being <u>led</u> <u>on by the subtle influence of the adversary,</u> he convinces himself that it is his solemn duty to undo all the things that Brother Russell taught and to turn the church's vision in the right way. He prepares a manuscript and charts in support of same, setting forth his views. Submitting it to others and being advised that his thoughts are wrong, he construes this to mean a desire to prevent him from permitting his light to shine, and disregards such advice. So thoroughly is he impressed that he must thus teach the people and undo that which has been taught, that he begins the publication of his thoughts and to send these forth to the consecrated. His arguments seem plausible to those who make only a <u>superficial examination, and especially to</u> <u>those who have forgotten what they were taught.</u> Doubt arises in the minds of some who thus read. Now the test is on.

Loyalty to the Society's teachings, received from Russell, was equated with loyalty to God and Christ. To deny Russell's teachings was to deny Christ. This amazing claim is plainly stated in the same issue of the *Watch Tower:*

> Jesus clearly indicated that during his second presence he would have amongst the church a <u>faithful and</u> <u>wise servant,</u> through whom he would give to the household of faith meat in due season. The evidence is overwhelming concerning the Lord's second presence, the time of the harvest, and that the office of "that servant" has been filled by Brother Russell. This is not man-worship by any means. It matters not who Charles T. Russell was—whether he was a doctor, a hod-carrier or a seller of shirts. St. Peter was a fisherman; St. Paul a lawyer. But these matters are immaterial. Above all, these men were the chosen vessels of the Lord. Regardless of his earthly avocation, above all, Brother Russell was the Lord's servant. <u>Then to repudiate him and</u> <u>his work is equivalent to a repudiation of the Lord,</u> <u>upon the principle heretofore announced.</u>

This line of argument is precisely the same as that used half a century later, in the 1980s, in condemning those called "apostates." Then as now, chronology was a major factor, made a "Test of Faith" as to the genuineness of one's Christianity. This same issue of the *Watch Tower* also warned that doubting the Society's date system, including 1799, 1874, 1914 and 1925, would lead eventually to a "repudiation of God and our Lord Jesus Christ and the blood with which we were bought." It said:

> Again the test is on. This time it is on chronology. And following this lead, it will be found that the road of doubt and opposition will carry one into doubting the second presence of the Lord, the time of the harvest, the office of "that servant" and the one who filled it, the evidences of the end of the world. the inauguration of the kingdom, the nearness of the restoration of man, and finally to a repudiation of God and our Lord Jesus Christ and the blood with which we were bought.

Now, issue after issue of the *Watch Tower* magazine focused on the Society's chronology, speaking deprecatingly of any contrary evidence, and exalting the accuracy of the organization's own date system. 1914 was only one feature of that date system, and the *Watch Tower* argued insistently that *all* the dates (and the accompanying claims about them) were right, the product of divine guidance; hence there was no need to doubt any of them. From the May 15, 1922, *Watch Tower:*

CHRONOLOGY

WE HAVE no doubt whatever in regard to the chronology relating to the dates of 1874, 1914, 1918, and 1925. Some claim to have found new light in connection with the period of "seventy years of desolation" and Israel's captivity in Babylon, and are zealously seeking to make others believe that Brother Russell was in error.

The apostle James assures us that "if any of you lack wisdom, let him ask of God, that giveth to all men liberally, and upbraideth not; and it shall be given him". We believe that promise and daily petition for heavenly wisdom and grace to be guided aright. We also believe that the prayers of the saints ascend daily to the throne of heavenly grace for divine guidance as to what shall appear in THE WATCH TOWER, and we are very appreciative of that fact.

Readers were warned not to be easily swayed in favor of evidence from secular history that contradicted the Society's chronology. Note the closing statement of this paragraph:

Some of their best "authorities" are found at times to be unreliable; as, for instance, Josephus and Ptolemy. These men lived during the first two centuries after Christ. They had difficulty in compiling their records; for complete data were not accessible to them. No doubt they did the best they could under their limited circumstances. They are accepted as among the best that secular history can produce. From these and from others, certain dates have been generally accepted by historical writers; but to be generally accepted does not necessarily imply absolute accuracy. However, to impress the weight of their wisdom upon their readers, these conclusions are often stated in positive language, and the student is inclined to accept them at their face statement without further investigation.

Compare that final statement with the kind of language the *Watch Tower* itself uses in urging acceptance of its system of dates:

STAMPED WITH GOD'S APPROVAL

It was on this line of reckoning that the dates 1874, 1914, and 1918 were located; and the Lord has placed the stamp of his seal upon 1914 and 1918 beyond any possibility of erasure. What further evidence do we need?

Using this same measuring line, beginning with the entry of the children of Israel into Canaan, and counting the full 70 cycles of 50 years each, as clearly indicated by Jehovah's sending of the Jews into Babylon for the full 70 years, it is an easy matter to locate 1925, probably the fall, for the beginning of the antitypical jubilee. There can be no more question about 1925 than there was about 1914. The fact that all the things that some looked for in 1914 did not materialize does not alter the chronology one whit. Noting the date marked so prominently, it is very easy for the finite mind to conclude that all the work to be done must center about it, and thus many are inclined to anticipate more than has been really foretold. Thus it was in 1844, in 1874, in 1878 as well as in 1914 and 1918. Looking back we can now easily see that those dates were clearly indicated in Scripture and doubtless intended by the Lord to encourage his people, as they did, as well as to be a means of testing and sifting when all that some expected did not come to pass. That all that some expect to see in 1925 may not transpire that year will not alter the date one whit more than in the other cases.

Once again the failed expectations resulting from earlier time prophecies are all charged up to the Lord's account, as of his doing, used by him, "doubtless intended by the Lord to encourage his people." Nothing strange is seen in this concept that God and Christ would use falsehood as a means of encouragement for their servants. Yet in Scripture we read that "God is light and there is no darkness at all in union with him."[2] The idea that God or his Son employ error in their guidance of Christians is foreign to Scripture. It is clearly an attempt to put the questioning one on the defensive, cast him in the role of complainer against God.

Great stress was laid on the claim that to change the chronology presented by *even one year* would be disastrous, "would destroy the entire system of chronology" advanced by the Society.[3] The fact is that most of the dates used for the B.C.E. period have been changed substantially by the Society in more recent times.

No adjective seemed too extreme and no claim too extravagant to be used in insisting on the rightness of what was then called "present-truth chronology." Keeping in mind that the great bulk of it has since been rejected, consider these claims made in the June 15, 1922, *Watch Tower*:

FURTHER PROOF OF PRESENT-TRUTH CHRONOLOGY

There is a well known law of mathematics called "the law of probabilities". Applications of this law are frequent in everyday life in settling matters of doubt. In a family of children, if a certain kind of mischief is committed, the probabilities— indeed, the certainty— are that it was done by a certain one, and that the others assuredly did not do it. If some peculiar damage is done by night to a single house, then by the law of probabilities it may have been a pure accident; if done to two houses in the same manner it probably was not accidental but by design of some person; but if done to three or more houses in the same manner it passes out of the possibility of accident into the *certainty* of design.

The chronology of present truth might be a mere happening if it were not for the repetitions in the two great cycles of 1845 and 2520 years, which take it out of the realm of chance and into that of certainty. If there were only one or two corresponding dates in these cycles, they might possibly be mere coincidences, but where the agreements of dates and events come by the

2   1 John 1:5.
3   *Watch Tower*, June 15, 1922, p. 187

> dozens, they cannot possibly be by chance, but must be by the design or plan of the only personal Being capable of such a plan—Jehovah himself; *and the chronology itself must be right.*
> In the passages of the Great Pyramid of Gizeh the agreement of one or two measurements with the present-truth chronology might be accidental, but the correspondency of dozens of measurements proves that the same God designed both pyramid and plan—and at the same time proves the correctness of the chronology.
> The agreement of the chronology with certain measurements of the Tabernacle and the Temple of Ezekiel further stamps the chronology as true.
> It is on the basis of such and so many correspondencies—in accordance with the soundest laws known to science—that we affirm that. *Scripturally. scientifically, and historically, present-truth chronology is correct beyond a doubt.* Its reliability has been abundantly confirmed by the dates and events of 1874, 1914, and 1918. Present-truth chronology is a secure basis on which the consecrated child of God may endeavor to search out things to come.—1 Peter 1: 11, 12; John 16: 13.

The chronology stood "firm as a rock, based upon the Word of God," the article said, stressing that belief in it was a "matter of faith in Jehovah and in his inspired Word."[4] The "divine" nature of the now largely rejected chronology was insisted upon, not for certain parts or elements of it, but for *all of it,* "absolutely." It bore the "stamp of approval of Almighty God." Thus the July 15, 1922, *Watch Tower,* under the heading "The Strong Cable of Chronology," said:

> The chronology of present truth is, to begin with, a string of dates, like other chronologies. That is to say, the dates are each known to be so many years before and after the succeeding and preceding dates, each step being proved by the most reliable evidence in existence. But if this were all the proof of the trustworthiness of the chronology, it could not truthfully be claimed to be more reliable than are the secular chronologies. Thus far, it is a chain, and no stronger than its weakest link.
> There exist, however, well established relationships among the dates of present-truth chronology. These internal connections of the dates impart a much greater strength than can be found in other chronologies. Some of them are of so remarkable a character as clearly to

4   *Watch Tower,* June 15, 1922, p. 187.

indicate that this chronology is not of man. but of God. Being of divine origin and divinely corroborated, present-truth chronology stands in a class by itself, absolutely and unqualifiedly correct.

INCONTESTABLY ESTABLISHED

When a date is indicated by several lines of evidence it is strongly established. The scientific law of probabilities imparts a united strength to the strands of the cable of chronology far greater than the sum of the individual lines of evidence. This is a law which is implicitly relied upon in important affairs: viz., that when a thing is indicated in only one way it may be by chance; if it is indicated in two ways, it is almost certain to be true; and if in more than two ways, it is usually impossible that it is by chance, or that it is not true; and the addition of more proofs removes it entirely from the realm of chance into that of proven certainty.

This principle is applied daily in the weightiest matters in courts of law. The testimony of a single witness may be considered doubtful, but that of only two or three witnesses incontestably establishes the truth. "In the mouth of two or three witnesses shall every word be established."—2 Corinthians 13:1.

In the chronology of present truth there are so many inter-relationships among the dates that it is not a mere string of dates, not a chain, but a cable of strands firmly knit together—a divinely unified system, with most of the dates having such remarkable relations with others as to stamp the system as not of human origin.

PROOF OF DIVINE ORIGIN

It will be clearly shown that present-truth chronology displays indisputable evidence of divine foreknowledge of the principle dates, and that this is proof of divine origin, and that the system is not a human invention but a discovery of divine truth.

The proof resides in the many connecting inter-relationships among the dates. Without these relations the chronology would not differ from secular systems, but with them we believe that it bears the stamp of approval of Almighty God.

"Parallelisms" were relied upon heavily as evidence of the divine origin of the date system advanced, parallel periods of 1,845 years and of 2,520 years being applied to a considerable number of dates and events in history. Of this system of using parallelisms the article in this issue of the *Watch Tower* stated:

> Parallelisms of this nature are proof of divine origin of present-truth chronology, because they show foreknowledge. In the instance cited, the division of Israel and that of Christendom, 2520 years apart, are evidence that when the first division was permitted, the latter one was foreknown. This is true because of the relationship between the two events as regards both time and nature.
>
> When it is found that there is a series or system of parallel dates composed of pairs of dates 2520 years apart, the foreknowledge becomes obvious. It would be absurd to claim that the relationship discovered was not the result of divine arrangement. God alone has such foreknowledge, and this proves that he so overruled times and events that they should be knit together into a beautiful and harmonious whole too sublime to be the result of chance or of human invention.

Once again, what genuine difference is there between speaking of "the *divine origin* of present-truth chronology" and describing that chronology as "inspired"? Ironically, though here presented as so obviously the product of divine foreknowledge that to deny their reliability and significance would be "absurd," the whole system of using parallelisms has since been discarded by the organization.

All of this material, hammering away against any tendency to question the time prophecies that formed such a vital part of the doctrinal structure of the organization seems to have been preparing the *Watch Tower* readers for a coming event. It apparently was designed to build up a certain spirit and attitude before the holding of that year's convention in Cedar Point, Ohio. Regularly referred to as a major milestone in the organization's history, that 1922 convention had as its principal talk a discussion that built on the foundation already laid by the earlier *Watch Tower* articles. Today the organization quotes a small portion of that talk in support of 1914. It ignores the fact that 1799 and 1874 figured with equal strength in the argument advanced and in the conclusion the audience was then called upon to reach, as seen in the following portions published in the November 1, 1922, *Watch Tower*:

Bible prophecy shows that the Lord was due to appear for the second time in the year 1874. Fulfilled prophecy shows beyond a doubt that he did appear in 1874. Fulfilled prophecy is otherwise designated the physical facts; and these facts are indisputable. All true watchers are familiar with these facts, as set forth in the Scriptures and explained in the interpretation by the Lord's special servant.

Jesus himself declared that in the time of his presence he would conduct a harvest of his people, during which he would gather unto himself the true and loyal ones. For some years this work has been in operation and is nearing completion. He stated that during his presence he would have one who would fill the office of a faithful and wise servant, through whom the Lord would bring to his people meat in due season. All the facts show that those prophecies have been fulfilled.

DAY OF PREPARATION

Why has the King come? To set up his kingdom and reign as King. But he had a work to do before his reign began, and that is a preparatory work. Since there are to be associated with him in his reign his body members, these must be gathered together and prepared for the beginning of the reign. The gentile times under the supervision of the god of this world ended August 1, 1914. Before that date it would not have been consistent for the Lord, the King of glory, to take unto himself his great power and reign. (Ezekiel 21:27) Since he has been present from 1874, it follows, from the facts as we now see them, that the period from 1874 to 1914 is the day of preparation. This in no wise militates against the thought that "the time of the end" is from 1799 until 1914. The period from 1799 to 1874 could not be said to be a day of preparation, but a day of increasing light. It is not reasonable to think that the King began to make preparations until he was present.

For six thousand years God has been preparing for this kingdom. For nineteen hundred years he has been gathering out the kingdom class from amongst men. Since 1874 the King of glory has been present; and during that time he has conducted a harvest and has gathered unto himself the temple class. Since 1914 the King of glory has taken his power and reigns. He has cleansed the lips of the temple class and sends them forth with the message. The importance of the message of the kingdom cannot be overstated. It is the message of all messages. It is the message of the hour. It is incumbent upon those who are the Lord's to declare it. The kingdom of heaven is at hand; the King reigns; Satan's empire is falling; millions now living will never die.

> Do you believe it? Do you believe that the King of glory is present, and has been since 1874? Do you believe that during that time he has conducted his harvest work? Do you believe that he has had during that time a faithful and wise servant through whom he directed his work and the feeding of the household of faith? Do you believe that the Lord is now in his temple, judging the nations of earth? Do you believe that the King of glory has begun his reign?
>
> Then back to the field, O ye sons of the most high God! Gird on your armor! Be sober, be vigilant, be active, be brave. Be faithful and true witnesses for the Lord. Go forward in the fight until every vestige of Babylon lies desolate. Herald the message far and wide. The world must know that Jehovah is God and that Jesus Christ is King of kings and Lord of lords. This is the day of all days. Behold, the King reigns! You are his publicity agents. Therefore advertise, advertise, advertise, the King and his kingdom.

Despite the fierce calls for "loyalty" to Pastor Russell's teachings and chronology, this 1922 convention talk is remarkable in that it reveals the first sign of a gradual edging away from those very teachings. In *The Time Is At Hand*, Russell had taught that "1878, being the parallel of his [Christ's] assuming power and authority in the type, clearly marks the time for the actual assuming of power as King of kings, by our present, spiritual, invisible Lord—the time of his taking to himself his great power to reign." By Rutherford's talk at Cedar Point these acts—invisible acts—were moved up from 1878 to 1914, a date that had proved empty of all the things forecast and hoped for. It was the start of what would later become an almost wholesale transferal of events assigned to pre-1914 dates up to 1914 and post-1914 dates.

In harmony with the *Millions Now Living Will Never Die* booklet, the organization was now teaching that the Jubilee cycle (which, according to God's law through Moses, involved consecutive periods of fifty years, with a Jubilee year coming each fiftieth year) pointed to 1925 as the time for the full manifestation of Christ's rule and the return of the prophets of old to earth. In 1924, the organization published a booklet designed to be used by young people titled *The Way to Paradise*. Note how confidently these predictions were offered to those young minds, including the description of earthly Jerusalem as the world capital of restored mankind:

privilege of the heavenly invitation. God proved that he could easily find enough from the Gentiles to fill all the places of highest honor in his kingdom. This will be very humiliating to the Jews when they see what they have missed.

The Jewish legal year begins in the fall, about our October first. The year 1926 would therefore begin about October first, 1925. It would be very reasonable to expect to see some beginning of God's favor returning to the Jewish people, as a part of the world, shortly after that date. Many of the Jews are already looking longingly towards their old home-land, Palestine. God's limit of time to the Gentiles as nations expired in 1914, as we have already seen. Thus as the Jewish nation, as a nation, lost favor with God when they crucified Jesus, and the Gentile nations have no further recognition by God as nations, Christ will soon begin to deal with the world as individuals, commencing with the Jew first, through the ancient worthies. We should, therefore, expect shortly after 1925 to see the awakening of Abel, Enoch, Noah, Abraham, Isaac, Jacob, Melchisedec, Job, Moses, Samuel, David, Isaiah, Jeremiah, Ezekiel, Daniel, John the Baptist, and others mentioned in the eleventh chapter of Hebrews.

These will form a nucleus of the new kingdom on earth. One of the first things necessary will be to put Jerusalem in condition to be the capital of the world. This will necessitate a great deal of work, but there will be many willing

workers. Current news informs us that attention is already being centered upon Palestine, and thousands of Jews are trying to return there. Already considerable work has been done in the way of building better roads and cultivating the fields. However, we should not expect to see much systematic work under way until these "princes" have been awakened and placed in charge.

The capital of every country should be in direct and quick communication with all parts of its territory. If Jerusalem is to be the capital of the world, it should be able to get into quick touch with every locality. Christ's kingdom is to undo in one thousand years all the evil brought about in the previous six thousand years. Old-fashioned methods will not suffice. Already we see great changes coming in. The wireless and radio can carry messages half way around the world now; and by the time the princes are brought forth these inventions will be perfected to reach all the way around.

Everybody in the world will be "in one room," so to speak. The room will be a little larger than we may have been accustomed to hold meeting in; but what of that? Now when we read Isaiah 2:3 and Zechariah 14:16, 17 we see how easy it will be for all the people to go "up to Jerusalem." The princes can easily radio their instructions to any part of the world. Think of Prince Abraham having some general instructions to give, calling "Attention"; and all the

226   *The Way to Paradise*

people everywhere listening, and hearing every word he speaks, as easily as though he were addressing them from the platform of a public hall!

Of course if any one desires to visit Jerusalem and personally interview the princes, or if the princes should desire to make a personal inspection of some public work, aeroplanes will soon be so perfected that it will be a matter of but a few hours ride to any part of the earth to or from Jerusalem. This will indeed be a new world, made glorious in every way.—Zechariah 14:20, 21; Revelation 21: Psalms 72 and 145.

These ancient worthies will also have the power to use the "rod of iron," if necessary, to deal with the wilful and disobedient. All must learn that unrighteousness will not be permitted. Justice is the foundation law of the new kingdom.—Psalm 37:9, 10, 2, 38.

No doubt many boys and girls who read this book will live to see Abraham, Isaac, Jacob, Joseph, Daniel, and those other faithful men of old, come forth in the glory of their "better resurrection," perfect in mind and body. It will not take long for Christ to appoint them to their posts of honor and authority as his earthly representatives. The world and all the present conveniences will seem strange to them at first, but they will soon become accustomed to the new methods. They may have some amusing experiences at first; for they never saw telephones, radios, automobiles, electric lights, aeroplanes,

Princes in All the Earth   227

steam engines, and many other things so familiar to us.

What a privilege to be living just at this time and to see the ending of the old and the coming in of the new! Of all the times in earth's history, today is the most wonderful.

Needless to say, the boys and girls to whom this publication was addressed are now old men and old women, at least in their nineties.

Although the Society has occasionally employed the catchy slogan "Millions now living will never die," and called attention to the fact that Witness membership has reached the multimillion range, they gloss over an obvious misrepresentation. The claim that "Millions now living will never die" was not made to people living in the 1990s or the 2000s. It was made to people in the first half of the 1920s. Only a fraction of the approximately 5.9 million members of Jehovah's Witnesses were living then. Only if there were today [in the year 2008] more than two million Witnesses around 85 years of age or older could there be any pretense that the prediction was in any way substantiated. This is clearly not the case.

1925, on which the prediction and slogan were based, proved empty of all the things foretold. The teaching was without substance, mere fluff, prophetic fantasy.

Yet all of this material, appearing in the *Watch Tower* magazine and other publications, was supposedly "food in due season" being provided through God's channel of communication, a channel claiming the special approval and direction of Christ Jesus as the now reigning King. As they themselves say, they spoke as God's "genuine prophet."

The passing of 1925 and the failure of these latest predictions, however, proved that the predictors had not acted as a "faithful and discreet slave." They had not held faithfully and humbly to the inspired Word of God, which alone merits such terms as "indisputable," "absolutely and unqualifiedly correct," "incontestably established." Nor had they been discreet during all the years they published such dogmatic claims earthwide, that indiscretion being, in effect, acknowledged by Judge Rutherford's recognition that he had made an "ass" of himself.

The intimidating language used in the proclaimed "channel" of God, the *Watch Tower,* the insinuations of ambition, pride, and disloyalty to Christ it directed at any who did not want to take the same presumptuous course, doubtless influenced the majority to 'follow the leader' as he made admittedly asinine claims. Many, however, found they could not continue to support such an irresponsible course and the organization experienced a major loss in adherents after 1925.[5]

How do publications of the organization depict the 1925 situation? Typical is the statement in the *1975 Yearbook of Jehovah's Witnesses* on page 146 which attributed the problem, not to the organization that published the information, but to "the brothers" who read it, saying:

> The year 1925 came and went. Jesus' anointed followers were still on earth as a class. The faithful men of old times—Abraham, David and others—had not been resurrected to become princes in the earth. (Ps. 45:16) So, as Anna MacDonald recalls: "1925 was a sad year for many brothers. Some of them were stumbled; their hopes were dashed. They had hoped to see some of the 'ancient worthies' [men of old like Abraham] resurrected. Instead of its being considered a 'probability,' they read into it that it was a 'certainty,' and some prepared for their own loved ones with expectancy of their resurrection.

---

5   Among these was Alvin Franz, my father's brother and the youngest of the four Franz brothers.

Does a review of the published statements in the *Watch Tower,* as found in the preceding pages of this book, in any way justify this shifting of responsibility onto the "brothers" for having developed such high hopes and seeing those hopes dashed?

The 1980 *Yearbook* (published the same year that Rutherford's private remark was recounted to the headquarters family by Frederick Franz) similarly gave this slant to the matter.

It tells of Judge Rutherford's visiting Switzerland in May of 1926 for a convention and his participation in a question meeting in which this interchange took place:

> "**Question:** Have the ancient worthies returned?
> "**Answer:** Certainly they have not returned. No one has seen them, and it would be foolish to make such an announcement. It was stated in the 'Millions' book that we might reasonably expect them to return shortly after 1925, but this was merely an expressed opinion."

Everyone has the right to express opinions. But men who claim to be God's spokesmen on earth surely do not have the right to express mere opinions while claiming that what they say is backed up by God's own Word and should be accepted as such. When statements are spread around the globe as God's message for mankind, as spiritual "food in due season," those publishing them are certainly neither "faithful" nor "discreet" if they irresponsibly express fallacious opinions, argue tenaciously for them, belittle any who disagree or, worse, question their loyalty and humility before God.

In 1930, the house called Beth-Sarim was constructed by the organization in San Diego, California. Of this, the book *The New World,* written by Fred Franz, states:

104   THE NEW WORLD

were promptly thereafter defeated in battle and cast out of heaven and down to the earth. That wicked one and his demons now bring great woes upon the earth and sea to drive all nations into a totalitarian system and to turn all people in bitterness against God. The Lord Jesus has now come to the temple for judgment, and the remnant of the members of "his body" yet on earth he has gathered into the temple condition of perfect unity with himself (Malachi 3:1-3), and hence those faithful men of old may be expected back from the dead any day now. The Scriptures give <u>good reason to believe that it shall be shortly before Armageddon breaks.</u>

<u>In this expectation the house at San Diego, California, which house has been much publicized with malicious intent by the religious enemy,</u> was built, in 1930, and named "Beth-Sarim", meaning "House of the Princes". [6] It is now held in trust for the occupancy of those princes on their return. The most recent facts show that <u>the religionists of this doomed world are gnashing their teeth because of the testimony which that "House of the Princes" bears to the new world.</u> To those religionists and their allies the return of those faithful men of old to rule with judgment over the people shall not bring any pleasure.

As shown in an earlier chapter, it was in 1941, just sixteen years after 1925, at a convention in St. Louis, Missouri, that the organization's head, President Rutherford, again was assuring young children that very soon the faithful men and women of Bible times would return. They would direct the young people in their selection of marriage mates, making it advisable for them to postpone marriage until such time. The *Watchtower*

---

6   A few years after the book *The New World* was published (1942), Beth-Sarim was sold. At a 1950 assembly in Yankee Stadium, New York City, Fred Franz gave a talk in which the predicted return of the "princes" before Armageddon was officially abandoned, replaced with the view that the Society's appointees in the congregations already filled that princely role.

describing the event then made its comment about the book *Children,* there released, as, "the Lord's provided instrument for most effective work *in the remaining months before Armageddon."*

Approximately three hundred months later, in 1966, a new date came to the fore: 1975.

9

1975: 'THE APPROPRIATE TIME FOR GOD TO ACT'

It is not for you to know the times or dates the Father has set
by his own authority
— Acts 1:7 *New International Version.*

DURING the second half of Rutherford's presidency most of the older time prophecies so strenuously argued for in the first half were gradually dropped or relocated.

The start of the "last days" was moved up from 1799 to 1914.

The 1874 presence of Christ was also moved up to 1914 (as had already been done in 1922 with the 1878 official start of Christ's active Kingdom rule).

The beginning of the resurrection was moved from 1878 to 1918.

For a time it was even claimed that 1914 had indeed brought the "end of the world" in the sense that God had 'legally' terminated the worldly nations' lease of power on the earth. This, too, was dropped and the "end" in that sense is now held to be future.

All of the things claimed being *invisible;* the acceptance of them obviously depended entirely upon one's faith in the interpretations offered. After one session in which these time prophecies and changes came up for discussion, Governing Body member Bill Jackson smilingly said to me, "We used to say, you just take the date from this shoulder and put it on the other shoulder."

It was not until after Rutherford's death in 1942 that a change was made regarding the year 606 B.C.E. as the starting point for the 2,520 years. Strangely, the fact that 2,520 years from 606 B.C.E. actually leads to 1915 C.E., and not 1914 C.E., was not acknowledged or dealt with for over 60 years.

Then, quietly, the starting point was moved back one year to 607 B.C.E., allowing for the retention of the year 1914 C.E. as the ending point for the 2,520 years. No historical evidence had come forward to indicate that the destruction of Jerusalem had occurred a year earlier than believed. The organization's desire to retain 1914 as a marked date pointed to by them for so many years (something they had not done with 1915) dictated moving Jerusalem's destruction back one year, a simple thing to do—on paper.

By the mid-1940s it had been decided that the chronology used during Russell's and Rutherford's presidencies was off some 100 years as regards the count of time back to Adam's creation. In 1966, the organization said that, instead of coming in 1874 as previously taught, the end of six thousand years of human history would arrive in 1975.

This was published in the summer of 1966 in a book written by Fred Franz, titled *Life Everlasting in Freedom of the Sons of God.* In its first chapter, the book drew upon the Jubilee arrangement, which had also featured prominently in the predictions relating to 1925, and it argued (as had also been done back then) in favor of belief in six "days" of a thousand years each, during which mankind was to experience imperfection, to be followed by a seventh "day" of a thousand years in which perfection would be restored in a grand Jubilee of liberation from slavery to sin, sickness and death. The book said on pages 28 and 29:

> [41] Since the time of Ussher intensive study of Bible chronology has been carried on. In this twentieth century an independent study has been carried on that does not blindly follow some traditional chronological calculations of Christendom, and the published timetable resulting from this independent study gives the date of man's creation as 4026 B.C.E.† According to this trustworthy Bible chronology six thousand years from man's creation will end in 1975, and the seventh period of a thousand years of human history will begin in the fall of 1975 C.E.

⁴² So six thousand years of man's existence on earth will soon be up, yes, within this generation. Jehovah God is timeless, as it is written in Psalm 90:1, 2: "O Jehovah, you yourself have proved to be a real dwelling for us during generation after generation. Before the mountains them- selves were born, or you proceeded to bring forth as with labor pains the earth and the productive land, even from time indefinite to time indefinite you are God." So from the standpoint of Jehovah

God these passing six thousand years of man's existence are but as six days of twenty-four hours, for this same psalm (verses 3, 4) goes on to say: "You make mortal man go back to crushed mat- ter, and you say: 'Go back, you sons of men.' For a thousand years are in your eyes but as yester- day when it is past, and as a watch during the night." So in not many years within our own generation we are reaching what Jehovah God could view as the seventh day of man's existence.

What would be the significance of this? The book goes on to make this application of the points developed:

30   LIFE EVERLASTING—IN FREEDOM OF THE SONS OF GOD

⁴³ How appropriate it would be for Jehovah God to make of this coming seventh period of a thou- sand years a sabbath period of rest and release, a great Jubilee sabbath for the proclaiming of liberty throughout the earth to all its inhabitants! This would be most timely for mankind. It would also be most fitting on God's part, for, remember, mankind has yet ahead of it what the last book of the Holy Bible speaks of as the reign of Jesus Christ over earth for a thousand years, the mil- lennial reign of Christ. Prophetically Jesus Christ, when on earth nineteen centuries ago, said con- cerning himself: "For Lord of the sabbath is what the Son of man is." (Matthew 12:8) It would not be by mere chance or accident but would be according to the loving purpose of Je- hovah God for the reign of Jesus Christ, the "Lord of the sabbath," to run parallel with the seventh millennium of man's existence.

Had the organization said "flat out" that 1975 would mark the start of the millennium? No. But the above paragraph was the climax to which all of the involved, carefully constructed argumentation of that chapter had been building.

No outright, unqualified prediction was made about 1975. But the writer had been willing to declare it to be "appropriate" and "most fitting on God's part" if God would start the millennium at that particular time. It would seem reasonable that for an imperfect man to say what is or what is not "fitting" for the Almighty God to do would call for quite a measure of certainty, surely not the mere 'expression of an opinion.' *Discretion* would require, rather, would *demand* that. Even stronger is the subsequent statement that "it would be according to the loving purpose of Jehovah God for the reign of Jesus Christ, the 'Lord of the sabbath,' to run parallel with the seventh millennium of man's existence," which seventh millennium had already been stated as due to begin in 1975.

Once again, the Watch Tower's recent history book, *Jehovah's Witnesses—Proclaimers of God's Kingdom* had an opportunity to demonstrate the objectivity and candor its foreword promises. In a very brief presentation of the matter, it said this (on page 104), focusing on the 1966 convention at which Fred Franz presented the new book which introduced the information about 1975:

> At the convention held in Baltimore, Maryland, F. W. Franz gave the concluding talk. He began by saying: "Just before I got on the platform a young man came to me and said, 'Say, what does this 1975 mean?'" Brother Franz then referred to the many questions that had arisen as to whether the material in the new book meant that by 1975 Armageddon would be finished, and Satan would be bound. He stated, in essence: 'It could. But we are not saying. All things are possible with God. But we are not saying. And don't any of you be specific in saying anything that is going to happen between now and 1975. But the big point of it all is this, dear friends: Time is short. Time is running out, no question about that.'
>
> In the years following 1966, many of Jehovah's Witnesses acted in harmony with the spirit of that counsel. However, other statements were published on this subject, and some were likely more definite than advisable. This was acknowledged in *The Watchtower* of March 15, 1980 (page 17). But Jehovah's Witnesses were also cautioned to concentrate mainly on doing Jehovah's will and not to be swept up by dates and expectations of an early salvation.

Typically, the material quotes the one cautionary statement made at this time. It acknowledges that "other statements were published on this subject, and some were likely more definite than advisable."[1] Approximately two-thirds of the present organizational membership has entered since 1975 and therefore did not have the experience of knowing what followed. They have no knowledge of the *extent* and *intensity* of the emphasis given to the date of 1975 and the significance attached to it. But the members of the Governing Body do know this. At least some of those on the Writing Committee must have read and approved what appears in the 1993 history book. They had to have known what an incomplete and watered down picture it offers. What actually happened?

That same year of 1966, the October 8 issue of *Awake!*, the companion magazine to the *Watchtower*, carried an article titled "How Much Longer Will It Be?" and under the subheading "6,000 Years Completed in 1975," it too reasoned that the millennium would be the last 1000 years of a 7000-year rest day of God. It went on to say (pages 19, 20):

> Hence, the fact that we are nearing the end of the first 6,000 years of man's existence is of great significance.
>
> <u>Does God's rest day parallel the time man has been on earth since his creation? Apparently so.</u> From the most reliable investigations of Bible chronology, harmonizing with many accepted dates of secular history, we find that Adam was created in the autumn of the year 4026 B.C.E. Sometime in that same year Eve could well have been created, directly after which God's rest day commenced.

---

1   The Watch Tower's history book, in a footnote, cites as evidence of other cautionary material certain publications. Only one of them appeared in the 1960s. (the May 1, 1968, *Watchtower*), and, as was true in the case of other cautionary statements involving earlier predictions, the two others were published as 1975 was already *imminent* or *present* (the June 15, 1974, and May 1, 1975, issues of the *Watchtower*). The footnote then goes back *before* the release of the book announcing 1975 and quotes from the 1963 book *All Scripture Is Inspired and Beneficial*, which states: "It does no good to use Bible chronology for speculating on dates that are still future in the stream of time.—Matt. 24:36." It does not explain why the author of the book pointing to 1975 in connection with the start of the millennium so obviously failed to follow the principle set out three years before.

> In what year, then, would the first 6,000
> years of man's existence and also the first
> 6,000 years of God's rest day come to an
> end? The year 1975.* This is worthy of no-
> tice, particularly in view of the fact that
> the "last days" began in 1914, and that the
> physical facts of our day in fulfillment of
> prophecy mark this as the last generation
> of this wicked world. So we can expect
> the immediate future to be filled with
> thrilling events for those who rest their
> faith in God and his promises. It means
> that within relatively few years we will
> witness the fulfillment of the remaining
> prophecies that have to do with the "time
> of the end."

The May 1, 1968, *Watchtower* is cited in the Society's 1993 history book as an example of caution given on the subject. In actuality, it helped continue this stimulation of anticipation. Using much the same argument as the *Awake!* article last mentioned, it then said (pages 272, 273):

> ⁷ The immediate fu-
> ture is certain to be
> filled with climactic
> events, for this old
> system is nearing its
> complete end. Within
> a few years at most
> the final parts of Bi-
> ble prophecy relative
> to these "last days"
> will undergo fulfill-
> ment, resulting in the
> liberation of surviv-
> ing mankind into
> Christ's glorious
> 1,000-year reign.
> What difficult days,
> but, at the same time,
> what grand days are
> just ahead!
> ⁸ Does this mean
> that the year 1975
> will bring the battle
> of Armageddon? No
> one can say with cer-
> tainty what any par-
> ticular year will
> bring. Jesus said:
> "Concerning that day
> or the hour nobody
> knows." (Mark 13:
> 32) Sufficient is it for
> God's servants to
> know for a certainty
> that, for this system
> under Satan, time is
> running out rapidly.
> How foolish a person
> would be not to be
> awake and alert to the
> limited time remain-
> ing, to the earth-
> shaking events soon
> to take place, and to
> the need to work out
> one's salvation!

The paragraphs above appeared in columns bordering each side of a large chart of dates, beginning with the year 4026 B.C.E, listed as the date for the "Creation of Adam (in early autumn)." The chart ended in this way:

1975	6000	End of 6th 1,000-year day of man's existence (in early autumn)
2975	7000	End of 7th 1,000-year day of man's existence (in early autumn)

In that context, how "cautionary" would be the effect of references to "the *immediate* future," to "a few years *at most*," and the "*certainty*" of these bringing the fulfillment of the final parts of last-days prophecies? What rational, normal thinking person would view this as having any other intent than that of exciting expectations and hopes centered around a date, 1975?

In an article titled "What Will the 1970s Bring?" the October 8, 1968, *Awake!* again emphasized the shortness of the remaining time, saying at the start (page 13):

> THE fact that fifty-four years of the period called the "last days" have already gone by is highly significant. It means that only a few years, at most, remain before the corrupt system of things dominating the earth is destroyed by God. How can we be so certain of this?

Later, drawing on the year 1975 as the close of six thousand years of human history, the article said (page 14):

> **6,000 Years Nearing Completion**
> There is another way that helps confirm the fact that we are living in the final few years of this "time of the end." (Dan. 12:9) The Bible shows that we are nearing the end of a full 6,000 years of human history.

Again and again the Watch Tower publications quoted statements made by people of prominence or "experts" in any field who made some reference to 1975, for example, the statement made in 1960 by former U.S. Secretary of State Dean Acheson, who said:

> I know enough of what is going on to assure you that, in 15 years from today [hence, by 1975], this world is going to be too dangerous to live in.

The book *Famine—1975!*, published in 1967 by two food experts, was quoted repeatedly, particularly these statements, in many ways reminiscent of Russell's predictions regarding 1914:

> By 1975 a disaster of unprecedented magnitude will face the world. Famines, greater than any in history, will ravage the undeveloped nations.
>
> I forecast a specific date, 1975, when the new crisis will be upon us in all its awesome importance.
>
> By 1975 civil disorder, anarchy, military dictatorships, runaway inflation, transportation breakdowns and chaotic unrest will be the order of the day in many of the hungry nations.

Three years after the original focusing on 1975 in the book *Life Everlasting in Freedom of the Sons of God,* the author, Fred Franz, wrote another publication titled *The Approaching Peace of a Thousand Years.*[2] If anything, the language in it was even more definite and specific than in the previous publication. Released in 1969, it contained these statements on pages 25, 26:

> More recently earnest researchers of the Holy Bible have made a recheck of its chronology. According to their calculations the six millenniums of mankind's life on earth would end in the mid-seventies. Thus the seventh millennium from man's creation by Jehovah God would begin within less than ten years.

> In order for the Lord Jesus Christ to be "Lord even of the sabbath day," his thousand-year reign would have to be the seventh in a series of thousand-year periods or millenniums. (Matthew 12:8, *AV*) Thus it would be a sabbatic reign.

---

2   This same material also appeared in the October 15, 1969, *Watchtower.* The 1930-1985 Index to Watch Tower Publications, however, does not list it under the heading "1975" simply ignoring it despite its strong focus on that date.

The argumentation here is quite clear and direct: As the sabbath was the seventh period following six periods of toil, so the thousand-year reign of Christ would be a sabbatical seventh millennium following those six millenniums of toil and suffering. The presentation is in no sense indefinite or ambiguous.

Even as it had been determined what would be "appropriate" and "fitting" for God to do, so also a requirement is now set out for Jesus Christ. For him to be what he says he will be, 'Lord of the sabbath day,' then his reign "would *have to be*" the seventh millennium in a series of millenniums. Human reasoning imposes this requirement upon God's Son. Six thousand years would end in 1975; Christ's rule, according to the argument, "would have to be the seventh" period of a thousand years following the previous six. The "faithful and discreet slave" had, in effect, outlined the program he expected his Master to adhere to if he was to be true to his own word.

Though the writing is more polished, the expressions more refined, this material in essence is remarkably like that set forth in Judge Rutherford's booklet *Millions Now Living Will Never Die,* in which he admittedly made foolish claims. Aside from the specific date being publicized, it was as if the clock had now been turned back about a half a century to the pre-1925 days. The difference was that the things said then were now being said of 1975.[3]

When the 1970s arrived, the buildup of expectation kept on. The October 8, 1971, *Awake!,* spoke yet again of six periods of toil and labor followed by a seventh (sabbath) period of rest and then presented the following chart:

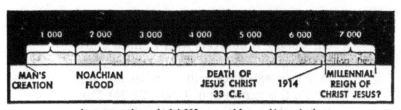

As we near the end of 6,000 years of human history in the
mid-1970's there is the thrilling hope of a grand relief

---

3   It is true that (on page 25 of the booklet) the less specific phrase "the mid-seventies" is used, but the year 1975 had already been presented as a Biblically marked date and that date was now firmly imprinted on the minds of all of Jehovah's Witnesses earthwide.

All this steady flow of information was clearly designed to foment and build up hope, anticipation. It was not designed to calm or defuse a spirit of excited expectation. True, most statements were accompanied by some qualifying statement to the effect that 'we are not saying positively' or are not 'pointing to a specific date,' and that 'we do not know the day and the hour.' But it must be remembered that the organization was not a novice in this field. Its whole history from its very inception was one of building up people's hope in certain dates only to have those dates pass with the hope unrealized. In past cases the publications of the Society subsequently sought to place the responsibility for any disillusionment on the receivers, not the givers, of the information, as inclined to expect too much. Surely, then, the responsible men of the organization should have realized the danger, realized what human nature is, realized how easily great hopes can be excited.

Yet, while carefully avoiding any *explicit* prediction that a *specific* date would see the start of the millennium, those responsible men approved the use of the phrases, "within relatively few years," "the immediate future," "within a few years at most," "only a few years, at most," "the final few years," all used in the *Watchtower* and *Awake!* magazines with reference to the beginning of the millennial reign and *all in a context that included the date 1975.* Do such words mean anything? Or were they used loosely, carelessly? Are people's hopes and plans and feelings something to be toyed with? To fail to be concerned about those factors would be both irresponsible and insensitive. Yet the *Watchtower* of August 15, 1968, even implied that one should be careful about putting too much weight on Jesus Christ's own cautionary words.

> " One thing is absolutely certain, Bible chronology reinforced with fulfilled Bible prophecy shows that six thousand years of man's existence will soon be up, yes, within this generation! (Matt. 24:34) This is, therefore, no time to be indifferent and complacent. This is not the time to be toying with the words of Jesus that "concerning that day and hour *nobody* knows, neither the angels of the heavens nor the

Son, but only the Father." (Matt. 24:36) To the contrary, it is a time when one should be keenly aware that the end of this system of things is rapidly coming to its violent end. Make no mistake, it is sufficient that the Father himself *knows* both the "day and hour"!

How could a "faithful and discreet slave" possibly say this—in effect, say that, "True, my master said thus and so, but don't make too much of that; to the contrary, realize that what *I* am telling you should be the guiding force in your life"?

Some of the most direct statements came from the Brooklyn Service Department which produces a monthly paper called "Kingdom Ministry," a paper which goes only to Witnesses and not to the public. The March, 1968, issue of the U.S. edition urged getting into full-time preaching activity ("pioneer service") saying:

In view of the short period of time left, we want to do this as often as circumstances permit. Just think, brothers, there are only about ninety months left before 6,000 years of man's existence on earth is completed.

The May, 1974, issue of *Kingdom Ministry,* having referred to the "short time left," said:

Reports are heard of brothers selling their homes and property and planning to finish out the rest of their days in this old system in the pioneer service. Certainly this is a fine way to spend the short time remaining before the wicked world's end.—1 John 2:17.

Quite a number of Witnesses did just that. Some sold their businesses, gave up jobs, sold homes, farms and moved with their wives and children to other areas to 'serve where the need was greater,' counting on having sufficient funds to carry them through 1975.

Others, including some older persons, cashed in insurance policies or other valuable certificates. Some put off surgical operations in the hope that the millennium's entrance would eliminate the need for these.

When 1975 passed and their funds ran out or their health worsened seriously, they now had to try to cope with the hard realities and rebuild as best they could.

What was the thinking within the Governing Body during this time?

Some of the older men on the Body had personally experienced the failed expectations of 1914, 1925, as well as the hopes excited in the early 1940s. The majority, from my observation, took a 'wait and see' attitude. They were reluctant to call for restraint. Big increases were taking place. Consider the record of baptisms for the period from 1960 on up to 1975:

Year	Number Baptized	Year	Number Baptized
1960	69,027	1968	82,842
1961	63,070	1969	120,805
1962	69,649	1970	164,193
1963	62,798	1971	149,808
1964	68,236	1972	163,123
1965	64,393	1973	193,990
1966	58,904	1974	297,872
1967	74,981	1975	295,073

From 1960 up until 1966, the rate of increase had diminished to a near standstill. But following 1966, when 1975 was highlighted, there came a phenomenal period of growth, as the chart reveals.

During the years 1971 to 1974 while I was serving on the Governing Body I do not recall hearing any strong expressions of concern from Body members about the excited expectations that had been generated. I would not pretend that I did not initially feel stirred myself in 1966 when the book *Life Everlasting in Freedom of the Sons of God* came out with its glowing picture of the nearness of a millennial jubilee. Nor would I claim to have had no part whatsoever in the early part of the campaign to focus attention on the target date of 1975. But each passing year from 1966 on made the idea seem more and more unreal. The more I read the Scriptures the more the whole concept seemed out of line; it did not square with the statements of Jesus Christ himself, statements such as:

> Concerning that day and hour nobody knows, neither the angels of the heavens nor the Son, but only the Father.
>
> Keep on the watch, therefore, because you do not know on what day your Lord is coming.
>
> On this account you too prove yourselves ready, because at an hour that you do not think to be it, the Son of Man is coming.
>
> Keep looking, keep awake, for you do not know when the appointed time is.
>
> It does not belong to you to get knowledge of the times or seasons which the Father has placed in his own jurisdiction.[4]

As part of a headquarters organization that was flushed with joy because of riding a crest of remarkable growth, there was not much that could be done, however. Some articles on the subject that came to me for editing I tried to moderate but that was about all. In my personal activity I did try to draw attention to the scriptures just mentioned, both in private conversations and in public talks.

One Sunday evening in 1974, after my wife and I had returned from a speaking engagement in another part of the country, my uncle, then vice president, came over to our room. (His eyesight being extremely poor, we usually read the *Watchtower* study material out loud to him each week.) My wife mentioned to him that in my talk that weekend I had cautioned the brothers about becoming unduly excited over 1975. His quick response was, "And why *shouldn't* they get excited? It's something to be excited about."

There is no question in my mind that, of all the Governing Body members, the vice president was most convinced of the rightness of what he had written, and on which writing others had built. On another evening in the summer of 1975, an elderly Greek brother named Peterson

---

4   Quoted from Matthew 24:36, 42, 44; Mark 13:33; Acts 1:7.

(originally Papagyropoulos) joined us in our room for our reading, as was his custom. After the reading, my uncle said to Peterson, "You know, it was very much like this in 1914. Right up into the summer months everything was quiet. Then all of a sudden things began to happen and the war broke out."

Earlier, toward the start of 1975, President Knorr had made a trip around the world, taking Vice President Franz with him. The vice president's speeches in all countries visited centered on 1975. Upon their return, the other members of the Governing Body, having heard reports from many countries of the stirring effect of the vice president's talk, asked to hear a tape recording of it, made in Australia.[5]

In his talk, the vice president spoke of 1975 as a "year of great possibilities, tremendous probabilities." He told his audience that, according to the Hebrew calendar, they were "already in the fifth lunar month of 1975," with less than seven lunar months remaining. He emphasized several times that the Hebrew year would close with Rosh Hashanah, the Jewish New Year, on September 5, 1975.

Acknowledging that much would have to happen in that short time if the final windup was to come by then, he went on to talk about the possibility of a year or so difference due to some lapse of time between Adam's creation and Eve's creation. He made reference to the failure of expectations in 1914 and 1925 and quoted Rutherford's remark, "I made an ass of myself." He said that the organization had learned not to make "very bold, extreme predictions." Toward the close, he urged his listeners not to take an improper view, however, and assume that the coming destruction could be "years away," and focus their attention on other matters, such as getting married and raising families, building up a fine business venture or spending years at college in some engineering course.

After hearing the tape, a few of the Governing Body members expressed concern that if indeed no "very bold, extreme predictions" were being made, some subtle predictions were, and the effect was palpably evident in the excitement generated.

---

5   This was in the session of February 19, 1975.

This was the first time that concern was expressed in the Governing Body discussions. But no action was taken, no policy decided upon.

The vice president repeated many of the points of the same talk on March 2, 1975, at the following Gilead School graduation.[6]

1975 passed—as had 1881, 1914, 1918, 1920, 1925 and the 1940s. Much publicity was given by other sources as to the failure of the organization's expectations surrounding 1975. There was considerable talk among Jehovah's Witnesses themselves. In my own mind, most of what was said did not touch upon the major point of the matter.

I felt that the real issue went far beyond that of some individual's accuracy or inaccuracy or even an organization's reliability or untrustworthiness or its members' sensibleness or gullibility. It seemed to me that the really important factor is how such predictions ultimately reflect on God and on his Word. When men make such forecasts and say that they are doing it on the basis of the Bible, build up arguments for these from the Bible, assert that they are God's "channel" of communication—what is the effect when their forecasts prove false? Does it honor God or build up faith in Him and in the reliability of his Word? Or is the opposite the result? Does it not give added inducement for some to feel justified in placing little importance upon the Bible's message and teachings? Those Witnesses who made major changes in their lives in most cases could, and did, pick up the pieces and go on living in spite of being disillusioned. Not all could. Whatever the case, however, serious damage had been done in more ways than one.

In 1976, a year after the passing of that widely publicized date, a few members of the Governing Body began urging that some statement should be made acknowledging that the organization had been in error, had stimulated false expectations. Others said they did not think we should, that it would "just give ammunition to opposers." Milton Henschel recommended that the wise course would be simply not to bring the matter up and that in time the brothers would stop talking about it. There was clearly not enough support for a motion, favoring a statement, to carry. That year, an article in the July 15 *Watchtower* did refer to the failed

---

6   See the *Watchtower*, May 1, 1975.

expectations but the article had to conform to the prevailing sentiment within the Governing Body and no clear acknowledgement of the organization's responsibility was possible.

In 1977, the subject again surfaced in a session. Though the same objections were raised, a motion passed that a statement should be included in a convention talk that Lloyd Barry was assigned to prepare. I understand that afterward Governing Body members Ted Jaracz and Milton Henschel talked with Lloyd about their feelings on the matter. Whatever the case, when the talk was prepared, no mention of 1975 was included. I recall asking Lloyd about this and his reply was that he had just not been able to make it fit in with his subject. Almost two years went by and then in 1979 the Governing Body again considered the matter. By then everything indicated that 1975 had produced a serious "credibility gap."

A number of members of the headquarters staff expressed themselves in that vein. One described 1975 as an "albatross" hanging around our necks. Robert Wallen, a Governing Body secretary, wrote as follows:

> I have been associated as a baptized Witness well over 39 years and with Jehovah's help I will continue to be a loyal servant. But to say I am not disappointed would be untruthful, for, when I know my feelings regarding 1975 were fostered because of what I read in various publications, and then I am told in effect that I reached false conclusions on my own, that, I feel, is not being fair or honest. Knowing that we are not working with infallibility, to me it is but proper that when errors are made by imperfect, but God-fearing men, then corrections will be made when errors are found.

Raymond Richardson of the Writing Department said:

> Are not persons drawn to humility, and more willing to place confidence where there is *candor?* The Bible itself is the greatest example of candor. This is one of the most outstanding reasons why we believe it to be truthful.

Fred Rusk, also of the Writing Department, wrote:

Despite any qualifying statements that might have been made along the way to admonish the brothers not to say that Armageddon would come in 1975, the fact is there were a number of articles in the magazines and other publications that more than hinted that the old system would be replaced by Jehovah's new system in the mid-1970s.

Merton Campbell of the Service Department wrote:

A sister called the other day on the phone from Massachusetts. She was at work. Both the sister and her husband are working to pay up bills that have accumulated because of sickness. She expressed herself as feeling so confident that 1975 would bring the end that they both were having trouble facing up to the burdens of this system. This example is typical of many of the brothers we meet.

Harold Jackson, also of the Service Department, said:

What is needed now is not a statement to the effect that we were wrong about 1975 but rather a statement as to why the whole matter has been ignored so long in view of the fact that so many lives have been affected. Now it is a credibility gap we are faced with and that can prove to be disastrous. If we are going to say something at all, let us speak straightforwardly and be open and honest with the brothers.

Howard Zenke, of the same department, wrote:

We certainly do not want the brothers to read something or listen to something and then say in their own mind that the approach that we have taken amounts to a "Watergate."

Others made similar comments. Ironically, some who now spoke the strongest criticism had themselves been among the most vocal before 1975 in stressing that date and the extreme "urgency" it called for, had even written some of the articles earlier quoted, had approved of the *Kingdom Ministry* statement commending those who were selling homes and property as 1975 drew near. Many of the most dogmatic statements about 1975 were made by traveling representatives (Circuit and District Overseers) all of whom were under the direct supervision of the Service Department.

In the March 6, 1979, session of the Governing Body, the same argu-ments against publishing anything were advanced—that it would lay the organization open to further criticism from opposers, that at this late date there was no need to make an apology, that nothing really would be accomplished by it. However, even those so arguing were less adamant than in previous sessions. This was because of one factor in particular: the worldwide figures had registered serious drops for two years.

The yearly reports reveal the following:

Year	Total Number Reporting Activity	% Increase Over Previous Year
1970	1,384,782	10.2
1971	1,510,245	9.1
1972	1,596,442	5.7
1973	1,656,673	3.8
1974	1,880,713	13.5
1975	2,062,449	9.7
1976	2,138,537	3.7
1977	2,117,194	-1.0
1978	2,086,698	-1.4

This drop, more than any other factor, seemed to carry weight with the Governing Body members. There was a vote of 15 to 3 in favor of a statement making at least some acknowledgement of the organization's share in the responsibility for the error. This was published in the March 15, 1980, *Watchtower.*

It had taken nearly four years for the organization through its admin-istration finally to admit it had been wrong, had, for an entire decade, built up false hopes. Not that a statement so candid, though true, could be made. Whatever was written had to be acceptable to the Body as a whole for publishing. I know, because I was assigned to write the statement and, as in similar cases before, I had to be governed by—not what I would have liked to say or even what I thought the brothers needed to hear—but by what could be said that would have some hope of approval by two-thirds of the Governing Body when submitted to them.

Today, all the decade-long buildup of hopes centered on 1975 is discounted as to being of any particular importance. The essence of Russell's word in 1916 is once again expressed by the organization: It "certainly did have a very stimulating and sanctifying effect upon thousands, all of whom can praise the Lord—even for the mistake."

10

1914 AND "THIS GENERATION"

For the couch has proved too short for stretching oneself on,
and the woven sheet itself is too narrow when wrapping
oneself up. — Isaiah 28:20.

FOR more than three decades the year 1914 was pointed forward to as the terminal point for the Watch Tower organization's time prophecies. Now, for some eight decades, that same date has been pointed backward to as the starting point for the time prophecy that constitutes the major stimulus to "urgency" in the activity of Jehovah's Witnesses.

Perhaps no other religion of modern times has so much invested in, and dependent on, a single date. The Witness organization's claim to be the unique earthly channel and instrument of God and Christ is inseparably linked to it, for the claim is that in that year Christ began his "invisible presence" as a newly enthroned ruler, and that thereafter he examined the many religious bodies of earth and selected that which was connected with the Watch Tower as his choice to represent him before all mankind. In correlation to this, he gave his approved recognition of that same body of people as a "faithful and wise servant" class, which he appointed over all his earthly belongings. The Governing Body of Jehovah's Witnesses derives its claim to authority from this, presenting itself as the administrative part of that "faithful and wise servant" class. Take away 1914 and its claimed significance, and the basis for their authority largely evaporates.

The evidence shows that the Governing Body felt a considerable degree of discomfort as regards this major time prophecy. The time-frame allotted for its fulfillment proved embarrassingly short and narrow as to covering the things foretold. The passing of each year only served to accentuate the discomfort felt.

Since the 1940s the Watch Tower publications have represented the words of Jesus Christ, "Truly I say to you that this generation will by no means pass away until all these things occur," as having begun to apply as of the year 1914. The "1914-generation" was spoken of, and was presented as referring to the period in which the final fulfillment of the "last-days prophecies" would take place and a new order would enter.

In the 1940s the view held was that a "generation" covered a period of about 30 to 40 years. This lent itself to the constant insistence on the extreme

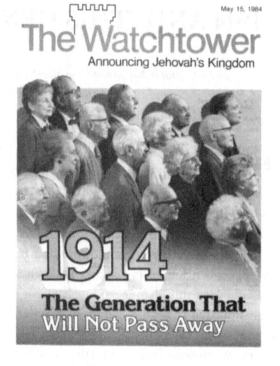

shortness of time left. At least some Bible examples could also be cited as corroboration. (See, for example, Numbers 32:13.)

With the arrival of the 1950s, however, the time period provided by that definition had effectively elapsed. Some "stretching" was needed, and hence in the September 1, 1952 Watchtower, pages 542, 543, the definition was changed and, for the first time, the time period covered by a "generation" was defined as representing an entire lifetime, thus running—not just for 30 or 40 years—but for 70, 80, or more years.

For a time this seemed to provide a comfortable span of time in which the published predictions might occur. Still, with the passing of the years the application of the term "1914-generation" underwent further adjustment and definition. Note the statements here underlined from an article in the Awake! magazine of October 8, 1968 (pages 13, 14):

> Jesus was obviously speaking about those who were old enough to witness *with understanding* what took place when the "last days" began. Jesus was saying that some of those persons who were alive at the appearance of the 'sign of the last days' would still be alive when God brought this system to its end.
>
> Even if we presume that youngsters 15 years of age would be perceptive enough to realize the import of what happened in 1914, it would still make the youngest of "this generation" nearly 70 years old today. So the great majority of the generation to which Jesus was referring has already passed away in death. The remaining ones are approaching old age. And remember, Jesus said that the end of this wicked world would come *before* that generation passed away in death. This, of itself, tells us that the years left before the foretold end comes cannot be many.

When the Awake! magazine discussed this more than thirty years ago in the pre-1975 days the stress was on how soon the generation of 1914 would be running out, how little time was left for that generation's life span. For any of Jehovah's Witnesses in 1968 to have suggested that things might go on for another thirty years or more would have been viewed as manifesting a poor attitude, one not indicative of strong faith.

When 1975 passed, however, the emphasis changed. Now the effort was made to show that the 1914-generation's span was not as narrow as one might think, that it could stretch for quite a long ways yet.

Thus, the October 1, 1978, Watchtower now spoke, not of those witnessing "with understanding what took place" in 1914, but of those who "were able to observe" the events beginning that year. Mere observation is quite different from understanding. This could logically lower the minimum age limit for the ones forming "this generation."

Continuing this trend, two years later, the Watchtower of October 15, 1980, cited an article in the U. S. News & World Report magazine, which suggested that ten years of age could be the point at which events start creating "a lasting impression on a person's memory." The news article said that, if such be true, "then there are today more than 13 million Americans who have a recollection of World War I."

'Recollecting' also allows for a more tender age than does understanding, earlier suggested as being found among "youngsters 15 years of age" in the 1968 Awake!. (Actually, World War I continued up into 1918, with American involvement beginning only in 1917. So the suggested 10-year-old age given in the news magazine quoted does not necessarily apply to 1914.)

Though different systems of measuring may have gained a year or so here and there, the fact remained that the generation of the 1914 period was shrinking with great rapidity, since the death rate is always highest among those of older age. The Governing Body was aware of this, for the matter came up for discussion a number of times.

The issue arose during the June 7, 1978, session of the Body. Earlier factors led to this. Governing Body member Albert Schroeder had distributed among the members a copy of a demographic report for the United States. The data indicated that less than one percent of the population who were out of their teens in 1914 were still alive in 1978. But a more attention-getting factor had to do with statements Schroeder had made while visiting certain countries in Europe.

Reports drifted back to Brooklyn that he was suggesting to others that the expression "this generation" as used by Jesus at Matthew 24:34 applied to the generation of "anointed ones," and that as long as any of these were still living such "generation" would not have passed away. This was, of course, contrary to the organization's teaching and was unauthorized by the Governing Body.

When the matter was brought up, following Schroeder's return, his suggested interpretation was rejected and it was voted that a "Question from Readers" be run in a forthcoming issue of the Watchtower reaffirming the standard teaching regarding "this generation."[1] Interestingly, no rebuke or reproof whatsoever was directed to Governing Body member Schroeder for having advanced his unauthorized, contradictory view while in Europe.

The issue emerged again in both the March 6 and November 14, 1979, sessions. Since attention was being focused on the subject, I made Xerox copies of the first twenty pages of the material sent in by the Swedish elder which detailed the history of chronological speculation and revealed the actual source of the 2,520-year calculation and the 1914 date. Each member of the Body received a copy. Aside from an incidental comment, they did not see fit to discuss the material.

Lyman Swingle, as head of the Writing Department, was already familiar with this material. He directed the Body's attention to some of the dogmatic, insistent statements published in several 1922 issues of the Watch Tower, reading portions of these aloud to all the members. He said that he had been too young in 1914 (only about four years old then) to remember much about it.[2] But he said that he did remember the discussions that took place in his home regarding 1925. That he also knew what had happened in 1975. He said he personally would not want to be misled regarding another date.

In the course of the session, I pointed out that the Society's 607 B.C.E. starting date had no historical evidence whatsoever for support. As for 1914 and the generation then living, my question was: If the organization's traditional teaching is valid, how can we possibly apply Jesus' accompanying words to the people living in 1914? He said: "When you see all these things, know that he is near at the doors," and "as these things

---

1   See the *Watchtower*, October 1, 1978.

2   Among the Governing Body members at the time discussed, only Fred Franz was out of his teenage years in 1914, being 21 years old then. As to the other members, Karl Klein and Carey Barber were 9, Lyman Swingle was 4, Albert Schroeder 3, and Jack Barr was 1 year old. Lloyd Barry, Dan Sydlik, Milton Henschel, and Ted Jaracz had not yet been born, their births coming after 1914, as is true of the seven latest members added since to the Body.

start to occur, raise yourselves erect and lift your heads up, because your deliverance is getting near." The publications regularly stated that those words began applying from 1914 onward, to those Christians living in 1914. But if so, then to whom among them could this apply? To those who were then 50 years old? But such ones if still alive would now (that is, in 1979, the time of the discussion) be 115 years old. The 40-year-olds? They would be 105. Even the 30-year-olds would be 95 and those just out of their teens would already be 85 in 1979. (Even these would be over 100 if still living today.)

If then those stirring words 'lift up your heads because your deliverance is getting near, it's at the doors' indeed applied to people in 1914 and meant that they could hope to see the final windup, reasonably that exciting announcement would need to be qualified by saying: "Yes, you may see it—that is, provided you are now quite young and live a very, very long life." As an example, I pointed to my father who, born in 1891, was just a young man of twenty-three in 1914. He lived, not just threescore years and ten, or fourscore years, but reached eighty-six years of age. He had been dead for two years by this time and died without seeing the predicted things.

So I asked the Body how meaningful the application of Jesus' words in Matthew 24:33, 34, could have been in 1914 if the only ones who could hope to see them fulfilled were children just in their teens or younger? No specific reply was offered.

A number of members, however, did voice their continued support for the organization's existing teaching about "this generation" and the 1914 date. Lloyd Barry expressed personal dismay that doubts existed within the Body regarding the teaching. Referring to Lyman Swingle's reading of statements from the 1922 Watch Towers, he said that he saw nothing to be concerned about in these, that they were "present truth" for the brothers at that period.[3] As to the advanced age of the 1914-generation, he pointed out that in some parts of the Soviet Union there are

---

3   The expression "present truth" was popular in the time of Russell and Rutherford and was based on a faulty translation of 2 Peter 1:12. The *New World Translation* there reads more accurately, "the truth that is present in you."

regions where people live to be 130 years old. He urged that a united position be expressed to the brothers so that they would maintain their sense of urgency. Others expressed concurring views.

When later recognized by the Chairman, my comment was that it seemed we would need to keep in mind that what is today taught as "present truth" may also in time become "past truth," and that the "present truth" that replaces such "past truth" may itself become replaced by "future truth." I felt that the word "truth" used in such a manner became simply meaningless.

A couple of the Body members said that if the current explanation was not the right one, then what was the explanation of Jesus' statements? Since the question seemed aimed at me, my response was that I felt there was an explanation that harmonized with Scripture and fact, but that anything presented should surely not be some "spur-of-the-moment" idea, but something carefully researched and weighed. I said that I thought there were brothers capable of doing that work but that they would need the Governing Body's authorization. Was the Governing Body interested in having this done? There was no response and the question was dropped.

At the discussion's end, with the exception of a few members, the Body members indicated that they felt that 1914 and the teaching about "this generation" tied to it should continue to be stressed. The Writing Committee Coordinator, Lyman Swingle, commented, "All right, if that is what you want to do. But at least you know that as far as 1914 is concerned, Jehovah's Witnesses got the whole thing—lock, stock and barrel—from the Second Adventists."

Perhaps one of the most disturbing things to me was knowing that, while the organization urged the brothers to maintain unwavering trust in the interpretation, there were men in responsible positions within the organization who had themselves manifested that they did not have full confidence in the predictions based on the 1914 date.

As a notable example, at the time of the February 19, 1975, session, in which the Governing Body listened to Fred Franz's taped talk on 1975, there followed some discussion about the uncertainty of time prophecies. Nathan Knorr, then the president, spoke up and said:

There are some things I know—I know that Jehovah is God, that Christ Jesus is his Son, that he gave his life as a ransom for us, that there is a resurrection. Other things I'm not so certain about. 1914—I don't know. We have talked about 1914 for a long time. We may be right and I hope we are.[4]

At that session the date primarily under discussion was 1975, so it came as a surprise that the far more fundamental date of 1914 should be referred to in such context. As stated, the president's words were spoken, not in private conversation, but before the Governing Body in session.

Previous to the major discussion of 1914 (in the November 14, 1979, full Governing Body session), the Body's Writing Committee in a committee meeting had discussed the advisability of continuing to stress 1914.[5] In the committee discussion it was suggested that we might at least refrain from "pushing" the date. As I recall, Karl Klein reminded us of the practice sometimes followed of simply not mentioning a certain teaching for a time, so that if any change came it would not make such a strong impression.

Remarkably, the Writing Committee voted unanimously to follow basically that very policy in the publications with regard to 1914. This position, however, was short-lived, since the November 14, 1979, full session of the Governing Body made clear that the majority favored emphasizing the date as usual.

That questions about this teaching were not limited to Brooklyn was brought home to me by an incident occurring while I was on a trip to West Africa in the fall of 1979. In Nigeria, two members of the Nigerian Branch Committee and a longtime missionary, took me to see a property the Society had purchased for constructing a new Branch headquarters. On the return trip I asked when they expected to be able to move to the new site. The reply was that, with the clearing of the land, obtaining approval of plans and getting necessary permits, and then the actual construction, it might well be in 1983 before the move was made.

---

4   This does not seem to have been just a momentary thought on President Knorr's part, for the same viewpoint was expressed in virtually the same words by one of his closer associates, George Couch. Knowing the two, it seems more likely that Couch acquired the view from Knorr than vice versa.

5   The Writing Committee membership was then composed of Lloyd Barry, Fred Franz, Raymond Franz, Karl Klein and Lyman Swingle.

Because of this, I asked, "Do you get any questions from the local brothers as to the length of time that has passed since 1914?" There was a momentary silence, and then the Branch Coordinator said, "No, the Nigerian brothers seldom ask questions of that kind—but WE do." Almost immediately the longtime missionary said, "Brother Franz, could it be that Jesus' reference to 'this generation' applied only to persons back there who saw the destruction of Jerusalem? If that were the case, then everything would seem to fit."

Quite evidently not everything did seem to fit in his mind, the way the existing teaching had it. My reply was simply that I supposed that such was a possibility but that there was not much more that could be said for the idea. I repeated this conversation to the Governing Body after my return, for it gave evidence to me of the questions existing in the minds of men throughout the world, respected men in positions of considerable authority. The comments the men in Nigeria made and the way that they made them indicated clearly that they had discussed the question among themselves before ever my visit took place.

Shortly after my return from Africa, in a Governing Body session on February 17, 1980, Lloyd Barry again voiced his feelings about the importance of the teaching regarding 1914 and "this generation." Lyman Swingle said that the "Questions from Readers" material published in 1978 had not settled the matter in the brothers' minds. Albert Schroeder reported that in the Gilead School and in Branch Committee seminars, brothers brought up the fact that 1984 was now being talked about as a possible new date, 1984 being seventy years from 1914 (the figure seventy evidently being looked upon as having some special import). The Body decided to discuss the matter of 1914 further in the next session."[6]

The Chairman's Committee, consisting of Albert Schroeder (Chairman), Karl Klein and Grant Suiter, now produced a most unusual document. They supplied a copy to each member of the Governing Body. Briefly put, these three men were suggesting that, rather than applying to

6   Contrary to what is alleged by some, the Governing Body itself never gave importance to the date of 1984 and, as I recall, this occasion was the only time that date was even mentioned, and that only in connection with rumors.

people living in 1914, the expression "this generation" would begin applying as of 1957, forty-three years later!

This is the material exactly as these three members of the Governing
Body supplied it to us:

To Members of the Governing Body -- On Agenda for Wednesday Mar.5 '80

Question: What is "this generation (genea')?"(Mt. 24:34; Mr. 13:30;
                                                 Luke 21:32)

TDNT (many Commentaries) say: genea' "mostly denotes the sense of
     contemporaries." Vol. 1, p. 663

     Most all say genea' differs from genos, genos means offspring,
        people, race. See TDNT Vol. 1 p. 685 (genos at 1 Pet. 2:9)

Answer may be tied to question on Mt. 24:33. What is meant by: "When
     you see all these things"?

     Lange's Commentary (Vol. 8) suggests that "these things" do not
        refer to C.E. 70, nor the parousia 1914 but to vss. 29,30 the
        celestial phenomina that we now see began with the space age
        1957 onward. In that case it would then be the contemporary
        generation of mankind living since 1957.

Three Sections

     Lange's Commentary divides Matthew 24th chapter into "three cycles."
        His 1st cycle-- Matt. 24:1-14
             2nd cycle-- Matt. 24:15-28
             3rd cycle-- Matt. 24:29-44 (synteleia or conclusion)
        (See Vol. 8 pp 421, 424 and 427)
        Based on Matt. 24:3 question in three parts.

     The Watchtower and God's Kingdom of a Thousand Years (ka)
        Have now also divided Matthew 24 into three parts so to speak

        (1) Matt. 24:3-22 Has parallel fulfillments in 1st century
               and today since 1914. (See w 75 p. 273, ka p. 205)

        (2) Matt. 24:23-28 Period into Christ's parousia of 1914.
               (See w 75 p. 275)

        (3) Matt. 24:29-44 "Celestial Phenomina"have literal application
               since the space age began in 1957 and onward to include
               Christ's erkhomenon (coming as the executioner at the
               beginning of the "great tribulation.")
               (See w 75 p 276 par. 18; ka pp 323 to 328)

"All these things" would have to throw back in the context to the nearest
     items listed in the composite sign, namely, the celestial phenomina
     of verses 29 and 30.*

If this is true: to
     Then "this generation" would refer/contemporary mankind living
     as knowledgeable ones from 1957 onward.

*Confirmed in thought by C.T.Russell in Berean Commentary, p. 217:
     "Genea, people living contemporaneously which witness the signs
     just mentioned." Vol. 4 p. 604.

                              Chairman's Committee, 3/3/80

1957 marked the year when the first Russian Sputnik was launched into earth's outer space. Evidently the Chairman's Committee felt that that event could be accepted as marking the start of the fulfillment of these words of Jesus:

> The sun will be darkened, and the moon will not give its light, and the stars will fall from heaven, and the powers of heaven will be shaken.[7]

Based on that application, their conclusion would be as they stated:

> Then 'this generation' would refer to contemporary mankind living as knowledgeable ones from 1957 onward.

The three men were not suggesting that 1914 be dropped. It would stay as the "end of the Gentile Times." But "this generation" would not begin applying until 1957.

In view of the swiftly diminishing numbers of the 1914-generation, this new application of the phrase could undoubtedly prove even more helpful than some person allegedly living to be 130 years old in a certain section of the Soviet Union. As compared with starting in 1914, this new 1957 starting date would give an additional 43 years for the period embraced by the expression "this generation" to reach.

Governing Body standards required that for any Committee to recommend something to the full Body there should be unanimous agreement among the Committee members (otherwise the divided viewpoint should be presented to the Body for settlement). The presentation of the novel idea regarding 1957 was therefore one upon which the three members of the Chairman's Committee, Schroeder, Klein and Suiter must have agreed.

I would think that, if asked about this presentation today, the response would be, "Oh, that was just a suggestion." Possibly, but if so it was a suggestion seriously made. And for Albert Schroeder, Karl Klein and Grant Suiter to bring such a suggestion to the Governing Body they must have been willing in their own minds to see the suggested change made. If, indeed, their belief and conviction as to the Society's longtime teaching

---

7   Matthew 24:29.

about "this generation" (as applying from 1914 onward) had been strong, firm, unequivocal, they certainly would never have come forward with the new interpretation they offered.

The Governing Body did not accept the new view proposed by these members. Comments made showed that many considered it fanciful. The fact remains, however, that Governing Body members Schroeder, Klein and Suiter presented their idea as a serious proposition, revealing their own lack of conviction as to the solidity of the existing teaching on the subject.

Despite all this evidence of divided viewpoint as to the validity of the claims regarding 1914 and the "1914-generation," bold, positive, forceful statements regarding 1914 and "this generation" continued to be published as Biblically established fact by the "prophet" organization, and all of Jehovah's Witnesses were urged to put full trust in this and carry the message about it to other people earthwide. In an apparent effort to calm concern about the diminishing ranks of the 1914-generation, the same Watchtower (October 15, 1980, page 31) that implied that the age limit for that generation's members could be lowered to ten years of age, also said:

> And if the wicked system of this world survived until the turn of the century, which is highly improbable in view of world trends and the fulfillment of Bible prophecy, there would still be survivors of the World War I generation. However, the fact that their number is dwindling is one more indication that "the conclusion of the system of things" is moving fast toward its end.

That was written in 1980. Twenty years later, by the turn of the century, the ten-year-olds of 1914 would be ninety-six years old. Still, there might be a few of them yet around and evidently that was viewed as all that was necessary for Jesus' words to be fulfilled—depending, of course, on the acceptance of the idea that Jesus was directing his words particularly to ten-year-old children. This illustrates the extremes to which the organization was willing to go to hold on to its definition of the "1914-generation."

More years passed and now no mention was made of "ten-year-olds" but instead the reference was simply to "those living in 1914" or similar. This, of course, allowed for newborn babies to be included in the "1914-generation." But with the arrival of the 1990s, and with the third millennium about to begin, even this "adjustment in understanding" provided only momentary relief for the problem. Even a newborn in 1914 would be approaching 90 by the year 2000.

One thing I can say with positiveness about the matter is that I personally found the reasoning employed within the Governing Body to be incredible. I found it tragic that a time prophecy could be proclaimed to the world as something solid upon which people could and should confidently rely, build their hopes, form their life plans, when the very ones publishing this knew that within their own collective body there did not exist a unanimity of genuine, firm conviction as to the rightness of that teaching. It may be that when viewed against the whole background of the organization's decades of date-fixing and shifting of dates, their attitude becomes more understandable.

Perhaps more incredible to me is that the Chairman's Committee members, Albert Schroeder, Karl Klein and Grant Suiter, within about two months of their submission of their new idea on "this generation" listed the teaching about the start of Christ's presence in 1914 as among the decisive teachings for determining whether individuals (including headquarters staff members) were guilty of "apostasy" and therefore merited disfellowshipment. They did this knowing that just months before they themselves had placed in question the corollary, companion doctrine regarding "this generation."

Throughout the half century in which the organization promulgated the concept of a "1914-generation," its span consistently proved like a couch that is too short for comfort, and the reasoning used to cover that doctrinal "couch" proved like a woven sheet that is too narrow, not able to shut out, in this case, the cold facts of reality.

The leadership had made numerous adjustments and now had few remaining options. There was the 1957 starting date for "this generation" proposed by members Schroeder, Klein and Suiter, but that seemed an unlikely choice. There was Albert Schroeder's idea of applying the phrase to the "anointed" class (an idea that had been floating around the organization for many, many years) which offered certain advantages—there are always additional persons (some fairly young) who each year decide for the first time that they are of the "anointed" class. So this would offer an almost limitless extension of time for the teaching about "this generation."

There was another option. They could acknowledge the historical evidence placing Jerusalem's destruction twenty years later than the Society's 607 B.C.E. date. This would make the Gentile Times run out (using their 2,520-year interpretation) about 1934. But such enormous importance has been placed on 1914 and, as has been shown, so much of the doctrinal superstructure is linked to it, that this also seemed an unlikely step.

The inevitable signs of yet further "adjustment of understanding" began to appear with the February 15, 1994, Watchtower. In it the beginning of the application of Jesus' statement about "signs in sun and moon and stars, and on the earth anguish of nations" was moved up from the year 1914 to a point following the start of the yet future "great tribulation." Likewise, the foretold 'gathering of the chosen ones from the four winds,' previously taught as running from 1919 onward, was now also moved to the future, following the start of the "great tribulation" and subsequent to the appearance of the celestial phenomena. Each of the now-abandoned positions had been taught for some fifty years. (See, as but one of numerous examples, the Watchtower of July 15, 1946.)

Though heralded as "new light," the changes simply moved Watch Tower teachings closer to understandings presented long ago by those the organization disdains as "Christendom's scholars."

In September 1994, the eighth printing of Crisis of Conscience discussed this February 15, 1994 issue of the Watchtower and its moving the application of portions of Matthew 24 forward to the start of the "great tribulation." In that discussion I included the following thoughts:

What is perhaps most notable is that the phrase "this generation"—which the *Watchtower* so constantly emphasizes and which is found in Matthew 24:34 and Luke 21:32—nowhere appears in these articles, being conspicuous by its absence. It is hard to say whether the organization will now be able to assign Matthew 24:29-31 to a point *after* the start of the future "great tribulation" and still continue to apply Jesus' statement about "this generation" three verses later to the time period beginning in 1914. But as has been shown, it is reasonable to believe that the Governing Body would welcome some means of escape from the increasingly difficult position created by tying the phrase "this generation" (along with the accompanying words that it "will not pass away until all these things have taken place") to the steadily-receding date of 1914.

Whether this new interpretation is simply preparing the ground for a crucial change in the application of the phrase "this generation" remains to be seen. Undoubtedly, the most desirable escape would come with an explanation that both *retained* 1914 as the "start of the last days" and at the same time successfully *disconnected* the phrase "this generation" from that date. As stated, the organization can hardly give up 1914 completely without undermining a host of teachings based on that date. But if the phrase "this generation" could be unlinked from 1914 and be applied to some future period of unknown date, then the passage of time, the arrival of the third millennium in the year 2000, and even the approach of the year 2014, might not prove too difficult to rationalize, particularly with a membership trained to accept whatever the "faithful and discreet slave class" and its Governing Body may offer them.

As stated, that information in Crisis of Conscience was printed in September 1994. Just thirteen months later articles appeared in the November 1, 1995 Watchtower which did almost precisely what had been pointed to in that 1994 edition of Crisis of Conscience. As indicated, they now unlinked the phrase "this generation" (Matthew 24:34) from the date of 1914, but still retained the date as Biblically significant.

This was accomplished by a new definition of the sense of "generation" in this text. About 70 years ago, The Golden Age magazine of October 20, 1926, connected Jesus' words about "this generation" to the date of 1914 (as did subsequent Watchtower magazines). Some 25 years later, the June 1, 1951, Watchtower, page 335, in connection with 1914, stated, "Hence our generation is the generation that will see the start and finish of all these things, including Armageddon." In the July 1, 1951, issue, page 404, "this generation" was again linked to 1914. Of Matthew 24:34, it said:

> The actual meaning of these words is, beyond question that which takes a "generation" in the ordinary sense, as at Mark 8:12 and Acts 13:36, or for those who are living at the given period.

It then added:

> This therefore means that from 1914 a generation shall not pass till all is fulfilled, and amidst a great time of trouble.

For over forty years thereafter Watch Tower publications continued to assign a temporal sense to the "generation" of Matthew 24:34. The aging of the 1914-generation was pointed to again and again as clear evidence of the shortness of the remaining time.

In the revised 1995 definition, however, rather than having parameters of time limitations or any set starting point, the "generation" is instead said to be identified, not temporally, but qualitatively, by its characteristics, as in the reference to an "evil and adulterous generation" in Jesus' time. "This generation" is now said to be "the peoples of earth who see the sign of Christ's presence but fail to mend their ways."

1914 is not discarded, however, something the organization could not do without dismantling the major theological structure and distinctive tenets of the religion. 1914 remains as the claimed date of Christ's enthronement in heaven, the beginning of his second, invisible, presence, as also the start of the "last days." And it still figures, though obliquely, in the new definition of "this generation," since the "sign of Christ's presence"—which the doomed ones see and reject or ignore—supposedly began to be visible worldwide from and after 1914.

What then is the significant difference? It is that now, to qualify as part of "this generation," a person need no longer have been alive in 1914 to form part of "this generation." Anyone can see the supposed "sign of Christ's presence" at any time—even if for the first time in the 1990s, or for that matter in the third millennium—and still qualify as part of "this generation." This allows the phrase to float free of any starting date and reduces considerably the need to explain the embarrassing length of time that has elapsed since 1914, and the rapidly diminishing ranks of persons who were alive at that date.

Perhaps the most graphic evidence of this change is seen in the masthead of the Awake! magazine. Up until October 22, 1995, it read:

Awake!®

Why Awake! Is Published *Awake!* is for the enlightenment of the entire family. It shows how to cope with today's problems. It reports the news, tells about people in many lands, examines religion and science. But it does more. It probes beneath the surface and points to the real meaning behind current events, yet it always stays politically neutral and does not exalt one race above another. Most important, this magazine builds confidence in the Creator's promise of a peaceful and secure new world before the generation that saw the events of 1914 passes away. ◀━━

The statement that "this magazine builds confidence in the Creator's promise of a peaceful and secure new world before the generation that saw the events of 1914 passes away," appeared year after year from 1982 until October 22, 1995. With the November 8, 1995 issue, the statement was altered to read:

Awake!®

Why Awake! Is Published *Awake!* is for the enlightenment of the entire family. It shows how to cope with today's problems. It reports the news, tells about people in many lands, examines religion and science. But it does more. It probes beneath the surface and points to the real meaning behind current events, yet it always stays politically neutral and does not exalt one race above another. Most important, this magazine builds confidence in the Creator's promise of a peaceful and secure new world that is about to replace the present wicked, lawless system of things. ◀━━

All reference to 1914 is now deleted, presenting graphic evidence of this crucial change—as well as, in effect, indicating that "the Creator" had somehow reneged on his "promise" tied to the 1914-generation.

It remains to be seen what the ultimate effect of this change will be. I would think that those feeling its effects most acutely would be those older, longtime members who had embraced the hope of not dying before the realization of their expectations regarding the complete fulfillment of God's promises. Proverbs 13:12 says that "hope deferred [expectation postponed, NW] makes the heart sick, but a desire fulfilled is a tree of life." (NRSV) Any feelings of heartsickness these may now experience are not the responsibility of the Creator but of the men who implanted and nourished in them false expectations tied to a date.

Those younger or more recently affiliated will not likely feel as severely the impact of the change. It is, after all, clothed in language that makes no acknowledgment of error on the organization's part, but which shrouds the change in terms of 'progressive understanding' and 'advancing light.'

The May 1, 1999 Watchtower (page13) says; "Our progress in under-standing the prophecy in Matthew chapters 24 and 25 has been thrilling," this, while contemporaneously discarding one interpretation after another taught for years as divine truth! The many newer ones may not be aware of the intense insistence with which, for decades, the "1914-generation" concept was advanced, how positively it was presented as a certain indica-tor of the "nearness of the end." They may not realize how adamantly the "1914-generation" teaching was presented as being, not of human origin, but of divine origin, not a timetable based on human promise, but based on "God's promise." This 40-year-long, implicit tying of God and his Word to a now-failed concept only adds to the heaviness of the responsi-bility. One is reminded of Jehovah's words at Jeremiah 23:21:

> I did not send the prophets, yet they ran; I did not speak to them, yet they prophesied.

This basic change can only have come as the result of a Governing Body decision. As shown, the essential issue involved came up for discus-sion as far back as the 1970s. One cannot but wonder as to the thoughts of the Governing Body members today, what sense of responsibility they feel. Every member of that body knew then and knows now what the organization's record has been in the field of date-setting and predicting. Through the publications this is excused on the basis of "a fervent desire to realize the fulfillment of God's promises in their own time," as if one cannot have such fervent desire without presuming to set a timetable for God, or to make predictions and attribute them to God, as based on his Word. They know also that, despite mistake after mistake, the organiza-tion's leaders kept on feeding its membership new predictions. They know that the leadership has consistently failed to shoulder full responsibility for the errors, to admit that it, the leadership, was simply and plainly wrong. They have sought to protect their image and their claim to authority by endeavoring to make it appear that the errors were those of the member-ship as a whole. In an article on "False Predictions or True Prophecy," the June 22, 1995 Awake! (page 9) said:

Bible Students, known since 1931 as Jehovah's Witnesses, also expected that the year 1925 would see the fulfillment of marvelous Bible prophecies. They surmised that at that time the earthly resurrection would begin, bringing back faithful men of old, such as Abraham, David, and Daniel. More recently, many Witnesses conjectured that events associated with the beginning of Christ's Millennial Reign might start to take place in 1975. Their anticipation was based on the understanding that the seventh millennium of human history would begin then.

The November 1, 1995, Watchtower magazine presenting the new teaching regarding "this generation" follows the same tactic, saying (page 17):

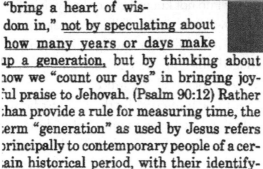

Eager to see the end of this evil system, Jehovah's people have at times speculated about the time when the "great tribulation" would break out, even tying this to calculations of what is the lifetime of a generation since 1914. However, we "bring a heart of wisdom in," not by speculating about how many years or days make up a generation, but by thinking about how we "count our days" in bringing joyful praise to Jehovah. (Psalm 90:12) Rather than provide a rule for measuring time, the term "generation" as used by Jesus refers principally to contemporary people of a certain historical period, with their identifying characteristics.

The leadership thus shrugs off the responsibility that rightfully rests with them, piously counseling the membership on their spiritual outlook as if it were their wrong spiritual viewpoint that produced the problem. They do not acknowledge that the membership originates nothing and that the membership embraced hopes as to various dates solely because the leaders of the organization fed them material clearly designed to stir up such hopes, that every date mentioned and all the 'surmising,' 'conjectures' and 'speculations' and 'calculations' connected to those dates, originated, not with the membership, but with the leaders. It is somewhat like a mother, whose children become ill with indigestion, saying of such children, "They weren't careful about what they ate," when in fact the children simply ate what the mother served them. And not only served them but insisted that the food should be accepted as wholesome, part of a superior diet unobtainable elsewhere, so much so that any expression of dissatisfaction with what was fed them would bring threat of punishment.

The men now on the Governing Body all know that, for as long as any of the organization's teachings connected with the 1914 date were in effect, any open questioning or disagreement regarding these could and did bring disfellowshipment. They know that the very "heart of wisdom" that the Watchtower article now urges—a heart that avoids speculation based on dates and which focuses instead on simply living each day of our lives as unto God—is the very same "heart" that some members of the Brooklyn headquarters staff sought to convey, and that it was their position in this exact regard that formed a principal part of the accusation on which they were judged as "apostate." What the thoughts of the Governing Body members involved are today I do not know. I can only say that, had I been a party to the presentation now made and its failure to make an open and manly acknowledgment of responsibility for having seriously misled, and for having seriously misjudged other sincere Christians, I do not see how I could escape feeling some sense of moral cowardice.

It is difficult not to be impressed by the contrast between this course and that taken within another religion guilty of making similar time predictions, the Worldwide Church of God. After the death of its longtime leader, Herbert W. Armstrong, in the late 1980s, the new leadership published an article in the March/April issue of the religion's main publication, The Plain Truth magazine. The article was titled "Forgive Us Our Trespasses," and began by saying, "The Worldwide Church of God, sponsor of The Plain Truth magazine, has changed its position on numerous long-held beliefs and practices during the past few years." In detailing these, it also said:

> At the same time, we are acutely aware of the heavy legacy of our past.
>
> Our flawed doctrinal understanding clouded the plain gospel of Jesus Christ and led to a variety of wrong conclusions and unscriptural practices. We have much to repent of and apologize for.

> We were judgmental and self-righteous—condemning other Christians, calling them "so-called Christians" and labeling them "deceived" and "instruments of Satan."
>
> We imposed on our members a works-oriented approach to Christian living. We required adherence to burdensome regulations of the Old Testament code. We exercised a strongly legalistic approach to church government.
>
> Our former old covenant approach fostered attitudes of exclusivism and superiority rather than the new covenant teaching of brotherhood and unity.
>
> We overemphasized predictive prophecy and prophetic speculation, minimizing the true gospel of salvation through Jesus Christ.
>
> These teachings and practices are a source of supreme regret. We are painfully mindful of the heartache and suffering that has resulted from them.
>
> We've been wrong. There was never an intent to mislead anyone. We were so focused on what we believed we were doing for God that we didn't recognize the spiritual path we were on. Intended or not, that path was not the biblical one.
>
> As we look back, we ask ourselves how we could have been so wrong. Our hearts go out to all whom our teachings have misled in the Scriptures. We don't minimize your spiritual disorientation and confusion. We earnestly desire your understanding and forgiveness.

> We make no attempt to cover up the doctrinal and scriptural errors of our past. It is not our intention to merely paper over the cracks. We are looking our history squarely in the face and confronting the faults and sins we find. They will always remain a part of our history, serving as a perpetual reminder of the dangers of legalism.

Such frank admission and acceptance of responsibility for harm are not found in Watch Tower publications. Knowing them personally, I am satisfied that many of the men on the Governing Body are sincere in the belief that they are serving God. Unfortunately, that belief is accompanied by a parallel belief that the organization they head is God's channel of divine communication, superior to all other religious organizations on earth—a belief that gives evidence of a state of denial, in which they do not allow themselves to face the reality of the organization's flawed course and record. Whatever their sincerity in their desire to serve God, it regrettably has not protected them from a remarkable insensitivity to the potential disillusioning effect of their failed apocalyptic predictions, the weakening effect this can have on people's confidence in the reliability and worth of the Scriptures.

11

POINT OF DECISION

*But whatever was to my profit I now consider loss for the sake
of Christ. What is more, I consider everything a loss compared
to the surpassing greatness of knowing Christ Jesus my Lord,
for whose sake I have lost all things.*
— Philippians 3:7-8 *New International Version.*

BY THE end of 1979 I had arrived at my personal crossroads. I had
spent nearly forty years as a full-time representative, serving at every
level of the organizational structure. The last fifteen years I had spent at
the international headquarters and the final nine of those as a member of
the worldwide Governing Body of Jehovah's Witnesses.

It was those final years that were the crucial period for me. Illusion
there met up with reality. I have since come to appreciate the rightness of
a quotation I recently read, one made by a statesman, now dead, who said:

> The great enemy of the truth is very often not the lie—deliberate, con-
> trived and dishonest—but the myth—persistent, persuasive and unrealistic.

I now began to realize how large a measure of what I had based my
entire adult life course on was just that, a myth—"persistent, persuasive
and unrealistic." It was not that my view toward the Bible had changed.
If anything, my appreciation of it was enhanced by what I experienced. It
alone gave sense and meaning to what I saw happening, the attitudes I saw
displayed, the reasoning I heard advanced, the tension and pressure I felt.
The change that did come was from the realization that my way of looking
at the Scriptures had been from such an essentially sectarian viewpoint,
a trap that I thought I had been protected against. Letting the Scriptures

311

speak for themselves—without being first funneled through some fallible human agency as a "channel"—I found they became immensely more meaningful. I was frankly astonished at how much of their import I had been missing.

The question was, what should I now do? My years on the Governing Body, the things I heard said in and out of sessions, the basic spirit I saw displayed, steadily brought me to the awareness that, as regards the organization, the 'wineskin had grown old,' had lost whatever flexibility it might have had, and that it was stiffening its resistance to any Scriptural correction either as to doctrinal beliefs or its methods of dealing with those who looked to it for guidance.[1] I felt, and still feel, that there were many good men on the Governing Body. In a long-distance phone call, a former Witness said to me, "We have been followers of followers." Another said, "We have been victims of victims." I think both statements are true. Charles Taze Russell followed the views of certain men of his time, was victimized by some of the myths they propagated as "revealed truth." Each successive part of the organizational leadership has followed along, at times contributing additional myth in support of, or in elaboration of, the original myth. In place of rancor, I feel only compassion for those men I know, for I too was such a "victim of victims," a "follower of followers."

Though each year on the Governing Body, particularly from 1976 onward, became increasingly difficult and more stressful for me, I clung to the hope that things would improve. In time I was obliged to recognize that was a hope which the evidence did not support.

I was not opposed to authority. I was opposed to the extremes to which it was carried. I could not believe that God ever purposed for men to exercise such all-pervading authoritarian control over the lives of fellow members of the Christian congregation. My understanding was that Christ grants authority in his congregation only to serve, never to dominate.[2]

Similarly, I did not object to "organization" in the sense of an orderly arrangement, for I understood the Christian congregation itself to involve

---

1   Compare Jesus' words at Luke 5:37-39.
2   Matthew 20:25-28; 23:8-12; 2 Corinthians 4:5; 1 Peter 5:3.

such an orderly arrangement.[3] But I believed that, whatever the arrangement, its purpose and function, its very existence, was only as an aid for the brothers; it was there to serve their interests, not the other way around. Whatever the arrangement, it was to build men and women up so that they would not be spiritual babes, dependent on men or on an institutionalized system, but able to act as full-grown, mature Christians. It was not to train them to be simply conformists to a set of organizational rules and regulations, but to help them to become persons "having their perceptive powers trained to distinguish both right and wrong."[4] Whatever arrangement there was, it must contribute toward a genuine sense of brotherhood, with the freeness of speech and mutual confidence true brotherhood brings—not a society composed of the few who are the governors and the many who are the governed. And finally, whatever the arrangement, the way to 'take the lead' therein must be by example, by holding firmly to the Word of God, passing on and inculcating the instructions of the Master the way he gave them, not "adjusting" these to fit what seemed to be in the interests of a humanly created organization, not by 'making people feel the weight of one's authority' in the way the great men of the world do.[5] It must result in the exaltation of Christ Jesus as the Head, never in the exaltation of an earthly authority structure and its officers. As it was, I felt that the role of Christ Jesus as active Head was overshadowed and virtually eclipsed by the authoritarian conduct and constant self-commendation and self-praise of the organization.

Furthermore, I did not deny the value and need for teaching. But I could not accept that organizational interpretations, based on shifting human reasoning, could ever be made equal in authority to the actual statements found in God's unchangeable Word. The great importance given to traditional views, the bending and slanting of God's Word to accommodate it to those views, and the inconsistencies that resulted in double standards were a source of serious emotional upset to me. What I found unacceptable was, not teaching, but dogmatism.

---

3   1 Corinthians 12:4-11, 25; 14:40.
4   Hebrews 5:14; 1 Corinthians 8:9; 16:13, 14.
5   Matthew 20:25.

The convictions I held I tried to reflect during my years of service on the Governing Body. From the beginning I found that this brought me difficulty, animosity. In the end it brought rejection, expulsion.

In the autumn of 1979, I had an assignment to go on a "zone visit" to certain branch offices in West Africa. Some were in countries where the government had placed an official ban on the activity of Jehovah's Witnesses. Knowing how easily something could happen that might result in my being detained, possibly imprisoned, I felt an obligation to discuss some of my concerns with my wife. (In view of her previous health problems, including a blood condition that nearly caused her death in 1969, I felt it best to make the trip alone.) Though she could not help but be aware of the emotional strain I felt, I had never discussed with her the actual circumstances that produced that strain, what the real issues were that affected me. I had not felt free to do so. Now I felt not only that it was proper but that I had an obligation to consider with her what I had become aware of, particularly in the light of the Scriptures. How could I let men hold me back from discussing with my own wife truths that I saw in the Word of God?

By that time we concluded that the advisable course for us was to terminate our activity at the international headquarters. We felt that our peace of mind and heart, as well as our physical health, required it. We also had faint hopes that it might yet be possible to have a child and we had, in fact, talked to two doctors about this, including one of the staff doctors, Dr. Carlton, on a confidential basis.[6] I was fifty-seven and I knew that it would be very difficult to find secular employment due to that factor. But I trusted that somehow things would work out.

The decision was not easy. I felt torn between two desires. On the one hand, I felt that by remaining on the Body at least I could speak up on behalf of others' interests, on behalf of the truth of the Scriptures, on behalf of moderation and balance, even though my voice was heard with irritation or ignored. I sensed that the time-span in which I could do

---

6   My wife is thirteen years younger than I. We recognized the risks the doctors brought to our attention but were willing to face these.

Former hotels
now owned by
Watch Tower

Personal room at headquarters

that was rapidly shortening, that whatever voice I had in Governing Body discussions would soon be shut out, silenced. The desire to be free from the suspicious atmosphere I saw developing, to be free from participation in an authority structure I could not Scripturally defend and decisions I could not morally condone, weighed equally heavy with me.

If security and comfort were my aim, I certainly would have opted for staying where I was, for all our physical needs would have been provided us as part of the headquarters staff. Our long years of "seniority" would give us the choice of some of the better rooms that periodically became available in the Society's many large buildings.[7] Our vacation time would increase to the equivalent of some six weeks a year and, because of being a Governing Body member, it would always be possible to combine this with speaking engagements that carried one to points all over the United States and Canada, or with zone visits that took one to points all over the earth. (Governing Body members can regularly take their vacations in places the average person could only afford to dream about.) In 1978, my wife and I found ourselves boarding planes over fifty times in that one year, and over the years we had traveled to Central and South America, Asia, Europe, Africa and the Middle East.

---

7   The Society had not long before purchased the fifteen-story Towers Hotel, complementing other ten-story residences already owned in the Brooklyn Heights area. Since then the Society has purchased (through agents) the Standish Arms Hotel and the Bossert Hotel, both in Brooklyn, as well as erecting a new 30-story residential building in the area.

If prestige or prominence were what was sought, I could not reasonably have asked for more. I was already declining, on a monthly basis, about three or four invitations for speaking engagements for every one that I accepted. Internationally, if traveling to Paris, Athens, Madrid, Lisbon, Mexico City, Sao Paulo, or almost any other major city, it was only necessary to advise the Branch Office and a meeting would be arranged to which thousands of Jehovah's Witnesses would flock. It became almost commonplace to address audiences ranging in size anywhere from five thousand up to thirty thousand persons.

Speaking in Madrid

Practically anywhere a Governing Body member goes he is the guest of honor among his fellow Witnesses.[8]

As for the Governing Body itself, it was quite evident to me that esteem from one's peers on the Body could be assured simply by regularly voicing total support for the organization and, with rare exceptions, by noting which way the majority inclined in discussions and speaking and voting that way. I am not being cynical in saying this. Those few others on the Body who on occasion felt compelled to voice conscientious objections to certain traditional positions, policies or teachings, know—even if they do not express it—that this is so.

Even as it was, I had been assigned to membership on what might be called two of the more influential Governing Body committees, the Writing Committee and the Service Committee. The Writing Committee saw fit to assign me to oversee the development (not to do the actual

---

8   I found Jesus' words at Matthew 23:6 brought to mind by all this.

writing thereof) of a number of publications printed eventually in many languages in the millions of copies.[9]

The "formula," if it may be called that, for maintaining a position of prominence in the organization was easily discernible. But I could not find it conscientiously acceptable.

I would have had to have been blind not to have seen that my expressions on certain issues, motivated by what I felt were clear Scriptural principles, did not please many on the Body. There were times when I went to Governing Body sessions having decided simply not to speak rather than see animosity build. But when issues arose that could seriously affect the lives of people, I found I could not hold back from making some expression. I would have felt guilty not to have done so. I had no illusions that what I said would carry particular weight—in fact I knew from experience that it would more probably only make my own situation more difficult, more precarious. But I felt that if I did not stand for something, for certain principles that I felt were crucial to Christianity, then there was no purpose in being there, for that matter, not much real purpose in life.

It has been mentioned that from about 1978 onward a changed climate began to manifest itself in the Body. The initial euphoria that accompanied the dramatic change in the administration had faded. The spirit of brotherly "comradeship" that seemed to prevail for a time, along with its accompanying expressions of moderation, greater flexibility in viewpoint, had also noticeably diminished. The members had settled into their respective positions on the various Committees and after a time there seemed to be some "muscle flexing" shown on the part of certain ones. Fairly discernible lines began to be evident within the membership, so that it was often not difficult to foresee what the vote was likely to be on an issue.

---

9   These included the books *Is This Life All There Is?* (actual writing by Reinhard Lengtat); *Life Does Have a Purpose* (by Ed Dunlap); *Making Your Family Life Happy* (written principally by Colin Quackenbush); *Choosing the Best Way of Life* (by Reinhard Lengtat); and *Commentary on the Letter of James* (by Ed Dunlap). At the time of resigning I was assigned to oversee the development of a book on the life of Jesus Christ that Ed Dunlap was assigned to write.

If for example, the hands of Milton Henschel, Fred Franz, Ted Jaracz and Lloyd Barry went up, one could *generally* be sure that the hands of Carey Barber, Martin Poetzinger, William Jackson, George Gangas, Grant Suiter and Jack Barr would go up as well. If the hands of the former stayed down, the hands of the latter would generally stay down also. Some others would *likely* vote with these but their vote was not as predictable. With rare exceptions, this pattern prevailed.

The pattern held particularly true if any traditional policy or position was under discussion. One could know beforehand those members who would almost certainly vote in favor of maintaining that traditional policy and against any change therein. Even in the case of the "alternative service" issue, already discussed in a previous chapter, though here outnumbered, these members were still able to prevent a two-thirds majority vote from altering the position on that issue.

In certain controversial cases there seemed to be at least some evidence of "lobbying" on the part of some members. I felt that if anyone wanted to present information apart from the actual session, the better way was to put it in writing and submit copies to all members. Then at least everyone heard the same thing and, in effect, the 'cards were all on the table.' But such written submissions were usually quite rare and, when made, were seldom discussed to any extent.

The Governing Body session of November 14, 1979, was, I believe, a precursor of the traumatic events that violently shook the headquarters in the spring of 1980, resulting in a number of members of the staff being disfellowshipped for "apostasy," and also my own resignation from the Body and from the headquarters staff.

That day we handled four minor issues; each motion carried unanimously. Any sense of harmony that might have existed was quickly broken by a jarring note, however. Grant Suiter said he wished to bring up a matter about which he stated there was "considerable gossip." He said that he had heard reports that some members of the Governing Body and the Writing Department had given talks in which they made comments not in accord with Society teaching and that this was causing confusion. He had also heard, he said, that within the headquarters family staff some were making expressions such as, "When King Saul dies then things will change."[10]

I had never heard anyone in the headquarters family make such a remark. Grant Suiter did not say where he obtained his information or who was the source of the "gossip" he referred to, but he became very intense and both his words and facial expressions reflected strong and heated emotion. And, for the first time, the term "apostasy" surfaced in a Governing Body session.

Considerable discussion followed, with most members indicating they were hearing such things for the first time. In my own expression, I stated that I had given talks all over the United States and in many countries and that in not one of them had I ever made statements contradicting published teachings of the organization. It was rare that talks by a Governing Body member would not be taped by at least someone and, had anything out of line been said, the evidence would be there. In that case, I pointed out, the Body would surely not have to rely on rumor to know about it, for someone would certainly write in about it, asking questions. I asked if Grant Suiter knew personally of any such case on the part of any member of the Body or of the Writing Department? His comment was simply that 'these matters were being talked about,' and that some Branch Committee members attending seminars at the headquarters had said they were "confused" because they had heard some conflicting views from those conducting classes.

The decision was that the Teaching Committee (which had oversight of the seminars) should investigate. At a later session, they reported that they had found no evidence of the things spoken of, that the only "confusion" among the Branch men was about a point developed in a class conducted by Governing Body member Carey Barber. He dealt with Christ's kingdom having commenced in 33 C.E. upon his ascension to heaven and some had difficulty in reconciling this with the teaching about 1914.[11]

---

10   Presumably the reference was to the corporation president (Fred Franz), some apparently believing (mistakenly so) that the presidency still represented the power base it had occupied up until 1976.

11   The official teaching is that upon his ascension, Christ began ruling as king toward his congregation only; that in 1914 he took full power to reign toward all the earth.

The resolution of the matter was an agreement that all Governing Body members would exercise care when speaking on assignments; it was clearly stated in the session, however, that this did not imply any attempt to control private conversations by the members, as among personal friends. This latter stand did not hold up under test.

I found the discussion significant. Although Grant Suiter had not indicated knowing of any case where a Governing Body member had, when on assignment, made comments contrary to published teachings, I knew that some could have been cited. The Body had already considered the occasion of Albert Schroeder's visit to some European branches and his advancing the view that the expression "this generation" might have a meaning different from the published one. Word had reached us about this from more than one place. It was also known that the president, Fred Franz, had introduced a new view regarding the "keys of the kingdom" (referred to at Matthew, chapter sixteen, verse 19) when teaching certain classes in the Gilead School, a view that contradicted published teachings of the organization. This had been done without previous consultation with the Body and the view was presented, not as a suggestion, but as the *correct* view.[12] Entire classes of Gilead graduates went to their assignments with this new view that none of the rest of the brotherhood had even heard about.

None of these cases were brought up in the Governing Body session, however, and I felt no inclination to do so.[13] But I sensed that a definite undercurrent was running that sooner or later would come into the open. And I had no doubt that when it did its force would be directed, not against any such persons, but against myself and, outside the Body, Edward Dunlap.

---

12 Eventually this came before the Body and, after much debate, was finally approved *(not unanimously)* and published in the *Watchtower* of October 1, 1979, pages 16-29.

13 At a meeting (in Chicago I believe) of witness attorneys and doctors, another Governing Body member, Grant Suiter, had invited them to express themselves as to the rightness of the Society's then current position on the use of the term "ordained minister." Though no open statement of disagreement was expressed at that meeting by him, he had made such before the Body, and the response that followed his invitation indicated clearly that those hearing it felt free to criticize that current position.

Due to the sentiment that I could discern on the part of several members, I had already been weighing the advisability of resigning from the Service Committee, thus limiting my participation in committee membership to just the Writing Committee. One day in conversation with Robert Wallen, who acted as secretary for the Service Committee (not himself a Governing Body member), I mentioned that I had about decided to drop off that committee.[14] His response was, "You can't do that. There has to be some balance on the committee." He urged me to change my mind.

However, the same adverse sentiment expressed in the November 14, 1979, session, surfaced in another session and, as I had thought, I now came in for specific mention. In the course of the session, Lloyd Barry, who had the responsibility of seeing that each issue of the *Watchtower* magazine was put together and ready for publishing, voiced strong concern over the fact that I had not placed my initials on a considerable number (he gave the number) of *Watchtower* articles circulated in the Writing Committee. (Each article due to be published was first circulated among the five committee members and their initials written at the top indicated approval.) While not understanding his reason for bringing the matter up in a full session, rather than speaking first to me privately or at a Writing Committee meeting, I acknowledged that what he stated was true. (I was actually surprised to hear the exact number of articles I had not signed since I had kept no count; he had.)

I explained that I had not signed in those cases simply because I could not do so conscientiously. At the same time I had made no effort whatsoever to impede the publication of the particular articles (some of them being articles written by the president on the prophecy of Jeremiah and laying much stress on the 'prophetic role' of the organization and on certain dates, such as 1914 and 1919), nor had I made any effort to create an issue of the matter. The absence of my initials represented abstention, not opposition. I stated before the entire Body that if this was viewed as a problem, if having someone refrain from signing for conscientious reasons was viewed as undesirable, then there was a simple solution. They could

---

14   The other Committee members then were Ted Jaracz (Coordinator), Milton Henschel, Albert Schroeder, William Jackson and Martin Poetzinger.

appoint someone else to serve on the Writing Committee who would not feel such conscientious restraint about approving material. I mentioned at that time my thoughts about resigning from the Service Committee so as to spend more time contributing to the needs of the Writing Department. So I placed the matter in their hands and made it clear that whatever disposition they chose to make would be acceptable to me.

After the session, Lyman Swingle, then the Coordinator of both the Writing Committee and the Writing Department, spoke to me in his office and said: "You can't do that to me. If they decide on their own to replace you on the Writing Committee, all right. But *don't you offer to resign."* He spoke with considerable force. I told him I was simply leaving it up to the Body, but that I was tired of controversy and would be happy for anything that would lessen some of the strain I felt. He repeated his urging.

The Body made no change in my assignment.

Nonetheless I had a strong presentiment of trouble brewing. But I had no way of knowing that within six months I would find myself in the midst of a storm of near fanatical intensity, with the Governing Body reacting with harsh measures to what it viewed as a "conspiracy" of serious proportions, one that threatened the very heart of the organization. Consider, now, what this "dangerous conspiracy" actually was, just how "massive" its proportions were, how great the "criminality" of those involved was, what the justification was for the state of "siege mentality" that developed within the organization and which continues to this day, the events that led up to the "purge" in the spring of 1980.

The day before I took off for Paris on the first leg of my trip to West Africa (November 16, 1979), the Society's president, Fred Franz, was presiding at the morning Bible text discussion (that being his week to serve as chairman). In his comments, he stated that some were questioning the Society's position (set forth in a recent *Watchtower)* that Jesus Christ is the mediator only for the "anointed" ones and not for the other millions of Jehovah's Witnesses.[15] He said of such ones:

---

15   See the *Watchtower* of April 1, 1979, p. 31; November 15, 1979, pp. 21-27.

They would merge everyone together and make Jesus Christ the mediator for every Tom, Dick and Harry.

I could not help but think of all the Toms and Dicks and Harrys there present in the headquarters family and wondered how those words would sound to them. I knew that there was considerable discussion within the family on this subject, some of it definitely unfavorable.

The president went on to affirm that the Society's teaching was right. The one text he referred to in Scripture was Hebrews, chapter twelve, and the words:

> It is for discipline you are enduring. God is dealing with you as sons. For what son is he that a father does not discipline? But if you are without the discipline of which all have become partakers, you are really illegitimate children, not sons.

He then gave the illustration of a horse whose master uses discipline to teach it to walk around in a circle and he stated, "Sometimes it may take a few lashes with the whip to get it to do this." He urged anyone who had doubts about the Society's teaching on this point to hold on, take the discipline and "show that he has the *guts* to stick with it!"[16]

That evening I took off for Paris but for days I felt sickened, not merely by these words, but by the whole approach and spirit I had been witness to for the last few years. For me it was evident from Scripture that Jesus Christ did offer his mediation to bring about reconciliation with God for every Tom, Dick and Harry and that his laying down his life for all persons, his providing the ransom sacrifice and making its benefits available to any and all who might choose to accept them, was the very opposite of the attitude expressed in that headquarters discussion. It seemed that we were hearing "a different good news," not the good news as it was presented by the inspired writers of the first century.

---

16 Ed Dunlap's comment on this afterward was, "I always thought that what enabled us to endure was faith, not 'guts'."

In Africa, the next-to-the-last country I visited was Mali. Most of the missionaries there were French nationals. After working my way through a presentation in French of some points I was covering with missionaries in each country, I asked if they had any questions. The second question presented was, "The *Watchtower* says that Jesus is the mediator only for the anointed, not for the rest of us. Can you clear this up for us? Not even in prayer is he our mediator?"

If it had been my interest to sow doubts, this would have been an obvious opportunity. Instead I tried to calm them, pointing to the First Letter of John, chapter two, verse 1, which speaks of Jesus as the "Helper" of those for whom he is a "propitiatory sacrifice for sins," including those of "the whole world." I said that even if they were not to think of Jesus as their Mediator, they could surely think of him as their Helper. And, that of one thing they could be sure: that his interest in them was as great as his interest in any other persons on earth.

"Witnessing" in Africa

I felt that I had managed to keep the matter from becoming a serious issue with them, and I had said nothing that in any way placed in question the *Watchtower's* statements.

However, a few days later, on going to the airport to depart for Senegal, the missionaries came out to see me off. One of the women missionaries approached and asked me, "But not even in prayer is Jesus our mediator?" I could do nothing but repeat

Locomotive of derailed train.

and reemphasize basically the same points I had presented earlier in their missionary home meeting.

I returned to Brooklyn after about three weeks, the only difficulty encountered in Africa being the derailment of the train on which I was making a twenty-hour, overnight trip from Ouagadougou, Upper Volta, to Abidjan in the Ivory Coast.

Upon my return, the following morning at the breakfast table a visiting Branch Committee member and his wife were seated next to me. Breakfast had barely begun when the wife wanted to know if she could ask me a question. I replied, "You can ask it. I don't know if I can answer it." She said that the previous night they had attended the study of a *Watchtower* dealing with the mediatorship of Christ, and she then asked virtually the same question that the French missionary in Mali had asked. I gave the same answer.

That weekend, I went to New Jersey on a speaking assignment and following the talk a woman in the audience came up (an active Witness) and said she had some questions. There were three questions and the second was about Christ's mediatorship. Once again I gave the same response.

These incidents are cited because they represent my standard practice when questions arose from such persons, questions involving published teachings of the organization. Any question as to the Scriptural backing for the organization's teachings that I myself had, I discussed only with personal acquaintances of long association, every one of them (in the case of men) being elders. Up until 1980, aside from my wife I do not believe there were more than four or five persons on earth who knew to any real extent the concerns I had, and none of these knew all the reasons that caused these concerns. It would have taken a book such as this for them to have known that.

I had not the slightest doubt, however, that many, many others among Jehovah's Witnesses had a number of the same concerns that I did.[17] From my years on the Governing Body I saw no evidence that those concerns would be frankly faced or given the consideration they merited by means of careful, thorough research of the Scriptures, and decided, not on the basis of traditional views long held, but on the basis of the Biblical proof or lack of it.

The evidence pointed instead to the conclusion that any open discussion of these difficulties was viewed as a great danger to the organization, as disloyal to its interests. Unity (actually uniformity) was apparently counted more important than truth. Questions about organizational teachings could be discussed within the inner circle of the Governing Body but nowhere else. No matter how heated the debate on an issue within that inner circle, the Body must present a face of unanimity toward all those on the outside, even though such "face" actually masked serious disagreement on the point in question.

I found nothing in the Scriptures to justify this pretense, for those Scriptures commended themselves as truthful by their very frankness, openness and candor in acknowledging the differences existing among early Christians, including apostles and elders. More importantly I found nothing in Scripture to justify the restricting of discussion to such a secretive, closed society of men, whose two-thirds majority decisions must then be accepted by all Christians as "revealed truth." I did not believe that truth had anything to fear from open discussion, any reason to hide from careful scrutiny. Any teaching that had to be shielded from such investigation did not deserve to be upheld.

From the time of the writing of the reference work called *Aid to Bible Understanding*, I had had close association with Edward Dunlap. I first met

---

17   One day a longtime member of the Service Department approached me, raising a question about an article written by the president. I said I could not answer for the article and suggested he write in his query. He replied. "No, I did that before and got burned." I said that unless people did write in no one would know their concerns. His response was, "If you really want to know how people feel about these articles, tell the Circuit and District Overseers to write in how they feel about some of the articles. But you must tell them NOT to sign their names, otherwise they'll only write what they feel is wanted." He said the same would be true if Bethel Elders were invited to write.

him in 1964 when attending a ten-month course at Gilead School. He was then the Registrar of the School and one of its four instructors. Our class (the 39th) was composed of about one hundred persons, the majority of them men from Branch Offices. It can be truthfully stated that most of them considered Dunlap's classes by far the most instructive as regards gaining understanding of the Scriptures.[18] Originally from Oklahoma, of somewhat rough-hewn appearance, Ed was of ordinary education but had the ability to take very difficult, complex subjects and put them in understandable language, whether it was the functions of the Mosaic Law or a scientific study of genetics. However, more important to me was his unpretentiousness. Aside from a penchant for loud ties, he was a basically low-key, low-profile person, in appearance, demeanor and speech. No matter what responsibility was assigned him, he stayed the same person.

One incident that typified for me his personality was a remark he made to me in connection with a semestral exam. We were going through the various letters of Paul in our classes and each week there was an exam on points studied. Among the points there were generally questions about the likely time and place of writing for each letter. Taken one letter at a time this was not difficult to remember. But when time came for exams at the end of the semester, I realized that now we would have ALL the thirteen Pauline letters involved, and how to remember the different suggested times and places of writing posed a fair-sized problem. They followed no chronological order in the Bible canon. I worked for a long time at it and finally came up with a mental system for recalling these.

The exam came, with a two-hour period for completing it. I finished somewhat early and on leaving the classroom I met Ed coming in. He asked, "How was it?" I replied, "Oh, it wasn't bad. But I'll never forgive you." He asked what I meant. I said, "I worked and worked and worked to develop a system for remembering the times and places of writing of each letter and then you didn't ask a *single* question on that." Taking my remark somewhat more seriously than it was intended, he said, "You

---

18 Lloyd Barry was also in this class and made such expression on more than one occasion while a Governing Body member. I doubt that any others of the students ever had any question as to Ed's deep love for, and knowledge of, the Scriptures.

know the reason I don't put questions on that in the semester exams? I can't keep that stuff in mind myself." There were four instructors for the school, Ulysses Glass, Bill Wilkinson, Fred Rusk and Ed Dunlap. I think it is fair to say that of the four only Ed would have made the reply he did. It was typical of his unassuming personality.

Edward Dunlap

He had always been thoroughly devoted to the organization; his full-time service record equaled mine in length. Another circumstance that tells something about him relates to an illness he developed in the late 1960s. Commonly called *tic douloureux* (a French term meaning "painful spasm"), the medical name for it is *trigeminal neuralgia*, the inflammation of a large, three-branched facial nerve that produces one of the most painful ailments known to humans. The stabbing, blinding pain can be provoked by anything, a slight breeze, a touch, anything that excites the nerve, and as the ailment worsens the victim can hardly do such ordinary things as comb his hair, brush his teeth, or eat, without risking an attack. Some so afflicted are driven to suicide.

Ed suffered with this for seven years, having some temporary remissions and then worsening. During this time, the president, Nathan Knorr, somehow acquired the opinion (based perhaps on others' comments) that this was something emotional on Ed's part, not genuinely of physical origin. One day he talked with Ed, questioning him about his married life and other matters in relation to this ailment. Ed assured him that that had absolutely nothing to do with the problem, that he could be thoroughly enjoying himself on vacation and yet the attacks could strike without warning. The president did not give any weight to Ed's explanation, however, and informed him that he had decided to send him over to the factory for a while to give him more exercise. He was to work in the bindery department.

Ed was then in his sixties, for some time had been taking strong medication prescribed by the staff doctor designed to suppress the painful attacks, at times had been bedridden for days or a week with the ailment.

But he was now sent to the bindery and was there assigned to feed a machine on the bindery line. He did this for months and quietly endeavored to make the best of this "theocratic" assignment. But as he confided to me, it made him realize for the first time the absolute control the organization exercised over his life. His attempts at explaining were ignored and, contrary to all good sense, he was placed in the least desirable situation for one with that kind of ailment.

It was some years later, when he was at the point of absolute despair, that he learned of a neurosurgeon in Pittsburgh who believed he had discovered the cause of this age-old ailment and had perfected microsurgery to remedy it. Ed had the operation (involving the removal of a portion of the skull and remedial operation in connection with the main artery to the brain, which artery runs parallel to the inflamed nerve). He was thus finally cured. He expected no apology from the organization for its serious error in judgment in its viewing and handling of his agonizing problem. He received none.

Since our places of work, both during the *Aid* project and thereafter, were never more than an office apart, we conversed regularly, sharing with each other any interesting items we came across in research. The Writing Committee of the Governing Body assigned us to work together on a number of projects, such as the *Commentary on the Letter of James*. In our conversations we did not always agree on all points, but this did not affect our friendship or mutual respect.

I mention all this because Edward Dunlap was one of the few persons who knew how deep my concerns ran as to what I saw in the organization and particularly within the Governing Body. He shared that concern. Like myself, he did so because he could not harmonize much of what he saw, heard and read with Scripture.

Though associated with the organization since the early 1930s, during most of that association he did not count himself as among the "anointed." I was talking to him about this one day in the late 1970s, and he related that when he began associating in the 1930s the *Watch Tower* then taught that there were two classes who would inherit heavenly life: the "elect" (composed of the 144,000) and the "great company" (or "great crowd" of Revelation chapter seven). The "great company" were said to be Christians of *lesser faith* than the elect and hence, though likewise destined for heavenly life, the "great company" would not be among those who would reign with Christ as kings and priests. Since, of the two classes, one was clearly superior and the other inferior, Ed typically assumed that he must be of the inferior class, the "great company."

Came 1935 and Judge Rutherford, at the Washington D.C., assembly, announced the "revealed truth" that those of the "great company" were Scripturally destined to live, not in heaven, but on earth. As Ed stated, he had always had the hope of heavenly life, felt there could be nothing more wonderful than to serve in the presence of God and in company with his Son. But because of the announced change in organizational viewpoint, he subdued those hopes and accepted what he was told should be his hope as part of the "great company."

It was not until 1979 that he clearly arrived at the decision that no human organization could change the invitation found in Scripture, as by setting a date for a change in the hope the Bible presented as open to any person embracing that hope, whether his name was Tom, Dick, Harry, or Ed. So, forty-four years after 1935 he began to partake of the emblems, the bread and the wine, at the Lord's Evening Meal, something only the "anointed" among Jehovah's Witnesses do.

When a Witness or any one else asks, "How does one know whether he or she is of the 'anointed' class with heavenly hopes?" the standard response is to refer to Paul's statement at Romans 8:16-17:

> The spirit itself bears witness with our spirit that we are God's chil-
> dren. If, then, we are children, we are also heirs, heirs indeed of God, but
> joint heirs with Christ, provided we suffer together that we may also be
> glorified together.

The official teaching has been, and is, that only those of the 144,000 "anointed" can have such 'witness of the spirit,' and that this would tell them that they were of the select group of 144,000 who alone could hope for heavenly life. All others could only be classed as "prospective" children of God and their hopes must be earthly.

In reading the context, from the very start of the chapter, it was evident to Ed that the apostle Paul was indeed writing about two classes. But *not* two classes divided by their hope of either heavenly or earthly life in the future.

The two classes instead clearly were: those guided by God's spirit, on the one hand, and those ruled by the sinful flesh, on the other.

The contrast the apostle set forth was not between hope of life in heaven or of life on earth, but between life and death themselves, between friendship with God or enmity with God. As verses at Romans 8:6-9 state:

> For the minding of the flesh means death, but the minding of the spirit means life and peace; because the minding of the flesh means enmity with God, for it is not under subjection to God, nor, in fact can it be. So those who are in harmony with the flesh cannot please God.
>
> However, you are in harmony, not with the flesh, but with the spirit, if God's spirit truly dwells in you. But if anyone does not have Christ's spirit, this one does not belong to him.

There was no question about heavenly or earthly life in Paul's discussion but simply whether one was living by God's spirit or was instead living according to the sinful flesh. Paul made it clear that it was one thing or the other: Either one had God's spirit and produced its fruitage or he was at enmity with God and did not belong to Christ. Without that spirit there could be no "life and peace," only death. If the person *did* have God's spirit, then he was a son of God, for Paul states (verse 14):

> For all who are led by God's spirit, these are God's sons.[19]

As Ed noted, Paul says, not some, but "ALL who are led by God's spirit" are his sons, his children. Those led by that spirit would have the "witness" of the spirit to that effect, including the evidence of its fruitage in their lives,

---

19 Romans 8:14 — Compare the apostle's use of the same phrase "led by the spirit" in a similar contrast between sinful flesh and God's spirit at Galatians 5:18, where it is stated that those "led by spirit" are "not under law." To deny that this applies to *all* Christians, rather than to a select group, would be to leave all the others still under law and law's condemnation.

somewhat similar to the way the Bible says that Abel, Enoch, Noah and others had "witness borne to them" that they were pleasing to God.[20]

The relevance of these points will become evident as later developments are considered.

Suffice it to say here, that Ed Dunlap shared with me the same basic concerns and particularly the concern over the dogmatism and authoritarian spirit being manifested. His view, like mine, was that human authority, when pushed beyond its proper limits, inevitably detracts from the role of Christ Jesus as Head of the congregation.

Not long after my return from Africa, a longtime friend came by our room at the headquarters. His name was René Vázquez and I had known him for about thirty years. I had first met him in Puerto Rico, in the town of Mayagüez where he lived with his father, who had remarried. René was then a high school student in his teens. Both his father and his father's wife strongly opposed René's studying with Jehovah's Witnesses. Their opposition became so intense that one evening, after having studied at the home of some Witness missionaries, René felt he could not endure any more. He spent the night on a park bench in a public plaza. The following morning he went to the home of an uncle and aunt and asked to be allowed to live with them, to which they agreed. Though not in favor of Jehovah's Witnesses, they were tolerant people. Upon graduation from high school, René immediately took up full time "pioneer service."

Attending an assembly in New York in 1953, he decided to remain in the United States, married, and he and his wife "pioneered" together. They were invited into traveling work among Spanish congregations in the western United States, later attended Gilead School and were sent to Spain. René was soon assigned as District Overseer in that country. The work of Jehovah's Witnesses was under official ban and he and his wife traveled all over Spain, having to be on constant watch for the police and conscious of the danger of being discovered and arrested or deported. All meetings held were clandestine. After years of such "underground" activity, René's nerves had worn thin to the point of breaking. By now he and

20 Hebrews 11:1-7

his wife had been in Spain seven years. Due to his health and some needs within his wife's family, they returned to the United States, paying their own way and arriving with virtually no funds.

On his return, the only job René could find was in a steel mill, lifting heavy loads. A small person, his frail frame gave way the second day, putting him in the hospital. He later found other work and once they had settled their financial problems, he and his wife were right back into "pioneer" service, then into Circuit and District work and finally were asked to become part of the Brooklyn headquarters staff where René was given supervision of the Service Desk caring for all the Spanish congregations in the United States, composed of about thirty thousand Witnesses. He served there until 1969 when his wife became pregnant, requiring them to give up their "Bethel service."

René told me he would try to remain in New York, not because he liked the city, but with the thought that, should his circumstances allow, he could be of some service to the headquarters organization. It turned out that way, and in a few years he was donating his time two days a week to help out, doing Spanish translation, directing the taping of Spanish-language dramas for conventions, as well as doing part-time Circuit and District Overseer work among the scores of Spanish congregations in the New York area. He had spent some time in Portugal and when Portuguese congregations developed, he brushed up on the language and served them also.

In his thirty some years of association with the organization, I seriously doubt that anyone in Puerto Rico, Spain or the United States ever found cause for complaint about René's service. Of a quite gentle nature, he was at the same time a person of principle; he had learned the art, however, of being firm without being hard or harsh. Even given his later situation, which will be presented farther along, I doubt that any of those persons who worked with René Vázquez in any of the places he served would deny that the above is an honest assessment of him as a person. If he had a notable fault, it was, as he himself acknowledges, that he was perhaps too compliant when asked to do something for others, particularly by the Society. He feels today that his family life suffered unnecessarily because of this.

As one example, he and his wife had gone for some years without a true vacation and he had lined up a trip that would take them back to Spain for a visit. Shortly before the time arrived, Harley Miller, then the head of the Service Department, called and asked René to do some Circuit work at that particular time. René felt that the right thing to do was to accept, for he had never turned down an assignment from "the Lord's organization." His wife made the trip to Spain, accompanied by her mother.

René lived near La Guardia airport and members of the Service Department, Harley Miller among them, when traveling by plane on weekend speaking engagements, regularly arranged for René to meet them and transport them to Bethel on their return. Some of the flights arrived near midnight, others even later. René had insisted on providing such service for me and I had accepted on the basis of our long friendship, until I learned to what extent others were making use of his willingness to be helpful. To my mind, his good nature was imposed upon and with rare exceptions; I sought other means of transportation thereafter.

I would think that if the view of the Governing Body were obtainable as to whom they would list as the principal figures in the "conspiracy against the organization" that they took such radical action to wipe out, they would point to us three—Ed, René and myself. Yet there was never an occasion when the three of us spent any time together. During the period involved I had extended conversations with René on perhaps two occasions; the same was true of Ed and René.

What were the supposedly sinister activities we engaged in? Simply this, we discussed the Bible as friends and with friends of long standing.

The night René came by our room, he had been attending a seminar for elders arranged by the Society. We discussed his impressions, which were basically favorable. At one point in the conversation, however, he said, "It seems to me as if we almost worship *figures*. Sometimes I wish we would do away completely with reports." By reports he was referring to the system of having each Witness turn in report slips each month listing what "witnessing" activity was done, including hours spent, literature distributed, and so forth.[21]

I recalled some points made in the previous District Assembly program about "faith and works" and we talked about this and the apostle's statements in Romans on the subject. As I saw it, the apostle's teaching called first of all for building people up in faith; when that was done the works would follow—for genuine faith is productive and active in the same way that genuine love is. One can keep constantly at people to perform certain works and they may do this as a result of pressure. But where is the evidence that the works are generated by faith and love? And if not so motivated, how pleasing would they be to God anyway?

It seemed evident that deeds of faith had to be spontaneous, not systematized or made to conform to a certain mold, just as acts of love should be spontaneous, not something performed out of mere compliance with some scheduled activity programmed by others. Orderly arrangements are fine, but they should be for the purpose of convenience, not as a means of subtle compulsion, used to create a guilt complex in any not 'fitting into the mold.' The more closely men try to supervise the lives and activity of fellow Christians, the more they actually squeeze out the opportunity for faith and love to motivate and control. I acknowledged that it is more difficult and far harder work to build up people's faith and appreciation through Scripture than simply to give "pep talks" or make people feel guilty, but, from what the apostle wrote, that harder way seemed to me to be the only Scripturally right and wise way.

That was the essence of the conversation. The subject of report slips sparked the conversation but thereafter did not figure therein. On meeting up with René in the lobby of one of the buildings sometime later, he

---

21 The importance given to these reports is undeniable. Every Witness reports to the congregation, every congregation reports to the Branch Office of their country, every Branch Office sends a detailed monthly report to the international headquarters where these monthly reports are compiled, averages are figured, percentages of increase are noted. They are studied with the same avid interest that a large corporation would study the figures of its production records, its business growth; any fluctuations or downward trends in the number of Witnesses reporting time, the hours reported or the distribution of literature, become causes for concern. Branch representatives become uneasy if the monthly reports for their country fail to show increase or, worse, show a decrease.

said he found that approaching matters in the light of Paul's writings in Romans made his Circuit and District Overseer work far more enjoyable, his discussion with elders more meaningful.

Some weeks later my wife and I went to his home for a meal. Though we two couples had been together in the same Spanish-speaking congregation in Queens, New York, during our first years in the city, since then our getting together had been quite sporadic. Both before and after the meal, René wanted to discuss the message of Romans. Though to a lesser degree than with my wife, I felt an obligation to respond to his questions rather than evade issues. I had known him for thirty years; I knew him to be a serious student of the Scriptures. I spoke to him as a friend, not as an organizational official, and in discussing the Word of God with him I felt my prime responsibility was to God, not to men, not to an organization. If I held back from speaking to persons like this on what I saw to be clear-cut teachings of Scripture, how could I say as Paul did in his words to the Ephesian elders, recorded at Acts, chapter twenty, verses 26 and 27:

> I call you to witness this very day that I am clean from the blood of all men, for I have not held back from telling you all the counsel of God.

Paul knew that it was doing this that had resulted in his being spoken of injuriously within the synagogue of Ephesus.[22] I knew, as well, that my speech could produce similar results.

Among other sections, we discussed the first portion of the eighth chapter of Romans (considered earlier in this chapter of this book). I was interested to know how he viewed verse 14, as to the sonship relation to God, when considered in the light of the context. He had never examined it contextually (as is probably true of practically all of Jehovah's Witnesses). When he did, his reaction was both spontaneous and stirring. What to others might seem obvious, can strike one of Jehovah's Witnesses as if it were a revelation. René's comment was, "For years I have had the feeling that I was resisting holy Spirit when reading the Christian Scriptures. I would be reading along and applying to myself everything I read, then

---

22 Acts 19:8, 9.

suddenly I would stop and say, 'But these things do not apply to me, they apply only to the anointed.'"

I know, he knows and God knows that I used no persuasion to cause him to see matters differently. It was the apostle's own words in the Bible, read contextually, that did the persuading. His expression on a later incidental contact was that the Scriptures as a whole came alive with far greater meaning to him from that point forward.

Though it may seem strange, for one of Jehovah's Witnesses (not of the about 9,100 "anointed") to come to the conclusion that the words found from Matthew to Revelation *are* directed to him and *do* apply, not merely "by extension," but actually and directly, causes a door to open to a whole host of questions, questions that have often been longing for an answer but which did not dare to be asked.

When I review what has been done in recent times in an effort to uphold the organization's interpretations, the manipulation of Scripture and fact, I can only feel grateful that I did not let concern for an organization's favor hold me back from pointing at least some persons to the Scriptures on these points.

On March 4, 1980, I submitted a request to the Personnel Committee of the Governing Body for a leave of absence to extend from March 24 to July 24. My wife and I both felt that our health demanded an extended change. During that period I also hoped to investigate what possibility there was of finding employment and somewhere to live if we were to terminate our headquarters service. We had about $600 in a savings account and a seven-year-old car as our major assets.

When attending District Assemblies in Alabama, we had previously met and become acquainted with a Witness named Peter Gregerson. Later he had invited us to visit Gadsden, Alabama, on a couple of occasions so that I could speak to the local congregations. Peter had developed a small chain of supermarkets in the Alabama-Georgia area. In 1978, when a "zone trip" took my wife and me as far as Israel, Peter and his wife joined us there and we spent parts of two weeks touring that Bible land.

At that time Peter expressed serious concern about the effects the 1975 predictions had had. He said he thought it would be a grave error if the Society pushed strongly on their 1914 date; that the disillusionment resulting from 1975 would be nothing compared with what would come if the Society was forced to move away from that 1914 chronology. I acknowledged his assessment as undoubtedly correct but we went no further into the matter.

When Peter learned of our proposed leave of absence, he urged us to spend some time with them and fixed up a mobile home belonging to one of his sons for us to stay in. He offered to let me do yard work on his property to help cover some of our expenses and at the same time get some of the vigorous exercise that had been medically recommended for me at a recent physical exam.[23]

Peter's father had become one of Jehovah's Witnesses when Peter was a small child, and from about the age of four he had been taken by his parents to meetings. As a young man he had become a full-time "pioneer" and even after marriage and the arrival of his first child he had struggled to keep on in that full-time activity, doing janitorial work for income.[24] He had been sent by the Society into "problem" areas in Illinois and Iowa to help solve difficulties and build up certain congregations. In 1976 he was one of a representative group of elders invited to Brooklyn for discussions with the Governing Body.

A year or so after this seminar, however, he decided to relinquish his eldership. He had recently turned over the presidency of the grocery company to one of his brothers and had made use of his increased free time to do more Bible study. He was troubled by some of the organization's teachings and wanted to reaffirm his convictions as to their rightness, reestablish his confidence in his lifelong religion. (He was then in his early fifties.)

The result was exactly the opposite. The more he studied the Scriptures, the more convinced he became that there were serious errors in the organization's theology. This led to his decision as to ceasing his eldership. As he put it in talking with me about it, "I just can't bring myself to stand before people and conduct studies on things that I cannot see have a Scriptural backing. I would feel like a hypocrite doing that and my conscience won't

---

23   See Chapter 12, "Aftermath" footnote #5.
24   He and his wife now have seven children and about seventeen grandchildren.

let me do it." Although when first hearing his decision, I had encouraged him to reconsider it, I could not deny the validity of his serious questions, and I had to respect his conscientiousness and his distaste for hypocrisy. He had reached his personal crossroads before I reached mine.

This was the man that organizational policy later categorized as a "wicked man" with whom one should not even eat and my having a meal with him in a restaurant in 1981 resulted in my trial and banishment from the organization.

It was in April, 1980, while we were in Gadsden on leave of absence that I first began to hear of what seemed to me to be strange occurrences back in Brooklyn. The expected storm had begun to break upon us.

INQUISITION

When he left the house, the scribes and the Pharisees began a furious attack on him and tried to force answers from him on innumerable questions, setting traps to catch him out in something he might say.
— Luke 11:53, 54, *Jerusalem Bible.*

An inquisition, in the religious sense, is an *inquiry* into individuals' personal convictions and beliefs.

Historically, its aim has been—not to aid the individual, or to provide basis for reasoning with him—but to incriminate, to convict as heretical.

The initiating cause for the inquiry often has nothing to do with the individual's being disruptive, malicious or even being particularly vocal about his beliefs. Mere suspicion is sufficient cause to set in motion the inquisitory action. The suspect is viewed as, in effect, having no rights: even his personal conversations with intimate friends are treated as something the inquisitors have full right to delve into.

It was not solely the atrocious acts of punishment meted out in the Spanish Inquisition that earned it such a despised name in history. It was also the authoritarian approach and arrogant methods of interrogation employed to gain the incrimination so often zealously pursued by the religious judicial court. The torture and the violent punishment meted out then are outlawed today. But the authoritarian approach and arrogant methods of interrogation can still be practiced with apparent impunity.

I am reminded here of an article in the January 22. 1981, issue of the *Awake!* magazine, titled "Searching Out Legal Roots." It emphasized the superb legal precedents found in the Mosaic Law and, among other things, said:

> Since the local court was situated at the city gates, there was no question about the trial being public! (Deut. 16:18-20) No doubt the public trials helped influence the judges toward carefulness and justice, qualities that sometimes vanish in secret star-chamber hearings.

This principle was praised in the Society's publication. In actual practice it was totally rejected. As Jesus said, "They say one thing and do another."[25] The "secret star-chamber hearings" were preferred, as the evidence clearly shows. Only fear of the power of truth prompts that kind of proceedings. Those methods serve, not the interests of justice or mercy, but the cause of those who seek to incriminate.

The *Awake!* magazine of April 22, 1986 also relates:

> Anyone—man, woman, child or slave—could accuse a person of heresy, without fear of being confronted with the accused or of the latter even knowing who had denounced him. The accused rarely had someone to defend him, since any lawyer or witness in his behalf would himself have been accused of aiding and abetting a heretic. So the accused generally stood alone before the inquisitors, who were at the same time prosecutors and judges.

Four weeks after starting my leave of absence, while in Alabama, a phone call came from Ed Dunlap. After some general conversation, he told me that two members of the Governing Body, Lloyd Barry and Jack Barr, had come into his office and had interrogated him about his personal beliefs for about three hours. At one point Ed asked, "What's the purpose

---

25   Matthew 23:3, *NEB.*

of this 'third degree'?" They assured him that it was not a "third degree" but that they simply wanted to hear how he felt about some matters.

They gave him no explanation as to what motivated their interrogation. Despite their claim that the discussion was simply informative, Ed's distinct impression was that it was the start of an organizational action that would prove both inquisitorial and punitive. Their questions inquired into his view of the organization, the teachings about 1914, the two classes of Christians and the heavenly hope, and similar points.

As regards the organization, he told his interrogators that his major concern was the obvious lack of Bible study on the part of the members of the Governing Body, that he felt that they had an obligation to the brothers to make such study and research of the Scriptures a primary concern, instead of allowing themselves to become so preoccupied with paper work and other affairs that Bible study got crowded out. As to 1914, he frankly acknowledged that he felt it was something that one should not be dogmatic about, and he asked them if the Governing Body itself believed this was something completely solid, certain. The reply from the two men was that 'while there were one or two who had doubts, the Body as a whole supported the date fully.' He told them that if others in the Writing Department expressed themselves it would be evident that almost all had different views on certain points.

On another day, Albert Schroeder and Jack Barr began a person-by-person interrogation of each member of the Writing Department. None of these acknowledged the uncertainty they felt about specific teachings, though in personal conversation virtually every one had some point that he had expressed a different view on.

The ironical feature of this was the diversity of viewpoint existing within the Governing Body itself, something that the interrogators themselves personally knew but never mentioned or acknowledged to those they questioned.

I knew that Lyman Swingle, the coordinator of the Writing Committee of the Governing Body and the coordinator of the Writing Department, was away on a zone trip. I found it puzzling that such an intensive investigation should be initiated in his absence. Yet the Governing Body members doing the investigating had given no indication that anything out of the ordinary had arisen that should call for such a full-scale inquiry. From experience with the organization, I felt that this absence of any explanation for their action was indicative, not of something innocuous or benign, but of something that, when it came into the open, could prove quite devastating to those affected by it. For that reason, on Monday, April 21, 1980, I phoned the Brooklyn headquarters from Alabama and asked to speak to Governing Body member Dan Sydlik. He was not available, the Society's telephone operator informed me. I then asked to speak to Governing Body member Albert Schroeder, who was acting Chairman of the Body that year. He likewise was not available. I left a message with the operator that I would appreciate it if one or the other would phone me.

The next day, a call came from Albert Schroeder.

Before considering the conversation and the way he, as the Chairman of the Governing Body answered my questions, consider what I eventually learned had already happened and was in the process of happening at the time he talked to me.

On April 14, eight days before Schroeder returned my call, a Witness in New York named Joe Gould phoned the Brooklyn Service Department and talked to Harley Miller, a member of the five-man Service Department Committee.[26] He told Miller that a fellow employee, a Cuban Witness named Humberto Godínez, had told him of a conversation in his home with a friend who was a Bethel family member. He said that the Bethel family member expressed himself on a number of points that differed from the organization's teachings. Miller recommended to Gould that he try to find out from Godínez the name of the Bethel family member. This was done and the name of Cris Sánchez was supplied. Godínez also said that my name and those of Ed Dunlap and René Vázquez came into the conversation. Miller did not recommend to Gould and Godínez that they endeavor to clarify matters with those involved nor to seek a solution through brotherly discussion. Miller did not speak to Ed Dunlap who was well known to him and in an office just across the street from him. He did

---

26   This committee supervises the Service Department, at that time composed of a staff of about forty persons.

not make a phone call to René Vázquez whom he had known for years and whose services as voluntary chauffeur he regularly employed. He did not endeavour to contact Cris Sánchez who worked in the Society's factory and was accessible by telephone.

Instead, he first spoke to the members of the Service Department Committee asking them if any of them could supply any similar information. He then went to the Chairman of the Governing Body, Albert Schroeder.

He was told to arrange for Godínez and his wife to come to the headquarters for an interview with Miller. Nothing was said to Cris Sánchez, Ed Dunlap or René Vázquez, nor was anything communicated to me. The Chairman's Committee of the Governing Body evidently felt that to have acted in such a friendly way, thereby endeavoring to keep the matter from becoming a major issue, was not the desirable way to proceed.

During Miller's interview with the Godínezes, he suggested to Humberto Godínez that he phone René Vázquez and "tactfully" see if he would express himself about the matter. Miller himself did not see fit to do so, nor did he consider it advisable to phone Ed Dunlap or walk across the street to talk to him about the matter. The phone call to René was made and the apparent goal was achieved, René responded in a way that could be viewed as incriminating. Another interview with the Godínez couple was arranged, this time with the Chairman's Committee, composed of Governing Body members Schroeder, Suiter and Klein, present. This was held on Tuesday, April 15. Still nothing had been said to René, Ed, Cris or myself. The interview ran two hours and was taped. Through Godínez' recollections and impressions, they heard of his conversation with fellow Cuban and longtime friend Cris Sánchez, following a meal in the Godínez home. A number of controversial points were discussed. Godínez' presentation included numerous references to René, Ed Dunlap and myself. At the close of the taping, each of the three Governing Body members, Schroeder, Suiter and Klein, commended the Godínez couple for their loyalty and expressed (on tape) their disapproval of those who had been implicated by the interview.

Like Miller, the Chairman's Committee of the Governing Body had made no effort to talk to Cris Sánchez, about whom they had heard only hearsay evidence. They had made no effort to talk with René Vázquez, Ed Dunlap or myself, about whom they had heard only third-hand information. Yet the next day, Wednesday, April 16, 1980, at the regular Governing Body session, the Chairman's Committee played the entire two-hour tape of the interview to the Body (Milton Henschel, Lyman Swingle and myself being absent).

All this had taken place one week before Schroeder spoke to me on the phone, a phone call that he made only at my request.

It was after this playing of the tape to the Governing Body that the questioning of Ed Dunlap and, subsequently, of the entire Writing staff took place. It was that tape that motivated the questioning. The Governing Body members who did the questioning, Barry, Barr and Schroeder, knew that was the case. Yet they said nothing about it, even when Barry and Barr were asked by Ed Dunlap the reason for the interrogation. Why?

The action taken was swift, extensive, coordinated. Both Cris Sánchez and his wife and also Nestor Kuilan and his wife were now interrogated. Cris and Nestor both worked in the Spanish Translation Department where René served two days a week.

Harley Miller now phoned René and asked him if he would come to the office, saying, "We just want to pick your brains a little on some points."

The Chairman's Committee had arranged for investigating committees to be formed to handle the interrogation of these different ones. With the exception of Dan Sydlik, all the men on these committees were staff members outside the Governing Body. The Governing Body through its Chairman's Committee directed all the actions but from this point on remained in the background. They now arranged to have the various men serving on these investigative committees listen to portions of the two-hour tape that had been played to the Body so as to equip them for their committee action. That is why these committees subsequently used my name and Ed's name repeatedly in their questionings of Sánchez, Kuilan and Vázquez. Yet the Chairman's Committee had still not seen fit to inform *us* that the tape even existed. Why?

The objective of the investigating committees was evident from the direction their questionings took. The committee interrogating Nestor

Kuilan asked him to describe his personal conversations with Ed Dunlap and myself. He replied that he did not think his personal conversations were something others had a right to inquire into. He made clear that if he felt that anything wrong or "sinful" had been said he would not hesitate to inform them, but that this was certainly not the case. His questioners told him he should 'cooperate or he would be subject to possible disfellow-shipping.' His response was, "Disfellowshipping? For what?" The reply was, "For covering over apostasy." Kuilan said, "Apostasy? Where is the apostasy? Who are the apostates?" They answered that this was still being determined, but that they were quite sure that such existed.

This is somewhat like a man's being threatened with imprisonment unless he cooperates by giving information about certain persons, and when he asks why, he is told that the imprisonment would be for complic-ity in a bank robbery. When he asks, "What bank was robbed and who are the robbers?" he is told, "Well, we don't know yet what bank was robbed or who did it, but we're quite sure there was a bank robbery somewhere and unless you answer our questions we will find you guilty of complicity and you will be subject to imprisonment."

Nestor explained that he had studied in Gilead School under Ed Dunlap as one of his instructors and so knew him since then, and that he had known me from the time I served as a missionary and Branch Overseer in Puerto Rico. He acknowledged that he had conversed with each of us on occasion but that those conversations involved nothing sin-ful or bad and were his personal affair.

By April 22, when Albert Schroeder responded to my request and phoned me, the judicial machinery of the organization was in full opera-tion and moving rapidly. As Chairman of the Governing Body he, better than anyone else, knew all these facts, for all the investigating committees involved were under the direction of the Chairman's Committee.

He knew that his Committee had had the earlier-mentioned two-hour tape played to the Governing Body one week before his phone call.

He knew that the various investigating committees had all been "briefed," hearing portions of the tape and that, at the very time he spoke to me, they were using my name, along with that of Ed Dunlap, in their interrogations.

He knew that the extremely grave charge of "apostasy" was included in the committee hearings. He had to know the very serious effect this could have on us two men he had known for decades, men he called his "brothers."

What, then, was said to me in his phone conversation? Consider:

After a brief exchange of greetings, I said, "Tell me, Bert, what's going on in the Writing Department?"

His reply was:

> Well—the Governing Body thought it well that some of us make an investigation of the Department to see what could be done to improve the coordination, cooperation and efficiency of the Department—and— to see if any of the brothers had reservations on some points.

This final expression, as to persons having reservations, was stated in a rather offhand way as if of secondary importance. He had had a clear opportunity to tell me the facts as to what was taking place. He chose not to do so.

I then asked what reason there could be for such a full-scale investigation? He now had a second opportunity to give me an honest explanation of the situation. His answer was:

> Well, the Department isn't operating as efficiently as it should. The book for this summer's convention is going to be late getting to the factory.

A second time he chose to give an evasive answer rather than a straightforward reply to my question. As to his statement, I replied that this was nothing new, but that the previous year both the *Commentary on the Letter of James* (written by Ed Dunlap), and the book *Choosing the Best Way of Life* (written by Reinhard Lengtat) had reached the factory by the first part of January, in good time. (I knew this since it was my assigned responsibility to see that these books were developed on time. The book for 1980, titled *Happiness, How to Find It,* was being written by Gene Smalley, who had never written a book before, and the project was not under my supervision.) I added that I didn't see why this should be cause for such an investigation.

Schroeder continued:

> And then some of the brothers aren't very happy about the way their
> articles are being reworked. Ray Richardson said he had turned an article
> in [here he gave the subject of the article] and he was very unhappy with
> the way it was worked over.

I said, "Bert, if you know anything at all about writers you know that
no writer likes to have his material undergo 'surgery.' But that is nothing new either; as long as there's been a Writing Department it's been
that way. What does Lyman [Swingle, the Coordinator of the Writing
Department] think about this?"

He replied, "Oh, Lyman isn't here now."

"I know he isn't there," I answered, "he's on a zone trip. Have you
written to him?"

"No," he said.

I then stated, "Bert, I find this very strange. If for example, Milton
Henschel [the Coordinator of the Publishing Committee which supervises
all factory operations] were away and another member of the Publishing
Committee were away, let's say Grant Suiter, and reports came to the
Governing Body that the factory there was not functioning as efficiently
as it should—do you think that the Governing Body would begin a full-
scale investigation of the factory and its operations in the absence of those
two brothers?" (I knew such an action would not even be contemplated.)

He hesitated somewhat and said, "Well, the Governing Body asked us
to do this and we're simply making a report to them. We're going to make
our report tomorrow."

My response was, "Well, I'd appreciate it if you would express my feelings on the matter. I think it's an insult to Lyman Swingle, to the man, to
his years of service and to his position to take an action like this without
consulting him or even letting him know."

Schroeder said he would convey this expression. I added that if there
was anything of genuinely great importance that required discussion, I
could always go up there. He said, "You could?" I replied, "Of course I
could. It would simply be a matter of taking a plane and going up there."
He asked if I could come the following Wednesday. I replied, "What

would be the purpose if Lyman Swingle won't be there then?" The conversation ended there.

The Chairman of the Governing Body of Jehovah's Witnesses had had multiple opportunities to respond openly and honestly to my requests for information by saying, "Ray, what we feel is a very serious matter has come up and there are even charges of apostasy being made. We think you should know that your name has been involved and before we do anything we thought the only Christian thing to do was to talk to you first."

He could have done that. Instead he said nothing, not one word, to indicate that this was the case. Of course, he could not very well have made the latter part of that statement since he and the other members of the Chairman's Committee had already put into motion a large-scale operation of tapings, investigating committees and interrogations. The picture given me by the Governing Body representative was, plainly put, deceptive, fictitious. But I had no way of knowing then just how deceptive and fictitious it was. I soon began to learn, but primarily from sources outside the Governing Body.

If the conduct of the Governing Body and its Chairman's Committee in this regard is difficult to understand, I consider it even more inexplicable—and unjustifiable—that they were not open and above board with Ed Dunlap who was right there at the headquarters. When he asked Barry and Barr what the purpose of their interrogation was, simple fairness should have moved them to tell him why the Governing Body assigned them to question him, what serious, even grave charges were being made. Certainly Scriptural principles, including the statement of the Lord Jesus Christ that we should do to others as we would have them do to us, would have *demanded* that someone say to his face what accusations of "apostasy" were being made behind his back. The ones who knew this chose not to do so at that time. They chose not to do so for *nearly a month thereafter.* Yet his name, like mine, was passed on to the members of investigating committees and then of judicial committees—to at least a dozen or more men—and *still* no one from the Governing Body approached him to tell him what grave charges were being linked to his name. *Yet many of them saw him on a daily basis.*

I do not understand how that course of action can be considered worthy of the name Christian.

On Friday, April 25, just three days after Schroeder's phone call in response to my request, judicial committees, operating under the sanction and direction of the Chairman's Committee of the Governing Body, disfellowshipped Cris Sánchez and his wife and Nestor Kuilan. René Vázquez and his wife were also disfellowshipped by another committee as was an elder of a congregation adjoining that in which René served. The names of all except the congregation elder were read out to the entire headquarters staff, stating that they had been disfellowshipped. The Governing Body thus informed well over a thousand five hundred persons. They did not see fit to inform me. I eventually heard it, of course, but from phone calls from those so treated, not from any of my fellow members on the Governing Body.

Diane Beers, who had been serving as a member of the headquarters staff for ten years and who was well acquainted with the Sánchezes and Kuilans, described her impression of the events of the week of April 21 to 26 in this way:

> I think the thing that was impressed on my mind the most during that week was the cruel way these friends were being treated. They never knew when they would be required to go to a committee meeting. Suddenly the phone would ring and there would go Cris. Then he would come back, the phone would ring and there would go Nestor. On and on it went. They were kept constantly up in the air during that week. One day when I was talking to Norma [Sánchez], she told me that the committee wanted her to talk to them without Cris there and she didn't know what to do. I suggested that Cris should be there at all times because otherwise she would never have a witness to what they said to her and how she replied. They could say anything, and she would have no way of proving that it was different. It was becoming apparent that they were trying to pit Norma against Cris.
>
> Finally on Friday afternoon [April 25] at 4:45 pm, the Committee came marching on to the 8th floor where we all worked and headed for the conference room that was directly behind my desk. Shortly, everyone

began to leave work and go home, but I stayed around to see what the outcome would be. They called Cris and Norma and Nestor and Toni in and as they each came out, I went to see what the 'verdict' was. I remember that when I went into Nestor's office to talk to Toni and him, they told me I had better leave before I too got into trouble for being seen with them. I walked home by myself fighting all the way not to break down in tears. I was just devastated. I couldn't believe what was happening. It's a feeling I will never forget. This place had been my home for many years and I had enjoyed my time there—now it was like I was in a place totally foreign to me. I thought about Christ saying that by their fruits you will know them and I just couldn't reconcile what I had seen and heard about during that week as being Christian. It was so harsh and unloving. These were people who had given years and years of service to the Society, had good reputations and were much loved by everyone. And yet no mercy could be shown to them. It was incomprehensible to me.

I had a meeting that evening, but I refused to go as I was just too upset. Later on that evening when Leslie [Diane's roommate] had come home from the meeting, we were talking and we heard a knock at the door. This was around 11:00 pm. It was Toni Kuilan: She didn't even get in the door before she broke down and just sobbed. She didn't want Nestor to know how upset she was. We all sat there and cried together and talked. We let her know that she and Nestor were our friends now the same as always and tried to encourage her as best we could. I couldn't sleep very good that night and got up once around 2:00 or 3:00 in the morning. I just sat in the bathroom thinking about what had happened and felt like it was a nightmare—it didn't seem real to me.

Saturday morning I went to see Nestor and Toni and Cris and Norma and when I got to Kuilan's room, they had just had a visit from John Booth [a member of the Governing Body]. He was sent to tell them that their appeal had been rejected by the Governing Body. The committee had told them Friday evening that they had to have the appeal in by that next morning at 8:00 am. This in itself was ridiculous, but they complied and had an appeal in by 8:00 am. Booth was sent to tell them No. Nestor asked him why and he told him that he [Booth] was just a 'messenger boy'—he made it obvious that he did not want to discuss anything with any of them.

Here were people who had been associated for decades, had given many years of their life wholesouled and full time to what they believed was God's service, and yet in the space of six days, from Monday, April 21 to April 26, all that was set aside and they were disfellowshipped. During that week, when Scriptures were employed by their interrogators, it was in an accusatory, condemnatory way, not in the way that the apostle Paul describes at Second Timothy, chapter two, verses 24 and 25, when he instructs:

> And the Lord's servant must not quarrel; instead he must be kind to everyone, able to teach, not resentful. Those who oppose him he must gently instruct, in the hope that God will give them a change of heart leading them to a knowledge of the truth.—*New International Version.*

I believe it speaks poorly for any religion if it is unwilling to take time to reason with persons by means of God's Word—not for a few hours or even a few days, but for weeks or months—when those persons question the Scripturalness of that religion's teachings. When those being interrogated at the headquarters brought up Scriptural points, they were told in so many words, "We are not here to discuss your Bible questions." Harley Miller told René Vázquez, "I don't claim to be a Bible scholar. I try to keep up with the Society's publications and that is about all I can do." In the minds of the interrogators the prime issue was, not loyalty to God and his Word, but loyalty to the organization and its teachings. In this, as has already been shown; they had ample backing from the publications of the Society.

It can be truthfully said that none of the persons disfellowshipped had had any thought of separating themselves from Jehovah's Witnesses nor had they any thought of encouraging others to separate. Their attitude is poignantly expressed in this letter written by René Vázquez in appealing the disfellowshipping action taken against him and his wife:

Rene Vazquez
31-06 81 Street
Jackson Heights, NY 11370

May 4, 1980

Judicial Committee
c/o Claudius Johnson
1070 E 174 Street   Apt. 6 A
Bronx, NY 10472

Dear brothers:

I find it necessary once again by this means to appeal to your
sound reasoning and impartial judgement and see that we are not
guilty of the accusation brought against us, my wife and I. We, in
fact do not really understand or know who our accusers are.

During our hearing, time and again, we stated from the heart,
in all truthfulness before Jehovah God that the very idea of
promoting a sect or being apostate is utterly unthinkable on our
part. Is this not borne out by my dedicated service to Jehovah God
for the past 30 years, to the extent of giving minimal attention to
my own family and to my secular work? Why should my recent actions
in regard to discussing some Bible points in private conversation
with some dear brothers and friends, all of a sudden be taken as an
attack on the organization or as apostasy? Why should such extreme
action as disfellowshiping be taken, when sound reasoning, kindness,
true christian love and mercy, could mend and heal any miunderstandings
or heartache that resulted from imprudent talk or repetition of things
not in harmony with what has been published by the Society? Where
is the evil, wicked person, the hater of Jehovah, the rebellious
individual, the unrepentant doer of wicked acts that should be
stamped out? Why should a legalistic definition of apostasy be used
in such a cold and unmerciful way to condemn people who have done
nothing but serve faithfully and pour out their souls in behalf of
the brothers for so many years?

Who are the ones causing reproach on Jehovah's name and giving
a bad name or image to the organization? Are not the drastic actions
that are being taken, and the unloving methods being used, and the
slanderous rumors being spread, and the lack of mercy and christian
love, the suspicion, fear and terror of inquisitory investigations,
multiplying a thousand times any misunderstanding or unintentional
harm due to people repeating improperly some things said?

Brothers, there is nothing but love in our hearts for the entire
association of our brothers, and in no way has my wife or I ever wanted
to act with or had any evil design to cause confusion or disturbance of
their faith. How would Christ Jesus handle a situation like this?

It appears that the main objective of the committee was to establish
guilt by establishing that there was apostasy. In spite of our repeated
expressions from the heart, that pursuing a course of apostasy is

Judicial committee
May 4, 1980
Page 2

unthinkable, that such a thing never came into our heart, that charge continued to be pressed. The committee appears to have been committed to proving that we were apostates by showing that private personal conversations we had with some of our dear friends, were in fact part of an evil scheme to form a sect or cause a division by apostasy. In two different occasions Brother Harold Jackson used the illustration of a young girl who committed fornication, but the idea of doing that was so rejected by her mind, that she in fact believed that she did not commit fornication, but she was pregnant. The application would be that no matter how abhorrent is to us the idea of being apostates, that no matter if our heart and conscience tell us that it is unthinkable for us to do such a thing, still we are apostates.

But brothers, we know the difference between our right and left hand. This is not the case of a young girl lacking in understanding and experience. But for the sake of argument, even if such were the case, that we are something that we are not, because we are not in our heart, mind and conscience, how would Christ Jesus handle the matter? Would he not extend his lovingkindness and mercy to that girl, so that sin may not rule as king because he died so that we may be shown mercy?

On the other hand, would it be the wisdom from above to use the example of that girl as a principle to judge another case where the girl is sure that she did not commit fornication but her belly is big? What if proper examination shows that she had a cyst in her womb, so that she was in fact telling the truth, but was so pressed by questionings and mental anguish that she would be made to suffer, and in addition to that, slanderous rumors would begin to circulate saying that she was pregnant, that she was going to have twins, that she already gave birth to triplets, and so on. Would that not be a great injustice? Who would be the ones causing the real harm? Would not the love and mercy of Christ Jesus avoid such a great injustice?

For this very same reason Christ Jesus told those who condemned him for doing works of healing on the Sabbath: "Stop judging from the outward appearance, but judge with righteous judgement."--John 7:24

Brother Episcopo, as one on the judicial committee, stated, by a number of leading questions, that an apostate could be very sincere in what he would be teaching, but he still was an apostate. The application would be that in spite of our continued expressions indicating that such an apostate course of action is unthinkable on our part, that we have never engaged in any evil design against the organization, nor in forming a sect, that we still are to be dealt with as apostates because of the things we discussed in our private conversations with our friends.

However, if we were to use that definition of apostasy, then we would have to conclude that our history as an organization as Jehovah's witnesses is full of acts of apostasy. When we were teaching that the invisible presence of Christ Jesus began in 1874, we were very sincere. But Jehovah knew that what we were teaching was not in harmony with bible truth. Then He would have to have considered us apostates, by the definition put forth by Brother Episcopo. Time and again, as an

Judicial Committee
May 4, 1980
Page 3

organization we have taught, with godly devotion and sincerity, what resulted not to be in harmony with the Word of God, and the faith of many was disturbed when things did not turn out to be the way we taught. Would it be in harmony with mercy and love to judge the organization as apostate on that basis? Would it be sound reasoning to put the organization in the class of Hymeneaus and Philetus, who were subverting the faith of others, saying that the resurrection had already occurred?

The basis of the action against us is our having discussed certain points from the Bible with a few brothers in private conversation with them. One of the fundamental privileges each one has as an individual is that of talking confidentially to a friend or trusted person. If this privilege is taken away, or if we are told that we have to confess such confidential talk and then be judged on the basis of such expressions, or if the individuals we took into our confidence are forced by fear of action against them, to accuse us of talking to them, what sort of subjection are we demanding as an organization? Would not that become total subjection or absolute subjection? Would'nt that be in effect violating the headship of Christ Jesus over the congregation?

We can give various examples of such kind of conversations in the past on the part of many, including some of those in our committee, of things not published or taught by the organization. If I know of such conversations, how many more know or knew about them? To how many did they speak about those things? Should we now start an inquisitory investigation to determine that, and to argue that they are apostate? The very reason that I did not mention such examples, giving names, is that I know it would be unjust to do such a thing. We did not want to give the idea that we were pointing the finger at someone else. Are the brothers now to be under an atmosphere of terror so that the very mention of reading the Bible at home would be viewed as suspicious and possible apostasy, or should we say "heresy."?

In our hearing, when I expressed that we were very sorry for the disturbance that somehow was traced back to us due to a very imprudent repetition of some points to a number of brothers, and when we gave the assurance that we would in no way again talk about such things to others, but rather tell anyone who would mention such things that such talk should be stopped, brother Harold Jackson strongly stated that I had to give them some kind of assurance about that, and then proceeded to say that we were a danger to the organization, and to imply that I was following a pattern of covering up things, and that he did not personally believe what I was saying. What is the direction given in the bible in this regard? How can that "assurance" be given? Even if there were valid reason for someone to be accused of promoting a sect, Titus 3:10 says: "As for a man that promotes a sect, reject him after a first and second admonition." The second admonition would be due to the individual's _continuing_ with _new offenses_ indicating that he insisted on promoting a sect. Even if we were viewed as that kind of persons, from the very first unfortunate misunderstanding, we have

Judicial Committee
May 4, 1960
Page 4

even become abnormally non-comunicative in order to avoid any further
misunderstanding. Since a mere verbal assurance would not be enough,
as implied by the counsel of Paul, the conduct of the individual,
not necessitating a second admonition, and then a re-ocurrence of the
wrong, would be the assurance needed. Even that benefit of the doubt
is not given to us.

More than one time it was stated by brother Jackson that the
things comented constituted an attack on the very heart of the
organization. But in the first place, such attack does not exist,
and I personally do not know of anyone conducting an attack. Could
it be that an expression is being used which was coined by an
undiscerning person who made a hasty judgement and made a complaint?
Should a statement, or hasty judgement like that, all of a sudden
be taken as an absolute truth and measure everybody by that? Brothers,
the extreme and strange actions taken in this situation are very
disturbing and perplexing.

We appeal on the basis of righteousness and mercy, because we
have been judged on a wrong we have not committed.

Be assured of our prayers to Jehovah for this matter to be
clarified for the blessing of his name and the spiritual well-being of
his people.

Your brothers,

René Vázquez

Elsie Vázquez

Some thirty years earlier, René had left his father's home to escape
what he felt was an oppressively intolerant atmosphere, narrow-mindedness. He sought freedom to pursue his interest in Jehovah's Witnesses.
From then on he had given himself, heart and soul, to service among
them. Now, in the space of two weeks, he saw those thirty years set aside
as of no particular weight, he was subjected to intense interrogation, his
sincerity of motive was impugned, and he had been labeled a rebel against
God and Christ. His letter voices his painful anguish on finding himself
in the same atmosphere of religious intolerance and narrow-mindedness
he thought he had escaped.

René was granted an appeal and again met with a committee (formed
of five other Elders). Every effort he made to be conciliatory, to show that
he was not seeking to make an issue of specific doctrinal matters, that he
had no desire to be dogmatic about such, was rejected as evasive, as evidence of guilt.

At one point, after hours of being plied with questions, he was interrupted by Sam Friend, a member of the Appeal Committee (as well as of the Brooklyn headquarters staff), who said, "That is a lot of hogwash. Now I'm going to read this list of questions to you and I want you to answer them yes or no." To René, whose native language is Spanish, the term "hogwash" was unfamiliar and, although afterward deciding it was simply some regional expression, he says that at the time it hit him with such a literal image of filth that something "gave" inside him and he responded, "No! I'm not going to answer any more of your questions. You men are trying to sift my heart and I'm not going to endure any more of it." A recess in the session was called; René walked out and on reaching the street broke down in tears.

The committee upheld the disfellowshipping decision.

Of all the persons René had known and worked with in the Brooklyn Service Department, including those who had been willing to make use of his kindness and helpfulness over many years, not one appeared to say at least something in his behalf, to express any request for a similarly kind treatment toward him.[27] On the organization's scales of justice his undeniable sincerity, his unmarred record of the past thirty years—none of this carried any weight if he did not totally agree with the organization and maintain unquestioning silence. Somewhere in all this it would seem that the words of the disciple James have application, when he writes:

> Talk and behave like people who are going to be judged by the law of freedom, because there will be judgment without mercy for those who have not been merciful themselves; but the merciful need have no fear of judgment.[28]

Finally, on May 8, 1980, the Governing Body officially informed me that my name was involved in all of this. A phone call came from Chairman Albert Schroeder and he said that the Governing Body wanted me to go to

---

27   While it is true that all these proceedings were carried on in "secret star-chamber" style, there were many in the Department who knew what was taking place, either through direct knowledge or by departmental "gossip."

28   James 2:12, 13, *JB*.

Brooklyn to appear before them. This was the *first time* they gave me any indication whatsoever of my being in any way under question.

Fifteen days had passed since our previous conversation in which the Chairman repeatedly evaded telling me what was actually taking place. I still was unaware of the existence of the two-hour taped interview or that it had been played to the Governing Body in full session. *Twenty-three days* had passed since that was done.

In those twenty-three days they had not only played that tape to the Governing Body but had played portions of it containing my name and that of Ed Dunlap to at least seventeen persons outside the Governing Body (those forming investigative and judicial committees), they had disfellowshipped three members of the headquarters staff and three person outside, one of them a friend of mine for thirty years, they had taped another interview with a man named Bonelli (a tape that will be discussed later), and in general had not only invited but had actively sought any evidence of an incriminating nature that could be obtained from members of the Bethel family or others, the threat of disfellowshipping even being used to extract information from some.

Only after all this did the Governing Body through its Chairman's Committee think it advisable to let me know that they viewed me as in any way implicated in what was taking place. Why?

What I knew I had learned entirely from other sources, not from the Governing Body of which I had been a member for nine years. The Bethel headquarters members who were grilled and put on trial had phoned me, voicing their dismay at the unkind, intolerant attitude shown. They expressed their belief that the ones directing the whole process were simply going through them in order to reach their true objective, Edward Dunlap and myself. They felt that such ones were taking what they considered to be the more strategic course of beginning with the "small people," the lesser known and less prominent ones, establishing their "guilt," making it seem as if the situation was of great and dangerous proportions, and then, having laid as strong a foundation as possible, proceeding to deal with the better known and more prominent ones. Rightly or wrongly, this was the impression they had. It would be interesting to hear from those of the Chairman's Committee, to whom all reports ultimately went and who answered all requests for direction by the investigating and judicial committees—to hear what possible reasons that Committee could have had for proceeding in the manner they did.

When Chairman Schroeder phoned me on May 8, I expressed my feelings, how difficult I found it to understand why, after living and working together, week in and week out, for nine years with the members of the Governing Body (fifteen years with some), not one of them had the brotherly considerateness to communicate with me as to what was taking place. (In all fairness to the members as a whole, it must be granted that they may not have known in detail how the Chairman's Committee was handling matters. They may not have known the content of Albert Schroeder's phone conversation with me on April 23 and the misleading responses my questions received—though it seems possible, even probable, that the conversation was taped, as later developments would indicate. Either way, it must be acknowledged that some or many of the members may have expected and believed that the Chairman's Committee was conducting matters on a high level, in accord with Christian principles, doing to others as they would have done to themselves.)

I then asked Albert Schroeder what his feelings would have been if, at the time he was in Europe conveying his thoughts of a different application of the critical phrase "this generation," some in Brooklyn, on hearing of this, had brought accusations of "apostate leanings" on his part, and then had begun gathering together any other expressions he might have made anywhere at any time to anyone as evidence to substantiate that grave charge—and had done all this without even communicating with him to advise him of what was taking place. How would he feel?

He gave no reply. I told him I would go to Brooklyn as requested and the conversation came to a close.

By the time I arrived in Brooklyn on May 19, the continual toll on my nerves had brought me to a state of near shock. There seemed to be something so irrational about what was happening, the methods used. Some called it a "nightmare." Others felt a stronger term was needed, namely, "paranoia." Innocent Christians were being treated as if they were dangerous enemies.

Some time ago I ran across an item I had read and clipped years before from the *New York Times*. Headed "Mistrust Found in Nixon's Staff," among other things it said:

> A psychiatrist on the White House staff from 1971 to 1973 says the inner group around Richard M. Nixon deeply mistrusted the motives of other people, viewed concern for people's feelings as a character flaw, and could not respect loyal opposition or dissent.
>
> "Dissent and disloyalty were concepts that were never sufficiently differentiated in their minds." Dr. Jerome H. Jaffe said. "That really was the tragic part. To dissent was to be disloyal. That is the theme that recurred again and again." . . .
>
> "The Administration admired people who could be cold and dispassionate in making personnel decisions," he said. "To make concessions to people's feelings, to recognize that a particular objective was not worth destroying people in the process of its attainment, was not something that elicited any admiration. Such a concern was viewed as a fatal flaw."
>
> "They deeply distrusted the motives of other people and were unable to believe that people could rise above selfish motives," he said."[29]

I find a frighteningly close parallel between this and the attitudes shown in Brooklyn in the spring of 1980. Quoting from the above article, "To dissent was to be disloyal. That is the theme that recurred again and again." The kindness of Jesus Christ seemed so seriously missing. Any warmth of friendship, and the compassionate understanding that gives friendship its warmth, seemed replaced by a cold organizational approach that assumed the worst, gave no benefit of doubt, and viewed forbearance and patience as a weakness, inimical to the interests of the organization, to its goals of uniformity and conformity. It was as if some massive legal machine had been put in motion and was grinding along in an unfeeling, unrelenting way toward its ultimate objective. I found it hard to believe it was actually happening.

---

29   *New York Times*, January 12, 1976, p. 12.

On arriving at the headquarters, among other things on my desk I found an item prepared by the Chairman's Committee back on April 28, 1980. (See the next page.) Some of the points were surprising to me, since I had never even considered them, much less discussed them with others. I was repelled by the dogmatic terms in which all the points were stated. And I thought the "Notes" at the bottom really presented the true issue. For those notes focused repeated emphasis on the *"basic Biblical 'framework' of the Society's Christian beliefs,"* the *"'pattern of healthful words' that have come to be Biblically accepted by Jehovah's people over the years."*

This had a familiar ring, for it was an argument so frequently used in Governing Body sessions, the argument that long-standing traditional teachings of the Society must be adhered to, as if the years they had been believed necessarily gave proof of their rightness. Those traditional teachings, and not the Word of God itself, lay at the crux of the issue.

On May 20, I met with the Chairman's Committee and they played me a tape of the report they gave to the Governing Body with regard to the interviews with members of the Writing Staff, and about the Chairman's Committee's subsequent steps in getting investigative and judicial processes in motion. They then gave me two tapes to take and listen to, one being the two-hour interview with the Cuban couple (the Godínezes) and the other a shorter taped interview with a Witness named Bonelli. I learned for the *first time* of the existence of the two-hour tape and that they had played it to the Governing Body over a month before. I find it almost ludicrous that after all the havoc that had been wreaked on people's lives since the time of playing that tape, they were just now getting around to letting me hear it, *the day before* my hearing in a plenary session of the Governing Body.

(To Governing Body) RECENT EVIDENCES OF WRONG TEACHINGS BEING SPREAD ABOUT

Following are some of the wrong teachings being spread as eminating from Bethel. These have been brought to the attention of the Governing Body from the field from April 14 onward.

1. That Jehovah does not have an organization on earth today and its Governing Body is not being directed by Jehovah.

2. Everyone baptized from Christ's time (C.E. 33) forward to the end should have the heavenly hope. All these should be partaking of the emblems at Memorial time and not just those who claim to be of the anointed remnant.

3. There is no proper arrangement as a "faithful and discreet slave" class made up of the anointed ones and their Governing Body to direct affairs of Jehovah's people. At Matt. 24:45 Jesus used this expression only as an illustration of faithfulness of individuals. Rules are not needed only follow the Bible.

4. There are not two classes today, the heavenly class and those of the earthly class also called "other sheep" at John 10:16.

5. That the number 144,000 mentioned at Rev. 7:4 and 14:1 is symbolic and not to be taken as literal. Those of the "great crowd" mentioned at Rev. 7:9 also serve in heaven as indicated in vs. 15 where it is claimed that such crowd serves "day and night in his temple (naọ̄)" or K. Int says: "in the divine habitation of him."

6. That we are not now living in a special period of "last days" but that the "last days" started 1900 years ago C.E. 33 as indicated by Peter at Acts 2:17 when he quoted from the Prophet Joel.

7. That 1914 is not an established date. Christ Jesus was not enthroned then but has been ruling in his kingdom since C.E. 33. That Christ's presence (parousia) is not yet but when the "sign of the Son of man will appear in heaven" (Matt. 24:30) in the future.

8. That Abraham, David and other faithful men of old will also have heavenly life basing such view on Heb. 11:16.

Notes: The above Biblical viewpoints have become accepted by some and now being passed on to others as "new understandings." Such views are contrary to the basic Biblical "framework" of the Society's Christian beliefs. (Rom. 2:20; 3:2) They also are contrary to the "pattern of healthful words" that have come to be Biblically accepted by Jehovah's people over the years. (2 Tim. 1:13) Such "changes" are condemned at Prov. 24:21,22. Hence the above are 'deviations from the truth that are subverting the faith of some.' (2 Tim. 2:18) All considered is this not APOSTASY and actionable for congregational discipline. See ks 77 page 58.

Chairman's Committee   4/28/80

I took the tapes to my office and played them. It made me feel ill. Everything was given such an ugly cast. I had no doubt that the Godínezes were seeking to repeat things as they had heard them, for I knew them and had always found them to be decent persons. But, as Harley Miller led them through the interview, I kept asking, "Were the things said to them actually presented in the extreme way that they here sound?" I was effectively cut off from determining this since the Chairman's Committee had already directed the formation of the judicial committees that had produced the disfellowshipping of those involved.

At the end of the tape, I heard the three members of the Chairman's Committee individually express themselves as though satisfied that they now had a clear picture of matters and, first, commending the couple interviewed for their loyalty, while, thereafter, condemning those implicated. This increased my feeling of illness. How could they do this without even having talked with Cris Sánchez? Why was he not there? Why was René Vázquez in effect "set up" by Harley Miller's suggestion (expressed on this very tape) that Godínez phone René and "tactfully" see if he would commit himself? What was the interest that these men had, what were they seeking to accomplish? Was it sincerely to help people, to understand their viewpoint and work toward a peaceful solution, to seek to clear matters up with a minimum of difficulty and hurt, through kind counsel, through exhortation to moderation and prudence if these were lacking—or was it to build up a case against persons? I found nothing in the entire tape to indicate anything but the latter goal.

If the contents of that first tape were bad, the second was far worse. The Godínezes had expressed their recollections of a conversation in their home and the way the things said had struck them and, as stated, I believe they did so sincerely. The second tape was filled largely with rumor. But the most disheartening aspect of the whole recording were the expressions made by the headquarters interviewers.

Bonelli was a member of a Spanish-speaking congregation adjoining that of René's. The tape began with Albert Schroeder introducing Bonelli as a man who had been a "ministerial servant" (or "deacon") in two previous congregations but who was not presently such. He quoted Bonelli as having said that he was not appointed as a ministerial servant in his present congregation because of an adverse attitude of one of the elders there, named Angulo.

Bonelli then gave testimony against this same elder that he said had contributed toward his not being appointed as a ministerial servant. (Angulo was one of those who was disfellowshipped.) He also said that after the Memorial service (the Lord's Evening Meal) at the Kingdom Hall on March 31, he had gone to René Vázquez' home where he saw René's wife and mother partake of the emblems of bread and wine.[30] Bonelli said he himself also partook of the emblems.

This last statement produced surprised comments from his interviewers, Albert Schroeder and, from the Service Department, Dave Olson and Harold Jackson. Bonelli went on to say in explanation, and I here quote his exact words as they are recorded on the tape: "I'm sneaky." He said he had gone to René's home to get information about them.[31]

He went on to say that he understood from another Witness that the elder named Angulo had already obtained a building in which he and René would hold meetings, that they had already baptized persons in their new belief.

There was, in reality, *not a single word of truth* in those rumors. The interrogators did not ask where the supposed location of meetings was, or what the names of the persons supposedly baptized were. None could have been supplied if they had asked, for they did not exist.

Farther along in the tape, Bonelli had difficulty expressing one point in English and Harold Jackson, who speaks Spanish, had him state it in Spanish and then Jackson put it into English. Bonelli chuckled and said: "My English is not so good, but the information I am giving is." Dave Olson's voice then came in quickly saying, "Yes, Brother, you're giving us just what we need. Go on."

When I heard those words it was as if a crushing weight came down on my heart. In the whole interview, this man had not said one thing that could possibly be viewed as helpful if the aim was to try to aid persons who had a wrong understanding of Scripture. Only if the aim was to build up a case, to obtain incriminating, damning evidence, then only could he

---

30 Previous to my departing on my leave of absence, René told me that he and his wife and mother all felt conscientiously that they should partake of the emblems. He said he was certain that if all three did so at the Kingdom Hall it would cause a lot of talk (it is rare for any of the Spanish-speaking congregations to have even one person professing to be of the "anointed" among them). He said he felt the course that would cause the least problem would be for his wife and mother to wait until after the congregation meeting and partake quietly at home. He said that Bonelli was not in their congregation and was not asked to accompany them home but asked to do so himself. (René's mother had at one time conducted a Bible study with Bonelli and knew him well.)

31 I personally doubt that that was his motivation at the time.

be said to be 'giving just what was needed.' But even the evidence supplied was half rumor, unfounded, utterly false, and the other half could be viewed as significant only if one upheld the view that a religious organization has the right to prohibit private conversations about the Bible among personal friends if these conversations do not adhere totally to that organization's teachings, as also the right to judge the conscientious actions of persons even when done in the privacy of their own home.

At the close of Bonelli's taped testimony, Dave Olson asked him if he could supply names of other "Brothers" who might give similar information. Bonelli had claimed that a large number of persons were spoken to about the "apostate" beliefs. He replied to Olson's request by saying that he thought he knew a "Brother" in New Jersey who might be able to give some information. Olson asked his name. Bonelli answered that he didn't remember but thought he could find out. Olson said, "But there must be many others who could supply information." Bonelli then said he thought he knew some "Sisters" who might be able to do that. What were their names? That too, he would have to find out.

Albert Schroeder then expressed gratitude to Bonelli for his cooperation in testifying and counseled him to 'keep himself spiritually strong by attending the meetings regularly,' and added that if Bonelli heard any other information to come to them with it.

In my opinion, nothing expresses more clearly and forcefully the direction taken in the entire process of investigation, interrogation and ultimate condemnation than does this particular tape. I can think of nothing that would be more helpful to all of Jehovah's Witnesses everywhere to enable them to have a balanced, not a one-sided, view of what took place, the "climate" that prevailed, how the men connected with God's "channel" at headquarters conducted themselves, than for them to hear this tape and compare it with what has thus far been told them by the organization or what they have heard through gossip. But they should also have the right to ask questions as to what was done to verify the testimony of this man, to separate fact from rumor, and also the right to ask why this kind of testimony was viewed by the headquarters men as of such value, *"just what we need."*

The likelihood of the organization's doing that, allowing this tape to be heard (with no portions erased) and for questions to be asked is, I believe, virtually nonexistent. I personally think they would destroy it rather than allow that to happen. I still do not understand why the Chairman's Committee did not feel ashamed to let me hear it as they did.

The Governing Body had ample opportunity to know that within days after the disfellowshipping of the headquarters staff members, rumors of the same kind contained in this tape began circulating within the Bethel family. The "apostates" were forming their own religion, had been holding separatist meetings, baptizing people, their new belief went under the name of "Sons of Freedom"—these and similar expressions were common talk. They were also totally false. Governing Body members presiding at the morning Bible discussions made many comments about the "apostates" but did not see fit to expose the falsity of the rumors circulating.

Those rumors went unchecked and eventually spread all over the globe. Yet every Witness who passed these on was speaking, even if unwittingly, false testimony against his neighbor. The only ones in position to expose the falsity of those rumors and thus help stop the false testimony were those of the Governing Body. Why they did not choose to do so only they know. I do not doubt that among them there were some who honestly believed that the things they were hearing were factual. But I believe that in their position and with their weight of responsibility they had an obligation to investigate and to help others to realize that it was not factual, it was fiction, and not only fiction but hurtful, even vicious, fiction.

I would not argue that errors of judgment were all on one side. I do not doubt in the least that among those of us "brought to trial" there were cases of injudicious statements. The evidence indicates that some of the most extreme statements were made by a man who, on being approached, quickly offered to become a 'witness for the prosecution,' testifying against a fellow elder. I do not personally know that man, have never met him, nor do I know the other elder. They are total strangers to me.[32]

I do not think it was wrong for the headquarters to make at least some inquiry into the matter as a result of the information that was brought

---

32   These elders were in the congregation adjoining the congregation René attended.

to their attention. It would be entirely natural for them to do so. If they believe that what they teach is truth from God it would be wrong for them not to do so.

What I find very difficult to understand and to harmonize with Scripture is the *manner* in which this was done, the precipitous reaction and hastiness, the methods employed—covering over and withholding information from persons whose life interests were intimately involved, whose good name was at stake, the devious approaches employed to obtain damaging information, of coercion through threat of disfellowshipping to obtain "cooperation" in getting such incriminating evidence—and, above all, the spirit shown, the crushing despotism, the unfeeling legalistic approach, and the harshness of the actions taken. Whatever injudicious statements may have been made by a few of those 'put to trial,' I think the facts show them to have been far surpassed by the means used to deal with the matter.

As in the Inquisition, all rights were held by the inquisitors, the accused had none. The investigators felt they had the right to ask any question and at the same time refuse to answer questions put to them. They insisted on maintaining their judicial proceedings secret, entirely away from observation by anyone else, yet claimed the right to pry into the private conversations and activities of those they interrogated. For them, their judicial secrecy was proper, the exercise of "confidentiality," their evasiveness was simply being "practical," strategic, but the efforts of the accused to maintain the privacy of their personal conversations was labeled as being devious, as evidence of a hidden conspiracy.

The investigators expected their own actions to be taken as evidence of zeal for God, for "revealed truth," while at the same time they suspected the worst in all that the accused had done, made no allowance for their sincerity in wanting to put God first, or for their love of truth even when that truth was contradicted by traditional teachings.

When René Vázquez, for example, on being interrogated, endeavored to express himself moderately, undogmatically, to show that he had no desire to make flaming issues of minor doctrinal matters, and to make clear that he was not being insistent that anyone else see things as he did or adopt his views, he found that this was very unsatisfactory to the judicial committee members. They sought to pin him down on his inner feelings, his personal beliefs. As he put it, when a question from one direction did not accomplish this, then a question from another direction attempted to force him into some categorical reply. In his hearing before the first judicial committee, another elder, named Benjamín Angulo, was also "on trial." Angulo was very positive, even adamant in many of his expressions. When René spoke in moderate terms, one of the Committee members, Harold Jackson, told René, "you are not even a good apostate." Saying that René did not clearly defend his beliefs, Jackson continued:

> Look at Angulo, he defends them. You talked to Angulo about these things and look how he now talks about them. He may be disfellow-shipped, and yet you are not definite about these points.

In the second hearing with the appeal committee, as has been shown, René's efforts at being moderate brought forth the expression "hogwash." Mildness, moderateness, a willingness to yield where the issues permit yielding, these qualities do not make good evidence for disfellowshipping persons as rebellious "apostates." Yet they are qualities that are part of René Vázquez' nature, and those who know him know that this is true.

Two years after his disfellowshipping I talked to René about the whole affair and asked him how he now felt about having spoken to others on what he saw in the Scriptures. What would he say to someone who advanced the argument that, as in the case of someone working for a business organization, as long as he is part of that organization he should uphold all its policies and if he could not he should first leave before saying anything. His reply was:

> But that is a business organization and I did not think of matters in those terms. I viewed the matter as involving a higher relationship, one with God. I know what my feelings were then and what was in my heart, and no one can tell me otherwise. If I were in some scheme, why should I now deny it? When the hearings came, I prayed that I would not be disfellowshipped. Others did the same. Yet it happened.
>
> If I had wanted to stay in the organization just to proselytize, I would now be a militant. Where is the 'sect' that I was working for? Where is the afterfact to prove that is what I was working for? To this day, even

when people have approached me to talk with me, afterward I prefer to let them call *me* rather than take the initiative.

If I had it all to do over again I would be facing the same dilemma. I feel that so much good came from what I learned from the Scriptures, that it proved such a blessing to have things cleared up and brought me closer to God.

If I had had some 'scheme,' I could have programmed the way I would do things. But what I did was simply human and I was acting according to human reaction. That human element took precedence over fear of an organization. It was never my idea to disassociate myself from the Witnesses. I was just rejoicing in what I was reading in the Bible. The conclusions I came to were as a result of my personal reading of the Bible. I was in no way trying to be dogmatic.

The question I ask is, after all these thirty years as a Witness, the feelings I had of mercy and compassion—why were these not felt by *them?* Why the conniving way of framing questions? The hearings were held as if to gather information proving guilt, not to aid an 'erring' brother.

One rumor that circulated widely, in fact internationally, was that these three men (Vázquez, Sánchez and Kuilan), all of whom worked in the Spanish Translation Department, were deliberately making changes in material when translating and that I knew of this and had condoned it. (In French-speaking countries the rumor was adjusted to apply to French translation work.) René's comments on this were:

> That is ridiculous. It would have been impossible to do. There were no changes made and that never came into our minds. No one ever accused us of that. Everything translated had to go through about five different persons for checking, Fabio Silva being the last one to read it. In translating it was always necessary to strive to be faithful to the original idea.[33]

---

33 Not only was everything checked by a number of different persons in Brooklyn, but a large percentage of Branch Office personnel in Spanish-speaking countries know English and read the publications in both languages. Had such charge of deliberate alteration been true, it would have been quickly reported. To think otherwise simply betrays an ignorance of the facts or a lack of concern for facts on the part of those originating and spreading the rumors.

Probably the most vicious rumor, passed on as "truth" by elders and others in various parts of this country, was that there was homosexuality being practiced among the "apostates." Where such a blatant lie originated is difficult to imagine. The only explanation I can think of is that, about a year before the inquisition tactics began, an organizational member in a position of considerable responsibility had been accused of homosexual tendencies. The Governing Body handled the case and endeavored to keep the matter quiet. Nonetheless, it seems that some talk did circulate. In the rumor mills this man's actions were now transferred over to the "apostates." This was easy to do since spreaders of rumors are seldom concerned about facts. I can think of no other possible explanation.

Why would people priding themselves on their high Christian principles pass on such vicious rumors when they had absolutely nothing but gossip on which to base them? I believe that in many cases it was simply because many felt a need somehow to justify in their own minds and hearts what had happened. They had to have reasons other than the true ones to explain why such summary and harsh actions were taken against people with unblemished records, people whom even their closest associates knew to be peaceful, unaggressive persons. To see the ugly label of "apostate" suddenly placed on these people required *something more* than the facts of the matter provided. Without such, those who knew these people, and others who heard of them, would have been obliged to face up to the possibility that the organization they viewed as God's sole channel of communication and guidance on earth was perhaps not what they thought it to be. For many this was to think the unthinkable. It would severely disturb their feeling of security, a security that rests largely (far more so than most would acknowledge) on their unquestioning reliance on a human organization.

SANHEDRIN EXPERIENCE

Now it is required that those who have been given a trust must prove faithful. I care very little if I am judged by you or by any human court; indeed, I do not even judge myself. My conscience is clear, but that does not make me innocent. It is the Lord who judges me.
— 1 Corinthians 4:2-4, *New International Version.*

When I arrived in Brooklyn, all the information that had been withheld from me was given in one large dose. The next morning I was due to appear before the Governing Body in full session.

Afterward, I could review it and see just what had been done, the program of action followed, the methods employed. But at the time it only created a sense of shock. There was no opportunity to ask those involved about the accuracy of what was now given to me—they were already disfellowshipped, their testimony now unacceptable to the Body.

I still found it hard to believe that people, the people within whom I had my lifelong religious heritage, would ever do what I saw being done. My feelings on going to the Brooklyn headquarters were strangely comparable to my feelings when making trips to the Dominican Republic during the regime of the dictator Trujillo. In Puerto Rico, my point of departure, everything was so free and open, people on the street or in public conveyances talked with no sense of restraint. But as soon as my plane landed at the airport of what was then Ciudad Trujillo (now Santo Domingo), the change was almost palpable. People were so guarded in their speech, in public conveyances conversation was minimal, people were concerned lest any remark be taken as unfavorable to the dictator and be reported by the spy system that proliferated during that regime. Conversation and interchange of ideas that were viewed as completely normal in Puerto Rico were dangerous in the Dominican Republic, liable to bring upon one the label of an enemy of the state. In the one country, a man could express an opinion that differed from that of the majority and feel no sense of concern if he later learned that he had been quoted. In the other, a man expressing any thought that did not conform to the existing ideology afterward found himself engaging in self-recrimination, feeling as if he had committed some wrong, something over which to feel guilt, and the thought of being quoted was a foreboding one. In this latter case, the issue was not whether what one had said was true; it was not whether his saying it was honestly motivated and morally proper. The question was, how would it be taken by those in power?

Any feeling of this latter kind that I had had at the headquarters before the spring of 1980 had been only fleeting, momentary. Now it surrounded me, seemed overwhelming. The view those exercising governing authority had already taken was obvious from the "briefing" given me by the Chairman's Committee, and by the remarks they and the Service Department men expressed on the tapes. In the highly emotional atmosphere and the climate of suspicion that had developed, it was difficult to keep in mind that what I or others had said could be viewed in any other light than the harsh way these men had expressed it. To keep in mind that what might be condemned from an organizational standpoint as heretical, could, from the standpoint of God's Word, be right, proper and good, was hard to do, particularly after a life of intense service in the organization. I knew that I had not sought out people to whom to speak on these matters; they had approached me and I felt an obligation to point them to God's Word for answers, even if the answers found there differed from those of men in authority.

I felt sure that by far the majority of the men before whom I would appear would see the matter from the organizational viewpoint only. If, from the start, there had been any other point of view taken, I was satisfied that the whole affair could have been quietly, peacefully and simply worked out, through friendly, brotherly conversation, encouraging moderation if any immoderate speech had been made, urging considerate restraint if inconsiderate restraint had been shown. By avoiding condemnatory confrontations, refusing to resort to high-handed methods and legalistic approaches, it would not have been necessary for private conversations and incidents that involved a small handful of persons to have blown up to such proportions that they became a *cause célèbre*, a full-scale affair with violent impact on the lives of many persons, one that produced reverberations and gossip on an international scale.

On going before the Governing Body, I felt no desire to add fuel to the fire already raging. It had already consumed some much-loved friends. I was willing to acknowledge that something I personally deplored—statements of an extreme or dogmatic nature—might have been made by a few of those involved, though I had no way of determining at this time to what extent this was true, for it related primarily to persons with whom I had had no Scriptural discussion, some of whom I did not even know.

On Wednesday, May 21, the Governing Body session opened with Albert Schroeder as Chairman. He first stated that the Chairman's Committee had asked me if I was willing to have the Governing Body's discussion with me taped and that I had agreed, with the provision that a copy of the taping be provided to me.

The Governing Body conference room contained one, long oval table capable of seating about twenty persons around it. The full Body of seventeen members was present. Aside from Lyman Swingle, who sat to my left, no member had conversed with me; the day before, no one (not even the member related to me) had visited me, either in my office or in my room. If there was any warmth or brotherly compassion in the Governing Body conference room, I failed to discern it. I felt only the feelings I had experienced when appearing in secular court trials of the past, with the exception that in those cases I felt freer to speak and knew that other persons were present who could witness what was said, the attitudes expressed. This instead was a closed secret session; the attitude displayed seemed only to confirm what René Vázquez had told me of the attitude manifested toward him.

The Chairman said that the Body first wanted me to express myself on each of the eight points the Chairman's Committee had drawn up as evidences of apostasy (in their memo of April 28). I did, in each case endeavoring to be moderate, undogmatic, as yielding and conciliatory as I could be without going against my conscience by being either dishonest or hypocritical. The absolutist form in which the points were presented by the Chairman's Committee in their memo—as if one either accepted fully the organization's teaching on these points or else viewed them in the dogmatic way expressed in the memo—simply did not fit my case. None of their eight points expressed what I felt were the true issues. The issue was not whether God had an "organization" on earth but *what kind* of organization—a centralized, highly structured, authoritarian organization, or simply that of a congregation of brothers where the only authority is authority to help, to guide, to serve, never to dominate? Thus my response was that I believed that God had an organization on earth in the sense that He had a congregation on earth, the Christian congregation, a brotherhood.

The issue was not whether God had guided (or would guide) those forming this Governing Body, but to what extent, under what conditions? I did not doubt or question that God would give his guidance to these men if that was sincerely sought (I felt that some of the decisions made, particularly in earlier years, had been good decisions, compassionate decisions), but I certainly did not think this was automatic; it was always conditional, contingent on certain factors. So my response included the statement that I believed such guidance always was governed by the extent to which God's Word was adhered to; that to that extent God grants his guidance or withdraws it. (I think that that is true for any individual or any collective group of people, whoever they are.)

My responses to all the questions were made in this manner. If any of those accused had spoken about these matters in the dogmatic, absolutist way that the Chairman's Committee presented them, then I felt a desire to do whatever I could to restore a measure of reasonableness and moderation, to conciliate rather than exacerbate, and I bent as far as I could bend.

Other questions asked me were relatively few. Lyman Swingle asked about my view of Bible commentaries, from which I gathered that this had been a subject of discussion in the Body. I replied that I had begun to use them more extensively as a result of my uncle's encouragement (during the *Aid* project) and that if the view was that they should not be used then there were entire sections of the Bethel library that would need to be emptied, since there were dozens, scores of sets of commentaries there.

Martin Poetzinger, who had spent several years in concentration camps during the Nazi regime, expressed dissatisfaction with my responses to the set of eight doctrinal points. How could it be, he asked, that I felt as expressed if these other people were making such strong statements? (As was true of the others, he had never talked personally to any of them.)[34] I answered that I could not be responsible for the way others might express things, and I directed his attention to Romans, chapter three, verse 8 and Second Peter, chapter three, verses 15 and 16, as examples of how even the apostle Paul's expressions were wrongly expressed or understood by some. Though I did not say so, I frankly felt my circumstance was like that described at Luke, chapter eleven, verse 53, as among men who were try-ing to 'draw me out on a great many subjects, waiting to pounce on some incriminating remark.'[35] The conduct of the Body during the preceding weeks gave basis for no other feeling.

Poetzinger went on to make known his view of the disfellowshipped "apostates," saying, with strong feeling, that they had shown their real attitude by "throwing their Watch Tower literature into the garbage before leaving!" (This was one of the rumors that circulated most widely in the Bethel family; in fact, it was reported to the entire Bethel family by a Governing Body member one morning.) I told Martin Poetzinger that I would never want to arrive at a conclusion when I had not talked with those involved to learn the facts. I said that in the fifteen years I had been at the headquarters it was a rare thing to go into one of the closets containing "dirt hoppers" without seeing quantities of Society literature— older magazines and books—discarded by members of the family; that, from what I knew, some of the disfellowshipped ones of the Bethel staff were departing by plane for Puerto Rico and that the heaviest items, and the most easily replaceable, would be such books. I repeated that I did not think it right to make a judgment on the basis of hearsay and that I thought it was especially unfitting for one sitting as a judge to do so. He stared at me but said nothing further.

Another question was asked with regard to the Memorial service (the Lord's Evening Meal) I had conducted the month before (April) at Homestead, Florida.[36] Was it true that I had not discussed the "other

---

34   Lloyd Barry also expressed similar dissatisfaction, saying that I had "equivocated" on every one of the 8 points the Chairman's Committee had drawn up as proof of "apostasy."

35   *Phillips Modern English translation.*

36   Jehovah's witnesses hold this service as an annual celebration only, approximately at the time of Passover.

sheep" (those with earthly hopes) in my talk there? I said that was true, and related to them my experience the first year I had come to Brooklyn from the Dominican Republic. My wife and I had attended a Memorial service at a congregation that held this meeting quite early in the evening. Thus we returned to the Bethel headquarters in time to hear my uncle, then the vice president, give his entire talk. After the talk we were invited, along with my uncle, to the room of staff member Malcolm Allen. My wife immediately said to my uncle, "I noticed that you didn't mention the 'other sheep' anywhere in your talk. Why was that?" He replied that he considered the evening one that was special for the "anointed" and said, "So, I just concentrate on them." I informed the Body that I still had my notes from that talk by the vice president and had used them many times in conducting Memorial services. They were welcome to look at them if they wished. (Fred Franz was, of course, present if they cared to question him about his talk.) The subject was dropped.[37]

My regret at what had happened, based on the premise that some persons had apparently been extreme in their statements, was sincere. I told the Body that if I had been informed I would have done all in my power to bring such to a halt. I did not deny that injudiciousness had been shown, nor did I exclude myself in saying this, but I stated that I felt it was wrong to equate what is injudicious with what is malicious. I expressed my respect for and my confidence in the Christian qualities of those I personally knew who had been so viewed and treated. I told them of what I knew of the thirty years of service of René Vázquez, his sincere devotion, his unblemished record in Puerto Rico, Spain and the United States. I also expressed dismay that, after having lived and worked with them as fellow Body members for so many years, not one of them had seen fit to communicate with me and convey the honest facts as to what was taking place.

---

37 Typical of the rumors circulated (and I had questions written to me about this from as far away as New Zealand) was that I had given a talk encouraging everyone to partake of the emblems and that an entire congregation had done so (which would be a truly spectacular event for Jehovah's Witnesses). The fact is, however, that at the talk I gave in Florida in April 1980, there were exactly two partakers, myself and a woman attending who was not a Witness but a member of a local church.

Chairman Schroeder was the only one to respond. He quickly said, "But Ray, you didn't level completely with us either. You didn't say [in the phone conversation] how you knew about the investigation of the Writing Department." I replied, "Did you ask me?" "No," was his answer. I said, "If you had I would have told you without hesitation. Ed Dunlap phoned me and mentioned it." Shortly afterward, Karl Klein, another member of the Chairman's Committee, smilingly acknowledged that "We didn't level fully with Ray," and added that "if René Vázquez had responded to the questions the way Ray did he would not have been disfellowshipped." Since neither Karl nor any other member of the entire Governing Body had made any effort to talk with René, to attend the first "investigative" interview held with him, or the first judicial hearing with him, or the appeal hearing with him, they could only judge his responses by the reports passed on to them by those who had carried out such activity for them. How they felt they could judge or compare on such second-hand basis I did not know. The Chairman's Committee, which included Karl Klein, had been willing to take the time to meet with accusers, to hear accusations brought, including the adverse testimony given by the Godínez couple and Bonelli, but they had *not found the time to talk to a single one of those accused.* I hardly find this an exemplary expression of brotherly love, of fellow feeling or compassion.

The majority of those on the Body simply sat and listened, asking no questions, making no comments. After two or three hours (I was too affected emotionally to be aware of the time) I was informed that I could leave the conference room and that they would get in touch with me. I went to my office and waited. Noontime came and looking from the window I saw Governing Body members walking through the garden en route to the dining rooms. I had no appetite for food and remained waiting. By the time three o'clock came I felt too drained to remain there and went to my room. The preceding weeks, the phone conversation with the Chairman and the shock that came on finding out how misleading it had been, the distress expressed in a flow of phone calls from those who were being subjected to intense interrogation and pressure, the rapidity and relentlessness of the disfellowshippings that followed, and, most of all, the continued silence on the part of the Governing Body as to informing me of a single one of the developments in all this, had now been culminated by my experience that morning, the coldness of the attitude shown, and the hours of waiting that followed. By evening I had become physically ill.

That same evening a phone call came to our room from Chairman Schroeder asking me to meet with the Body for an evening session of further questioning. My wife had answered the phone for me and I told her to inform him that I was simply too sick to go and that I had said what I had to say. They could make their decision on what they had heard.

Later that evening, Lyman Swingle, who lived in rooms two floors above ours, came by to see how I was feeling. I appreciated this and told him what a strain the period of many weeks had been. I stated to him that what concerned me most deeply was not what action the Body might decide to take toward me, but that beautiful truths of God's Word had been made to appear ugly. I meant that then and still feel that the most serious aspect of all that took place was the way an array of organizational teachings were used as a standard against which to evaluate plain statements in the Bible, and that those plain statements (because they did not conform to the organizational "pattern" of interpretation) were depicted as distorted teachings giving evidence of "apostasy."

I had in mind such plain yet beautiful statements of God's Word as:

> One is your teacher, whereas all you are brothers.
> You are not under law but under undeserved kindness.
> All who are led by God's spirit, these are God's sons.
> One body there is, and one spirit, even as you were called in the one hope to which you were called; one Lord, one faith, one baptism; one God and Father of all persons, who is over all and through all and in all.
> For as often as you eat this loaf and drink this cup, you keep proclaiming the death of the Lord, until he arrives.
> For there is one God and one mediator between God and men, a man, Christ Jesus.
> It does not belong to you to get knowledge of the times and seasons which the Father has placed in his own jurisdiction.[38]

---

38 Matthew 23:8; Romans 6:14; 8:14; Ephesians 4:4-6; 1 Corinthians 11:26; 1 Timothy 2:5; Acts 1:7.

By contrast, the eight points used by the Chairman's Committee as a sort of "Confession of Faith" by which to judge people had *not one single point* where the Society teaching involved could be supported by simple, clear-cut statements in Scripture. What plain statement in Scripture could anyone, Governing Body member or anyone else, point to and say, "Here, the Bible clearly says":

1. That God has an "organization" on earth—one of the kind here at issue— and uses a Governing Body to direct it? *Where does the Bible make such statements?*

2. That the heavenly hope is not open to anyone and everyone who will embrace it, that it has been replaced by an earthly hope (since 1935) and that Christ's words in connection with the emblematic bread and wine, "Do this in remembrance of me," do not apply to all persons putting faith in his ransom sacrifice? *What scriptures make such statements?*

3. That the "faithful and discreet slave" is a "class" composed of only certain Christians, that it cannot apply to individuals, and that it operates through a Governing Body? *Again, where does the Bible make such statements?*

4. That Christians are separated into two classes, with a different relationship to God and Christ, on the basis of an earthly or a heavenly destiny? *Where is this said?*

5. That the 144,000 in Revelation *must* be taken as a literal number and that the "great crowd" does not and *cannot* refer to persons serving in God's heavenly courts? *Where do we find those statements in the Bible?*

6. That the "last days" began in 1914, and that when the apostle Peter (at Acts 2:17) spoke of the last days as applying from Pentecost on, he did not mean the same "last days" that Paul did (at 2 Timothy 3:1)? *Where?*

7. That the calendar year of 1914 was the time when Christ was first officially enthroned as King toward all the earth and that that calendar date marks the start of his *parousia? Where?*

8. That when the Bible at Hebrews 11:16 says that men such as Abraham, Isaac and Jacob were "reaching out for a better place, that is, one belonging to heaven," this could not *possibly* mean that they would have heavenly life? *Where?*

Not a single Society teaching there dealt with could be supported by any plain direct statement of Scripture. Every single one would require intricate explanations, complex combinations of texts and, in some cases, what amounts to mental gymnastics, in an attempt to support them. Yet these were used to judge people's Christianity, set forth as the basis for deciding whether persons who had poured out their lives in service to God were apostates!

The morning after my hearing before the Governing Body, Chairman Schroeder came to my room with a tape recorder to tape my response to some additional testimony from a staff member, Fabio Silva, who recounted things said to him by René Vázquez when René was providing him transportation from the airport one day. I said I had nothing to comment with regard to such hearsay evidence.

The morning hours passed. I felt a need to get out from the place and the oppressive atmosphere it contained. When I knew the lunch period was ended, I left my room and walked upstairs and was able to speak to Lyman Swingle as he was walking from the elevator to his rooms. I asked how much longer I had to wait. He told me a decision had been reached and that I would be notified that afternoon. His remarks gave me reason to believe that some members had pushed strongly for disfellowshipping and, while speaking with me, his face suddenly became very drawn and he said, "I can't understand how some men think. I fought, oh how I fought—" and then his lips compressed, his shoulders began to heave, and he began to sob openly. I suddenly found myself trying to comfort him, assuring him that it really did not matter that much to me what their decision was, that I simply wanted the matter to come to an end. Since his tears kept coming, I walked away so that he could go on to his rooms.

I know that there was no person on the Governing Body more devoted to the organization of Jehovah's Witnesses than Lyman Swingle. I had felt admiration and affection for him because of his honesty and courage. I have no idea what his attitude toward me would be in the years that followed. It might have been

Lyman Swingle

totally opposite. I only know that, if for no other reason, I will always love the man for the sincere feeling he expressed that day in the hallway. In his sadness I found strength.[39]

That afternoon Chairman Schroeder brought the Governing Body's decision to me. Evidently those seeking disfellowshipping had not attained a two-thirds majority, for he simply informed me that I was being asked to resign from the Body and also as a member of the headquarters staff. The Body offered to place me (and my wife) on what is known as the "Infirm Special Pioneer list" (an arrangement often offered to Circuit and District Overseers who have to leave traveling work due to old age or poor health). Those on this list report each month to the Society and receive monthly financial help, but are not required to reach any particular "quota" of hours in preaching work.[40] I informed him that neither of us felt we wanted to be under any arrangement that carried any obligation, even an implied one. He then made a few remarks about "what a marvelous piece of work" the *Aid to Bible Understanding* book had been. Then he left.

I wrote out my resignation, set out on the following page. I have not failed to do what I there said up to the present time.

---

39 In the months that followed, Lyman Swingle, though continuing as a Governing Body member, was removed from his position as the Coordinator of the Writing Committee and of the Writing Department, being replaced by Lloyd Barry. Lyman died in 2001.

40 At that time I believe the monthly allowance was about $175 per person.

May 22, 1980

Governing Body

Dear Brothers:

By means of this letter I submit my resignation as a member of the Governing Body.

I will also be terminating my Bethel service.

My prayers will continue to be offered on your behalf as well as for Jehovah God's servants earthwide.

Your brother,

RV Franz

My wife and I went away for a couple of days to get our emotions under control and then returned to move out what belongings we would take with us. I left the bulk of my files behind, bringing primarily the files on matters in which I had been most personally involved. I felt a need to be able to document my position on such issues should that position be misrepresented in the future, as in several cases it was.

On our return, I saw Ed Dunlap standing outside one of the headquarters buildings. He was to meet that day with a judicial committee.

Ed was now sixty-nine years old. The year before, in 1979, he had talked seriously about leaving the headquarters. He knew he had been the object of personal attack both within the Governing Body and outside thereof. At one point he had asked the Writing Committee to give him relief from harassment. The Writing Committee assigned three of its members, Lyman Swingle, Lloyd Barry and Ewart Chitty, to speak to Governing Body member Karl Klein (not then a member of the Writing Committee, though he became such after Chitty's resignation). They urged him to refrain from going into Ed's office and speaking critically to him as well as to refrain from talking to others about Ed in such manner. This seemed to have effect for a time as to expressions outside the Body, though not within the Body and its sessions.

When, in late 1979, I informed Ed of our thoughts about leaving, he said that he had weighed the idea but had come to the conclusion that it was not feasible for him. At his advanced age and in his economic situation he did not see how he could reasonably hope to support himself and his wife. By remaining, at least they would have a place to live, food, and medical care when needed. So, he said, he had decided to stay and added, "If they give me too much hassle in the Writing Department I'll just ask for a transfer to the carpenter shop or some other kind of work."

Less than a year later he found himself cited for a judicial committee hearing. The day I saw him he said, "I'm going to be very frank with them. It's against my nature to hedge." He said he had little doubt as to what the committee would do.

It was now near the end of May. About six weeks had elapsed since the Chairman's Committee had played the Godínez tape to the Governing Body in which Ed's name was used several times. Nearly that length of time had passed since Barry and Barr had interviewed him, assuring him that they were 'just seeking information.' During all those weeks—although Ed Dunlap was right in their midst, even up to the very last working on a Governing Body assignment to prepare a book on the life of Jesus Christ—not a *single one* of the Chairman's Committee approached him to discuss these matters with him, to inform him of the grave charges being made. These men were exercising full direction of the whole affair, they all knew Ed intimately, yet to the end they said not one word to him on the subject.[41]

---

41   Albert Schroeder had been a fellow instructor with Ed at Gilead School for many years; Karl Klein worked in the same Writing Department with him, his office being right next door to Ed's; Grant Suiter, a year or so before these events, had come to Ed with an assignment he (Suiter) had received to prepare (an outline for one of the Branch seminar class discussions) and asked Ed to prepare it for him, saying that he was very busy and was sure Ed would "do a better job anyway."

After Barry and Barr's initial interview with him, for nearly six weeks *no one in the entire Governing Body* went to Edward Dunlap to talk about the matter, to reason with or discuss God's Word with this man who had been associated for nearly half a century, had spent some forty years in full-time service, professed the heavenly hope, and was now nearly seventy years of age. They themselves are witnesses that this is true. How unlike the shepherd who would leave the ninety-nine to search out and help a "strayed" sheep, for such he was in their eyes.

Again, it may well be that some injudicious words had been spoken by a few individuals among those disfellowshipped. The above actions by those in authority, to my mind, spoke far, far louder than did any such words.[42]

A committee of five headquarters staff men was assigned to do the work of judging Ed Dunlap. The Governing Body remained in the background. All of the five men assigned were younger than Ed, none professed to be of the "anointed." After just one day's deliberations they arrived at their decision.

Fairly typical of the attitude shown were these expressions:

When asked about his views on the organization's teachings about two classes of Christians, Ed called their attention to Romans, chapter eight, verse 14, that "ALL who are led by God's spirit" are God's sons. He asked, "How else can you understand it?" Fred Rusk, who had served as a Gilead School Instructor for several years while Ed was Registrar, said, "Oh, Ed, that's just your interpretation of it." Ed asked, "Then how else would you explain it?" Fred Rusk's reply was, "Look, Ed, you're the one that's on trial, not me."

When questioned about the organization's forming of rules, he stressed that the Christian is not under law but under undeserved kindness (or grace). He said that faith and love were greater forces for righteousness than rules could ever be.

Robert Wallen said, "But Ed, I *like* to have someone tell me what to do." Having in mind the apostle's words at Hebrews, chapter five, verses 13 and 14, that Christians should not be like babes but like mature persons "who through use have their perceptive powers trained to distinguish

---

42   1 John 3:14-16, 18.

both right and wrong," Ed answered, "Then you need to read your Bible more." Robert Wallen smiled and said, "Me and two million others." Ed replied, "The fact that they don't do it doesn't excuse you from doing it." He stressed that this was the major problem, the brothers simply did not study the Bible; they relied on the publications; their consciences were not genuinely *Bible* trained.

Evidently the major factor that developed in all the session was that on two occasions Ed had had Bible discussions with some of those who had now been disfellowshipped. The judicial committee had no evidence that this had been the case but Ed voluntarily offered the information, having said from the start that he intended to be perfectly open with them on all points. These persons had approached him and on two occasions had had a meal with him after which they discussed portions of the book of Romans.[43]

The judicial committee wanted to know if he would talk to anyone else on these points. He replied that he had no intention of "campaigning" among the brothers. But he said that if persons came to him privately seeking help and he could direct them to the Scriptures for the answers to their question, he would do so, would feel an obligation to help them. In all likelihood, this was the determinative factor. Such freedom of private Scriptural discussion and expression was not acceptable, was viewed as heretical, as dangerously disruptive.

One statement made seemed particularly paradoxical. Ed had told them plainly that he had no desire to be disfellowshipped, that he enjoyed the brothers and had no desire or thought of cutting himself off from them. The committee urged him to "wait on the organization," saying, "Who knows? Perhaps five years from now many or all of these things you are saying will be published and taught."

They knew the fluctuating nature of the organization's teachings and doubtless on that basis felt they could say this. But how much conviction as to the rightness, the solid Scriptural basis for these teachings at issue, did this show on their part? If they were willing to accept the possibility

---

43   Ed was assigned by the Governing Body's Teaching Committee to conduct a regular class on Romans for the Branch Committee members in their seminars.

that the organization's teaching on these points might be no more solid and enduring than that, how could they possibly use them as the basis for deciding whether this man was a loyal servant of God or an apostate?

If they considered that these teachings (to which the Chairman's Committee had attached such major importance) were so subject to change that it would be worth while to wait and see what five years would bring, why was it not also worth while to postpone any judicial action against this man who had given, not five years, but half a century of service to the organization?

The logic of such an approach can be understood only if one accepts and embraces the premise that an individual's interests—including his good name, his hard-earned reputation, his years of life spent in service— are all expendable if they interfere with an organization's objectives.

I feel sure that every man on that judicial committee recognized that Edward Dunlap had a deep love for God, for Christ and for the Bible— yet they felt they had to take action against him. Why? They knew the temperament prevailing within the Governing Body, expressed through its Chairman's Committee. Organizational loyalty required such action by them, for this man did not, could not, accept all the claims and interpretations of that organization.

So they disfellowshipped Ed Dunlap, and he was asked to leave what had been his home at the Bethel headquarters. He returned to Oklahoma City where he had grown up and where, now 72 years of age, he supported himself and his wife by hanging wallpaper, a trade he had practiced before he began his 40 years of service as a full-time representative of the Watch Tower Bible and Tract Society.[44]

Edward Dunlap and his wife

---

44 Edward Dunlap continued secular employment up until he was 86 (though physically unable to keep up his wallpaper hanging work). He died on September 17, 1999 at the age of 88.

How those responsible—genuinely and primarily responsible—for all this can approach God in prayer at night and say, "Show us mercy as we have shown mercy to others," is difficult for me to understand.

12

AFTERMATH

I know that after my going away oppressive wolves will enter in among you and will not treat the flock with tenderness.
— Acts 20:29.

THERE is an old expression, "An iron hand in a velvet glove."
I do not believe that the events of the spring of 1980 produced the hardhandedness manifested by the authority structure. I believe the hardness was already there, that history shows it was. What took place in the spring of 1980 merely caused the velvet glove to be removed, exposing the unyielding hardness underneath. What followed supports that conclusion.

When the judicial committee of five Bethel elders that, by any standard of rightness, did for the Governing Body what the Governing Body should have done for itself, finally met with Ed Dunlap and informed him of their decision to disfellowship him, Ed said to them:

All right, if that is your decision. But *don't you say that it's for "apostasy."* You know that apostasy means rebellion against God and Christ Jesus, and *you know that that is not true of me.*

In the August, 1980, edition of the monthly paper called *Our Kingdom Service,* sent to all congregations, the front page contained the statement that a number of persons in the Bethel family had been disfellowshipped and then spoke of "apostasy against the organization." This phrasing, though still false (for there had been no rebellion even against the organization) was at least closer to the truth than statements made elsewhere.

On May 28, 1980, my letter of resignation was read to the headquarters family. On May 29, a meeting of all Bethel elders was called.

387

Jon Mitchell was among these. He was serving as a secretary in both the Service Department and the Governing Body offices. My only contact with him had been when he obtained visas for me for my trip to Africa. He had never conversed with any of those who were disfellowshipped. He had, however, seen some of the correspondence from judicial committees passing through the offices and had heard the departmental gossip about the "heresy" trials. Relating his impressions of the elders meeting, and the talks given by Governing Body members Schroeder and Barry, he says:

> Schroeder's talk focused on the subject of organization. He spoke about our "finely tuned organization" and how certain ones who seemed to feel that they couldn't go along with its rules and regulations "ought to be leaving and not be involved in the further progressive work here." (The publication *Branch Organization* was held up to illustrate how "finely tuned" the organization was, and he said that this publication contained over 1,000 rules and regulations regarding the operations of the Branches and the Brooklyn headquarters.) He stressed that this was not a "witch hunt," but there appeared to be a "pruning" going on.
>
> Of those who had left, he said, "It's not that they don't believe the Bible, you'd have to be an atheist to think that way," but "they understand it differently."
>
> He concluded his part by opening it up to questions from the Bethel elders. Harold Jackson raised his hand and suggested that there be a "forum" or open discussion of what the issues were. Schroeder replied that they had no plans to do this. If we had a question we could send in a letter. Another elder, Warren Weil, asked if the possibility of having the brothers take "loyalty oaths" had been considered. Brother Schroeder replied that that avenue was not being pursued at that time.
>
> Lloyd Barry's talk seemed to be an effort to refute some of the beliefs apparently held by those viewed as apostates and to sound a call for loyalty to the organization. He read Proverbs 24:21, 22, and warned that we should beware of "those who are for a change." He spoke disparagingly of certain ones who were getting together to study the Bible in an independent fashion, claiming that some were even doing this instead of going to the *Watchtower* study on Monday evening.

He likewise spoke in unfavorable terms of those inclined to use commentaries by writers of Christendom. (Barnes' *Notes on the New Testament* were possessed by men in the Service Department and kept in open display; this remark prompted them to remove these and put them in drawers.) Barry spoke about our "rich heritage" as Jehovah's Witnesses and was visibly upset by the possibility that some did not hold it in as high esteem as he did and seemed inclined toward thinking which could be detrimental to the organization's growth and prosperity.

Though he had never discussed any Scriptural points or any of the issues involved with any of us who were the target of these talks, Jon writes:

This meeting and the events that followed had the effect of augmenting the sickening feeling developing in me since I first heard of the startling news of the disfellowshippings and Brother Franz's dismissal.

The August 1, 1980, *Watchtower* was to contain an article which listed what were considered to be various "signs of apostasy." But I already had some very clear-cut ideas of what the *actual* signs were. I was deeply distressed by the realization that the organization more and more seemed to be displaying these signs itself, as follows:

1) The suppression of free Bible reading. Though I knew it was not likely there would be Bible burnings, nonetheless, it was apparent that complete freedom to read the Scriptures and enjoy open Bible discussions was being curtailed. Why wouldn't the Governing Body permit an open discussion of the issues as suggested, especially since it involved individuals who had contributed much to the organization and who were greatly respected as good Bible scholars? What were they trying to hide? Couldn't the 'truth' stand up to such examination?

2) The apparent shift in emphasis from the Bible to our "rich heritage" or organizational traditions. I knew quite well that this had been the failing of many religious sects, including the Pharisees. Matthew 15 and Mark 7 contain the words of Jesus wherein he denounced them for giving greater weight to tradition than to God's word. The suggestion that a "loyalty oath" be required to ensure loyalty to an organization and its traditions was absolutely appalling to me. Yet it had been made in all seriousness.

3) Inquisition tactics. It seemed clear that the Governing Body, which I had considered to be there more for the purpose of serving the brothers, was wielding a very powerful authoritarian hand and was determined to act quickly and decisively in its handling of the matter. Would it not have been far wiser and judicious for them to act carefully and deliberately, thoroughly weighing and considering matters and then *slowly and cautiously* reaching a decision?

I remember thinking to myself at the Elders' meeting, "Stop! Slow down! Can't you see what you're doing?" I felt this way, not because of being disloyal to the organization, but because I loved it and wanted more than anything else for it to be solidly based on a firm foundation of truth.[1]

Like him, I initially retained hope that after the nightmare had passed, perhaps more rational thinking would begin to prevail, that the emotional, almost hysterical, "siege mentality" which treated a small number of conscientious individuals as if they constituted a mammoth threat to the worldwide organization, would be replaced by calmer, more judicious thought and action. The opposite took place.

Perhaps nothing illustrates so clearly the incredible demands now made for total conformity as does the following letter, sent out to all traveling representatives, Circuit and District Overseers, by the Service Department of the international headquarters, dated September 1, 1980. Here presented is material from the first two pages of the letter, the section under the heading "Protecting the Flock" being of special interest in this discussion (particularly relevant points are underlined).

---

1   In 1992 Jon Mitchell authored a booklet, *Where is the "Great Crowd" Serving God?*, sharing his research and observations from his time in Bethel in 1980. It has been included in this 2018 edition of *Crisis of Conscience* in its entirety in Appendix C.

WATCHTOWER
BIBLE AND TRACT SOCIETY OF NEW YORK, INC.

CABLE WATCHTOWER

117 ADAMS STREET, BROOKLYN, NEW YORK 11201, U.S.A.   PHONE (212) 625-1240

SCG:SSF   September 1, 1980

TO ALL CIRCUIT AND DISTRICT OVERSEERS

Dear Brothers:

We know that you and your wives benefitted greatly from the "Divine Love"
District Conventions. They impressively brought to our attention why love is
the most beneficial quality that we can develop. (1 Cor. 13:13) Love enables us
to remain united in spite of the limitations and shortcomings we manifest.
--Col. 3:12-14.

You can be sure that by your loving example, the brothers you serve will be
uplifted and strengthened in the faith. We have received a number of letters
informing us of the love you brothers and your wives have displayed. One body
of elders wrote concerning their circuit overseer: "(He) is truly devoted to do
Jehovah's will . . . being of spiritual assistance to all . . . approachable
in discussing any matter. (He) has a listening ear, showing empathy for the
brothers. Such brothers we can rely upon when future problems we know will come,
set in."

You can be confident that the brothers treasure your friendship, association
and love when you 'genuinely care for the things pertaining to them.' (Phil. 2:19-23,
29) Therefore, continue exerting yourselves to deal lovingly with them. Never
pressure them or scold them. Lead them, work hard with them, exhort them in accord
with their needs. Be patient if their progress appears slow. Such loving,
patient treatment will refresh the brothers.--Matt. 11:28-30.

PROTECTING THE FLOCK

A major responsibility of an overseer as he 'shepherds the flock of God in
his care' is to protect it from dangers. (Acts 20:28) Acts 20:29, 30 indicates that
one of those dangers can be men who apostatize. There is a fine study of this
subject in the August 1, 1980, Watchtower. All of you want to get thoroughly
familiar with the contents of the study articles. Encourage all of the elders and
ministerial servants, especially, to do likewise. Include key points in your
"Continue in the Things You Have Learned" program.

Help the elders discern between one who is a trouble-making apostate and
a Christian who becomes weak in faith and has doubts. (2 Peter 2; Jude 22, 23)
The former one should be dealt with decisively after extended efforts have been
put forth to readjust him. (2 John 7-10) On the other hand, one weak in faith
should be patiently and lovingly assisted to get the accurate knowledge that will
solidify his faith.

Page 2

Keep in mind that to be disfellowshiped, an apostate does not have to be a promoter of apostate views. As mentioned in paragraph two, page 17 of the August 1, 1980, Watchtower, "The word 'apostasy' comes from a Greek term that means 'a standing away from,' 'a falling away, defection,' 'rebellion, abandonment. Therefore, if a baptized Christian abandons the teachings of Jehovah, as presented by the faithful and discreet slave, and persists in believing other doctrine despite Scriptural reproof, then he is apostatizing. Extended, kindly efforts should be put forth to readjust his thinking. However, if, after such extended efforts have been put forth to readjust his thinking, he continues to believe the apostate ideas and rejects what he has been provided through the 'slave class, then appropriate judicial action should be taken.

This is not to say that you or the elders should go on 'witch hunts,' as it were, inquiring into the personal beliefs of your brothers. Rather, if something reasonably substantial comes to the attention of the elders along this line, it would be appropriate to make a kindly, discreet inquiry so as to protect the flock. We cannot overemphasize the need to be cautious, discreet and kindly as such situations are dealt with.--James 1:19, 20.

COOPERATION BETWEEN BODIES OF ELDERS

In some of our larger cities it has been noticed that, at times, when wrongdoing is uncovered, several congregations may be involved. There is a need for full cooperation between the bodies of elders of these congregations. The elders should be alert to the need to quickly pass on to the bodies of elders of other congregations any information about publishers in their congregations that may necessitate an investigation. Any who have indiscreetly gotten themselves involved in wrong conduct need to be assisted right away. Any who have allowed themselves to become hardened in sin need to be severely reproved and if unresponsive to this, expelled from the congregation. It would be good for you to alert the bodies of elders in your circuit to the material that was presented to you in your seminar in the fall of 1979 in outline #13 under the heading "Elders Still Need Assistance in Handling Intercongregational Problems." Whatever information is needed and available should be passed on quickly to the elders of the congregation involved.

You want to help elders feel keenly the obligation before God to prevent wrongdoing from infiltrating and spreading within the congregation. (1 Cor. 5:6-8) The judicial committee should make great effort to see if the individual is genuinely repentant before extending forgiveness to him for the bad name that he has given to the congregation. Usually a person who is truly repentant can point to some "fruit that befits repentance." (Matt 3:8) We want to have in mind that no matter how good the counsel or reproof, if the person's heart is unresponsive, given the same circumstances he will repeat the sin. To protect the flock the elders must be willing to take decisive action in such cases.

The letter presents an official policy. It actually says that a person's believing—not promoting, but simply *believing*—something that differs from the teachings of the organization is grounds for taking judicial action against him as an "apostate"!

The letter makes no qualifying statements limiting such differences of belief to fundamental teachings of God's Word, such as the coming of God's Son as a man, the ransom, faith in Christ's shed blood as the basis for salvation, the resurrection, or similar basic Bible doctrines. It does not even say that the person necessarily disagrees with the Bible, the Word of God. Rather, he disagrees with "the teachings of Jehovah, *as presented by the faithful and discreet slave.*" Which is something like saying that a man's accepting and obeying a King's written message is no guarantee that he is loyal; it is his accepting and obeying what a slave messenger claims the ruler meant that decides this!

The symbol at the top of the September 1, 1980 letter ("SCG") identifies the composer of it as Leon Weaver. But it should not be thought that this "thought-control" policy was the thinking of one individual, nor was it some momentary off-the-cuff expression of extremism which a person might make and afterward feel ashamed of as a rash, harsh and utterly unchristian position to take. The composer was a member of the Service Department Committee whose members, such as Harley Miller, David Olson, Joel Adams, Charles Woody and Leon Weaver, were all longtime representatives of the organization, with decades of experience behind them. They were agents of the Governing Body in supervising the activity of about 10,000 congregations and the activity of all the elders, Circuit and District Overseers in the United States, where nearly one million Jehovah's Witnesses live. They were in regular contact with the Service Committee of the Governing Body and were supposed to be thoroughly familiar with the Governing Body policies, attuned to its thinking and viewpoint and spirit.

But this only adds to the appalling aspect of the position the letter took. As I know from years on the Service Committee, any letter of this importance *must* be submitted to the Governing Body Service Committee for approval before being sent out.[2] Objection by even one member of that Committee would have resulted in the letter's going before the entire Governing Body for discussion.

Whatever the case, the letter and its policy—which evokes memories of the position of religious authorities in the Inquisition—had to have been approved by a number of headquarters representatives, including several Governing Body members. Since people's friendships, family

---

2   The members at that time were Ted Jaracz (Coordinator), Milton Henschel, Albert Schroeder, William Jackson and Martin Poetzinger.

relationships, personal honor and other life interests were all at stake, it should be presumed that these men gave long, careful thought to that statement of September 1, 1980, before approving it as an official expression from the "faithful and discreet slave" of Jesus Christ. What they there said was no light matter to be explained away later by saying, "Well, we really didn't mean it exactly the way it sounded." As the facts show, people, many persons, were actually disfellowshipped and continue to be disfellowshipped solely on the basis of this very thought-control policy sent out. The denigrating label of "apostate" is placed on their name simply because in their own hearts, they cannot accept all of the Society's interpretations.

Possibly this policy resulted from or was influenced by something that developed earlier that year in one of the New York congregations. Jon Mitchell, mentioned previously as working part time in the Service Department, relates:

> Somewhere around this time period [referring to the early summer of 1980] a memo came down from F. W. Franz, apparently in response to a question that had been sent in by Harold Jackson [part of the Service Department staff].
>
> It seems there was a pioneer (full-time preaching) sister in a Spanish congregation who felt she could not conscientiously teach that the 144,000 of Revelation 7 and 14 was a literal number. She said she would not proselytize or seek to publicize an opposing view, but she did not want to teach that the 144,000 was a literal number to those with whom she studied the Bible.
>
> Brother Jackson's question apparently was to the effect of wanting to know whether or not such a person could be classified as an "apostate." The memo confirmed that such a person could indeed be viewed as an apostate and should be disfellowshipped if she did not agree to teach what the Society instructed her to teach. I recall someone in the Service Department referring to the outcome of this case and stating that the girl had "recanted." I was amazed that such terminology could be used without any sense of shame.

One might think that the extreme position taken in the September 1, 1980, letter, earlier quoted, conveyed to all elders by the traveling representatives, would produce, if not a storm of protest, at least some measurable expression of dismay from elders and others. They were too well trained for that to be the case. Some few individuals did express themselves, but cautiously, lest they also receive the label of "apostate." Certainly the lack of protest was not because they had 'proved to themselves that this was the good and acceptable and perfect will of God,' as the apostle urges.[3] Rereading the paragraph on page two, one finds not a single scripture advanced as proof that such thought-control policy has any Scriptural support. The Christian's thoughts are to be 'brought into captivity to the Christ,' not to men or an organization.[4] Why then this willingness to surrender one's conscience to such total control?

It is the concept of "the organization" that produces this. That concept creates the belief that, to all intents and purposes, whatever the organization speaks; it is as if God himself were speaking. Perhaps epitomizing the spirit that the Society's pronouncements, including this letter, produced is an incident occurring at a Circuit Assembly meeting for elders of a section of Alabama. The District Overseer, Bart Thompson, held up a Society publication that had a green cover. He then said to the assembly of elders, "If the Society told me that this book is black instead of green, I would say, 'Y'know I could have sworn that it was green, but if the Society says it's black, then it's black!'" Others have used similar illustrations.

True, there are many thinking Witnesses who are repelled by such blatant expressions of blind faith. Yet most are still willing to conform, even to take "judicial action" against any who express doubts about the Society's interpretations. Why?

I try in my own mind and heart to understand the feelings of all these persons, including those on the Governing Body. Based on my own experience among them I believe that they are, in effect, the captives of a concept. The concept or mental image they have of "the organization" seems almost to take on a personality of its own, so that the concept itself controls them, moves them or restrains them, by molding their thinking, their attitudes, their judgments. I do not believe that many of them

---

3   Romans 12:2
4   2 Corinthians 10:5.

would take the position they now take if they thought only in terms of God, Christ, the Bible, and the interests—not of an organization—but of their Christian brothers, fellow humans. The insertion of the existing concept of "the organization," however, radically alters their thinking and viewpoint, becomes, in fact, the dominant, controlling force.

I believe that when the men on the Governing Body think about and refer to "the organization" they likewise think of the *concept* rather than the reality. They think of "the organization" as something far bigger and grander than themselves, thinking of it in its numerical aspect, in the extent of its scope of control, as something international, worldwide. They do not realize—apparently—that this aspect relates more to the organization's *domain* than to what it itself actually is. When, however, they urge "loyalty to the organization" they must know, they certainly *should* know, that they are not talking about that domain—about the thousands of congregations and their members that the organization directs. They are talking about loyalty to the *source* of the direction, the *source* of the teachings, the *source* of the authority. Whether the Governing Body members acknowledge it or whether they prefer not to think about it, the fact remains that in these crucial respects *they, and they alone, are "the organization."* Whatever other authority exists—that of the Branch Committees, that of the District or Circuit Overseers, that of Congregational Elder Bodies—that authority is totally dependent on that small body of men, subject to adjustment, change or removal at their decision, unilaterally, with no questions asked.

The June 22, 2000 *Awake!* earlier referred to makes these comments:

Slogans are vague statements that are typically used to express positions or goals. Because of their vagueness, they are easy to agree with.

For example, in times of national crisis or conflict, demagogues may use such slogans as "My country, right or wrong," "Fatherland, Religion, Family," or "Freedom or Death." But do most people carefully analyze the real issues involved in the crisis or conflict? Or do they just accept what they are told?

The propagandist also has a very wide range of symbols and signs with which to convey his message—a 21-gun salvo, a military salute, a flag. Love of parents can also be exploited. Thus, such symbolisms as the fatherland, the mother country, or the mother church are valuable tools in the hands of the shrewd persuader.

So the sly art of propaganda can paralyze thought, prevent clear thinking and discernment, and condition individuals to act en masse. How can you protect yourself?

I believe that for most of these Governing Body members, like the rest of Jehovah's Witnesses, "the organization" takes on a symbolic nature, something rather undefined, abstract, a concept rather than a concrete entity. Rather than the "mother church" it is the "mother organization." Perhaps because of such an illusory view of "the organization" a man can be a member of such a Body that has virtually unrestricted power and authority, and yet not feel a keen sense of personal responsibility for what the Body does, for whatever hurt or whatever misleading information and consequent misdirection results. "It was *the organization* that did it, not us," seems to be the thinking. And, believing that "the organization" is God's chosen instrument, the responsibility is passed on to God. It was His will—even if later the particular decision or the particular authoritative teaching is found wrong and changed. People may have been disfellowshipped or otherwise hurt by the wrong decisions. But the individual member of the Governing Body feels absolved of personal responsibility.

I express the above points, not as a means of condemnation but as a means of explanation, an attempt to understand why certain men that I consider to be honest, basically kind individuals could be party to what I feel that they in their own hearts, would normally have rejected. I think the concept earlier described is tragically wrong, as pernicious as it is tragic. I believe the drastic actions taken toward those persons accused of "apostasy" were, in almost all cases, not only unjustified but repugnant, unworthy not only of Christianity but of any free society of men. Yet this effort at comprehension enables me to be free from brooding or harboring bitterness toward the persons involved, either individually or collectively. Bitterness is both self-defeating and destructive. I do not know any person among those men that I would not be willing to express hospitality to in my home, with no questions asked, no issue of apology raised. Neither I nor any of my personal friends had any thought of cutting them, or any other persons, off from association because of a difference in understanding. The cutting off was not our thought, not our action.

When I met with the Governing Body the meeting was taped and I had been promised a copy of the tape. What happened to this? I believe what occurred is illustrative of points that have just been made.

About three weeks after returning to Alabama, I had occasion to write the Governing Body and took the opportunity to ask about my copy of the tape. I received a reply dated June 26, 1980.

PHONE (212) 625-1240

WATCH TOWER
BIBLE AND TRACT SOCIETY OF PENNSYLVANIA

CABLE WATCHTOWER

124 COLUMBIA HEIGHTS, BROOKLYN, NEW YORK 11201, U.S.A.

June 26, 1980

R. V. Franz
c/o P. V. Gregerson
Route 4, Box 444
Gadsden, AL 35904

Dear Brother Franz:

Your letter of June 14 has been received.

We checked with the shipping department and they inform us that your furniture has been crated and it was shipped out from Brooklyn on Tuesday, June 24. So you should be receiving it soon.

As for the tape about which you write this matter is being given attention and it will be sent to you just as quickly as a copy can be made and shipped on to you.

We will look forward to receiving the two procedure books that you will be sending to us. Your letter also enclosed the convention talk material you mentioned returning to us.

May Jehovah's blessing be with you and we send Christian love.

Your brothers,

Watch Tower ... T. Society
OF PENNSYLVANIA
For the Chairman's Committee

Two weeks passed and then this letter came:

PHONE (212) 625-1240

WATCH TOWER
BIBLE AND TRACT SOCIETY OF PENNSYLVANIA

CABLE WATCHTOWER

124 COLUMBIA HEIGHTS, BROOKLYN, NEW YORK 11201, U.S.A.

July 10, 1980

Mr.Raymond V. Franz
c/o P. V. Gregerson
Route 4, Box 444
Gadsden, AL 35904

Dear Brother Franz:

Further with regard to our letter of June 26:

We thank you for the return of the Branch Organization and Governing Body Procedure books, which arrived the other day. Also, the shipping department has notified us that your furniture items were sent and that they have been received by you.

While the Chairman's Committee had mentioned that the matter of sending you the tape of May 20 (although it may be the tape of May 21st that you have in mind of the Governing Body meeting) was "being given attention," the Governing Body has now thought it well not to make up and give out any copies of the tapes for either of such dates. Also, in view of a confidential item which had been sent to the Governing Body members in April somehow coming into the hands of one of the members of the Bethel family who was disfellowshiped, and which was further circulated, the Governing Body has determined that it would not be advisable to open the records of its sessions (be it by tapes or minutes in writing) to anyone off the Society's premises. Furthermore, a change of status as to yourself has occurred. If in the future you would wish to obtain information from the tape we would not object to making such available to you to hear at Bethel.

While we did verbally mention, and also write, that a copy of the tape would be available to you, now the situation has seriously changed. As you no doubt can appreciate the Governing Body feels that this would be a more discreet course. We trust that you will find this arrangement a reasonable one.

It is hoped all is well with you and we send our Christian love and greetings.

Your brothers,

Watch Tower B.&T. Society
OF PENNSYLVANIA

For the Chairman's Committee

A NONPROFIT CORPORATION

The letter unavoidably brought back memories of the way matters had been handled from the start, from the time the Chairman's Committee had first put in motion the judicial machinery and actions that produced the various disfellowshippings. I had hoped all that was passed. I had no way of knowing what they were referring to in writing of "a confidential item which had been sent to the Governing Body in April." While in Brooklyn I had not seen any of the disfellowshipped persons, nor did I see them between then and my return to Alabama. So I replied as follows:

                                        July 19, 1980

Watchtower Society
Attention: Chairman's Committee

Dear Brothers:

    This will acknowledge receipt of your letter of July 10.
Yes, the furniture items were received by us in good condition
and we appreciate the work of the brothers in shipping in caring
for this.

    I note what you say about the decision not to send the
tape of May 21 (incorrectly stated by me as May 20). As you
must realize, the agreement was, and it was stated by the
Chairman of the body before the session, that such would be
provided to me. There were no qualifications stated, such as
my status, my being at Bethel or outside of Bethel. It was
a simple acknowledgement of the one provision that I required
before agreeing to having the session taped, and you accepted
that stipulation and agreed to it. Since you have acknowledged
in writing that this is the case then it seems you should hold
true to your agreement. What others have done cannot be used
as a basis for breaking your agreement with me. If you do not
intend to hold true to that agreement then it is plain that the
only fair thing for you to do is to destroy that tape and any
transcripts or copies thereof. For if I am not entitled to a
copy of it then neither should you be, for I only agreed to it
on the provision that I would receive a copy of it.

    I have not completed my review of my papers but believe that
I have some further material that should be returned to you and
I will do this as soon as possible.

    I will look forward to hearing from you at an early date
on the matter of the tape. I will expect to receive either the
tape or your letter to the effect that the tape and any copies or
transcripts thereof have been destroyed.

    Thank you for your attention to the above and may God aid
you in loyally upholding the high principles of his Word and
the good news about his Kingdom.

                    Yours in Jehovah's service,

                    R. V. Franz

This is the answer the Governing Body sent me three weeks later.

PHONE (212) 625-1240

WATCH TOWER
BIBLE AND TRACT SOCIETY OF PENNSYLVANIA

124 COLUMBIA HEIGHTS, BROOKLYN, NEW YORK 11201, U.S.A.

CABLE WATCHTOWER

August 8, 1980

Raymond Franz
c/o P.V. Gregerson
Route 4, Box 444
Gadsden, AL 35904

Dear Brother Franz:

Your letter of July 19 with reference to the Chairman's Committee letter to you of July 10, has been received.

The Governing Body decided for the time being not to send you the tapes of the May 21 meeting as mentioned in our letter to you of the 10th of July. As described in our letter if you desire to hear the information on these tapes they are available to you for listening at Bethel.

We send our greetings.

Your fellow servants of Jehovah,

Watch Tower B. & T. Society
OF PENNSYLVANIA

For the Chairman's Committee

They answered not a single point I had raised. The sense of unreality I had experienced before now came back. It seemed difficult to believe that men in responsible positions could act so irresponsibly. The letter's tone conveyed the attitude that all rights belonged to them (to "the organization") and that the rights of individuals could simply be ignored, if that appeared desirable and advantageous, summarily set aside as of no particular consequence. I wrote once more, as follows:

August 28, 1980

Chairman's Committee
Brooklyn, New York

Dear Brothers:

I have received your letter of August 8 which is in
response to mine of July 19 with regard to the tape you
agreed to send me.

Your letter is a response but not a reply. It simply
repeats in abbreviated form your letter of July 10 and makes
no reply to the points presented in my letter of July 19.

The fact is that you have in your possession tapes of
the May 21 meeting only as a result of an unkept agreement.
To set up new conditions after an agreement has been made,
doing so unilaterally and arbitrarily, is certainly not fair
by any standards. In your letter of June 26 you acknowledged
in writing that you had made an agreement to provide me a
copy of the tape of the meeting and stated your intention of
preparing such copy and sending it to me. My status had already
changed at that time, yet this was subsequently used as one
basis for not keeping your agreement. The reasons given for
not carrying out your agreement, as stated in your letter of
July 10, are in no way a justification for a breach of contract.

May I urge you to meditate upon the consequences of such
a course, keeping in mind the principle set forth at Leviticus
19:15; Romans 1:31. In view of your evident concern about
releasing a copy of the tape, I have offered you the only
honorable alternative, that of eliminating the tape and any
copy or transcripts thereof. If you wish to keep the tape then
the only just thing to do is to keep the agreement by which you
obtained it. I have no doubt that if the circumstances were
reversed, with the tape being in my possession and you being the
petitioners for an agreed-upon copy, you would take the same
position that I have taken.--Matthew 7:12.

Please accept the above as an expression of concern for
your own spiritual interests as well as for that of brothers
everywhere. Though my status may be viewed as a lowly and not
a high one, I will appreciate your manifesting consideration for
the points made in this letter and my letter of July 19.

Your brother,

R. V. Franz

Nearly one month later, another letter came:

WATCH TOWER
BIBLE AND TRACT SOCIETY OF PENNSYLVANIA

PHONE (212) 625-1240

CABLE WATCHTOWER

124 COLUMBIA HEIGHTS, BROOKLYN, NEW YORK 11201, U.S.A.

GT/A   September 24,1980

Raymond V. Franz
Route 4, Box 440F
Gadsden, AL 35904

Dear Brother Franz:

Your letter of August 28, 1980 has been received and has been given consideration.

This is to inform you that the tapes of the May 21, 1980, meeting to which you have made reference have now been destroyed. There are three witnesses of the Governing Body who were present when such tapes were destroyed. There were no written transcripts made of the material that was taped, nor were any taped copies made of the recordings. The tapes have been totally destroyed.

This is in accordance with your wishes as set out in your correspondence to us.

Your brothers,

Watch Tower B. & T. Society
OF PENNSYLVANIA

For the Chairman's Committee

As the correspondence already presented shows, my "wishes" actually were for the copy of the tape to be sent as promised. Since they clearly were unwilling to part with it (recalling somewhat the "Watergate" attitude), I had offered them an option, which they finally exercised. At any rate, I was glad to have the matter settled and hoped that was the end of any further dealings with the Body. It was not.

Some weeks after my return to Alabama, and prior to the exchange of letters set out above, the Society had sent me a check for $10,000, as a gift 'to aid in reestablishing in the South.' I had made no request for money and the action taken was both unexpected and appreciated. It took a loan of another $5,000 to obtain a mobile home, and Peter Gregerson allowed us to park this on his property. I was grateful to be able (as well as economically obliged) to do strenuous physical labor for Peter in yard work. Each day was spent mowing lawns, cutting weeds, trimming hedges, being stung by wasps and yellow jackets, bitten innumerable times by fire ants, sweating through one period when for 30 consecutive days the temperature out in the sun passed 100° Fahrenheit (38° C.). I cannot recall any other time in my life till then when I had experienced the constant physical pain that I did during those months. Yet I was glad for it, as it served to offset the emotional hurt I felt.[5]

The greatest help, for both my wife and myself, was, however, our daily reading of the Scriptures. Each morning we read four of the Psalms, doing this consecutively until completing them. Though read many times before, they seemed almost new to us now. We could relate to them so much more. For if any one part of the Bible makes clear the very *personal* relationship that can and should exist between God's servants and himself, the Psalms seem to do this, outstandingly so. The emotional upset, the sighing, the feeling of helplessness and despair that the writers so often expressed, their ultimate acknowledgment in each case that their full and final hope was and must be, not in men, but in Jehovah God as their Rock and high place of protection, struck a very responsive chord in both of us.

My determination on leaving the international headquarters had been not to precipitate problems. I did not go looking for trouble. The trouble came looking for me.

For a number of months we enjoyed a pleasant relationship with the members of the East Gadsden Congregation of Jehovah's Witnesses, sharing in their meetings and in the "field activity." A few months after

---

5   The present copyright owner of *Crisis of Conscience*, had discussions with both Raymond Franz and Peter Gregerson about Ray's preference to do yard work at this time. Peter's original intention was that Ray would have an office job in his business. Nevertheless, Ray strenuously insisted that he do yard work! With great reluctance Peter acquiesced to his request. Ray said that he needed to "sweat" some things out! In the end, Peter observed that the hard labor was therapeutic for Ray as he sought to emotionally process all that had occurred at Brooklyn headquarters.

my arrival the local body of elders wrote to Brooklyn recommending my appointment as an elder in the congregation. The brief reply that came back said succinctly that the Society did not think it advisable for the elders to recommend me as such (or as a ministerial servant). The only reason given was that the notice of my resignation (published in the same *Our Kingdom Service* as the information about the disfellowshipping of several staff members) was still recent. The presiding overseer of the congregation seemed upset by the spirit of the letter but I recommended he simply forget about it.

With this letter, plus the information given out to elders as a result of the September 1, 1980, Society letter (stating that mere *belief* that differed from the published teachings of the Society was grounds for disfellowshipping), the atmosphere gradually began to change. The *Watchtower* magazine began publishing articles clearly designed, not to calm matters, but to focus discussion on the supposed "apostasy" taking place. From then till now, by word and by printed page, a concerted campaign has apparently been under way to justify the extreme treatment meted out to those brothers in Brooklyn who were so swiftly expelled, and more particularly the viewpoint and policy behind this that continue to operate. Rather than a lessening of dogmatism the claims of divine authority and the accompanying calls for unquestioning loyalty became more strident. Issue after issue of the *Watchtower* magazine focused on points that had been questioned, insisted on their rightness, and in general produced a definite entrenchment of position rather than a moderating thereof. The argumentation used to achieve this seemed to reach new lows in misrepresentation of any contrary views.

An atmosphere of both suspicion and fear developed. Elders who were by nature moderate men felt hesitant about calling for moderation lest this be viewed as evidence of disloyalty. Those who were inclined toward tough action found favorable opportunities to express their hardline attitude. It recalled the McCarthy period in the United States, when anyone who spoke on behalf of civil rights and freedom and expressed disapproval of ruthless methods of crushing unpopular ideologies was in real danger of being classed as a "Communist sympathizer," a "fellow traveler" of radical elements.

Under these circumstances, meeting attendance for me became more and more depressing, as it meant hearing God's Word misused, made to say things it did not say, as well as hearing the constant self-authentication and self-commendation of the organization. It made one wish that there was at least the freedom of expression found in the first-century synagogues that granted persons, such as the apostles, opportunity to speak out in favor of truth (though even there this inevitably led to a hardening of attitude that eventually would close the doors of the synagogue to them). But, as I remarked to Peter Gregerson, I considered myself simply a guest at the Kingdom Hall; it was their Hall, their meetings, their programs, and I had no desire to put a "damper" on their carrying them out. So, I limited my comments to the reading of relevant scriptures, simply emphasizing whatever portion was applicable. It was a rare meeting that someone, often an older member, did not come up afterward and make some expression of appreciation.

The "crusade" atmosphere developing, however, gave me reason to believe it was just a matter of time until some further action would be taken toward me. And so it happened.

THE CRIME AND THE SENTENCE

Both the Pharisees and the scribes kept muttering, saying: "This man welcomes sinners and even eats with them."
— Luke 15:2.

One meal was all the evidence needed. It happened this way:

Within about six months of my return to northern Alabama, the Society sent a new Circuit Overseer into the area. The previous man had been a moderate person, inclined to play down problems rather than make issues of them. The man who replaced him had a reputation for greater aggressiveness. This was about the time the Society's letter to District and Circuit Overseers had come out saying that "apostasy" included persons who even *believed* something different from the organization's teachings.

On his second visit to the East Gadsden Congregation (March 1981) the new Circuit Overseer, Wesley Benner, arranged to meet with Peter

Gregerson, going to his home along with a local elder, Jim Pitchford. The reason? Benner told Peter that there was a "lot of talk" about him in the city and in the circuit. Peter said he was very sorry to hear that. Where was the "talk" coming from? Benner was reluctant to say, but Peter pointed out that he needed to know to remedy the situation. Benner then said the source was an in-law of Peter's family.

Peter made clear that he had put forth every effort to be circumspect in his expressions and that any conversations on Scriptural matters he had had with anyone in the area were strictly with his own relatives. He was deeply concerned that persons outside his family relationship were now engaging in "a lot of talk," as the Circuit Overseer had said. "How could that be?" he asked. Wesley Benner offered no explanation.

What, then, were they talking *about?* Benner brought up a point in a certain *Watchtower* article that Peter had reportedly objected to. Under no circumstances could the point be called a "major teaching" of Scripture; it actually involved a technicality.[6] Nonetheless, since Peter had not agreed with the organization it became important. After long discussion, the Circuit Overseer was finally obliged to acknowledge that the point might indeed be in error. (In actual fact, the Watchtower Society acknowledged the error in a letter dated May 11, 1981, sent in response to an inquiry. The letter stated that "point three in the summary that appears at the bottom of page 15 was deleted in translating this article for publication in foreign language editions of The Watchtower." (This statement, however, was not true.)[7]

Peter said afterward, "I was determined not to let a 'confrontation' situation develop and I did everything I could to keep the conversation calm and reasonable." When the Circuit Overseer and the local elder left,

---

6   The article, in the August 15, 1980, issue of the *Watchtower,* endeavored to show that the Greek term *naos* (temple or sanctuary), used in Revelation 7:15 with regard to the "great crowd," could apply to the temple courtyards. In doing so it said that Jesus chased the moneychangers out of the *naos.* (See page 15, box at the bottom of the page.) Since the Bible account itself, at John 2:14-16, clearly uses another term (*hieron*), the claim was obviously false, as one elder expressed it, "either an example of intellectual dishonesty or intellectual ignorance."

7   For full documentation of this matter, see the booklet *Where Is the "Great Crowd" Serving God?* by Jon Mitchell, which has been placed in Appendix C of this 2018 edition of *Crisis of Conscience* in it's entirety.

Peter felt the matter had ended on a friendly basis and was glad that was the case. It was not.

The following week, the Circuit Overseer sent word that he wanted a second meeting to pursue the matter further.

Peter told me he felt that the time had come to make a decision. The spirit that had been generated by the Governing Body, its Service Department and its letter of September 1, 1980, and a succession of *Watchtower* articles, had built up to the point where a "witch hunt" atmosphere prevailed. He felt it would be naïve on his part if he failed to recognize the strong likelihood that efforts were under way to bring about his disfellowshipment. His befriending me, he felt, was at least a contributing factor. As he saw it, he had two choices: either voluntarily disassociate himself from the congregation or let the efforts under way continue to their goal of disfellowshipping him. He found neither choice desirable but of the two he believed he should take the first, voluntarily disassociate himself.

When I expressed doubt as to whether things had reached that stage yet, he said he had weighed the matter, prayed about it, and felt it was the wiser course. The factor that most concerned him, he said, was his family. Of his seven children, three were married, some had children, and he had three brothers and two sisters living in the area and many nephews and nieces. All of them were Jehovah's Witnesses.[8] If he allowed the organization's representatives to push matters to the point of disfellowshipping, it would make for a very difficult situation for all these family members. It would put them in a serious dilemma as to whether to associate with him as their father or grandfather or brother or uncle, or, instead, to be obedient to the organization and shun him. Additionally, there were about thirty-five Witnesses in the employ of his grocery company. Voluntary disassociation seemed better since, as he understood it, it simply meant that he was no longer a member of the congregation. But it did not call

---

8   His wife's family also included many witnesses.

for the rigid cutting off of relations that organizational policy required in cases of disfellowshipping [9]

Peter submitted his letter of resignation on March 18, 1981. It was read to the congregation. Although normal comment followed, inasmuch as Peter had been a Witness from childhood and had taken the lead for many years in local congregation activity, the letter seemed to clear the air since it calmly presented his reasons and expressed no animosity. With rare exception, Jehovah's Witnesses in Gadsden, on meeting up with Peter, treated him in a manner that was at least cordial. I think they would have kept on doing so had they been governed by their own sense of right and wrong. It seemed that a crisis situation had been averted.

Within six months the *Watchtower* magazine published articles changing the whole picture. Some commented to me, "They did everything but put your name and Peter Gregerson's in the magazine." I do not believe the situation in Gadsden was solely responsible for the articles. I do believe, however, that it did have some effect on the ones motivated to prepare these. What was the change made in these articles?

Back in 1974 the Governing Body assigned me to write articles on the treatment of disfellowshipped persons. (The Body had just made a decision that made this advisable.)[10] Those articles, duly approved by the

---

9   I knew personally that the Governing Body had till then equated disassociation and disfellowshipment *only* in the case of persons entering politics or the military, *not* for a simple resignation from the congregation. I had, in fact, been assigned to undertake a revision of the *Aid to Answering Branch Office Correspondence* manual which spelled out all such policies and I knew that no such extreme position had been reached on disassociation. Persons who resigned were not treated the same as those disfellowshipped, with the sole exception that if they desired to re-enter the congregation they had to submit a request to that effect. After hearing that the Service Department had sent out some letters that, in effect, equated disassociation with disfellowshipment, I talked with a member of the Service Department Committee and pointed out that the matter had never been presented to the Governing Body and that any such action had to be of the Service Department's own doing (an example of the Department's occasional unauthorized "policy-making" actions). He acknowledged that nothing on this had come through from the Governing Body.

10   Two cases had come before the Body of disfellowshipped persons who wanted to attend meetings but needed assistance. One was a young girl living in a rural area in New England, the other a woman in a drug rehabilitation center in the Midwest. Neither could get to meetings without assistance as to transportation. The Governing Body's decision was that it would be acceptable to provide transportation in such cases.

Body, greatly moderated the attitude that had prevailed up to that time, encouraged Witnesses to manifest a more merciful attitude in many areas of their contacts with disfellowshipped persons, reduced the rigidity of policies governing dealings with a disfellowshipped family member.

The September 15, 1981, *Watchtower* not only reversed this, on some points it carried the matter backward to an even more rigid position than had existed previous to 1974. (An example of "tacking" backwards, this time to a point *behind* the starting place.)[11]

A major change made was with regard to any voluntarily disassociating themselves (as Peter Gregerson had done a few months previous). For the first time the policy was officially published that anyone doing this was to be treated in the same way as if he had been expelled from the congregation.[12]

When I read the material, viewing it against my background of experience on the Governing Body (and particularly in the light of my recent experiences with the Chairman's Committee) I had little doubt as to where this would lead. I did not have long to wait.

What is now related is given in detail not because my own case is involved or because it is so unusual, but instead because it is so typical of what others experienced, the methods and actions of elders of Jehovah's Witnesses in case after case of this kind. It is illustrative of the thinking and spirit inculcated in them, a thinking and spirit derived from a central source.

Though published with a September 15 date, the *Watchtower* magazine in question arrived over two weeks before that date. Within a few days, came a visit from a local elder of the East Gadsden Congregation of Jehovah's Witnesses, Dan Gregerson, Peter's youngest brother. He asked

---

11   The *Watchtower* of December 1, 1981, carried an article attempting to justify all the shifting back and forth on various doctrinal points on the Society's part. It used the analogy of a boat tacking against the wind. The problem is that the shifting of teaching often brings them back virtually to the point where they began.

12   This was directed primarily toward those who resigned. While those entering politics or the military were classed as "disassociated," this was not some voluntary action on their part, not on their request. It was an automatic action taken by the elders in accord with Society policy. So the new position dealt with those *voluntarily* withdrawing.

if he and a couple of other elders could come out and speak to me. I said that would be all right; what did they want to talk about? After some hesitation, he said first that it was to discuss my having made remarks of an adverse nature about the organization. When I inquired who was the source of such a claim, he said the person preferred to remain anonymous. (This 'shooting of spears out of the fog' is quite common and the one accused is supposed to take this all as quite normal and proper.)

I asked him, however, if he did not think that Jesus' counsel at Matthew, chapter eighteen, verses 15 to 17, should apply (the counsel there being that one with a complaint against a brother should first go himself and talk with his brother about the problem)? Dan agreed it did apply. I suggested that as an elder he see the individual and recommend that he come and talk to me about the matter and thus apply Jesus' counsel. He replied that the person did not feel "qualified." I pointed out that that really was not at issue, that I had no interest in arguing with anyone, but that if I had disturbed someone I would appreciate that person's telling me personally so that I could apologize and set matters straight. (I still do not know of whom he was speaking.) Dan's reply was that I had to realize that the elders also had "a responsibility to protect the flock and watch out for the interests of the sheep." I agreed fully and said I was sure he realized that doing this certainly meant that elders should encourage everyone in the flock to hold carefully to God's Word and apply it in their lives. In this case, they could help the party involved to see the need to apply Jesus' counsel and come and speak with me, then I could know what had offended the person and make whatever apology was needed.

He said he would drop that point and went on to say that they wanted to discuss my "associations" with me. They would be welcome to do that, I said, and it was agreed that he and another elder would come two days later. Dan and an elder named Theotis French came. The conversation started with Dan's reading Second Corinthians, chapter thirteen, verses 7 to 9, and informing me that they were there to "readjust" my thinking in connection with the September 15, 1981, *Watchtower,* particularly as regards my association with his brother, Peter Gregerson, now disassociated. Dan had been in a restaurant in August when Peter and I and our wives had a meal there.

I asked them if they realized they were right then on Peter's property, that in that sense he was my landlord. That I was also in his employ. They knew that.

I explained that, as in all matters, I was governed by conscience as regards my associations and I discussed Paul's counsel about the importance of conscience in his letter to the Romans, chapter fourteen. Whatever the Scriptures instructed, I would be happy to do, but I saw no evidence to support the view now adopted as to disassociated persons. What Scriptural support was there?

The conversation now followed an easily predictable course: Dan referred to First Corinthians, chapter five, in support of the position. I pointed out that the apostle there spoke of not associating with persons called brothers who were fornicators, idolaters, revilers, drunkards and extortioners. I had no such persons among my associates and would not want them in my home. But surely they did not consider Peter Gregerson as included among that kind of people? Neither responded.

Dan then referred to the apostle John's words at First John, chapter two, verse 19: "They went out from us, but they were not of our sort; for if they had been of our sort, they would have remained with us." When asked what the context showed as to the kind of persons John spoke of, they acknowledged that he was speaking of "antichrists." I pointed out that the same was true in John's Second Letter, verses 7 to 11, which deals with association with such ones. I assured them that I would never fellowship with an antichrist, one who had rebelled against God and Christ, but that again I had none such among my acquaintances. Surely they were not saying that Peter Gregerson was an antichrist? Again, no response.[13]

This was, *actually,* the extent of the Scriptural "readjustment" that I received from these two shepherds of the flock. From that point on their only references were to the *Watchtower* magazine. Did I accept what it said on this subject, did I submit to the organization's direction? I stated that in the end the real question was what God's Word says on any matter,

---

13   Dan Gregerson acknowledged that he had never made the effort to speak to his brother, Peter, about Peter's differences of viewpoint, although Dan was fully aware of them.

that some teachings are clearly solid, founded immovably on God's Word; other teachings can be subject to change.

In illustration, I asked Dan if he thought it possible that the organization could, at some future time, change its view as to the application of Jesus' expression about "this generation" in Matthew, chapter twenty-four? (I did not tell them that Governing Body members Schroeder, Klein and Suiter had in fact suggested a change that would have moved the start of that "generation" from 1914 up to 1957.) Dan's reply was, "If the organization sees fit to change it at some future time, then I will accept it." While not a direct answer, that indicated he recognized the possibility of a change. I then asked him if he thought the organization could possibly change as regards the teaching that Jesus Christ gave his life as a ransom for mankind? He just looked at me. I said I was sure that he did not think that could take place, for that teaching was solidly based on Scripture. The other teaching was a "current understanding," subject to change, certainly not on the same level with the teaching of the ransom sacrifice. I viewed the material in the September 15, 1981, *Watchtower* and its prohibitions regarding association with disassociated persons in the same light.

Dan now began speaking of the "need to be humble" in accepting God's direction. I could wholeheartedly agree to that and said I was sure they would also agree that those who preach humility should be the first in exemplifying it.

Again to illustrate, the example was given them of a group of people in a room, conversing. One person expresses his views very emphatically on a variety of matters. When he finishes, another person in the room comments, saying he agrees wholeheartedly with the initial speaker on several points; however, he feels differently on a couple of them, giving his reasons. At this the first individual becomes incensed and calls on the group to expel this person from the room as unfit company—because he did not agree with him on *every* point. Who, I asked, is the one needing to learn humility? Again, no response. The conversation ended not long thereafter and they left.

Peter visited me that evening to find out the results. He was very sorry about the position taken toward me and knew to what it could lead. He said he wanted me to know that if I thought it advisable not to have any further association with him that he would understand.

I reminded him of an incident that took place a year and a half earlier one evening shortly before I went to Brooklyn in May, 1980, for my final session with the Governing Body. He and I were alone in his car and I told him that Cynthia and I had talked things over and decided it would be better not to return to Alabama after the session, but instead go to the home of members of Cynthia's family. I said that I did not know what might come of the meeting, perhaps "the worst," and I did not want to create problems for him and his family.[14] We felt there was less likelihood that problems would be made for my wife's family if we went there. He replied that they very much wanted us to return, were counting on it. I told him we appreciated that greatly, but that he had a large family—wife, sons and daughters, brothers and sisters, grandchildren and in-laws, all Witnesses—and that if disfellowshipped, my returning could result in considerable difficulty and unpleasantness for them on the part of the organization.

His response was, "I realize that, and don't think I haven't thought a lot about it. But we've talked it over among ourselves and we've crossed that bridge. We want you to come back no matter what."

It would be difficult to say how much those words had meant to me at that particular time. Now the situation was the other way around and I now told Peter that I did not see how I could do any less than he had done for me. I could not be party to something that labeled a man wicked who had simply acted according to conscience, out of concern for truth and for the interests of others, as he had done.

After the "readjustment" meeting with the two elders of the East Gadsden Congregation, nothing further was said to me until the arrival of Circuit Overseer Wesley Benner, some weeks later. He arranged to come to my home with Dan Gregerson. Tom Gregerson, also a brother of Peter and the second of the four sons of the Gregerson family, was also present at his own request.

The discussion followed the same predictable pattern, except that the Circuit Overseer was inclined to interrupt my statements to the point that

---

14   Peter at that time had not yet disassociated himself. His disassociation came nearly a year later.

I finally had to request that, as a guest in my home, he at least wait until I had finished an expression before breaking in. The "readjustment" was once more based on the *Watchtower*, not on Scripture. Again, when asked if they really considered Peter Gregerson to be a "wicked" man of the kind described at First Corinthians, chapter 5, or an "antichrist" as described by the apostle John, neither had any comment.

I drew their attention to Romans, chapter fourteen, where the apostle stressed the need to be true to conscience, that anyone who does something while doubting that it is approved of God thereby sins, since "everything that is not out of faith is sin." Since the Scripture states that, "Anyone pronouncing the wicked one righteous and anyone pronouncing the righteous one wicked—even both of them are detestable to Jehovah," I could not conscientiously violate that principle by viewing or treating Peter Gregerson as a wicked person, when all I knew about him told me otherwise.[15]

Benner's response was that, if I had to be guided by my conscience, so did the elders have to be guided by theirs. That if this was my position then "they would have to take action accordingly." (Evidently the conscience of the elders did not allow for respecting the conscience of another man, showing tolerance.) What kind of "action" was meant was made quite clear by his further expression. He said he simply viewed himself as one who conveyed the things provided by the organization. Quoting his own words, he said, "I parrot what the Governing Body says." This was stated with evident pride, for what reasons I could not understand. I have never viewed being a parrot as an achievement of any great merit.

Not long after this the conversation ended and they left. Tom Gregerson shook his head in disbelief, saying the experience had been revealing but depressing; that he would not have believed that men would say things such as he had heard.

By the first of November the same judicial machinery that had functioned in Brooklyn, began functioning in Gadsden. Phone calls asking one thing after another came from the elders. I was advised that a judicial committee would meet with me.

---

15   Proverbs 17:15.

I had been planning to write to the Governing Body to submit my resignation to membership in the Society's corporations. (I had been a voting member of both the Pennsylvania and the New York corporations for several years.).[16] Along with informing the Body that I was resigning from such membership, on November 5, I wrote:

```
        Locally, certain elders have taken the information in the
September 15, 1981, Watchtower as authorization to demand a change
in my relationship with the man on whose property I live and for
whom I work, Peter Gregerson.  They state that, since he has dis-
associated himself, I should view him as among those with whom one
should not eat--wicked persons and antichrists--and that failure to
conform to this position requires disfellowshiping.  Approaching 60,
having no financial resources, I am in no position to move or to
change my employment.  So I would very much appreciate knowing if the
intent of your statements in that issue of the magazine is truly
as they present it, namely that my accepting an invitation from my
landlord and employer to eat with him is grounds for disfellowshiping.
If, instead, they have exceeded the intent of what was published,
some counsel of moderation would grant me relief from a situation
that is potentially oppressive.  I will appreciate whatever clarifi-
cation you can give, whether directly or through one of your depart-
ments.
```

That same day a phone call came from the elders. Their calls had been so numerous and the approach so unbrotherly that my wife and I both began to feel emotionally upset every time we heard the phone ring. I instructed my wife that if the elders phoned and I was not there that she should inform them that anything they had to say to put it in writing. So, she now passed this information on. The next day the appointed judicial committee wrote, the letter arriving November 10, 1981.

Many of Jehovah's Witnesses find it incredible that I was actually disfellowshipped because of eating a meal with a man, Peter Gregerson. Some insist that this could not be the case. I believe the correspondence that now developed makes the matter plain. The first letter, sent by the judicial committee, was dated November 6, 1981.

---

16   That membership continued after I left the headquarters. Both in 1980 and 1981 I received the usual "Proxies" for voting at the annual meeting. The first year I mailed the proxy in, but in 1981 I could not find it in myself to do so, particularly in view of the material being published in the society's magazines.

2822 Fields Avenue
East Gadsden, AL   35903
November 6, 1981

Raymond V. Franz
Route 4, Box 440F
Gadsden, AL   35904

Dear Brother Franz:

As per your instructions given us by Sister Franz on Thursday,
November 5, this is to ask you to meet with a judicial committee
on Saturday, November 14, at 2:00 p.m. at the East Gadsden Kingdom
Hall. The purpose of the meeting is to discuss with you your
continued association with a person disassociated from the congregation.

If you are unable to meet with us on the above date, please contact
one of us to arrange another meeting.

Your brothers,

Theotis French
Theotis French

Edgar Bryant
Edgar Bryant

Dan Gregerson
Dan Gregerson

This letter makes clear that one charge, and one charge only, formed
the basis for their "judicial action," namely, my "association with a disassociated person."

In my written response, I pointed out to the Gadsden elders that, I
had written to the Governing Body for clarification of the meaning of the
material published in the September 15, 1981, *Watchtower,* and wondered
why they had given no consideration to this, evidently being unwilling to
allow time for me to receive a reply. I also pointed out the unreasonable-
ness of having Dan Gregerson serve on the judicial committee when he
had already presented himself as my accuser. I expressed the hope that

the judicial committee might be enlarged to make more likely a fair and impartial discussion of this new policy and its application.[17]

I sent this letter and a week later, on Friday, November 20, when I arrived home from work, my wife told me that Elder Theotis French had phoned. They would be meeting as a judicial committee the very next day, Saturday afternoon, he said. They had sent me a letter to that effect.

In that afternoon's mail there was a notice of a certified letter. I hurriedly drove to the Post Office and was able to obtain the letter before closing time. The letter was dated November 19, 1981.

```
2622 Fields Avenue
East Gadsden, AL   35903
November 19, 1981


Raymond V. Franz
Route 4, Box 440-F
Gadsden, AL   35904

Dear Brother Franz:

As a body of elders, we have reviewed your letter and
would like to respond.  First, we would like to let you
know that the body of elders had been made aware that you
had mailed a letter to the Watchtower Society and we had
determined that we should proceed with the judicial committee
hearing.  Second, in view of Dan Gregerson's being an accuser
the body of elders has decided to replace him on the judicial
committee with Larry Johnson.

Third, there are persons other than Dan who could serve as
witnesses regarding the matter in question, but we feel that
it is not necessary to disclose their names in view of your
acknowledging that you have been fellowshipping with persons
who are dissassociated from the congregation.

Fourth, the body of elders has determined that three elders
will serve on the committee.  We would like to assure you that
the brothers designated have not prejudged you and that they will
approach the meeting objectively.

Finally, Brother Franz, the appointed judicial committee would
like to schedule a meeting with you on Saturday, November 21,
at 4:00 p.m. at the Kingdom Hall.  If you are unable to attend
we request that you notify one of the brothers shown below to
arrange a more convenient meeting.

Your brothers,
```

Larry Johnson

Edgar Bryant

Theotis French

---

17   For the reader's information my letter is presented in full in Appendix A.

The letter was not merely formal. It might as well have come from some civil court, for, although signed "Your brothers," it conveyed none of the warmth of a Christian brotherhood. Cold legalism dominated its tone. Yet, unless I had already been prejudged (which they affirmed was not the case), there surely should have been a brotherly spirit expressed, a sense of compassionate concern for the life interests of the man to whom they wrote. Setting aside my entire adult life's service among Jehovah's Witnesses or my having served on their Governing Body or my age and existing circumstances—setting all that aside, they still should have manifested some measure of loving interest, even if they viewed me as *'one of the least* of Christ's brothers.' (See Matthew chapter twenty-five, verse 40.) I do not believe the unfeeling spirit expressed originated with these men. It had another source. The letter was typical.

My wife had already informed Elder French in the phone conversation that we had guests arriving from out of state on Saturday and that there was no way to communicate with them or change our plans.

The following Monday, November 23, I again wrote to express my dismay at the hurried and inconsiderate manner in which the judicial committee was proceeding.

That very afternoon a phone call came from Elder French stating that the judicial committee would meet two days later, on Wednesday evening (November 25) and make their decision whether I was present or not. I decided that it was useless to mail the letter I had written to them. They seemed to be in an enormous hurry, a "rush to judgment." I do not personally think that this was of their own initiative. As the chairman of the committee later acknowledged, they were in communication with the Society's representative, Circuit Overseer Wesley Benner. Many of their expressions and attitudes reflected remarkably those made by him in my home. He, in turn, was almost certainly in touch with the Service Department of the Brooklyn headquarters, and that department was—beyond any doubt—in communication with the Governing Body. This is not unusual; it is the usual way in which things work. The methods employed were not surprising to me; they were simply depressing.

When Wednesday (November 25) came, I decided that, rather than be tried *in absentia,* I would go to their meeting which Elder French said would be held "Wednesday evening." That afternoon I called the home of one of the committee members to ascertain the exact time. The man's wife said that he was already at the Kingdom Hall. I phoned the Hall and found that they were going to have the meeting in the afternoon—to them the "evening" apparently meant any time after 3 p.m. I told them that I had not understood that, that no specific time had been given me and asked it they could postpone their meeting till after 6 p.m. They agreed.

Tom Gregerson had said that he wanted to accompany me and I now phoned him. On arriving at the Kingdom Hall we went into the conference room where the judicial committee, Elders French (chairman), Bryant and Johnson were. They informed Tom that he could not be present except to give testimony. He said he wanted to be present since about thirty-five Jehovah's Witnesses worked for the company (Warehouse Groceries) of which he was an officer. He wanted to know just what position was being taken on this issue. Their answer was still, No.

After his departure, the committee opened the hearing and called in the witnesses. There were two: Dan Gregerson and Mrs. Robert Daley.

Dan spoke first. He said he had seen me in the Western Steak House along with Peter Gregerson (and our wives). This was the essence of his testimony. When he finished, I asked him when this was and he acknowledged that it was in the summer and hence before the September 15, 1981, *Watchtower,* with its new ruling that called for treating anyone voluntarily disassociating himself the same as though he were disfellowshipped. I told the committee that unless they believed in *ex post facto* laws, Dan's testimony was irrelevant.

The other witness was then asked to present her testimony. She testified to essentially the same thing as Dan, except that the occasion in the restaurant was after the publishing of the September 15, 1981, *Watchtower.*

I readily acknowledged that I had indeed had a meal with Peter at the time she referred to. I also asked her if it was not the case that she and her husband (an elder in the East Gadsden congregation) had similarly eaten a meal with Peter? (Peter had gone to Morrison's Cafeteria one day and found himself in line right behind Elder Daley and his wife. Since, previous to his present marriage, Daley had been Peter's stepfather, having married Peter's mother after his father's death, Peter now nudged Daley and Daley turned, began talking with Peter and asked Peter to sit with them and the three conversed throughout the meal. This, too, was after the September 15, 1981, *Watchtower's* appearance.)

The witness became quite excited at this and said that while that was true, afterward she had told some of the "Sisters" that she knew it was not right and would never do it again. (Later, after the hearing, I mentioned this to Peter and he said, "But they ate with me twice! Another day I went into Morrison's and they were already seated and when they saw me they waved to me to come and sit with them." The witness said nothing of this second occasion, which was unknown to me at the time of the hearing.)

That was the absolute sum and substance of the "evidence" against me. The two witnesses left.

The judicial committee then began asking me about my position toward the September 15, 1981, *Watchtower*. I inquired why they had not been willing to wait for the Governing Body's response to my inquiry on this, written on November 5? The chairman, Theotis French, brought his hand down on the September 15 *Watchtower* open before him and said, "This is all the authority we need."

I asked if they would not feel more confident if they had confirmation of their viewpoint from the Governing Body? He repeated that 'they had to go by what was published,' and that, anyway 'they had called Brooklyn on the matter.' This was the first I had heard anything about such a call. Evidently that was why, when I spoke to the committee chairman, Elder French, on the phone two days earlier he had said that the body of elders "did not feel it was necessary" to wait for the Governing Body to answer my letter! They followed the same secretive course followed earlier by the Chairman's Committee and apparently did not feel any need whatsoever to let me know that they had already communicated by telephone with the Brooklyn headquarters.

I asked if they spoke with someone on the Governing Body. The answer was, No, that they talked with a member of the Service Department. What had they been told? French said they were told, "Nothing has changed and you can go ahead."

French said that his understanding was that "the Society has taken a hard look at the previous position [in the 1974 *Watchtower*] and they are now going back to the way it was before." (This is basically the way Circuit Overseer Benner expressed himself in my home.) Theotis went on to say that "the *Watchtower* helps us to see where to draw a fine line" in these matters. Elder Edgar Bryant added, "We are all trying to put ourselves in line with what the *Watchtower* requires."

Up to this point none of the three men had made any reference to the Bible. I stressed that this was my guide. On what *Scriptural* basis should I consider Peter Gregerson as a person unfit to eat with?

Elder Johnson turned to First Corinthians, chapter five, began reading a couple of verses, hesitated and stopped, making no application of the information. I asked each member of the committee individually, if he himself could say he honestly believed Peter Gregerson was the kind of person described in such texts, including John's writings about "antichrists"? Theotis French reacted with some agitation, saying 'it wasn't up to him to make a judgment of the man,' that 'he didn't know everything about Peter so as to make such a judgment.' I asked him how, then, they could possibly ask me to make such a judgment and be governed by it, when they themselves were not willing to do so?

His response was, "We didn't come here to have you teach us, Brother Franz." I assured him that I was not there to "teach" them, but that my whole course of life as a Christian was being put in question, was at issue, and I felt I had a right to express myself. Neither Edgar Bryant nor Larry Johnson would make any clear statement as to how they viewed Peter Gregerson, eating a meal with whom was now being treated as a "criminal" act.

The chairman then said he saw no purpose in further discussion. Tom Gregerson was called in to see if he had any testimony to give. When he asked what effect this *Watchtower* position would have on Witness employees in his company who periodically might travel with, or attend a meal in company with, a disassociated person, Larry Johnson said they were not there to answer that question, Tom could bring the question up at another time.[18] Tom replied that he had been asking the question for some time, had asked the Circuit Overseer, and still had no answer. There was no response, the meeting concluded and we left. The judicial committee remained behind to discuss the "evidence."

About a week later, the phone rang and Larry Johnson informed me that the committee's decision was for disfellowshipping. I had seven days from the date of his phone call in which to appeal their decision.

I wrote them a lengthy letter, my "appeal" letter. I felt that whatever I had to say it would be best to put it in writing. What is spoken can be easily changed, twisted or simply forgotten; what is written remains and is not so easily ignored. My experience at the previous hearing made it obvious that a very unhealthy climate prevailed and that even in an appeal hearing the likelihood of any calm, reasoned Scriptural discussion of matters was quite remote.

In the letter I called their attention to the Society's published counsel that elders on a judicial committee should "weigh matters carefully," that they should not look for "rigid rules for guidance," but "think in terms of principles," that they should "be sure the counsel is based solidly on God's Word," should "take sufficient time and endeavor to reach the heart of the person," should "discuss the application of the scriptures that apply and be sure that he [the one accused] understands." That was what was said; it was not what was being done (yet what was being done was known to the ones responsible for the publishing of that same counsel). The essence of my position is perhaps summed up in these two paragraphs:

> Perhaps it may be said that I have not expressed repentance for having eaten with Peter Gregerson. To express repentance I need first to be satisfied that doing so is a sin before God. The only means for providing such conviction must rightly come from God's Word, which alone is inspired and unfailingly reliable. (2 Timothy 3:16, 17) My understanding from the Scriptures is that loyalty to God and to his Word is of supreme importance and supercedes any other loyalty of whatever kind. (Acts 4:19, 20; 5:29) My understanding also is that it is not for me or any other human or group of humans to add to that Word, under pain of being "proved a liar" or even receiving divine plagues. (Proverbs 30:5, 6; Revelation 22:18, 19) I cannot take such scriptural warnings lightly. In view of all the scriptural admonition against judging others, I have a healthy fear of setting myself (or any human or group of humans) up as legislator and feel compelled to let God's Word alone do such judging. To do that I need to be certain that I am not

---

18   Tom Gregerson was at that time the president of Warehouse Groceries.

simply following some humanly devised standard that poses as a
divine standard but which is in fact uninspired, unsupported by
God's Word. I do not wish to be guilty of presumption and imper-
tinence in judging someone whom God by his own expressed Word has
not so judged.--Romans 14:4, 10-12; James 4:11, 12; see also
Commentary on the Letter of James pages 161 to 168.

        I assure you that if you will help me to see from the Scrip-
tures that the act of eating with Peter Gregerson is a sin I will
humbly repent of such sin before God. Those who have talked with
me thus far have not done this but have cited the above-mentioned
magazine as their "authority" (the term used by the chairman of
the judicial committee). My understanding is that all authority
within the Christian congregation must derive from and be solidly
based on the Word of God. Proverbs 17:15 states that "Anyone
pronouncing the wicked one righteous and anyone pronouncing the
righteous one wicked--even both of them are something detestable
to Jehovah." I have no desire to be detestable to God and hence
am very concerned about this matter.

I closed making yet another appeal that they honor my request to wait
for a reply from the Governing Body to my letter of November 5.[19]

By now, however, I had little doubt but that the Governing Body
had no intention of answering my letter. One month had already passed
and they were well aware of my circumstances and how critically some
statement from them was needed. From my years of experience on the
Body I knew that, though preferring to remain in the background, they
were very definitely kept informed of every development in my case. The
Service Department would be expected to pass on all information, and it
in turn would be supplied with reports from the Circuit Overseer. Both
the actions and the expressions made by the local elders indicated that
procedures were orchestrated from the center of authority, through the
Circuit Overseer. The center of authority, the Governing Body, was willing to communicate with those who were judging me, doing so through
their Service Department, but they were not willing to respond to my
petition written to them, not even to acknowledge receipt of the letter.

So, on December 11, seven weeks after my initial letter, I again wrote
the Governing Body, sending them a copy of my "appeal letter" and
reminding them of my letter to them dated November 5.[20]

Exactly seven days after submitting my appeal letter, Elder French
phoned to tell me an appeal committee had been formed, naming the

19   See Appendix A for the letter in its entirety.
20   See Appendix A.

members selected. Three days passed and another phone call came; he was informing me that the appeal committee would meet with me on Sunday. I told him I had written him asking for the specific names of the committee members (he had only given me family names of a couple of them) and said I would be asking for a change in the committee membership. When I inquired why these particular men had been selected, his reply was that Wesley Benner, the Society's representative, had selected them.

Those he had chosen as appeal committee members were Willie Anderson, Earl Parnell and Rob Dibble. In view of the fact that the principal charge against me was my association with Peter Gregerson I found this selection incredible.

Every one of these men was very unlikely to show objectivity where Peter was concerned.

As I pointed out in a letter to the Gadsden elders (although they themselves already knew it), Willie Anderson had been at the head of a committee that created a considerable stir in Gadsden in its handling of issues involving a large number of young people in the local congregations. Peter Gregerson had appealed to the Brooklyn headquarters to send in a review committee and when this was done the committee headed by Willie Anderson was found to have been excessive in a number of its actions. This had a noticeable effect on the relationship between Elder Anderson and Peter Gregerson thereafter.

Circuit Overseer Benner's selection of Earl Parnell was even harder to fathom. One of Peter Gregerson's daughters had been married to a son of Elder Parnell but had recently obtained a divorce from him. The strained relations between the two sets of parents was obvious; Circuit Overseer Benner knew of the divorce action and, one would think, would also have been sensitive enough to have realized how inappropriate it would be to assign Elder Parnell to a case in which Peter Gregerson was a central figure.

Similarly with Rob Dibble. He was Elder Parnell's son-in-law, his wife being the sister of the Parnell son recently divorced by Peter Gregerson's daughter.

As I wrote to the Gadsden elders, I found it difficult to think of a committee of three men that would have less to recommend it for an unbiased, objective hearing. (The only way I could see any logic to the selection would be if an adverse decision was somehow being deliberately sought.) In my letter I requested that a totally different appeal committee be selected.[21]

The same day I wrote these letters (December 20), yet another phone call came from Elder French. The appeal committee wanted to inform me that they would meet on the next day, Monday, and 'would hold the hearing whether I was present or not.' I told Elder French I had written requesting a change in the committee and had written to the Brooklyn headquarters as well. I delivered copies of these letters directly to his home the next day, Monday.

Two days later, Wednesday, December 23, the following note came by registered mail:

> RAY FRANZ,
> THE MEETING THAT WAS SET FOR THURSday
> DEC. 24 AT 7:00 P.M AT THE EAST GADSdEN
> CONgERATION HAS BEEN CHANged, To DEC. 28ᵘ
> 1981 AT 7:00 PM AT THE EAST GADSdEN CONg.
> Would VERY MUCH like To SEE you THERE.
>
> Theotis French

No one had said anything to me about a proposed meeting on Thursday. But the above note was my official notice of a December 28 meeting, Monday.

During the two days after delivering the letters to Elder French's home, I learned that he was trying to obtain information to support a new and totally different charge.

Mark Gregerson, another of Peter's brothers, informed Peter that Theotis French had called long distance to Mark's home in Florida where he had moved from Alabama. Elder French spoke to Mark's wife and asked

---

21   See Appendix A.

if she could recall ever hearing me make any remarks against the organization. She told him she never had heard me make remarks against anybody, including the organization. Why did he want to know? He replied that he was 'just seeking information.' He did not ask to speak with her husband.

This, too, brought memories of the nightmarish situation I had experienced a year and a half before, and of the conduct of the Chairman's Committee of the Governing Body then.

Approximately seven weeks had passed since I first wrote the Governing Body asking for an expression on the material in the September 15, 1981, *Watchtower,* telling them why it was of serious importance to me. I had now written them two more times, petitioning them to make some expression. They did not see fit to answer or even to acknowledge *any* of this correspondence.

Is it unbelievable that the leadership of a worldwide organization with millions of members, one that claims to be the outstanding example of adherence to Christian principles, could conduct itself in such manner? No, not if one is familiar with the attitude prevalent among its leadership. I have personally been witness to similar ignoring of letters when the Governing Body felt it was not to their advantage to provide an answer. They clearly felt so in my case.

From the beginning I had felt no doubt as to the ultimate goal of all that was being done. I was thoroughly sickened by the whole conduct of the affair, what I can only describe as a narrow-minded approach, an obvious determination to find something, no matter how trivial or petty, that could serve as a basis for bringing adverse action against me. So I wrote my last letter, dated December 23, 1981, sending copies to the Governing Body and to the East Gadsden Congregation Body of Elders.

December 23, 1981

East Gadsden Congregation Body of Elders
Gadsden AL

Dear Brothers:

By means of this letter I am withdrawing my appeal of the
decision to disfellowship me. My reason for doing so is as
follows:

On the basis of testimony that I had eaten a meal on one
occasion with Peter Gregerson since the publication of the
September 15, 1981, <u>Watchtower</u>, the initial judicial committee
decided to disfellowship me. That forty years of full-time
service could be discounted on such a petty basis indicates
to me that there is no real concern to take into account my
conscientious feelings, expressed in detail in my letter of
December 8, 1981, nor concern to show me from Scripture wherein
I have erred.

Additionally, the selection of the membership of the appeal
committee, as made by the circuit overseer, gives no real basis
for expecting a fair consideration in my case. The selection
made, as pointed out in my letter of December 20, 1981, was of
three persons who are obviously among those least likely to be
able to handle my case in an objective way, free from the
influence of personal feeling. I can think of no justification
for the selection made, and believe it makes a travesty of justice.

There seems to be no evidence to indicate that the Governing
Body is desirous of providing any aid or relief for me, since my
letter of November 5, 1981, has now gone approximately seven weeks
with no response to me. While the chairman of the initial
judicial committee has stated that he called the Service Department
on more than one occasion, the conversations give no indication
of relief since, according to the chairman, they said that 'nothing
has changed and to go ahead.'

Finally, I now know that effort is being made, by phone, even
by long distance, to try to find something to use against me in
an effort to incriminate me. This has been done in the last few
days, since my turning in my letter of December 20, 1981, requesting a different appeal committee. Even though the person contacted
has never made any complaint about me, the request is made to
see if they can remember anything I said that might be viewed as
improper. Surely if I were responsible for making a disturbance
in the congregation, one of a genuinely perverse or malicious
kind, it would never be necessary to resort to such methods to
substantiate such a charge.

East Gadsden Congregation Body of Elders
December 23, 1981, Page II

The continuation of such method can only result in further damaging of my good name and character. It is an open invitation to suspicion and gossip.

My feelings are as those of the apostle at Galatians 6:17: "Henceforth let no one be making trouble for me, for I am carrying on my body the brand marks of a slave of Jesus." For the past eight weeks my wife and I have been subjected to much mental anguish, not merely by the repeated visits and more than a dozen phone calls (to the point where the ring of the phone became an unpleasant sound), but more especially by the attitude manifested. Now there is added to all this the knowledge that a surreptitious inquiry is being carried on that is clearly adverse to my rightful interests. I experienced similar treatment last year in New York, where similar efforts were made for one month—and not one word was said to me during that time to indicate to me that my conduct was in any way under accusation, this despite the fact that a clear opportunity was given by me for those conducting the inquiry to express such. I have no desire to undergo similar mistreatment again, particularly since there is nothing to indicate that the truth of the matter can be made known in such a way as to remove the unwarranted stain produced. That must rest in God's hands. —Matthew 10:26.

My withdrawal of my appeal should in no way be construed as an acknowledgment of guilt or an acceptance of the disfellowshiping decision as being in any sense proper, just or Scriptural. Again with the apostle I can say: "Now to me it is a very trivial matter that I should be examined by you or by a human tribunal. Even I do not examine myself. For I am not conscious of anything against myself. Yet by this I am not proved righteous, but he that examines me is Jehovah." (1 Corinthians 4:3, 4) My confidence in his righteous judgment is implicit and my confidence in the rightness and truthfulness of his Word is only strengthened by what I have experienced. And as long as I have life I will endeavor to make the truth of that Word known to others for their blessing and God's praise.

As for my brothers among Jehovah's Witnesses, I can say that the good will of my heart and my supplication to God are on their behalf. I have labored conscientiously since 1938 in their spiritual interests and I assure you that if I saw any hope that my subjecting myself to further trial would result in benefit to them I would gladly endure such.—Compare Romans 9:1-3.

Respectfully,

There was little doubt in my mind that those directing the whole affair had begun to feel that the "evidence" used to disfellowship me—one meal with Peter Gregerson—might appear rather weak. Rather than seek to provide the evidence from God's Word (demonstrating that my act was truly sinful), which I had requested in my appeal letter, they tried to build a stronger "case" by soliciting adverse testimony. I saw no good in further submission to this.

Eight days later, a phone call came from Larry Johnson informing me that they had received my letter and that in view of my withdrawal of my appeal, the disfellowshipping action taken by the first committee was counted as remaining in force.

That the call came on the day it did, seemed rather appropriate. I had been baptized on January 1, 1939, and exactly forty-three years later, on December 31, 1981, I experienced excommunication—the only charge serving as the basis for this being testimony that I had eaten a meal with a disassociated person.

Do I personally believe that this was the true reason for their taking the action they did? No. I believe it was simply a technicality used to achieve an objective. The end justified the means in their minds. That an organization would make use of a technicality of such pettiness, to my mind betrays a remarkably low standard for conduct and a great insecurity.

Based upon my past experience on the Governing Body of Jehovah's Witnesses, upon the conduct of its Chairman's Committee during the spring of 1980, and also upon the material published from that time until the present, my personal belief is that it was considered "advantageous" that I be disfellowshipped so as to eliminate what they considered a "threat." If so, then this too, I think, reveals a very great sense of insecurity—particularly so for a worldwide organization that claims to be God's chosen instrument, backed up by the Sovereign power of the universe, the reigning King's appointee as supervisor of all his earthly interests. This would surely *not* be the action of an organization fully at ease with its own teachings, calmly confident that what it presents is truth, solidly supported by God's Word.

Nor is it the action of an organization having genuine confidence in its body of adherents, confidence that the instruction and training given have produced mature Christian men and women who do not need some maternal *magisterium* to prescribe what they shall read, discuss or think about, but who are instead capable of discerning for themselves between truth and error, through their knowledge of the Word of God.

The action *is* typical, however, of many religious organizations of the past, all the way back to the first century, organizations that felt a compelling need to eliminate anything that, *in their view*, threatened to diminish their authority over others.

In his book, *A History of Christianity,* scholar Paul Johnson writes of methods employed during the dark period of religious intolerance, which produced the Inquisition, and says:

> Convictions of thought-crimes being difficult to secure, the Inquisition used procedures banned in other courts, and so contravened town charters, written and customary laws, and virtually every aspect of established jurisprudence.[22]

The methods employed regularly by judicial committees formed of Witness elders would be considered unworthy of the court systems of any enlightened country. The same withholding of critically important information (such as the names of hostile witnesses) also the use of anonymous informers, and similar inquisitorial tactics, described by historian Johnson, have been employed with great frequency by these men in dealing with those not totally in agreement with the "channel," "the organization." What was true back then, is true in the vast majority of cases now, as Johnson puts it:

> The object, quite simply, was to produce convictions at any cost; only thus, it was thought, could heresy be quenched.[23]

Again, I do not think the coldness or the hardness, the aloof, superior attitude experienced, is owing to the normal personality of most of the

---

22   Paul Johnson, *A History of Christianity* (New York: Atheneum, 1979), p. 253.
23   Ibid., pp. 253, 254.

men involved. I believe it owes very definitely to the teaching that allows an organization to make claims of exclusive authority and unapproachable superiority that are both immodest and unfounded. That concept deserves not only to be questioned, it deserves to be exposed for the hurtful, God-dishonoring doctrine that it is. The October 15, 1995 *Watchtower* article "Watch Out for Self-Righteousness" said:

> When a Christian displays a spirit of su-periority because of his God-given abilities, privileges, or authority, he is in fact rob-bing God of the glory and the credit that only He deserves. The Bible clearly admon-ishes the Christian "not to think more of himself than it is necessary to think." It urges us: "Be minded the same way toward others as to yourselves; do not be minding lofty things, but be led along with the low-ly things. Do not become discreet in your own eyes."—Romans 12:3, 16.

What is true of an individual is equally true of a collective body. Reading the above, one cannot but think of the apostle's words to those who viewed themselves as in a superior relation to God:

> You are sure that you are a guide to the blind, a light to those who are in darkness, a corrector of the foolish, a teacher of children, having in the law the embodiment of knowledge and truth, you, then, that teach oth-ers, will you not teach yourself?—Romans 2:17-21, *NRSV.*

13

PERSPECTIVE

Therefore we do not lose heart. Though outwardly we are
wasting away, yet inwardly we are being renewed day by day.
For our light and momentary troubles are achieving for us an
eternal glory that far outweighs them all. So we fix our eyes
not on what is seen, but on what is unseen. For what is seen
is temporary, but what is unseen is eternal.
— 2 Corinthians 4:16-18 *New International Version.*

THIS, then, is my account and these are the fundamental issues that
produced in me a crisis of conscience. The effect they had, my feelings, reactions, conclusions reached, are set forth and the reader can assess
them for whatever they are worth. Simply put, my question is: How
would your own conscience have been affected?

What with nearly six thousand million people on earth and only God
knows how many generations in the past, the life of any one person is
but a minute fraction of the whole. We are very tiny drops in a very big
stream. Yet Christianity teaches us that, small and inconsequential as we
are, we can each contribute good to others that is out of proportion to our
own smallness.[1] Faith makes that possible, and, as the apostle expresses it,
"the love of Christ urges us on."[2]

We do not need the bulk of a big organization to back us up, nor
its headship, control, proddings and pressure, to accomplish this. Heart
appreciation for God's undeserved kindness in making life a "free gift,"

---

1   1 Corinthians 3:6, 7; 2 Corinthians 4:7, 15; 6:10.
2   2 Corinthians 5:14, *NRSV.*

not dependent on works but on faith, is sufficient, more than enough, to motivate us. If we respect and cherish our Christian freedom, we will respond to no other compulsion. Neither will we submit to any other yoke than the one offered in these words:

> Come to me, all you who are weary and burdened, and I will give you rest. Take my yoke upon you and learn from me, for I am gentle and humble in heart, and you will find rest for your souls. For my yoke is easy and my burden is light.[3]

I feel certain that when life comes to its close the only thing that will, in retrospect, bring any true sense of satisfaction is the extent to which life was used to contribute to the welfare of others, primarily spiritually, and, secondarily, emotionally, physically and materially.

I cannot believe that "ignorance is bliss," or that there is any kindness in encouraging people to live in illusions. Sooner or later, illusion must meet up with reality. The longer it takes for this to happen, the more traumatic the transition—brought on by disillusionment—can be. I am only glad it did not take any longer than it did in my own case.

That is why I have written what I have written. I have sincerely sought to be accurate throughout the account. Based on what has happened already and what has been published and circulated through rumors and gossip, I have no doubt but that effort will be made to disparage the significance of the information. Whatever may be said, I can only say that I am willing to stand by what I have presented. If there are errors, I will be grateful to anyone who will point such out to me and I will do whatever I can to make correction.

What does the future hold for the organization of Jehovah's Witnesses and its central Governing Body? Though often asked this, I have no way of knowing. Time alone will tell.

There are some things that I feel a measure of certainty about, but only a few. I do not personally foresee a mass movement out of the

---

3   Matthew 11:28-30, *NIV.*

organization. The reports worldwide at the start of the new millennium indicate problems, as shown in a previous chapter, yet there is still some measure of growth, even if diminished. The vast majority of Jehovah's Witnesses are simply unaware of the realities of the authority structure. From lifelong experience among them, in many countries, I know that for a large percentage the organization has a certain "aura," as though a luminous radiation surrounds it, giving its pronouncements an importance above and beyond that normally accorded the words of imperfect men. Most assume that Governing Body sessions are on an unusually high level, manifesting more than ordinary Scriptural knowledge and spiritual wisdom. As Witnesses, all are, in fact, admonished thus:

> After being nourished to our present spiritual strength and maturity, do we suddenly become smarter than our former provider and forsake the enlightening guidance of the organization that mothered us?[4]

There are constant admonitions to be humble, which translates into accepting whatever the organization provides as coming from a source of superior wisdom. The fact that the average Witness has only a misty idea of the way that the leadership arrives at its conclusions adds to the aura of esoteric wisdom. It is, they are told, "the only organization on earth that understands the 'deep things of God.'"[5]

Few of these Witnesses have ever confronted the issues dealt with in this book, the challenge to conscience they raise. I incline to believe that many, perhaps most, would prefer not to face those issues. Some have personally expressed their feeling to me that they enjoy their friendships within the organization and would not want to see these disturbed. I also enjoyed mine and had no desire to see them disturbed; I felt, and still feel, affection for the people with whom I spent most of my life. But I also felt that there were issues of truth and honesty, of fairness and justice, of love and mercy, that were bigger than those friendships and my enjoyment of them.

By this I am not saying that I think anyone should precipitate difficulty, seek or force a confrontation that is unnecessary. I can sympathize

---

4   *The Watchtower*, February 1, 1952, p. 80.
5   *The Watchtower*, July 1, 1973, p. 402.

wholeheartedly with those who are of families composed of Jehovah's Witnesses and who know full well the wrenching effect it could have on family relationships if the members were called upon to treat a son or daughter, brother or sister, father or mother, as an "apostate," a God-rejected, spiritually unclean person. I have never encouraged anyone to precipitate such a situation; I tried to avoid precipitating it in my own case.

But given the existing climate in the organization, it has become increasingly difficult to avoid this without compromising conscience, without 'acting a part,' pretending to believe what one may not believe, what one may actually be convinced is a perversion of the Word of God, producing unchristian fruitage, hurtful results.

I know a number of persons who have tried to withdraw quietly and some who have been, in a sense, "in hiding," persons who actually went to the extent of moving to another area and who sought to keep their whereabouts unknown (organizationally) so as to avoid harassment. I could cite case after case where, despite all efforts at avoiding confrontation, elders have sought the persons out, their only concern apparently being to extract from them some statement of their position—not toward God, Christ or the Bible—but toward "the organization." If the persons fail in this "loyalty test," presented as a clear ultimatum, they are almost always disfellowshipped, cut off from friends and family if these are members of the organization.

Typical is the experience of one young woman, a wife and mother, in southern Michigan. She had been interrogated by the elders because of her doubts about certain teachings and had been so emotionally affected by the experience that she had withdrawn from attending meetings. After some months, a phone call came from the elders requesting that she meet with them again. She said she did not want to undergo that experience again. They urged her to do it, saying that they wanted to 'help her with her doubts' and that this would be the last time they would ask her to meet with them. Her husband, not a Witness, recommended that she go and "have it over with." She went.

As she said, "Within the first ten minutes I could see the direction they were taking." Half an hour from the start of their questioning they had disfellowshipped her. She says the time factor alone stunned her. As she put it, "I couldn't believe they were doing this. I sat there the whole time sobbing and within thirty minutes they had 'kicked me out of the Kingdom.' I would have thought they would have got down on the floor with tears in their eyes, pleading with me for hours, to prevent that from happening." One of the five elders, a man who dozed off during the discussion, later said in her hearing, "The nerve of that woman to say that she wasn't sure if this was God's organization or not."

If efforts to avoid the unwanted confrontation fail, I think there is then consolation in knowing that the reason for any family distress and heartache rests on one side only. It is fully and entirely the fruitage of an organizational policy that calls upon members to report to the elders any expression of dissent, even if by family members, and a policy backed by the threat of expulsion for anyone who fails to treat disassociated or disfellowshipped persons as though they were rejected by God, no matter how sincere and devoted one may know them to be. The religious intolerance that acts as the divisive force, destructive of family oneness and affection, is not mutual therefore. Jesus said that it would be his *disciples* who would be handed over to religious judicial bodies for trial, not that *they* would be the ones handing others over to such bodies. He warned that *those who held true to his teachings* would be "betrayed even by parents and brothers, by relatives and friends," not that *they* would be the ones doing the betraying.[6] As in Jesus' day, so today, the divisive force comes from one side, one source, a source that equates conscientious disagreement with disloyalty. There is where the real responsibility for the broken family relationships, ruined friendships and the accompanying emotional hurt and distress ultimately rests.

Many Witnesses, though deeply concerned over what they see, find it difficult to adjust to the thought of serving God without being connected to some powerful organization, having the benefit of its largeness, its strength of numbers. True, Jehovah's Witnesses are a small organization compared to many, but they are widespread. Their visible structures are

---

6   Matthew 10:17, 21; Mark 13:9-12; Luke 21:16.

not as impressive as those of the Vatican or of some other major religions; nonetheless, the expanding international headquarters, which now owns a sizeable chunk of Brooklyn, the many Branch facilities, some with large printing establishments, all built or bought at the cost of millions of dollars and staffed by hundreds of workers (in Brooklyn, by around three thousand), the large Assembly Halls and the many thousands of Kingdom Halls (not a few costing more than a quarter million dollars to build), are sufficient to impress the average person. Every new acquisition or expansion of material properties is hailed as indicative of divine blessing and evidence of the organization's spiritual prosperity and success. Above all, the teaching that they are, exclusively, the one people on earth with whom God has dealings, and that the direction they receive from the Governing Body is from a divinely appointed "channel," helps produce a sense of cohesion, of specialness. The view of all other persons as "worldlings" contributes to this feeling of a close-knit relationship.

Because of this, I think it is equally as difficult for the average Witness to contemplate serving God without these things as it was for Jewish persons in the first century to contemplate such service apart from the religious arrangements they were accustomed to. The impressive temple buildings and courtyards at Jerusalem, with temple service carried out by a large staff of hundreds and thousands of dedicated workers, Levites and priests, their claim to be exclusively the chosen people of God, with all others viewed as unclean, stood in tremendous contrast to the Christians of that time, who had no large buildings, who met in simple homes, who had no separate priestly or Levite class, and who humbly acknowledged that 'in every nation the man that fears God and works righteousness is acceptable to him.'[7]

Quite a number, particularly among elders of Jehovah's Witnesses, express the sincere hope that some kind of "reform" will take place to correct the wrongs they are conscious of, both doctrinally and organizationally. Some have looked for this to come about by a change of personnel

---

7   Acts 10:35.

in the leadership. Even before I went on my leave of absence from the headquarters in early 1980, a member of a Branch Committee of a major country, a discerning person who realized the distress I felt over the existing attitudes and situation, said to me, "Ray, don't give up! These are old men, they will not live forever." This expression was not reflective of a hard, unfeeling, cynical personality, for the person who spoke it is just the opposite of that; he is a very kind, warmhearted man. Such expressions are often born of a belief that some change *must* come, that the trend toward an ever harder line and an increasingly dogmatic stance *must* give way to a more Christian approach, a more humble presentation of beliefs.

Personally, I do not believe that fundamental change is to be expected simply as a result of men in authority dying. I say *fundamental* change, for there have been changes in varying degrees throughout the history of the movement, some as a result of the deaths of Russell and Rutherford. During Russell's life a considerable measure of autonomy existed, and though disagreement with his views may have been deprecated, it was not crushed by his exercise of authority. Russell's death and the issue of control his successor faced led to the extreme focus on "organization" and organizational authority and control that has ever since characterized the Witness community. Whatever moderating changes that have followed Rutherford's death, the basic foundation has remained the same. The change in the authority structure in 1975-76 was as major an adjustment as has taken place in the whole history of the organization. Authority was spread out to a body of men, with many new faces coming to the fore. Yet the power of traditional beliefs and traditional policies has overcome any effort to bring about a genuine change from speculative interpretations, dogmatism, Talmudic legalism, control by an elite group, repressive measures, replacing these with a simple brotherhood, united in essentials, tolerant and yielding in nonessentials, both in belief and practice.

In questioning the validity of points made in this chapter with regard to prospects of reform, the book *Apocalypse Delayed* by M. James Penton (2nd edition, on pages 333, 334) refers to major changes in other organizations brought about by change in leadership. The book then states: "It is therefore wrong to discount the *possibility* of change from the top within Jehovah's Witnesses." As a review of the material found in this and previous editions of *Crisis of Conscience* shows, there is no denial of the *possibility* of change from that source but rather the point is made that the evidence points to an obstacle greater than the personnel of the leadership.

Of the eleven men who were on the Governing Body when I entered it in 1971, I am the only one yet alive. Of the seventeen members shown in the photo at the beginning of Chapter 4, of this edition, 2008, fifteen have died. The corporation presidency has passed from Nathan Knorr to Fred Franz, then to Milton Henschel and most recently to Don Adams. Seven new members have been added to the Governing Body. But despite all the changes in personnel the course of the organization has continued essentially the same, its essential character seems unaltered. As stated in this book, it is the concept that controls the men, the concept that the Watch Tower organization was divinely chosen by Christ Jesus and constitutes God's "channel of communication" for all his servants on earth, and that their functioning as a governing body is a divine arrangement. As evidence indicates, the changes in teaching or policy that *have* occurred, some discussed in this book, have resulted from force of circumstance rather than personnel changes.

From the other direction, those who feel that some kind of "grass roots" expression will bring about change are quite unaware of the spirit that characterizes Governing Body meetings. Having attended many hundreds of these, I know the disregard, often approaching disdain, with which questioning and objections from the "rank and file" are considered.

Concern about the benefits of preserving or attaining certain relationships with governments does manifest itself and so, too, does concern over numbers. The annual reports for the years since the year 2000 have revealed a notable decrease in growth in all of western Europe and in the United States. Japan, which for years was seen as a shining example of expansion, had zero growth in the year 2000 report and minus growth the following year. A continuance of this trend may produce additional changes. But as has been the case till now, the root cause of problems is rarely addressed and the changes often are designed to perpetuate a traditional stance.

Recently, in a seminar for elders called the Kingdom Ministry School, the organization altered its policy on "reporting" as a "publisher." Formerly the minimum amount of time for qualifying as an active "publisher" during a given month was one hour. For elderly and infirm Witnesses this has now been reduced to fifteen minutes. Presented as evidence of compassionate concern for such ones, it seems more likely that it is a measure taken to bolster the declining annual reports.

After all is said and done, it needs to be recognized that separating from the Watch Tower Society and its control—or any other flawed system—is of itself no solution, no guarantee of improvement. Some who separate are essentially no better off than before, have no idea how to use Christian freedom in a good and beneficial, God-honoring way; some exchange one set of combined true and false beliefs for another combined set of true and false beliefs. The purity of one's motivation is crucial. So, my interest is not in "getting people out of an organization" but in enhancing and deepening their appreciation of a genuine personal relationship with God and Christ.

The death of Fred Franz in 1992, at the age of 99, in a sense did indeed mark the end of an era—he was the only Governing Body member baptized as of 1914, the year so crucial to Witness beliefs. And he likely was the only member who had personally met the founder of the organization, Charles Taze Russell. He was the architect of by far the major part of the post-Rutherford doctrinal structure as well as the formulator of much of the policy relating to disfellowshipping matters. The divine "mantle" supposedly passed on by Rutherford (see pages 117 to 119 of this book) disappeared with him.

I had written to my uncle a few times since my resignation from the Governing Body, never with the thought of receiving a reply (and none ever came), nor as to an authority figure, but solely because of my feeling for him as a family member and as a person. I wrote to express interest in his health, and to assure him that my concern for him was not governed by policies of any human system. My main wish is that it might have been possible to sit down and talk with him person to person, for I am fully convinced in my own mind that he realized the fragility of the Scriptural foundation for many of the organization's teachings. He was a man of intellectual power and of mental discipline, and he was capable of writing sound Biblical exposition. But his unremitting devotion to a humanly-founded organization apparently allowed him to act as its prime apologist whenever its distinctive teachings were subjected to questioning or when its organizational interests appeared to be threatened, even when this meant "accommodating" the Scriptures in such a way that they appeared to support the organization's position. In such cases his intelligence was diverted into what ultimately was only imaginative inventiveness, an ability to lead readers' minds to desired conclusions by mere rhetoric and plausibility.

I find a definite sadness in all this. Although he witnessed the increase of organizational membership from a few thousands into several million, saw its headquarters property grow from a handful of buildings into entire city blocks of multi-storied structures, saw its publishing operations expand from a relatively modest status to that of an international printing empire, none of this goes with him to the grave—and none of these numerical and material factors surely has any bearing whatsoever on the way God will express either his commendation or his reproof. Already years before his death all the books written by him had been allowed to go out of print (though some are available on CD-ROM disks), essentially relegated to the status of mere memorabilia which the writings of Rutherford and Russell occupy. His very creative interpretations of prophecies, such as that of Daniel, in many cases are being replaced by other interpretations, made necessary by force of circumstance. (The dissolution of the Soviet Union, as one example, critically undermined his interpretation of the "king of the north" and the "king of the south" of Daniel 11:29-45.)

In 1988, after learning of his health problems, including the implantation of a heart pacemaker, I felt moved to write again to my uncle. I reviewed with him a few of what I considered his finest writings and talks, statements presenting valid principles which, if genuinely held to, would call for a reassessing of many of the organization's present positions and claims. Among other things, my letter said:

> For both of us life is in its final stages. I am very conscious of the certainty declared by the apostle that "we shall all stand before the judgment

seat of God" where "each one of us will render an account of himself to God." His Son, as judge, will then "both bring the secret things of darkness to light and make the counsels of the heart manifest, and then each one will have his praise come to him from God." (Romans 14:10-12; 1 Corinthians 4:5) Convinced of your knowledge of Scripture, I am unable to think that you believe organizational affiliation or loyalty to the interests of an organization will be a determining factor in that personal judgment, or that in most cases it will have any relevancy whatsoever. The more I advance into older age and the more imminent the end of life becomes, the more convinced I am that the most valuable thing any of us can leave behind is a moral legacy, and that the worth of that moral legacy will be determined by the principles for which we have stood, principles that can never be sacrificed or rationalized away in the interests of expediency. Those principles are primarily complete, unalloyed devotion to God, unqualified submission to his Son as our sole Head, integrity to truth, and compassionate concern for others, not as part of a favored system, but as individuals.

To leave such a moral legacy deeply concerns me; nothing else surpasses it in the thoughts of my heart. As Phillips renders Romans 14:7, "the truth is that we neither live nor die as self-contained units. At every turn life links us to the Lord and when we die we come face to face with him." I would hope that, if in no other matter, perhaps at least in this we share a mutual thought, a compatible depth of concern.

As with other letters, this one received no response. I am, nonetheless, glad today that I wrote it. Viewing the end of my uncle's life, the sadness felt is not only for what was, but more deeply for what might have been.

Fred Franz's death resulted in the naming of a new corporation president, and, as the material written in this book in 1983 indicated as a likely step, Milton Henschel was appointed as his replacement.[8] Franz's death did facilitate change. But this is not—as some would present the matter—because of a new corporation president, since the corporation presidency no longer carries with it any special power. Fred Franz's voice had

---

8   In the 1983 edition of *Crisis of Conscience*, this information appeared on page 344.

power, not because of the corporation office he occupied but because of his being viewed as the organization's major scholar. His successor, Milton Henschel, possessed none of that prestige. The change in the interpretation of the expression "1914-generation," considered in chapter 10 is perhaps the one major *doctrinal* adjustment that has been made since Fred Franz' death, and even this leaves the basic teachings regarding the date of 1914 in place.

If the ultimate effect of the restructuring of 1975-76 was like moving the inner walls of a house around, then whatever changes of personnel that take place within the administration might be compared to a rearranging of the furniture or adding new pieces—in both cases the house itself remains the same. As mentioned, of the 10 other men forming the Governing Body at the time of my appointment, none remains alive. Their deaths have produced no fundamental change in the essential character of the administration. For nearly two decades, those collectively exercising the most powerful influence among the members of the Governing Body, were Milton Henschel, Ted Jaracz and Lloyd Barry.[9] From 1999 to 2008, Lloyd Barry, Lyman Swingle, Karl Klein, Milton Henschel, Dan Sydlik, Albert Schroeder, and Carey Barber have died. Ted Jaracz is 83, and Jack Barr is 95 years old. With these lifetime members of the Body becoming aged, some becoming incapacitated and others dying; these factors have undoubtedly led to the appointment of seven new members. Beginning with Gerrit Lösch, from Austria, appointed in 1994, four others were appointed in 1999, Samuel Herd (the first African-American member), Stephen Lett, Guy Pierce, and David Splane. Then two more members were added in 2005, Geoffrey Jackson and Anthony Morris III, bringing the total membership to nine.

---

9   During my nine years on the Body it was unusual if anything these three members combined in favoring were not supported by sufficient members to control the result of a vote. Their positions were almost always unquestioningly supported by members Barr, Barber, Booth, Gangas, and Poetzinger. Lyman Swingle's voice was always heard with respect and certainly carried considerable weight. Yet when issues arose, his viewpoint and position were often overruled if they did not coincide with that of the three members mentioned. Dan Sydlik at times showed a willingness to favor a position other than the traditional one, but his voice did not carry the same weight as that of the three mentioned, or for that matter, of Lyman Swingle.

This highlights yet one more area where the use of special dates portends potential difficulty. These seven latest members are all of the professedly "anointed" class. *Watchtower* teaching is that the divine invitation to form part of such "anointed class" had accomplished the gathering of the full number of 144,000 as of the year 1935 and was replaced by the call to earthly life on the part of a "great crowd."[10] However, what is the case with Gerrit Lösch is evidently essentially true of the other new members. He was born in 1941, hence *27 years after 1914,* and was baptized in 1959, or *some 24 years after* the supposed change of the call from a heavenly to an earthly class in 1935. Basically the same is evidently the case with the six newest members and their average age indicates that they too were likely born *after* the supposed "cutoff" date of 1935 (David Splane was born in 1944). Logically, for anyone today to have been of the "anointed" as of 1935, such one would have to have been at least in his or her teens in that year to make such profession, which would mean, at the very least, being beyond 85 years of age today. One can but wonder how many of the 9,100 "anointed" today are of that age. Even as the passage of years made the claims regarding the "1914-generation" embarrassingly difficult to sustain, so, too, with the date of 1935 as the time when the formation of an "anointed" class supposedly reached its divinely appointed point of closure.

The introduction of new members to the Governing Body must meet the approval of the existing members and particularly of those with dominant influence and, rather than automatically increase likelihood of change, the selection process tends to maintain the status quo. There is no question but that it is becoming more and more difficult to find "suitable" candidates for membership on the Body in view of the dwindling number of "anointed" men. This *conceivably* could some day oblige the Governing Body to back away from its fundamental requirement that its membership is open only to those of such class. That would be difficult to

---

10   As has been noted in Chapter 7, early *Watch Tower* articles presented the year 1881 as the time when the invitation to be part of the "bride class" of 144,000 would cease, and the "closing of the door to the high calling" would have taken place. After 1881 came and then passed farther and farther into the past, this date's supposed significance was dropped, to be replaced in essence some half century later by the date of 1935.

harmonize, however, with their doctrine about the privileged status of the "faithful and discreet slave class."

Some viewed the announcement, in the April 15, 1992, *Watchtower*, page 31, as perhaps indicating a shift in this regard. Two main articles of this issue set forth the Watch Tower doctrine that Christians today fall into two main classes: "citizens" and "foreigners" or, put in other terms, "spiritual Jews" and "spiritual Gentiles." Thus, the about 9,100 members of the "anointed" are "citizens," the "spiritual Israelites," forming the "chosen race" and "royal priesthood" of 1 Peter 2:9, while the several million "other sheep" are the "foreigners," the "spiritual Gentiles," spiritual "alien residents," likened to those "foreigners" who would "build walls" or be "farmers" and "vinedressers" for Israel, the service in each of these cases being presented in the Bible accounts themselves as an evidence of subservience to the ones to whom it was rendered.

This is all in striking contrast to apostolic writings, which know of no such class separation and stress instead the equality of standing among Christians before God, even as Paul stated that in Christ there is 'no distinction between Jew and Greek, slave and free.' (Romans 10:12; Galatians 3:28; Colossians 3:11) Those literal racial and economic distinctions are replaced in Watch Tower teaching by distinctions of *spiritual* race and *spiritual* subservience or servitude. It does this by "overprinting" the Christian arrangement with Old Covenant circumstances and arrangements, in a sense spiritually "turning the clock back" to pre-Christian times and nullifying the radical change brought about by Christ.

The April 15, 1992, *Watchtower* articles in effect introduce yet a third class, or sub-class, the spiritual "Nethinim" and "sons of the servants of Solomon." The articles emphasize that these groups were elevated from mere slavery to a *higher status*, and quote reference works that speak of the 'raised social position, station or status' of the Nethinim and of their becoming "established as a sacred official class, [so] that privileges are accorded to them." With no Scriptural evidence to show that it should be so, the articles assert that these Old Testament circumstances should have a modern-day parallel. (Initially the material linked with the Nethinim the non-Levite "male and female singers" at the temple but thereafter mention of them is dropped, undoubtedly because they include women. So, the writer of the articles arbitrarily decides just how far the claimed "parallel" should go and what it should or should not include.) The articles proceed to place emphasis on a class of men having privileges involving "administrative responsibilities," and they thereafter represent the ancient "Nethinim" and "sons of the servants of Solomon" as typifying Witness men today who are traveling overseers, members of Branch Committees, men who prepare material for publication at the world headquarters, or who oversee Society residences and factories, or supervise construction work in various countries. Quite clearly, this leaves all the remaining "foreigners," the other millions of "spiritual Gentiles" or "other sheep" as of lesser privilege and of unequal status with this newly identified sub-class. The articles breathe an underlying spirit of love for special privilege and organizational position, a spirit that is embodied in the supremacy of privilege and authority held by the Governing Body members, who are undeniably 'in a class by themselves.'

The arrangement that evidently prompted the writing of these articles—that of having other men sit in on committee meetings of the Governing Body—is actually new only in the sense of the *number* involved. From early on, following the formation of Governing Body committees in 1976, men from the headquarters staff were appointed to serve as secretaries to the five Governing Body committees (Personnel, Publishing, Service, Teaching and Writing), and each of these five men (David Mercante, Don Adams, Robert Wallen, David Sinclair, and Karl Adams) were from the "non-anointed" class. These secretaries not only sat in on the respective committee meetings but were also allowed to *participate* in the discussions, though not to vote. Nothing is said of voting in the April 15, 1992, *Watchtower* announcement and it may be assumed that this remains the prerogative of the Governing Body members at the committee meeting. Only Governing Body members evidently continue to be present at sessions of the full body (where even the mentioned secretaries did not attend).

So, the new arrangement meant nothing more than that, instead of one non-Governing Body member present at the *committee* meetings, there would now be two or three. Only in an organization where position and privilege are viewed with such concern could this simple adjustment be presented as of notable significance, needing a worldwide announcement.

The organization could not actually introduce "non-anointed" men into the Governing Body itself without critically weakening its claims regarding a "faithful and discreet slave class" composed solely of "anointed" persons. From personal knowledge I would say that there is no question that there are scores of "non-anointed" men in various countries who are far more capable, who have a better knowledge of Scripture and greater ability to convey that knowledge, demonstrate more insight, even a higher level of spirituality, than many of the current members of the Governing Body. But to admit them to that elite body would be to place spiritual "foreigners" on an equality with the spiritual "citizens," move the spiritual "non-Levite temple helpers" up to equality with the spiritual "royal priesthood" class. That would blur and, in a practical sense, dissolve all the distinctions the Watch Tower's doctrine has called for during the past half century. I would think the Governing Body would resist doing that as long as it is humanly possible. As with 1914, the very traditional views so ardently advocated may thus become frustrating chains that hinder them from doing what prudence and practicality would normally call for. They may be helped by the fact that periodically down through the years younger members in the organization have decided that they were "of the anointed" (as was the case with the seven latest members) and thus have become possible candidates for membership in the Body.

A major mistake in looking for reform from the direction of personnel changes is, I believe, in thinking that the situation owes to the particular men in charge. Only in a secondary sense is that the case. Primarily, it is not the men. As stated, it is the *concept* that controls, the *premise* on which the whole movement is founded.

It can never be overlooked that what most markedly distinguishes the beliefs of Jehovah's Witnesses is not their disbelief of eternal torment or of the inherent immortality of the soul or of the trinity, nor their use of the name Jehovah, or their belief in a paradise earth. Every one of these features can be found in other religious organizations.[11]

What especially distinguishes their teachings from any other denomination is the keystone doctrine centered on 1914 as the date when Christ's active rulership began, his commencing judgment then and, above all, *his selecting the Watch Tower organization as his official channel,* his assigning *full control* of all his earthly interests to a "faithful and discreet slave class" while giving *ultimate authority* to its ruling body. Any abandoning of that keystone teaching would affect the whole doctrinal structure and is extremely unlikely, would be very difficult to explain. There is no reason at present to expect other than a determined effort through the columns of the *Watchtower* and other publications to shore up their defense of the interpretations supporting, or resulting from, that date, and to sustain faith in the claims based on it. Most important among those claims is that related to *organizational authority,* and here again there is presently a very intensive campaign to solidify support of, and loyalty to, that authority structure. If the past is any indication, the direction taken by the current leadership will follow that course, resisting whatever does not uphold and promote the traditional teachings, methods and policies now in force.

True, each year that passes places more of a strain on the 1914 teaching and those claims of divinely assigned authority coupled with it. As the evidence indicates, the teaching about the "generation" living in 1914 simply became too difficult to sustain with any credibility and so an "adjustment" was made. Despite this, with the advent of a new millennium, and particularly with the year 2014 approaching, the year 1914 is certain to seem quite ancient to many. The change in the teaching about the "1914-generation" may thus prove to be only a temporary postponement of the problem, a sort of "delaying action" in their struggle against the effects of the unrelenting advance of time.

---

11 Not only the various "Bible Student" associations, several of which are international, but also some Church of God affiliations hold nearly identical beliefs in these same areas; the Seventh Day Adventist churches believe in soul sleep, do not believe in eternal torment, do believe in a paradise earth ruled by Christ's kingdom.

There is a French expression that says, *Plus ça change, plus ça reste le même,* meaning basically, "The more things change, the more they remain the same." The changes that have been made in recent years ultimately only demonstrate the core nature of the organization, the unchanging character and mindset that dominates. As with the changes that have been made, so too with whatever future changes that may yet come, they will most certainly be heralded, not as the correction of error, but as the product of progressive revelation, and the past doctrines or arrangements that may be discarded will be depicted as 'God's will for that time.'

All this reminds me of some comments that Charles Davis, a former priest and leading Catholic theologian of Great Britain, wrote in his book *A Question of Conscience.* He said of the writings of the church's principal authority figures:

> The words are not alive. They are not at the service of living minds, but in slavery to a fixed unalterable pattern. . . . Any suggestion of questioning . . . or humble searching after truth not yet possessed is carefully avoided. Above all, there is never an admission of past error or a frank avowal that present statements contradict past teaching. . . . Official documents as an habitual rule cover over changes of attitude and teaching with specious claims to continuity with illustrious predecessors.

As the evidence has shown, that is essentially what the Watch Tower organization does whenever it acknowledges a change in its teachings. Showing the effects upon people within the system, Davis goes on to say:

> . . . all genuine love rests upon truth. Christian love is no exception. It rests upon faith as an entry into the truth of God and a liberation of man to all truth. Christians for whom doctrine is distorted into prejudice and who are rendered tense and fearful by the suppression of questioning, cannot love as they should. They are without the full basis of Christian truth for their love. They fear the freedom that would liberate them for love. They are too repressed and anxious to meet others with joy and tolerance. . . . Only those who shake off the pressure of the institution and manage largely to ignore it are able to release the full expansive dynamism of Christian love. . . .

People are, however, held by an institution in which they have no real part or say and in which they cannot be themselves. They are reluctant to release themselves from it because they see no alternative and instinctively they want some social structure in which to live as Christians. But the more earnest they are the greater the tension of living under a structure that simply does not correspond to their experience and needs. Recent changes have increased the tension by raising hopes without fulfilling them, and their chief effect has been to show that tinkering with the present structure is no solution. . . .

There is great talk of renewal, couched in high-flown spiritual language, but when the first tentative reforms begin to have practical effects, the authorities draw back, uttering warnings and issuing new restrictions. . . . The plain fact is that the present system cannot take more than superficial adjustments. I do not want to give the impression of disparaging the noble efforts of those working for reform. I admire their aims and determination. But it seems to me they cannot fully succeed within the present framework of the institutional Church. They are asking for more freedom than it can allow while retaining its present identity.[12]

Again, there seems to be a strong parallel with those among Jehovah's Witnesses who continue to hope, in spite of any evidence to the contrary, that some type of major reform will take place. As stated earlier, even the recent changes made seem to be simply a case of dealing with symptoms rather than the root cause of the illness or disease, which is the heavy emphasis on organizational authority and its right to dictate to human consciences and control personal thinking. As Davis puts it: "There is a possibility that the cause of the disease will be advocated as its remedy."

Thus, each *Watchtower* article setting out a major change, fails to face up to the problem of the original false reasoning and misuse of Scripture that makes change necessary. Rather, it consistently seeks to cast the change in the light of evidence for putting trust in, and being submissive to, *the system that gave the wrong understanding*, not only gave it but insisted on it and took action against any not accepting it. In each case,

---

12   *A Question of Conscience* (Hodder and Stoughton, London, 1967), pp. 65, 66, 77, 78, 81.

as well, one sees clear and regrettable evidence that the change results, not from pure love of truth or deep devotion to Scripture or compassionate concern for people, but comes instead when the previous position has become precarious, difficult to sustain, sometimes embarrassingly so, as with regard to certain teachings relating to 1914, or, in other cases, when interests in avoiding taxation or other restrictions are at stake.[13] That is why the hopes for genuine and fundamental reform, for the present at least, give evidence of being essentially wishful thinking.[14]

Turning to a source having a protestant or evangelical background, one finds these expressions in the book *The Myth of Certainty*, by scholar Daniel Taylor:

> The primary goal of all institutions and subcultures is self-preservation. Preserving the faith is central to God's plan for human history; preserving particular religious institutions is not. Do not expect those who run the institutions to be sensitive to the difference. God needs no particular person, church, denomination, creed or organization to accomplish his purpose. He will make use of those, in all their diversity, who are ready to be used, but will leave to themselves those who labor for their own ends.
>
> Nonetheless, questioning the institutions is synonymous, for many, with attacking God—something not long to be tolerated. . . . Actually, they are protecting themselves, their view of the world, and their sense of security. The religious institution has given them meaning, a sense of purpose, and, in some cases, careers. Anyone perceived as a threat to these things is a threat indeed.

---

13 As noted earlier, serious problems have arisen for the Witness organization in several European countries as to certain status and related benefits normally available to religious organizations. Governmental agencies in Germany, France, Russia and other countries have implemented policies or assessed fines that have given cause for concern. The change in policy regarding alternative service may relate to this. Disfellowshipping policies, and policies prohibiting blood transfusions are subject to criticism. Efforts to improve their public "image" has led to the formation of public relations staffs and considerable effort to portray a favorable impression in the news media.

14 See also pages 383, 384.

This threat is often met, or suppressed even before it arises, with power. . . . Institutions express their power most clearly by enunciating, interpreting and enforcing the rules of the subculture. Every institution has its rules and ways of enforcing them, some clearly stated, others unstated but no less real.[15]

It should be noted that the author was not writing about Jehovah's Witnesses but of religious institutions in the broader spectrum. People in many denominations fall into the common error of thinking that commitment to a religious system is equivalent to commitment to Christ as Lord.

I think here of a saying that was passed on to me by a friend. It says:

The mind which renounces, once and forever, a futile hope, has its compensation in ever growing calm.

I have found that saying true in my own case. I know that it has proved true in the case of many others.

Whatever the initial distress—a distress that sometimes follows the demeaning experience of being interrogated by men who, in effect, strip one of human dignity, make the weight of their authority felt, and presume to judge adversely one's standing with God—however torn one may feel inside, afterward there does come a distinct feeling of relief, of peace. It is not just knowing that one is finally outside the reach of such men, no longer subject to their ecclesiastical scrutiny and pressure. Truth, and the refusal to compromise truth, brings freedom in other fine and wonderful ways. The more responsibly one makes use of that freedom the finer the benefits.

The greatest freedom enjoyed is that of being able to serve God and his Son—as well as serve for the good of all persons—untrammeled by the dictates of imperfect men. There is freedom to serve according to the dictates of one's own conscience, according to the motivation of one's own heart. The sense of having a great burden lifted off, the lightening of a heavy load, comes with that freedom. If genuinely appreciated, this

15   Daniel Taylor, Ph.D., *The Myth of Certainty*, (Word Books, Waco, Texas, 1986), pp. 29, 30.

gives one the desire to do, not less, but more in service to the Ones giving that freedom.[16]

Traumatic as the initial transition may be, it can lead to the development of a truly *personal* relationship with these two greatest Friends. Perhaps nothing is more crucial or more helpful in making the transition than to come to a full appreciation of the need for that personal relationship with God and his Son. Without that, one may feel unable to have any sense of identity without membership in some system.

Christ clearly emphasized the *personal* nature of that relationship. (Matthew 10:32, 33) His call is, not "come to my organization" or "come to a certain church or denomination," but rather it is, "Come to *me.*" (Matthew 11:28) In giving the illustration of the vine and its branches, his words were not "I am the vine and religious organizations are the branches and you are the twigs or the leaves connected to those branches," but rather "I am the vine and *you* are the branches," connected directly to him. (John 15:5) In his beautiful description of the good shepherd, he says, "I am the good shepherd. I know my own and my own know me, just as the Father knows me and I know the Father. And I lay down my life for the sheep." (John 10:14, 15) Among Eastern shepherds of that time, a shepherd gave names to each of his sheep and so could "call his own sheep by name." (John 10:3, *NRSV)* It is wonderfully comforting and assuring to know that as our good Shepherd, God's Son knows each individual in his flock by name and cares for us personally and individually.

Whatever sense of "belonging" that membership in some religious system may create, it can never compare with the power and beauty and strengthening benefit of the intimate personal relationship the Scriptures present. The Son's love mirrors that of his Father, of whom the apostle writes, "Cast all your anxiety on him, because he cares for you."[17]

We need, as well, to recognize that to be genuine, faith must be truly personal, individually arrived at and attained. There is no group or collective faith—except as each *individual* therein has gained and expressed such faith on a personal, individual basis. So, too, with conviction, it has

---

16   Galatians 5:1, 13, 14; 1 Corinthians 9:1, 19; Colossians 3:17, 23-25.
17   1 Peter 5:7, *NRSV;* compare Matthew 6:26-33.

no meaning or validity unless it is individual, personal. To believe because others believe is to have a borrowed conviction and a borrowed faith. To be genuine and to lead to life, these must be the product of one's own mind and one's own heart.

The apostle puts the matter on that individual basis when he writes, "For one believes with the heart and so is justified, and one confesses with the mouth and so is saved. . . . For, 'Everyone who calls on the name of the Lord shall be saved.'" (Romans 10:10, 13, *NRSV*) Mouthing words that merely repeat traditional teachings of a religious system is not what is here described, but rather constitutes what the prophet calls worship based on a "human commandment learned by rote." (Isaiah 29:13, *NRSV*) At the time of divine judgment we do not appear before God and his Son as members of some church group or organization. We stand as individuals, and "each of us will be accountable to God."—Romans 14:10-12, *NRSV*.

Sadly, in the case of most Witnesses, the organization has so persistently pushed its own self to the fore, has occupied such a large place on the spiritual scene, focusing so much attention on its own importance, that it has kept many from the closeness of fellowship with the heavenly Father that should have been theirs. The figure of the organization has loomed so large that it has overshadowed the greatness of God's own Son, has clouded the vision of many from appreciating the warm relationship he invites persons to share with him, has distorted their perception of his compassionate personality.[18] It is not surprising, then, that many persons, if expelled from the organization, feel a sense of aloneness, of being adrift, floundering, due to no longer being tied to some visible authority structure, no longer having their lives channeled into its routine of programmed activity, no longer feeling the restrictive pressures of its policies and rulings.

In a sense, it seems that often one must undergo a measure of such painful adjustment to come to appreciate fully what complete dependence on God and his Son really means. I do not know personally of anyone who, in such circumstances, has recognized the need to draw closer to God, to give serious attention to the reading of his Word, to show interest

---

18   Matthew 11:28-30; Mark 9:36, 37; 10:13-16; Luke 15:1-7; John 15:11-15.

in others by trying to be of spiritual uplift and encouragement, who has not been able to weather the experience well, to come through it feeling greatly strengthened, more strongly fixed on the only solid foundation, faith in God's provision of his Son.[19] They have realized more than ever before the intimate relationship they have with their Master and Owner as *his* disciples, whom he treats as personal friends, not like sheep that men have penned off in a mass enclosure, but sheep to whom the Shepherd gives individual, personal attention and care. Whatever their age, whatever the length of time it took them to come to this realization, the feeling they have fits the well-known saying, "Today is the first day of the rest of my life." Their outlook is both happy and positive, for their hopes and aspirations are dependent, not on men, but on God.

To feel this way does not imply any failure to recognize that there is indeed a flock of God, a congregation headed by Christ Jesus. How does one become a member thereof? One factor and one factor only is determinative. It is not membership or affiliation with some denomination, church group or organization. Scripturally, this has no relevance or bearing on the matter. One shows that he or she is a member of that body of believers by being joined to its Head, God's Son, responsive to that Head's direction and guidance, and that alone is determinative. There is only one mediator in God's arrangement and that is Christ Jesus, and no human organization can insert itself into that picture as a co-mediator or supplementary mediator. (Ephesians 4:11-16; 1 Timothy 2:3-6) Between those in that congregation of believers there is an *interrelationship* and *interdependency*, not because they are subject to some organizational structure but because "we are members of one another," and so we are subject, not to some authority group but are "subject to one another out of reverence for Christ."—Ephesians 4:25; 5:21, *NRSV.*

God's Son gave the assurance that he would have true followers, not just in the first century or in this twentieth century, but in all the centuries in between, for he said, "I am with you *always, to the close of the age.*"[20] Intermixed though they were among all the "weeds" that were bound to

---

19   Psalm 31:11-16; 55:2-6, 12-14, 22; 60:11, 12; 94:17-22; Romans 5:1-11; 8:31-39.
20   Matthew 28:20, *RSV.*

come, he would know who these genuine disciples were, *not* because they belonged to some organization but because of what they *were,* as *persons.* Wherever they were, however indistinguishable from the human standpoint their being part of his congregation may have been, down through the centuries he has known them, not only collectively but *individually,* and led them as their Head, their Master. His apostle tells us, "But God's firm foundation stands, bearing this seal: 'The Lord knows those who are his.'"[21] Why should we doubt that this continues to be the case right up to the present time? God's Word shows that it is not up to men—not even possible for men—to separate people out so as to say that they have now gathered all the "wheat" into one neat enclosure. The Scriptures make clear that only when God's Son makes known his judgments will that identification become manifest.[22]

It is a pleasure now to be free to meet people and not feel obliged to look for some "label" in order to know how to view them. One feels no need to classify them automatically as either a Witness or a "worldling," as either "in the Truth" or "part of the Devil's organization," as either someone who, by virtue of having the Witness "label," is automatically one's "Brother" or "Sister" or, because of lacking such, is a person only to be "witnessed to" but unworthy to associate with on a friendly basis. In place of this, there is a healthful feeling of being able to do what is fair and just by assessing each person in an unbiased way for what he or she is—as a person. It is reassuring to be able to do this because of knowing that "God is not partial, but in every nation the man that fears him and works righteousness is acceptable to him."[23]

Certainly one of the most painful experiences for many who have tried to be true to conscience is to realize how quickly long-term friendships within the Witness community can end, how abruptly an atmosphere of apparent love can change to one of cold distrust. A Witness in a southern state, one of the most active in her congregation, began to see

---

21   2 Timothy 2:19, *RSV.*
22   Compare Matthew 13:37-43 with Romans 2:5-10, 16; 14:10-12; 1 Corinthians 4:3-5; 2 Corinthians 5:10; 10:12, 18; 2 Timothy 4:1.
23   Acts 10:34, 35.

how far the organization had strayed from Scriptural teaching. She told an acquaintance that, despite this, she had no thought of withdrawing. As she expressed herself, "There are so many people in our congregation that I personally studied the Bible with and helped to bring into association with the congregation. I feel a deep love for them and for others and for that reason I feel I should stay. I can't walk away from these people I love." Not long after this, the elders, becoming aware that she had reservations about some teachings, began questioning her "loyalty." Almost overnight, attitudes toward her underwent change. She found herself being convicted by congregational innuendo and gossip. As she said, "I discovered that the deep love I thought existed was actually a one-way thing. Without even talking to me to find out how I really felt, persons I had dearly loved suddenly turned cold to me."

When your very reverence, devotion and integrity toward God have been defamed—the greatest calumny possible—it is a chilling experience to hear someone that you considered a solid friend say, "I don't know what happened and I prefer not to know." Or to learn that such a one has said, "I don't know the facts but whatever the organization did there must have been a good reason."

All too often the vaunted love claimed as part of the "spiritual paradise" shows itself to be quite superficial. In a phone conversation, a Witness in a nearby state, still actively associated, told me that her husband, a prominent elder in their city, had for some time been under considerable pressure from other local elders. "If they could get anything at all against him, they'd hang him from the highest tree," she said. My comment was that this reminded me of the saying, "With friends like these, who needs enemies?" "You don't know how many times we've repeated that," she replied.

My feelings are like those contained in a letter from a person who had experienced cold rejection and who wrote:

> Even the hurt I felt when many former friends of many years chose to believe these stories rather than come to me and find out the truth, was dimmed by my joy . . . and also the knowledge that the reason they were acting this way was because of the fear in them. I can really forgive them from my heart because I truly know how they felt—at best that I had abandoned Jehovah (by leaving his organization) and at worst that I was

deceived and led astray by Satan. Either way put me in an unapproachable position. I am really sorry for any hurt that I have caused them or anyone in the organization. I really love them and would do anything in my power to reach them and try to explain the truth of what is happening to me.

My feelings coincide because I believe that the turning off of one's affection with the apparent ease of turning off a light switch is also a product of organizational indoctrination, not something normal to most persons' natural feelings.

Whatever the case, the Witness who follows his or her conscience may indeed find terminated virtually every friendship that he or she has had. In such circumstance, one surely needs to embrace the attitude voiced by the psalmist:

> In case my own father and my own mother did leave me, even Jehovah himself would take me up.[24]

Only an increased awareness of God's friendship and that of his Son can compensate, can put all other relationships in proper perspective as to their relative worth. Though it may take time, there is good reason to trust that other friendships will become available, if one is willing to make the needed effort. And there is a likelihood that they will prove more enduring, the affection being predicated, not on organizational membership, a sort of "club spirit," but on what one really is as a person, on the Christian qualities demonstrated, the realities of one's heart. I did not personally lose all my friends by any means. But for every one that I did lose I have found another. They are persons who have made clear that they are determined not to let differences of opinion or viewpoint have a disruptive effect on that friendship. This follows the counsel given:

> Accept life with humility and patience, generously making allowances for each other because you love each other. Make it your aim to be at one in the Spirit, and you will be bound together in peace.[25]

---

24   Psalm 27:10; compare Psalm 31:11; 38:11; 50:20; 69:8, 9, 20; 73:25, 28.
25   Ephesians 4:2, 3, *Phillips Modern English* translation.

The oft-quoted words at Hebrews 10:24, 25 are frequently made to say something different from what they actually say. If we love God and his Son we will also love those who share that love. We will want to associate with them, share companionship with them, benefit from them and seek to be of benefit to them. The writer of Hebrews says nothing as to time or place or manner. He does not speak of some formalized service or meeting, organizationally generated and supervised. Any of those things would have to be read into his words, superimposed on them. He speaks simply of getting together with other fellow believers, and doing so, not to absorb some particular format of church teachings but to be mutually upbuilt and to encourage one another to good deeds. Among early Christians this was customarily done in homes and, evidently, often in connection with shared meals.[26]

It may be difficult, because of being so long accustomed to the organization's extreme emphasis placed on numbers and the pretension that numerical growth is proof of divine direction and blessing, to take a humbler, more modest outlook, to scale down one's viewpoint in such areas. For the first time, one may come to appreciate and cherish Jesus' assurance that 'where two or three are gathered together in his name he is present with them.' In my own experience, I can say that sharing with only one or two others in reading and discussing the Scriptures has proved fully satisfying and rewarding. True, when at times a larger number of persons have shared with us, there has been a greater degree of interest and variety of comment. Yet the fundamental strengthening power and richness of God's Word have not been diminished on those occasions when we have been just "two or three." I can honestly say, in each case, that it has resulted in my carrying away with me things worth remembering to a greater extent than on so many occasions in the past when I met with hundreds, thousands, tens of thousands of persons in organizationally programmed functions.

It takes faith to trust that this can result. But this is related to another of the benefits of the freedom that upholding God's truth brings, namely, that in place of feeding on a strictly regimented "diet" prepared by a

---

26 1 Corinthians 16:19; Colossians 4:15; Philemon 1:2; Acts 2:46; Jude 1:12.

human authority structure, one can rediscover God's Word for what it really is, for what it actually says. It is surprising how refreshing it can be to read the Scriptures and simply let them speak for themselves, contextually, without being "overprinted" by the traditional teachings of men. One person, in a southern state, who said that in her association as a Witness she had never failed to report activity every month for forty-seven years, with equally regular attendance at all meetings, expressed how thrilling she now found her reading of the Scriptures, saying, "I never felt moved to stay up until 2 a.m. reading the *Watchtower* but now I find myself doing just that with the Bible."

After being accustomed to intricate interpretations, complex arguments, and imaginative allegorizing of the Scriptures, it may be difficult to recognize and accept the remarkable simplicity of the Bible's actual message. It may be hard to realize that Jesus meant just what he said when, after stating the principle that "whatever you wish that men would do to you, do so to them," he went on to say, "for this *is* the law and the prophets."[27] That shows that the essential thrust of all the inspired Scriptures then in existence was to teach men and women to love. This harmonizes with Jesus' declaration that on the two commandments of loving God and loving one's neighbor "depend all the law and the prophets."[28] Note, not only the law but also "the prophets."

Prophecy then has as its aim not the development of some speculative, highly imaginative application to certain dates and events in modern times (which application often changes as the passing of time makes it unsuitable), nor to supply the means for boasting of an organization's supposed superior relationship to God. All prophecy is designed to lead us to the "son of God's love," that we might learn love through him, and live in love as he lived in love. Thus, we read that, "The bearing witness to Jesus is what inspires prophesying."[29]

Whenever Scripture is employed in any other way, whenever dogmatism and sectarian argumentation becloud and complicate this simple

---

27   Matthew 7:12, *RSV.*
28   Matthew 22:40, *RSV.*
29   Revelation 19:10; compare 1 Peter 1:10, 11.

design of the Scriptures, it demonstrates that those so arguing have missed the whole purpose of the Bible.

Those who think that intricate, often perplexing interpretations of prophecy—that few can explain without a particular publication in their hands—constitute the "deep things of God," betray a lack of understanding of what that phrase Scripturally applies to. Letting the Bible speak for itself one finds that the truly "deep things" of Scripture relate to learning the "depth of the riches, the wisdom and the knowledge of God" expressed particularly in his mercy through Jesus Christ, so that "out of his glorious riches he may strengthen you with power through his Spirit in your inner being, so that Christ may dwell in your hearts through faith. And I pray that you, being rooted and established in love, may have power . . . to grasp how wide and long and high and deep is the love of Christ, and to know this love that surpasses knowledge—that you may be filled to the measure of all the fullness of God."[30]

That the "good news" centers on this very expression of mercy by God through Christ and his ransom can be demonstrated by anyone who will take the time to look up each occurrence of that phrase by means of a concordance. Of the more than one hundred occurrences of the expression "good news" in the Bible, there are eight references to the good news "of the kingdom," but there are scores of references to the good news "about the Christ." This is because God's kingdom, the expression of his royal sovereignty, is all centered in his Son and the things that God has done through him and will yet do through him. It is on Christ Jesus, and not on some human organization, that our attention and interest should focus, for "carefully concealed in him are all the treasures of wisdom and knowledge."[31] When compared with study, meditation and prayer that concentrate on a greater understanding of the depth of God's mercy and love and goodness, the writings found in some explanations of prophecy, however intriguing or mystifying or exotic, prove superficial indeed.

It is pleasant, then, to be able to read God's Word without feeling compelled to fix with absolute precision the meaning of every portion, or

---

30   Romans 11:33; Ephesians 3:16-19, *NIV.*
31   Colossians 2:3.

to explain every prophetic statement in an authoritative application. For what the apostle Paul wrote still holds true:

> For our knowledge and our prophecy alike are partial, and the partial vanishes when wholeness comes. . . . Now we see only puzzling reflections in a mirror, but then we shall see face to face. My knowledge now is partial; then it will be whole, like God's knowledge of me. In a word there are three things that last for ever: faith, hope, and love; but the greatest of them is love.[32]

If our love for God and his Son and for fellow humans is enhanced and upbuilt by our reading of the Scriptures, then that reading has undeniably served its major purpose. There are many points in the Scriptures that are so stated that they simply cannot be pinned down to one explanation as the only possible, right explanation. If there are alternative explanations, both of which allow for harmony with the rest of the Scriptures, both of which contribute to faith, hope and love, why fall into the sectarian trap of adamantly insisting on just one of these?

After all the arguing and debating is done over certain points or doctrinal issues that so often involve things not clearly spelled out in Scripture, what genuine good has been accomplished? The real question remains, what are we as persons? How well do we reflect the qualities of our heavenly Father and his Son? Does our life, our manner of dealing with others truly exemplify their teachings? Any teaching, organizational or individual, that does not genuinely contribute toward one's being compassionate, considerate and helpful in one's treatment of others, could never be from God, for "this commandment we have from him, that the one who loves God should be loving his brother also."[33]

In my account of events, I have referred to and sometimes quoted various individuals who went through experiences like my own. I do not offer them as some type of role model for others; even as I do not offer myself in that position. I do believe the account faithfully represents their position and spiritual attitude at the time of the events described. In any

---

32   1 Corinthians 13:9, 10, 12, 13, *NEB*.
33   1 John 4:21.

case, it should be kept in mind that we have only one role model and that is God's Son. Humans may disappoint us and prove unreliable, God's Son never will. In the Scriptures we have the record of his life and we also have the record of the lives of others, Paul, Peter, John, James and others, who proved themselves his faithful disciples and whose writing faithfully illuminate his teaching.

Some former Witnesses express concern that they are living lives that they feel are too quiet, that they should be "doing something," doing more, accomplishing more. It seems that having a background with the Watch Tower organization often leaves a residue of feeling that service to God and Christ and to humankind should have some aspect of the unusual, the special, activity that of itself distinguishes one from others. In a time when men might work from sunup to sundown, 12 hours a day; when women had none of today's labor-saving devices; and when many Christians were to be found among the estimated 60 million slaves in the Roman Empire, it is unlikely that the daily activities of the great majority of Christians in the first century were altered that much by their new-found faith.[34] The daily cycle and routine may have been essentially the same. But a new motivation was there, whether in the service a worker rendered to his master, or in the care a wife provided to her husband and children, or in any other relationship and feature of life. A new spirit was manifest, and by what they did and the way they did it, and by the spirit of love they showed they allowed the light of their faith to shine, opening up the opportunity to share the good news about God's Son with others. The difference quite evidently lay, not in an unusual program of activity, but in the faith they embraced in their heart and the effect of that faith on their attitude toward others and their daily dealings with others.

In one illustration Jesus gave about the kingdom, he likened it to the yeast placed in dough for breadmaking. (Luke 13:20, 21) Once placed there it disappears from sight. Yet it is accomplishing its purpose—quietly and unseen, with no fanfare, no brilliant display, nothing to draw

---

34   Matthew 20:1-8. The *Expositor's Bible Commentary*, in connection with Ephesians 6:5 cites the figure of 60 million slaves as likely.

attention to it. In a somewhat similar way, even if our lives and activity may seem quiet, simple, with little of the highly visible or notable about them, that does not mean that we are accomplishing nothing. The results of our faith and its influence will become evident in time. Whatever we do and whatever characteristics may attach to what we do, it seems we need to keep ever in mind that it is so very minute as compared with what is actually accomplished by God's spirit. As Paul expressed it: "Neither the one who plants nor the one who waters is anything"—essentially nothing by comparison, for it is "God who gives the growth." (1 Corinthians 3:5-7) God and his Son are the ones who take on the real burden, the heavier load to be carried.—Matthew 11:28-30.

We may need to free our minds of a stereotypical, conventionalized idea of what the Scriptures mean when they speak of "good works." The expression "works" comes from the Greek *ergon* and carries with it no implicit idea of something formal or programmed. "Good works" simply mean "good deeds," as the term is often rendered. The context of the expression can be revealing. When Paul, in his letter to Titus, speaks of being "a people zealous for good deeds," his preceding discussion has dealt with older men, older women, younger women, younger men, and slaves, and in all of his exhortation to all these groups he deals with—not some specialized, programmed activity—but features of everyday life and everyday conduct. (Titus 2:1-14) When James speaks of being "doers of the Word" and of the "religion that is pure and undefiled," he highlights "care for orphans and widows in their distress," along with being unstained by the world. (James 1:22, 26-28) And when he shows that genuine, live faith will motivate deeds of faith, he uses as his example the caring for the bodily necessities of fellow Christians in need. (James 2:14-17) John does the same in urging his brothers to love "not in word or speech, but in truth and action [*ergon*]." (1 John 3:17-18, *NRSV*) All these, then, are among the "good works" or "good deeds" or "good actions" that we can do to let the light within us shine and thereby cause others to give glory to our Father in heaven. — Matthew 5:14-16.

The question is asked, Where then do I go? What do I become?

I feel no need to "go" anywhere. For I know the One who has the "sayings of everlasting life."[35] I appreciate the strengthening companionship of those I have with whom to associate (either personally or by correspondence) and hope that the future will add to my acquaintance with yet other sincere persons whose concern is for truth, not simply in doctrine, in words, but as a way of life.[36]

I am simply trying, then, to be a Christian, a disciple of God's Son. I cannot see why anyone would want to be anything else. I cannot understand how anyone could hope to be anything more.

The past is now past. I have much to be grateful for, comparatively few things to regret. By this I am not minimizing the seriousness of error. When the sands of time in life's hourglass begin to run low, the damaging effects of having allowed any measurable degree of error to affect one's earlier decisions and life course can become rather painfully apparent. I have no regrets as regards hardships endured in the past. I feel I have learned valuable lessons from them. The trusting confidence I placed in a human organization, however, has proved to have been misplaced. Having spent the greater part of my life endeavoring to direct people to God and his Son, I found that that organization views such ones as if *their* flock, answerable to *them*, subject to their will. Nonetheless I am happy in the knowledge that I personally sought to encourage such ones to build their faith on God's Word as the sure foundation. My trust is that that labor will prove to have been not in vain.

At an age where other men contemplate retirement, I found myself just trying to make a start in providing for future needs of myself and my wife. Yet, along with the Bible writer, I could "say with confidence, 'The Lord is my helper; I will not be afraid. What can man do to me?'"[37] I do not regret in any way having held to conscience; the good that has resulted far outweighs any unpleasantness experienced.

Some early decisions, based on false presentations of God's will, produced effects that seem well nigh irreversible. I still get a hollow feeling

---

35   John 6:68.
36   1 John 3:18.
37   Hebrews 13:6, *NIV.*

inside whenever I think of leaving behind a wife with no son or daughter to supply emotional support and comfort. But there is a future beyond the immediate future and it is hope in that future, and the divine promises related to it, that calm the heart.

Though I find some of their actions incomprehensible, I feel no more authorized, or inclined, to pass judgment on those individuals who have rejected me than I feel they had the right to pass judgment on me. My sincere wish would be that the future might bring them better days, for I feel that there is so much that they could do that would broaden their outlook and lives and cause their days to become far richer in more meaningful ways.

I hope I have learned from mistakes of the past and, although I will certainly make more, I trust that at least there will be improvement, for the good of others as well as my own. I do regret that I cannot personally apologize to some whom I have wronged in one way or another, but my prayers are that no lasting hurt will come and I trust in God's providence in those areas that are beyond my ability to do anything about. Hopefully, the remaining years of my life may see a measure of peace for my wife and me and God's blessing on our united efforts to serve him all our days.

After his summary expulsion from the international headquarters, Edward Dunlap passed through Alabama on his way to Oklahoma City and his beginning life anew there at sixty-nine years of age. In talking with him, he said, "It seems to me that all one can do is try to lead a Christian life and help people within whatever sphere of influence he normally has. All the rest is in God's hands." He eventually had to discontinue his wallpaper-hanging work due to age, but he continued providing for himself and his wife by secular work until well past 80 years of age. He remained spiritually active, both through home Bible discussion with others in his area and through correspondence with persons writing to him from within the U.S. and from other countries. He expressed no regrets and his faith was strengthened by his experience. He died at age 88 in September 1999.

As of this present writing (2008), I am now 86. I rejoice, as did Ed, in the rich benefits that Christian freedom brings, the closer relationship with God and his Son which that freedom makes possible. Initially I felt that my only regret was that of not coming to the realization I did at an earlier age in life—perhaps a decade earlier (at age 47 instead of 57)—when starting life anew might have been less difficult. On reflection, I recognized that had that been the case I would not have had the experience of spending several years on the Governing Body and gaining the perspective that this made possible, something of potential benefit that could be conveyed to others who had not had this experience.

Life is a journey, and we cannot make progress in it if our focus is mainly on where we have been; that could lead to emotional inertia or even spiritual decline. What is done is done. The past is beyond our changing, but the present and future are things we can work with, focus on. The journey inevitably contains challenge, but we can find encouragement in knowing that we are moving on, making at least some progress, and can feel confident that what lies ahead can be fulfilling.—Psalm 5:8; Proverbs 3:6; 16:9; Jeremiah 29:11.

Whatever our individual circumstances may have been, we can each put confidence in the truth of these words of the apostle, "We know that by *turning everything to their good* God cooperates with all those who love him." (Romans 8:28, *JB*) By holding to conscience and staying true to our Head, God's Son, we suffer no lasting loss, but do gain that which is of immense and enduring value. Assured of that, we can feel as did the apostle:

> Whatever gain I had, I counted as loss for the sake of Christ. . . . one thing I do, forgetting what lies behind and straining forward to what lies ahead, I press on toward the goal for the prize of the upward call of God in Christ Jesus.—Philippians 3:7, 13, 14, *RSV*.

APPENDIX A:
Chapter References

For Chapter 3

WILL AND TESTAMENT OF CHARLES TAZE RUSSELL

Having at various times during past years donated to the WATCH TOWER BIBLE AND TRACT SOCIETY all of my personal possessions except a small personal bank account of approximately two hundred dollars, in the Exchange National Bank of Pittsburgh, which will properly be paid over to my wife if she survives me, I have merely love and Christian good wishes to leave to all of the dear members of the Bible House Family—and all other dear colaborers in the harvest work—yea, for all of the household of faith in every place who call upon the name of the Lord Jesus as their Redeemer.

However, in view of the fact that in donating the journal, ZION'S WATCH TOWER, the OLD THEOLOGY QUARTERLY and the copyrights of the MILLENNIAL DAWN SCRIPTURE STUDIES Books and various other booklets, hymn-books, etc., to the WATCH TOWER BIBLE AND TRACT SOCIETY, I did so with the explicit understanding that I should have full control of all the interests of these publications during my life time, and that after my decease they should be conducted according to my wishes. I now herewith set forth the said wishes—my will respecting the same—as follows:

AN EDITORIAL COMMITTEE OF FIVE

I direct that the entire editorial charge of ZION'S WATCH TOWER shall be in the hands of a committee of five brethren, whom I exhort to great carefulness and fidelity to the truth. All articles appearing in the columns of ZION'S WATCH TOWER shall have the unqualified approval of at least three of the committee of five, and I urge that if any matter approved by three be known or supposed to be contrary to the views of one or both of the other members of the committee, such articles shall be held over for thought, prayer and discussion for three months before being published—that so far as possible the unity of the faith and the bonds of peace may be maintained in the editorial management of the journal.

The names of the Editorial Committee (with such changes as may from time to time occur) shall all be published in each number of the journal—but it shall not in any manner be indicated by whom the various articles appearing in the journal are written. It will be sufficient that the fact be recognized that the articles are approved by the majority of the committee.

As the Society is already pledged to me that it will publish no other periodicals, it shall also be required that the Editorial Committee shall write for or be connected with no other publications in any manner or degree. My object in these requirements is to safeguard the committee and the journal from any spirit of ambition or pride or headship, and that the truth may be recognized and appreciated for its own worth, and that the Lord may more particularly be recognized as the Head of the church and the Fountain of truth.

Copies of my Sunday discourses published in the daily newspapers covering a period of several years have been preserved and may be used as editorial matter for The WATCH TOWER or not, as the committee may think best, but my name shall not be attached nor any indication whatever given respecting the authorship.

Those named below as members of the Editorial Committee (subject to their acceptance) are supposed by me to be thoroughly loyal to the doctrines of the Scriptures—especially so to the doctrine of the ransom—that there is no acceptance with God and no salvation to eternal life, except through faith in Christ and obedience to his Word and its spirit. If any of the designated ones shall at any time find themselves out of harmony with this provision they will be violating their consciences and hence committing sin if they continue to remain members of this Editorial Committee—knowing that so to do would be contrary to the spirit and intention of this provision.

The Editorial Committee is self-perpetuating, in that should one of these members die or resign, it will be the duty of the remainder to elect his successor, that the journal may never have an issue without a full Editorial Committee of five. I enjoin upon the committee named great caution in respect to the election of others to their number—that purity of life, clearness in the truth, zeal for God, love for the brethren and faithfulness to the Redeemer shall be prominent characteristics of the ones elected. In addition to the five named for the committee I have named five others from whom I prefer that selection should be made for any vacancies in the Editorial Committee, before going outside for a general selection—unless in the interim, between the making of this Will and the time of my death, something should occur which would seem to indicate these as less desirable or others as more desirable for

filling the vacancies mentioned. The names of the Editorial Committee are as follows:

> WILLIAM E. PAGE,
> WILLIAM E. VAN AMBURGH,
> HENRY CLAY ROCKWELL,
> E. W. BRENNEISON,
> F. H. ROBISON,

The names of the five whom I suggest as possibly amongst the most suitable from which to fill vacancies in the Editorial Committee are as follows: A. E. Burgess, Robert Hirsh, Isaac Hoskins, Geo. H. Fisher (Scranton), J. F. Rutherford, Dr. John Edgar.

The following announcement shall appear in each issue of THE WATCH TOWER, followed by the names of the Editorial Committee:

ZION'S WATCH TOWER EDITORIAL COMMITTEE

This journal is published under the supervision of an Editorial Committee, at least three of whom must have read and have approved as TRUTH each and every article appearing in these columns. The names of the Committee now serving are: (names to follow.)

As for compensation, I think it wise to maintain the Society's course of the past in respect to salaries—that none be paid; that merely reasonable expenses be allowed to those who serve the Society or its work in any manner. In harmony with the course of the Society, I suggest that the provision for the Editorial Committee, or the three that shall be actively engaged, shall consist of not more than a provision for their food and shelter and ten dollars per month, with such a moderate allowance for wife or children or others dependent upon them for support as the Society's Board of Directors shall consider proper, just, reasonable—that no provision be made for the laying up of money.

I desire that the OLD THEOLOGY QUARTERLY continue to appear as at present, so far as the opportunities for distribution and the laws of the land will permit, and that its issues shall consist of reprints from the old issues of THE WATCH TOWER or extracts from my discourses, but that no name shall appear in connection with the matter unless the same is required by law.

It is my wish that the same rules apply to the German, the French, the Italian, the Danish and the Swedish or any other foreign publications controlled or supported by the WATCH TOWER BIBLE AND TRACT SOCIETY.

I will that a copy of this paper be sent to each one whose name has appeared above as of the Editorial committee or the list from whom others of that committee may be chosen to fill vacancies and also to each member of the Board of Directors of the WATCH TOWER BIBLE AND TRACT SOCIETY. This shall be done immediately on my death being reported, so that within a week, if possible, the persons named as of the Editorial Committee may be heard from, their communications being addressed to the Vice-President of the WATCH TOWER BIBLE AND TRACT SOCIETY—whoever may be holding that office at that time. The answers of those appointed shall be to the point, indicating their acceptance or rejection of the provisions and terms specified. A reasonable time shall be allowed for any one mentioned who may be absent from the city or from the country. Meantime the remainder of the committee of at least three shall proceed to act in their capacity as editors. It shall be the duty of the officers of the Society to provide the necessary arrangements for these members of the Editorial Committee and to assist them in their duties in every possible manner, in compliance with the engagements made with me bearing on this matter.

I have already donated to the WATCH TOWER BIBLE AND TRACT SOCIETY all my voting shares therein, putting the same in the hands of five Trustees, as follows: Sr. E. Louise Hamilton, Sr. Almeta M. Nation Robison, Sr. J. G. Herr, Sr. C. Tomlins, Sr. Alice G. James.

These Trustees shall serve for life. In event of deaths or resignations successors shall be chosen by the WATCH TOWER SOCIETY Directors and Editorial Committee and the remaining Trustees after prayer for divine guidance.

I now provide for the impeachment and dismissal from the Editorial Committee of any member thereof found to be unworthy the position by reason of either doctrinal or moral laches, as follows:

At least three of the Board must unite in bringing the impeachment charges, and the Board of Judgment in the matter shall consist of the WATCH TOWER BIBLE AND TRACT SOCIETY'S trustees and the five trustees controlling my voting shares and the Editorial Committee, excepting the accused. Of these sixteen members at least thirteen must favor the impeachment and dismissal in order to effect the same.

DIRECTIONS FOR FUNERAL

I desire to be buried in the plot of ground owned by our Society, in the Rosemont United Cemetery, and all the details of arrangements respecting the funeral service I leave in the care of my sister, Mrs. M. M. Land, and her daughters, Alice and May, or such of them as may survive me, with the assistance and advice and coöperation of the brethren, as they may request the same. Instead of an ordinary funeral discourse, I request that they arrange to have a number of the brethren, accustomed to public speaking, make a few remarks each, that the service be very simple and inexpensive and that it be conducted in the Bible House Chapel or any other place that may be considered equally appropriate or more so.

MY LEGACY OF LOVE

To the dear "Bethel" family collectively and individually I leave my best wishes, in hoping for them of the Lord his blessing, which maketh rich and addeth no sorrow. The same I extend in a still broader sweep to all the family of the Lord in every place—especially to those rejoicing in the harvest truth. I entreat you all that you continue to progress and to grow in grace, in knowledge, and above all in love, the great fruit of the spirit in its various diversified forms. I exhort to meekness, not only with the world, but

with one another; to patience with one another and with all men, to gentleness with all, to brotherly kindness, to godliness, to purity. I remind you that all these things are necessary for us, necessary that we may attain the promised kingdom, and that the Apostle has assured us that if we do these things we shall néver fail, but that "so an entrance shall be ministered unto us abundantly into the everlasting kingdom of our Lord and Savior Jesus Christ."

It is my wish that this my last Will and Testament be published in the issue of THE WATCH TOWER following my death.

My hope for myself, as for all the dear Israel of God, is that soon we shall meet to part no more, in the first resurrection, in the Master's presence, where there is fulness of joy forevermore. We shall be satisfied when we awake in his likeness—

                    "Changed from glory unto glory."
(Signed)   CHARLES TAZE RUSSELL.
PUBLISHED AND DECLARED IN THE PRESENCE OF THE WITNESSES WHOSE NAMES ARE ATTACHED:
                    MAE F. LAND,
                    M. ALMETA NATION,
                    LAURA M. WHITEHOUSE.
DONE AT ALLEGHENY, PA., JUNE TWENTY-NINE, NINETEEN HUNDRED AND SEVEN.

The preceding document is the Will prepared by Charles Taze Russell, founder of the Watch Tower Society and its magazine, as published in the *Watch Tower* of December 1, 1916.

For Chapter 5

Following are paragraphs from the May 1, 1996, *Watchtower* presenting a reversal of position regarding the "alternative service" issue discussed in Chapter 5.

Civilian Service

[16] However, there are lands where the State, while not allowing exemption for ministers of religion, nevertheless acknowledges that some individuals may object to military service. Many of these lands make provision for such conscientious individuals not to be forced into military service. In some places a required civilian service, such as useful work in the community, is regarded as nonmilitary national service. Could a dedicated Christian undertake such service? Here again, a dedicated, baptized Christian would have to make his own decision on the basis of his Bible-trained conscience.

[17] It seems that compulsory service was practiced in Bible times. One history book states: "In addition to the taxes and dues exacted from the inhabitants of Judea, there was also a corvée [unpaid labor exacted by public authorities]. This was an ancient institution in the East, which the Hellenistic and Roman authorities continued to maintain. . . . The New Testament, too, cites examples of corvée in Judea, showing how

widespread it was. In accordance with this custom, the soldiers pressed Simon of Cyrene into carrying Jesus' cross [torture stake] (Matthew 5:41; 27:32; Mark 15:21; Luke 23:26)."

[18] Similarly, citizens in some countries today are required by the State or by local authorities to participate in various forms of community service. Sometimes this is for a specific task, such as digging wells or building roads; sometimes it is on a regular basis, such as weekly participation in cleaning up roads, schools, or hospitals. Where such civilian service is for the good of the community and is not connected with false religion or is not in some other way objectionable to the consciences of Jehovah's Witnesses, they have often complied. (1 Peter 2:13-15) This has usually resulted in an excellent witness and has sometimes silenced those who falsely accuse the Witnesses of being antigovernment.—Compare Matthew 10:18.

[19] What, though, if the State requires a Christian for a period of time to perform ci-

vilian service that is a part of national service under a civilian administration? Here again, Christians must make their own decision based on an informed conscience. "We shall all stand before the judgment seat of God." (Romans 14:10) Christians faced with a requirement of Caesar should prayerfully study the matter and meditate on it.* It may also be wise to talk the matter over with mature Christians in the congregation. After this a personal decision must be made. —Proverbs 2:1-5; Philippians 4:5.

[20] While engaged in such research, Christians would consider a number of Bible principles. Paul said that we must "be obedient to governments and authorities as rulers, . . . be ready for every good work . . . be reasonable, exhibiting all mildness toward all men." (Titus 3:1, 2) At the same time, Christians would do well to examine the proposed civilian work. If they accept it, will they be able to maintain Christian neutrality? (Micah 4:3, 5; John 17:16) Would it involve them with some false religion? (Revelation 18:4, 20, 21) Would performing it prevent or unreasonably limit them from fulfilling their Christian responsibilities? (Matthew 24:14; Hebrews 10:24, 25) On the other hand, would they be able to continue to make spiritual progress, perhaps even sharing in the full-time ministry while performing the required service?—Hebrews 6: 11, 12.

[21] What if the Christian's honest answers to such questions lead him to conclude that the national civilian service is a "good work" that he can perform in obedience to the authorities? That is his decision before Jehovah. Appointed elders and others should fully respect the conscience of the brother and continue to regard him as a Christian in good standing. If, however, a Christian feels that he cannot perform this civilian service, his position should also be respected. He too remains in good standing and should receive loving support.—1 Corinthians 10:29; 2 Corinthians 1:24; 1 Peter 3:16.

[22] As Christians we will not cease to render "to him who calls for honor, such honor." (Romans 13:7) We will respect good order and seek to be peaceful, law-abiding citizens. (Psalm 34:14) We may even pray "concerning kings and all those who are in high station" when these men are called upon to make decisions that affect our Christian life and work. As a result of our paying back Caesar's things to Caesar, we hope that "we may go on leading a calm and quiet life with full godly devotion and seriousness." (1 Timothy 2:1, 2) Above all, we will continue to preach the good news of the Kingdom as mankind's only hope, conscientiously paying back God's things to God.

* See *The Watchtower* of May 15, 1964, page 308, paragraph 21.

For sake of comparison, sample portions of the 14-page memorandum I submitted to the Governing Body in 1978 are here reproduced. This is, obviously, only a small fraction of the evidence presented then, some 18 years before they finally acknowledged that alternative service should be a matter of conscience.

OBSERVATIONS ON THE FOLLOWING QUESTIONS:

THE POSITION IS TAKEN THAT ALTERNATIVE SERVICE SHOULD BE REJECTED IF THE ORDER TO PERFORM IT PROCEEDS FROM A MILITARY AUTHORITY OR FROM AN AUTHORITY IN SOME WAY ASSOCIATED WITH MILITARY PURPOSES, SUCH AS A DRAFT BOARD. DO THE SCRIPTURES SUPPORT THIS?

Matthew 5:41 says: "And if someone under authority impresses you into service for a mile, go with him two miles."

Other translations read:

"If a man in authority makes you go one mile, go with him two." (NE
"If anyone orders you to go one mile, . . ." (Jerusalem)
"And whoever shall force you to go with him . . ." (New American)
   Standard; Goodspeed and Berkely similar)

The expression "impress . . . into service" translates the Greek word angareuo. Greek-English lexicons give definitions such as:

"denotes to compel one to go on a journey, to bear a burden, or to perform any other service"--Thayer's
"[noun]: impressment for the public service . . . impressed workman, labourer"--Liddell-Scott
"put to compulsory labor"--Moulton-Milligan
"[noun] compulsory service . .. [verb] press into service, compel to serve"--Patristic Greek Lexicon

Bible commentaries present information such as:

"The word in the original properly implies a legal requisition, being taken from the compulsory service employed in Persia for carrying royal dispatches. In a secondary sense, however, it is used for any forced service, as that of Simeon the Cyrenian who was compelled to bear our Lord's cross. . . . this compulsory service to foreign governments was particularly distasteful to the Jews."--The Bible Commentary by Cook.

The International Critical Commentary cites Josephus' Antiquities (xiii, 52 [2,3 in some versions] with reference to the use of the term as describing "the compulsory transportation of military baggage."

The Greek Testament, a commentary by Dean Alford, states: "The Jews particularly objected to the duty of furnishing posts for the Roman government . . . . The epistathmia, or billeting of the Roman soldiers and their horses on the Jews, was one kind of the angareia."

M'Clintock and Strong's Cyclopædia, on Simon of Cyrene, states: ". . . he was pressed into the service (angareusan, a military term) to bear the cross."

Matthew recorded both Jesus' words (5:41) and the account about Simon of Cyrene (27:32), using the same term in both cases. The account about Simon says: "This man they impressed into service to lift up his torture stake." It is obvious that the "they" here refers to the military forces carrying out the execution.

So the 'impressing into service' spoken of by Jesus could come from a military source and, in the only specific case mentioned in the Bible, evidently did. As Greek lexicons have shown, the term is not limited to carrying a load or baggage. It can apply to any type of compulsory service or labor.

DOES THE "SUPERIOR AUTHORITY" HAVE THE RIGHT TO CALL UPON ITS SUBJECTS TO PERFORM CERTAIN SERVICE OR WORK? WHAT DO THE SCRIPTURES INDICATE ABOUT THIS?

When Israel requested a king, the prophet Samuel told them: "This will become the rightful due of the king that will reign over you: Your sons he will take and put them as his in his chariots and among his horsemen, and some will have to run before his chariots; and to appoint for himself chiefs over thousands and chiefs over fifties, and some to do his plowing and to reap his harvest and to make his war instruments and his chariot instruments. And your daughters he will take for ointment mixers and cooks and bakers. . . . And your menservants and your maidservants and your best herds, and your asses he will take, and he will have to use them for his work." (1 Sam. 8:10-16) History shows that similar exactment of service and labor was done by many nations in all periods, including the present time.

CAN THIS BE VIEWED AS A FORM OF TAXATION OR DOES THE EVIDENCE SHOW
THAT TAXATION IS RESTRICTED, ABSOLUTELY AND UNEQUIVOCALLY, ONLY TO
MONETARY PAYMENTS?
There is no question that money payments are,
and for some time have been, the most COMMON form of taxation. In
the minds of most persons the term "tax" or "tribute" first calls
up the thought of a money payment. Money has the advantage of
facilitating the payment and of being usable in many ways and thus
governments have generally preferred such form of payment. But
basically they are calling for what they view as their "due," the
fulfillment of an obligation to them for services rendered. That
that obligation may be fulfilled in ways other than by money payments
is a matter of record, both in Scriptural and secular history.

Thus under "tax" the World Book Encyclopedia Dictionary includes
not only this definition:

> "money taken from the public by their rulers, as for the cost
> of government and public works; money paid by people for the
> support of the government; an assessment; levy"

but also this definition:

> "work or goods required from people by the government"

Money is earned by work and represents work. Thus people are
often spoken of as spending 30% (often more) of their time
"working for the government," because the money paid in taxes
represents that much work. In English the word "tax" comes from
the Latin taxare through the Middle English tasken. The word
"task" comes from the same source. Of the word "task," Webster's
New World Dictionary says:"1. originally, a tax. 2. a piece of
work assigned to or demanded of a person." Thus work and taxation
are related in this term, both being within its meaning. In each
case the same idea is basic: the fulfilling of a demand or assignment, payment of an obligation.

WHAT IS THE MEANING OF THE GREEK WORD THAT THE APOSTLE USED
AND WHICH IS RENDERED "TAX"? IS IT SOLELY A MONETARY TERM?

The word Paul used for "tax" (NW) is phoros. This Greek word comes
from the verb phero meaning to bear or carry, being used at Luke 23:26
when it speaks of Simon being made to "bear" Jesus' stake. (See
Kingdom Interlinear.) As Liddell and Scott's Greek Lexicon shows
it can also mean to "pay something due or owing." That something
could be a monetary tax but it is not limited to that. So, although
phoros came to be a very common term for a monetary tax, there is
no money aspect implicit in the term itself. That is why the
Kingdom Interlinear gives its literal meaning as simply the "thing
brought." (Rom. 13:7) The "thing brought" could be and often was
money, but it could also be goods or service rendered in payment of
an obligation.

... addition to what we read at 1 Samuel 8:10-16 about the rightful
due of the king, there are many other Scriptural references to the
enforcement of labor upon subject peoples by the ruling authority.
When the Israelites conquered Canaan, the inhabitants of cities sur-
rendering to them became theirs for "forced labor" to serve them.
(Deut. 20:11; Judg. 1:28, 30, 33, 35) When the kingdom was set up
in Israel, the Bible shows that the kings not only subjected foreign
peoples to compulsory labor but also subjected certain of the
Israelites to such labor, even as Samuel had prophesied. During
the reigns of kings David and Solomon they set up various departments of government--secretarial, military, household and also
conscription of forced labor. Adoniram (called Adoram and Hadoram)
was over the conscription of forced labor until the time of Rehoboam.
(2 Sam. 20:24; 1 Ki. 4:6; 12:18; 2 Chron.10:18) Solomon conscripted
persons for forced labor to build the temple, his own palace and
other works.--1 Ki. 9:15.

Describing how this worked, 1 Kings 5:13-18 says: "And King Solomon kept bringing up those conscripted for forced labor out of all Israel; and those conscripted for forced labor amounted to thirty thousand men. And he would send them to Lebanon in shifts of ten thousand a month. For a month they would continue in Lebanon, for two months at their homes; and Adoniram was over those conscripted for forced labor. And Solomon came to have seventy thousand burden bearers and eighty thousand cutters in the mountain, besides Solomon's princely deputies who were over the work, three thousand three hundred foremen over the people who were active in the work. Accordingly the king commanded that they should quarry great stones, expensive stones, to lay the foundation of the house with hewn stones. So Solomon's builders and Hiram's builders and the Gebalites did the cutting, and they kept preparing the timbers and the stones to build the house."

In all the above cases the Hebrew term mas (מַס), meaning compulsory labor, is used. This term of itself does not imply slavery. Thus 1 Kings 9:15-23 makes a distinction between the Israelites performing such labor and the Canaanites. The terms "slave" and "slavish" are introduced and in the Hebrew this is shown by the introduction of the word ébed (slave). (See also Genesis 49:15 where mas does not stand alone but ébed is added.)

WAS SUCH COMPULSORY SERVICE IN EFFECT UNDER THE ROMAN SYSTEM OF RULE?

Again, history shows that it was. The Encyclopædia Britannica presents the following information (the first portion being from the Micropedia and the second from the Macropedia):

statute labour, unpaid work on public projects required by law. Under the Roman Empire, certain classes of the population owed personal services to the state or to private proprietors—for example, labour in lieu of taxes for the upkeep of roads, bridges, and dikes; unpaid labour by coloni (tenant farmers) and freedmen on the estates of landed proprietors; and labour requisitioned for the maintenance of the postal systems of various regions. The feudal system of corvée—regular work that vassals owed their lord—developed from this Roman tradition. (The term corvée, meaning contribution, is now used synonymously with statute labour.)

Similar labour obligations have existed in other parts of the world. In Japan the yō system of imposing compulsory labour on the farmers was incorporated in the tax system in the 7th century. The Egyptians used the corvée for centuries to obtain labour to remove the mud left at the bottom of the canals by the rising of the Nile River. In various times and places the corvée has been used when money payment did not provide sufficient labour for public projects. In wartime the corvée was sometimes used to augment regular troops in auxiliary capacities.

CORVÉE, a term used in feudal law to designate the regular work that vassals owed their lord. It came to mean a contribution and in medieval Latin it meant labour exacted by the authorities. From this was derived the Old French corvée, adopted without change by the English.

In France the distinction was made between the corvées réelles (genuine), those days of work due in return for the property right, and corvées personnelles (personal), due by reason of residence and usually confined to road work. The term has retained its meaning as a payment in kind or in work levied on the inhabitants of a parish for the upkeep of local roads. It has also come to be used figuratively as a military term to describe fatigue duty, and thence extended to describe any drudgery or any work done reluctantly.

The use of the corvée as a system of obtaining labour dates from ancient. .... Under the Roman empire, personal services were due from certain classes of the population to the state and also to private proprietors. Obligations were imposed on freedmen as a condition of their enfranchisement and in the country usually took the form of unpaid work on the landlord's domain. The semiservile coloni were bound, besides paying rent in money or kind, to do a certain number of days' unremunerated labour on that part of the estate reserved by the landed proprietor. The state also exacted personal labour from certain classes in lieu of taxes for such purposes as the upkeep of roads, bridges and dikes. The inhabitants of the various regions were responsible for the maintenance of the posting system, for which horses, carts or labour would be requisitioned. Under the Frankish kings, who followed the Roman tradition, this system was preserved. Between the 6th and 10th centuries the Gallo-Roman estates were converted to the feudal model, and the officials of the Frankish empire developed into hereditary feudal nobles. They evolved the system of the corvée as it existed throughout the middle ages in Europe. |

---

1   As stated, this is only a small sampling of the 14-page memorandum supplied each member of the Governing Body in 1978. Though not as extensive, several branch offices offered similar evidence. The Governing Body allowed the traditional policy to remain in effect for another 18 years, at a cost of years in prison for thousands of young Witnesses.

For Chapter 10

As noted, the approach of the year 2014, marking 100 years since the prominent Watch Tower date of 1914, certainly presents a problem for the organization and its concern to maintain a mindset of date-related urgency among its members.

What appears to be an attempt to introduce a new time-factor that will serve that purpose appears in the December 15, 2003 *Watchtower* (shown on the following page) which contains major articles that seek to draw a parallel between conditions in Noah's day and leading up to the Flood and the conditions existing from 1914 on up to the final time of judgment.

As can be seen in the photocopied material, reference is made to the period of "120 years" at Genesis 6:3 and this is followed by the statement, "What about us? Some 90 years have passed since the last days of this system began in 1914." It requires only elementary arithmetic to discern that 90 subtracted from 120 years leaves 30 years and that 30 years added on to the year 2003 (when the article was published) *would lead to the year 2033*. Hence, if the parallel drawn had basis in fact and held true, the final act of God's divine judgment upon the world would be due to occur by that date. Though the publishers of the *Watchtower* magazine know, from their long experience with failed date predictions, that they should avoid saying precisely that this means that only 30 years remain before divine destruction, they clearly plant the seed for speculation, perhaps seeking to mitigate the effect of the approach of the year 2014, now just a decade away.

A former presiding overseer in Germany, had communication with a Witness who attended an annual meeting at the German branch office and said this man remarked that such implication was already being talked of. The former presiding overseer personally commented on this presentation, saying, "I don't expect to be alive in 2033. But if I were and nothing happened to support the focus on that date, I have no doubt that a *Watchtower* article would soon appear, saying, 'Now remember, it rained 40 days and 40 nights prior to the Flood. So, if we take the rule of "a day for a year" (Ezekiel 4:6) that indicates that we may expect the final destruction to come within 40 years.' There is a certain viciousness that allows men to play with people's hopes and lives in that way.

One effort to solve the problem resulting from the passage of time since 1914 is found in the February 15, 2008 issue of the Watchtower. With regard to Jesus' statement in Matthew 24:34, an article in this issue says that, while people 'who don't have spiritual understanding' think that there is nothing of "stunning observableness" as to the signs of Jesus' presence, the faithful brothers of Christ, the present class of John, 'recognize the sign and understand its real meaning.' And that 'as a group. those anointed comprise the present "generation" of contemporaries who won't pass away "until all these things come to pass." [2]

This change in the assigned identity of the "generation" of Matthew 24:34 is clearly one more attempt to hold on to the 1914 date and to cope with the approach of the year 2014. Remarkably, as shown in Chapter 10 of this book, this latest interpretation is one Albert Schroeder (now deceased) made some 30 years ago when on a trip to Europe. As shown in that chapter, on his return, he was reprimanded by the Governing Body and a Watchtower article was published reaffirming the traditional position.

The advantage of this latest interpretation is that it leaves the fulfillment of the Watchtower's claims about 1914 with no definable terminal point, effectively open-ended. For example, among the members of the Governing Body (all of whom are classed as among the "anointed") some were not even baptized until after 1950. More significantly, rarely does a year now go by without some persons among Jehovah's Witnesses newly making profession of being of the "anointed" class. In this way this "class" and the organization's application of "this generation" could extend almost interminably.

For Chapter 12

This is the letter sent in response to the citation for a judicial hearing by the East Gadsden Congregation of Jehovah's Witnesses:

---

2   A footnote at the bottom of the page says that 'this indicates that some of the anointed brothers of Christ will still be alive on earth when the foretold great tribulation begins.

November 12, 1981

Body of Elders
East Congregation of Jehovah's Witnesses
2822 Fields Avenue
East Gadsden, AL 35903

Dear Brothers:

Your letter of November 6 arrived Tuesday afternoon, November 10. This letter I am writing may or may not reach you before Saturday, so I will contact Theotis by phone in order that the brothers will not make an unnecessary trip to the Hall then.

I asked Dan to let you know that I was writing a letter to the Governing Body requesting information and would appreciate your waiting until an answer was received before following through on your judicial proceedings. Your letter does not make mention of this. Perhaps you can write me as to your decision on that request, if it was indeed given consideration. As you perhaps know, forty years of my life were spent in full-time service, as pioneer, special pioneer, circuit overseer, district overseer, missionary, Branch overseer, Bethel family member, Governing Body member. I do not know if you consider those forty years as allowing for a measure of forbearance on your part in the sense of patiently waiting whatever period of time it takes for Brooklyn to respond. I would hope that such would be the case and that your interest in their response would equal mine.--James 2:12, 13.

Do the three signatures at the end of the letter represent those forming the judicial committee? If so, then may I respectfully petition the body of elders to reconsider their selection? From what was stated at the meeting with Wesley Benner and Dan Gregerson, Dan presented himself as the accuser in the matter, stating at the beginning of the conversation that 'he had seen me eat with Peter Gregerson' (the occasion being some months ago, previous to the publication of the September 15, 1981, Watchtower). Till now I know of no other accusation of a supposed offense. Are there such? (I would need to know what such are--and by whom raised--if I am to be in position to have witnesses on my behalf.) Whatever the case in that respect, by any standard of justice it would hardly seem proper for the accuser to form part of the judging body. There are additional reasons for viewing Dan as not qualifying to serve in that capacity but I see no need to add them to that which is stated.

In your consideration of the above point, it would be much appreciated by me if you would weigh the advisability of enlarging

Body of Elders
East Gadsden Congregation
November 12, Page Two

the judicial committee. The charge involves a new position taken by the Governing Body (the placing of disassociated persons in the same class with disfellowshiped persons has heretofore been limited in publications only to those entering military service or political activity). Besides this, I have heard comments regarding condemnatory remarks about me made by some elders on the body. Since they have not spoken personally to me, I cannot know to what extent this testimony is accurate. But since it does raise the question of prejudgment it would be viewed as a kindness if additional elders in the congregation were included so as to contribute toward a fair and impartial discussion.

This letter is somewhat lengthy but perhaps you will pardon this considering that my devotion to God, his Son and his inspired Word are all being called in question. Accept my thanks for considering the points raised and may Jehovah God and our Lord Jesus Christ be with the spirit you show.--2 Timothy 4:22; Philemon 25.

Your brother,

R V Franz

Following is the complete letter sent as an appeal from the decision of the Gadsden judicial committee to disfellowship me:

December 8, 1981

East Gadsden Congregation Body of Elders

Dear Brothers:

By means of this letter I would like to appeal the decision to disfellowship me that was made by the judicial committee you appointed.

Speaking of judicial matters, one of the Society's publications says that "elders serving as a judicial committee must weigh matters carefully, knowing that certain factors may distinguish one situation from another. Instead of looking for rigid rules for guidance, you will need to think in terms of principles and judge each case on its own merits." As to giving counsel, the same publication says, "Be sure the counsel is based solidly on God's Word. Take sufficient time, and endeavor to reach the heart of the person. Take time to listen. Be sure you have all the facts. Discuss the application of the scriptures that apply and be sure that he understands. Take time for research, if that is needed, before you give counsel or answer his questions. If you cannot take the necessary time, it would be well to let another elder handle the matter." (Xerox copies enclosed.)

I do not feel that these things have thus far been done in my case. I find it saddening that an attitude of unusual haste has been shown and an apparent reluctance or inability to 'discuss the application of the scriptures that apply for full understanding.' I feel that a brotherly approach would call for patience rather than haste; compassion and understanding rather than a rigid application of rules.

My circumstances should not be unknown to you. After forty years of full-time service, in which I endured privation, poverty, hunger, thirst, cold, heat, fever, dysentery, jailings, dangers of mob violence, of gunshots and war, the risk of life and liberty in dictatorial lands, along with constant toil, I found myself at the age of 58 facing the problem of finding a home and employment to provide for myself and my wife. Since I began pioneering upon graduation from high school in 1940, I had no experience in secular employment and no financial resources to sustain me. The funds given me by the Society (evidently viewed as some type of compensation for my forty years of service) were less than most persons earn in one year of secular employment and covered no more than a portion of our initial expenses.

Peter Gregerson provided me with employment and a place to park the mobile home I obtained and am still in debt for. He thus became both my landlord and employer. About six months ago, under pressure, he resigned from the local congregation. As you know, the sole basis for the judicial hearing with me was the accusation that I had eaten at a local restaurant with Peter Gregerson.

East Gadsden Congregation Body of Elders
December 8, 1981, Page II

Some elders in the area feel that their employment with
Warehouse Groceries allows for their remaining free from accusation when eating with Peter Gregerson, who is Chairman of the
Board. Yet my relationship is closer, more involved than theirs,
since I not only work for Warehouse Groceries but also work for
him personally, doing work on his property and home in a way that
calls for regular conversation and discussion, often in his home,
at mealtimes and on other occasions. I am unable to understand
why a brotherly approach would not call for a compassionate,
understanding attitude, weighing my circumstances and recognizing
the "factors that distinguish one situation from another."

At the judicial hearing, only one of the two witnesses gave
testimony that relates to anything subsequent to the publication
of the September 15, 1981, Watchtower, which places disassociated
persons in a category with disfellowshiped persons. One witness
stated that he had seen me at the restaurant with Peter and Janet
Gregerson but acknowledged that the occasion was in the summer,
hence previous to the publication of that magazine. Unless one
believes in ex post facto laws, his testimony would hardly seem
relevant.

The other witness testified to a more recent occasion, having
seen me enter a restaurant in company with my wife and Janet Gregerson (who is not disassociated) and then subsequently seeing Peter
enter. This same witness, along with an elder of the East Gadsden
congregation, ate at a restaurant with Peter Gregerson on two
occasions subsequent to the publication of the September 15, 1981,
Watchtower. In neither case did Peter ask to sit with them but
in both cases he was invited to sit at their table and to engage
in free conversation with them. Apparently this was not viewed
as meriting a judicial hearing, but the one occasion in my case
was viewed as meriting such. I mention this only because your
letter of November 19 assured me that the elders handling my case
were free from prejudgment and would be objective in their approach.
The inconsistency apparent makes it difficult for me to feel satisfied that such was the case. It raises serious questions as to the
motivation for the judicial action itself and the decision rendered.

I find it equally hard to understand the accusation directed
at me when viewing it against the background of what is happening
in the Gadsden area. To list the occasions when elders and others
have eaten or otherwise had social contact with disassociated and
disfellowshiped persons would be difficult since they are numerous.
Yet for some reason I have been singled out for accusation. If the
view be taken that it is simply a matter of starting with someone,
why should the testimony of only one witness to one occasion since
the appearance of the September 15, 1981, Watchtower, result in my
being selected as the one to begin with? This too raises questions
as to objectivity and impartial motivation.

Perhaps it may be said that I have not expressed repentance

East Gadsden Congregation Body of Elders
December 8, 1981, Page III

for having eaten with Peter Gregerson. To express repentance I
need first to be satisfied that doing so is a sin before God. The
only means for providing such conviction must rightly come from
God's Word, which alone is inspired and unfailingly reliable.
(2 Timothy 3:16, 17) My understanding from the Scriptures is that
loyalty to God and to his Word is of supreme importance and super-
cedes any other loyalty or whatever kind. (Acts 4:19, 20; 5:29)
My understanding also is that it is not for me or any other human
or group of humans to add to that Word, under pain of being "proved
a liar" or even receiving divine plagues. (Proverbs 30:5, 6; Revelation 22:18, 19) I cannot take such scriptural warnings lightly.
In view of all the scriptural admonition against judging others,
I have a healthy fear of setting myself (or any human or group of
humans) up as legislator and feel compelled to let God's Word alone
do such judging. To do that I need to be certain that I am not
simply following some humanly devised standard that poses as a
divine standard but which is in fact uninspired, unsupported by
God's Word. I do not wish to be guilty of presumption and imper-
tinence in judging someone whom God by his own expressed Word has
not so judged.--Romans 14:4, 10-12; James 3:11, 12; see also
Commentary on the Letter of James pages 161 to 168.

I assure you that if you will help me to see from the Scriptures that the act of eating with Peter Gregerson is a sin I will
humbly repent of such sin before God. Those who have talked with
me thus far have not done this but have cited the above-mentioned
magazine as their "authority" (the term used by the chairman of
the judicial committee). My understanding is that all authority
within the Christian congregation must derive from and be solidly
based on the Word of God. Proverbs 17:15 states that "Anyone
pronouncing the wicked one righteous and anyone pronouncing the
righteous one wicked--even both of them are something detestable
to Jehovah." I have no desire to be detestable to God and hence
am very concerned about this matter.

I fully accept the scriptural teachings at 1 Corinthians 5:11-13
and 2 John 7-11 and have assured those with whom I spoke that I
have no desire to associate with or eat with or have in my home
persons of the kind there described, wicked persons and antichrists.
My problem is seeing how these scriptures apply to the person who is
at the crux of the case directed against me, Peter Gregerson.
Under pressure he resigned from the congregation of Jehovah's
Witnesses, but, as you know, he stated the following in his letter:

"It was brought to my attention yesterday that I have caused
many brothers throughout Gadsden and our circuit to be disturbed.
I had tried very hard to prevent that.

It is true that I have been experiencing serious doubts
regarding certain teachings of the Watchtower Society. However,
I would like to make clear two points of importance. First, I
have not been actively discussing these matters within the congregation. I have not even discussed them with the Body of Elders for
fear of accidentally causing conversation within the congregation.
I have had "confidential talks" with very few people, almost all in

East Gadsden Congregation Body of Elders
December 8, 1981, Page IV

my own family.

Secondly, my views have not changed regarding Jehovah God Jesus Christ and the plain teachings of the Bible such as resurrection.

As Jehovah God is my judge, I am conscious of no conduct unbecoming a Christian. For almost 50 years, since the winter of 1931-1932, when my dad started taking me to meetings, I have been a regular and hard working Jehovah's Witness. My good name and reputation is of great value to me, both among you and in the community at large.

So that my "good name" can be preserved, and so that there will be no further trouble and disturbance within and among you, I hereby resign from association with the organization.

This does not change my respect for the good done by the Watchtower Society. It does not change my friendship and love for you as individuals. Of course, I will accept whatever attitude you choose to show me.

Respectfully,

Peter V. Gregerson

[End of the copy of Peter Gregerson's letter. What follows is the continuation of my appeal letter.]

He states that he is "conscious of no conduct unbecoming a Christian" which would mean that he is not the kind of person described at 1 Corinthians 5:11-13. He expresses his faith in Jehovah God, his Son and the plain teachings of the Bible which would rule against his being among the kind of persons described at 2 John 7-11. To my knowledge no one has disputed those claims or refuted them. For me to treat him as a wicked man or an antichrist without clear scriptural basis for doing so would, I believe, make me liable for divine disapproval.

I have asked each of the elders who has spoken with me, including the three members of the judicial committee, if they themselves view Peter Gregerson as the kind of person described at 1 Corinthians 5:11-13 and 2 John 7-11, namely a wicked person or an antichrist. They themselves were obviously hesitant to say that these scriptures apply to him, yet these are the only scriptures that set out the injunction identifying persons with whom a Christian should not eat. Is it truly fair to ask of me that I apply these scriptures to him and thereby judge him as an unfit person with whom to eat when those sitting in judgment upon me are themselves either unwilling or unable to do so? As of now I do not see that these scriptures apply to Peter Gregerson. In order to see that they do I would need your assistance.

East Gadsden Congregation Body of Elders
December 8, 1981, Page V

I can understand why the elders would be reluctant to say
that they themselves would place Peter Gregerson among the kind
of persons described by the inspired apostle at 1 Corinthians 5:11-13,
fornicators, greedy persons, idolaters, revilers, drunkards and
extortioners. I seriously doubt that any one of you on the body
of elders would admit that as even a remote possibility. Please
correct me if I am wrong.

That leaves those described at 2 John 7-11, antichrists. Can
you understand why in my heart I feel the need for genuine conviction before I could apply these verses to anyone? The apostle John,
who is the sole user of the term, describes such a one in these
words: "Who is the liar if it is not the one that denies that Jesus
is the Christ? This is the antichrist, the one that denies the
Father and the Son." (1 John 2:22) "But every inspired expression
that does not confess Jesus does not originate with God. Furthermore, this is the antichrist's inspired expression . . . ." (1 John
4:3) "For many deceivers have gone forth into the world, persons
not confessing Jesus as coming in the flesh. This is the deceiver
and the antichrist." (2 John 7) On this basis, some commentaries
(used on a number of occasions in Society publications) make these
points:

> Barnes' Notes on the New Testament says: "From this it is
> clear, that John understood by the word all those who
> denied that Jesus is the Messiah, or that the Messiah had
> come in the flesh. . . . They arrayed themselves against
> him, and held doctrines which were in fact in entire
> opposition to the Son of God."

> From Lange's Commentary: "$\dot{\alpha}\nu\tau\iota$ [anti] may mean both
> hostility and substitution. In the former case it denotes
> the antagonist of Christ, the antichrist, in the latter the
> pretender-Christ or pseudo-Christ . . . . The antichrists
> deny that Jesus is the Christ; that He did not come in the
> flesh, that He is not the Son of God, that He is not of God.
> The doctrine is the denial of the truth, the lie, they
> themselves are LIARS, and according to John viii.44, the
> children of the devil, of the father of the lie ([1 John]
> iii.3-10) . . . . The antichrist and the antichrists are
> to be taken 'as expressly connected with Satan,' and the
> two words here denote not substitution but hostility to
> Christ . . . ; the antichrist is pre-eminently the instru-
> ment and tool of Satan."

Do any of you on the body of elders seriously believe that
Peter Gregerson is to be classed among such kind of persons?

Jesus Christ said that "whoever addresses his brother with
an unspeakable word of contempt will be accountable to the
Supreme Court; whereas whoever says, 'You despicable fool!' will
be liable to the fiery Gehenna." (Matthew 5:22) For myself, I

East Gadsden Congregation Body of Elders
December 8, 1981, Page VI

had far rather be called a "despicable fool" than to be labeled an
"antichrist." Surely there is no uglier term to be found in the
Bible. Since even the unjust application of the expression "despicable fool" can make one liable for Gehenna, how much more so the
application of "antichrist" if unjustly used? I am very concerned
not to run such grave risk and I trust that you as individuals
will weigh that risk with equal concern. At Matthew 12:36, Jesus
says: "I tell you that every unprofitable [careless, RSV;
unfounded, Jerusalem Bible] saying that men speak, they will
render an account concerning it on Judgment Day." How could any
of us take such warnings lightly? Or how could we feel that we
can let the responsibility for our action rest with others if we
erroneously, without genuine foundation, declare someone a person
unfit to eat with as a person 'hostile to Christ'? Emphasizing
our personal relationship and responsibility to himself, as to his
Father, God's Son says: "Know that I am he who searches the inmost
thoughts and hearts, and I will give to you individually according
to your deeds."--Revelation 2:23.

Loyalty to God obliges me to be guided by my conscience which
is molded by these scriptures. Does such a conscientious course
make me subject to condemnation? It is true that the circuit
overseer said in my home that 'the Governing Body can overrule
our conscience.' While he stated--to use his own words--that he
"parrots what the Governing Body says," it would seem that in
this case he spoke of his own originality, for I know of no publication of the Society that makes a statement like his. More importantly, I know of no scripture that supports such view. The inspired
apostle tells us that, even where an action is right in itself, if
a person does it having doubts "he is already condemned," since
"everything that is not out of faith is sin." (Romans 14:23) If
my conscience is to change, it must be by the power and force of
the Word of God, not by mere human reasonings, for I am determined
to "let God be found true, though every man be found a liar," and
hence determined to be among those not "adulterating the word of
God, but by making the truth manifest recommending ourselves to
every human conscience in the sight of God."--Romans 3:4; 2 Corinthians 4:2.

I have set out this information in detail to enable you to
see the problem I face in accepting unquestioningly and with no
qualms of conscience the view advanced, namely, that the letter
written by Peter Gregerson (copied herein)--by itself and with no
other justifying evidence in support--gives anyone the right to
say that he automatically has become a wicked person unfit for
Christians to eat with. Have I missed the sense of the scriptures
that now restrain me from making such automatic judgment? Do they
not say what I understand them to say? And does my conscientious
concern to be true to God's Word now make me subject to condemnation
as also a wicked person, unfit to eat with? Three men among you
have rendered such judgment. I write this as much for their benefit,
and out of concern for them, as for the rest of you. If I am wrong
and God's Word says something different than what I see there, then

East Gadsden Congregation Body of Elders
December 8, 1981, Page VII

your reproving me by setting forth the proof from that inspired
Word of God will not only be accepted but welcomed.

I am supplying a copy of this letter for each member of the
body of elders since the judicial committee that rendered its
decision against me received its appointment from you. I am
also sending copies to the Governing Body and its Service Department
since your appointment as elders comes from them. As you know,
I wrote the Governing Body on November 5, 1981, requesting information as follows:

"Locally, certain elders have taken the information in the
September 15, 1981, Watchtower as authorization to demand a change
in my relationship with the man on whose property I live and for
whom I work, Peter Gregerson. They state that, since he has disassociated himself, I should view him as among those with whom one
should not eat--wicked persons and antichrists--and that failure to
conform to this position requires disfellowshiping. Approaching 60,
having no financial resources, I am in no position to move or to
change my employment. So I would very much appreciate knowing if the
intent of your statements in that issue of the magazine is truly
as they present it, namely that my accepting an invitation from my
landlord and employer to eat with him is grounds for disfellowshiping.
If, instead, they have exceeded the intent of what was published,
some counsel of moderation would grant me relief from a situation
that is potentially oppressive. I will appreciate whatever clarification you can give, whether directly or through one of your departments."

I have repeatedly petitioned you to allow them time to answer
this request for information. Thus far you have not seen fit to
honor that plea. I hope that you will now do so.

                              Sincerely,

A copy of the appeal letter was sent to the Governing Body along with
the following letter:

                                        December 11, 1981

Governing Body of Jehovah's Witnesses
Brooklyn, New York

Dear Brothers:

    On November 5, 1981, I wrote to you seeking some clarification
as to the position taken in the September 15 Watchtower and its
placing of disassociated persons in the same category with disfellowshiped persons and detailing the manner in which all of
Jehovah's Witnesses should view and treat such persons. In that
letter I expressed concern over the probable consequences of the
material.

    Since then local elders in the congregation where I have
been associated have taken that material as "authority" to take
disfellowshiping action toward me, the charge being that I had
eaten a meal with a disassociated person at a restaurant, the
person being my landlord and employer.

I am enclosing a copy of the appeal letter I have turned in to the local body of elders. If the judicial committee's action meets with your approval and is in accord with the intent of the material you have published, then the appeal letter may be of no interest to you. If, however, that is not the case and you do feel concern over this action (not solely as relates to me but as it is indicative of the probable reaction generally to that published material) then you may wish to do something to moderate the effect of that material. The company I work for, Warehouse Groceries, employs from thirty-five to forty Witnesses in its offices and ten stores. The Chairman of the Board is disassociated as is the head of the Non-Foods section; other personnel, including the manager of one of their larger stores, are disfellowshiped persons. So the clarification requested in my letter could be of benefit to a number of persons in this area.

It seems clear that the position taken in your published material will have a progressively cumulative effect, with more and more persons being affected. If applied consistently, rather than in a selective, arbitrary manner, in the way it has been applied to me, it could easily lead to the disfellowshiping of dozens of persons in just this area whose names come readily to mind. Do you genuinely feel that such action is justified scripturally?

Since the responsibility for the results of the earlier mentioned material rests ultimately with you brothers, it seems of benefit to pass this information on to you and to your Service Department.

Sincerely,

RW Franz

Following is my letter of December 20, requesting a change in the appeal committee selected by Circuit Overseer Wesley Benner:

December 20, 1981

East Gadsden Congregation Body of Elders
Gadsden AL

Dear Brothers:

By means of this letter I am requesting that a different appeal committee be appointed. I am sending a copy of this letter to the Service Department of the Governing Body and of the Watchtower Society since I am requesting that a committee be formed of brothers outside of this area and outside of this circuit. My reasons are as follows:

On December 15 I received a phone call from Theotis French saying that an appeal committee had been selected, composed of Willie Anderson, either Earl or Felix Parnell (he wasn't sure which) and Brother Dibble (whether the father or the son was not said to my knowledge). I told him that I would write a letter and that I would have something to say about the composition of the committee. I asked why elders from the East Gadsden congregation were not used and he said that that was not the way it was done anymore and that he had called on the circuit overseer to make the selection.

On December 18, Friday, I wrote to Theotis asking him to
supply me in writing the names of those definitely selected to
serve on the committee. I mailed the letter that morning. That
evening Theotis called saying that the appeal committee would
meet on Sunday. I informed him that I had written a letter which
he should receive in a day or so. Saturday evening he called
again, saying he had received the letter and that the committee
wanted to meet with me on Monday, evidently December 21. He did
not state either time or place, as he had not done when informing
me of the planned Sunday meeting. He gave me the names of the
proposed committee members: Willie Anderson, Earl Parnell and
Rob Dibble. I again requested he send the information in writing.
This morning he phoned yet again, stating that the appeal committee
was going to meet on Monday (again failing to state either time or
place). I told him that the proposed committee ought to write me
direct rather than have him phone me and told him that I objected
to the composition of the committee as selected and would be writing
this letter requesting a new committee. He said that the proposed
committee would meet anyway on Monday. I stated that in my forty
years of experience I had never seen such an obvious rushing of
matters, to which he replied that the last school provided by the
Society had brought changes (what these were he did not say).
Despite my objections to such inconsiderate haste he said that the
committee would meet anyway and that anything I had to say should
be said then. I again stated that I was requesting a different
committee.

East Gadsden Congregation Body of Elders
December 20, 1981, Page II

    I believe my reasons for such request are substantial. I
will detail them for your benefit and that of the Service Department as well as as a matter of record.

    I was serving on the Service Committee of the Governing Body
at the time that Gadsden experienced a very disturbing period for
many families, one involving a large number of the young people
in the area. By way of the Service Department I was made aware
of serious mishandling of matters by the local committee, requiring
the sending in of a special committee to straighten matters out.
The matter is fresh enough in my mind to assure you that I could
not feel confident of a competent hearing if the appeal committee
included one who played as prominent a role as Brother Anderson did
in the committee responsible for such serious errors. Additionally
I know, both through information from the Service Department at
that time and from personal knowledge since, that Peter Gregerson
was active in seeking the review of the local committee's action
and thus contributed substantially to the bringing in of the outside
committee assigned by the Society. When the whole picture is put
together, the selection of Brother Anderson to serve on my case,
in which my relationship with Peter Gregerson is the central issue,
is a selection not conveying great likelihood either of judicious-
ness, impartiality or objectiveness. While it might be hoped that
Brother Anderson profited from the correction given by the review
committee, the present conduct of the proposed appeal committee,
their haste to 'rush to judgment,' the irregularity of their
methods, only strengthen the memory of the past mishandling of
matters. I think you can understand why I would rightly object to
such a selection and find it completely unacceptable.

As to the selection of Earl Parnell, the reasoning that led to such choice is indeed hard to fathom. May I say once more, that my relationship with Peter Gregerson is the point on which this whole cases revolves, about which the whole testimony of the adverse witnesses was based, and because of which relationship the first committee decided that I should be disfellowshiped. How then could there be any rational justification for the selection of Earl Parnell to serve on my appeal committee? He is, as you well know, and as the circuit overseer knows, the father of Dana Parnell who was recently divorced by Vicki Gregerson, Peter Gregerson's daughter. Without going into matters in detail, it should be sufficient to say that for some time now very strained feelings have developed between the two families and more particularly between the two fathers. The circuit overseer was certainly aware of the very strong feeling that exists in this regard, since Dana was brought up in his conversation with Peter during his previous visit to Gadsden. It would seem clear to anyone of even average comprehension that the selection of Dana's father to serve in a matter where Peter Gregerson is involved, would be flying in the face of all that good judgment, fairness and just plain common sense would lead one to expect. What possible reasoning or proper motivation could lead to such a choice?

East Gadsden Congregation Body of Elders
December 20, 1981, Page III

The circumstances involving Brother Parnell unavoidably affect the third member of the proposed committee, Rob Dibble. He is Earl Parnell's son-in-law, being the husband of Dana's sister Dawn. If necessary, I believe that testimony is available showing that Rob's wife has been very much affected by Peter Gregerson's daughter's divorcing of her brother and has been fairly vocal about the matter. It seems most unlikely that what she has expressed to others has not also been expressed to her own husband. To expect that he could enter a case in which one's association with Peter Gregerson is a central issue and do so with the necessary freedom from personal feelings and the needed objectiveness is, I believe, asking more than good judgment would indicate.

In view of all this, I am respectfully requesting that a different committee be formed, made up of brothers outside this area and outside the circuit. With perhaps one exception I cannot conceive of a comittee of three individuals that would have less to recommend itself for an objective, unbiased hearing of my appeal than the one that has been selected. Perhaps the circuit overseer's selection was the product of a hurried decision without due consideration of the factors here stated. While attempts could be made to argue or explain away those factors, a love of fairness and justice would certainly rule out such a course. It will, I hope, move you to acknowledge that the appeal committee should be one that does not require such attempted justification but, rather, be one that can stand on its own, free from serious question.--1 Timothy 5:21, 22.

You may also wish to write to the Society about these points and I would welcome your doing so.

For your information, I am expecting today the arrival of some guests who are traveling over 500 miles to visit us and who have only a few days to spend with us. Monday afternoon I have an appointment in Birmingham (made some days ago) that will likely result in my getting home late that evening. Later that week we are scheduled to go on a trip out of the state, one planned some time ago, with arrangements made by those with whom we will be staying. During the days before and after New Year's day, a family of friends

will be visiting us, flying in from out of state to do so. However,
after January 5 I should have time to meet with the new committee
selected and this should also give time for the Society to arrange
for such.

May I also request that your communication with me be in writing
so that the frequent omissions and difficulties already experienced
may not continue to multiply. Thank you for your consideration of this.

                              Sincerely,

Copies of that letter were sent to the Governing Body and to the
Service Department along with the following letter:

                                        December 20, 1981

Watchtower Bible and Tract Society
Brooklyn N Y

          Attention: Service Department

Dear Brothers:

        By means of this letter I am appealing to you to arrange
for an appeal committee to hear my appeal, a committee formed
of brothers outside the Gadsden area and the circuit in which
it lies. My reasons for making such appeal are set out in
the enclosed letter directed to the East Gadsden Congregation
Body of Elders, under this same date.

        The chairman of the original judicial committee has informed
me of conversations with you so you are not unaware of the case.

        I am requesting that the committee be formed of brothers
outside the circuit, in part because of the large amount of rumor
and gossip that has circulated, much of which has filtered back
to me. But I also believe that the selection made by your
appointed representative, the circuit overseer, when compared with
the information presented in the enclosed letter, shows that
his judgment is, put simply, quite deficient.

        As mentioned in the appeal letter sent to you earlier and
dated December 8, 1981, when visiting me in my home Brother Benner
manifested a rigidity of attitude that provides little basis for
confidence as to his judgment in matters of this kind. As he
stated, he believes that one's conscience 'can be overruled by the
Governing Body' (whereas only Scripture should do such overruling)
and described himself at length as one who 'parrots' whatever the
Governing Body says. That attitude gives cause for concern, being
disturbingly reminiscent of the mentality that led to so many in-
justices in the German nation during a recent period, not to mention those religious persons through the centuries who have rendered
unquestioning acdeptance and adherence to the directives of what
they called the "Mother" church. The selection of appeal committee
members he has made does nothing to dispel such concern but rather
it heightens it. I believe the enclosed letter makes this clear.

        I urge you to take action to correct this obvious mishandling
of matters in this case. Thank you.

                              Respectfully,

I had now written to the Governing Body three times requesting some expression from them (on November 5, December 11 and December 20), as well as sending letters to the Brooklyn Service Department. In the eight weeks that passed from the time of writing the first letter until my ultimate disfellowshipment, none of these letters were answered. They were not even acknowledged.

APPENDIX B:

Excerpts from *In Search of Christian Freedom*

* **The following 6 pages published in *In Search of Christian Freedom*, 2007 pages 72-77 are referred to on page vi of this 2018 edition of *Crisis of Conscience*, footnote 1. The document below is from the *Watch Tower*, April 1882.**

are members of it, and should be properly recognized by those names. But if we were baptized into the one body or church of which Jesus is the one and only Head, then we are *members* in particular of his body, and the only name appropriate would be his; Scripturally called the "Church of Christ," "Christians," "Church of the first born," and such like general names. Again we would remark that ours is the only Scriptural basis of Christian *union*, viz: We have no creed (fence) to bind us together or to keep others out of our company. The Bible is our only *standard*, and its teachings our only *creed*, and recognizing the progressive character of the unfolding of Scriptural truths, we are ready and prepared to add to or modify our *creed* (faith—belief) as we get increase of light from our *Standard*.

We are in fellowship with all Christians in whom we can recognize the Spirit of Christ, and especially with those who recognize the Bible as the only standard. We do not require, therefore, that all shall see, just as we do in order to be called Christians; realizing that growth in both grace and knowledge is a gradual process. Nor do we see reason to expect that any but the *watchmen* of Zion will "see eye to eye" (Isa. 52:8.) until that which is perfect is come, when "that which is in part shall be done away." (1 Cor. 13:10.)

If all Christians were to thus free themselves of prescribed creeds, and study the Word of God without denominational bias, truth and knowledge and *real* Christian fellowship and unity, would result. The Spirit of the Head would pervade the unfettered members of the body, and sectarian pride would vanish.

It did not take long, however, for human reasoning to suggest something more "practical." The question was raised if it would not be good to have an "earnest, aggressive organization" (built, *of course,* "upon Scriptural lines"!) to accomplish more effectively the preaching of the good news? The *Watch Tower* in March, 1883, presents the question and the answer:

491

Q. "Would not an earnest, aggressive organization (or sect), built upon Scriptural lines, be the best means of spreading and publishing the *real* Good Tidings? We must have fellowship and sympathy. Union is strength. It is not the skirmishers that win the battle, but the disciplined and solid battalions."

A. We believe that a visible organization, and the adopting of some particular name, would tend to increase our numbers and make us appear more respectable in the estimation of the world. The natural man can see that a visibly organized body, with a definite purpose, is a thing of more or less power; therefore, *they esteem* the various organizations, from which we have come out, in obedience to the Master's call. But the natural man cannot understand how a company of people, with no organization which they can see, is ever going to accomplish anything. As they look upon us, they regard us simply as a few scattered skirmishers—a "peculiar people" —with very peculiar ideas and hopes, but not worthy of special notice.

But, though it is impossible for the natural man to see our organization, because he cannot understand the things of the Spirit of God, we trust that you can see that the true Church is most effectually organized, and in the best possible working order. (See the plan of our organization, as stated in October issue, under the caption "The Ekklesia.") The Apostle Paul urges all to unity of faith and purpose (Phil. 3:15, 16—*Diaglott*.) All led by the *same Spirit* may and do come to a knowledge of the *same truth*. Under our Captain, all the truly sanctified, however few or far separated in person, are closely united by the Spirit of Christ, in faith, hope and love; and, in following the Master's command, are moving in solid battalions for the accomplishment of his purposes. But, bear in mind, God is not dependent upon numbers (See Judges 7, as an illustration).

Recognizing this organization, which is of the Spirit, and desiring no assimilation whatever with the worldly, who cannot see or understand it, we are quite willing to bear the reproach of a peculiar people. We always refuse to be called by any other name that that of our Head—Christians—continually claiming that there can be no division among those continually led by his Spirit and example as made known through his Word.

The view that a strong visible organization was desirable was thus portrayed as the product of fleshly thinking, typical of the "natural man" who seeks numerical growth, who admires the power that a visible organization with its own distinctive name can generate. It was thus typical also of the unspiritual man who "cannot understand how a company of people, with no organization which they can see, is ever going to accomplish anything." The only organization they belonged to, these Bible students again affirmed, was a spiritual one, "invisible to the world." There was nothing to "go and see" to impress people with any organizational bigness and efficiency and strength and ownership of property and buildings. In place of organizational unity, unity of spirit was the proclaimed goal. They were encouraging people to free themselves from denominational religions with their visible organizations. So how, they asked, could they call on others to do this if they did not do it themselves?

It was, therefore, misleading for the *Watchtower* magazine of March 1, 1979, under the heading "Modern Day Theocratic Organization," to quote from a February, 1884, issue of the *Watch Tower* as though the quotation supported the *existing view* of organization prevailing among Jehovah's Witnesses. Notice how the material (page16) prefaces its quotation so as to allow for this idea:

> [16] The aforesaid congregation earnestly sought to prove worthy of being Jehovah's visible organization and his instrument. So it kept free from any alliance with the sectarian organizations of Christendom, as well as from the political organizations of this world. Voicing itself in this regard, that Christian congregation said, in the issue of February 1884 of its official magazine *Watch Tower:*
>
> > "New readers in all parts of the country are constantly inquiring: By what *names* do you call yourselves? Are you 'Primitive Baptists'? Are you 'Missionary Baptists'? Are you 'Universalists'? Are you 'Adventists'? Are you 'Primitive Methodists'? etc., etc. We have several times tried to make clear our position, and now endeavor in a few words again to do so.

> "We belong to NO *earthly organization;*
> hence, if you should name the entire list of
> sects, we should answer, No, to each and
> to all. We adhere only to that *heavenly
> organization*—'whose names are written in
> heaven.' (Heb. 12:23; Luke 10:20.) All the
> *saints* now living, or that have lived during
> this age, belonged to OUR CHURCH ORGANI-
> ZATION: such are all ONE Church, and there
> is NO OTHER recognized by the Lord. Hence
> any earthly organization which in the least
> interferes with this union of saints is con-
> trary to the teachings of Scripture and
> opposed to the Lord's will—'that they may
> be ONE.' (Jno. 17:11.)"

In an attempt to explain away beforehand the statement "We belong
to NO *earthly organization*," the writer of the March 1, 1979, *Watchtower*
presents this as if it referred only to separateness from "sectarian organizations of Christendom, as well as from political organizations." They
were separate from these—though the thought of "political organizations" does not even come into the discussion; its insertion by the later
Watchtower writer is simply the drawing of a "red herring" over the trail,
diverting attention from the actual significance of the statements. In the
blunt statement, "We belong to NO *earthly organization*," the "NO"
plainly means *none,* not just none of the sectarian ones but none that
they themselves had set up. They clearly taught that to set up such an
organization themselves, with its own authority structure and its own
distinctive name, would be to create yet another sectarian system. The
only organization they belonged to was the "*heavenly organization*"
whose members' names are written in heaven. This is made evident by
the context. In the following paragraphs, not quoted by the 1979 writer,
the 1884 article contained these points:

> By what name may this Church be called? We answer, By
> the name of its *founder* and *instituter*—Christ. Hence it is
> the "Church of Christ" or "Church of God," for God founded
> it on the *Rock* Christ Jesus; or "Christians," as they were
> known in early times. (Acts 11:26; 26:28, and 1 Pet. 4:16.;
> But because Paul and the other disciples were not followers
> of Calvin's teachings, therefore they were not called Calvin-
> ists; because they were not followers of Luther's teachings and
> example, therefore they were not called Lutherans; but be-
> cause they followed the ONE example and teachings of CHRIST
> only, therefore they gladly acknowledged it when they were
> called "Christians."

> What think you, do we not occupy the *only ground for union?* Or suppose that all man-made creeds, and forms, and prayer-books, and liturgies, and names were laid aside, or that all Christians met in the one name of Christ, and in earnest simplicity studied HIS words under the direction of God's Spirit and the explanations furnished in the Apostle's writings, would there long be serious differences even of opinion in the Church?

> And so, by whatsoever names men may *call us,* it matters not to us; we acknowledge none other name than "the only name *given* under heaven and among men"—Jesus Christ. We call ourselves simply CHRISTIANS and we raise no fence to separate from us any who believe in the foundation stone of our building mentioned by Paul: "That Christ died for *our sins* according to the Scriptures"; and those for whom this is not broad enough have no right to the name Christian.

This makes quite clear that Russell and his associates did not then present an exclusivistic viewpoint, as if considering themselves the only Christians. They rejected the narrow viewpoint that would deny the Christianity of other religious persons because of their not coming within some organizational "fence." Any who believed in the foundation truth "that Christ died for our sins according to the Scriptures" would not be denied the name "Christian" by them.

That this is the meaning of their statements is obvious from earlier issues of the magazines, several of which have already been quoted. An openness to others beside themselves as fellow "Christians" is expressed, for they had said "We are in fellowship with all Christians in whom we can recognize the Spirit of Christ, and especially with those who recognize the Bible as the only standard. We do not require, therefore, that all shall see just as we do in order to be called Christians; realizing that growth in both grace and knowledge is a gradual process."[1] The 1979 *Watchtower* writer who looked up the 1884 quotation reasonably should have seen these other statements. If so, he would have known that the use he made of the quotation was misleading, contrary to fact.

That this attitude continued is seen a decade later, when the September 15, 1895, issue the *Watch Tower* stated in quite blunt terms the attitude toward human organization. Responding to inquiries from those wanting

---

1   The *Watch Tower*, April 1882.

advice as to the most profitable way to conduct group meetings, it presented this as one of its initial points:

> (2)   Beware of "organization." It is wholly unnecessary. The Bible rules will be the only rules you will need. Do not seek to bind others' consciences, and do not permit others to bind yours. Believe and obey so far as you can understand God's Word today, and so continue growing in grace and knowledge and love day by day.[3]

These were the early statements, the early positions.[2] How then did such a remarkable metamorphosis take place, producing an almost complete reversal of position, one that prevails to this day? In the 1980s, Ron Frye, a former circuit overseer and a Witness for 33 years, having spent "years of agonizing" over the Watch Tower's teaching as to its authority, did intensive research into its validity. Contrasting the past and the present, he wrote:

> Today, more than a hundred years from Russell's start, the Witnesses are outstandingly organization-minded. The organization always comes first. In the *Watchtower* of March 1, 1979, the article "Faith in Jehovah's Victorious Organization" the expression "theocratic organization" appears *fifteen times* in just the first eleven paragraphs.[3] This kind of mesmerizing repetition is constantly used by the Society to condition Jehovah's Witnesses to think that it is wrong for them to question anything the Society ever published as truth. In contradiction to this attitude toward the organization, Russell and his early associates were actually anti-earthly organization.

---

2   When the book *The New Creation* was published in 1909 the viewpoint of organization remained as has been presented. It said, for example: "The test of membership in the New Creation will not be membership in any earthly organization, but union with the Lord as a member of his mystical body; as saith the Apostle, 'If any man be in Christ, he is a New Creature ...'"

3   The term "Theocratic organization" has been used since the December 1, 1939 *Watchtower* in particular.

* This page was published in *In Search of Christian Freedom*, 1991, page 149 which is referred in Chapter 3, footnote 27 of this 2018 edition of *Crisis of Conscience*.

Watch Tower headquarters staff celebrating Christmas in Brooklyn Bethel dining room, 1926. J.F. Rutherford at head of center table.

* **Pages 498-505 are from *In Search of Christian Freedom* 2007, pages 78-84, referred to in Chapter 3, footnote 28 of this edition of *Crisis of Conscience.***

Yet here was a man whom, Jehovah's Witnesses still argue, God used to revive the great teachings of Jesus and his apostles. Why don't they study his books today in the congregations of Jehovah's Witnesses, even from a historical standpoint? Because much of it, if not most of it, would be considered heresy today.

That there is a basis for such an assessment can be seen in what did happen while Russell was yet alive. If one looks back over the various quotations earlier presented in this chapter, it may seem difficult to believe that the man who was the source of them all was the same man who in 1910—when he had become recognized by thousands of persons internationally as their "Pastor," when the *Watch Tower* magazine he had founded had attained a history of three decades, and when his writings were circulating by the thousands of copies in many nations—now said that the person who read the Bible alone without using the *Scripture Studies* he had written would, according to experience, 'go into darkness within two years,' whereas the one reading his *Scripture Studies* without reading any of the Bible itself would still be "in the light" at the end of that time. Though a man might spend "weeks and years" in personal Bible study without the use of Russell's writings, "the chances even then are that when he does light on something he will have it all wrong."[4]

There were qualifying remarks made in connection with these claims. Nonetheless, the fact remains that the ability of the individual Christian to understand God's Word by personal study was deprecated and the whole thrust was to represent the Watch Tower publications as God's exclusive channel for light and truth. It is difficult to conceive of a more immodest, sectarian attitude, to conceive of a sadder departure from the lofty principles earlier advocated.

Nor was the attitude a onetime, momentary expression. That it had been developing is evident from material published in the *Watch Tower*

---

4   *Watch Tower*, September 15, 1910.

the year previous, 1909. In its October 1 issue, Russell, the founder and editor of the magazine, the sole "Pastor" recognized by the Bible Students, discussed Matthew chapter twenty four, verse 45, and its reference to "that servant" and his "fellow servants." Using, as he commonly did, the editorial "we" in place of "I," he acknowledged that fourteen years earlier the term "that servant" (referring to the faithful and wise servant of the parable) had been applied to him by another Watch Tower affiliate (actually his wife, according to the July 15, 1906 issue of *Zion's Watch Tower*) and that he had not entered into the discussion that developed over this application. But he states that the person who had first applied this designation to him now asserted that "while we did occupy such position we have forfeited it, lost it to a successor." He then presents a discussion of the issue but does it indirectly by the method of presenting first what his "friends" say and then what his "opponents" say, limiting his own direct comments to the close. He presents his "friends" as saying:

> Our friends insist that this Scripture indicates that in the end of this Gospel age the Lord would use not many channels for the dissemination of the truth, but one channel, and that it would be the privilege of others of the Lord's faithful ones to be "fellow-servants" (co-laborers). They insist that the facts connected with this harvest time abundantly substantiate this interpretation. They hold that all of them received their knowledge of present truth directly from the Watch Tower Bible and Tract Society's publications, or indirectly through those who have received their enlightenment through this channel. They are glad correspondingly to co-operate as "fellow-servants" with the Society's work, believing that thereby they are following the leadings of the divine providence, as well as the instructions of the divine Word. They believe that such as do otherwise, oppose the divine word, antagonize the harvest work, and will bring injury upon themselves.

> They declare that, to their judgments, there is no other interpretation of the facts before us than that presented in our Lord's promise; that at the appropriate time in the end of the age, in the time of his presence, he would bring forth from the storehouse of Grace, Wisdom and Truth things "new and old," and that he would select at that time one special channel through which those blessings would be called to the attention of the household of faith—indicating also that a privilege would be granted to others who might join the service as "fellow-servants." They point out that such as have thus become "fellow-servants" have been blest and used in the harvest work, whilst others opposing have gone into the "outer-darkness" of nominalism as respects "harvest" truth and its service.

It must be remembered that the *Watch Tower* was Russell's own maga-zine. He started it, he controlled it, he determined what went into it as its sole editor.[5] It was essentially a vehicle for his writings. Previous to his death, in a "last will and testament" he stated that, while he had donated the magazine to the Watch Tower Bible and Tract Society (a corporation which he also controlled as by far the dominant shareholder), this was done "with the explicit understanding that I should have full control of all the interests of these publications during my life time, and that after my decease they should be conducted according to my wishes."[6] So, when he speaks of attitudes toward the magazine or the Society, or applies the term "channel" to the Society or the magazine, he is actually referring these things to himself in the most personal sense. The entire context of the article confirms this. That he was the only one recognized as "Pastor" adds force to this application. He had earlier referred to himself as "God's mouthpiece" and "agent" for revealing truth.[7] So, when he speaks of the "one channel" through which persons (his "friends") had received their enlightenment, he clearly means the writings of Charles Taze Russell. He shows this also by saying that "it would be the privilege of others of the Lord's faithful ones to be 'fellow servants' (co-laborers)" with this "one special channel" chosen by the Lord.[8]

That this is so is clearly evident from statement after statement appear-ing in the *Watch Tower* magazine in the years following Russell's death. Giving a totally different picture from the very slanted version modern *Watchtower* material presents, the March 1, 1923, *Watch Tower* quotes Russell as saying that some spoke of him as the "faithful and wise servant" and others spoke of the Society as such. The magazine then adds:

---

5   The *Watch Tower*, December 1, 1916, page 356.
6   Charles Taze Russell's will and testament is presented in full on the first and second page of Appendix A of this 2018 edition of *Crisis of Conscience*.
7   The *Watch Tower*, July 15, 1906, page 229. See Chapter 3 footnote 19 of this book.
8   It is worthy of note that when the December 15, 1981, *Watchtower* (page 25) quoted this article it left out entirely the reference to other Watch Tower associates being "fellow servants" along with "that servant" who is the "one channel." This allowed the magazine to give the false impression that the "faithful slave" was understood as applying to the *Watch Tower* maga-zine rather than to Charles Taze Russell. This type of editing can only be termed journalistic dishonesty.

Both statements were true; for Brother Russell was in fact the Society in the most absolute sense, in this, that he directed the policy and course of the Society without regard to any other person on earth.

In fact, a biographical issue of the *Watch Tower* published after his death on October 16, 1916, stated:

Thousands of the readers of Pastor Russell's writings believe that he filled the office of "that faithful and wise servant," and that his great work was giving to the household of faith meat in due season. His modesty and humility precluded him from openly claiming this title, but he admitted as much in private conversation.[9]

Of those classed as "opponents" to his being "that servant" used as God's "channel," in the October 1, 1909 *Watch Tower* referred to, Russell represents them as saying:

Our opponents are often bitter and sarcastic after taking the antagonistic position. They retort that the expression "that servant" should be understood to mean all the members of the church of Christ, and that the expression, "his fellow-servants," is meaningless, because it refers to the same class. They declare that although it is true that they got their first enlightenment respecting the value of Christ's death as a "ransom for all," and their first knowledge of the "times of restitution of all things," and their first appreciation of the "high calling," and their first knowledge of the parousia and the harvest time of this age, and their first knowledge of the fulfilment of prophecies in connection with this harvest time, and their first understanding of the nature of man and the work of redemption, atonement and regeneration from this Society's publications, nevertheless they are of the opinion that all of these things were previously published by others, and they are seeking to find the books. They claim further that to apply this Scripture to us would signify that we are infallible.

But, retort the opponents, while we do not deny the service rendered, yet if we grant the application of Matthew 24:45 to be correct, then we are forced to apply the other part, the context, which says, "Verily I say unto you, he shall make him ruler over all his goods." That would mean that the "fellow-servants" and the "household of faith" in general might not expect to receive their spiritual meat from any other quarter than "that servant." We are opposed to this thought and hence opposed to the entire matter.

---

9   The *Watch Tower*, December 1, 1916, page 356. See also this 2018 edition of *Crisis of Conscience*, Chapter 3, for photocopied documentation of the Society's insistence during the 1920's that Russell was the "faithful and wise servant."

Note that those he calls "opponents" *then took the same position that the Watch Tower Society today upholds,* namely, that "the faithful and wise servant" should be understood to mean "all the members of the church of Christ," not one man. To view Russell as "that servant" and call all others his "fellow servants" was therefore "meaningless," since they were all part of "that servant." They saw a clear danger in looking to any human source as the sole channel through which to receive truth and understanding. In Russell's eyes, to question in such way the special relationship with the Lord which his holding the position of "that servant" and of being the chosen "channel" implied, was being "antagonistic" and making "bitter and sarcastic" expressions. All of this has a very familiar ring.

Twenty-three years earlier, in 1886, in his book *The Divine Plan of the Ages* (page 23), Russell had said that the development of a heirarchical organization has its roots in "an undue respect for the teachings of fallible men."

> Then by degrees there came into existence a special class called "the clergy," who regarded themselves, and were regarded by others, as the proper guides to faith and practice, aside from the Word of God. Thus in time the great system of Papacy was developed by an undue respect for the teachings of fallible men and a neglect of the Word of the infallible God.
>
> Serious indeed have been the evil results brought about by this neglect of truth. As all know, both the church and the civilized world were almost wholly enslaved by that system, and led to worship the traditions and creeds of men.

Now, however, when some were expressing less than total support for his writings as constituting "the one special channel" chosen by the Lord, he endeavored to attribute great, even vital, importance to those writings. He thus represents his "friends" as saying of his publications:

> They point out that they themselves and their forefathers for generations had Bible classes and Bible studies all to no purpose until the Lord, in due time, sent them the "Bible Keys," through the Society. They point out that to ignore this leading of the Lord and to exclude from their study of the Bible the teacher sent of the Lord would be to dishonor the Lord who sent the same and to reject His helping hand; and that the only result that could be expected of such a course would be a gradual loss of light—a proportionate loss of the holy Spirit, the Spirit of the truth, and eventually to reach the "outer darkness" of the world and

the nominal-church, from which they were rescued by the truth.
They declare that this would correspond to a sow returning to
her wallowing in the mire and the dog to his vomit, as the Apostle declares. They declare that to take such a course, to them
would mean a lack of appreciation of having been called out of
darkness into this marvelous light, a lack of appreciation of the
light of "the day star" promised by the Lord as a precursory of
the glorious sunrise of the new dispensation.—2 Pet. 1:19-21.
    They point out further that the <u>"Dawn-Scripture Study"
Volumes are practically the Bible itself in an arranged, systematic form; and that it is this very systematization of the Bible
which brought them to their present enlightenment and joy in
the holy Spirit.</u> They declare that wranglings and speculations
and guesses respecting things not revealed in God's Book are
what is often styled "Bible study," and that they are afraid of
these and desire to keep close to the Lord and to the message
which they believe that he has sent to them, and that. therefore, <u>they prefer to study the Bible in the light and under the
leading of the "Berean Studies" and the "Studies in the Scriptures," and to look for further light in the same direction and
without expecting special revelations to their own brains or
from a variety of directions.</u> [10]

Note that the "friends" are presented as saying that all the Bible study
they and their forefathers had engaged in had been *completely ineffectual*
until the Watch Tower publications came along. Evidently God's holy
Spirit was either inactive or simply ineffective in providing them and
their forefathers the help they needed. Whatever prayers they had made
to God for understanding during those "generations" apparently simply
went unanswered, because His time had not yet arrived to produce His
"channel."[11] Note as well that after this statement of the crucial role of that
Society, Russell presents his "friends" as saying that "to ignore this leading
of the Lord and to exclude from their study of the Bible *the teacher* sent of
the Lord *would be to dishonor the Lord who sent the same and to reject His
helping hand*," all this leading to "gradual loss of light," loss of holy Spirit
and ultimate entry into "outer darkness." All this from the pen of the man

10 Three months later, in the December 15, *Watch Tower*, page 371, he warned the magazine's
    readers that a test was on and that the "wily adversary" was attempting to "prejudice them
    against the very instrumentalities God provided to keep the 'feet' [the final body members] of
    Christ in this evil day." This was being done through certain class leaders who were attempt-
    ing to supplant the Watch Tower publications with the Bible and Russell states that in so
    doing they were endeavoring "to come between the people of God and the divinely provided
    light upon God's Word."

11 Compare John 14:26; 1 John 2:27; 5:20.

who had earlier said that it was "the undue respect for the teachings of fallible men" that led to a hierarchy and to enslavement.

In the latter part of the article Russell abandons the "friends versus opponents" literary device and expresses himself directly. Commendably, he urges an avoidance of quarreling or name-calling. He urges the importance of "meekness" and "humility." At the same time, in the article he himself portrays those who believe it unscriptural to view him and his magazine as God's unique channel as "disloyal 'fellow servants,'" "crafty," having a "contentious spirit," that they seem "inoculated with madness, Satanic hydrophobia." Any who do not continue in affiliation with his Watch Tower Society are described as 'sifted-out ones.' While saying that one should not be unkind to persons who have gone "blind," he goes on to speak of these dissenters as persons "who in this hour of temptation are being smitten down by the arrows of the adversary because, from the Lord's standpoint, they are not deemed worthy of the necessary succor." Clearly, in his mind, to qualify as among those showing 'meekness, humility and teachableness' required a humble recognition that Christ had chosen just one special "servant," "one special channel," and a meek receptiveness to the writings of that "servant" as unquestionably superior to all other sources of knowledge on God's Word. In reading the article I could not but wonder at the incredibly warped reasoning that can develop in the human mind no matter how religiously oriented it may be. How can an individual write such extreme praise of himself and his writings, attach such enormous, crucial, vital importance to those writings, argue for his being a special, one-of-a-kind, never-before-seen, never-to-be-repeated agent of God and then impute a lack of meekness and humility and teachableness to those who doubt this? I view it as a form of mental illness, an infection from the germs of self-centeredness that breed wherever an atmosphere of personal importance and power develops. None of us have a natural immunity to it. Our protection comes from a clear and constant recognition of the headship reserved solely to Christ, from remembering that, if we have a personal relationship with God, so does every other person who shares a common faith, and from a deep respect for the fact that before God we all stand as equals.

Compare all the foregoing history and expressions with the statements of Ignatius, Cyprian and other leaders of the early centuries in their push for greater adherence and loyalty to the bishop as the God-selected religious teacher, their equation of any lack of submission or receptiveness with a 'dishonoring of the Lord,' and their warnings of dire consequences to any who questioned the privileged position that being so chosen by the Lord implied. In the words of Lightfoot, the bishop then became "the indispensable channel of divine grace." In the case at hand, we have a man presenting himself as the "one special channel" of God for receiving understanding of God's message and direction. The parallel is evident.

The centuries-old pattern of elevating human importance and, by implication, human authority, was surfacing once again. It soon received fresh and powerful impetus.

The Centralizing Process Intensifies

With Russell's death in 1916, a period of uncertainty ensued. By then the wholesale collapse of his intricately developed time-prophecies system (which had its starting point in 1874 and its ending date in 1914) threw matters into disarray and produced a fallout of much questioning.[12]

Russell's successor, Joseph F. Rutherford, had to deal with this. Any devotion Rutherford felt for the high principles that early issues of the *Watch Tower* had enunciated was now put to the test.

The book *Crisis of Conscience* has already documented the means he chose to employ to bring order to the ranks.

* The following information contained from this point to page 523, was published in *In Search of Christian Freedom*, 2007, pages 255-270 which are referred to in this 2018 edition of *Crisis of Conscience*, Chapter 5, footnote 13 and Chapter 6, footnote 17.

By saying "As a Christian he could not do that," the manual simply means that if he does he will be subject to disfellowshipping. This, too, is

---

12   See this 2018 edition of *Crisis of Conscience, Chapter 8.*

not hypothetical in the least. In the chapter that follows the extremes to which this policy can be carried are illustrated.

Such policies illustrate clearly that the organization is indeed run "from the top down and not from the bottom up." What this actually results in is a usurping of the individual's exercise of personal conscience, accomplished by superimposing on his conscience the rulings legislated by the organizational leadership, rulings made binding and "enforceable" through disfellowshipping decrees.[13]

The examples given only touch the surface. Since then, many additional rules have been made. There seems to be nothing on which the organization is not willing to legislate. A "Question from Readers" in the June 15, 1982, *Watchtower* (page 31) even rules on whether a Witness can submit to medical treatment in which (to reduce the risk of stroke by blood clot or for other purposes) a leech is used to draw off blood. The answer, based on a very wandering type of argument, is "No."[14]

Unbalanced Thinking

By legalistic thinking, a comparatively innocent minor action can be transformed into a major one of great culpability. In life there is need for balance, since the rightness or wrongness of many things really comes down to a matter of *degree*. As a simple example, a gentle pat with one's hand on another's cheek signifies affection, whereas a strong slap on the cheek tells of anger, even hatred. The action of the hand and fingers is the same in both cases; it is the difference in the *degree* of force that converts an expression of affection into one of hatred. So, too, in more complex aspects. While the element of degree may not enter notably into such clear-cut offenses as murder (a murderer does not "slightly kill" or "moderately kill" or "strongly kill" someone), or theft, or adultery, it does play a deciding

---

13   As shown earlier, this sometimes, particularly where military issues are involved, comes in the form of automatic "disassociation."

14   Though saying initially that such "use of leeches would conflict with what the Bible says, "the only Scriptures referred to thereafter are God's words to Noah that humans should not eat blood (Genesis 9:3, 4), and his command through Moses that the *blood of slain animals* be poured onto the ground. (Leviticus 17:10-14) Since no human will eat the leech, and no one will likely retain the blood the leech sucks, it is difficult to see what possible connection there is here.

role in a wide variety of life's affairs. Thus, people commonly work to earn money. This does not, however, justify classing them as "greedy." But if the *degree* of concern for money passes a certain point, then greed is evident. Who can specifically identify that "certain point" so as to draw a clear line of demarcation, one that divides precisely between the proper and improper concern for gain? It is only when the evidence *clearly points to excess* that one can feel justified in assessing another as greedy. This is true in a whole host of matters.

Again, in Bible times the religious leaders failed to exercise such balance, to distinguish between actions of a minor nature and those which might be termed major. Thus, when they saw Jesus' disciples, on the Sabbath day, picking grains of wheat, rubbing them in their hands to remove the chaff and eating them, they accused them of violating the Sabbath law against work. How could they? Because, in their unbalanced, extremely scrupulous thinking, the men were, in effect, both harvesting and threshing. Indeed, if they had picked large quantities of grain, loading up their cloaks with the wheat, and then rubbed the chaff off, producing piles of such grain, they would have been doing just that. But they were not. And Jesus reproved the religious leaders for 'condemning the innocent.' — Matthew 12:1-7.

This same unbalanced thinking seems to be the only explanation for the positions taken by the Watch Tower organization in a number of the policies already described. Perhaps nothing demonstrates this more forcefully than does the issue of alternative service to be performed in place of military service.

Submission to the Superior Authorities

Remind them to be submissive to the government and the authorities, to obey them, and to be ready for any honourable form of work. — Titus 3:1, *New English Bible*.

In many enlightened countries, the government provides for a nonmilitary form of service to be performed instead of military service and training. They do this specifically to show consideration for the conscientious objections of some citizens to participation in war or military service, a concession that is surely commendable. In *Crisis of Conscience* this subject was discussed in part.[15] As explained there, the organization's policy was that no Witness can accept an order from a draft board (or any other governmental agency other than a court) to perform alternative service—which generally consisted of hospital work, rendering services to elderly people, work in libraries, in a forest camp, or in some other field that would benefit the community at large.

Since any of these is clearly an "honourable form of work" why was a Witness not to accept it? Because in its being "*alternative* service" it is a "substitute" for military service, and because such work stands *in the place of* military service then, by some process of reasoning, to accept an alternative service assignment from a draft board was deemed the *equivalent* of having accepted military service and therefore one had "compromised," had "violated his neutrality," and he had thereby become bloodguilty. If that reasoning seems remarkably convoluted, there is yet more that follows.

At the same time, when the Witness refusing was arrested and brought to trial for his refusal to comply with the draft board's orders, and is found guilty, if the judge in the trial then *sentenced* the individual to perform such alternative service he could now obey the court order, do the work assigned, and be free from compromise and bloodguilt. The reasoning behind this? The person, having been convicted, was now a prisoner and hence had not "voluntarily" given up his freedom of action and choice of occupation. In actuality, there was nothing "voluntary" to begin with about the government-assigned service, no more than the payment of money as taxes is "voluntary." It was an obligatory, compulsory service, and that is why the man refusing was arrested in the first place. And it might also be said that he had really given up his freedom and choice when he submitted to the Watch Tower organization's deciding for him that obedience to an order from the draft board to perform hospital work or other such service is wrong. In doing that he allowed his conscience to become a prisoner and removed the possibility of making a choice based on personal conscience.

---

15   See this 2018 edition of *Crisis of Conscience*, Chapter 5.

But yet another technicality was introduced. The organization even took the position that if, *previous to the actual sentence* being passed, the Witness was asked by the judge if his conscience would allow him to accept an assignment from the court to do hospital work or similar service, he could not answer in the affirmative but must say, "that is for the court to decide." If he answered, "Yes" (which would have been a truthful answer), he was considered to have "compromised," having made a "deal" with the judge, and thus had broken his integrity. But if he gave the prescribed, approved response already quoted, and then the judge *in sentencing him* assigned him to do hospital work or similar service, he could comply.[16] He was now not guilty of violating the apostolic exhortation to "stop becoming the slaves of men." (1 Corinthians 7:23) Surely such technicalities are truly casuistic and the application of the term "Pharisaical" does not seem too harsh.[17]

This is no light matter. During World War II, in the United States alone some 4,300 young Jehovah's Witnesses went to prison, with sentences ranging as high as 5 years, not simply because of conscientious objection to war, but primarily because, in adhering to the Society's policy, they refused governmental provisions allowing them to perform other service of a non-military nature provided for conscientious objectors. In England, there were 1,593 convictions, including those of 334 women.[18] Though the policy was rescinded in 1996, there still remained hundreds in prisons in various lands, the imprisonment resulting from their obeying the Society's policy. In 1988, in just the countries of France and Italy there were some 1,000 Jehovah's Witnesses in prison for this reason.[19]

---

16   See this 2018 edition of *Crisis of Conscience*, Chapter 6, footnote 10.

17   All of these technical distinctions were worked out from the 1940s on through the 1960s. While final approval unquestionably rested with Nathan Knorr, and while the Society's attorney Hayden Covington was involved during the 1940s and 1950s, the style of reasoning is not typical of either man but *is* typical of Fred Franz, then vice president. I believe that the later technical distinctions were designed to moderate somewhat the organization's position, thereby reducing the number of those going to prison (in cases where judges were willing to sentence them to hospital or other work) and yet allow for appearing to be upholding the original position in its basic premise as having been right, God-directed. This elaborate policy remained in effect until the May 1, 1996 *Watchtower* declared it a matter of conscience.

18   See *Jehovah's Witnesses in the Divine Purpose*, page 157.

19   *Amnesty International Report for 1988*, pages 199, 206.

In *Crisis of Conscience*, when relating the discussion of this issue by the Governing Body in numerous sessions over a period of years, only brief mention was made of a resulting survey taken among all the Branch Committees operating throughout the world under the direction of the Governing Body. The survey was suggested by Milton Henschel since, as he put it, 'perhaps it would reveal that only a relatively few countries had alternative service provisions.' If such were the case, then that would militate against the need for making any policy change. Apparently the fact that men in those "few countries" were in prison and that other hundreds of men would yet go to prison (if the policy continued as it was) would not be of sufficient weight or gravity to make the issue a crucial one.

In the survey the Branch Committees were to be asked whether the Witnesses in their country understood the reasoning behind the policy and its Scripturalness and also what the committee members' own views were of the existing policy. Since the Governing Body assigned me to carry out the survey correspondence with the 90 or more Branch Committees, I have in my files copies of all their replies. The responses received were revealing.

Before considering them, I might here quote a portion of a memorandum submitted to the Governing Body by member Lloyd Barry. Warning against any change in the existing policy he wrote:

> Those who have studied out the matter on the basis of the Bible and who have been through the experience, have no question about maintaining a stand of "no compromise"—unless someone comes along and tries to plant such a question. A change of viewpoint sponsored by the Governing Body would be very upsetting for these countries and brothers, where they have fought for so long in behalf of their uncompromising stand.

What do the facts show as to the *actual* thinking of those affected? Does the picture portrayed in the memorandum fit the reality? The information that follows is fairly extensive (though only a fraction of the whole). I believe it merits the space. The reason is that it so graphically demonstrates the power of indoctrination to cause people to sacrifice liberty, years of life and livelihood and family association, in order to obey something that they do not understand or really believe—doing this purely out of a sense of loyalty to an organization. Anything that produces such a blindly submissive state of mind is fraught with potential danger of even greater consequence.

Since disagreement with any position of the organization is generally viewed as indicating a lack of loyalty and even a lack of faith and confidence in God's direction, it is not at all surprising that the majority of the Committees expressed full support for the organization's policy. What *is* surprising is the significant number of Branch Committees that spoke of serious difficulties of Witnesses in their country either as to understanding the policy or seeing any Scriptural basis for it. Not that they were not complying with the policy. Witness men were going to jail rather than act contrary to it. But did they feel as Governing Body member Barry put it that 'there was no question' about the policy that led to their being put in prison? Here are direct quotations from the letters sent by some Branch Committees:

> **Austria**: "Many of the brothers do not fully understand the Scriptural position why we should not render such alternative service."

> **Brazil**: "We believe that the brothers would have no difficulty to prove their stand if the work involved direct support to the military machine, say, working in a munitions factory or constructing barracks or digging trenches, etc. They would use the same scriptures that they use for objecting to direct military service. The brothers <u>would</u> have difficulty if the work involved building a road for civilian use, or work on some agricultural project or other work of that kind."

> **Italy**: "From direct contacts made with the brothers faced with a military service problem we found that <u>in the majority of cases</u> they did not understand why they could not accept alternative civilian service. They maintained that no longer being under the direct jurisdiction of the military authorities because of having been assigned to another ministry, they could accept alternative civilian service just as long as they did not engage in any activity having to do with militarism, but doing nonmilitary work

such as in museums or hospitals, etc. they would not be guilty of any violation of their neutrality."

Spain: "As a part of the research for this report, a member of the branch committee spoke extensively with three brothers who were exemplary in their neutral stand years ago. He also conversed with three mature elders, two of them from other countries, who have not personally faced the issue in Spain. Varying viewpoints surfaced on many aspects of this matter, but there was complete agreement on one point:

Practically none of our young brothers really understand why we cannot accept 'substitute service' if it is of a civic nature and not under the control of the military. It seems clear that most of the elders do not understand it either, and therefore they often send youngsters to the [branch] office to get information. So the question comes up, Why don't they understand? Is it lack of personal study? Or is it because the arguments and reasonings we have used are not convincing enough or do not have a clear and firm Bible stand?"[20]

In addition to the sampling presented, Branch Committees in Australia, Belgium, Canada, Fiji, France, Germany, Greece, Hawaii, Malaysia, Nigeria, Norway, Portugal, Puerto Rico, Rhodesia, Thailand, Trinidad, Uruguay and Zaire all expressed problems among Witnesses in their lands as to understanding the organization's policy or seeing its Scriptural basis.

Yet throughout the world Jehovah's Witnesses *did* take an adamant stand in rejecting alternative service (unless sentenced by a judge to perform it). Some may still be in jail in some lands for that reason. That this is really not the result of loyalty to God's Word and their personal conviction of the unscripturalness of the course is evident from what follows. Conformity to an organizational policy, and concern that they not be viewed adversely by that organization and by their peers, seems to be the determinative factor for these young men. While some of the quotations just made touch on this aspect, other letters from the committees were

---

20   In these, and in the quotations that follow, key points have been underlined.

quite explicit, revealing the *basic reason why* Witnesses rejected alternative service provisions made by the governments in their lands.

Belgium: "Few brothers are really in position to explain with the Bible why they refuse ... basically, they know it is wrong and that <u>the Society views it as such</u>. For that reason some courts said to the brothers that they were pushed by the Society to refuse the provision of the civil service."

Denmark: "While many young brothers seem able to grasp arguments and think them out and explain them to a degree, it is felt that the majority of young brothers today follow the example of others and <u>take the stand expected of them by the brotherhood</u> without really understanding the basic principles and arguments involved, and without being able to explain their stand clearly."

Hawaii: "Generally speaking, the brothers here have trouble seeing Bible principles governing the maintaining of strict neutrality. <u>Once they know the Society's stand on such issues, they fully cooperate, but do not see the principles too clearly upon which our stand rests.</u>

Norway: "The brothers in Norway do not accept civilian work without a court sentence, <u>mainly because they know that this is the Society's policy and they are loyal to the Society.</u> It is difficult for them to understand why it is wrong to accept civilian work when the work itself is not wrong and condemned by the Bible. <u>They cannot support their stand properly from the Scriptures.</u>"

Spain: "When an elder discusses the matter of substitute service with someone, that person generally accepts [the position] that substitution amounts to equivalence. But this idea is not usually truly understood. Rather, <u>it is taken to be the organization's viewpoint, and the elders present it as well as they can and the brothers loyally follow through as they know is expected of them</u>. But it seems to us that many brothers find our reasoning somewhat artificial."

Thailand: "From our experience many in the past have had problems when trying to maintain their neutrality. Many have refused work out of

<u>a kind of group loyalty.</u> They did not know the reason or principle why, but they heard a certain thing was wrong, so they refused."

Lloyd Barry's memorandum spoke of "planting" ideas in the minds of the brothers. The evidence clearly indicates that any planting done was by the Watch Tower Society itself, since it is plain that these Witnesses would never have arrived at the policy laid down by the organization from their own reading of the Scriptures or as a product of their personal conscience. Nor was it only those of the so-called "rank and file" or the younger Witnesses who had such serious difficulty with the policy. Men on the Branch Committees themselves found it difficult to support, either on the basis of reason or Scripture.

Referring again to Lloyd Barry's memorandum, he also stated:

> In this, the issue is not taxation, employment, etc., but COMPROMISE. We are agreed that we should not take up arms for the military. Then we should be agreed, too, that if the military or any other agency asks us to do something as a substitute therefore, we do not accept the alternative. That is our action. Then, if we are handed over to a court, and a judge sentences us, that is his action. We accept the sentence. We have not compromised. We are integrity keepers. It is as simple as all that. — Job 27:5.

Yet, along with most other Witnesses, many of the Branch Committee members themselves did not find the stated position by any means "simple." They saw no logic in the position that it would be wrong to accept a work order from a draft board but all right to accept the identical order to do the identical work under identical circumstances if that order was given by a court. They could not see how this could be so inasmuch as these agencies are all simply *branches of the same government,* of the same "superior authority." Thus the Chilean Branch Committee pointed out some of the inconsistencies, saying:

> If the work itself does not contribute toward the military objective, does it matter what agency orders that [it] be accepted? Here in Chile it is not clear just how independent courts are. This is a military government

and many of the civilians who serve in the Cabinet are just "show" pieces. The military run the show.... It is all just one system.

From then Communist Poland came this expression:

As far as we know, the German brothers take up such work upon the basis that the administrative authorities direct them to the work and not the military. Would this mean that they would not take up the same work, <u>under the same conditions</u>, if the military authorities would direct them to do it? <u>Is it not the same Caesar?</u>

In a very lengthy letter, the Canadian Branch Committee focused especially on this point. Referring to the existing policy as a "confusing 'agency' approach," they said:

... we feel that officials would find it hard to see where we draw the line. We would complicate matters for them and for the brothers as well. If, for example, we tried to make a point of the draft board or induction center being a part of the <u>political</u> setup and that we are neutral in matters of politics, they would wonder why the courts are not also viewed as an arm of the same governmental political setup.

On the other hand, if we try to make it a matter of the agency being a part of the <u>military</u> setup and argue our neutrality from that point of view, they might concede that they appreciate our desire to have nothing to do with the military, but if the actual work assigned is the same, regardless of the agency involved, then what's the difference? We would find that a problem to argue successfully.... Today, courts, councils, police, induction centers and the military are all manifestations of Caesar's authority. All are, in one way or another, his agencies.

The matter seemed summed up in this simple question from the Nigerian Branch Committee:

If something is wrong Scripturally, then why should a court order make it all right to do it?

The questions themselves illustrate how the organization's policies have led to technical complexities as well as to confusion on the part of men sincerely seeking to be guided by God's own Word. Illustrating to what extremes the organization's concept could and did lead, consider this remarkable situation and stand presented by the Branch Committee in Sweden:

> Even in such instances where our brothers have been offered to perform their National Service training <u>at their ordinary place of work</u>, for example, at a County Administration or the State Railways, they refused, because they have held that they could not accept any substitute whatsoever for the National Service training, not <u>even if this was purely civil, or even meant that they could stay on in their ordinary daily occupations</u>.

Incredible as it may seem, that is actually the stand taken in that country on the basis of the organization's policy, namely, that even where the authorities, bending over backwards to accommodate the Witnesses' religious position, in some cases offered to let their regular, customary job be counted as done in place of such training, they must refuse!

This is not due to convictions personally arrived by the Swedish Witnesses. It is due to being so sensitized by the organization's policy decreeing that substitute work was the *equivalent* of military service, that any offer of *any kind* had to be refused.[21] Following a "zone trip" to branch offices in Scandinavian countries, Robert Wallen, the secretary for the Service Committee of the Governing Body, expressed his concern to me on this matter. He related a conversation with one Scandinavian Witness who said:

'If I accept the government's assignment of alternative service they will assign me to work in a hospital here in my area and I will be able to live at home with my family. But the Society's policy is that I cannot do this and must refuse. I will then be arrested, tried and sentenced and the court will again assign me to work in a hospital. But this time it will be in another part of the country. I will be doing exactly the same work *but* I will be separated from my home and family. Does this really make sense?'

Branch Committee members did not only question the *logic* of the organization's policy. They also presented *Scriptural evidence* in favor of a

---

21   The Swedish government finally solved the matter by exempting Jehovah's Witnesses totally from all service.

different approach. As just one example, the Branch Committee in Brazil expressed the view of the committee, saying:

> The point is that the young man has made clear his stand to the military authorities, showing Scripturally why he cannot participate in any war or even be trained for it. So, what Scriptures could be used to show that it would be improper to do civilian work ordered by the authorities, since he has made clear his Scriptural stand? This [that is, doing such assigned civilian work] seems to be supported by Matth. 5:41; Rom. 13:7; Titus 3:1-3; 1 Peter 2:13, 14 and others.

The Scriptures they referred to read as follows (*New World Translation*):

> Matthew 5:41: "If someone under authority impresses you into service for a mile, go with him two miles."

> Romans 13:7: "Render to all their dues, to him who calls for the tax, the tax; to him who calls for the tribute, the tribute; to him who calls for fear, such fear; to him who calls for honor, such honor."

> Titus 3:1-3:"Continue reminding them to be in subjection and be obedient to governments and authorities as rulers, to be ready for every good work, to speak injuriously of no one, not to be belligerent, to be reasonable, exhibiting all mildness toward all men. For even we were once senseless, disobedient, being misled, being slaves to various desires and pleasures, carrying on badness and envy, abhorrent, hating one another."

> 1 Peter 2:13, 14: "For the Lord's sake subject yourselves to every human creation; whether to kings as being superior or to governors, as being sent by him to inflict punishment on evildoers but to praise doers of good."

Reading the letters of these Branch Committee members I could not help but contrast the thoughtfulness and breadth of viewpoint many of their expressions revealed as compared with the narrowness and rigidity of the assertions made by several of the Governing Body members. I had already submitted to the Governing Body a 14-page, carefully documented discussion of the Biblical and historical evidence relative to submission to

government authority when that authority orders a citizen to perform
certain work or service of a nonmilitary nature. Among other things, I felt
that the evidence clearly showed that performance of such service came
within the Scriptural designation of taxation, since taxation from ancient
times has included compulsory forms of labor. As just one example, at
1 Kings 5:13-18 we read (*New World Translation*) of Solomon's "bringing up those conscripted for forced labor out of all Israel." The Hebrew
expression rendered "forced labor" is the word *mas*, meaning compulsory
labor. When the translators of the *Septuagint Version* (of the third century B.C.) translated this Hebrew term— not only here but in other texts
where it appears—what Greek term did they employ? They rendered it by
the Greek term *phóros*. That is the identical term used by Paul at Romans
13:6 when he speaks of paying tax to the superior authorities.[22] While the
term can and undoubtedly does in most cases apply to a money tax, *it is
in no way restricted to this*, as the *Septuagint's* use of it for "compulsory
labor" forcefully demonstrates.[23] I regret that in view of its lengthiness it
is not possible to present here the complete discussion and the Scriptural,
historical, lexicographical, and etymological documentation provided.

What was the result of all this? Remember that any decision made
would affect the lives of thousands of persons. The existing policy had
already resulted in imprisonments representing tens of thousands of years.
Again, I believe the way the matter was handled is remarkably revealing.
It illustrates dramatically the way long-standing, traditional policies can

---

22   It may also be remarked that Paul is notable among the writers of the Christian Scriptures in
his frequent use of the *Septuagint* renderings when quoting from the Hebrew Scriptures, and
this is particularly true in his letter to the Romans.

23   The November 1, 1990, *Watchtower*, page 11, gives a typically one-sided presentation of
the matter, stating that Paul's references to "tax" (and "tribute") at Romans 13 "refer specifically to money paid to the State." It cites Luke 10:22 as proof, as if the single reference to a
monetary tax there is binding on the sense of *phóros* everywhere. Evidently the writer made
only a cursory study of the subject, yet writes with great definiteness. Even the organization's
own *Kingdom Interlinear Translation* acknowledges the breadth of application of the term
phóros. For the term's basic meaning, its interlinear reading shows—not "money paid," or
even "tax"—but simply "the thing brought." The "thing" brought could have been money,
or produce or service in the form of compulsory labor. In Biblical times tax could and did
involve any of these.

exercise overruling power on the thinking of men who have declared their determination to let God's Word be their sole and supreme authority.

The Governing Body met and discussed the issue in four separate sessions extending from September 26 to November 15, 1978. In all these four days of discussion the letters submitted received only cursory attention; none of the arguments or questions received careful analysis or point-by-point discussion, and this was equally true of the fourteen pages of Biblical and historical evidence I had personally supplied. The meetings were typical of most Governing Body sessions in that there was no particular order of discussion, no systematic consideration of one question or point at issue before moving on to consideration of another point at issue. Discussion could jump, as it typically did, from one aspect of the problem to another entirely different and relatively unrelated aspect. One member might conclude with the question, "What Scriptural basis is there then for saying that because a service is 'alternative' it therefore becomes the equivalent of what it substitutes for?" The next member recognized by the chairman might take up a totally different point, leaving the previous member's question hanging in midair.[24]

Those favoring retention of the existing policy referred to the Branch Committee letters primarily to discount their importance. Thus, Ted Jaracz said, "Regardless of what the brothers may say, it is the Bible that guides us." He then went on to discuss some points, not from the Bible, but from certain *Watchtower* articles dealing with the issue.

Yet many of the Branch Committee men had brought up serious points from the Bible and these had neither been refuted nor clearly answered, at least not to the satisfaction of the majority of the Governing Body members themselves, as subsequent voting revealed. Ted Jaracz, however, urged that we should ask ourselves, "Just how much of a problem is it all over the world? He asked this because the survey showed that

---

24 The question of substitution equaling equivalency had been raised in the letter (from Belgium) that initiated the whole discussion. The writer, Michel Weber, was an elder who had visited Witnesses in prison in his country and realized their inability to grasp the reasoning behind the Society's policy. Among other things, he asked why, after refusing a blood transfusion, we did not consistently also refuse any *substitute* given in *place of* blood? Should not the reasoning apply in the same way?

the majority of the countries had no provision for alternative service. Acknowledging that perhaps "a hundred or so are disfellowshipped" as a result of the existing policy, he asked, "What of all the other brothers in the world-wide organization who rejected alternative service and what of the suffering already undergone by those who took such stand?" This question would seem to say that, because a past wrong view caused considerable suffering, this would somehow justify the continuance of the wrong view—and the suffering it would continue to produce! It exemplifies how traditional policies can, in the minds of some, override both Scripture and logic. As a further reason for maintaining the policy that led to this "suffering," he added, "If we allow the brothers this latitude we will have serious problems, similar to those where latitude is shown in matters of employment." In reality, the only "problems" that latitude in matters of employment had produced were problems for those seeking to maintain tight control over the activities of fellow Christians. Whatever risk there might be was not truly to the morality or Christian integrity of the congregation; what was at risk was the exercise of ecclesiastical authority.

Indicative of this, the Society's president, Fred Franz, also expressed doubt as to the weight to be given to the expressions of the Branch Committee members. He reminded the Body that he had not voted in favor of the worldwide survey and then, sharply increasing the force of his tone, asked: "Where does all this information come from anyway? Does it come from the *top down*? Or from the *bottom up*?" He said that we should not build our decision around the situations found in different countries.

As noted, this phrase regarding "top" and "bottom" was not new to me. As recently as 1971 in a *Watchtower* article, Fred Franz had used it, along with reference to the "rank and file" members of the organization. But the whole tone of the discussion was extremely upsetting to me, particularly such expressions as "If *we* allow the brothers this latitude." When recognized by Chairman Klein, I reminded the members that it was the Governing Body's decision to write the Branch Committee members, that those men were among the most respected elders in their respective countries, and if we could not give weight to their expressions then to whose expressions could we do so? I felt compelled to add that my understanding was that we considered ourselves as a **brotherhood** and had no reason to look on ourselves as the "top" of anything, that we should even find the concept personally repelling.

What, then, was the final outcome? At the October 11, 1978, meeting, of the sixteen members then on the Body, thirteen were present and nine voted for a change in the traditional policy, four (Henschel, Jackson, Klein, and Fred Franz) did not. This not being a two-thirds majority of the total membership, no change was made. On November 15, the vote showed eleven of sixteen in favor of a change, a two-thirds majority. The motion voted on was one of several suggested and happened to be one I had submitted. It read:

MOTION

That where the superior authorities in any land, acting through whatever constituted agency they use, order a brother to perform some form of work (whether because of his conscientious objection to military service or for other reasons), there will be no congregational action taken against such a brother if he submits to that order, provided always that the work he is ordered to do is not in violation of direct commands or clear Scriptural principles found in God's Word, including that at Isaiah 2:4. — Matt. 5:41; 22:21; 1 Cor.13:1-7; 1 Pet. 2:17; Titus 3:1; Acts 5:29.

We will continue to exhort our brothers to guard against becoming a part of the world and that in whatever circumstances they find themselves they must keep God's kingdom foremost, never forgetting that they are slaves of God and of Christ. Thus they should seek to avail themselves of any provision that allows them the greatest freedom to use time, strength and funds for that Kingdom. — John 15:17-19; Acts 25:9-11; 1 Cor. 7:21, 23.

A two-thirds majority had voted in favor of the motion—but the two-thirds majority did not last long. During a momentary break in the session, a member remarked that there evidently was going to be a change in the vote. He quoted President Franz (who was among those not favoring any change) as saying, "It isn't over yet; Barry has had second thoughts."

Lloyd Barry had been among the eleven voting in favor of the motion. Why the change? Since the decision could make the difference between men going to prison or not going to prison, I think it is enlightening to realize just what sort of things can happen in a religious governing body holding power to affect the lives of thousands of persons.

You will note that in the cited texts at the end of the first paragraph of the Motion the citation "1 Cor. 13:1-7" appears. I had meant to put "Rom. 13:1-7" but, perhaps because of familiarity with Paul's well-known description of love in First Corinthians chapter thirteen, I mistakenly wrote it down as I did. Someone called the matter to my attention during the intermission and the Body was informed of the need to correct this one reference.

When we reconvened, however, Lloyd Barry stated that he would not vote in favor of the motion with Romans chapter thirteen listed in the citations. Given the opportunity to speak, I suggested to Lloyd that we could simply eliminate the reference completely or even remove *all* the cited texts if need be to make the motion acceptable for him. Without explaining the basis for his objection, he said he would still not vote for the motion and that he was withdrawing his previous vote. Other members endeavored to find some conciliatory adjustment but were unsuccessful. Though no provision had existed for withdrawal of one's vote after a motion had passed, we acceded to Barry's action. The two-thirds majority was gone. After further discussion, when another vote was taken it read: Nine in favor, five against, one abstention.[25] Though still a definite majority it was no longer a *two-thirds* majority. Though only a *minority* of the Governing Body favored the continuance of the existing policy and the sanctions it applied toward any who accepted alternative service (unless sentenced thereto), that policy remained in effect. Year after year, hundreds of men, submitting to that policy although neither understanding it nor being convinced of its rightness, would continue to be arrested, tried, and

---

25 Lloyd Barry had left on some business matter and so was not present for this vote made necessary by his withdrawal of his previous vote. The five voting against change were Carey Barber, Fred Franz, Milton Henschel, William Jackson and Karl Klein. Ted Jaracz abstained. See this 2018 edition of Crisis of Conscience, Chapter 5, footnote 14.

imprisoned—because one individual on a religious council changed his mind. Witness men could exercise their conscientious choice of accepting alternative service only at the cost of being cut off from the congregations of which they were a part, being viewed as unfaithful to God and Christ.

Surely such instances make clear why no Christian should ever be expected to mortgage his conscience to any religious organization or to any body of men exercising virtually unlimited authority over people's lives. I found the whole affair disheartening, tragic. Yet I felt that I learned more clearly just to what ends the very nature of an authority structure can lead men, how it can cause them to take rigid positions they would not normally take. This case illustrated the way in which the power of tradition, coupled with a technical legalism and a mistrust of people's motives, can prevent one from taking a compassionate stand.

The matter came up on one other occasion and the vote was evenly split. Thereafter it was dropped and for most members it seemed to become a non-issue. The organization, following its voting rules, had spoken. The Branch Committees' arguments need not be answered—they could simply be informed that "nothing had changed" and they would proceed accordingly. The men in prison would never know that the matter had even been discussed and that, consistently, half or more of the Governing Body did not believe they needed to be where they were.

Illustrating the frequent flaw of inconsistency found in such reasoning is the way a parallel issue was later handled. It originated in Belgium; the country from which the whole issue of alternative service had arisen. The Belgian branch office asked for a ruling on another issue. Belgian law provided for the selecting and assigning of certain persons, generally attorneys, to serve at voting locations during political elections, to assure that the voting procedures were carried on properly. The Branch Committee wanted to know if this was permissible for Witness attorneys. Remarkably, the Governing Body ruled that to serve in this manner would not disqualify one as an approved Witness—though it is difficult to imagine an assignment that would place one in closer contact and involvement with the political process than this.

APPENDIX C:

Where is The "Great Crowd" Serving God?

A discussion of Revelation 7:9–17 in light of events
at the Watchtower Society's headquarters in 1980

As told by
Jon A. Mitchell
1951 – 2004

Former Secretary to
The Governing Body of Jehovah's Witnesses

Jon Mitchell spent ten years in the full-time ministry of Jehovah's Witnesses from February, 1971 to February, 1981. The first five years and four months of that period were devoted to "regular pioneering," and the balance was served at the World Headquarters of the Watchtower Society in Brooklyn, New York, as a member of the "Bethel family."

As part of the "Bethel family", Mr. Mitchell served initially as a receptionist in the lobby of 117 Adams Street, where he organized tours for visitors from 1977 to 1978. From 1979 to 1981, he worked in the Service Department and "Tenth Floor Offices" (later known as the "Executive Offices") where his responsibilities included doing secretarial work for members of the Governing Body of Jehovah's Witnesses.

Much of the research contained in this treatise was completed from 1980 to 1981, while Jon Mitchell was still at the Brooklyn headquarters of Jehovah's Witnesses. Jon's conscience troubled him as he reflected on this material, especially in light of Biblical texts like Revelation 22:18–19. Ultimately this motivated him to leave the headquarters staff in February of 1981.

Appendix C contains Jon Mitchell's story of the events he observed at Brooklyn Bethel in 1980 to 1981.

Preface

The Scriptures teach that Christians are to worship God "with spirit and truth." (John 4:24) They also indicate that the search for truth must be an ongoing, continuous process, which never ends during the believer's lifetime. Jesus taught his followers to "keep on asking, ... keep on seeking, ... keep on knocking, ..." (Matthew 7:7, *New World Translation of the Holy Scriptures*) Paul wrote at 1 Thessalonians 5:21 that we should "make sure of all things; hold fast to what is fine." John admonishes us to "test the inspired expressions to see whether they originate with God ..." (1 John 4:1) And the Beroeans are commended at Acts 17:1, for "carefully examining the Scriptures daily as to whether [the things taught by Paul and Silas] were so."

Unfortunately, many people confuse Christian faith with un-questioning acceptance of the things they have been taught by the religious organization to which they belong. This attitude has even been praised by religious leaders as the proper one to have. For example, in the year 1541, "Saint" Ignatius Loyola, founder of the Roman Catholic religious order known as the Jesuits, wrote in *Exercitia spiritualia (Spiritual Exercises)*:

> We should always be disposed to believe that that which appears to us to be white is really black, if the hierarchy of the Church so decides.

Possessing genuine Christian faith, however, does not mean reaching a point in life where you no longer question the validity of your present religious views. It is, instead, an inner assurance that no matter how many questions we ask, no matter how much "seeking," "knocking;" "test[ing]," and "examining" we do, our basis for a substantive faith will be strengthened and not undermined. (Compare Hebrews 11:1 in the *New World Translation* where faith is defined as "the *assured* expectation of things hoped for" [Emphasis added.]

While this treatise discusses portions of the Bible that are commonly understood to relate to the subject of where redeemed mankind will enjoy their eternal reward, it is not intended to establish the answer to this question with finality. Instead, the discussion limits itself specifically to the more narrow focus of the location of "great crowd" described at Revelation 7:9-17 which may or may not have relevance to the future of the earth in God's great plan for blessing the faithful. The primary purpose of what follows therefore is to examine the methods of Biblical interpretation employed by the Watchtower Society in its explanations of these texts, and to allow the reader the opportunity to determine whether these are in accordance with the principles of sound and honest Biblical scholarship.

Below is page 1080 of the 1985 edition of the Watchtower Society's publication, *The Kingdom Interlinear Translation of the Greek Scriptures*. Note the circled word *naos* (*naō* in this instance since it is in the dative case) translated by the expression "divine habitation" in the literal translation of Revelation 7:15. It is here that the Bible teaches the "great crowd" is serving God.

(*Note To Reader*: In Biblical Greek. noun endings change according to case. A singular, masculine noun of the second declension may appear with the endings -*os*, -*ou*, -*ō*, -*on*, or -*e* as it appears in the nominative, genitive, dative, accusative and vocative cases, respectively. At Revelation 7:15, *naos* appears in the dative case [expressing location] and thus is spelled *naō*. The general, nominative form, of this word. however, is *naos*.)

Where Is The "Great Crowd" Serving God?

In the summer of 1988, the Watchtower Society released a commentary on the entire last book of the Bible, entitled *Revelation—Its Grand Climax At Hand!* It is enlightening to consider the information this book contains against the backdrop of events that occurred at the world headquarters of Jehovah's Witnesses during the early part of the 1980's. When this is done, it appears that one of the purposes of this book is to shore up the foundations for some of the unique interpretations advanced by Jehovah's Witnesses relative to this part of the Bible, and to rework some information found in previous commentaries on John's Apocalypse which may actually be somewhat embarrassing to those who advocate the Society's explanations.

In the spring and early summer of 1980 several long-time members of the Society's headquarters staff (including members of the Writing Department who had researched and written most of the *Aid To Bible Understanding*[1] book) were either dismissed, disfellowshipped or reassigned to another job after lengthy interrogations. One of the first doctrinal matters about which there seemed to be some dispute that became known to other members of the Bethel family pertained to the "great crowd" of Revelation 7:9. Apparently some were questioning the basis for the Society's teaching that this is an earthly class, instead of a heavenly one, as most Bible commentators believe and as the Society itself taught until the year 1935.

At this time I was splitting my hours between working in the Service Department and the "Tenth Floor Offices" (later known as the "Executive Offices") where I did secretarial work for men who handled correspondence, including Governing Body members like **Milton Henschel** and **Ted Jaracz** who worked in the Executive Offices.

The congregation I was assigned to was a local one, called "Fort Greene" and it met in the Kingdom Hall found in one of the Society's factory buildings. **Harold Jackson,** one of the "section men" in the Service Department (who handled correspondence relating to congregational matters in a specific section of the United States) was scheduled to give a

---

1   Revised in a two-volume work published in 1988 entitled *Insight On The Scriptures.*

talk at our hall on one of the last Sundays in May of 1980. But **Jackson** informed us that he might have to cancel due to being assigned to take care of some serious judicial cases, which had arisen. As matters worked out, however, he was able to give the talk and in the course of delivering it, he appeared to be a bit shaken. One point he tried to make was in connection with the Greek word *naos*, the word used at Revelation 7:15 (translated by the word "temple" in the *New World Translation* and by the expression "divine habitation" in the literal translation under the Greek text in *The Kingdom Interlinear Translation of the Greek Scriptures*) to describe where the "great crowd" is serving God. To show that this did not refer to God's heavenly temple, **Jackson** read a verse out of the book of Matthew where the term is used in connection with the earthly temple that was in Jerusalem, and then stated that this showed the term *naos* could be used in referring to an earthly temple. He then cautioned us against listening to those who might come along and try to make a case for a heavenly "great crowd" instead of an earthly one on the basis of this term *naos*.

Later when I reported to work in the Service Department one morning the following week, a group of men were huddled around **Harold Jackson** plying him with questions about the nature of the judicial cases he was involved with. He was cautious about giving out details, but did remark that "this is *big*, this is *big*."[2] These events were the start of the rude awakening, which I would soon

---

2   **Jackson** apparently had been assigned to sit in on hearings involving Spanish-speaking members. Though cautious with us, it seems he had been less discreet in his dealings with the Governing Body members under whose direction he had been acting, and he later felt it advisable to apologize to them in a letter. In correspondence which happened to pass through my hands in the Executive Offices, he said he felt horrified by some of the remarks he had made to members of the Governing Body and that, although his appreciation of their way of handling things had not been there at first, by the time of now writing, that appreciation had "blossomed" out to the full measure it should have been all along. In retrospect, however, it would appear from remarks I overheard him make to his stenographer at that time (**Lee Waters**) that he was mainly concerned with protecting himself. **Jackson** told **Waters** that he felt the serious judicial problems which had arisen could be attributed, at least in part, to the failure of the Governing Body to truly 'devote themselves to the Word' as the Scriptures say the apostles did at Acts 6:4. (Most Governing Body members have no direct involvement in the research and writing of published Biblical materials.)

experience after nearly ten years of mostly pleasant and happy experiences in my full-time service as a pioneer and then as a member of the Bethel family.

I had tentatively decided to remain on at the Brooklyn headquarters for about eight months after some of the startling disfellowshippings and dismissals subsequently took place. In part, this was because we had been assured by members of the Governing Body that answers to some of the questions which had arisen would be forthcoming. These were to be presented in the Society's publications as well as in the form of special, televised comments, which would be given at the morning breakfast table by members of the Writing Staff and others who would endeavor to respond to questions, which had come in. This was to start in September of 1980.

However, the month before this, an article appeared in the August 15, 1980 edition of *The Watchtower* entitled "The 'Great Crowd' Renders Sacred Service Where?" Probably most of the Bethel family knew this article was written in response to some of the issues, which had arisen earlier that year when the disfellowshippings and dismissals took place. And most everyone sensed the gravity of this article since by this time the lives of long-time members of the headquarters staff had been irrevocably changed; they had been branded as "apostates" and portrayed as being worse than persons without faith. It was generally assumed that Fred Franz was the author of this article, which was undoubtedly a correct assumption since he was the one who was looked to for answers during this organizational crisis when serious doctrinal issues had arisen.

The article endeavored to support the Society's teaching that the "great crowd" is in fact an *earthly* group by showing that the word **naos** could actually be applied not just to the inner sanctuary of the temple (consisting of the Holy and Most Holy), but also to the outer courts of the temple, including the "courtyard of the Gentiles" where Jehovah's Witnesses have been taught to believe the "great crowd" is serving in an antitypical fashion. This is important because in the Bible's symbolism, the innermost part of the temple represents heaven, so those serving there would likewise have to be in heaven. (See for example, Hebrews 8:5; 9:11-12, 23-24; Revelation 11:19; 14:15, 17; 15:5-6, 8; 16:1,17.) This article presented a summary chart on page 15 as reproduced below to show how the

Bible could use the term **naos** in a broader sense to apply not just to the inner sanctuary of the temple, but also to the outermost courtyard.

The Greek word *na·os'* refers often to the inner sanctuary representing heaven itself
- BUT it was the entire temple (*na·os'*) that had been 46 years in the building
- It was the entire temple (*na·os'*) that was destroyed as a judgment from God
- It was from the courts of the outer temple (*na·os'*) that Jesus drove the money changers
- It was in the outer temple (*na·os'*) that Judas threw back the 30 pieces of silver
- HENCE it is consistent that the "great crowd" serve God in the earthly court of the spiritual temple

THE WATCHTOWER — AUGUST 15, 1980   15

The chart above[3], published in *The Watchtower*, August 15, 1980 issue, serves to explain how the "great crowd" could be in God's *naos* (Revelation 7:15) and still be on earth.

Those at Bethel who made a careful examination of this article (few though they may have been), however, found something extremely disturbing about it, especially because of knowing that it was written to refute the conclusions formerly loved and respected members of the Bethel family may have arrived at as a result of their personal study of the Scriptures. Looking up the Biblical texts to which the summarized statements referred in the Society's *Kingdom Interlinear Translation of the Greek Scriptures* revealed that the word *naos* is apparently not even used in some of the verses alluded to by the *Watchtower*.

What follows is a point-by-point discussion referring to the points made in the above *Watchtower*, August 15, 1980 chart:

- It was from the courts of the outer temple *(na·os')* that Jesus drove the money changers[4]

---

3   Bullet points in this chart are referenced in this treatise, in order to offer another Biblical interpretation to these arguments.

4   Third bullet point. Ibid footnote 3.

The Biblical verses which describe how Jesus drove the money changers out of the temple are Matthew 21:12, Mark 11:15, Luke 19:45 and
John 2:14-15. Checking the *Kingdom Interlinear Translation of the Greek
Scriptures* showed that the word *hierón,* not *naos* is used in these texts. *(Naos*
is consistently rendered "divine habitation" in the Society's *Interlinear*
translation in the literal, word-for-word translation found under the
Greek. *Hierón* is the word commonly used in the Scriptures to denote the
whole temple area. As *Vine's Expository Dictionary of New Testament Words*
states on page 115 [Seventeenth edition, 1966]: "HIERON ... signifying
the entire building with its precincts, or some part thereof, as distinct
from the *naos,* the inner sanctuary ...")

This same point is also made on page 493 of the August 15, 1960
issue of *The Watchtower* in its discussion of the second chapter of John and
how it was that the temple could have had room for the money changers
and all the animals which were being sold there. It states:

> **What kind of building could this be that had room for all this
> traffic? The fact is that this temple was not just one building but a
> series of structures of which the temple sanctuary was the center. In
> the original tongue this is made quite clear, the Scripture writers
> distinguishing between the two by the use of the words *hierón* and
> *naós. Hierón* referred to the entire temple grounds, whereas *naós*
> applied to the temple structure itself, the successor of the tabernacle
> in the wilderness. Thus John tells that Jesus found all this traffic in
> the *hierón.***

(The *Kingdom Interlinear Translation of the Greek Scriptures* translates
hierón by the word "temple" in the literal translation under the Greek text.)

the TEMPLE of
the apostles' time

T HE passover of the year 30 (A.D.) was drawing on apace as Jesus Christ "went up to Jerusalem. And he found in the temple those selling cattle and sheep and doves and the money-brokers in their seats. So, after making a whip of ropes, he drove all those with the sheep and cattle out of the temple and he poured out the coins of the money-changers and overturned their tables. Therefore . . . the Jews said to him: 'What sign have you to show us, since you are doing these things?' In answer Jesus said to them: 'Break down this temple, and in three days I will raise it up.'"—John 2:13-15, 18, 19.

It may well be asked, What kind of building could this be that had room for all this traffic? The fact is that this temple was not just one building but a series of structures of which the temple sanctuary was the center. In the original tongue this is made quite clear, the Scripture writers distinguishing between the two by the use of the words *hierón* and *naós*. *Hierón* referred to the entire temple grounds, whereas *naós* applied to the temple structure itself, the successor of the tabernacle in the wilderness. Thus John tells that Jesus found all this traffic in the *hierón*. But when Jesus likened his body to a temple he used the word *naós*, meaning the temple "sanctuary," as noted in the footnote of the *New World Translation*.

This series of structures of the apostles' time was rebuilt by King Herod. That sensual and bloodthirsty Idumean ruler was loathed by his Jewish subjects as much for his outraging their religious susceptibilities as for his wanton murders, such as that of his wife Mariamne, a Hasmonaean princess. Wanting to ingratiate himself with them, and at the same time to feed his inordinate pride, he proposed the rebuilding of their temple, which, after about five hundred years, was showing signs of decay.

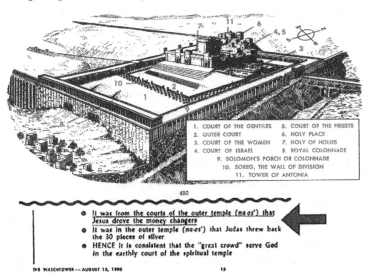

1. COURT OF THE GENTILES
2. OUTER COURT
3. COURT OF THE WOMEN
4. COURT OF ISRAEL
5. COURT OF THE PRIESTS
6. HOLY PLACE
7. HOLY OF HOLIES
8. ROYAL COLONNADE
9. SOLOMON'S PORCH OR COLONNADE
10. SOREG, THE WALL OF DIVISION
11. TOWER OF ANTONIA

493

● It was from the courts of the outer temple (*na·os'*) that Jesus drove the money changers
● It was in the outer temple (*na·os'*) that Judas threw back the 30 pieces of silver
● HENCE it is consistent that the "great crowd" serve God in the earthly court of the spiritual temple

THE WATCHTOWER—AUGUST 15, 1960   13

The above photocopy is from page 493 of the August 15, 1960 issue of *The Watchtower.* It correctly identifies the outer part of the temple area (where the Bible says the money changers were located) by the Greek word *hierón.* Twenty years later, however, page 15 of the August 15, 1980 issue of *The Watchtower* misleadingly implied that the money changers were located in the area of the temple described by the word *naos.* This was done in an article designed to uphold the Society's teaching that the "great crowd" is an earthly class despite their being located in God's *naos* according to Revelation 7:15. (The sanctuary of the temple, the *naos,* pictures heaven in the Bible. The subject matter and writing style indicate that Frederick W. Franz was the author of both articles.)

- **It was the entire temple (na·os´) that was destroyed as a judgment from God[5]**

Matthew 24:1-2; Mark 13:1-3 and Luke 21:5-6 relate the words of Jesus where he prophesied concerning the destruction of Jerusalem and its temple, and again the *Kingdom Interlinear* shows the word *hierón,* not *naos* is used in these verses.

- **It was in the outer temple *(na·os´)* that Judas threw back the 30 pieces of silver[6]**

While it is true that some reference works will point to Matthew 27:5; (which describes how Judas threw back the 30 pieces of silver into the temple or *naos)* as a possible exception to the rule that *naos* always has reference only to the innermost part of the temple area, others point out that this is not necessarily the case. For example, Thayer's *Greek-English Lexicon* (1889, Harper & Brothers) says on page 422 in its definition of the word *naos:*

> **"[U]sed of the temple at Jerusalem, but *only of the sacred edifice (or sanctuary) itself, consisting of the Holy place and the Holy of holies. ... : Mt xxiii. 16 sq. 35; xxvii.40; Mk. xiv.58; xv.29; Jn. ii. 19 sq.; Rev. xi.2; nor need Mt. xxvii.5 be regarded as an exception, provided we suppose that Judas in his desperation entered the Holy place, which no one but the priests was allowed to enter ..."* (Emphasis added.)**

From this it can be seen the use of the term *naos* in Matthew 27 is not necessarily an exception to the rule that this term always refers to the innermost sanctuary of the temple, since it may very well be that Judas,

---

5   Second bullet point. Ibid footnote 3.
6   Fourth bullet point. Ibid footnote 3.

in his desperate frame of mind, did indeed enter into an area normally forbidden to all except the priests.[7]

In his commentary on the book of Matthew (Augsburg Publishing House, Minneapolis, Minnesota, 1961), on pages 1079 and 1080, R.C.H. Lenski also comments on how Judas may have been able to have thrown the silver coins into the actual sanctuary building itself and not one of the outer structures of the temple complex:

> **Judas ... hurls the silver "into the [*naos*] or Sanctuary." Some think that this was the place (they call it the room) in the Temple where the receptacles for the receipt of money stood in the court of the women. But then [*hierón*] would have been the proper word. The term [*naos*] refers to the Sanctuary which included the Holy and the Holy of Holies.[8] Judas went up to the top of the priestly court, took the sack of silver, and flung it into the open entrance of the Holy Place.**

7   While Judas, in tossing his coins, may have entered into the courtyard of the priests (which was not normally accessible to non-priests), it seems unlikely that he actually went into the sanctuary or naos itself. The Greek word *eis* ("into") would seem to preclude that possibility. If Judas "threw the silver pieces into (eis) the temple," this Greek word presupposes that he himself was outside of the building. Hence, Judas may have gone into the portion of the courtyard immediately in front of the door to the Holy Place and, from this position, thrown his coins into the open door of the sanctuary. (Please see comments by R.C.H. Lenski.)

The word *eis* may also be rendered "toward" as shown in *The Anchor Bible*, translated by W.F. Albright and C.S. Mann (copyright 1971 by Doubleday & Co.). In this translation, Matthew 27:5 reads: "... Throwing down the silver pieces toward the Most Holy Place, he withdrew and went away and hanged himself." (Emphasis added.) If Matthew merely intended to say that Judas cast the money "toward" the sanctuary, then, of course, he would not necessarily have had to have entered any restricted areas of the temple. Simply throwing the coins in the direction of the sanctuary from one of the temple precincts would have been sufficient for Matthew's description of the incident to have been accurate. (Examples of eis being translated by the word "toward" may be found at Acts 24:15 and 2 Corinthians 9:8 in the *New World Translation*.)

8   According to page 1081 of the extensive work *Der Tempel Von Jerusalem* by Th. A. Busink (Leiden, E.J. Brill, 1980), Josephus uses the word "neōs (=naos)" to indicate the "whole inner sanctuary," including the courtyard of the priests with its walls, but excluding the outer courtyards like the courtyard of the Gentiles. He cites Josephus' *Wars of the Jews,* Book V, Chapter 5, section 3, clause number 201 as an example of this usage. If Matthew 27:5 uses naos in this same sense, then Judas may have cast the silver pieces "into" the naos without having to have gone into a restricted area. Simply tossing the coins into the courtyard of the priests from a location he would normally have been permitted to enter would have been sufficient for Matthew's account to have been accurate.

• **BUT it was the entire temple *(na·os')* that had been 46 years in the building**[9]

John 2:19-20 are apparently the verses referred to here by *The Watchtower.* In these verses Jesus likens his own body to a sanctuary and tells the Jews "Break down this temple *(naos)* and in three days I will raise it up." To this they responded, "This temple *(naos)* was built in forty-six years, and will you raise it up in three days?" The Jews, of course, either by mistake or because of captiousness, were thinking that Jesus was talking about the literal temple rebuilt by Herod. Flavius Josephus reports in *Antiquities of the Jews* that the sanctuary of Herod's temple was built in one and one-half years and the courtyards were under construction for an additional eight years. *(Antiquities of the Jews,* Book XV, Chapter XI, sect ions 5 & 6) Thus, the Watchtower Society publications *Insight on the Scriptures* (Volume 2, page 1079) and *Aid To Bible Understanding* (page 1584) make this observation:

> **When certain Jews approached Jesus Christ in 30 C.E., saying, "This temple was built in forty-six years" (John 2:20), these Jews were apparently talking about the work that continued on the complex of courts and buildings up until then.**

While it may be true that the work which continued after the first one and one half years up until the time Jesus spoke the words recorded at John 2:19 largely involved the outer complex of courts and buildings, this does not in itself prove that *naos* must in this instance refer to more than the sanctuary. Certainly, at least one reason the Jews used the term *naos* in this case instead of *hierón* was because they were quoting Jesus who had used the term metaphorically in describing his body.

The basic structure of the sanctuary was apparently complete and in usable form after only one and one-half years of building, but the writings of Josephus also indicate that this structure remained in an unfinished state even at the time of its destruction by Roman armies

---

9   First bullet point. Ibid footnote 3.

in the year 70 C.E. (or A.O.) *The Interpreters Dictionary of the Bible* (Abingdon Press, copyright 1962) notes the following on pages 551 and 552 with regard to the temple rebuilt by Herod:

> **The work of rebuilding was begun in the eighteenth year of Herod's reign (20/19 B.C.). Herod thought, according to Josephus, that Solomon's temple was 120 cubits high (cf. II Chr. 3:4); its successor was only half as high; Herod wished to redress the deficiency and restore the former glory (Antiq. XV.xi.1)... .**
>
> **The old foundations were removed and new ones laid. The new building was 100 cubits long, and the same in height; a structural difficulty prevented attainment of the full height of 120 cubits. ...**
>
> **In Antiq. XX.ix.7 we read that the construction of the temple precincts [hierón] was "finished" during the time of Agrippa II ... during the procuratorship of Albinos, ca. 63. ... Later, Agrippa gathered material to increase the height of the sanctuary building by 20 cubits to bring it to the supposed Solomonic height, but the war intervened before this work could be begun (War V.i.5).**

Josephus' *Antiquities of the Jews* says the following regarding this in Book XV, Chapter XI, section 3 (as translated by William Whiston, A.M. in *The Life And Works of Flavius Josephus,* published by Holt, Rinehart and Winston, New York):

> **So Herod took away the old foundations, and laid others, and erected the temple upon them, being in length a hundred cubits, and in height twenty additional cubits, which [twenty], upon the sinking of their foundations fell down; and this part it was that we resolved to raise again in the days of Nero.**

(Nero was emperor during the years 54 C.E. to 68 C.E., according to *Insight on the Scriptures*, Volume 1, page 382.)

Josephus adds to this in Book V, Chapter I, section 5 of *Wars of the Jews*. The materials which had been gathered to rebuild the sanctuary to its intended height were instead used by John of Gischala to support the war effort. Josephus writes (according to the Whiston translation cited above):

> Nay, John abused the sacred materials, and employed them in the construction of his engines of war; for the people and the priests had formerly determined to support the temple, and raise the holy house twenty cubits higher; for king Agrippa had at very great expense, and with very great pains, brought thither such materials as were proper for that purpose, being pieces of timber very well worth seeing ....

A footnote in the Whiston translation of this part of *Wars of the Jews* says the following:

> This timber, we see, was designed for the rebuilding [of] those twenty additional cubits of the holy house above the hundred, which had fallen down some years before.

This evidence shows that the sanctuary may very well have been considered to have been still "in the building" when the Jews spoke the words recorded at John 2:20 to Jesus. Since it appears that the sanctuary was never successfully brought to its intended height of 120 cubits, it may very well have been considered to have been still "under construction" at that time (either literally or in an anticipatory sense). Details are not given as to the manner in which this upper most portion of the sanctuary underwent the "sinking" process described by Josephus or the time span over which this occurred, but it very well may have been a gradual deterioration which began shortly after its construction and lasted over a period of years. Repeated efforts to shore up and save the defective structures may have been made by the temple builders before these efforts were abandoned and the work of removing and planning for the replacement of the fallen structures was undertaken. If this were the case, it is understandable how the Jews could have been referring specifically to the *sanctuary* when saying the *naos* had been 46 years in the building. (Many translators, in fact, use the word "sanctuary" in their renderings of this verse. See for example, *The Jerusalem Bible, An American Translation* by Goodspeed and Smith, *Young's Literal Translation* and the translations by Moffatt and Lenski.) Maintenance work (and possibly work of an ornamental or embellishing nature) very well may have been done on the sanctuary throughout the 46-year period described as well.

This explanation may be helpful in understanding John 2:20 if it truly has the sense commonly conveyed by both old and recent translations that the building process was still continuing. (The *Berkeley Version* makes this understanding explicit by translating this verse, "This temple has been in process of building for forty-six years.") However, some scholars find this rendering of the original Greek text unacceptable. B.F. Wescott (who helped compile the Greek master text that *New World Translation* is based on) and Leon Morris feel instead that the Jews were referring to the completion of a definite stage of the work and that no building was going on when these words were spoken. (This is not to say that the work was totally completed at this time. As previously noted on page 8, Josephus reports in *Antiquities of the Jews,* Book XX, Chapter IX, section 7, that this did not take place until the procuratorship of Albinus in A.D. 62-64. Of course, the intended rebuilding of the uppermost part of the sanctuary building never was completed.) Thus, they feel that the Greek text may be accurately translated to carry the sense that "the Jews were asking Jesus how He would be able to raise up in three days the temple edifice which had stood for forty-six years." (See the book *Chronological Aspects of the Life of Christ* by Harold W. Hoehner, page 42, published in 1977 by the Zondervan Publishing House in Grand Rapids, Michigan.)

The Handbook of Biblical Chronology by Jack Finegan (Princeton University Press, 1964) further explains this view on page 279:

> **Perhaps [*oikodomēthē*], which is an aorist indicative passive ... meaning literally "was built," does not refer to a building enterprise that was still going on, as it had been for forty-six years, but to a building enterprise that had been completed long before so that it could be said that the building had stood for forty-six years. On this interpretation the Jews ask Jesus in effect, "How can you possibly raise in three days a Temple which has stood for forty-six years?"**

If this was the intended sense of the words spoken by the Jews to Jesus, it is apparent that they would not have had to have anything more than the innermost sanctuary of the temple structure in mind when referring to the *naos*. If the priests began to build the *naos* at the same time Herod began the construction of the entire *hierón*, the sanctuary had surely stood for those forty-six years so the Jews would again have been perfectly accurate in asking Jesus how he, was going to raise in only three days a structure which had stood for forty-six years. *The Handbook of Biblical Chronology* makes this same observation on pages 279 and 280:

> **In this connection it may also be noticed that there seems to be a clear distinction in the Fourth Gospel between [*naos*] and [*hieron*] ... ... Therefore this reference [at John 2:20] *could be specifically to the temple edifice proper.* (Emphasis added.)**

Page 41 of *Chronological Aspects of the Life of Christ* is more emphatic on this point:

> **There are two Greek words for temple which are distinguished by Josephus. The first term [*hieron*] refers to the whole sacred area which includes three courts or enclosures. ... The second term for the temple is [*naos*] which is the sacred building alone. ...**
>
> **The Gospels make the same distinction. ... [I]n 2:19-20 John uses [*ho naos*] when the Jews were talking about the destruction of temple edifice. Therefore, the Jews were speaking of the temple edifice and not the whole sacred precints.**

In actuality, however, it matters little whether or not the gospel accounts do at times use the word *naos* in the broader sense the Society would like this term to have (to allow for its interpretation of an earthly "great crowd" serving in the outer courtyard of the spiritual temple according to their explanation of Revelation 7:15). What is important is *how the apostle John uses the term* in Revelation, and what Scriptural basis there is for even saying that there is such a thing as 'an earthly courtyard of the Gentiles.'

It seems apparent that, throughout the book of Revelation, John uses the term *naos* to refer to the innermost part of the temple, the heavenly sanctuary in its figurative application. Noting verses where this Greek word appears, the 1986 edition of *The New International Dictionary of New Testament Theology* (Vol. 3, page 784) says: "The Apocalypse speaks often of the heavenly temple (Rev. 7:15; 11:19; 14:15ff; 15:5-8; 16:1, 17), clearly on the basis of Ps. 11:4." One of the Society's own commentaries on the Apocalypse, *Then Is Finished the Mystery of God* (1969), states the following on page 260 in its discussion of Revelation 11:2:

The temple sanctuary or *naos* occupied only part of the temple area.

While the location of the temple mentioned in this verse may not be as clear as the numerous other references in Revelation, the Society's own publication acknowledges that here John uses this term in referring to the sanctuary only and not to the outermost courtyard of the Gentiles where the "great crowd" is said to be serving. This may be one more reason why the Governing Body felt it would be advisable to produce an updated commentary on the book of Revelation. In *Revelation—Its Grand Climax At Hand!*, it does not point out that *naos* is the term used at Revelation 11:2 in its comments on this verse, as the previous book does. It would be embarrassing to do so because it is plain in this text that John uses the term in reference to the sanctuary only, and not to the entire temple area.

Below is the Watchtower Society's conception of "Jehovah's Temple Arrangement." Note the portrayal of the court of the Gentiles as a place where happy worshippers of God render sacred service day and night. This contrasts sharply with the Bible's use of this courtyard to symbolize a period of oppression by those not numbered among true worshippers at Revelation 11:2. (The February 1, 1998 issue of *The Watchtower* (see page 21) indicates that the Society associates this courtyard with the outer courtyard of Solomon's temple instead of Herod's.)

> "This beautiful vision presents the international 'great crowd' as serving Jehovah in his temple, that is, in the earthly courtyards reserved for those who are not spiritual Israelites, as it were in the 'courtyard of the Gentiles.'"
>
> —*The Watchtower*, Dec. 1, 1972, p. 722

> "As foretold, the great crowd 'are worshiping [God] day and night in his temple.' . . . Since they are not spiritual, priestly Israelites, John likely saw them standing in the temple in the outer courtyard of the Gentiles."
>
> —*The Watchtower*, July 1, 1996, p. 20

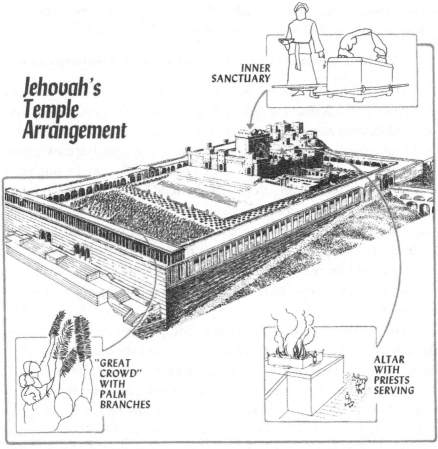

Jehovah's Temple Arrangement

INNER SANCTUARY

"GREAT CROWD" WITH PALM BRANCHES

ALTAR WITH PRIESTS SERVING

What makes this text at Revelation 11:2, even more disconcerting to the Society is the fact that this verse also uses the courtyard of the Gentiles in a figurative or symbolic sense, and it is the only verse in the book of Revelation which does so in a relatively clear and direct manner. This is not as easily seen in *The New World Translation* because it uses the word "nations" instead of "Gentiles," but it is more easily seen in other translations like that of James Moffatt, the *King James* version and *The New English Bible*. The *NEB* renders this verse as follows:

> **But have nothing to do with the outer court of the temple; do not measure that; for it has been given over to the Gentiles, and they will trample the Holy City underfoot for forty-two months.**

It is generally recognized by Bible scholars that the courtyard here spoken of as being "outside the temple sanctuary *(naos)*" in the *New World Translation* must refer to an earthly courtyard since it seems unlikely that such trampling of the holy city by the nations or Gentiles could take place in heaven. However, it is quite evident that, by and large, the ones occupying this courtyard are *oppressors* of true worship, not supporters of it. Albert Barnes, a nineteenth-century Bible scholar who has been quoted as authoritative in Watchtower publications (See for example *The Watchtower*, May 1, 1983, page 3), makes the following comments about Revelation 11:2 on page 1643 of *Barne's Notes on the New Testament* (Kregel Publications, Grand Rapids, Michigan 49501, Tenth Printing, 1978):

> **There is undoubtedly reference here to the "court of the Gentiles," as it was called among the Jews—the outer court of the temple to which the Gentiles had access, and within which they were not permitted to go. ... In forming an estimate of those who, according to Hebrew notions, were true worshippers of God, only those would be regarded as such who had the privilege of access to the inner court, and to the altar. In making such an estimate, therefore, those who had no nearer access than that court, would be omitted; that is, they would not be reckoned as necessarily any part of those who were regarded as the people of God. ... They occupied it, not as the people of God, but as those who were *without* the true church ...**

Commenting on this same verse in the *Tyndale New Testament Commentaries* (William B. Eerdmans Publishing Company, Grand

Rapids, Michigan; Seventh Printing, April, 1979) Leon Morris observes on page 146 of his commentary on the book of Revelation:

> **The starting-point for John's imagery is the Jerusalem temple, where the outer court might be used by Gentiles, but the inner courts, including the sanctuary, by Israelites only. The church, the true Israel, is the sanctuary in the vision. ... Though they are not permitted to destroy the church, the Gentiles are permitted for a limited time to oppress it.**

R.C.H. Lenski's commentary on the book of Revelation *(The Interpretation of St. John's Revelation,* Augsburg Publishing House, Minneapolis, Minnesota, copyright assigned in 1961) explains Revelation 11:2 in similar terms on page 330:

> **The outer court, that of the Gentiles in the Jewish Temple, symbolizes all that is unholy, that belongs to the world! It is ... "outside," John is to "throw it out," to reject it as profane, is not to measure it, to draw no boundary to mark any part of it as belonging to the *Una Sancta* [the church]. "It was given to the heathen," ... to whom it belongs, who also freely enter this outside court. ... Here we must render "to the heathen," to all those outside of the church who cannot be accepted as worshippers at God's and Christ's altar.**

The same basic understanding of this verse is taught in the 1930 Watch Tower Society publication *Light* by J. F. Rutherford. Book One of this two-volume work says on page 189, paragraph one:

> **The instruction is not to measure the court outside the temple but to "cast [it] outside" *(Roth.),* because it symbolizes those who merely profess to be God's children but who are not. ... Those who merely pretend to be followers of the Lord are represented as in the court and are left out.**

Regardless of whether or not these commentators are accurate in their explanation of the significance of this verse, several points seem apparent:

1) John uses the term *naos* in referring to the inner part of the temple only because the courtyard is spoken of as being "outside the temple [sanctuary] *(naos)*":

Although Revelation 11:1-2 are the very next verses in Revelation where *naos* appears after its usage in connection with the "great crowd" at 7:15, the Society totally ignores and even covers this up in *Revelation—Its Grand Climax At Hand!*, the plain evidence that John is using this term in referring to the sanctuary only.

***The Kingdom Interlinear Translation of the Greek Scriptures* (1985) (above) makes a clear distinction between the outer courtyard of the (temple and the *naos* ("temple [sanctuary]" or "divine habitation"). — See photocopy below:**

1089   REVELATION 11:2—6

τὸν	ναὸν	τοῦ	θεοῦ	καὶ	τὸ	the temple [sanctuary]
the	divine habitation	of the	God	and	the	of God' and the altar
θυσιαστήριον	καὶ	τοὺς	προσκυνοῦντας	ἐν		and those worshiping
altar	and	the (ones)	worshiping	in		in it. 2 But as for
αὐτῷ.	2 καὶ	τὴν	αὐλὴν	τὴν	ἔξωθεν	the courtyard that is
it.	And	the	courtyard	the (one)	outside	outside the temple
τοῦ	ναοῦ		ἔκβαλε	ἔξωθεν,	καὶ	[sanctuary], cast it
of the divine habitation			throw you out	outside,	and	clear out and do not
μὴ	αὐτὴν	μετρήσῃς,		ὅτι	ἐδόθη	measure it, because
not	it	you should measure,		because	it was given	it has been given to
τοῖς	ἔθνεσιν,	καὶ	τὴν	πόλιν	τὴν ἁγίαν	the nations, and they
to the	nations,	and	the	city	the holy	will trample the holy
πατήσουσιν	μῆνας		τεσσεράκοντα		καὶ	city underfoot for
they will trample on	months		forty		and	forty-two months.
δύο.	3 καὶ	δώσω	τοῖς	δυσὶν	μάρτυσίν	3 And I will cause
two.	And	I shall give	to the	two	witnesses	

2) The outer, earthly courtyard of this temple is used to depict a period of oppression of true worship because those occupying it "trample the holy city underfoot." It is not pictured as a location where a "great crowd" of true worshipers might joyously carry on sacred service day and night, but instead as a place, which does not allow for such complete devotion to be offered.

3) Those occupying this courtyard are apparently not numbered among true worshipers because John is told to 'cast out' or reject this courtyard and not to measure it for the purpose of finding

out how many worshipers are in it as in verse one where he is told to measure the sanctuary. The people of the nations or "Gentiles" portrayed in this verse are not 'non-anointed' Christians, but, instead, non-Christians, who are separate and distinct from God's people who have access to the sanctuary.

So in the Bible's symbolism, the courtyard of the Gentiles is used to portray a time of oppression of true worship by those not numbered among God's people. In the Watchtower Society's made-up symbolism, it is used to picture a place where happy worshipers of God render sacred service to Him day and night, and where "[t]hey will hunger no more nor thirst anymore ... [a]nd God will wipe out every tear from their eyes." (Rev. 7:16-17) It is plainly a case of adding a contrived significance to the Scriptures and ignoring or taking away what they actually teach. I was well aware of the Bible's warning against this type of thing at Revelation 22:18-19, and this, along with other similar factors, helped me make the difficult decision to leave Bethel in February, 1981. I felt I had no other choice since I knew I could not knowingly be a party to advancing such obviously inaccurate representations of what the Scriptures actually teach.

Who then, are those who comprise the "great crowd" of Revelation 7:9? In the Society's publication *The Finished Mystery* they are identified as being one and the same as the group later described by the *New World Translation* as "a great crowd in heaven" at Revelation 19:1. (See page 289 of the 1917, 1918 and 1924 editions; also pages 136 and 138) It seems that there is a great deal of evidence which points to this conclusion. Some reference works link quite a number of texts pertaining to those who dwell in heaven with verses which refer to the "great crowd." Some of these texts are included in the chart on the next page:

WHERE IS THE "GREAT CROWD"? *

	Verses About Great Crowd	Verses To Compare
Out of all tribes and peoples and tongues	Rev. 7.9	Rev. 5:9-10
"before[10] the throne"	Rev. 7:9, 15	Rev. 1:4; 4:5-6, 10; 7:11; 8:3; 9:13; 11:16; 14:3
"before the lamb"	Rev. 7:9	Rev. 5:8
dressed in white robes	Rev. 7:9	Rev. 3:4, 18; 4:4; 6:11
great crowd attributes salvation to God	Rev. 7:10	Rev. 19:1
washed robes and made them white in the blood of the Lamb	Rev. 7:14	1 Peter 1:2, 18-19; 1 Cor. 6:11; Rev. 22:14; 1 John 1:7; Eph. 2:13

* These are but a portion of literally dozens of verses in which characteristics of those associated with the "great crowd" are shared with those who enjoy heavenly residency with Jesus Christ. So some have suggested that the 144,000 and the great crowd are in fact the same group. (See footnote #11)

---

10 Page 123 of *Revelation—Its Grand Climax At Hand!* states that "the Greek word here translated "before" *(enopion)* literally means "in [the] sight [of]" and is used several times of humans on earth who are "before" or "in the sight of" Jehovah. (1 Timothy 5:21; 2 Timothy 2:14; Romans 14:2; Galatians 1:20)" The implication is then made of Matthew 25:32, where it speaks of all the nations being gathered "before" the Son of Man, somehow supports this. However, the Greek word translated "before" in this text is *emprosthen,* not *enopion.* (This is indirectly acknowledged in the footnote at the bottom of page 123, which admits the Greek word used here means literally, "in front of him," not "in [the] sight [of]".) Rather than searching elsewhere for examples of how *enopion* ("before") is used, it would seem far more logical and scholastically honest to see how this word is used in context—in the book of Revelation itself. As indicated in the above chart, *enopion* ("in [the] sight [of]") is consistently and repeatedly used of things and persons in heaven (often times "before the throne"). — Revelation 1:4; 4:5-6, 10; 7:11; 8:3; 9:13; 11:16; 14:3; also see chart "How the Bible Uses "Before" *(enopion)* in the Book of Revelation" found on the page before the "References" at the end of this treatise.

Using the terminology common to that time period, page 289 of the 1917, 1918 and 1924 editions of the Watch Tower Society publication, The Finished Mystery, identifies the "great crowd" of Revelation 7:9 as being one and the same as the "great crowd in heaven" described at Revelation 19:1. (See also pages 136 and 138.)

The unlikelihood of the number 144,000 referring to a literal number of "spiritual Israelites" or members of the Christian congregation can be seen by the context in which this number first appears at Revelation 7:4-8. The number 144,000 is first presented as the total of twelve twelve-thousands. Each of those twelve-thousands are said to come out of one of the tribes of Israel. By pointing out that this is not the usual listing of these tribes and that James refers to anointed Christians by the expression "the twelve tribes that are scattered about" at James 1:1, the Society endeavors to establish that this is not referring to literal Israel on pages 117 and 118 of *Revelation—Its Grand Climax At Hand!*:

> Could this not be a reference to literal, fleshly Israel? No, for Revelation 7:4-8 diverges from the usual tribal listing. ...
> The Christian congregation is "a chosen race, a royal priesthood, a holy nation." (1 Peter 2:9) Replacing natural Israel as God's nation, it becomes a new Israel that is "really 'Israel.'" (Romans 9:6-8; Matthew 21:43) For this reason, it was quite proper for Jesus' half brother James to address his pastoral letter "to the twelve tribes that are scattered about," that is, to the worldwide congregation of anointed Christians that in time would number 144,000. — James 1:1

In establishing that the comments regarding the 144,000 at Revelation 7:4-8 are not "a reference to *literal,* fleshly Israel" however, the Society is acknowledging that this is to be taken in a figurative or symbolic sense. Those who believe it applies to a multiracial group of Christians and not to natural Israel have no choice but to admit this because *there simply is no* Christian tribe of Judah, or Reuben or Gad or Asher, etc. But if these 12 tribes of 12,000 are figurative or symbolic elements, it would seem only logical that their total (144,000) is also figurative or symbolic.[11]

Whatever conclusions our personal study of the Scriptures may lead us to concerning the identities of the "great crowd" and the 144,000, we must be careful to always let the Bible speak for itself. We must not let preconceived notions cause us to arrive at forced explanations, which actually misrepresent its teachings, as has the Watchtower Society. The concluding part of this fascinating book assures faithful ones who handle God's Word properly of grand blessings. But to those who add to or subtract from it, it promises the most serious of consequences. — Rev. 22:18-19.

Summary

The Watchtower Society explains the "great crowd" of Revelation 7:9-17 to be an earthly class even though they are spoken of as being in God's *naos* in verse 15 of this chapter. Although the Society (like other commentators) acknowledges that *naos* refers to the sanctuary of the temple which represents heaven in the Bible, Jehovah's Witnesses try to justify this explanation by saying that this term can also refer to the outermost portion of the temple—specifically, the courtyard of the gentiles. (*The Watchtower* February 1, 1998, changed this teaching, to the outer

---

11   It would be far easier to argue for a literal application of the number 144,000 if the 12 tribes of 12,000 were understood in a literal sense as a reference to fleshly Israel. If this were done, the interpretation would at least be consistent with itself throughout this whole passage of scripture.

Regarding the symbolic nature of the number "144,000" *The Interpreters One-Volume Commentary On The Bible* notes on page 955: "The 2nd vision in this interlude [the "great crowd"] is not intended as a contrast to the first. The 144,000 symbolize the church as the true Israel while still militant on the earth. The great multitude which no man could number from all national, racial, and linguistic groups is the church triumphant in heaven. ..." It is worth noting (as this commentary observes) the 144,000 are presented first as an *earthly* group in Revelation chapter 7. The "four angels standing upon the four corners of the earth" are instructed not to "harm the earth or the sea or the trees" until the 144,000 are "sealed ... in their foreheads" while still on earth. It isn't until Revelation 14 that the 144,000 are pictured in heaven, perhaps, (as pointed out by some commentators) to stress a note of fulfillment here. In the seventh chapter of Revelation, 144,000 were sealed on earth while they were confronted by their enemies. Now, in the fourteenth chapter, the complete number of 144,000 (representing the whole church) are saved and are in heaven, not one of them being lost.

courtyard of Solomon's temple.) However, the only verse in the book of Revelation which is recognized as using the outer courtyard of the temple as a symbol is Revelation 11:2, and it is obvious in this verse that those occupying this portion of the figurative temple are mainly *oppressors* instead of *supporters* of true worship. Additionally, this verse plainly states that the courtyard is "outside the temple [sanctuary]" (*or naos*), so it is impossible to conclude that *naos* could refer to more than the sanctuary or innermost part of the temple in John's usage of the term here.

Hence, it is unscriptural to teach that the "great crowd" could be serving in "the earthly court of the spiritual temple" of God.

Concluding Notes

In the years since the events at Watchtower headquarters in 1980, the Society's publications seemed understandably reluctant to link the location of the "great crowd" with the courtyard of the Gentiles. While still placing this group in "the earthly courtyard of [God's] great spiritual temple" (*Revelation—It's Grand Climax At Hand!*, page 126) it seemed that efforts were being made to disassociate the "great crowd" with a specific location of the typical temple which was once in Jerusalem. (Thus, page 107 of the 1983 publication *United In Worship of the Only True God* placed this assembled multitude "in God's temple, or universal house of worship," but did not specify which part of the temple they are in.)

However, in an article entitled, "The Triumph Of True Worship Draws Near," the July 1, 1996 issue of *The Watchtower* reaffirmed the teaching that the "great crowd" is serving in the antitypical, earthly courtyard. Page 20 states, "Since they are not spiritual, priestly Israelites, John likely saw them standing in the temple in the outer courtyard of the Gentiles."[12] Page 23 refers to "the earthly courtyards of Jehovah's temple." Then, in a surprising doctrinal shift, only nineteen months after *The Watchtower* restated this doctrine, the February 1, 1998 edition of *The Watchtower* changed this teaching. Page 21 of this issue says:

> **The great crowd worships with anointed Christians in the earthly courtyard of Jehovah's great spiritual temple. (Revelation 7: 14, 15; 11:2) There is no reason to conclude that they are in a separate Court of the Gentiles. When Jesus was on earth, there was a Court of the Gentiles in the temple. However, in the divinely inspired plans of Solomon's and Ezekiel's temples, there was no provision for a Court of the Gentiles. In Solomon's temple, there was an outer courtyard where Israelites and proselytes, men and women, worshiped together. This is the prophetic pattern of the earthly courtyard of the spiritual temple, where John saw the great crowd rendering sacred service. (Emphasis added)**

What is particularly striking about this change in teaching, aside from stating the "great crowd" is not in "a separate Court of the Gentiles," is the fact that the Society has very clearly made a definite link between Revelation 7:15 and 11:2. The "courtyard that is outside the temple [sanctuary] *(naos)*" described at Revelation 11:2 is now positively identified as the "earthly courtyard of Jehovah's great spiritual temple" occupied by both the "great crowd" and anointed Christians. When Fred W.

---

12   The other courts of the literal temple were accessible only to Jews and therefore would not appropriately picture those not considered to be "spiritual Jews." Those of the "great crowd" are not really included among the 144,000 "spiritual Jews," according to Watchtower Society teachings but only "hold ... the skirt of a man who is a Jew" according to their figurative application of Zechariah 8:23. (See the April 15, 1986 issue of *The Watchtower*, Page 20, paragraph 21; also the January 1, 1988 edition of *The Watchtower.* pages 17 and 18, paragraph 18.) Hence, the 1972 publication *Paradise Restored To Mankind—By Theocracy!*, states on page 80: "[T]his 'great crowd' of 'other sheep' are already at the spiritual temple of Jehovah God. ... ... Not being the sealed spiritual Israelites, they are, as it were, in the Court of the Gentiles such as was a part of the temple at Jerusalem in the days of Jesus Christ and his apostles." (See also Ephesians 2:14 which undoubtedly alludes to the wall in the outermost courtyard of the Jerusalem temple beyond which non-Jews were forbidden to pass.)

Franz was alive (and even during the intervening years since his death on December 22, 1992) the Society seemed to carefully avoid making this connection. This apparently was because of the evident distinction between the sanctuary *(naos* or "divine habitation") and the outer court-yard mentioned in this text. Perhaps this can be seen most clearly in the way the first part of this verse is rendered in the word-for-word transla-tion beneath the original Greek text in the Society's *Kingdom Interlinear Translation of the Greek Scriptures:*

καὶ	τὴν	αὐλὴν	τὴν	ἔξωθεν	τοῦ	ναοῦ
And	the	courtyard	the (one)	outside	of the	divine habitation

Now, however, the organization has placed the "great crowd" squarely inside of the courtyard depicted at Revelation 11:2 and clearly defined it as part of the same "spiritual temple" Jehovah's Witnesses are taught that Revelation 7:15 refers to when it places the "great crowd" in God's temple [*naos*].

Attempting to change the widely accepted prophetic type of the courtyard from the Court of the Gentiles to the outer courtyard of Solomon's temple does not solve the Society's interpretative problem how-ever. Regardless of which temple one chooses to link to Revelation 11:2, be it Solomon's, Ezekiel's or Herod's, the plain fact of the matter is that this earthly courtyard is "outside the temple [sanctuary] *(naos)"* while the "great crowd" of Revelation 7:15 is described as being *inside* the temple sanctuary or *naos*.

It is evident that throughout the book of Revelation the term *naos* is used repeatedly to refer exclusively to the innermost part of the temple, the heavenly sanctuary in its figurative application. As noted previously, the Watchtower Society publication *Then is Finished the Mystery of God* (1969) says on page 260 in its comments on Revelation 11:2:

The temple sanctuary or *naos* occupied only part of the temple area.

The 1986 edition of *The New International Dictionary of New Testament Theology* (Vol. 3, page 784) refers to other verses in the book of Revelation where the Greek word *naos* appears and comments:

> **The Apocalypse speaks often of the heavenly temple (Rev. 7:15; 11:19; 14:15ff; 15:5-8; 16:1,17), clearly on the basis of Ps. 11:4.**

And the August 15, 1980 *Watchtower* correctly observed on page 15:

> **The Greek work *naos* refers often to the inner sanctuary representing heaven itself.**

Proving the "great crowd" is not located in God's heavenly sanctuary would therefore require somehow demonstrating that the term *"naos"* can also include the "courtyard that is outside the temple [sanctuary] *(naos)"* described at Revelation 11:2. But, as the Society's own above-quoted publication has pointed out, this verse itself makes it plain that it does not since it makes a clear distinction between the courtyard and the temple sanctuary. John obviously uses the term *naos* in a limited sense as applying to God's "divine habitation" only. — See these verses in *The Kingdom Interlinear Translation of the Greek Scriptures.*

Again it is a case of the Society reasoning, from their traditional beliefs and interpretations and endeavoring to make the Bible align with these, instead of starting with the Scriptures and then changing its teaching to conform to the Bible. (Compare Matthew 15:1-9 and Mark 7:6-9 where Jesus condemned the scribes and Pharisees for allowing tradition to take precedence over God's Word.)

The only way, therefore, to resolve this problem would be by acknowledging that the book of Revelation applies *naos* strictly to the sanctuary of the temple in the verses under consideration, and then to accept the obvious conclusions, which would result therefrom.

Appendix

On page 882 of the *Theological Dictionary of the New Testament,* (Wm. B. Eerdmans Publishing Company, Grand Rapids, Michigan, Vol. IV, edited by Gerhard Kittel; Geoffrey W. Bromiley, D. Litt., D.D., translator and editor), Dr. O. Michel writes: "In the N[ew] T[estament], in addition to [*hieron, hagion*] ... we also find [naos] ... with no real distinction between the terms in either meaning or range." He further states on page 884 in support of this view: "If [*naos*] is taken to mean the temple in the narrower sense, one may ask how Judas could bring the money into it, since only priests were allowed access. We may thus assume that it is used in a broader sense, as in Jn."

However, as already demonstrated in footnotes number 7 and 8, there is more than one way to explain this text without having to conclude that Matthew was using *naos* in a broader sense to include the entire temple area. *The Expositor's Bible Commentary* (Frank E. Gaebele in and J.D. Douglas, editors; copyright 1984 by the Zondervan Publishing House, Grand Rapids, Michigan), specifically addresses the comments found in the *Theological Dictionary of the New Testament* and states on page 566 of Volume 8:

> **O. Michel (TDNT, 4:882-5) and G. Schrenk (TDNT, 3:235) argue that there is no necessary difference between ... (*naos,* "temple [sanctuary]") and ... (*hieron,* "temple [and its precincts]"). If so, then the use of the former in this verse means no more than that Judas threw the money somewhere in the temple area. But a fairly strong case can be made for maintaining a distinction between the words in Matthew's usage: *naos* is used only of the temple proper, the sanctuary, in 23:16-17, 21; 27:51, and, metaphorically, in 26:61; 27:40; whereas *hieron* is used of the temple and its precincts in 4:5; 21:12, 14-15, 23; 24:1; 26:55 (cf. Garland, p. 199, n.117). It is possible that *hieron* is a trifle forced in 12:5; but since it is the encompassing term and not all the priests' functions took place in the temple proper, the use still admits the traditional distinction between the terms. That leaves only 27:5; but in the narrow sense of *naos,* Judas would normally not have been allowed to enter. That may be just the point:**

feeling damned already, he has nothing more to lose; and in desperation he runs into the temple proper and flings down his money before he can be stopped. Thus he deeply incriminates the priests, a further example of 23:35.

* Note — The following correspondence was exchanged with the Watchtower Society regarding the August 15, 1980 issue of *The Watchtower*.

1075 B

April 6, 1981

Watchtower Bible & Tract Society
117 Adams Street
Brooklyn, New York 11201

Dear Brothers,

I am writing concerning a question I have on the article "The Great Crowd Renders Sacred Service Where?" in the August 15, 1980 Watchtower, particularly the fourth and fifth paragraphs and the outlined dotted statements at the bottom of page 15.

I've been trying to locate the exact scriptures referred to in the different statements. I can see the first point refers to John 2:20 and the fourth one to Matthew 27:5, but I have been unable to locate the whereabouts of the use of the word naos in the manner described in points 2 and 3. I've noticed by examining the Emphatic Diaglott and the Interlinear translation that at Matthew 24:1, Mark 13:1 and 3, and Luke 21:5 where Jesus prophesied concerning the destruction of Jerusalem and its temple, that the word hieron is used. The same is true of Matthew 21:12, Mark 11:15, Luke 19:45 and John 2:14, 15 where the moneychangers were driven out of the temple by Jesus. I examined the Aid book and noticed that hieron is used for temple also, and I am somewhat confused by the use of the word naos used in the fourth paragraph of the Watchtower, when I am unable to find it anywhere in the described instances of the paragraph. Likely, I am overlooking something or have made a mistake in my understanding, but I would appreciate your help in this area.

Could you please give me the specific scripture points the second and third statements refer to, namely: "It was the entire temple (naos) that was destroyed as a judgement from God," and "It was from the courts of the outer temple (naos) that Jesus drove the money changers". I would really appreciate an answer as soon as possible, as I have really researched this matter and am anxious to really come to an "accurate understanding" of it. I know you are busy, but I am thanking you in advance for your early reply.

Thank you so very much for your help in this matter.

Your sister,

Margaret
1075 B

P.S. Regarding Revelation 11:2, it is widely recognized by Bible scholars (e.g. The New American Bible) that the "courtyard that is outside the temple" (naos) alludes to the courtyard of the Gentiles in Herod's Temple. This being the case, would it be proper to use the scripture to support the view that the great crowd is serving in the anti-typical "courtyard of the Gentiles?"

WATCHTOWER
BIBLE AND TRACT SOCIETY OF NEW YORK, INC.

CABLE WATCHTOWER

25 COLUMBIA HEIGHTS, BROOKLYN, NEW YORK 11201, U.S.A.   PHONE (212) 625-3600

EW:ESE   May 11, 1981

Margaret
1075 B

Dear Sister

    Your letter of April 6, 1981, now has our attention. You write
regarding a point made in paragraph 4, on page 15, of the August 15,
1980, issue of The Watchtower.

    Your question is understandable, since, as you say, the apostle
John, in giving the account about the driving of the money changers
and merchantmen out of Herod's temple, did use the Greek word hieron,
w h e n t h e article refers to "the Bible account of where Jesus
Christ drove the money changers and merchantmen out of Herod's temple,"
have in mind that this account involves not only verses 13-17 of
chapter two, but also verses 18-22. That is why the article goes
on to state: "There [that is, in the account as a whole] we read:
'Jesus answered, "Destroy this sanctuary [naos], and in three days
I will raise it up." The Jews replied, 'It has taken forty-six
years to build this sanctuary [naos]: are you going to raise it up
in three days?' But he was speaking of the sanctuary [naos] that was
his body." Then verses 19-21 were cited.

    We recognize that the way this is worded in the paragraph one
might conclude that the word naos was used in verses 13-17. To
avoid this impression, point three in the summary that appears at
the bottom of page 15 was deleted in translating this article for
publication in foreign language editions of The Watchtower. Thank
you for your comments on the article as a whole. As you recognize
in your letter, hieron is most often used in referring to the entire
temple complex, but it is evident from how the Jews replied to Jesus
and other Scriptural references that there was no problem in Bible
times in also applying the word naos to the whole temple area and
not just to the sanctuary.

    With respect to your final question, the Court of the Gentiles
is one of the outer courts as shown in the illustration on page 1585
of the Aid book. It would be part of the entire temple area, to
which the word naos was at times applied and would appropriately
picture or foreshadow where the "great crowd" is serving, as stated
at Revelation 7:15.

    We trust the above comments will prove helpful to you, and please
be assured of our best wishes.

            Your brothers,

            Watchtower B.&T. Society
            OF NEW YORK, INC.

How the Bible Uses "Before" (*enopion*) in the Book of Revelation

Page 123 of the book *Revelation—It's Grand Climax At Hand!* points out that "the Greek word here translated [at Revelation 7:9] 'before' (enopion) literally means 'in [the] sight [of]' and is used several times of humans on earth who are 'before' or 'in the sight of' Jehovah. (1 Timothy 5:21; 2 Timothy 2:14; Romans 14:22; Galatians 1:20)" When considered in context in the book of Revelation, however, the sense in which this word is used becomes more plain:

Revelation 1:4   "seven spirits that are before (*enopion*) his [God's] throne, ..."

Revelation 4:5   "seven lamps of fire burning before (*enopion*) the throne [of God], ..."

Revelation 4:6   "And before (*enopion*) the throne [of God] there is, as it were, a glassy sea like crystal."

Revelation 4:10   "the twenty-four elders fall down before (*enopion*) the One seated upon the throne ... and they cast their crowns before (*enopion*) the throne, ..."

Revelation 7:9   **"a great crowd, ... standing before (*enopion*) the throne and before (*enopion*) the Lamb. ... "**

Revelation 7:11   "And all the angels were standing around the throne and the elders and the four living creatures, and they fell upon their faces before (*enopion*) the throne and worshiped God, ..."

Revelation 7:15   **"That is why they [the great crowd] are before (*enopion*) the throne of God; and they are rendering him sacred service. ..."**

Revelation 8:3   "And another angel arrived and stood at the altar, having ... incense ... to offer ... with the prayers of all the holy ones upon the golden altar that was before (*enopion*) the throne."

Revelation 9:13   "And I heard one voice out of the horns of the golden altar that is before (*enopion*) God"

Revelation 11:16   "And the twenty-four elders who were seated before (*enopion*) God ... "

Revelation 14:3   "And they [the 144,000] are singing as if a new song before (*enopion*) the throne and before (*enopion*) the four living creatures and the elders ..."

Clearly, when considered within the entirety of the book of Revelation there seems little reason to doubt that the "great crowd" is "before the throne" in the same manner as the seven lamps of fire, the glassy sea like crystal, the crowns of the 24 elders, the angels, the elders themselves, the four living creatures, the golden altar, and the 144,000.[13]

---

13   Fifth bullet point. Ibid footnote 3.

References

1. John 4:24
2. Matthew 7:7
3. 1 Thessalonians 5:21
4. 1 John 4:1
5. Acts 17:11
6. *A New Dictionary of Quotations* On Historical Principles From Ancient And Modern Sources (New York, Alfred A. Knopf, 1942). p. 378. (Third quotation on page.)
7. *The Kingdom Interlinear Translation of the Greek Scriptures* (1985 edition), p. 1080. (Note the expression "divine habitation" for the Greek word *noas* [*naō* in this instance since it is in the dative case] in the literal translation under the Greek text in Revelation 7:15.)
8. *The Watchtower*, August 15, 1980, pp. 14-20 (Note particularly the summary chart on the bottom of page 15.)
9. Hebrews 8:5; 9:11-12, 23, 24; Revelation 11:19; 14:15, 17; 15:5-6, 8; 16:1,17
10. Matthew 21:12; Mark 11:15; Luke 19:45; John 2:14-15. (Note the expression "divine habitation" for the Greek word *naos* does not appear, but instead the word "temple" for the Greek word *hieron* in *The Kingdom Interlinear Translation of the Greek Scriptures*.)
11. *Vine's Expository Dictionary of New Testament Words* (Seventeenth edition, 1966). p 115. (Note definition of the word HIERON.)
12. *The Watchtower*, August 15, 1960, p. 493.
13. Matthew 24:1-2; Mark 13:1-3 and Luke 21:5-6. (Note in *The Kingdom Interlinear Translation of the Greek Scriptures* the word used is *hieron*, not *naos*)
14. Matthew 27:5. (*The Kingdom Interlinear Translation of the Greek Scriptures* shows the Greek word *naos* [accusative form– *naon*] or "divine habitation" does appear in this verse.)
15. *Thayer's Greek-English Lexicon* (Harper & Brothers, 1889), p. 422 (Note definition of word *naos.*)
16. *The Anchor Bible* by W. F Albright and C. S. Mann (Doubleday & Co., copyright 1971). Observe use of "toward" in translation of Matthew 27:5
17. *The Interpretation of St. Matthew's Gospel* by R.C.H. Lenski (Augsburg Publishing House. copyright 1961) pp. 1079 and 1080 (See comments regarding Matthew 27:5.)
18. *The Life and Works of Flavius Josephus* translated by William Whiston. (Holt, Rinehart and Winston, New York) *Antiquities of the Jews*, Book XV. Chapter XI, sections 5 & 6.
19. *Insight on the Scriptures*, Volume 2, p. 1079. (Note second paragraph under section entitled "The Temple Rebuilt by Herod." or see same paragraph on page 1584 of *Aid To Bible Understanding.*)
20. *Der Temple Von Jerusalem* by Th. A. Busink (Leiden, E. J.Brill. 1980), page 1081 Comments on Josephus' use of word *naos* to include "whole inner sanctuary."
21. *The Interpreter's Dictionary of the Bible* (copyright 1962), p. 551. paragraphs 1 - 3 under "Josephus references," and p. 552. paragraph 4.
22. *Antiquities of the Jews*, Book XV. Chapter XI, section 3
23. *Insight on the Scriptures*, Volume 1, p. 382. (Reference to length of Nero's emperorship from 54 C.E. to 68 C.E.)
24. *The Life and Works of Flavius Josephus*, translated by William Whiston. *Wars of the Jews*, Book V, Chapter I, section 5. (Note also the second footnote at the bottom of page 774.)
25. John 2:20 in *The Jerusalem Bible, An American Translation* by Goodspeed and Smith, *Young's Literal Translation* and the translations by Moffatt and Lenski. (Note how these translations use the word "sanctuary" in this verse.)

26. *Chronological Aspects of the life of Christ* by Harold W. Hoehner (Zondervan Publishing House, Grand Rapids, MI, 1977), page 42.

27. *The Handbook of Biblical Chronology* by Jack Finegan (Princeton University Press, 1964), pages 279, 280.

28. *Chronological Aspects of the Life of Christ* by Harold W. Hoehner (Zondervan Publishing House, Grand Rapids, MI, 1977), page 41.

29. *The New International Dictionary of New Testament Theology* (1986 edition), Volume 3, p. 784. (See definition of *naos*.)

30. *Then Is Finished The Mystery of God* (Watch Tower Bible & Tract Society, 1969), page 260. (Note comments on *naos* in discussion of Revelation 11:2.)

31. *The Watchtower*, December 1, 1972, p. 722, paragraph 22. *The Watchtower*, July 1, 1996, p. 20, paragraph 4

32. Revelation 11:2. Note how translations like *The New English Bible*, the *King James Version* and that of James Moffatt use the word "Gentiles" when discussing outer court of the temple.

33. *Barnes Notes on the New Testament* (Tenth Printing, 1978), p. 1643. (See comments on Revelation 11:2.)

34. *Tyndale New Testament Commentaries*, commentary on The Revelation of St. John by Leon Morris (1979 edition), p. 146. (Comments on Revelation 11:2.)

35. *The Interpretation of St. John's Revelation* by R.C.H. Lenski (Augsburg Publishing House, Minneapolis, Minnesota, copyright 1961) p. 330, paragraph 1.

36. *Light*, Book One by J. F. Rutherford (The Watch Tower Bible & Tract Society, 1930), page 189. paragraph 1.

37. Revelation 22:18-19

38. *The Finished Mystery* (The Watch Tower Bible & Tract Society, 1924), p. 289. (Note how "Great Company" of Rev. 7:10 is associated with heavenly group of Rev. 19.1)

39. Revelation 7:9 (Compare Revelation 5:9-10 and note both groups come from all tribes and peoples and tongues)

40. Revelation 7:9, 15 (Compare Revelation 1:4; 4:5-6, 10; 7:11; 8:3; 9:13: 11:16; 14:3 and consider how expression "before the throne" is illuminated by these verses. Notice also how comments on this expression on page 123 of *Revelaion—Its Grand Climax At Hand!*, do not take into account how "before" [*enopion*] is used in context throughout the book of Revelation.)

41. Revelation 7:9 (Compare Revelation 5·8 and note common expression "before the lamb.")

42. Revelation 7:9 (Compare Revelation 3:4, 18; 4:4; 6:11 and note references to being dressed in white.)

43. Revelation 7: 10 (Compare Revelation 19:1 and note how this "great crowd" [NW] also attributes salvation to God.)

44. Revelation 7:14 (Compare 1 Peter 1:2, 18-19; 1 Corinthians 6:11; Rev. 22:14; John 1:7; Ephesians 2:13. Notice who is cleansed by blood of the Lamb.)

45. Revelation 7:4-8. Note how comments on these verses on pages 117 and 118 of *Revelation—Its Grand Climax At Hand!*, establish this is not a reference to "literal, fleshly Israel." Showing 12,000's are not literal would indicate their total (144.000) is not literal.

46. Revelation 22:18-19

47. *The Expositor's Bible Commentary*, edited by Frank E. Gaebelein and J. D. Douglas (Zondervan Publishing House, 1984), "Notes" on page 566.

INDEX

SCRIPTURE INDEX

THE COPYRIGHT OWNER'S
STORY

I felt completely empty inside as I returned home from a 12 hour encounter that I knew would surely change the course of my life. I had received credible information showing me that my 29 years involved with Jehovah's Witnesses had been based on an illusion. In a state of shock and exhaustion, I arrived home with my back covered with stress-induced hives.

I had been introduced to the beliefs of Jehovah's Witnesses as a young child. I was taught that Jehovah's Witnesses were the only true Christians in the whole world. As I went through my teen years, I embraced the beliefs published by the Watchtower Bible and Tract Society with all my heart, being baptized in 1969, at the eight-day, International '*Peace on Earth*' Convention in Buffalo, New York, on July 11th, at 17 years old. In my young adulthood I was a regular pioneer and then a temporary special pioneer. I often say that I believed that Jehovah's Witnesses exclusively had the "truth" from my nose to my toes. Every life decision that I made was influenced by what they taught; from decisions on whether to go to college, who to marry, postponing having children, or even a simple thing like whether to purchase a two or four-door car, were all influenced by the Watchtower Society. They were my present and future as I looked forward to life with them on a paradise earth in the near future, just around the corner. Throughout life's problems and challenges I considered the teachings of Jehovah's Witnesses as a rock under my feet. I believed I had a firm foundation in life because I had the "truth." Through the teachings of the Watchtower Society, I was sure that I had the answers to almost everything or anything concerning the Bible or my life.

Even though I believed that I had the truth; it did not mean that I did not see problems within the local congregations. I did. Over the years there were many things that deeply troubled me. I knew of several elders that had been removed for sexual sins with adults and children, and within a few years were back to being elders again. I knew of teenagers that used illegal drugs and others that had abortions. I witnessed an elder abusively yelling at the congregation with everyone accepting it as normal behavior. In all of it, I found it hard to understand how these situations could occur within our "spiritual paradise." Nevertheless, I carried on, feeling the problems were merely local and due to imperfect men, being confident that in time Jehovah would surely straighten all matters out.

In 1988, I had many religious discussions with someone that I met through my place of employment. This person was confident that my views as one of Jehovah's Witnesses were wrong. To the contrary, I trusted that my beliefs were solidly founded and were true. After reaching an impasse in our discussions, this person asked me to meet with some former Jehovah's Witnesses that regularly attended their church. I emphatically insisted that I would not under any circumstances meet with people who once had the "truth" and then abandoned it. This person persisted in a desire to inform me that my beliefs were not true, as I believed them to be. I was asked if I would meet with the pastor of the church they attended. (The church was First Baptist Atlanta and the pastor was Charles Stanley.) To their surprise I said, "*yes, I would.*" I explained that I would be more than happy to share the "truth" with Charles Stanley. In spite of him being a famous Christian pastor, I was confident that I would be able to enlighten him with the teachings of Jehovah's Witnesses. The next week this person called me to ask if instead of meeting with Charles Stanley, would I meet with someone else; a man named David Henke and his wife, Carole? I was informed that David was a businessman who had never been one of Jehovah's Witnesses and was a Christian who simply enjoyed talking with them. I agreed to meet with them. I explained that just as I would have been more than happy to share the "truth" with Charles Stanley, I would likewise be happy to share that "truth" with these people. The only obstacle to my meeting with them was that they lived in Columbus, Georgia, which was more than a two hour drive from my home. I said that I would make the drive, explaining that I had a lifetime dedication to share the beliefs of Jehovah's Witnesses with others. With Armageddon just around the corner, it may mean someone's life. If the Henke's were willing to listen to what I had to say, I was willing to share it, even if that meant driving over two hours to convey it.

When I called David Henke to set up a time to meet, he told me that in discussions he had with Jehovah's Witnesses in the past, the subject jumped around so much that progress was not made in any direction. He asked if he could suggest three subjects that we might want to explore, and we could discuss whatever we wanted to afterwards. I agreed. He then went on to suggest the three subjects to be:

1. The deity of Christ
2. The bodily resurrection of Jesus
3. The prophetic record of the Watchtower Bible and Tract Society

David suggested that in the time before we would meet, we could both research each subject and be prepared for a thorough discussion. I thought this was a thoughtful, reasonable and logical approach.

For the first two subjects, I was armed and prepared with answers from Watchtower Society literature. However the third subject, having to do with the prophetic record of the Watchtower Bible and Tract Society was a concern. Six months prior to this time, I had been questioned about the prophetic record of Jehovah's Witnesses and I did not have any clear answers for it. In preparation for my discussion, I called Tom, a well-respected elder in my congregation. I told him that I had difficulty with this question in the past and I was going to have another discussion with someone about the same subject and wanted to have a good answer. I shared with him that I had a piece of paper to make notes for reference later. Tom mentioned that the first thing I will want to put on my paper was: "We never call ourselves a prophet." This was great, as I knew I was not ever calling myself a prophet and I never heard anyone in the Kingdom Hall or door to door call themselves a prophet, therefore, that made sense. I happily put "We never call ourselves a prophet" at the top of my paper. Tom went on to list scripture after scripture where first century Christians were looking forward to the second coming of Christ in their day. He said that we as Jehovah's Witnesses have shown the same kind of faith and hope that the first century Christians had. At the end of my dialogue with Tom, I felt equipped for the discussion ahead of me.

On the morning of July 23, 1988, I loaded many Watchtower Society reference books into the trunk of my car in order to be prepared for my discussion. I wanted to be ready for whatever would come up in my time with the Henke's. Before leaving for Columbus, Georgia, I said a heartfelt prayer that I would in some way bring blessings to David and Carole. Confident, I went on my way.

Upon my arrival at the Henke home, I was pleased to meet a pleasant couple that lived in a modest home with their two children, a boy and a girl. We carried my trunk full of books into their kitchen dining area. For easy reference, we lined the books up on the floor against the wall just behind the chair that I would be sitting in. Before we sat down, David motioned to me to come into his library, just off the kitchen area. I was surprised to be met with a whole bookcase of Watchtower Society books! Many of the books were very old, going back to the inception of the Watchtower Bible and Tract Society. Some of the books had been written by Charles Taze Russell. I picked up and looked at *Studies in the Scriptures, Millions Now Living Will Never Die, Vindication* and so forth. I was happy to see these books, as I knew few people had them. Looking at him in amazement, I asked where he had acquired all these extraordinary books. He said he had collected them over the years from various garage sales and other places. Delighted, I said, "*I can see I did not need to bring all my books from home and I think your collection of books could be helpful in our discussion.*" David smiled and replied, "*Yes, I think they will.*" All the while I was thinking that this man has an interesting hobby of collecting Watchtower Society books.

For the first two hours of our discussion we discussed the first two subjects on our list, the deity of Christ and the bodily resurrection of Jesus. Around and around the discussion went. David did not make any headway with me and I did not make any headway with him. Then the discussion turned to the prophetic record of the Watchtower Society. I confidently got out my notes from my previous conversation with the elder, Tom, and read the heading at the top of my paper: "*We never call ourselves a prophet.*" David started to get up from his chair to head over to his bookcase. I stopped him and asked him to hear me out as I finished my list of scriptures, demonstrating that Jehovah's Witnesses are no different than the first century Christians as they eagerly anticipated the return of Christ. Once I finished sharing my references, he quietly went over to his bookcase and pulled out the *Watchtower* bound volume 1972. He turned to the April 1st Watchtower page 197 to an article entitled "*They shall know that A PROPHET WAS AMONG THEM.*" The article went on to say:

> "So, does Jehovah have a prophet to help them, to warn them of dangers and to declare things to come? These questions can be answered in the affirmative. Who is this prophet? ... This "prophet" was not one man, but was a body of men and women. It was the small group of footstep followers of Jesus Christ, known at that time as International Bible Students. Today they are known as Jehovah's Christian witnesses. They are still proclaiming a warning, and have been joined and assisted in their commissioned work by hundreds of thousands of persons who have listened to their message with belief. ... **Of course, it is easy to say that this group acts as a "prophet" of God. It is another thing to prove it. The only way that this can be done is to review the record. What does it show?**" (Bolding added.)

This article was actually inviting the reader to examine the record of the Watchtower Society. Then David asked me if I was willing to examine the record of the Watchtower Society as a prophet? I told him that I was. We examined prediction after prediction by Charles Taze Russell, the International Bible Students and Jehovah's Witnesses from 1874 to the present. Time after time a prediction was made and nothing happened. (Today these predictions are easy to look up on the Internet, however in 1988 this information was not readily available.) As we went from one date to the next, I became progressively more uncomfortable. Prior to this, I had not realized how from the very leadership of the Watchtower Society, prophecy after prophecy, for Armageddon's arrival had been made. Not only that, but each and every prophecy had failed! Example after example, of Watchtower Society prophecies were presented, all from their own publications. I was astounded! It was hard to believe but there they were right in front of me and in the original publications. I thought there must be a good explanation for them being God's modern day prophet, even with one failed prophecy after another. Turning to my library of books that I had right behind my chair, I picked up the Watchtower Society's book *Reasoning from the Scriptures*. I turned to page 136 under the subheading "Have not Jehovah's Witnesses made errors in their teachings?" The first paragraph said:

> "Jehovah's Witnesses **do not claim to be inspired prophets.** They have made mistakes. Like the apostles of Jesus Christ, they have at times had some wrong expectations. — Luke 19:11; Acts 1:6" (Bolding added.)

I was so relieved that the *Reasoning from the Scriptures* book had addressed this issue. Before I could even think much about the above answer to the failed prophecies of the past, I presented it promptly in defense. I concluded that although the Watchtower organization was a prophet, they certainly were not "inspired." David responded: "*Does this then mean that since they are not claiming "inspiration", they are not responsible for their prophetic mistakes?*" Following with an example of a person claiming to be a surgeon, yet refusing to accept responsibility for the patients who die on the operating table due to their mistakes. Who in response might say, "*You can't blame me, I didn't go to medical school and, I'm not licensed to practice medicine. So I made a few mistakes, don't expect me to have the track record of a 'real' surgeon!*" In essence stating: Just like a fake doctor who takes the physical lives of their patients, the fake prophet takes the spiritual lives of their followers.

I wanted to have an answer for the above analogy, but I just could not come up with one. I was troubled. Although I did not acknowledge this to David, I knew that the Bible talked about two kinds of prophets, true prophets and false prophets. I also knew the Bible did not have a third category for a "true but uninspired prophet"; unaccountable for whatever they say in God's name. No sooner had I thought that thought, when David had me turn to my Bible to read Deuteronomy 18:20-22:

"'However, the prophet who presumes to speak in my name a word that I have not commanded him to speak or who speaks in the name of other gods, that prophet must die. And in case you should say in your heart: "How shall we know the word that Jehovah has not spoken?" when the prophet speaks in the name of Jehovah and the word does not occur or come true, that is the word that Jehovah did not speak. With presumptuousness the prophet spoke it. You must not get frightened at him.'" NWT

The only thing that seemed logical for me to do was to go straight to the second part of the *Reasoning from the Scriptures* book about how the apostles made mistakes, having at times "wrong expectations." David's response was that the apostles did not "teach" or "promote" false ideas, which I agreed.

I brought up the point that we all make mistakes because of imperfection. Were not God's prophets of old guilty of making mistakes? David agreed that God's prophets were imperfect. They did make human mistakes. However, when we examine the record we find that, when they spoke a prophecy in God's name, they made no mistakes. Every prediction came true. I could not disagree.

At this point, the Henke's had no idea how very upset I was as I pondered these things. I was deeply unsettled. I began squirming in my chair because my back was breaking out in hives. I realize now that it was an emotional reaction to what I was learning; yet in the moment, I did not connect it. Carole took mercy on me, taking me into the restroom and put soothing cream on my back.

I had now been at the Henke's home for 6 hours. They asked me to stay to have some supper with them. Afterwards they wanted to show me a documentary movie about Jehovah's Witnesses. My curiosity was piqued. I was also hungry, so I agreed. They ordered pizza and we all sat down to eat. I was relieved to have a momentary oasis of time not to think about issues with Jehovah's Witnesses. To engage in light conversation, I decided to ask David what he did for a living? To which he replied, "*this.*" I responded with, "*What do you mean 'this'?*" He went on to say that he was the founder of Watchman Fellowship, a ministry outreach to Jehovah's

Witnesses and other cults.[1] In fact, he said that local Jehovah's Witnesses in Columbus, Georgia consider him to be part of the "evil slave" and anyone spending the time I just spent with him would probably be disfellowshipped. At that moment, I didn't know what to do with the bite of pizza in my mouth—whether to swallow it or to spit it out. Nevertheless, stressed as I was; I decided to stay because I wanted to see the documentary that David had promised to show me.

After eating, we went into the living room to watch a video called *Witnesses of Jehovah* produced by Jeremiah Films in 1987. The video is one hour long, but it took at least two hours to view it because I kept having David stop the video. A statement would be made in the video that I disagreed with and I would exclaim: "*Stop it, stop the movie! That's not true! I can tell you because I have spent all my life as a Jehovah's Witness and that is NOT true!*" He would calmly ask me to write it down on my paper and after the video, he promised to give me all the proof I needed. The whole video was stop and go, with my objections, David's calm assurances of proof and my writing items down for later reference.

Once the video was over, I needed to go for a walk to get myself together to be able to process any proof that David might present me with. Many things were presented in the video that if true... would change my whole perspective of Jehovah's Witnesses as the only true Christians on the earth. Could I face it, if these things were true? I came back from my walk and asked for "proof" of everything I had written down on my paper. Some of the things I wanted confirmation of were:

- Did the Watchtower Society change the date of when Jesus established his enthroned heavenly presence over time? Did they indeed believe until 1925 that Jesus established his enthroned heavenly presence in 1874? Also I wanted proof that they established 1914 as the date of his enthronement, only after 1925.

---

1   The Henke's did not realize that I had been told that David was a businessman and that I had no idea whatsoever that he was the founder of Watchman Fellowship and had an outreach ministry to Jehovah's Witnesses, Mormons, Scientologists and other groups. They thought I had been informed, however I had not.

- I wanted proof that there was a mansion in San Diego, California, (built in 1929), called Beth Sarim, "house of the princes." Was this mansion cared for by the Watchtower Society and deeded to the anticipated resurrection "princes" of the Old Testament patriarchs, including Abraham, Isaac, Moses, Samson, Samuel, David, etc.? Did J. F. Rutherford use the mansion for himself, while waiting for the resurrection of the "princes" to arrive? Was there proof that he died there himself, in 1942?

- Did the Watchtower Society ever use Johannes Greber, a known spiritualist, who translated the New Testament "with help from spirits" as a scholarly reference in support of the *New World Translation*?

- Did the Watchtower Society change being baptized in the name of "the Father, the Son and the Holy Spirit" to being baptized in the name of "the Father, the Son and the 'spirit directed organization'"?

- Did the Watchtower print an article in August 1968 called "*Why are You Looking Forward to 1975?*"

- Was Jerusalem destroyed as the Watchtower Society claims in 607 B.C.E. or in reality 586/587 B.C.E. negating the basis for 1914 as the date Jesus was enthroned in heaven? (The answer to this one was found in an Encyclopedia.)

- And many other questions.

Line item, after line item, David went to his bookcase and pulled out a Watchtower Society book, opened it and let me read it for myself. There it was, right in front of me, not in a book about Jehovah's Witnesses but in one of their very own books published by the Watchtower Society themselves. The Henke's were unaware of how profoundly these "proofs" were being received by me. As each confirmation was given, I moved on to the next item until all of them were answered.

It had now been 12 hours since I arrived in the Henke's home and in that time David was able to show me that what I had believed to be true all my life was not true. I was devastated. As I prepared to leave to go home, the Henke's prayed with me and sent me on my way with a large stack of literature. In that stack was a copy of *Crisis of Conscience* by Raymond Franz.

In only 12 hours, everything I had believed and built my life on had vanished. As I said at the beginning of this account, I felt empty, hollow. The compass for my life had disappeared. I found the rock I thought I had under my feet, had crumbled to dust. My confident future was gone and I was without "truth." I was in extraordinary emotional pain! For three days I felt as if I were in a nightmare. On the third day, I found myself pleading with Jehovah in prayer, asking him to please tell me what is the way and the truth? As I prayed, the scripture in John 14:6 came to my mind; "Jesus said to him: "I am the way and the truth and the life. No one comes to the Father except through me." This was a defining moment for me. I had put my hope in an "organization" for most of my life. Now I was amazed as I pondered this scripture. I had read that verse countless times, and yet on this day it was fresh and new. Jesus is the "way and the truth." Incredible! How could I have missed it? "Truth" is not an "organization" it is Jesus!

After that clarifying moment of realizing that Jesus is the "truth," I immersed myself in Bible reading at every possible moment. I used a minimum of four translations other than the *New World Translation* and at times up to 11 translations. It was an amazing time of discovery. I got much out of comparing other translations. Before reading a given translation, I read about the translators and/or translation committee. I wanted to know who they were and what ancient texts were relied upon. I also wanted to know what was their translation methodology, whether they implemented a 'word for word' or 'thought for thought' rendering. (This information is found in the front of most Bibles.) I was not then and am not now an expert in these fields, however I wanted to know about them and understand the concepts. I gave weight to 'consensus' among scholars and not so much to the 'exception' in translation. As I read, studied and researched; I felt enriched and was learning more about the Bible than I had ever known.

Even though I was enjoying my new discoveries, I was finding the need to discuss them with someone else. This was prior to the Internet, Google and social media, which were not an option then. The Henke's lived 135 miles away. Telephone rates per minute at the time were prohibitive for me to afford. It was important to me to have friends that shared my journey nearby. I knew I could not share this with any of my friends in the congregation or else risk being labeled as a doubter at best, or an "apostate" at worst. I wanted a friend or friends that knew the struggles of leaving the organization, that would be able to leave it and retain high moral and ethical standards, at the same time coming out of it better, stronger and with a resilient faith in God. But how would I ever find such friends?

In the beginning of September 1988, I read *Crisis of Conscience*. (It had only been six weeks since my meeting with the Henke's.) As I read Ray's story, I was impressed with his demeanor, as he presented himself in the book, expressing love toward those who hurt him. Even under extraordinary pressure and stress, Raymond Franz presented himself as I imagined a Christian should conduct himself. As I read his story, I admired the way he behaved under such circumstances. I wanted to meet this person of integrity and his wife. After a bit of research, I was able to find a telephone number for the Franz' and I called it. Raymond Franz' wife, Cynthia, answered my call. We talked for two and a half hours. She told me where they lived, which was to the west of metro Atlanta. I lived in the northeast metro Atlanta area, which was a one hour drive from my home and yet within a toll free telephone calling area. At the end of our conversation she invited me to supper at she and Ray's home. I accepted.

On Friday evening September 9, 1988, I rang the doorbell to the Franz' home. A smiling Ray, who warmly invited me into his home, greeted me. Cynthia was busy in the kitchen cooking. They had other guests there, Jon Mitchell, a former secretary to the Governing Body, a couple visiting from Australia, and Harrison Carlton, a former elder. As Cynthia busied herself in the kitchen, they all let me tell my story about meeting David and Carole Henke and my realization that Jesus is "the way, the truth and the life." I also shared the journey of my Bible reading and many of my discoveries from my studies. They listened with kindness and thoughtfulness. At that point, Cynthia let everyone know supper was ready and we all gathered around the dining room table. We shared a meal, our hearts and our struggles. None of us needed to fear saying or being anything but ourselves. The air seemed to be filled with extraordinary freedom and a joy.

Thereafter, Cynthia Franz invited me to come to their home every Sunday for a Bible study and lunch. I was delighted to accept the invitation. As I came to the Franz home week after week, Ray would always greet me with a big smile at the door and Cynthia was always busy in the kitchen. Ray would engage anyone that was there in light conversation, sharing stories or a joke or two. While he was busy being the host, Cynthia preferred preparing everything in the kitchen. She almost always refused any help as she prepared a meal or cleaned up afterwards. She wanted to be the one to take care of everyone else. Every week would be the same, Ray would greet and visit, and Cynthia would put on a tasty lunch. Ray would then lead everyone in reading and discussing a chapter of the Bible. Jon Mitchell was almost always there. Others might attend sporadically, however Jon was there consistently. Many times it would be Ray and Cynthia, Jon Mitchell, my five-year-old daughter and me.

A few times Ray and Cynthia had a large gathering of former Jehovah's Witnesses from several states. I had the pleasure of meeting Ed and Betty Dunlap, Peter and Janet Gregerson, and many others. Additionally some people that read *Crisis of Conscience* would contact the Franz', inquiring if they could come to visit them. Ever welcoming, ever hospitable, Ray and Cynthia enjoyed their roles as they opened their home to any and all that would come to them. Many would travel great distances to visit them, from other states and countries. Most were seeking answers to many questions, others would share their painful journey and to inquire if there could be a fulfilling future after their experience with the Watchtower Society? They opened their home and their hearts to them. Ray was a patient listener, thoughtful and understanding. He both comforted and encouraged person after person. I have often said, "Raymond Franz ministered to the brokenhearted."

2

As for me, I came to Ray and Cynthia primarily for friendship, and that is what I received. Even so, I did learn many things from both of them and I am thankful for it. Nevertheless, it was friendship that I was seeking and I gained a treasure in them as dear loving friends.

At the time I met the Franz', I was not married. I had gone through a divorce in 1986 and I had a little girl from that marriage. My daughter was five years old when I met them. She was small for her age, which allowed Ray to pick her up easily. Around and around, Ray would spin her in his arms, to the delight of her giggles. The Franz' enjoyed having my daughter join us. Jon Mitchell was pleased to have a child join us too. After lunch, Jon would get out a game of blocks and play with my daughter for a couple of hours at a time. One and all seemed happy to have a small child visit so often.

It was through connections with the Franz' that Dan Dykstra began to court me. They had been friends with Dan since 1982. They both always took responsibility for matchmaking my husband and me. They loved to tell and retell the story. Once Dan started writing to me, we had a whirlwind romance with a courtship of only a few months. Dan and I married in mid-August 1989. Ray and Cynthia were happy for me, however they were not pleased that both my daughter and I would be moving away to Michigan as a result.

---

2   Raymond & Cynthia Franz as they were in the late 1980's.

3

4

5

---

3   From left to right: Cynthia Franz, Deborah & Dan Dykstra and Raymond Franz.

4   In August 1989, as we were posing for this wedding picture, Ray joked that he still was not too sure about whether he should approve of my marriage to Dan Dykstra or not. Ray liked to lighten a situation with a joke. The Franz' were both happy for my marriage and sad I was moving to Michigan.

5   We stayed with the Franz' for a couple of days upon our return from our honeymoon. We wanted a little time with them before departing for Michigan. This picture was our goodbye photo taken in front of the Franz home before we left for our new home in Michigan.

Even though I moved away, we stayed in contact with each other over the years. We would visit whenever we came to Georgia and they came to visit us in Michigan on three occasions. As the years went by, it became more difficult to keep up with one another's lives as Ray and Cynthia, as well as Dan and I, had escalating health issues.

In the spring of 2007, Dan and I moved to Georgia. We moved for several reasons including being near our daughter (from my first marriage) and her husband. We also needed to be in a warm climate for my husbands' health.

We ended up moving to the east of metro Atlanta. Ray and Cynthia lived to the west of metro Atlanta. We were pleased that we could be near our daughter and her husband as well as the Franz'. At the time Ray was 85 years old, and Cynthia was 72 years old. My husband and I wanted to be available to them as they aged. We were happy to be within driving distance where we could easily visit them whenever the need would arise.

Back in the year 2000, Ray had suffered a moderate stroke, without paralysis, but it left him tired and low on energy. As a result, his right carotid artery was completely blocked. It was important that he undergo surgery on his left carotid artery to keep it open, as it was in process of becoming blocked too. He underwent successful surgery to address this in September 2007. It greatly relieved his mind, as he was feeling very vulnerable concerning the probability of another stroke. His general countenance appeared to improve after this surgery allowing him to travel to Europe on a 16 day trip the next month in October.

In early 2008, Ray reestablished regularly getting together for a home Bible study including both my husband and me. Because of both Ray and Cynthia's health issues, the Bible study had been meeting sporadically with a few friends for a couple of years; now however, the Bible study was back on a regular schedule. Besides Ray and Cynthia and my husband and me, there was one other married couple and two single people regularly participating in Ray's Bible study, with an occasional guest. There were no children attending. Because we were all scattered around the metro Atlanta area, as a group we agreed to meet once every two weeks. For a while we took turns having the Bible study and lunch each in a different home. However we most often met at one person's home that was centrally located for all of us. We would have lunch and then sit down to read a Bible chapter or two and discuss it. Ray was delighted that the Bible study and gathering with others was a regular occurrence again.

Another blessing in our relocating to Georgia was our opportunity to visit with Peter and Janet Gregerson. As you may recall, as reported in this book, *Crisis of Conscience,* Ray was disfellowshipped for having a meal with Peter Gregerson, his employer, landlord and friend. Nevertheless, over the years, the Gregerson's remained constant and loyal friends to the Franz'. My husband, Dan, also had been a friend of Peter's going back to 1982. Now that we were living in Georgia, we would get together periodically to have a meal in a restaurant with the Gregerson's and the Franz'. Since Ray and Cynthia lived halfway between the Gregerson's and us, we usually met at a restaurant near the Franz'. It was a delightful time. We greatly enjoyed one another's company and deepened our friendship.

Ray found deep gratification in contributing to the wellbeing of his fellowman; therefore he spent his old age working without ceasing, day after day to the benefit of others. He would be up early in the morning each day to embrace the day's work. Keeping his supply of books in his garage, he mailed out orders for his books one by one. He found the need to continuingly refine his books as the Watchtower Society changed positions on various subjects, updating the footnotes and appendix. Letters came in daily, either by email or postal mail. He spent much of his time reading and answering a multitude of letters, which to my knowledge he answered every one. He also researched various theological subjects. Even in his advanced age, he had a brilliant mind.

Knowing that Ray was such a kind, thoughtful, and compassionate person, some people thought that he would not mind if they published and sold his books themselves, infringing on his copyrights. Every time he became aware of an infringement he was deeply saddened. He occasionally found evidence that some people were changing the words of what he wrote as well. In each and every instance that he knew of, Ray worked to put an end to the infringement. He was direct, forthright, and honest. He was an honorable man. He expected other people to treat him and his works the same way.

Ray's indulgences were few. He always wanted a dog by his side. He enjoyed a good dog tremendously! In his life after leaving Bethel, he and his wife had three dogs, one following the other, Lobo, Muchacho, and Niño. Cynthia shared his passion for dogs. Since they never had children, their dogs became their children. He liked to both sing and dance. Some of his wife's most treasured memories were of Ray singing to her. They also enjoyed dancing together. Ray's favorite meal was Cynthia's spaghetti, which she was proud to tell was her mother's recipe.

And no meal was complete without hot sauce. He enjoyed a daily walk with his dog, on the wooded lot, behind his garage. At the end of the day, life was not complete without a glass of wine and a big bowl of popcorn, and it was a great pleasure to share his popcorn with his dog.

Even though Raymond Franz was 88 years old when he died, it was a shock to all of us that were close to him. His uncle Frederick Franz had lived to 99 years old and everyone had hoped that he would share the same life span. Although Ray's energy was declining and his aches and pains were increasing, there was no reason to believe that his life was about to end. On May 30, 2010, I received a phone call that Ray had fallen, hit his head, was in the hospital and it did not look good. Dan and I immediately drove out to the hospital. Ray had the best medical attention possible, however the hemorrhaging in his brain was beyond recovery. On June 2, 2010, he died. My husband and I were profoundly sad and grief stricken. If Ray had lived as long as his uncle Frederick, we would all have had him with us until 2021. Nevertheless, it was not to be.

6

7

Cynthia's grief was deep and persistent. She could not get over the loss of Ray until the day she died, three and half years later on December 29, 2013. She and I had been friends for 22 years prior to Ray's death; however after he passed we became closer than ever. Her grief moved me to very deep compassion for her as we spent much time together on the telephone as well as visits to her home.[8] I went from feeling that Cynthia was a friend, to feeling that she was an extension of my family. I know she felt the same. It was her wish that she would share her large family of brothers and sisters and their families with me. Her wish came true, as her family is very dear to my heart.

After Raymond died, I assisted Cynthia in selling the thousands of books stocked in her garage. I set up an Amazon.com account, gave her the labels and she shipped cases of books to Amazon. I actually wanted to take the burden off her and do it all for her, but she wanted to do it herself. She felt that she was doing something for Ray. She insisted that labeling

---

6   Ray studying in his home office. He loved to wear sweaters. This one was his favorite.
7   Ray enjoyed daily walks on his wooded lot. This photo was taken behind his garage.
8   I now know the challenges and difficulties of being a widow first hand, as my darling husband, Dan Dykstra died of cardiac arrest on May 11, 2017.

and shipping the books helped her with her grief. We did that until her entire stock of *Crisis of Conscience* books were gone in the fall of 2013. Eight months prior to Cynthia death, she surprised me by stating that she wanted to transfer the copyrights to Ray's works right away. She did not want to wait until her death to transfer the copyrights. She said that she wanted me to own them. Papers were drawn up and Cynthia signed them on June 1, 2013. I was then the legal copyright owner to all of Raymond Franz works. I immediately took the appropriate steps to establish this with the Library of Congress of the United States of America.

Late afternoon, on December 21, 2013, I received a call that Cynthia had fallen in her home. Her neighbor had looked in on her, saw that she had fallen earlier that day and decided to tell me about it. I immediately called Cynthia. She insisted she was okay; all she needed was a wheelchair. On the telephone she sounded like that might be true. My husband and I knew of a store located just 2 minutes from our home that rents medical equipment. We quickly drove over and rented a wheelchair for her and were on our way to her home to rescue her. Upon seeing her physical condition, we could see she needed medical attention so we took her to the hospital. After many tests were run, she was admitted just after midnight and stayed in the hospital for the next eight days. On December 29th, while in the hospital, Cynthia had a massive heart failure and died. It is difficult for me to fully express my grief at her passing. I miss her greatly.

One way I am expressing my love for both Raymond and Cynthia Franz is with my plan of covering the world with this fifth edition of *Crisis of Conscience* in multiple languages. I also intend on protecting the copyrights, preserve the integrity, and legally defend the works of Raymond Franz.

Raymond and Cynthia Franz are not far from my thoughts as I go about my various tasks each day. As close as we were, we did not always agree on everything. All of us were of strong personal opinions. Nevertheless, what we did agree on was that we loved God, and loved, valued, and mutually respected each other. We were dear friends who became "family" to each other and I will carry them in my heart always.

Deborah Dykstra

To contact the writer of the Foreword of this book:

David Henke
Email: dhenkewatchman@gmail.com

Watchman Fellowship of Georgia
PO Box 7681
Columbus, GA 31908

Website: www.watchman-ga.org

NU LIFE
P R E S S

www.NuLifePress.com

Made in United States
North Haven, CT
27 February 2024

49200666R00333